Lecture Notes in Computer Science 10659

Commenced Publication in 1973
Founding and Former Series Editors:
Gerhard Goos, Juris Hartmanis, and Jan van Leeuwen

More information about this series at http://www.springer.com/series/7407

Dora B. Heras · Luc Bougé (Eds.)

Euro-Par 2017: Parallel Processing Workshops

Euro-Par 2017 International Workshops
Santiago de Compostela, Spain, August 28–29, 2017
Revised Selected Papers

 Springer

Editors
Dora B. Heras
University of Santiago de Compostela
Santiago de Compostela
Spain

Luc Bougé
ENS Rennes
Rennes
France

Workshop Editors *see next page*

ISSN 0302-9743   ISSN 1611-3349   (electronic)
Lecture Notes in Computer Science
ISBN 978-3-319-75177-1   ISBN 978-3-319-75178-8   (eBook)
https://doi.org/10.1007/978-3-319-75178-8

Library of Congress Control Number: 2018931883

LNCS Sublibrary: SL1 – Theoretical Computer Science and General Issues

Printed on acid-free paper

This Springer imprint is published by the registered company Springer International Publishing AG
part of Springer Nature
The registered company address is: Gewerbestrasse 11, 6330 Cham, Switzerland

Workshop Editors

Auto-DaSP
Gabriele Mencagli
University of Pisa
Italy
mencagli@di.unipi.it

COLOC
Emmanuel Jeannot
INRIA
France
emmanuel.jeannot@inria.fr

Euro-EDUPAR
Rizos Sakellariou
University of Manchester
UK
rizos@manchester.ac.uk

F2C-DP
Rosa M. Badia
Barcelona Supercomputing Center
Spain
rosa.m.badia@bsc.es

HeteroPar
Jorge G. Barbosa
LIACC & Universidade do Porto
Portugal
jbarbosa@fe.up.pt

LSDVE
Laura Ricci
University of Pisa
Italy
laura.ricci@unipi.it

Resilience
Stephen L. Scott
Tennessee Technological University
    and Oak Ridge National Laboratory
USA
sscott@tntech.edu

ROME
Stefan Lankes
RWTH Aachen University
Germany
slankes@eonerc.rwth-aachen.de

UCHPC
Josef Weidendorfer
Technische Universität München
Germany
Josef.Weidendorfer@in.tum.de

Preface

Euro-Par is an annual international conference in Europe covering all aspects of parallel and distributed processing. These range from theory to practice, from small to the largest parallel and distributed systems and infrastructures, from fundamental computational problems to full-fledged applications, from architecture, compiler, language, and interface design and implementation to tools, support infrastructures, and application performance aspects. The Euro-Par conference itself is complemented by a workshop program, where workshops dedicated to more specialized themes, to cross-cutting issues, and to upcoming trends and paradigms can be easily and conveniently organized with little administrative overhead.

This year, 16 workshop proposals were submitted, and after a careful review process, which was led by the workshop co-chairs, 13 workshops were accepted. Three workshops had to be cancelled later due to a low number of submissions.

The workshops took place on the two days before the Euro-Par conference and the program included the following ten workshops:

1. Workshop on Advanced Parallel Processing Technology for Artificial Intelligence (APPT)
2. Workshop on Autonomic Solutions for Parallel and Distributed Data Stream Processing (Auto-DaSP)
3. Open Workshop on Data Locality (COLOC)
4. European Workshop on Parallel and Distributed Computing Education for Undergraduate Students (Euro-EDUPAR)
5. Workshop on Fog-to-Cloud Distributed Processing (F2C-DP)
6. Workshop on Algorithms, Models, and Tools for Parallel Computing on Heterogeneous Platforms (HeteroPar)
7. Workshop on Large-Scale Distributed Virtual Environments (LSDVE)
8. 10th Workshop on Resiliency in High-Performance Computing with Clouds, Grids, and Clusters (Resilience)
9. 5th Workshop on Runtime and Operating Systems for the Many-Core Era (ROME)
10. Workshop on Unconventional High-Performance Computing (UCHPC)

All workshops together received a total of 119 submissions from 41 different countries. Each workshop had an independent Program Committee, which was in charge of selecting the papers. The workshop papers received more than three reviews per paper on average (390 reviews in total). Out of the 119 submissions, 71 papers were selected to be presented at the workshops. One of the presented papers was not included in the final proceedings because it was considered short paper. Thus, the acceptance rate was 58%.

The success of the Euro-Par workshops depends on the work of many individuals and organizations. We therefore thank all workshop organizers and reviewers for the time and effort that they invested. We would also like to express our gratitude to the members of the Organizing Committee and the local staff, especially the volunteer PhD students, who helped us. Sincere thanks are due to Springer for their help in publishing the proceedings. This volume includes the 55 selected papers of nine workshops and also a section called Complementary Papers that includes four selected papers originally sent to the three cancelled workshops. The 11 papers accepted by the APPT workshop were also published in a separate volume by Springer.

Lastly, we thank all participants, panelists, and keynote speakers of the Euro-Par workshops for their contribution to a productive meeting. It was a pleasure to organize and host the Euro-Par workshops 2017 in Santiago de Compostela.

September 2017   Dora B. Heras
                                                                                      Luc Bougé

Organization

Euro-Par Steering Committee

Chair

Luc Bougé — ENS Rennes, France

Vice-chair

Fernando Silva — University of Porto, Portugal

Full Members

Dora Blanco Heras	CiTIUS, Santiago de Compostela, Spain
Emmanuel Jeannot	LaBRI-Inria, Bordeaux, France
Christos Kaklamanis	Computer Technology Institute, Greece
Paul Kelly	Imperial College, UK
Thomas Ludwig	University of Hamburg, Germany
Tomàs Margalef	Autonomous University of Barcelona, Spain
Wolfgang Nagel	Dresden University of Technology, Germany
Francisco F. Rivera	CiTIUS, Santiago de Compostela, Spain
Rizos Sakellariou	University of Manchester, UK
Fernando Silva	University of Porto, Portugal
Henk Sips	Delft University of Technology, The Netherlands
Domenico Talia	University of Calabria, Italy
Jesper Larsson Träff	Vienna University of Technology, Austria
Denis Trystram	Grenoble Institute of Technology, France
Felix Wolf	Technische Universität Darmstadt, Germany

Honorary Members

Christian Lengauer	University of Passau, Germany
Ron Perrott	Oxford e-Research Centre, UK
Karl Dieter Reinartz	University of Erlangen-Nuremberg, Germany

Observers

Marco Aldinucci	University of Turin, Italy
Ramin Yahyapour	GWDG/University of Göttingen, Germany

Euro-Par 2017 Organization

Co-chairs

Francisco F. Rivera   CiTIUS, Santiago de Compostela, Spain
Tomás F. Pena   CiTIUS, Santiago de Compostela, Spain
José C. Cabaleiro   CiTIUS, Santiago de Compostela, Spain
Dora B. Heras   CiTIUS, Santiago de Compostela, Spain

Workshops

Dora B. Heras   CiTIUS, Santiago de Compostela, Spain
Luc Bougé   ENS Rennes, France

Local Organization

Elisardo Antelo
Francisco Argüello
Antonio G. Loureiro
Juan C. Pichel
Natalia Seoane
David L. Vilariño

Additional Reviewers

Amoretti, Michele
Baiardi, Fabrizio
Brogi, Antonio
Caíno-Lores, Silvina
Christgau, Steffen
Di Francesco Maesa, Damiano
Dutot, Pierre-Francois
Ferrucci, Luca
García-Valls, Marisol
Graffi, Kalman
Guidi, Barbara
Ibeid, Huda
Jing, Chen
Kahvazadeh, Sarang
Kimovski, Dragi
La Gala, Massimiliano
Li, Jiajun
Lu, Wenyan

Lulli, Alessandro
Macedo, Jose
Maiterth, Matthias
Marino, Andrea
Marozzo, Fabrizio
Marques, Diogo
Misale, Claudia
Mommessin, Clement
Mordonini, Monica
Mori, Paolo
Neves, Nuno
Nicodemus, Carlos
Palazzi, Claudio
Peng, Zhang
Petcu, Dana
Renso, Chiara
Rey, Antón
Rossetti, Giulio

Rotta, Randolf
Schepke, Claudio
Serrapica, Flavio
Shijun, Gong
Soldani, Jacopo
Song, Mingcong
Su, Li
Tao, Dingwen

Tomaiuolo, Michele
Tremblay, Guy
Vieira, Alexandre
Wang, Xiaoyang
Xie, Yuan
Zhang, Weiqi
Zhang, Xian

Contents

COLOC – Workshop on Data Locality

Euro-EDUPAR – European Workshop on Parallel and Distributed Computing Education for Undergraduate Students

F2C-DP – Workshop on Fog-to-Cloud Distributed Processing

HeteroPar – Workshop on Algorithms, Models and Tools for Parallel Computing on Heterogeneous Platforms

LSDVE – Workshop on Large Scale Distributed Virtual Environments

Complementary Papers

Auto-DASP – Workshop on Autonomic Solutions for Parallel and Distributed Data Stream Processing

Workshop on Autonomic Solutions for Parallel and Distributed Data Stream Processing (Auto-DaSP)

Workshop Description

Auto-DaSP is a forum for researchers and practitioners working on parallel and autonomic solutions for Data Stream Processing applications, frameworks, and programming support tools. The data streaming domain belongs to the Big Data ecosystem, where the so-called *data velocity*, i.e., the rate at which data arrive at the system for processing, represents one of the most challenging aspects to be addressed in the design of applications and frameworks. High-volume data streams can be efficiently handled through the adoption of novel high-performance solutions targeting today's commodity parallel hardware. However, despite the large computing power offered by the affordable hardware available nowadays, high-performance data streaming solutions need to be equipped with smart logics in order to adapt the framework/application configuration to rapidly changing execution conditions and workloads. This turns out in mechanisms and strategies to adapt the queries and operators placement policies, intra-operator parallelism degree, scheduling strategies, load shedding rate and so forth, and fosters novel interdisciplinary approaches that exploit Control Theory and Artificial Intelligence methods. The workshop calls the attention of the data stream processing and the distributed and parallel computing research communities in order to stimulate integrated approaches between these two disciplines.

The first edition of the International Workshop on Autonomic Solutions for Parallel and Distributed Data Stream Processing (Auto-DaSP 2017) was held in Santiago de Compostela, Spain. The workshop was organized in conjunction with the Euro-Par annual series of international conferences. The format of the workshop included a keynote followed by technical presentations. The workshop was attended by around 25 people on average.

The workshop received 20 submissions for reviews, from authors belonging to more than 15 distinct countries. After an accurate and thorough peer-review process, we selected 12 papers for presentation at the workshop. The review process focused on the quality of the papers, their scientific novelty and applicability to existing Data Stream Processing problems and frameworks. The acceptance of the papers was the result of the reviewers' discussion and agreement. All the high quality papers were accepted, and the acceptance rate was 60%. The accepted articles represent an interesting mix of techniques to solve recurrent problems in Data Stream Processing, such as the identification of parallel streaming patterns, strategies, and mechanisms to support elasticity and resource scaling in Stream Processing and Fog Computing scenarios, and scheduling algorithms for load balancing in presence of stateful streaming applications.

Last but not least, we would like to thank the Auto-DaSP 2017 Program Committee, whose members made the workshop possible with their rigorous and timely review process. We would also like to thank Euro-Par for hosting the workshop and our emerging community, and the Euro-Par workshop chairs Luc Bougé and Dora B. Heras for the valuable help and support.

Auto-DaSP Chairs

Valeria Cardellini	University of Rome Tor Vergata, Italy
Gabriele Mencagli	University of Pisa, Italy
Massimo Torquati	University of Pisa, Italy

Program Committee

Marco Aldinucci	University of Torino, Italy
Daniele Bonetta	Oracle Labs Wien, Austria
Daniele Buono	IBM T. J. Watson Research Center, USA
Marco Danelutto	University of Pisa, Italy
Tiziano De Matteis	University of Pisa, Italy
Daniele De Sensi	University of Pisa, Italy
J. Daniel Garcia	University Carlos III of Madrid, Spain
Dalvan Griebler	Pontifícia Universidade Católica do Rio Grande do Sul, Brazil
Christoph Hochreiner	TU Wien, Austria
Yuanzhen Ji	SAP and TU Dresden, Germany
Supun Kamburugamuve	Indiana University, USA
Francesco Lo Presti	University of Rome Tor Vergata, Italy
Matteo Nardelli	University of Rome Tor Vergata, Italy
Yongluan Zhou	University of Southern Denmark, Denmark

Moderated Resource Elasticity for Stream Processing Applications

Michael Borkowski$^{(\boxtimes)}$ ⓘ, Christoph Hochreiner ⓘ, and Stefan Schulte ⓘ

Distributed Systems Group, TU Wien, Vienna, Austria
{m.borkowski,c.hochreiner,s.schulte}@infosys.tuwien.ac.at

Abstract. In stream processing, elasticity is often realized by adapting the system scale and topology according to the volume of input data. However, this volume is often fluctuating, with a high degree of noise, which can trigger a high amount of scaling operations. Since these scaling operations introduce additional overhead and cost, systems employing such approaches are at risk of spending a significant amount of time scaling up and down, nullifying the positive effects of scalability.

To overcome this, we propose an approach for moderating the scaling behavior of stream processing applications by reducing the number of scaling operations, while still providing quick responses to changes in input data volume. Contrary to existing approaches, instead of using linear smoothing techniques, we show how to employ non-linear filtering techniques from the field of signal processing to pre-process the raw volume measurements, mitigating superfluous scaling operations, and effectively reducing the number of such operations by up to 94%.

Keywords: Stream processing · Elasticity · TVD · EKF

1 Introduction

A major aspect of modern stream processing systems is elasticity [11], a feature well-established in cloud computing [6]. In short, an elastic system is capable of scaling up during times of increased load, and scaling down during times of reduced load, instead of constantly over- or under-provisioning computational resources. This allows the system to adapt to new situations, reducing cost while maintaining Quality of Service (QoS) [10]. A system with less capacity than the volume is said to be under-provisioned, whereas on the other hand, a system with more capacity than is needed is called over-provisioned [14]. Scaling is not limited to cloud computing, but has also been applied in stream processing [12].

In order to make scaling decisions, certain properties of the system are observed. On the one hand, these properties may be intrinsic to the system, i.e., its CPU utilization [10], memory usage [5], network traffic [26], or its performance [3]. On the other hand, the observed properties may be extrinsic to the system, for instance, the amount of incoming data to be processed [12,25], as observed in our work. Generally, every scaling operation requires resources

ⓒ Springer International Publishing AG, part of Springer Nature 2018
D. B. Heras and L. Bougé (Eds.): Euro-Par 2017 Workshops, LNCS 10659, pp. 5–16, 2018.
https://doi.org/10.1007/978-3-319-75178-8_1

by itself, i.e., it incurs a delay, consumes energy without creating revenue, and leads to computational overhead [9,18], and therefore additional cost. This is especially the case for scaling up, since additional operators on corresponding resources must be activated. Therefore, scaling operations should be kept at a minimum [5,18].

In cloud computing, current approaches assume thresholds of utilization between which an operator must be [2]. In stream processing, this translates to the notion that an operator can only handle a certain amount of input data volume [13]. For any amount of data exceeding this volume, an additional operator is instantiated. However, using this threshold-based scaling in a simple way results in relatively frequent scaling operations, which causes an overhead of resource usage and cost, as discussed before [5,9,18]. In certain cases, this cost is necessary in order to benefit from the additional computing power made available by scaling up, avoiding under-provisioning, or saving power by scaling down, but on a large scale, excessively frequent scaling operations increase the risk of losing too much cost on the overhead of scaling.

We consider the volume of incoming data as a time series, and argue that both long-term trends in volumes, as well as short-term variances (spikes and valleys) are observable. The long-term trend, for instance, can be the development of input data depending on the time of day, time of year etc., while short-term spikes rather represent spontaneous and short-lived events, i.e., noise that we aim to ignore for scaling decisions.

Following this, we propose to improve classic threshold-based scaling by changing the way scaling mechanisms react to changes of the input volume. Instead of using the raw input value of the measured input volume, or using simple smoothing techniques, we employ advanced, non-linear noise reduction techniques from the field of signal processing. We apply these techniques to the raw input values, creating a filter. Using this approach, we aim to separate the actual data to be used for scaling (the long-term trend) from noise (the short-term variance), and focus on scaling only based on the long-term trend. The intuition is that this reduces the frequency of scaling decision while still being adaptive to the fluctuations in input data volume.

To this end, the remainder of this paper is structured as follows: In Sect. 2, we discuss work found in literature related to the topic of scaling in stream processing. In Sect. 3, we present in detail our approach of minimizing the number of scaling operations in stream processing systems, followed by a detailed description of our implementation in Sect. 4. We evaluate the approach and its implementation in Sect. 5. Finally, we conclude and give an overview of possible future work in Sect. 6.

2   Related Work

A fundamental assumption in our work is the claim that computational overhead caused by scaling, as explained in Sect. 1, causes significant cost. The general impact of overhead introduced by frequent scaling of cloud resources has been studied by Corradi et al. [5] (in the context of overhead within cloud data centers) and by Mao and Humphrey [18] (in the context of auto-scaling in cloud workflows) and the common result is that indeed, such overhead has significant impact and should be kept to a minimum. Other work in this field has been presented by Gong et al. [9], where the impact of scaling overhead is quantified by showing that the CPU consumption using shorter scaling intervals is up to four times as high, compared to longer intervals.

Scaling in stream processing systems has been thoroughly considered and surveyed in the literature [1,12]. Abadi et al. [1] present the Borealis stream processing engine, along with a flexible and QoS-based optimization model. However, the scaling mechanisms presented do not take into account the volume of input data. No detailed information is given about whether any pre-processing of recorded data (e.g., denoising) is used. Hochreiner et al. [12] present a model for elastic stream processing, and discuss the methodologies, advantages and drawbacks of scaling within stream processing systems.

Mencagli et al. [19] use the Model-based Predictive Control (MPC) technique to create a trade-off between reconfiguration stability and amplitude. While the context (streaming application) is the same, and the aim (reduction of reconfiguration overhead) is similar to ours (reduction of the amount of scaling operations), the authors focus on the use of a distributed and cooperative approach, while we focus on the noise reduction in the input signal.

The usage of input data volume for scaling decisions has repeatedly been considered in literature [12,25], as was using threshold-based systems to deduce concrete scaling decisions [4,13]. All of those approaches, however, suffer from the same overhead problem as described before.

Some work has been done specifically to tackle this problem of overhead due to fluctuating input. A general recommendation seems to be the usage of low-pass filters [5], with a concrete instance of such a filter proposed by Shen et al. [23]. In this work, the authors employ a moving-average filter, similar to linear smoothing (LS). However, the authors do not use advanced non-linear approaches, like Total Variation Denoising (TVD) or Extended Kalman Filters (EKF).

Another example of linear filters is found in the work by Gong et al. [9], where scaling decisions are based on a Fast Fourier Transform (FFT) and pattern recognition. To avoid overhead, the authors use a delayed scaling mechanism, i.e., hysteresis. We argue that this is a rather basic approach in the context of signal filtering, and has the disadvantage of a fixed delay with which even the most extreme changes in input data volume are processed to scaling decisions. In contrast, the TVD approach presented in the work at hand reacts quickly to clear edges in the input data volume signal.

To the best of our knowledge, the only approach explicitly using a non-linear approach is presented by Khan et al. [16], where workload time series processing using clustering is proposed. Variations of workload patterns are predicted using hidden Markov models. Nevertheless, the authors do not take into account any normalization methods for processing the time series.

3   Approach

As stated in Sect. 1, the goal of our work is to minimize the amount of scaling operations performed, based on the volume of incoming data, using methods from the field of signal processing referred to as noise reduction or regularization.

We consider a stream processing system, which is receiving incoming data, e.g., from a message queue, processing it using an arbitrary amount of operators, and forwarding the resulting data as output. As stated in Sect. 1, we observe the volume of incoming data. This is done at the operators initially ingesting the data, either explicitly by measuring the incoming data, or by utilizing already-available data, for instance, statistics stemming from the incoming message queue.

The primary input for our approach is the time series of recorded measurements of input data volume. We denote a volume measurement at a time t as v_t. Figure 1 presents the intuition behind our approach. The dashed line represents the trend of the volume of input data of a stream processing system. However, due to temporally local variance and fluctuation, the measured amount varies, as denoted by the solid line. It is visible that while the recorded data generally follows the long-term trend, there is a substantial amount of noise overlapping the signal.

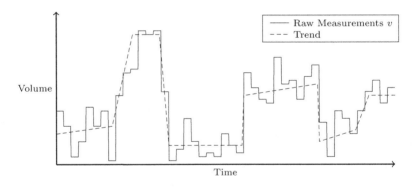

Fig. 1. Long-term volume trend (dashed) and actual, measured values (solid).

Naturally, if a stream processing system bases scaling decisions purely on the raw data, an excessive amount of scaling operations occurs [5,9,18]. In Fig. 2, this is shown in the lower graph. Our approach applies filters to this process to reduce the number of scaling operations, i.e., reduce the number of steps in the *operators* line in Fig. 2.

Therefore, we formally define our approach as follows. We regard a history of raw volume measurements, V, at various points in time t out of all measured times T, where v_t, as mentioned above, is the measured volume at time t:

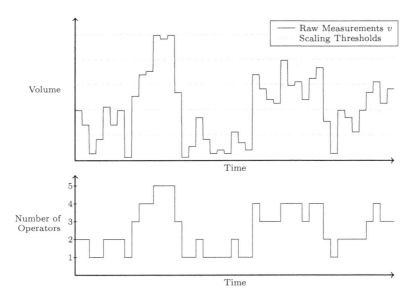

Fig. 2. Scaling of operator count according to thresholds of the actual volume, resulting in a high amount of scaling operations.

$$T = \{t_0, t_1, \ldots, t_n\} \tag{1}$$

$$V = \bigcup_{t \in T} v_t = \{v_{t_0}, v_{t_1}, \ldots, v_{t_n}\} \tag{2}$$

Based on the raw measurements $v \in V$, we define a filter f, which we apply to each value. The filter is applied at a given measurement time t and has access to all other measurement values in V, with the practical limitation that it can only access past measurements. We therefore define $f_V(t)$ as the filtered value for the time t, given all other values $v_i \in V$ where $i \leq t$. The concrete definition of f is not fixed, i.e., f is a parameter of our approach. Various concrete filters are described in the following section.

We then define the set of filtered measurements $\overline{V}$:

$$\forall v_t \in V : \bar{v}_t = f_V(t) \tag{3}$$

$$\overline{V} = \bigcup_{t \in T} \bar{v}_t = \{\bar{v}_{t_0}, \bar{v}_{t_1}, \ldots, \bar{v}_{t_n}\} \tag{4}$$

Figure 3 shows a possible resulting graph of the same volume measurement data, using a filter, along with the resulting scaling behavior of the system. When compared to Fig. 2, it becomes clear that the amount of scaling operations has decreased. Note that this approach does not guarantee that the volume is met with correct scaling at each point in time. There is the possibility of under-provisioning for short periods in time, depending on the used filter.

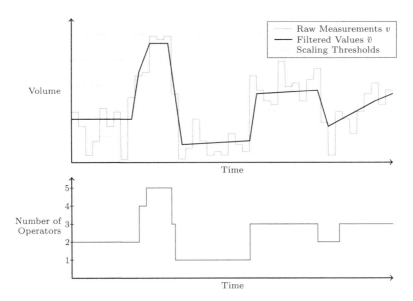

Fig. 3. The same scenario, with additional filtering of volume measurements. Instead of 23 scaling operations, the system only had to perform 7.

4   Implementation

We have implemented the approach described in Sect. 3 in different ways. The most important distinction between these approaches is the type of filter that is being used to reduce the noise in the signal, and to smoothen the time series of observed data volume used for scaling, i.e., the concrete function used for f. Stemming from the field of signal processing, a common approach of separating noise from signal is employing a low-pass filter [5]. We seek to improve the performance regarding detection of edges and separability in the Fourier domain [17] by proposing two non-linear filters: TVD [21] and EKF [15].

4.1   Linear Smoothing

Amongst the most basic methods in signal processing is linear smoothing (LS). Its essence is the smoothing of a noisy signal by setting each time series element to the arithmetic mean of its neighbors. In scenarios where live data is processed, only the past neighbors can be used, i.e., the window is set to *end* at the current element. Therefore, in its general variant, for a time series $v_0, v_1, \ldots, v_n$, and a given window width w, each filtered element $\bar{v}_x$ is set to the following:

$$f_V(t) = \bar{v}_t = \frac{1}{w} \sum_{x=t-w}^{t} v_x \qquad (5)$$

Alternative versions include weights for more recent elements or exponential smoothing. However, since all of those methods essentially build a mean over a window of past elements, we implemented LS as a baseline reference. A major flaw of all LS algorithms is the fact that they do not detect edges well. In the context of elasticity of stream processing, this means that changes in the volume are not detected immediately, and thus scaling operations are delayed by design.

4.2   Total Variation Denoising

A more advanced approach to smoothing is the approach originally proposed in [21], commonly called TVD [22], or ROF, after the authors' names [20]. The basic notion is that the total variation of a signal is to be minimized. Intuitively, TVD aims to remove the variation induced by noise while keeping the denoised signal as close to the original signal as possible, with respect to the least squares distance function. TVD is insensitive to the frequency ranges of noise and signal, making it more suitable to detecting sudden changes in near-real time, compared to linear methods like low-pass and high-pass filters or Fourier transforms.

Similarly to LS, TVD has one hyperparameter. In the case of TVD, this hyperparameter α determines the degree of smoothing. $\alpha = 0$ indicates no smoothing at all, i.e., the output of TVD is equal to its input, while $\alpha \to \infty$ means that more smoothing is performed, and this smoothing converges towards a steady state which is the denoised signal [21].

In its essence, the underlying TVD minimization problem proposed in the original work [21] is based on the assumption that the functional

$$v(x, y) = \bar{v}(x, y) + n(x, y) \tag{6}$$

expresses the raw signal v as a function of the actual (smooth) signal $\bar{v}$, and n, the additive noise[1]. Following this, the minimization problem is stated as a problem of minimizing the variation (i.e., the integral of changes in gradients):

$$\text{minimize} \int_{\Omega} (v_{xx} + v_{yy})^2 \tag{7}$$

where Ω is the variable domain, v_{xx} denotes the second derivative of v with respect to x. Two additional constraints provided in [22], binding the mean and variance of the raw and the reproduced signal to each other, are not shown here.

In our application of TVD, we have no multivariate functions, i.e., our v_0, v and n only depend on one (discrete) variable, which is the time t. Thus, we do not need to apply partial derivations. Since we record discrete, digital measurements, our definition of variation is also discretized and reduced, as shown in (8).

$$\text{minimize} \sum_{x=1}^{n} |v_x - v_{x-1}| \tag{8}$$

---

[1] Note that in the original work [21], the raw measured signal was named u_0, and the filtered signal was named u. We have adapted the names to v and $\bar{v}$, respectively, to maintain consistency within our work.

We have used this minimization problem, together with the original constraints, and applied the majorization-minimization algorithm described in [22], which majorizes the total variation minimization problem by its quadratic function, a methodology described in [7].

4.3   Extended Kalman Filter

The EKF is a nonlinear generalization of the Kalman filter [15]. Kalman type filters work by defining state transition and state observation models, and taking into account the noise and its (co-)variance. Again, since we do not have a multivariate function, we only have one variable, which simplifies the computation.

The EKF is based on the notion that there is a transition model F and an observation model G:

$$\frac{dx}{dt} = F(t)x + G(t)c(t) \tag{9}$$

$$z(t) = H(t)x(t) + n(t) \tag{10}$$

where $F(t)$ denotes the state transition, $G(t)$ is the control (input) transition, $c(t)$ is the control function, i.e., the input applied to a system, and x is the state. $H(t)$ is the observation model, i.e., the measurement transformation, $n(t)$ is the additive noise added to the signal, and z is the observed state[2].

In our application, we have simplified the model in that we do not apply any input to the system, but only observe it. Thus, the entire term $G(t)c(t)$ can be eliminated. As state x in the EKF notation, we have used the current volume (v in our notation), as well as the derivative (i.e., change in time, v') of the current volume. Therefore, in our application of EKF, $x = \begin{bmatrix} v \\ v' \end{bmatrix}$.

The term $z(t)$ from the EKF notation corresponds to the resulting, filtered volume measurement $\bar{v}$ in our notation. We have used this model in order to apply an unknown input to the estimation. In our case, the unknown input is the actual reason for the volume change, which is a factor we are not able to (generally) include in our model. We therefore allow the change in volume v' to be estimated by the EKF filter using only measurable data [8]. As a state transition, we use a matrix applying v' to v, i.e., we assume that without further input, the volume change will be constantly applied to the volume. The source of the change itself is, in this model, part of the noise, i.e., $n(t)$.

5   Evaluation

In order to evaluate our approach, we simulated a stream processing system using the three presented filters (LS, TVD, EKF) with varying input data volumes, and measured the resulting performance.

---

[2] Again, in the original approach [15], the control function is denoted as $u(t)$, and the noise is denoted as $v(t)$. We have changed the names to $c(t)$ and $n(t)$, respectively, in order to avoid overloading and maintain consistency.

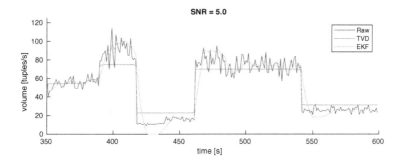

Fig. 4. Excerpt from a simulation with raw volume and filtered values.

To find commonly used and realistic values, we have surveyed literature, and decided to use values from [25]. Following this, we used volumes in the range of 200 to 500 tuples per second, and assumed a scaling threshold was 50 tuples per second. We introduced noise with varying signal-to-noise ratios (SNR). Since the *Rose criterion* states that an SNR of 5 is necessary to discern signal from noise with 100% confidence [24], we used various SNR values near that value for our evaluation (0.5, 0.8, 1.0, 5.0 and 10.0). All experiments were executed for a duration of 1,500 s. Volume measurements and filter applications were performed every second. An example is shown in Fig. 4, where a few characteristics are visible. Most prominently, the piecewise constant nature of TVD can be seen. TVD also visibly misinterprets the mean of certain segments, since TVD depends on the entire history of the data, not only the values of the range shown, and those values influence its operation. For EKF, a certain momentum is visible, with which it reacts to changes in value.

As metrics, we have used the filtered values for scaling decisions, as described in Sects. 3 and 4, and recorded (i) the number of scale-up and scale-down operations, denoted as s^+ and s^-, respectively, and (ii) the amount of time (in seconds) the system spent either over-provisioned, or under-provisioned, denoted as p^+ and p^-, respectively. The resulting metrics from the simulations are shown in Tables 1 and 2 (for SNR $= 0.5$ and 1.0), as well as Tables 3 and 4 (for SNR $= 5.0$ and 10.0). Note that in this work, we did not consider a cost model, but rather recorded the number of scaling operations performed throughout the simulation. For the work at hand, we consider each scaling activity as equally expensive, nevertheless we aim to refine the cost model in our future work.

The primary goal of reducing the frequency of scaling operations (s^+ and s^-) has been reached by both TVD and EKF, in high-noise environments even by over 93% (TVD) and 44% (EKF). However, the results clearly show that regarding scaling performance alone (p^+ and p^-), LS still outperforms EKF and TVD. This was expected, as LS has the tendency to scale without restriction (heavily impacting s^+ and s^-). Nevertheless, we argue that the advantages of reducing scaling frequency outweigh this drawback. For instance, in the case of SNR $= 1.0$, using TVD, a reduction of s^+ and s^- by around 90% causes an increase of p^+ and p^- of only around 8%, i.e., the positive impact in s^+ and s^- is still one order of magnitude higher than the negative impact in p^+ and p^-.

Table 1. Results for SNR = 0.5. Best result per metric printed in **bold**.

Filter	s^+	s^-	p^+	p^-
LS (baseline)	208	209	**262**	**332**
TVD	**13**	**13**	312	335
	−195	−196	+50	+3
EKF	115	114	373	335
	−93	−95	+111	+3

Table 2. Results for SNR = 1.0. Best result per metric printed in **bold**.

Filter	s^+	s^-	p^+	p^-
LS (baseline)	130	130	186	**220**
TVD	**8**	**7**	**154**	224
	−122	−123	+32	+4
EKF	79	78	319	224
	−51	−52	+133	+4

Table 3. Results for SNR = 5.0. Best result per metric printed in **bold**.

Filter	s^+	s^-	p^+	p^-
LS (baseline)	33	32	**54**	**72**
TVD	**7**	**6**	115	86
	−26	−26	+61	+14
EKF	26	25	110	86
	−7	−7	+56	+14

Table 4. Results for SNR = 10.0. Best result per metric printed in **bold**.

Filter	s^+	s^-	p^+	p^-
LS (baseline)	27	26	**44**	**64**
TVD	**7**	**6**	113	73
	−20	−20	+69	+9
EKF	23	22	100	73
	−4	−4	+56	+9

Considering the difference in performance between TVD and EKF, it becomes clear that TVD is a promising approach in high-noise situations, especially if SNR < 1.0. However, with increasing SNR, EKF starts to outperform TVD, especially in p^+ and p^-. We can observe this for SNR = 10.0. From a purely numeric point of view, this means that EKF is the most promising approach in low-noise situations. For s^+ and s^-, however, EKF, does not reach the performance of TVD, even in low-noise (high SNR) situations. However, looking in detail at the excerpt shown in Fig. 4, we also argue that the performance of EKF can be further fine-tuned if the dynamics of the system, expressed in the matrices of EKF, are studied better.

6   Conclusion and Future Work

In this work, we have presented a novel approach of scaling in stream processing systems. Contrary to current state of the art, which uses simple linear filtering to process the volume of incoming data and applies this to make scaling decisions, our approach exploits advanced non-linear filtering methodologies from the field of signal processing to pre-process these volume measurements. This reduces the amount of scaling operations by 15% for low-noise scenarios, and over 94% for high-noise scenarios, while maintaining a comparable provisioning performance.

The two filters presented in detail, TVD and EKF, have been used to show the feasibility of this approach. We therefore propose further research in this area. For EKF, we argue that deeper understanding of the dynamics of volume changes in stream processing would allow for modeling of increasingly precise transformation matrices, further increasing its performance. Therefore, we plan to invest more research into different variations of the EKF parameters, possibly adding QoS metrics from the system itself as inputs for EKF. Furthermore, our next focus is to investigate in detail the computational complexity of our approach, and to use a cost model, similar to existing literature [19]. Finally, we want to evaluate the approach in more detail, and use a real-world data set for the simulation.

Acknowledgements. This work is partially supported by the Commission of the European Union within the CREMA H2020-RIA project (Grant agreement no. 637066) and by TU Wien research funds.

References

1. Abadi, D.J., et al.: The design of the borealis stream processing engine. In: CIDR, vol. 5, pp. 277–289 (2005)
2. Beloglazov, A., Buyya, R.: Energy efficient allocation of virtual machines in cloud data centers. In: International Conference on Cluster, Cloud and Grid Computing, pp. 577–578. IEEE (2010)
3. Buyya, R., Ranjan, R., Calheiros, R.N.: InterCloud: utility-oriented federation of cloud computing environments for scaling of application services. In: Hsu, C.-H., Yang, L.T., Park, J.H., Yeo, S.-S. (eds.) ICA3PP 2010 Part I. LNCS, vol. 6081, pp. 13–31. Springer, Heidelberg (2010). https://doi.org/10.1007/978-3-642-13119-6_2
4. Castro Fernandez, R., et al.: Integrating scale out and fault tolerance in stream processing using operator state management. In: International Conference on Management of Data, pp. 725–736. ACM (2013)
5. Corradi, A., Fanelli, M., Foschini, L.: VM consolidation: a real case based on OpenStack Cloud. Future Gener. Comput. Syst. **32**, 118–127 (2014)
6. Dustdar, S., et al.: Principles of elastic processes. Internet Comput. **15**(5), 66–71 (2011)
7. Figueiredo, M.A.T., et al.: On total variation denoising: a new majorization-minimization algorithm and an experimental comparison with wavelet denoising. In: International Conference on Image Processing, pp. 2633–2636. IEEE (2006)
8. Ghahremani, E., Kamwa, I.: Dynamic state estimation in power system by applying the extended Kalman filter with unknown inputs to phasor measurements. Trans. Power Syst. **26**(4), 2556–2566 (2011)
9. Gong, Z., Gu, X., Wilkes, J.: PRESS: predictive elastic resource scaling for cloud systems. In: International Conference on Network and Service Management (CNSM), pp. 9–16. IEEE (2010)
10. Gulisano, V., et al.: StreamCloud: an elastic and scalable data streaming system. Trans. Parallel Distrib. Syst. **23**(12), 2351–2365 (2012)
11. Heinze, T., et al.: Online parameter optimization for elastic data stream processing. In: Symposium on Cloud Computing, pp. 276–287. ACM, New York (2015)
12. Hochreiner, C., et al.: Elastic stream processing for distributed environments. Internet Comput. **19**(6), 54–59 (2015)

13. Hochreiner, C., et al.: Elastic stream processing for the Internet of Things. In: International Conference on Cloud Computing (CLOUD), pp. 100–107 (2016)
14. Islam, S., et al.: How a consumer can measure elasticity for cloud platforms. In: 3rd International Conference on Performance Engineering, pp. 85–96. ACM/SPEC (2012)
15. Kalman, R.E., Bucy, R.S.: New results in linear filtering and prediction theory. J. Basic Eng. **83**(3), 95–108 (1961)
16. Khan, A., et al.: Workload characterization and prediction in the cloud: a multiple time series approach. In: Network Operations and Management Symposium (NOMS), pp. 1287–1294. IEEE (2012)
17. Little, M.A., Jones, N.S.: Sparse Bayesian step-filtering for high-throughput analysis of molecular machine dynamics. In: International Conference on Acoustics Speech and Signal Processing (ICASSP), pp. 4162–4165. IEEE (2010)
18. Mao, M., Humphrey, M.: Auto-scaling to minimize cost and meet application deadlines in cloud workows. In: International Conference for High Performance Computing, Networking, Storage and Analysis, pp. 1–12. IEEE (2011)
19. Mencagli, G., Vanneschi, M., Vespa, E.: A cooperative predictive control approach to improve the reconfiguration stability of adaptive distributed parallel applications. Trans. Auton. Adapt. Syst. (TAAS) **9**(1), 2 (2014)
20. Micchelli, C.A., Shen, L., Xu, Y.: Proximity algorithms for image models: denoising. Inverse Probl. **27**(4), 45009–45038 (2011)
21. Rudin, L.I., Osher, S., Fatemi, E.: Nonlinear total variation based noise removal algorithms. Phys. D: Nonlinear Phenom. **60**(1–4), 259–268 (1992)
22. Selesnick, I.: Total variation denoising (an MM algorithm). In: NYU Polytechnic School of Engineering Lecture Notes (2012)
23. Shen, Z., et al.: CloudScale: elastic resource scaling for multi-tenant cloud systems. In: 2nd Symposium on Cloud Computing, pp. 5–18. ACM (2011)
24. Thomas, P.J., Midgley, P.A.: Image-spectroscopy-I. The advantages of increased spectral information for compositional EFTEM analysis. Ultramicroscopy **88**(3), 179–186 (2001)
25. Xu, J., et al.: T-storm: traffic-aware online scheduling in storm. In: 34th International Conference on Distributed Computing Systems (ICDCS), pp. 535–544. IEEE (2014)
26. Zhang, Q., Cheng, L., Boutaba, R.: Cloud computing: state-of-the-art and research challenges. J. Internet Serv. Appl. **1**(1), 7–18 (2010)

Container-Based Support for Autonomic Data Stream Processing Through the Fog

Antonio Brogi⬤, Gabriele Mencagli⬤, Davide Neri$^{(\boxtimes)}$⬤, Jacopo Soldani⬤,
and Massimo Torquati⬤

Department of Computer Science, University of Pisa, Pisa, Italy
{brogi,mencagli,davide.neri,soldani,torquati}@di.unipi.it

Abstract. We present a container-based architecture for supporting autonomic data stream processing application on fog computing infrastructures. Our architecture runs applications as Docker containers, and it exploits the native features of Docker to dynamically scale up/down the resources of a fog node assigned to the applications running on it. Preliminary results demonstrate that Docker containers are appropriate for building migratable autonomic solutions on fog infrastructures.

Keywords: Data stream processing · Autonomic computing · Fog
IoT · Docker

1 Introduction

Fog computing [23] aims at distributing computing, storage and networking resources along the cloud-to-IoT continuum, closer to the edge of the network where millions of connected devices produce huge data flows. Many applications (e.g., intelligent transportation, emergency management or e-health) need to process such data flows by meeting compelling time requirements which cannot be satisfactorily met by traditional cloud+IoT solutions, typically because of latency and/or bandwidth limitations [6].

To suitably host autonomic data stream parallel applications on fog infrastructures, new solutions for the dynamic management of resources within and across fog nodes are needed. Container-based virtualisation can help solving this need [18,19], and the objective of this paper is precisely to investigate how to use it to dynamically manage autonomic applications on fog infrastructures.

We present a container-based architecture for supporting autonomic data stream processing applications on fog infrastructures. The architecture exploits containerisation to dynamically scale the resources assigned to each deployed application. Each fog node hosts a fog node controller, which interacts with the controllers of the autonomic applications deployed on such node. The objective of the interaction is to dynamically scale up and down the resources assigned to hosted applications. Fog node controllers of different nodes also interact to support the migration of deployed applications. Fog node controllers and applications are deployed as Docker containers.

© Springer International Publishing AG, part of Springer Nature 2018
D. B. Heras and L. Bougé (Eds.): Euro-Par 2017 Workshops, LNCS 10659, pp. 17–28, 2018.
https://doi.org/10.1007/978-3-319-75178-8_2

The rest of this paper is structured as follows. We first discuss two motivating examples that illustrate needs and benefits of dynamic resource management within/across different fog nodes (Sect. 2). After introducing Docker (Sect. 3), we describe the proposed architecture for supporting data stream processing on fog infrastructures (Sect. 4). We also present the results of two experiments that show the feasibility of the proposed container-based support (Sect. 5). We finally discuss related work (Sect. 6) and we draw some concluding remarks (Sect. 7).

2   Motivating Examples

We hereby describe two basic examples that motivate the development of our architecture. The first example describes a scenario of *intra-fog node* resource management and orchestration, through the synergical interaction between a fog node controller (FNC) and application controllers (ACs), which run the autonomic logic of the streaming applications deployed on such node. The second example focuses on the more complex and challenging case of *inter-fog node* adaptation.

Intra-fog node scenario. Each fog node, besides being interconnected to various data providers (e.g., sensors, IoT and edge devices), can be connected to an overlay of fog nodes and eventually to a traditional cloud system (Fig. 1, left).

Within a fog node, various streaming applications can run. Each streaming application is characterised by (i) a set of data providers that feed the application with a continuous flow of data items to be processed, and (ii) a set of data consumers that will retrieve real-time data analytics produced by the application. We also envision that *each application should be designed with an autonomic logic inside*, responsible for scaling up/down the resources utilised by the application and/or other application-dependent configuration knobs (e.g., load balancing policies, scheduling disciplines). While some reconfigurations are executed transparently to the fog infrastructure, other reconfigurations may need a proper interaction with the FNC (e.g., resource scaling).

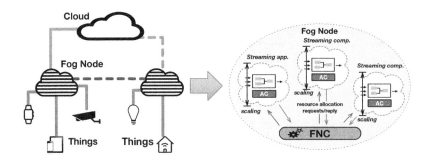

Fig. 1. Fog computing architecture and internal behaviour of a fog node.

Consider an application consuming a data stream generated by a set of mobile devices localised near to a fog node, and processing the most recent data items using a sliding-window model [2] according to a feasible parallel pattern (like those in [8]). To keep up with the arrival rate, the AC of the considered application may decide to increase the parallelism degree of such application in order to process input data faster. While the AC is in charge of reconfiguring the application to exploit additional resources (e.g., by spawning new processes/threads on-demand), the FNC is responsible for making the resources available to respond to the dynamic need of applications. To this end, the FNC is in charge of maintaining a complete vision of the node status (e.g., cores and cpu time available, memory utilisation [3]), and of processing the requests of AC by finding feasible agreements. For example, if the AC requires the exclusive utilisation of eight additional cores, the FNC can serve such request completely, if enough physical resources are available. Otherwise, the FNC can partially serve the request of the AC by allocating fewer cores. As *extrema ratio*, the FNC may *unilaterally* release some cores previously assigned to other running applications to serve completely the request, by informing the corresponding ACs of the decision taken. This scenario is depicted in Fig. 1 (right).

Inter-fog node scenario. Suppose that an application is a composition of two communicating components. The first (called *Filtering*) is a small graph of operators processing items produced by a set of data providers, by discarding inputs that are deemed to be irrelevant to the rest of the application. This component processes data items at high speed, thus it must exploit geographical proximity [21] with the data providers in order to leverage a reduced network cost. Instead, the *Selection* component runs a computationally demanding preference query like a skyline or a top-k query [25], in order to extract the best objects among the most recent data items received from the preceding phase.

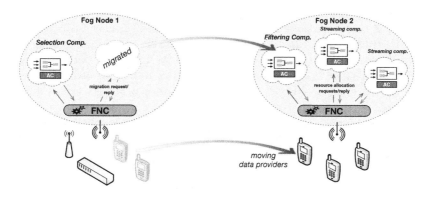

Fig. 2. Example of migration between fog nodes.

The infrastructure should be able to support the migration of streaming components from a fog node to another one properly chosen. This can be the result of an *internal* decision of the application itself, or *externally* triggered by the resource management control of the fog platform. As in the example of Fig. 2, the data providers feeding our *Filtering* component, which is initially deployed on FN1, are mobile devices that may enter in the proximity of FN2 at a certain time instant. The corresponding AC that continuously monitors the component's QoS may experience too high network latency and/or insufficient network bandwidth. Therefore, the AC may opportunistically decide to ask the FNC of FN1 to start the migration to FN2. As a second case, the decision can be triggered by the infrastructure itself, for example if the FNC is unable to meet the resource utilisation requests of the applications running in the first fog node, and some of them must be migrated to make further local resources available. In both cases, the underlying infrastructure should provide mechanisms for seamless migration with minimal intrusion and downtime in the processing flow.

3   Background: Docker

Container-based virtualisation is a lightweight virtualisation technology which provides near-native performances [24]. Container-based virtualisation exploits the kernel of the host OS for running multiple isolated user-space instances (called *containers*). Since containers share the same kernel of the host OS, container-based virtualisation adds minimal overhead to the guest applications.

Docker [9] is the de-facto standard technology exploiting container-based virtualisation. It provides the ability to package any application with all its dependencies (e.g., libraries, binaries, data files, etc.) into an isolated Docker *container*. Docker also (i) permits limiting the resources assigned to a container in term of memory and CPU (by default, a container has no resource constraints), and (ii) it provides functionalities for checkpointing and restoring a running container by exploiting *CRIU* [7,10,20].

A Docker container is created from a Docker *image*. From a single Docker image one or more Docker containers can be started. Docker also permits to look for existing images instead of building them from scratch. The images can be stored into *Docker registries* (e.g., Docker Hub [13]) where other users can retrieve and use them. Docker registries (as well as tools for automatically discovering Docker images—e.g., [4]) ease the distribution of images across different environment.

Docker containers can communicate by using Docker container networking [12]. Two containers attached to the same network can communicate with all other containers attached to the same network. Docker offers various network drivers depending if the containers reside on a single host or across a cluster of hosts. Standard sockets can also be used as low-level mechanisms for implementing a communication channel between containers.

Docker has also built-in orchestration tools to deploy multi-container applications. For instance, *Docker compose* [11] permits creating and managing Docker containers on a single host or in a cluster of hosts.

4 System Architecture

We hereby illustrate the main concepts of the high-level architecture we envision. Such architecture is composed by four main components: Fog nodes (FNs), fog node controllers (FNCs), autonomic applications (Apps), and autonomic application controllers (ACs). A sample instance of our proposal is depicted in Fig. 3.

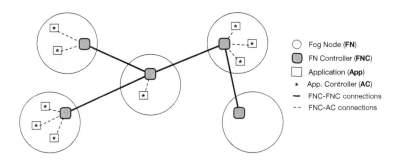

Fig. 3. An example of instance of the proposed architecture.

FNs are devices (e.g., smartphones, laptops, routers) with limited amounts of available computational resources, which are in charge of running containerised Apps. Therefore, FNs must be able to decide whether an App can run on a FN, and how many computational resources to assign to such App (e.g., cores, CPU time, memory, bandwidth). This is why FNs are equipped with FNCs that are in charge of scheduling containerised Apps on FNs and of assigning to each App a certain amount of resources available in the hosting FN.

Each App runs in a Docker container, or alternatively it can be split into various interacting components, each running in a Docker container. Each AC running within a container is also in charge of running the autonomic control loop of the corresponding App or component, and of interacting with the FNC of the corresponding FN to dynamically scale up/down the set of resources assigned to the container, and/or to support the migration to another FN (or to the cloud).

Accordingly, FNCs will have to support both FNC-FNC and FNC-AC communications. FNC-FNC communications are inter-node, hence requiring to be network communications. FNC-AC communications are instead intra-node, hence allowing to reduce communication latency by exploiting a shared memory or domain sockets. The latter seems more promising, as FNCs and ACs run in Docker containers, which can communicate using shared socket files (see Sect. 3).

In the following, we detail the behaviour of the architecture during the execution of the scenarios sketched in Sect. 2, by distinguishing those only concerning fog nodes from those also including autonomic applications[1].

---

[1] Due to space limitations, we hereafter abstract from the actual policies to be employed for coordinating FNCs and for deciding how to schedule containerised Apps within/across FNs depending on available resources.

Fog nodes. Our architecture is designed to account for FNs freely joining or detaching from the system. Whenever a new FN is willing to join the system, its FNC must connect to one or more of the FNCs already available in the system (e.g., those of the "geographically closest" FNs, or those that can guarantee a desired response time). It must then communicate the computational resources available in the new FN, and this information will be taken into account (by all FNCs) when deciding how to schedule containerised Apps within/across FNs. At this point, the new FN is considered to be part of the overlay of FNs, hence being eligible for deploying containerised Apps on it.

Whenever a FN wishes to detach from the system, its FNC should communicate to the other FNCs that such FN is going to detach. This will result in disconnecting FNC of the detaching FN from the overlay of FNs, and in migrating all Apps running on the detaching FN to the other FNs in the system.

It is worth noting that a FN may detach from the system without priorly advertising the FNCs of the other FNs (e.g., because the corresponding device unexpectedly crashes or shuts-down), and this should also result in migrating all Apps that were running on the crashed FN to the other FNs in the system. To enable this, the availability of each FN will have to be monitored (e.g., with watchdogs or heartbeat services connected to its FNC).

Autonomic applications. Data stream processing applications will be deployable on the proposed architecture after being properly containerised as (possibly multi-container) Docker applications. The images of the containers forming an application will have to be available on a remote, publicly accessible Docker registry (e.g., Docker Hub [13]).

The administrator of an application can issue the deployment of her application by connecting to one of the FNCs in the system, and by indicating the Apps to be executed. The administrator indicates the Docker images used to run the Apps along with the deployment constraints of each App. For example, the administrator can constraint the App to be deployed on a certain subset of FNs, or she can specify that the App must be migrated to cloud whenever all the FNs do not satisfy the requested resources by the App.

The FNCs will then coordinate themselves to identify a FN satisfying the deployment constraints of an App, and they will inform the corresponding FNC to enact the deployment of such App. The FNC will then download the image of the App from the remote registry, it will start the App by running a Docker container from the downloaded image, it will assign an initial set of computational resources to the App, and it will start interacting with the AC to scale the resources assigned to the App (when necessary).

A FNC can scale up and down the set of resources assigned to an App (e.g., by decreasing/increasing the cores, CPU time, and bandwidth assigned to such App) by simply changing the resources assigned to the corresponding Docker container (see Sect. 3). This may be driven by exploiting reactive or predictive control policies [17], and it happens: when a FNC needs to remove some of the resources that were assigned to an App and to re-assign such resources to other Apps, or when an AC realises that the App it is controlling requires less/more resources (e.g., to change the parallelism degree and adapt it to the data rate of the input stream). In the latter case, an AC sends a request to the FNC of the hosting FN, which decides how/whether to scale the resources assigned to the corresponding App.

It may happen that the computational resources available in a FN are no more capable of satisfying the requirements of all Apps running on it. If this is the case, the FNC of the overloaded FN will interact with the other FNCs in the system to decide which Apps can be migrated and on which FNs. To migrate them, it then send a migration request to the AC of each App to be migrated. The AC will then start preparing the migration by storing the current state of the App, and it will answer to the FNC by returning it the current state of the App. The FNC of the FN where the App must be migrated will then initiate the procedure for deploying such App, by exploiting the stored state of App as the initial application state.

It may also happen that no FN is capable of satisfying the requirements of a to-be-migrated App. If this is the case, the FNCs can decide to migrate an App to the cloud (with a migration approach very similar to that described above), or to reduce the resources assigned to an App as much as possible (if such App does not support fog-to-cloud migration).

Finally, an App can be undeployed from the system by simply informing the FNC of the FN where such App is running. This can either be done by the AC (if it realises that the App has ended its tasks), or by the administrator of the App. The FNC will then just have to remove the corresponding Docker container, hence freeing the resources assigned to it.

5   Preliminary Results

In this section we show two preliminary results aimed at illustrating that Docker can help deploying autonomic data stream processing applications in the Fog. First, we illustrate how Docker can be exploited by a FNC for limiting the physical resources (viz., CPUs) assigned to a containerised App running on a FN. Second, checkpoint and restore features offered by Docker (version *17.03.1-CE*) are used to freeze and restore a containerised App on a FN[2].

Intra-fog node test. In this first test, we considered a FNC and an App running in Docker containers on a FN. The goal of the experiment is to show (i) how a FNC and the AC of an App can communicate on the same FN, and (ii) how a FNC can exploit Docker for limiting the CPUs assigned to such App. In this perspective, the App and the FNC employed in this test work as follows:

– The App is an autonomic application equipped with its AC that consumes the CPUs of the FN running the *cpuburn* application (https://patrickmn.com/projects/cpuburn/). The AC periodically sends a request to the FNC asking for increasing or decreasing a random number of the CPUs assigned.

---

[2] The source code of the experiments is available on *GitHub*. https://github.com/di-unipi-socc/ffdocker.

- The FNC waits for incoming requests from the AC and (if available) increases or decreases the amount of CPUs assigned to the App.

The FNC and the App reside on the same FN and they communicate using a *socket* file, where the FNC is the server and the App the client.

As we anticipated above, the App and the FNC are shipped in their own Docker containers and their images are stored in the *Docker Hub* registry[3]. The App is packaged into the diunipisocc/app image while the FNC is packaged in the diunipisocc/fnc image. In order to run the experiment, the FNC must be first executed by running the diunipisocc/fnc image with the following command:

```
docker run -v /tmp/ffsocket.sock:/tmp/ffsocket.sock
           -v /var/run/docker.sock:/var/run/docker.sock
           diunipisocc/fnc
```

When the FNC starts, it waits for requests listening on the /tmp/ffsocket.sock socket file. The -v option is used to mount a folder from the host into a container. Instead, the /var/run/docker.sock is the socket used by the FNC for interacting with Docker to update the CPUs assigned to the App container. The App can be launched by running the diunipisocc/app image:

```
docker run  -v /tmp/ffsocket.sock:/tmp/ffsocket.sock
            diunipisocc/app
```

The App mounts the /tmp/ffsocket.sock file for communicating with the FNC.

Figure 4 (left) shows the result of the experiment executed on an Intel Linux machine with 48 cores. In the experiment, the FNC is configured to assign at most 20 cores to the App among the 48 cores available. The App, every 5 s, asks to the FNC to increase or decrease the cores assigned to it by a random number between 5 and 30. If the number of cores requested by the App are less or equal than 20, the FNC assigns to the App the cores requested, otherwise the FNC assign to the App at most 20 cores.

We measured the mean time required by the FNC to increase or decrease the cores assigned to a container. The time measured for updating the cores is about 80 ms with a standard deviation of 16 ms.

Inter-fog node test. In the second experiment we tested the possibility of exploiting Docker for implementing live migration of containers. The current version of Docker only allows to checkpoint and restore a running container into the same host, whereas it does not support live migration across different hosts yet. There are other projects that implements live migration on top of CRIU [1], but they are not yet integrated with Docker.

The experiment reproduces a simplified version of the *inter-fog* scenario proposed in Sect. 2. The *Filtering* component sends an integer every 10 ms (100

---

[3] The Docker images used to run the experiments are available in Docker Hub. https://hub.docker.com/u/diunipisocc/.

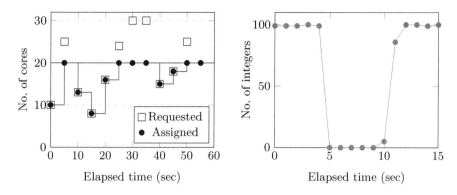

Fig. 4. Results obtained by running the *intra-fog node* experiment (left), and by running the *inter-fog node* experiment (right).

integers per second) to the *Selection* component that receives the stream of integers and prints them. *Selection*, *Filtering* and FNC run in their Docker container and they communicate via the default Docker bridge network (see Sect. 3). In our test we simulated the situation where the FNC checkpoints and restores the *Filtering* component in the same FN, evaluating the downtime experienced by the *Selection* component. This situation can happen, for example, if the FNC decides to temporarily suspend the execution of the *Filtering* component because it needs all the resources available on a Fog node to serve a higher priority request coming from another App.

The FNC triggers the migration of a component using the following steps:

1. The FNC sends a *migration request* to the *Filtering* component, notifying that the migration phase is willing to start.
2. The *Filtering* component receives the *migration request*, performs a clean up phase (e.g., it may notify the data sources to interrupt the data streaming), and sends a *migration reply* to the FNC.
3. The FNC receives the *migration reply* message and performs a checkpoint of the *Filtering* component,
4. Immediately after, the FNC restores the *Filtering* component into the same host and it continues to produce the stream of integers starting from the last checkpointed value.

The checkpoint of the *Filtering* saves both the application internal state (i.e., the last integer sent in the stream) and the sockets used for the communication. Figure 4 (right) shows the result of the execution of the experiment in a single node. The *Selection* component receives 100 integers every second on average. After five seconds the *Filtering* component is forced to perform a migration by the FNC. The downtime experienced by the *Selection* component is about 5 s which is still significant though compliant with the measurements described in https://criu.org/Performance_research. However, the checkpoint and restore mechanisms of Docker are still under development and not yet officially released. We expect to see further optimisations in the next stable releases.

6   Related Work

[21] proposes an architecture for processing streaming applications *near-to-the-edge*. The goal is to deploy latency-sensitive streaming operators near to the IoT devices that generate raw data streams. The infrastructure considers only two tiers, the first being traditional data centers and clouds, and the second featuring *cloudlets* near to IoT devices. The application programmer defines which tier will preferably execute the distinct operators of a streaming application. With respect to our work, the distinction in two tiers seems restrictive, and the applications do not provide any elastic/autonomic support or capability.

Recently, techniques to map streaming applications onto IoT environments have received a considerable attention, because existing IoT platforms still lack of advanced features in terms of dynamic resource management and data privacy that are needed by the streaming context. IoT devices are often considered as mere data providers, at most enabled to filtering the data in order to save network bandwidth. [15] envisions an interesting approach that has several common points with our research. Container-based technologies are used to encapsulate streaming operators and to easily deploy them on a distributed environment. One of the aspects that distinguishes our approach is that each containerised application should have both the processing logic and the autonomic logic inside, the latter directly connected to our infrastructure management entities. This makes each running container an autonomous and adaptive entity, and not a static running code as in [15].

[22] presents *Foglets*, a programming infrastructure for managing geo-distributed awareness applications in the Fog. Based on the mobility of the sensors and the requirements of an application, the paper proposes both algorithms for deploying the application components on the fog nodes and techniques for handling the migration of these components between fog nodes. While, *Foglets* migrates applications whenever the resources they require are no more available in a Fog node, our approach tries to accomplish the application requirements by increasing or decreasing the resources available in a fog node before starting the migration phase.

A nice application scenario has been described in [5] for a urban video surveillance system deployed on a fog infrastructure. The approach follows a divide-and-conquer design, where raw data from IoT devices is filtered by applications running in Fog nodes and forwarded to a centralised cloud for processing. Although an interesting example, the utilisation of the Fog infrastructure is limited and does not exploit the full potential of the paradigm.

Other recent papers mainly focus on extensions of the run-time support of existing and popular stream processing frameworks like Apache Storm and Flink, in order to make the frameworks able to deploy and run streaming applications in geographically distributed environments not limited to a single Cloud [14,16]. Differently, our approach is focused around a two-level adaptation approach, where applications are themselves adaptive with their logic, interacting with our infrastructure for negotiating agreements in the resource utilisation. Therefore, our approach is not limited to a single application running exclusively on the platform, and it is suitable to manage the execution of general applications and services, also outside the stream processing domain.

7 Conclusions

Fog computing is becoming a powerful enabler for IoT. Despite the growing interest, the implications and the advantages of Fog computing in streaming scenarios must still be explored and analysed. Furthermore, the availability of new emerging virtualisation concepts, like container-based technology, stimulates the research of new solutions for efficiently and flexibly deploy streaming applications in geographically distributed environments. In this paper we proposed a Docker-based architecture as an enabler for Fog deployment of autonomic applications. Besides the general overview of our idea, we presented also a concrete discussion of how the Docker technology can be exploited. Finally, first preliminary results confirmed our expectations about Docker as a viable approach for a new highly distributed and fog-oriented framework.

Acknowledgements. This work has been partially supported by the EU H2020-ICT-2014-1 project RePhrase (No. 644235).

References

1. Process HAULer. https://criu.org/P.Haul. Accessed 28 Apr 2017
2. Andrade, H., Gedik, B., Turaga, D.: Fundamentals of Stream Processing. Cambridge University Press, Cambridge (2014). Cambridge Books
3. Bertolli, C., Mencagli, G., Vanneschi, M.: Analyzing memory requirements for pervasive grid applications. In: 2010 18th Euromicro Conference on Parallel, Distributed and Network-Based Processing, Pisa, pp. 297–301 (2010). https://doi.org/10.1109/PDP.2010.71
4. Brogi, A., Neri, D., Soldani, J.: DockerFinder: multi-attribute search of Docker images. In: Proceedings of the 2017 IEEE International Conference on Cloud Engineering, IC2E 2017, pp. 273–278 (2017)
5. Chen, N., Chen, Y., You, Y., Ling, H., Liang, P., Zimmermann, R.: Dynamic urban surveillance video stream processing using fog computing. In: 2016 IEEE International Conference on Multimedia Big Data (BigMM), pp. 105–112 (2016)
6. Chiang, M., Zhang, T.: Fog and IoT: an overview of research opportunities. IEEE Internet Things J. **3**(6), 854–864 (2016)
7. CRIU: Criu integration with docker. https://criu.org/Docker. Accessed 28 Apr 2017
8. Matteis, T., Mencagli, G.: Parallel patterns for window-based stateful operators on data streams: an algorithmic skeleton approach. Int. J. Parallel Program. **45**(2), 382–401 (2017). https://doi.org/10.1007/s10766-016-0413-x
9. Docker Inc.: Docker. https://www.docker.com/. Accessed 28 Apr 2017
10. Docker Inc.: Docker checkpoint command. https://docs.docker.com/engine/reference/commandline/checkpoint/. Accessed 28 Apr 2017

11. Docker Inc.: Docker compose. https://docs.docker.com/compose/. Accessed 28 Apr 2017
12. Docker Inc.: Docker container networking. https://docs.docker.com/engine/userguide/networking/. Accessed 28 Apr 2017
13. Docker Inc.: Docker hub. https://hub.docker.com/. Accessed 28 Apr 2017
14. Hochreiner, C., Vögler, M., Schulte, S., Dustdar, S.: Elastic stream processing for the internet of things. In: 2016 IEEE 9th International Conference on Cloud Computing (CLOUD), pp. 100–107, June 2016
15. Hochreiner, C., Vögler, M., Waibel, P., Dustdar, S.: VISP: an ecosystem for elastic data stream processing for the internet of things. In: 2016 IEEE 20th International Enterprise Distributed Object Computing Conference (EDOC), pp. 1–11, September 2016
16. Mehdipour, F., Javadi, B., Mahanti, A.: FOG-engine: towards big data analytics in the fog. In: 2016 IEEE 14th International Conference on Dependable, Autonomic and Secure Computing, 14th International Conference on Pervasive Intelligence and Computing, 2nd International Conference on Big Data Intelligence and Computing and Cyber Science and Technology Congress (DASC/PiCom/DataCom/CyberSciTech), pp. 640–646, August 2016
17. Mencagli, G., Vanneschi, M.: QoS-control of structured parallel computations: a predictive control approach. In: 2011 IEEE 3rd International Conference on Cloud Computing Technology and Science, Athens, pp. 296–303 (2011). https://doi.org/10.1109/CloudCom.2011.47
18. Pahl, C., Lee, B.: Containers and clusters for edge cloud architectures - a technology review. In: 2015 3rd International Conference on Future Internet of Things and Cloud, pp. 379–386, August 2015
19. Pahl, C., Brogi, A., Soldani, J., Jamshidi, P.: Cloud container technologies: a state-of-the-art review. IEEE Trans. Cloud Comput. (2017, accepted for publication). https://doi.org/10.1109/TCC.2017.2702586
20. Pickartz, S., Eiling, N., Lankes, S., Razik, L., Monti, A.: Migrating LinuX containers using CRIU. In: Taufer, M., Mohr, B., Kunkel, J.M. (eds.) ISC High Performance 2016. LNCS, vol. 9945, pp. 674–684. Springer, Cham (2016). https://doi.org/10.1007/978-3-319-46079-6_47
21. Sajjad, H.P., Danniswara, K., Al-Shishtawy, A., Vlassov, V.: SpanEdge: towards unifying stream processing over central and near-the-edge data centers. In: 2016 IEEE/ACM Symposium on Edge Computing (SEC), pp. 168–178, October 2016
22. Saurez, E., Hong, K., Lillethun, D., Ramachandran, U., Ottenwälder, B.: Incremental deployment and migration of geo-distributed situation awareness applications in the fog. In: Proceedings of the 10th ACM International Conference on Distributed and Event-based Systems, pp. 258–269. ACM, June 2016
23. Shi, W., Dustdar, S.: The promise of edge computing. Computer **49**(5), 78–81 (2016)
24. Soltesz, S., Pötzl, H., Fiuczynski, M.E., Bavier, A.C., Peterson, L.L.: Container-based operating system virtualization: a scalable, high-performance alternative to hypervisors. In: SIGOPS Operating Systems Review (2007)
25. U, L.H., Mamoulis, N., Mouratidis, K.: Efficient evaluation of multiple preference queries. In: 2009 IEEE 25th International Conference on Data Engineering, pp. 1251–1254, March 2009

NOA-AID: Network Overlays for Adaptive Information Aggregation, Indexing and Discovery at the Edge

Patrizio Dazzi[1(✉)] and Matteo Mordacchini[2]

[1] ISTI–CNR, Pisa, Italy
`patrizio.dazzi@isti.cnr.it`
[2] IIT–CNR, Pisa, Italy
`matteo.mordacchini@iit.cnr.it`

Abstract. This paper presents NOA-AID a network architecture for targeting highly distributed systems, composed of a large set of distributed stream processing devices, aimed at adaptive information indexing, aggregation and discovery in streams of data. The architecture is organized on two layers. The upper layer is aimed at supporting the information discovery process by providing a distributed index structure. The lower layer is mainly devoted to resource aggregation based on epidemic protocols targeting highly distributed and dynamic scenarios, well suited to stream-oriented scenarios. We present a theoretical study on the costs of information management operations, also giving an empirical validation of such findings. Finally, we presented an experimental evaluation of the ability of our solution to be effective and efficient in retrieving meaningful information in streams on a highly-dynamic and distributed scenario.

Keywords: IoT · Stream · Adaptivity · Network overlay
Information aggregation in streams · Distributed indexing

1 Introduction

In recent times we are witnessing the emergence of pervasive computational environments in which a huge amount of distributed and heterogeneous devices produce, transmit and/or observe continuous streams of data. Such streams of data needs to be processed to detect faults, issue alerts, and trigger management operations. To achieve an efficient analysis of such data, it is gaining momentum the exploitation of high-performance solutions tailored on recent commodity parallel hardware and accelerators typically available on modern IoT and Edge devices. Even more recently, an increasing interest is coagulating around the methodologies enabling a fruitful cooperation of such devices, which are no longer limited to be independent stream processing entities but pieces of a complex and distributed system. Efficient and effective communication supports for information

© Springer International Publishing AG, part of Springer Nature 2018
D. B. Heras and L. Bougé (Eds.): Euro-Par 2017 Workshops, LNCS 10659, pp. 29–41, 2018.
https://doi.org/10.1007/978-3-319-75178-8_3

gathering, exchange, indexing and querying are of paramount importance in this context. As matter of facts, every information discovery process is strongly correlated to its query formulation and resolution mechanism. The query formulation process has to support an effective way to express needs, whereas the query resolution mechanism must be able to leverage the query expressiveness to efficiently find the information requested and to limit the overhead introduced by the process itself. A common technique for finding data and information, in a highly distributed and dynamic scenario is based on range queries over a set of different attributes [1–5]. However, the heterogeneous nature of distributed devices and the high dynamicity characterizing the information belonging to streams, often makes the task of query formulation very complex. For instance when an information is defined as the combination of many different attributes, it could not be easy to identify the most relevant and discriminating features. An interesting alternative consists in defining a *simulacrum*, representing the archetype of the information sought. This provides to the search system a mean to identify the desired set of information into data streams whilst relieving the requester from specifying complex queries. To this end, the discovery system needs to be organised accordingly. First, there is a need for a search system supporting approximated searches on data streams, enabling the system to deliver the best match against the provided simulacrum. Second, "information providers", which in our case are IoT or Edge devices devoted to stream processing, need an efficient discovery infrastructure, i.e., characterised by a reduced cost of maintenance, while ensuring that information can be easily found by requesters.

To date, several solutions, have been focusing on such approach. They try to let nodes to self-organise to disseminate the information toward groups of interested nodes [6] and/or they let each node to be in direct contact with the ones having similar data [7–12]. However, the local knowledge maintained by each device usually does not allow a proper identification of the features which characterise an entire community of nodes sharing a common set of information. Many existing approaches rely only on the information that each device owns, without providing any explicit identification of groups of nodes that can be considered as a community. This work presents a distributed architecture organised on two layers providing: (i) a flexible query-by-example (the aforementioned simulacrum) discovery mechanism and (ii) a solution for stream processing devices easing the information advertisement process. The focus is on scenarios in which IoT and Edge devices composing the discovery system consist in entities called *Advertising Nodes* (AN). Each AN has an associated succinct description of the information observed by such device: its *profile*. The proposed solution couples the flexibility of unstructured overlays with the power of structured networks. The former offer the advantage of a low maintenance cost, whereas the latter offer more guarantees on finding the requested resources but at the cost of a more expansive maintenance. The rest of this paper is organised as follows. Section 2 presents a review of the relevant literature. Section 3 presents the overall architecture of NOA-AID. Sections 4 and 5 describe the unstructured- and structured-layer, respectively. Section 6 presents the conducted evaluation. Finally, conclusions are given in Sect. 7.

2   Background and Related Work

The challenge of searching for information in highly distributed environment is very current and relevant. In spite of this, many work has been proposed so far. In this section we report some of the most relevant approaches facing this challenge. Multi-Attribute Addressable Network (MAAN) [1] consists in a structured system able to support multi-attribute range queries. In MAAN, items are identified by a set of attribute-value pairs, and each attribute is mapped on a bucket through a locality preserving function. The node target of such function stores the full item description so that each item is stored as many times as the number of its attributes. The resolution of a multi-attribute range query consists in executing a single one-dimensional query on the dominant (i.e. most selective) attribute, while the other attributes are checked using the replicated data. Although MAAN provides a smart routing technique and it has the ability to perform queries on subsets of the whole attributes domain, it requires large amount of memory to store resource indices, and a high computational cost to maintain them up-to-date. This class of solutions requires users to be aware of all the indexed attributes and their respective domains. Making queries exploiting only a small subset of them without specifying the other ones, or not defining the attributes range properly, it may happen that too many results are returned leading the user to iteratively refine her/his queries. More flexible queries can be expressed in DHT-based systems. MCAN [13], exploits the CAN architecture, where, in each dimension, coordinates are given by the distance from a given pivot. Although such solutions allow users to exploit the query-by-example paradigm, these proposals are other examples of ad-hoc solutions, though to be used for searching multimedia objects, and thus are unsuitable for more generic kinds of resources. Pirrò *et al.* [14] show an approach for a semantic-based service discovery in P2P networks. It couples a DHT layer with a SON (Semantic Overlay Network) overlay. Differently from our solution, here a DHT-based network allows peers to publish semantically annotated services. Then a SON is incrementally build by using the interactions between peers within the structured level during the service publication and searching processes. In our solution only the community representatives are registered in the DHT level. To have only a subset of the devices composing the network in the DHT layer leads to reduce the number of messages routed through the DHT to solve a query. GosSkip [15] is a self-organizing and fully distributed gossip overlay that provides a support to data storage and retrieval in highly decentralized environments. It is built using a epidemic protocol that organizes peers to form an ordered double-linked list. In the overlay network each peer is connected in a skip list where connection are similarity based. To this end, each node is associated with a single item of data and it has a name that describes the semantics of the associated object. These names follow a total and deterministic order. As a consequence, the position of an element is fully determined by its name. For information dissemination, its gossip protocol maintains $O(log(N))$ peer states, and has a message routing cost of $O(log(N))$. The association of links to the published object can lead to a very large number of connections. This is especially true in networks where the number of objects shared by each node is large. The main drawback of the above solutions is the lack of a broader, more recognized measure of similarity. Each peer only relies on its local view. Thus, it is not able to determine whether a peer not included in its similarity-based neighbourhood could be regarded as similar with respect to the overall network organization. More effective information dissemination cannot be implemented because peers are not able to determine whether or not there exist between them more latent forms of similarity, even when they do not consider each other as immediate neighbours. Another type of unstructured networks organization is given by Semantic Overlay Networks (SON). Crespo and Garcia-Molina [16] organize peers in clusters of semantically correlated nodes, on the basis of the semantic content of the document they share. Each cluster represent a semantic concept, i.e., peers belong to groups that go beyond their simple neighbourhood. The assignment of peers (and queries) to a given cluster is made using a hierarchical classifier organised as a tree, where each node is a concept. Nodes encountered descending such a tree represent semantic refinements of the concept of their father nodes. A SON is created for each node of tree of concepts. The main disadvantages of this class of solutions is the rigid predefined structure of the SON-based overlay network. Crespo and Garcia-Molina [16] assume that the concept of tree is pre-defined and peers must use the same classifier in order to join a group. We seek to create more dynamic, spontaneous communities, dynamically made by the interactions between nodes and without relying on a priori knowledge on how to classify the shared content.

3   Overall Architecture

The overall architecture of our proposed solution organized on two layers (structured and unstructured networks) and four different kinds of entities (advertising node, community representative, node belonging to the structured layer and requesters) realising the NOA-AID ecosystem. The unstructured layer is based on an highly scalable epidemic protocol, whereas the structured network is based on a properly defined Distributed Hash Table (DHT). The structured layer indexes profiles of Community Representatives (CR). Each CR is elected by a community of Advertising Nodes (AN). Each AN has an associated *profile*, i.e., a set of information continuously extracted during the stream processing phase. The unstructured layer is devoted to build communities by means of a similarity function applied on the profiles describing the data passed through of streaming processing devices. Each community elects its own representative, which is in charge of registering itself on the structured layer, that is the layer to query in order to search for the information sought. The query resolution process is organised on two stages. Firstly, it is queried the structured layer providing it a *simulacrum* of the information searched. This layer returns the CRs that are the closer to the simulacrum. Then, the selected CRs, acting as entry points, percolate the queries inside their own communities to search for ANs that actually satisfy the needs expressed by the query. Profiles are used to compare the information associated to different devices. To build profiles of streaming processing devices, many different functions and profile organizations can be exploited. This both depends on the ultimate aim of the system and on the type of information to manage and index. In this work we assume that the streams are made of textual data, thus the profiles represent collections of words. To measure the similarity between two different profiles, we adopted a slightly modified version of the Jaccard similarity coefficient [17], described in Sect. 5. It has proven to be an effective measure in distributed environments [18]. It is computed as the size of the intersection of two sets divided by the size of their union. However, traditional DHTs, providing mechanisms for exact matches, are not efficient for searching resources in highly heterogeneous and dynamic scenarios. To overcome this limitation, we instrumented our structured network to perform approximate matches between a user query and a community profile. To this end we leveraged a Locality Sensitive Hash (LSH) method. An appropriate representation of profiles is important to tailor an information discovery mechanism to a specific aim or application. However, such investigation is beyond the scope of this paper. In our study we limit our investigation to two profile representation:

- *Weighted Attribute Vector*: a collection of words, weighted according to their relevance with respect to a profile.
- *Attribute Adjacency Matrix* (hereafter Adjacency Matrix): a profile is represented with a weighted word of vector enriched with values estimating the correlation between attributes.

Among the two, the Weighted Attribute Vector is the simplest. It contains all the attributes describing the stream observed by a node along with their relevance weight values. Since it is a composition of all the attributes, the relevance weight value should be computed by taking into consideration all the single attribute values extracted from the stream. The exploitation of the Adjacency Matrix as profiles permits to represent a relational graph between attributes by using the co-occurrences of them in the set of information represented by a device. Each row of the resulting matrix is associated to an attribute $Attr_i$. Each entry j of such a row contains the co-occurrences proportion of $Attr_i$ with an attribute $Attr_j$. The i-th entry of the $Attr_i$'s row simply gives the relevance value associated to $Attr_i$. Entries are zero-valued when there is no relation between the referred pair of attributes.

4   The Unstructured Layer

The lower layer is aimed at the detection and the creation of self-emerging communities made up of Advertising Nodes. This layer is based on the GROUP protocol. GROUP is a protocol we conceived, designed and implemented for building communities in a completely decentralised way. An in-depth presentation of GROUP is beyond the goals of this paper. We refer interested readers to the original paper in which it has been presented and analyzed [19–21]. Here we briefly present its behaviour and approach. Group carries out communities of similar Advertising Nodes by achieving a logic partition $\mathscr{P}_I = \{P_1, \ldots, P_s\}$

of nodes belonging to a network, such that every P_i includes a subset of nodes characterised by similar profiles. Each distinct partition P_i represents a different community. To identify the communities GROUP exploits a distributed voting algorithm on the overlays built by other epidemic protocols. This process is driven by the consensus that a certain AN gathers among the other ANs. Each AN votes for the ANs it considers closer to itself, i.e. the ones with a profile similar to its own. Each elected AN, together with the ANs that contributed to its election, constitute a community, which is identified by the profile of the elected node.

5   Structured Layer

GROUP enables the creation, in a self-emerging, distributed way, of communities made of devices characterized by similar profiles, namely "communities" of similar data streams. However, the protocol does not provide any support for indexing such communities. To overcome this limitation, we introduce a further layer to our architecture. The idea is to provide a distributed index based on a DHT specifically instrumented to perform approximate matches between a query and a community profile. The approximate search is obtained by exploiting a Locality Sensitive Hash (LSH) approach. This approach allows to find the community of data streams that is the closest one to that provided by means of a simulacrum. In fact, traditional DHTs are very efficient to support the search for exact uni-dimensional data, but they are not conceived for supporting approximate searches. The idea for achieving a support for approximated multi-attribute searches on DHTs has been initially proposed by Zhu [18]. The approach consists in applying the Locality-Sensitive Hashing (LSH) method [22], Specifically, a family of hash functions $\mathcal{H} \in \mathbb{R}^d$ is locality-sensitive if, given a random hash function $h \in \mathcal{H}$, for any pair of points $a, b \in \mathbb{R}^d$ and a distance threshold r, we have:

- if $\|a - b\| \leq r$ then $Pr[h(a) = h(b)] \geq p_1$
- if $\|a - b\| \geq r$ then $Pr[h(a) = h(b)] \leq p_2$

In other words, fixed $p_1 > p_2$ the hash function allows to map with high probability a and b in the same bucket if they are very close (according to a given threshold r) or in different buckets if they are quite different. A detailed description of LSH can be found in the paper of Antoni and Indyk [23]. In this paper we exploit LSH as a mechanism for supporting efficient approximated searches in DHTs. In particular, for each profile we create n different indices, which are used to register a profile in a DHT. A submitted query is first indexed with the same LSH method. Then the community representatives' profiles registered under the same indices are retrieved and compared against the query in order to carry out the most similar representatives. Finally, such representatives forward the query to the related community of devices that likely manipulated a data stream close to the one represented by the simulacrum provided as a query. In order to exploit the potentials of this indexing mechanism, we test this structured layer with the two different types of profile representations described in Sect. 3.

All of them are built starting from the attributes collections characterizing the profile of a node. Clearly, to compare two profiles (and queries against profiles), proper similarity functions must be used. For the Weighted Attribute Vectors profile model we use the following function:

$$SIM_V(P_1, P_2) = \frac{\sum\limits_{obj \in P_1 \cap P_2} min\left[W_1(obj), W_2(obj)\right]}{max(|P_1|, |P_2|)} \tag{1}$$

where P_1 and P_2 are the two profiles to compare, and $W_1(obj), W_2(obj)$ are the weights associated to obj within P_1 and P_2, respectively. Like the Jaccard similarity measure, this similarity is computed only on the intersection of the attributes shared by P_1 and P_2. For each of them the minimum weight is considered. The sum of all those values is weighted with the size of the largest profile. This is done in order to avoid having a high similarity degree even in case of a profile is completely or largely contained in the other, or even when it represents only a small subset of other profiles. In order to compare matrix-based profiles, i.e. when Adjacency Matrices is used, the previous formula is changed in:

$$SIM_M(P_1, P_2) = \frac{\sum\limits_{obj \in P_1 \cap P_2} \left[min\left(W_1(obj), W_2(obj)\right) \cdot \delta_{Rel}(obj)\right]}{max(|P_1|, |P_2|)} \tag{2}$$

where

$$\delta_{Rel}(obj) = \frac{\sum\limits_{obj' \in P_1 \cap P_2} min\left(Rel_1(obj, obj'), Rel_2(obj, obj')\right)}{\max\limits_{i=1,2} |\{obj' \in P_1 \cap P_2 | \exists Rel_i(obj, obj')\}|}$$

In such a case, in addition to the two profiles sizes and attribute weights, we exploit the function $\delta_{Rel}(\cdot)$. It measures the degree of relationship of each attribute of the Adjacency Matrices-based profile, with the other ones. More precisely, given an object obj, we consider only the attributes that are in the P_1 and P_2 intersection. For each attribute we consider the sum over the minimum relevance weights existing in the two profiles. The relevance with an object obj' is given by the function $Rel(\cdot, \cdot)$. This sum is weighted with the maximum size of the set of objects having a relation with obj. Note that using an adjacency matrix, this set has the same size on both profiles, because all objects are considered to have a relation, even when they have a value equals to 0. In order to analyse the advantages deriving by the usage of all profile models, we performed a theoretical comparison between two different solutions, also comparing the LSH approach against a naive solution that would work by indexing, storing and retrieving every attribute of each profiles.

Theoretical Analysis. Table 1 shows the theoretical costs computed considering the LSH indexing approaches when applied to index node profiles expressed according to *Weighted Attribute Vector* and *Adjacency Matrix* profiles. Such costs are computed as function of the number of profiles' attributes, namely a cost $O(n)$ means n times the amount of memory required to store (or transfer) an attribute. In our analysis $|P|$ indicates the number of attributes composing a profile. X indicates the number of peers composing the DHT network, *Com* the total number of registered communities (i.e. groups of similar data streams). k is the maximum number of profiles returned by a node of the DHT when it resolves a query. R is the number of accesses performed to update the DHT when a community profile changes. Each access removes a copy of a community profile at a certain key (corresponding to a profile attribute) that is no longer contained in the community profile. n indicates the number of LSH identifiers associated with each profile.

Table 1. Complexity analysis for indexing profiles.

Operation	Profile	LSH cost	Naive cost
Query	A.M.	$O(n \cdot \frac{|P^2|}{2} \cdot \log(X))$	$O(\frac{|P^3|}{2} \cdot \log(X))$
	T.V.	$O(n \cdot |P| \cdot \log(X))$	$O(|P|^2 \cdot \log(X))$
Query resolution	A.M.	$O(k \cdot \frac{|P|^2}{2} \cdot n)$	$O(k \cdot \frac{|P|^3}{2})$
	T.V.	$O(k \cdot |P| \cdot n)$	$O(k \cdot |P^2|)$
Community insertion	A.M.	$O(n \cdot \frac{|P|^2}{2} \cdot \log(X))$	$O(\frac{|P|^3}{2} \cdot \log(X))$
	T.V.	$O(n \cdot |P| \cdot \log(X))$	$O(|P|^2 \cdot \log(X))$
Profile update	A.M.	$O((n \cdot \frac{|P|^2}{2} + R) \cdot \log(X))$	$O((\frac{|P|^3}{2} + R) \cdot \log(X))$
	T.V.	$O(n \cdot |P| + R) \cdot \log(X))$	$O((|P|^2 + R) \cdot \log(X))$
Descriptor removal	A.M.	$O(n \cdot \log(X))$	$O(|P| \cdot \log(X))$
	T.V.	$O(n \cdot \log(X))$	$O(|P| \cdot \log(X))$
Index size	A.M.	$O(n \cdot \frac{|P|^2}{2} \cdot Com)$	$O(\frac{|P|^3}{2} \cdot Com)$
	T.V.	$O(n \cdot |P| \cdot Com)$	$O(|P|^2 \cdot Com)$

Weighted Attribute Vector model. Following the **naive** approach, searching for a profile to requires to send to the DHT a request for each profile's attribute. Thus, the generation of $O(|P|^2 \cdot \log(X))$ messages. This derives from the DHT logarithmic routing approach: for each attribute a profile copy is transferred to a logarithmic subset of the set of nodes realising the DHT. Each queried node answers by sending a message of $O(k \cdot |P|)$ elements to the k communities with a profile that is similar to the received query. As a consequence the total amount of messages exchanged is $O(k \cdot |P^2|)$. The creation of the distributed index requires, for each community, to store a copy of its profile, for each profile's attribute. This leads to $O(|P|^2 \cdot Com)$ messages. When a community profile changes, the index is updated, $|P|$ copies of the new profile are sent, one for each profile's attribute. Moreover, R additional notifications are sent, one for each attribute that is no longer part of the community profile, aimed at removing old community's profiles. As a consequence, the number of exchanged messages is equal to $O(|P|^2 \cdot \log(X) + R \cdot \log(X))$. Storing a new profile requires to sent $|P|$ copies of that profile, one for each profile's attribute. Consequently, the total amount of generated messages is equal to $O(|P|^2 \cdot \log(X))$. Removing a community profile requires to send $|P|$ messages, which correspond to the number of profile's attributes that equals to $O(|P| \cdot \log(X))$; Using the **LSH** model a community search requires to generate a query for each one of the n LSH identifiers computed for a peer profile. As a consequence the generated number of messages is independent by the number of attributes within a community's profile. Since any message contains a community profile, the total number of generated messages is equal to $O(n \cdot |P| \cdot \log(X))$. Like the naive solution, to answer a query each peer sends a message having a maximum size equal to $(k \cdot |P|)$, but only n nodes of the DHT are involved. This leads to a total amount of generated messages of $O(n \cdot k \cdot |P|)$. The number of profile copies stored along the distributed index is equal to the number of the n LSH identifiers associated to a community's profile. This implies that the total number of generated messages for storing the whole distributed index is equal to $O(n \cdot |P| \cdot Com)$. When a community profile is updated, the DHT is requested to store n copies of the new profile, leading to an equivalent number of profiles to transfer, and, in the worst case, other n requests of profile removal are generated for deleting the old profile. However, due to the LSH properties the number of identifiers exchanged between the old and new profile is less than n on average. Then, the overall number of generated messages for updating a community profile is $O(n \cdot |P| \cdot \log(X) + n \cdot \log(X))$. The removal of a community descriptor requires to send n messages that generate a number of exchanged messages equal to $O(n \cdot \log(X))$.

Attribute Adjacency Matrix model. When a profiles is structured as an adjacency matrix, its behaviour in terms of complexity, for the various operations, is pretty similar to the Weighted Attribute Term Vector model. The only notable difference is on the amount of information required to represent the profile. In this case it goes from $|P|$ to $\frac{|P|^2}{2}$. As a consequence, almost all the complexities are scaled of a factor $\frac{|P|}{2}$, with the only exception on the removal of a descriptor, that is not directly proportional to the profile size but on the number of attributes.

6   Evaluation

The focus of our solution is on enabling approximate queries over textual data (coming from data streams) in a distributed system based on IoT and Edge devices. To this end, we firstly, we measured the ability of our system to maintain high-quality community representatives (representatives of a collection of data streams) when the indexed data changes. Figure 1 shows the average similarity of community members with the selected representatives, and with the other members of the same community. This experiment has been conducted by varying the actual composition of the information extracted by the stream processing devices starting from the simulation cycle #50. Every cycle we changed the 5% of the information content of a randomly selected set representing the 2% of the nodes. As can be observed, the similarity of nodes with their representative is essentially not affected by the changes. Thus the system is able to adaptively react to changes. Then, we analyse the ability of our system to

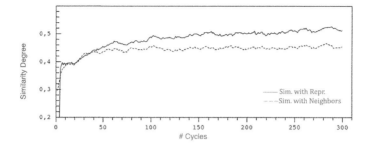

Fig. 1. Dynamic behaviour: internal homogeneity of communities

efficiently resolve textual queries in a distributed fashion. This evaluation is made in comparison against ERGOT [14]. ERGOT is a DHT-based Semantic Overlay Network aimed at service discovery structured on two layers (structured and unstructured). The main difference with our solution relies on the actual viewpoint. They use a DHT-based structured layer as lower-layer and a semantic-based unstructured network as higher-layer. To conduct an effective comparison we directly contacted the authors of ERGOT that provided us the dataset they used in their evaluation, the source code of their proposed solution and the complete set of information about the configuration of their testing environment. The dataset has been built by exploiting the WordNet ontology and the WordNet domain [24]. It consists of 200 domains labels organized in a hierarchical structure that categorizes WordNet synsets into domains. The content of this dataset has been used for generating textual descriptions, which has been assigned to profiles according to a Zipf distribution. The evaluation has been focused on the ability of retrieving relevant profiles given an input query.

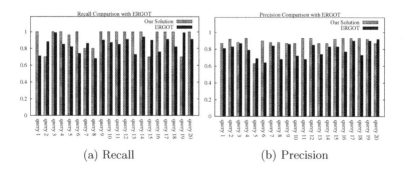

(a) Recall   (b) Precision

Fig. 2. Comparison against ERGOT

A result has been considered as *relevant* if its degree of similarity with the query is greater than 0.5. For achieving a fair trial, in our evaluation we compared the results obtained by ERGOT and NOA-AID, using the set of 20 queries presented in the original paper of ERGOT. Figure 2a shows the comparison between the results achieved by ERGOT and the ones provided by NOA-AID in terms of Recall. The Recall value for a given query has been computed as the ratio of the number of relevant profiles obtained on the total number of relevant results existing in the system. It can be noticed how our solution provides better results in almost all the submitted queries. Figure 2b shows the results obtained for the Precision metric by the two approaches. Precision has been computed as the ratio of the number of relevant peer profiles retrieved on the total number of profiles returned. Also in this case using our solution provide a clear advantage with respect to ERGOT in almost all cases. To validate the efficiency of our proposed system in providing access to the information sought by a requester (simulacrum describing the data stream), while minimizing the amount of data transferred through the network, we measure the actual cost associated with the LSH-based indexing and query resolution techniques. Their performance are strongly relevant for resource-constrained devices, like the ones we are focusing in this paper. Table 2 reports both the amount of data needed for storing the whole index of the communities as well as the communication costs associated with the query resolution process. Results are compared against the Naive solution. As can be observed, the experimental results validate the expected theoretical behaviour, following from the evaluation presented in Sect. 5.

Table 2. Comparison of the theoretical load with the actually measured one.

	Parameters	Naive	NOA-AID	Exp. Gain	Meas. Gain
Index size					
Term vector	n = 15; P = 300	3064	148	20	20.6
	n = 20; P = 300	3064	190	15	16.11
Adj. Matrix	n = 15; P = 300	257557	12728	20	20.2
	n = 20; P = 300	257557	16970	15	15.2
Query resolution					
Term vector	n = 15; P = 300	22165	1210	20	18.3
	n = 20; P = 300	22165	1544	15	14.35
Adj. Matrix	n = 15; P = 300	1572155	78684	20	19.98
	n = 20; P = 300	1572155	104810	15	15

7   Conclusions

In this paper, we propose NOA-AID, a network architecture aimed at providing a flexible query-by-example indexing and discovery mechanism targeting stream processing devices belonging to a highly dynamic and distributed environments. It is based on two overlay networks. At the lower level lies an unstructured, epidemic-based, network able to autonomously adapt and self-organize, aimed at grouping stream processing devices, collecting an heterogeneous set of information, into communities. The higher network layer indexes such communities and provides a query-by-example solution easing their discovery. We provided both a theoretical as well as a experimental evaluation of the approach showing its effectiveness and efficiency.

References

1. Cai, M., Frank, M., Chen, J., Szekely, P.: MAAN: a multi-attribute addressable network for grid information services. J. Grid Comput. **2**(1), 3–14 (2004)
2. Chang, R.S., Hu, M.S.: A resource discovery tree using bitmap for grids. Future Gener. Comput. Syst. **26**, 29–37 (2010)
3. Marzolla, M., Mordacchini, M., Orlando, S.: A P2P resource discovery system based on a forest of trees. In: 17th International Workshop on Database and Expert Systems Applications (DEXA 2006), pp. 261–265 (2006)
4. Mordacchini, M., Ricci, L., Ferrucci, L., Albano, M., Baraglia, R.: Hivory: range queries on hierarchical voronoi overlays. In: IEEE Tenth International Conference on Peer-to-Peer Computing (P2P2010). IEEE, pp. 1–10 (2010)
5. Gennaro, C., Mordacchini, M., Orlando, S., Rabitti, F.: Mroute: a peer-to-peer routing index for similarity search in metric spaces. In: Proceedings of the 5th International Workshop on Databases, Information Systems and Peer-to-Peer Computing (DBISP2P 2007), pp. 1–12 (2007)
6. Bruno, R., Conti, M., Mordacchini, M., Passarella, A.: An analytical model for content dissemination in opportunistic networks using cognitive heuristics. In: Proceedings of the 15th ACM International Conference on Modeling, Analysis and Simulation of Wireless and Mobile Systems. ACM, pp. 61–68 (2012)
7. Liu, L., Antonopoulos, N., Mackin, S., Xu, J., Russell, D.: Efficient resource discovery in self-organized unstructured peer-to-peer networks. Concurr. Comput. Pract. Exp. **21**, 159–183 (2009)
8. Ruffo, G., Schifanella, R.: A peer-to-peer recommender system based on spontaneous affinities. ACM Trans. Internet Technol. **9**, 4:1–4:34 (2009)
9. Baraglia, R., Dazzi, P., Guidi, B., Ricci, L.: Godel: Delaunay overlays in P2P networks via gossip. In: IEEE 12th International Conference on Peer-to-Peer Computing (P2P). IEEE, pp. 1–12 (2012)
10. Mordacchini, M., Dazzi, P., Tolomei, G., Baraglia, R., Silvestri, F., Orlando, S.: Challenges in designing an interest-based distributed aggregation of users in P2P systems. In: 2009 International Conference on Ultra Modern Telecommunications & Workshops, ICUMT 2009. IEEE, pp. 1–8 (2009)
11. Danelutto, M., Dazzi, P., et al.: A Java/Jini framework supporting stream parallel computations. In: PARCO, pp. 681–688 (2005)
12. Lulli, A., Ricci, L., Carlini, E., Dazzi, P., Lucchese, C.: Cracker: crumbling large graphs into connected components. In: 2015 IEEE Symposium on Computers and Communication (ISCC). IEEE, pp. 574–581 (2015)
13. Falchi, F., Gennaro, C., Zezula, P.: Nearest neighbor search in metric spaces through content-addressable networks. Inf. Process. Manag. **43**(3), 665–683 (2007)
14. Pirrò, G., Talia, D., Trunfio, P.: A DHT-based semantic overlay network for service discovery. Future Gener. Comput. Syst. **28**(4), 689–707 (2012)

15. Guerraoui, R., Sidath, B., Kermarrec, A., Fessant, F.L., Huguenin, K., Rivière, E.: GosSkip, an efficient, fault-tolerant and self organizing overlay using gossip-based construction and skip-lists principles. In: Sixth IEEE International Conference on Peer-to Peer Computing, 2006 Ratnasamy, pp. 12–22 (2001)

16. Crespo, A., Garcia-Molina, H.: Semantic overlay networks for P2P systems. In: Moro, G., Bergamaschi, S., Aberer, K. (eds.) AP2PC 2004. LNCS (LNAI), vol. 3601, pp. 1–13. Springer, Heidelberg (2005). https://doi.org/10.1007/11574781_1

17. Tan, P.N., Steinbach, M., Kumar, V.: Introduction to Data Mining, 1st edn. Addison-Wesley Longman Publishing Co., Inc., Boston (2005)

18. Zhu, Y., Hu, Y.: Efficient semantic search on DHT overlays. J. Parallel Distrib. Comput. **67**(5), 604–616 (2007)

19. Baraglia, R., Dazzi, P., Mordacchini, M., Ricci, L.: A peer-to-peer recommender system for self-emerging user communities based on gossip overlays. J. Comput. Syst. Sci. **79**(2), 291–308 (2013)

20. Baraglia, R., Dazzi, P., Mordacchini, M., Ricci, L., Alessi, L.: GROUP: a gossip based building community protocol. In: Balandin, S., Koucheryavy, Y., Hu, H. (eds.) NEW2AN/ruSMART -2011. LNCS, vol. 6869, pp. 496–507. Springer, Heidelberg (2011). https://doi.org/10.1007/978-3-642-22875-9_45

21. Carlini, E., Dazzi, P., Mordacchini, M., Ricci, L.: Toward community-driven interest management for distributed virtual environment. In: an Mey, D., et al. (eds.) Euro-Par 2013. LNCS, vol. 8374, pp. 363–373. Springer, Heidelberg (2014). https://doi.org/10.1007/978-3-642-54420-0_36

22. Gionis, A., Indyk, P., Motwani, R.: Similarity search in high dimensions via hashing. In: Proceedings of the International Confernece on Very Large Data Bases, pp. 518–529 (1999)

23. Andoni, A., Indyk, P.: Near-optimal hashing algorithms for approximate nearest neighbor in high dimensions. Commun. ACM **51**(1), 117–122 (2008)

24. Bentivogli, L., Forner, P., Magnini, B., Pianta, E.: Revising wordnet domains hierarchy: semantics, coverage, and balancing. In: Proceedings of COLING 2004 Workshop on Multilingual Linguistic Resources, pp. 101–108 (2004)

Nornir: A Customizable Framework for Autonomic and Power-Aware Applications

Daniele De Sensi$^{(\boxtimes)}$, Tiziano De Matteis, and Marco Danelutto

Department of Computer Science, University of Pisa, Pisa, Italy
{desensi,dematteis,marcod}@di.unipi.it

Abstract. A desirable characteristic of modern parallel applications is the ability to dynamically select the amount of resources to be used to meet requirements on performance or power consumption. In many cases, providing explicit guarantees on performance is of paramount importance. In streaming applications, this is related with the concept of *elasticity*, i.e. being able to allocate the proper amount of resources to match the current demand as closely as possible. Similarly, in other scenarios, it may be useful to limit the maximum power consumption of an application to do not exceed the power budget. In this paper we propose NORNIR, a customizable C++ framework for autonomic and power-aware parallel applications on shared memory multicore machines. NORNIR can be used by autonomic strategy designers to implement new algorithms and by application users to enforce requirements on applications.

Keywords: Autonomic · Power-aware · Quality of Service
Framework

1 Introduction

Nowadays, sensors, social network interactions and heterogeneous devices interconnected in the *Internet of Things* are continuously producing unbounded streams of data. In *Data Stream Processing* applications, this flow of information must be gathered and analyzed "on the fly" in order to produce timely responses. Systems for high-frequency trading, health-care, network security and disaster managements are typical examples: a massive flow of data must be processed in real-time to detect anomalies and take immediate actions.

Usually, the development of stream processing applications requires to exploit parallel and distributed hardware in order to meet *Quality of Service* (QoS) requirements of high throughput (i.e. applications must be able to cope with high volume of incoming data) and low latency (i.e. results must be computed in a short period of time). Due to their long-running nature (24 h/7 days), stream processing applications are naturally affected by "ebbs and flows" in the input rate and workload characteristics. These variations need to be sustained to provide the QoS required by the users without interruptions. However, run as fast

© Springer International Publishing AG, part of Springer Nature 2018
D. B. Heras and L. Bougé (Eds.): Euro-Par 2017 Workshops, LNCS 10659, pp. 42–54, 2018.
https://doi.org/10.1007/978-3-319-75178-8_4

as possible is not a viable solution in a world in which power consumption management has become a major concern for data centers due to economic cost, reliability problems and environmental reasons. In other cases, explicitly application's power consumption may be useful to do not exceed the available power budget. Not being able to enforce such requirement may lead to hardware failures and to a system outage. *Autonomicity* (sometimes referred as *adaptivity* or *elasticity*) is a fundamental feature: applications must be able to autonomously adjust their resources usage (i.e. their *configuration*) to accommodate dynamic requirements and workload variations by maintaining the desired QoS in terms of performance and/or power consumption.

Existing Stream Processing Systems (SPSs) fall short in handling this problem. Delegating the decisions to the user (like in [1]) or to applications (as in [19]) are not wise decisions since they will require a human intervention or a deep knowledge of the parallel computation to the application programmer. On the other hand, in the literature there are plenty of proposals of autonomic algorithms (e.g. [6,10,11,17,18]). Implementing such strategies is a cumbersome and error-prone duty for the application programmer, that has to deal with many architectural low-level issues related to hardware mechanisms management like voltage, frequency, cores topology, etc. Even interfacing with applications in order to collect monitoring data may not be an easy task. Indeed, in many cases the proposed strategies are only simulated or, even when actually implemented, they are embedded inside the application code and it is very difficult to port them on different applications. For these reasons, we believe that providing a customizable framework would allow the autonomic strategies designers to just focus on the algorithm, exploiting the infrastructure provided by the framework to collect the data and to apply the decisions. This is a fundamental step for building efficient autonomic techniques and for their wide adoption.

In this paper, we propose NORNIR, a customizable C++ framework for autonomic and power-aware parallel applications on shared memory multicore machines[1]. Our focus is on applications composed by a single, parallel functionality (an *operator*). The support for applications that can be expressed as the composition of different operators will be included in future releases of the framework. NORNIR can be used by different actors:

- Autonomic strategy *designers* can customize every aspect of NORNIR: the monitoring, the management of hardware mechanisms and the planning policies. The designer can just focus on the implementation of his new autonomic strategy by using the provided set of resource management mechanisms and the application monitoring infrastructure. *Designers* can develop strategies to explicitly control power consumption, performance or both of them.
- Application *programmers* can use it to interface an already existing application to NORNIR. NORNIR also provides a programming interface for parallel applications, to be used if the application needs to be written from scratch.

---

[1] The framework is released under open source license and publicly available at http://danieledesensi.github.io/nornir/.

– Application *users* specify requirements on performance and/or power consumption of their applications. NORNIR will be in charge of monitoring the application execution and selecting its appropriate configuration (e.g. number of cores, clock frequency, etc.) to enforce the imposed requirements.

Currently, different state of the art autonomic techniques have been already implemented in NORNIR, allowing the algorithm *designer* to compare his new algorithm with other existing ones.

The paper is organised as follows. In Sect. 2 we outline the related work. In Sect. 3 we describe how the *user* can express requirements on his application by using NORNIR. In Sect. 4 we show how the *programmer* can interface a new or an existing application to NORNIR and Sect. 5 describes how NORNIR can be customised by autonomic strategies *designers*. Some experimental results will be shown in Sect. 6 and conclusions are eventually drawn in Sect. 7.

2   Background and Related Work

An autonomic or autonomic system is able to alter his behavior according to QoS requirements and to the surrounding conditions in order to achieve some goal, without any human intervention. Altering the behavior usually implies changing the *configuration* of the application, e.g. the amount of used resources.

Existing algorithms are usually time-driven and, at each time step, act by following a generic *Monitor-Analyze-Plan-Execute* (MAPE) loop [14]. In the *Monitor* phase, various measurements are collected from the application (e.g. performance and power consumption). In the *Analyze* phase monitored data, collected at the current and previous time steps, is compared against the user's requirements. If requirements are violated, the *Plan* phase a new optimal resources allocation will be computed. This planned decision is communicated to the *Execute* phase, that applies the new resources allocation to the application.

Different autonomic strategies have been proposed, to satisfy user's requirements in terms of performance [11,16–18], power consumption [10] or both of them [6,9]. Such requirements are usually enforced even in presence of workload fluctuations or external interferences. However, in many cases, these techniques are only simulated or implemented for specific applications.

In literature, some proposed framework target a problem similar to the one we are addressing in this work [12,15,20]. However, they provide very limited customization opportunities, are quite outdated and the source code is not publicly available. Moreover, they do not provide any explicit support for streaming applications. The work most similar to ours is *SEEC* [13]. In this work, the authors describe the design of a framework for self-aware computing. Such framework is customizable, allowing the autonomic strategy *designer* to specify custom monitoring and execution mechanisms. Nevertheless, there are some limitations with respect to our work. First of all, there isn't an explicit concept of *stream*. As shown in [9] this can lead to unnecessary reconfigurations, since it would not be possible to know whether workload fluctuations are caused by intrinsic changes in the application or by changes in the arrival rate of data to the application. In addition to this SEEC allows the customisation of the *Monitor* and *Execute* parts but provides its own *Plan* algorithm. Albeit being a flexible strategy, it is not possible to replace it with a different one. On the other hand, in NORNIR this aspect is customizable as well. This is an important feature since allows the strategy *designer* to quickly prototype and validate his own planning strategies and to easily compare it with other existing ones. Lastly, the implementation of the *SEEC* framework is not publicly available.

3   User

The *user* needs to detail which kind of constraints should be enforced by NORNIR on his application by specifying them through an XML file. Requirements can be expressed on the metrics reported in Table 1.

Table 1. Parameters that can be controlled by the *user*. $\varpropto$ = Meaningful only if the stream has finite size. The *user* needs to specify the expected stream length.

Metric	S	Description
Bandwidth	B	Number of stream elements processed per second (number of iterations executed per second for non streaming, iterative, applications)
Latency	L	Time required to process a single stream element
Completion time	T	Time required to process all the elements on the stream$^\varpropto$
Utilisation factor	ρ	Percentage of time spent doing useful work (i.e. processing stream elements). $100 - \rho$ is the percentage of time wasted by the application waiting for new data to arrive from the stream
Power consumption	P	Since current operating systems don't provide mechanisms to monitor the individual power consumption of each application, this may correspond to the system level power consumption
Energy	E	Power integrated over time$^\varpropto$

Despite the target of this work is towards Data Stream Processing applications, NORNIR can manage generic iterative applications, for example by enforcing requirements on the latency of one iteration or on power consumption. It is possible to express constraints on more than one metric at the same time, for example by asking NORNIR to find the configuration characterized by the lowest power consumption among those with a bandwidth higher than a certain threshold. Similarly, the *user* can ask NORNIR to find the most performing configuration among those characterized by a power consumption lower than a specified bound.

The XML file can also be used to specify other parameters, like the autonomic strategy to be used, on which executors NORNIR should operate, the duration of the MAPE step (i.e. the *control step*), etc. The following code snippet shows a configuration file example, used to ask NORNIR to find the best performing configuration characterised by a power consumption lower than 50 W and using a control step of 500 ms:

```
<?xml version="1.0" encoding="UTF-8"?>
<nornirParameters>
    <requiredBandwidth>MAX</requiredBandwidth>
    <powerBudget>50</powerBudget>
    <samplingIntervalSteady>500</samplingIntervalSteady>
</nornirParameters>
```

4 Application Programmer

A controlled parallel application is coupled with a MANAGER, which is in charge of executing the MAPE control loop. The MANAGER runs in a separate thread/process and interacts with the application to gather monitoring data and to apply reconfiguration decisions (e.g. changing the number of threads) to enforce the user's requirements.

NORNIR offers different possibilities to the application *programmers* for realizing this interaction, allowing to chose the desired tradeoff between configuration optimality and required programming effort. In the following, we will discuss these different opportunities.

Application written from scratch. The *programmer* can write a parallel application by using the parallel programming interface provided by NORNIR. This interface allows the *programmer* to write both structured (i.e. parallel patterns based) and unstructured applications expressed as a graph of concurrent activities. By doing so, NORNIR can access many internal features of the runtime, thus extending its monitoring capabilities and being able to operate on additional executors. Details about this API can be found in [5].

Application written using a supported framework. NORNIR can easily interface with existing applications written in one of the supported parallel programming environments. At the time being, the only supported framework is FASTFLOW[2]. FASTFLOW is a pattern based parallel programming framework, particularly suited for parallel streaming applications. In this case is sufficient for the *programmer* to provide to the MANAGER a handler to the application, as shown in the following code snippet:

```
Parameters p("parameters.xml");  // Load Nornir parameters.
ManagerFarm<> m(&farm, p);       // farm = FastFlow Application.
m.start();                       // Start application.
m.join();                        // Wait for application end.
```

---

[2] http://calvados.di.unipi.it/.

Instrumented application. If the application is implemented with a non-supported framework, the *programmer* can interface it to a NORNIR MANAGER running in a separate process as a server. The application will act like a client, by inserting few instrumentation calls in his application, as shown in the following snippet:

```
StreamElement* s;
while(s = receive()){
  process(s);
}
```

```
1    Monitor r("parameters.xml");
2    StreamElement* s;
3    while(s = receive()){
4      r.begin();
5      process(s);
6      r.end();
7    }
8    r.terminate();
```

On the left, we have the original, already existing, streaming applications and on the right the same application after it has been instrumented. In line 1 the application opens a connection towards the manager and sends to it the parameters (e.g. QoS requirements). Then, for each stream element, after receiving it from the stream (line 3), the processing is wrapped between 2 calls (lines 4 and 6). By doing so, the performance of the application will be monitored and the data will automatically flow towards the MANAGER. Eventually, in line 8, the connection with the NORNIR MANAGER is closed. Note that this approach only requires inserting 4 instrumentation calls in the already existing application.

Black-box application. In some cases the *programmer* may not have the possibility to instrument and recompile his application. In such cases, the only way NORNIR has to monitor the application performances is to rely on performance counters, for example by monitoring the number of assembler instructions executed per time unit (i.e. instructions per second (IPS)). Accordingly, the *user* should express his performance requirements for the application in terms of IPS. Correlating the IPS to the actual application bandwidth is not an easy task and not so intuitive from the *user* perspective. Moreover, as shown in [13] performance counters may not be a good performance proxy. For these reasons, this approach should only be used if none of the previous ones can be adopted. Suppose that the *user* wants to specify some constraint on his `streamprocessing` application. Then, he can run it by using the NORNIR applications launcher:

```
manager-blackbox --parameters parameters.xml
               --application ./streamprocessing
```

Note that this doesn't require any intervention from the *programmer*.

To summarize, NORNIR provides different solutions to interact with applications. The optimal solution would be to program the streaming application with the provided programming API or to use a supported framework. By accessing the runtime support, NORNIR can also access other executors (Sect. 5.3) that would not be available otherwise (e.g. changing the number of threads), thus improving the quality of the selected configuration, as shown in [3]. If it is not possible to rewrite the application by using a different framework, the *programmer* can just insert few instrumentation calls inside the application, allowing NORNIR to monitor it. Eventually, if even the instrumentation is not feasible (e.g. because the *programmer* can't or doesn't want to change the application code and/or recompile it), NORNIR can still manage the application, not requiring any programming effort. However, we can only monitor system performance counters and we lose the concept of *stream*. Moreover, expressing performance constraints in this scenario could be not intuitive from the *user* perspective.

5   Strategy Designer

In this section, we describe the design of the framework, focusing on how it can be customized by the autonomic strategy *designer*. The general architecture of NORNIR is depicted in Fig. 1.

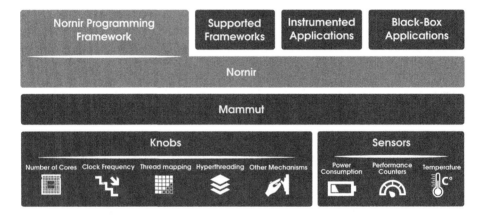

Fig. 1. General architecture of Nornir framework.

In the upper layer, we have the different types of applications that can be interfaced to NORNIR (Sect. 4). NORNIR interacts with the system knobs and sensors (e.g. power consumption one), by using MAMMUT [7][3]. MAMMUT is an object-oriented C++ framework allowing a transparent and portable monitoring of system sensors as well as management of several system knobs.

The following code snippet shows a simplified version of the main parts of NORNIR implementation[4]:

---

[3] http://danieledesensi.github.io/mammut/.
[4] Actual implementation consists of approximately 18000 lines of code.

```
1    typedef enum{
2      KNOB_VIRTUAL_CORES = 0,
3      ...
4      KNOB_NUM
5    }KnobType;
6
7    class Manager{
8      ...
9      void run(){
10       while(isRunning()){
11         sleep(_parameters.samplingInterval);
12         ApplicationSample s = getSample(); // Monitor
13         storeSample(s);
14         KnobsValues k = _selector->getNextKnobsValues(); // Analyze & Plan
15         for(uint i = 0; i < KNOB_NUM; i++){
16           _knobs[i]->changeValue(k[i]); // Execute
17         }
18       }
19     }
20     virtual ApplicationSample getSample() = 0;
21   };
22
23   class Knob{
24     ...
25     std::vector<double> _knobValues;
26     virtual void changeValue(double v) = 0;
27   };
28
29   class Selector{
30     ...
31     virtual KnobsValues getNextKnobsValues() = 0;
32   }
```

Source Code 1.1: Simplified version of the main parts of NORNIR implementation.

The meaning of this code snippet will become more clear after the end of this section. For the moment, we can focus on the MAPE (lines 10–18) loop. In the remaining part of this section, we describe how each of the 3 steps is designed and how they can be customized by the autonomic strategy designer.

5.1 Monitor

As we shown in Sect. 4, the *user* can get the highest benefits from using NORNIR, by using it on an application written with the NORNIR parallel programming interface or on an application written by using one of the supported frameworks. At the moment, this only includes FASTFLOW. To interface NORNIR with other runtimes, the *designer* needs to define a new manager for the new runtime support, by defining a subclass of the MANAGER class and implementing the getSample function (Code 1.1, line 20). In this function the *designer* should implement the retrieval of a new monitored sample from the runtime (i.e. the metrics in Table 1 and additional custom values). This function will be called by NORNIR (line 12) and the sample will be stored (line 13) in order to be accessible from the *Plan* phase (Sect. 5.3).

5.2 Execute

To implement a new executor, the *designer* must define a subclass of the KNOB class (Code 1.1, lines 23–27). In the constructor, the _knobValues vector must be populated with the set of values that the knob can assume. When the planning phase terminates, the function changeValue will be called by the manager on all the available knobs (lines 15–17), with the parameter v corresponding to the value that that specific knob must assume according to the planning algorithm. By implementing the function changeValue, the *designer* specifies the actual code to be executed when a request to change the value of that knob is received by the MANAGER. For example, if the *designer* wants to implement a knob to set the DRAM frequency, in the changeValue function he will insert the code to perform this action. The new KNOB object must then be created and added to the _knobs array (used in line 16). Moreover, a new enumeration value must be assigned to this knob (lines 1–5). Currently, the following knobs are implemented:

Number of Cores. Turns off (or on) some cores. If possible (e.g. for FAST-FLOW applications), it will also change the number of threads used by the application (without stopping or restarting it), to have one thread on each active core. Otherwise, more threads will contest for the same core. Threads will be allocated to cores through the *Threads Mapping* knob, while this knob only enforces the specified number of cores to be active. If the number of threads is changed, the *application programmer* must ensure the correctness of the computation (i.e. if the application maintains an internal state, the semantic of the computation must be preserved after a reconfiguration).

Hyperthreading Level. Number of hardware threads contexts to use on each physical core.

Threads Mapping. Once the number of cores to use has been decided, this knob can be used to apply a given placement. For example, to place them on a set of cores sharing some resources (e.g. last level caches) for minimizing power consumption, or to place them on a set of cores with the minimum amount of shared resources, wasting more power but improving performance.

Clock Frequency. Operates on the clock frequency (and voltage) of the cores, allowing to trade a decreased performance for a lower power consumption.

5.3   Analyze and Plan

To define a custom planning policy, the *designer* must define a subclass of the SELECTOR class (Code 1.1, lines 23–27) and implement the getNextKnobsValues function. In its own SELECTOR the *designer* can access different information provided by the superclass, like: parameters specified by the *user* through the XML file, the current configuration of the application and statistics about the previous monitored samples, to be used during the *Analyze* phase. This information is kept consistent by NORNIR and should be exploited by the algorithm *designer* to decide the next configuration. Once the decision is made, the next values of each knob are stored into a KNOBSVALUES object, an array of values (one for each knob) which can be accessed by using the enumeration values identifying the type of the knob (lines 1–5). The returned object will then be used to set the appropriate values on the available knobs (lines 9–11).

For example, the following code snippet show how to implement a simple selector that, when the monitored latency is lower than 100 ms, will force the application to run on the 25% of the available cores, setting them to work at 50% of their maximum clock frequency. When the latency is higher (or equal) than 100 ms, it will run the application on the 80% of the available cores and will set them to work at 100% of their maximum frequency.

```
1    class SelectorDummy: public Selector{
2      ...
3      KnobsValues getNextKnobsValues(){
4        KnobsValues k(KNOB_VALUE_RELATIVE);
5        if(_samples->average().latency < 100){
6          k[KNOB_VIRTUAL_CORES] = 25; k[KNOB_FREQUENCY] = 50;
7        }else{
8          k[KNOB_VIRTUAL_CORES] = 80; k[KNOB_FREQUENCY] = 100;
9        }
10       return k;
11     }
12   };
```

NORNIR will then automatically translate the percentage values for number of cores and frequencies in real values, according to the availability of resources on the target architecture. Alternatively, it is possible to directly express absolute values for the knobs. By replacing KNOB_VALUE_RELATIVE with KNOB_VALUE_REAL in line 4, NORNIR will interpret line 6 as "*Run the application on 25 cores and set their frequency to 100 Hz*". _samples contains the moving average (simple or exponential) of the monitored data. The type of moving average as well as the size of the moving window (or the exponential parameter) can be specified through the XML file.

This is the most flexible choice from the *designer* perspective since he can implement different strategies from scratch. However, it is also possible to customize some of the strategies already provided by NORNIR. The following state of the art autonomic strategies are already implemented in NORNIR: (i) Two online learning strategies to enforce requirement on bandwidth and power consumption [8,9]; (ii) A planning strategy mixing offline and online prediction [18]; (iii) An heuristic strategy [16] to enforce bandwidth requirements; (iv) Two heuristics for utilisation factor optimisation [4,5]. Being able to implement such a spectrum of different techniques, ranging from heuristics to online machine learning proves the generality and flexibility of our design.

6 Results

NORNIR already provides several autonomic strategies for streaming applications. We will show the results obtained by using the algorithm described in [9] on a network monitoring application [4]. This application analyses all the packets traveling over a network, applying *Deep Packet Inspection* techniques to identify possible security threats. For our experiment we used synthetic traffic data, while the arrival rates are those of a real backbone network[5]. We asked

---

[5] http://www.caida.org/data/realtime/passive/?monitor=equinix-chicago-dirA, 24 h of traffic between 03/01/2016 and 04/01/2016.

NORNIR to always guarantee a bandwidth equal to the input one, (i.e. to do not drop any input stream element), while minimizing power consumption. The application ran for 24 h, and the results are shown in Fig. 2.

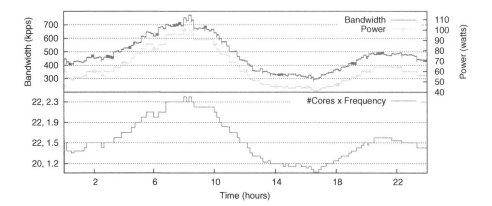

Fig. 2. Time behaviour of an application controlled by NORNIR, in presence of fluctuations in the input pressure. Bandwidth is expressed in thousands of packets per second.

No packets were dropped during this experiment and, as shown in the top part of the figure, NORNIR was able to reconfigure the application so to have a power consumption proportional to the actual input data workload to be processed. In the bottom part, we can see that this was possible since the number of used cores and the clock frequency was dynamically changed according to the workload intensity. When the autonomic strategy was not applied, the application was always characterized by the maximum power consumption during the 24 h.

7   Conclusions and Future Work

In this work we presented NORNIR, a framework to allow application's *users* to enforce performance and power consumption requirements on streaming applications. An application *programmer* will interface the *user*'s application to the NORNIR MANAGER. Moreover, thanks to a modular design, it is possible for an autonomic strategy *designer* to embed his own strategies inside NORNIR, by focusing only on the algorithmic part of his strategy, since the *monitor* and *execute* phases are managed by NORNIR. NORNIR already provides several autonomic strategies and supports different types of applications, proving its flexibility.

As a future work, we would like to support in NORNIR applications expressed as graphs of operators. In this case, decisions taken by an operator manager may influence the behavior of other parts of the computation, requiring to coordinate different managers to find agreements in reconfiguration decisions (e.g. *hierarchical managers*). Another important step would be extending the support to distributed memory architecture. Eventually, we will provide the user with information about the cost of reconfigurations, which may be helpful in mitigating their impact on performance [2].

Acknowledgements. This work has been partially supported by the EU H2020-ICT-2014-1 project REPHRASE (No. 644235).

References

1. Apache Storm (2017). http://storm.apache.org/
2. Bertolli, C., Mencagli, G., Vanneschi, M.: A cost model for autonomic reconfigurations in high-performance pervasive applications. In: Proceedings of the 4th ACM International Workshop on Context-Awareness for Self-Managing Systems, pp. 3:20–3:29 (2010)
3. Danelutto, M., De Matteis, T., De Sensi, D., Torquati, M.: Evaluating concurrency throttling and thread packing on SMT multicores. In: Proceedings of the 25th Euromicro International Conference on Parallel, Distributed, and Network-Based Processing (2017)
4. Danelutto, M., De Sensi, D., Torquati, M.: Energy driven adaptivity in stream parallel computations. In: Proceedings of 23th Euromicro International Conference on Parallel, Distributed, and Network-Based Processing, Turku, Finland, pp. 103–110. IEEE (2015)
5. Danelutto, M., De Sensi, D., Torquati, M.: A power-aware, self-adaptive macro data flow framework. Parallel Process. Lett. **27**(01), 1740004 (2017)
6. De Matteis, T., Mencagli, G.: Keep calm and react with foresight: strategies for low-latency and energy-efficient elastic data stream processing. In: Proceedings of the 21st ACM SIGPLAN Symposium on Principles and Practice of Parallel Programming (PPoPP), pp. 13:1–13:12 (2016)
7. De Sensi, D., Torquati, M., Danelutto, M.: Mammut: high-level management of system knobs and sensors. SoftwareX **6**, 150–154 (2017)
8. De Sensi, D.: Predicting performance and power consumption of parallel applications. In: Proceedings of 24th Euromicro International Conference on Parallel, Distributed, and Network-Based Processing, pp. 200–207, February 2016
9. De Sensi, D., Torquati, M., Danelutto, M.: A reconfiguration algorithm for power-aware parallel applications. ACM Trans. Archit. Code Optim. **13**(4), 43:1–43:25 (2016)
10. Gandhi, A., Harchol-Balter, M., Das, R., Kephart, J., Lefurgy, C.: Power capping via forced idleness. In: Proceedings of Workshop on Energy-Efficient Design (2009)
11. Gedik, B., Schneider, S., Hirzel, M., Wu, K.L.: Elastic scaling for data stream processing. IEEE Trans. Parallel Distrib. Syst. **25**(6), 1447–1463 (2014)
12. Goel, A., Steere, D., Pu, C., Walpole, J.: Swift: a feedback control and dynamic reconfiguration toolkit. Technical report (1998)
13. Hoffman, H.: SEEC: a framework for self-aware management of goals and constraints in computing systems. Ph.D. thesis, Cambridge, MA, USA (2013)
14. Kephart, J.O., Chess, D.M.: The vision of autonomic computing. Computer **36**(1), 41–50 (2003)

15. Li, B., Nahrstedt, K.: A control-based middleware framework for quality-of-service adaptations. IEEE J. Sel. Areas Commun. **17**(9), 1632–1650 (1999)
16. Li, J., Martínez, J.F.: Dynamic power-performance adaptation of parallel computation on chip multiprocessors. In: Proceedings of International Symposium on High-Performance Computer Architecture, pp. 77–87 (2006)
17. Lohrmann, B., Janacik, P., Kao, O.: Elastic stream processing with latency guarantees. In: The 35th International Conference on Distributed Computing Systems (2015)
18. Mishra, N., Zhang, H., Lafferty, J.D., Hoffmann, H.: A probabilistic graphical model-based approach for minimizing energy under performance constraints. In: ACM SIGARCH Computer Architecture News, vol. 43, no. 1, pp. 267–281 (2015)
19. Qian, Z., He, Y., Su, C., Wu, Z., Zhu, H., Zhang, T., Zhou, L., Yu, Y., Zhang, Z.: Timestream: reliable stream computation in the cloud. In: Proceedings of the 8th ACM European Conference on Computer Systems, pp. 1–14. EuroSys 2013. ACM, New York (2013)
20. Zhang, R., Lu, C., Abdelzaher, T.F., Stankovic, J.A.: Controlware: a middleware architecture for feedback control of software performance. In: Proceedings 22nd International Conference on Distributed Computing Systems, pp. 301–310 (2002)

Supporting Advanced Patterns in GrPPI, a Generic Parallel Pattern Interface

David del Rio Astorga$^{(\boxtimes)}$, Manuel F. Dolz⊙, Javier Fernández, and J. Daniel García⊙

Computer Science and Engineering Department,
University Carlos III of Madrid, 28911 Leganés, Spain
david.rio@uc3m.es, {mdolz,jfmunoz,jdgarcia}@inf.uc3m.es

Abstract. The emergence of generic interfaces, encapsulating algorithmic aspects in pattern-based constructions, has greatly alleviated the development of data-intensive and stream-processing applications. In this paper, we complement the basic patterns supported by GrPPI, a C++ General and Reusable Parallel Pattern Interface of the state-of-the-art, with the advanced parallel patterns Pool, Windowed-Farm, and Stream-Iterator. This collection of advanced patterns is basically oriented to some domain-specific applications, ranging from the evolutionary to the real-time computing areas, where compositions of basic patterns are not capable of fully mimicking algorithmic behavior of their original sequential codes. The experimental evaluation of the advanced patterns on a set of domain-specific use-cases, using different back-ends (C++ Threads, OpenMP and Intel TBB) and pattern-specific parameters, reports remarkable performance gains. We also demonstrate the benefits of the GrPPI pattern interface from the usability and flexibility points of view.

Keywords: Parallel programming framework
Domain-specific parallel pattern · Data and stream computing
High-level API

1 Introduction

The advent of the heterogeneous HPC architectures in the last decade paved the way in improving performance of data-intensive and stream-processing applications [21]. This fact, however, posed a number of challenges to developers for exploiting available resources of parallel hardware. An example among these challenges is the variety of programming frameworks existing for multi-/many-core CPUs, GPUs, co-processors, DSPs or FPGAs units present in heterogeneous platforms [8]. Therefore, it becomes clear that additional expertise is required, not only to develop applications using those frameworks, but also to select and tune them optimally to operate on these architectures. The lack of unified interfaces, integrating available processor-specific programming frameworks in a standalone layer, makes the development an even more complex task.

© Springer International Publishing AG, part of Springer Nature 2018
D. B. Heras and L. Bougé (Eds.): Euro-Par 2017 Workshops, LNCS 10659, pp. 55–67, 2018.
https://doi.org/10.1007/978-3-319-75178-8_5

With the recent emergence of pattern-based programming frameworks, encapsulating algorithmic aspects using a building blocks approach, this aspect has been relieved when programming for parallel platforms [16]. Basically, parallel patterns offer a way to implement robust, readable and portable solutions while hiding away the complexity behind concurrency mechanisms, e.g., thread management, synchronizations or data sharing. Numerous examples of pattern-based programming frameworks, such as SkePU [9], FastFlow [3] or Intel TBB [19], can be found in the literature. Nevertheless, most of these frameworks are not generic enough nor offer unified pattern interfaces [5]. To tackle these issues, the recent interface GRPPI [20], accommodates a unified layer of generic and reusable parallel patterns on the top of existing execution environments and pattern-based frameworks. However, we find that the core patterns offered by this interface do not fully match in some domain-specific use cases, e.g., evolutionary and symbolic algorithms.

To deal with this issue, we extend GRPPI with a collection of advanced parallel patterns targeted to domain-specific applications and evaluate their performance on a set of use cases from different computing areas. Specifically, this paper contributes with the following:

- We complement the core patterns supported by GRPPI with the advanced parallel patterns: Pool, Windowed-Farm, and Stream-Iterator.
- We demonstrate the flexibility and the composability of the advanced patterns in the GRPPI interface context.
- We assess the usability of the patterns with respect to the number of lines of code (LOCs) that have to be modified in order to parallelize the selected use cases.
- We evaluate the performance gains by using these patterns on a set of domain-specific use cases and varying configurations of parallelism degree and problem-specific parameters.

The remainder of this paper is organized as follows. Section 2 revisits some related works about parallel programming frameworks and domain-specific patterns. Section 3 states the formal definition of the advanced parallel patterns supported by GRPPI. Section 4 describes the interface adopted for the new patterns presented in this paper. Section 5 evaluates these patterns from the usability and performance points of view under three different use cases. Section 6 gives a few concluding remarks and future works.

2   Related Work

In the literature, we found numerous works proposing parallel patterns targeted to modern architectures for developing applications. In a first place, we find several open-source pattern libraries oriented exclusively to multi-core processors, e.g., Intel Thread Building Blocks (TBB) [19], RaftLib [4] or Kanga [14], and others supporting also accelerators, such as, SkePU [9], which allows hybrid

CPU–GPU configurations. We also encounter commercial solutions in the state-of-the-art, such as Thrust [17] and SYCL [13] for CUDA and OpenCL devices, respectively. Simultaneously, standardized interfaces are being progressively developed. This is the case of C++ STL algorithms, available in the forthcoming C++17, that start defining parallel versions of already existing STL algorithms [11]. Similar implementations to the parallel STL can also be found as third-party libraries, e.g., HPX [12] and GRPPI [20].

All in all, we observe that these frameworks provide a collection of classic parallel patterns targeted to data and stream-processing applications, e.g., the Map, Reduce, MapReduce, Pipeline and Farm patterns. However, none of them natively supplies advanced patterns. As stated in the previous section, we refer to advanced patterns to those constructions that match the algorithmic behavior of some particular domain-specific applications coming from, e.g., the symbolic computing, control theory, biology, wireless sensor networks or real-time stream processing domains. In this sense, we find that only some pattern-based frameworks in the literature have pushed forward the development of complex, high-level patterns. For instance, the FastFlow [3] library recently provided the Pool [2] and the Windowed-Farm [7] patterns, two commonly used structures in evolutionary and stream-intensive applications, respectively. On the other hand, the MALLBA library [1] offers a collection of high-level skeletons for combinatorial optimization which deals with parallelism in a user-friendly and efficient manner. In any case, the high-level patterns offered by these frameworks are not generic enough to be easily leveraged when developing parallel applications. The contribution of this paper is mainly focused on complementing the GRPPI library of basic parallel patterns with a new set of advanced patterns matching the algorithms that commonly appear in, e.g., genetic, sensor networks or real-time applications.

3   Advanced Parallel Patterns

Patterns have been generally defined as recurring strategies for solving problems from a wide spectrum of areas, such as architecture, object-oriented programming and software architecture [15, 16]. In our case, we take advantage of parallel software design patterns, since they provide a mechanism to encapsulate algorithmic features and are able to make applications more robust, portable and reusable. Also, if these patterns are properly tuned, they can achieve a good balance between parallel scalability and data locality.

As observed, several solutions in the state-of-the-art offer collections of basic parallel patterns as a "building blocks" modeling strategy for developing stream processing and data-intensive applications. However, while many of the algorithms found in general-purpose applications match directly those patterns, there exist situations in which those have to be composed among them in order to comply with the algorithm requirements. Furthermore, we identify some domain-specific algorithms, in which those basic patterns do not match any of these constructions or have to be composed in a very complex way in order to satisfy the problem prerequisites. This occurs in many algorithms that come from the evolutionary and symbolic computing [10] domain, wireless sensor networks algorithms [6] or in real-time processing engines [18]. Therefore, we determine the need for supporting advanced patterns in order to simplify the development of complex algorithms related to the aforementioned application domains.

In the following, we describe formally three new parallel patterns that can be eventually incorporated during the parallelization task of such applications: Pool, Windowed-Farm and Stream-Iterator.

Pool. This pattern models the evolution of a population of individuals matching many evolutionary computing algorithms in the state-of-the-art [2]. Specifically, the Pool pattern is comprised of four different functions that are applied iteratively to a population P of individuals of type α (see Fig. 1(a)). First, the *selection* function S: $\alpha^* \rightarrow \alpha^*$ selects a subset of individuals belonging to P. Next, the selected individuals are processed by means of the *evolution* function E: $\alpha^* \rightarrow \alpha^*$, which may produce any number of new or modified individuals. The resulting set of individuals computed by E are filtered through a *filter* function F: $\alpha^* \rightarrow \alpha^*$, and eventually inserted into the population. Finally, the *termination* function T: $\alpha^* \rightarrow \{true, false\}$ determines in each iteration whether the evolution process should be finished or continued. To guarantee the correctness of the parallel version of this pattern, both functions S and E should be pure, i.e., they can be computed in parallel with no side effects.

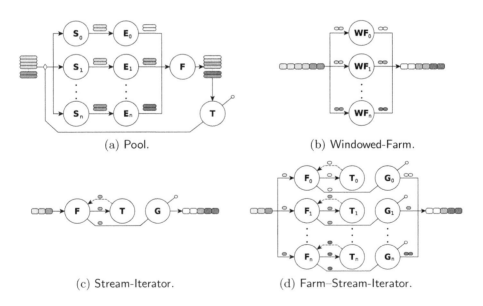

(a) Pool.

(b) Windowed-Farm.

(c) Stream-Iterator.

(d) Farm–Stream-Iterator.

Fig. 1. Advanced parallel patterns.

Windowed-Farm. This stream-oriented pattern delivers "windows" of processed items to the output stream. Basically, this pattern applies the function WF over consecutive contiguous collections of x input items of type α and delivers the resulting windows of y items of type β to the output stream (see Fig. 1(b)). Optionally, these windows can have an overlap factor, i.e., the number of items in the window w_i that are also part of the window w_{i+1}. The parallelization of this pattern requires a pure function WF: $\alpha^* \rightarrow \beta^*$ for processing item collections.

Stream-Iterator. This stream pattern is intended to recurrently compute the pure function F: $\alpha \rightarrow \alpha$ on a single stream input item until a specific condition, determined by the boolean function T: $\alpha \rightarrow \{true, false\}$, is met. Additionally, in each iteration the result of the function F is delivered to the output stream, depending on a boolean output guard function G: $\alpha \rightarrow \{true, false\}$ (see Fig. 1(c)). Note that this pattern, due to its nature, does not provide any parallelism degree by itself and can be classified as a pattern modifier. Therefore, the parallel version of this construction is only achieved when it is composed with some other core stream pattern, e.g., using Farm or Pipeline as for the function F. An example of Stream-Iterator composed with a Farm pattern is shown in Fig. 1(d).

4   Description

In this section, we extend our generic and reusable parallel pattern interface (GRPPI) for C++ applications, previously presented in [20], with the advanced parallel patterns described in Sect. 3. In general, GRPPI takes full advantage of modern C++ features, metaprogramming concepts and generic programming to act as switch between the parallel programming models OpenMP, C++ threads and Intel TBB. Its design allows users to leverage the aforementioned execution frameworks just in a single and compact interface, hiding away the complexity behind the use of concurrency mechanisms with negligible overheads. Furthermore, the modularity of GRPPI permits to easily integrate new patterns, while composing them to arrange more complex ones. Thanks to these properties, GRPPI can be used to implement a wide range of existing stream-processing and data-intensive applications with relative small efforts, having as a result portable codes that can be executed on multiple platforms.

Next, we describe in detail the interfaces of the advanced parallel patterns offered by GRPPI and demonstrate its composability.

Pool. The GRPPI interface designed for the Pool pattern, shown in Listing 1.1, receives the execution model, the population (**popul**), the selection (**select**), evolving (**evolve**), filtering (**filter**) and termination (**term**) functions, and the number of selections that will be performed. Initially, the parallel pattern implementation of GRPPI divides the number of selections among the concurrent processing entities that will select and evolve the population individuals. Afterwards, the resulting individuals are merged and forwarded to the sequential filtering and termination functions. Finally, only if the termination condition is met, the Pool parallel pattern finishes and delivers the resulting population. On the contrary, the whole process is repeated again with the evolved population.

The parallelism of this pattern is controlled via the execution model parameter, which can be set to operate in sequential or in parallel, through the different supported frameworks; e.g. to use C++ threads, the parameter should be set to `parallel_execution_thr`. In this case, any execution model can optionally receive, as an argument, the number of entities to be used for the parallel execution, e.g., `parallel_execution_thr{6}` would use 6 worker threads. If this argument is not given, the interface takes by default the number of threads set by the underlying platform.

Listing 1.1: Pool interface.

```
1 template <typename EM, typename P, typename S, typename E, typename F, typename T>
2 void Pool(EM exec_mod, P &popul, S &&select, E &&evolve, F &&filt, T &&term, int num_select);
```

Windowed-Farm. The interface for the Windowed-Farm pattern, described in Listing 1.2, receives the execution model, the stream consumer (`in`), the Farm (`task`) and the producer (`out`) functions. This pattern also receives the size and the overlap factor of the windows.[1] Specifically, the `in` function reads from the input stream as many items as required to fill the window buffer. Next, this buffer is forwarded to one of the concurrent entities, which will compute the function `task` in a Farm-like fashion. Therefore, the parallel implementation of this GRPPI pattern is offered by the Farm construction. Finally, the items collections resulting from the `task` function are delivered to the output stream. Note that, depending on the user requirements, this pattern can deliver items windows in an ordered way by properly configuring the execution model.

Listing 1.2: Windowed-Farm interface.

```
1 template <typename EM, typename I, typename WF, typename O>
2 void WindowedFarm(EM exec_mod, I &&in, WF &&task, O &&out, int win_size, int overlap);
```

Stream-Iterator. The GRPPI interface for the Stream-Iterator pattern, detailed in Listing 1.3, takes the execution model, the stream consumer (`in`), the kernel (`task`) and the producer (`out`) functions. This pattern also receives two boolean functions: the termination (`term`) and output guard (`guard`) functions. In the first step, the `in` function reads items from the input stream and a worker thread executes the kernel `task` function for each item. Next, the termination function `term` is evaluated with the resulting item to determine if the kernel should be re-executed on the same input item. Additionally, the output `guard` function decides whether an item should be delivered to the output stream or not.

Listing 1.3: Stream-Iterator interface.

```
1 template <typename EM, typename I, typename F, typename O, typename T, typename G>
2 void StreamIteration(EM exec_mod, I &&in, F &&task, O &&out, T &&term, G &&guard);
```

As stated in the previous section, the parallelism of the Stream-Iterator pattern is only obtained when it is composed with a basic GRPPI parallel pattern, e.g., Farm or Pipeline. As an example of composition, the code in Listing 1.4

---

[1] Note that while the current Windowed-Farm pattern only supports count-based windows, in the future we plan to extend its interface to cover time-based, slide-by-tuple and delta-based windowing models.

implements a Stream-Iterator, in which the kernel `task` function has been composed with the Pipeline pattern. Therefore, the kernel is computed in parallel by 2 worker threads. Note that the `optional`, as for the return type in the consumer function lambda, is used to indicate the end of the stream when constructed without arguments. As can be seen, thanks to GRPPI, it is possible to compose advanced with basic parallel patterns in order to increase the parallelism degree.

Listing 1.4: Example of **Stream-Iterator-Pipeline** composition.

```
 1  StreamIteration( parallel_execution_thr{4},
 2      [&]() -> optional<int> { // Consumer function
 3          auto value = read_value(is);
 4          return ( value > 0 ) ? value : {};
 5      },
 6      Pipeline( // Kernel function
 7          []( int e ) { return e + 2*e; },
 8          []( int e ) { return e - 1; }
 9      ),
10      [&]( int e ){ os << e << endl; }, // Producer function
11      [] ( int e ){ return e < 100; }, // Termination function
12      [] ( int e ){ return e % 2 == 0; } // Output guard function
13  );
```

5 Evaluation

In this section, we perform an experimental evaluation of the three novel advanced patterns from the usability and performance points of view. To do so, we use the following hardware and software components:

- *Target platform.* The evaluation has been carried out on a server platform comprised of 2× Intel Xeon Ivy Bridge E5-2695 v2 with a total of 24 cores running at 2.40 GHz, 30 MB of L3 cache and 128 GB of DDR3 RAM. The OS is a Linux Ubuntu 14.04.2 LTS with the kernel 3.13.0-57.
- *Software.* To develop the parallel versions and to implement the proposed interfaces, we leveraged the execution environments C++11 threads and OpenMP 4.5, and the pattern-based parallel framework Intel Threading Building Blocks (TBB). The C++ compiler used to assemble GRPPI is GCC v5.0.
- *Use cases.* To evaluate the advanced patterns, we use three different synthetic use cases targeting problems from different domains.
    - The Pool pattern has been evaluated on a benchmark that solves the *traveling salesman* problem (TSP) using a regular evolutionary algorithm. This NP-problem computes the shortest possible route among different cities, visiting them only once and returning to the origin city.
    - To evaluate the Windowed-Farm, we use a benchmark that computes average window values from an emulated sensor readings.
    - For the Stream-Iterator, we leverage a benchmark that reduces the resolution of the images appearing in the input stream, and produces the images with concrete resolutions to the output stream.

In the following sections, we analyze the usability, in terms of lines of code, and the performance of the GRPPI advanced patterns using the above-mentioned benchmarks with varying configurations of parallelism degree, problem size and execution frameworks.

5.1 Usability Analysis

In this section we analyze the usability and flexibility of the advanced pattern interfaces. To analyze these aspects, we assess the number of modified lines of code (LOCs) required to implement the parallel versions of the use case algorithms. Then, we compare the modified LOCs leveraging the GRPPI interface with respect to using directly the supported frameworks. Table 1 summarizes the percentage of modified LOCs in the sequential algorithm in order to implement the parallel versions of the use cases algorithms. As observed, the OpenMP and TBB versions require less LOCs, given that these frameworks provide high-level interfaces hiding away the complexity behind concurrency mechanisms. For instance, OpenMP 4.5 offers the `depend` clause in `task` directives which enforces additional constraints on the scheduling of tasks. However, the analogous implementation in C++ threads requires the use of explicit communication channels (e.g. multiple-produce/multiple-consumer queues) and synchronization mechanisms (e.g. locks, condition variables and atomic variables). On the other hand, using the GRPPI interface for parallelizing a given application is simpler than using directly the above-mentioned programming frameworks. On average, the LOCs that have to be modified in order to incorporate an advanced GRPPI pattern, is 28%. An additional advantage of GRPPI is its capability to easily switch among execution frameworks, since it is only required to replace a single argument in the pattern function call.

Table 1. Percentage of modified lines of code w.r.t. the sequential version.

Advanced pattern	% of modified lines of code			
	C++ Threads	OpenMP	Intel TBB	GRPPI
Pool	+55.0%	+70.0%	+55.0%	+22.5%
Windowed-Farm	+152.1%	+75.8%	+51.7%	+31.0%
Stream-Iterator	+153.5%	+56.4%	+46.1%	+30.8%

5.2 Performance Analysis of the Pool Pattern

Next, we evaluate the Pool pattern on a benchmark that solves the TSP problem using a population of 50 individuals representing feasible routes. We also set the benchmark to perform a total of 200 iterations, each of them making 200 selections. Figure 2(a) shows the performance gains when varying the number of threads, from 2 to 24, and using the three available GRPPI back-ends: C++ threads, OpenMP and Intel TBB, with respect to the sequential version. As can be seen, the speedup increases roughly at a linear rate when increasing the number of threads for all frameworks. Concretely, we observe that between 2 and 12 threads the efficiency is sustained in the range of 91%–98%. However, for 24 threads the frameworks OpenMP and Intel TBB deliver an efficiency of 80%, while for C++ threads it slightly decreases to 77%. This is mainly due to the better resource usage made by the OpenMP and Intel TBB runtime schedulers.

As a complementary evaluation, we set the number of threads to 12 and vary the number of selections from 10 and 200. According to the results shown in Fig. 2(b), the speedup grows hand in hand with the number of selections, since the Pool pattern only parallelizes the selection and evolution functions. This indicates that increasing the number of selections improves the load balance among the worker threads and pays off the parallelization overheads related to thread synchronizations and communications.

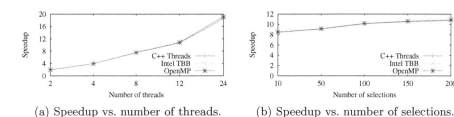

(a) Speedup vs. number of threads.   (b) Speedup vs. number of selections.

Fig. 2. Pool speedup varying with varying number of threads and selections.

5.3 Performance Analysis of the **Windowed-Farm** Pattern

In this section, we evaluate the performance of the Windowed-Farm using a synthetic benchmark that computes average window values from an input stream of sensor readings. Specifically, the sensor in this benchmark has been configured to read samples at 1 kHz and the pattern window size has been set to 100 elements with 90% of overlap among windows. Figure 3(a) shows the speedup when the number of threads increases from 2 to 24. The main observation is that all execution frameworks scale with the increasing number of threads and behave similarly, given that the OpenMP and Intel TBB runtime schedulers do not provide any major advantage over the C++ threads implementation in this concrete use case. This is because the internal Farm pattern leads, by nature, to well balanced workloads among threads. Note that a Farm is comprised of a pool of threads that constantly retrieve items from the input stream and apply the same function over them. On the other hand, we also observe an almost linear scaling for increasing number of threads. This is mainly caused because the Farm pattern can theoretically scale up to $\frac{T_f}{T_a}$, being T_f the computation time of the window average value and T_a the interarrival time of windows in the input stream. To demonstrate this strong scaling, we experimentally measured the computation time of the average function, which was, on average, 220 ms

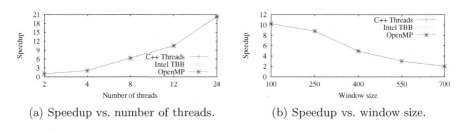

(a) Speedup vs. number of threads.   (b) Speedup vs. window size.

Fig. 3. Windowed-Farm speedup with varying number of threads and window size.

and the interarrival window time that was 10 ms. Therefore, applying the afore-mentioned formula, we get 22 as for the maximum theoretical speedup.

As an additional experiment, we evaluate the behavior of the Windowed-Farm pattern when increasing the window size, using 12 threads and the aforementioned configuration that uses a fixed overlapping factor of 90%. As can be observed from Fig. 3(b), the speedup decreases for increasing window sizes, as the number of non-overlapping items among windows also increases. This basically occurs because the interarrival time of window T_a increases, restricting proportionally the maximum parallelism degree.

5.4 Performance Analysis of the Stream-Iterator Pattern

Finally, we analyze the performance of the GRPPI Stream-Iterator pattern using the above-mentioned benchmark, in charge of processing square images and halving their sizes on each iteration until reaching concrete resolutions. Specifically, the size of the input images is fixed to 8,192 pixels, and the output images, for each input, have sizes of 128, 512 and 1,024. Figure 4(a) illustrates the benchmark speedup when varying the number of threads from 2 to 24 for the different GRPPI back-ends. In this case, when the number of threads ranges between 2 and 12, the efficiency attained is roughly 75%, while for 24 this is degraded to 48% for all programming frameworks. This effect is mainly caused by the fact that each of the threads involved in the Farm pattern, part of the Stream-Iterator, are simultaneously accessing to different input images. Therefore, these memory accesses become a bottleneck due to constant cache misses when the threads perform the computation of the `task` function of the pattern. In general, these results suggest a memory bandwidth limitation in this particular benchmark.

To gain insights into the performance degradation detected in the previous analysis, we perform an additional experiment in which we set the number of threads to 24 and vary the input image sizes from 2,048 to 16,384. Figure 4(b) depicts the performance gains for the different execution frameworks when varying the image size in the preceding range. Again, we observe a slight speedup decrease for increasing image sizes, which confirms our prior impressions. As an example, if we assume 22 worker threads in the internal Farm pattern, individually processing images with resolution of 2,048 × 2,048 pixels (represented with matrices of integers), these require about 352 MiB of memory. Therefore, not

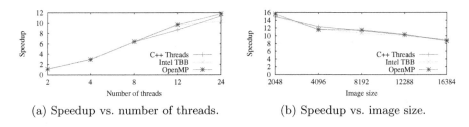

(a) Speedup vs. number of threads.   (b) Speedup vs. image size.

Fig. 4. Stream-Iterator speedup with varying number of threads and image size.

fitting in any of the available cache levels and leading to an increased L2/L3 cache miss rate when they are simultaneously accessed. All in all, this issue is mainly due to the inherent memory-bound nature of this specific use case.

6 Conclusions

In this paper, we have extended GRPPI, a generic and reusable parallel pattern interface, with the advanced parallel patterns Pool, Windowed-Farm and Stream-Iterator, targeted to domain-specific applications. With the unified interface, thanks to the use of C++ templates and metaprogramming techniques, these patterns can be executed in parallel using any of the currently supported back-ends: C++ threads, OpenMP and Intel TBB. Furthermore, their compact design facilitates the development of the domain-specific applications, improving at the same time their portability and maintainability.

As demonstrated through the experimental evaluation, the use cases implemented with the proposed patterns attain remarkable speedup gains compared with their corresponding sequential versions. Although in some cases, the parallelism degree is limited by the pattern nature. We also proved that leveraging GRPPI reduces considerably the number of LOCs that have to be modified in the original codes to turn them parallel with respect to using the parallel frameworks directly. In general, we believe that these advanced patterns can eventually be incorporated in domain-specific applications so as to easily parallelize them, without having a deep understanding of existing parallel programming frameworks or third-party interfaces.

As future work, we plan to support other advanced parallel patterns in GRPPI, such as the *keyed stream farm*, *stream pool* and *image convolution*. Furthermore, we intend to include other execution environments as for the offered parallel frameworks, e.g., FastFlow or SkePU. An ultimate goal is to provide support for accelerators via CUDA Thrust and OpenCL SYCL.

Acknowledgements. This work was partially supported by the EU project ICT 644235 "REPHRASE: REfactoring Parallel Heterogeneous Resource-Aware Applications" and the project TIN2013-41350-P "Scalable Data Management Techniques for High-End Computing Systems" from the *Ministerio de Economía y Competitividad*, Spain.

References

1. MALLBA geographically distributed environments: combinatorial optimization library (2000). http://www.cs.upc.edu/~mallba
2. Aldinucci, M., Campa, S., Danelutto, M., Kilpatrick, P., Torquati, M.: Pool evolution: a parallel pattern for evolutionary and symbolic computing. Int. J. Parallel Program. **44**(3), 531–551 (2016)
3. Aldinucci, M., Danelutto, M., Kilpatrick, P., Torquati, M.: Fastflow: High-Level and Efficient Streaming on Multicore, pp. 261–280. Wiley, Hoboken (2017)
4. Beard, J.C., Li, P., Chamberlain, R.D.: RaftLib: a C++ template library for high performance stream parallel processing. In: Proceedings of the Sixth International Workshop on Programming Models and Applications for Multicores and Manycores, PMAM 2015, pp. 96–105. ACM, New York (2015)
5. Belikov, E., Deligiannis, P., Totoo, P., Aljabri, M., Loidl, H.W.: A survey of high-level parallel programming models. Technical report HW-MACS-TR-0103. Department of Computer Science, Heriot-Watt University, December 2013
6. Bucur, D., Iacca, G., Squillero, G., Tonda, A.: An evolutionary framework for routing protocol analysis in wireless sensor networks. In: Esparcia-Alcázar, A.I. (ed.) EvoApplications 2013. LNCS, vol. 7835, pp. 1–11. Springer, Heidelberg (2013). https://doi.org/10.1007/978-3-642-37192-9_1
7. De Matteis, T., Mencagli, G.: Parallel patterns for window-based stateful operators on data streams: an algorithmic skeleton approach. Int. J. Parallel Program. **45**(2), 382–401 (2017)
8. Diaz, J., Muoz-Caro, C., Nio, A.: A survey of parallel programming models and tools in the multi and many-core era. IEEE Trans. Parallel Distrib. Syst. **23**(8), 1369–1386 (2012)
9. Enmyren, J., Kessler, C.W.: SkePU: a multi-backend skeleton programming library for multi-GPU Systems. In: Proceedings of the Fourth International Workshop on High-level Parallel Programming and Applications, HLPP 2010, pp. 5–14. ACM, New York (2010)
10. Gajda-Zagórska, E.: Multiobjective evolutionary strategy for finding neighbourhoods of pareto-optimal solutions. In: Esparcia-Alcázar, A.I. (ed.) EvoApplications 2013. LNCS, vol. 7835, pp. 112–121. Springer, Heidelberg (2013). https://doi.org/10.1007/978-3-642-37192-9_12
11. ISO/IEC: Programming Languages - Technical Specification for C++ Extensions for Parallelism, July 2015. iSO/IEC TS 19570:2015
12. Kaiser, H., Heller, T., Adelstein-Lelbach, B., Serio, A., Fey, D.: Hpx: a task based programming model in a global address space. In: Proceedings of the 8th International Conference on Partitioned Global Address Space Programming Models, PGAS 2014, pp. 6:1–6:11. ACM, New York (2014)
13. Khronos OpenCL Working Group: SYCL: C++ Single-source Heterogeneous Programming for OpenCL. https://www.khronos.org/sycl. (Accessed May 2015)
14. Kist, D., Pinto, B., Bazo, R., Bois, A.R.D., Cavalheiro, G.G.H.: Kanga: a skeleton-based generic interface for parallel programming. In: 2015 International Symposium on Computer Architecture and High Performance Computing Workshop (SBAC-PADW), pp. 68–72, October 2015
15. Mattson, T., Sanders, B., Massingill, B.: Patterns for Parallel Programming, 1st edn. Addison-Wesley Professional, Boston (2004)
16. McCool, M., Reinders, J., Robison, A.: Structured Parallel Programming: Patterns for Efficient Computation, 1st edn. Morgan Kaufmann Publishers Inc., San Francisco (2012)

17. NVIDIA Corporation: Thrust. https://thrust.github.io/
18. Popovic, V., Seyid, K., Pignat, E., Çogal, Ö., Leblebici, Y.: Multi-camera platform for panoramic real-time HDR video construction and rendering. J. Real-Time Image Process. **12**(4), 697–708 (2016)
19. Reinders, J.: Intel Threading Building Blocks - Outfitting C++ for Multi-Core Processor Parallelism. O'Reilly, Sebastopol (2007)
20. del Rio Astorga, D., Dolz, M.F., Fernández, J., García, J.D.: A generic parallel pattern interface for stream and data processing. Concurr. Comput.: Pract. Exp. **29**, e4175-n/a (April 2017)
21. Shan, A.: Heterogeneous processing: a strategy for augmenting Moore's law. Linux J. **2006**(142), 7 (2006)

A Topology and Traffic Aware Two-Level Scheduler for Stream Processing Systems in a Heterogeneous Cluster

Leila Eskandari[✉], Jason Mair, Zhiyi Huang, and David Eyers

University of Otago, Dunedin, New Zealand
{leila,jkmair,hzy,dme}@cs.otago.ac.nz

Abstract. To efficiently handle a large volume of data, scheduling algorithms in stream processing systems need to minimise the data movement between communicating tasks to improve system throughput. However, finding an optimal scheduling algorithm for these systems is NP-hard. In this paper, we propose a heuristic scheduling algorithm for a heterogeneous cluster—T3-Scheduler—that can efficiently identify the communicating tasks and assign them to the same node, up to a specified level of utilisation for that node. Using three common micro-benchmarks and an evaluation using a real-world application, we demonstrate that T3-Scheduler outperforms current state-of-the-art scheduling algorithms, such as Aniello et al.'s popular 'Online scheduler', improving throughput by 20–72% for micro-benchmarks and 60% for the real-world application.

Keywords: Stream processing · Scheduling · Big data
Heterogeneous cluster

1 Introduction

The increasing amounts of data generated by new applications such as social networks, low latency stock trading and real-time search, have necessitated the development of new data processing frameworks. Data Stream Processing Systems (DSPSs) process unbounded streams of data in real-time, as the data arrives without the need to store it first. Over the last few years, a broad range of research has advanced stream processing systems [1,2,11]. In a DSPS, an application is structured as a DAG, where data streams flow from one processing element to the next. Each processing element, represented as a vertex in the DAG, contains multiple tasks in order to perform parallelism. The tasks of two communicating processing elements are fully connected. The flows of data within the DAG are represented by the edges.

Task allocation policies in DSPSs have a significant impact on performance metrics such as data processing latency, maximal memory requirements for processing and system throughput [6]. Static data processing systems that store and later process data, such as Hadoop, consider the issue of data locality during scheduling, *i.e.*, stored data and processing tasks are placed close to each

© Springer International Publishing AG, part of Springer Nature 2018
D. B. Heras and L. Bougé (Eds.): Euro-Par 2017 Workshops, LNCS 10659, pp. 68–79, 2018.
https://doi.org/10.1007/978-3-319-75178-8_6

other. In a DSPS, the equivalent optimisation is for the scheduling policy to put the communicating tasks near each other to avoid unnecessary data movement. A stream processing cluster, usually grows over time as new systems are added, resulting in multiple generations of hardware, with varying capacities within a single cluster [13]. Therefore, heterogeneity of a stream processing cluster should also be taken into account in the scheduling policies in order to improve the performance. A number of scheduling algorithms have been proposed in the literature to improve the performance of DSPSs. The common practice in these heuristic algorithms is to find communicating tasks and put them in the same node. However, these methods inspect each communicating pair of tasks or groups of tasks in isolation, which can leave some nodes underutilised in a heterogeneous cluster. To address the above issues, we propose T3-Scheduler, a Topology and Traffic aware Two-level Scheduler for typical DSPSs. T3-Scheduler finds highly communicating tasks and assigns them to the same compute node in a heterogeneous cluster such that each node remains fully utilised. This paper makes the following contributions:

- We propose T3-Scheduler which can efficiently assign the tasks to the compute nodes in a heterogeneous cluster where each node is fully utilised. In the first level of scheduling, T3-Scheduler uses a heuristic algorithm to divide the application graph into multiple parts where each part has a size relative to the capacity of the compute node hosting that part of the graph. This ensures T3-Scheduler utilises each compute node, helping reduce the inter-node communication. In the second level of scheduling, T3-Scheduler assigns highly communicating tasks to the same worker process in order to minimise the communication between the workers within a compute node.
- We run experiments using three micro-benchmarks and one real-world application to evaluate T3-Scheduler and compare it with a popular and performant adaptive scheduler: Aniello et al.'s 'Online scheduler' [4]—for brevity we refer to this scheme as OLS in this paper. The results show that T3-Scheduler outperforms OLS, increasing throughput by 20–72% for the micro-benchmarks and 60% for the real-world application.

2   T3-Scheduler Algorithm

In order to efficiently assign the logical view of a stream application, DAG, to the physical compute nodes with different capacities, the DAG should be divided into a number of parts, where each part is sized relative to the capacity of the respective node, while minimising the number of edge cuts. This problem has been proven to be NP-hard [10]. While it is possible to use existing graph partitioning algorithms in a heterogeneous environment, such as those used by METIS [3], these algorithms are dependent upon *a priori* information. That is, they rely on knowing the number of tasks to be assigned to each node before the graph can be partitioned. This is a barrier to practical deployments as it is difficult to reliably know this information at scheduling time. Many heuristic algorithms have been proposed that reduce the amount of communication between nodes [4,7,12,14]. However, they inspect each communicating pair of tasks or groups of tasks separately and in isolation. Additionally, in these methods the heterogeneity of a cluster is not fully considered and nodes may not be fully utilised. T3-Scheduler improves upon this situation by inspecting communicating tasks at a larger scale by building a simplified graph, representing all the communications between the tasks. T3-Scheduler consists of five main steps, the following subsections provide a detailed discussion of each step.

2.1 Monitoring

As the first step, T3-Scheduler monitors the execution of the stream application. This involves measuring the data transfer rate between each of the task pairs, providing a profile of all communications and also the task loads. The collected values are stored regularly in a monitoring log which T3-Scheduler can read periodically when rescheduling.

2.2 Constructing a Simplified Graph

T3-Scheduler constructs a weighted simplified graph, initially similar to the application graph, using the online profile, collected from the monitoring step. T3-Scheduler initially aggregates all of the tasks within each processing element into a single group, representing a vertex in the graph. The weight of the new group/vertex in the simplified graph is found by summing the load of each task within the group. Each edge in the graph, connecting two groups, is the aggregation of all the communications between two groups, weighted with the sum of the data transfer rates of their communicating tasks. This has been made possible because of the fact that tasks between two communicating processing elements are fully connected in typical DSPSs.

The simplified graph has the advantage of having a view of the connectivity between all the tasks. Therefore, a sub-graph, consisting of highly communicating tasks, can be found and assigned to the same compute node. Additionally, by considering communicating groups of tasks instead of communicating tasks, a slight change between some data transfer rates of communicating tasks within the communicating groups will not result in rescheduling, making the scheduling more stable. Vertices and edges are updated regularly if any vertex has to be partitioned in order to fit in a compute node.

2.3 Node Selection

T3-Scheduler considers the capacity and resource availability of each node, selecting the highest capacity node. This allows T3-Scheduler to take steps towards minimising the inter-node communication as a result of placing more communicating tasks in the higher capacity nodes. If multiple nodes have the same capacity, ties are broken by selecting a node randomly among the potential nodes. T3-Scheduler fills a node with as many communicating tasks as possible, up to its capacity, and then moves to the next highest capacity node.

2.4   First Level of Scheduling

The goal of first level of scheduling in T3-Scheduler is to divide the simplified graph into multiple parts where each part consists of highly communicating groups of tasks. T3-Scheduler takes a heuristic approach to divide up the graph into multiple parts which are sized according to the capacity of the heterogeneous node to be scheduled on. For every empty compute node, T3-Scheduler begins by finding a starting point in the simplified graph and expanding it by repeatedly selecting the most highly communicating neighbouring groups, forming a sub-graph, until the node is full. Once the node becomes full, a new compute node is selected for which a new starting point is found and the same procedure is applied. By following this approach, T3-Scheduler can find highly communicating tasks and place them in the same compute node. In the following, we provide further details of the first level of scheduling.

Forming a Sub-graph. After locating the group pair with the highest weight as the starting point, we evaluate if the pair of groups is able to fit within the current compute node. This condition is checked by comparing the sum of the tasks' load of each group, and the capacity of the selected compute node. This will have two possible outcomes. If the compute node has sufficient capacity to accommodate the group pair, it is assigned to the compute node. However, in the event of the compute node having insufficient capacity, a fine-grained partitioning will be performed on the group pair, where the number of tasks within one or both groups is reduced. This will enable a new, smaller group pair to be assigned to the current compute node which would not otherwise be possible. Partitioning a group pair will be explained in more detail shortly.

If the node still has some remaining capacity, we expand the starting point by finding the most highly communicating neighbours. Having located the immediate neighbour with the highest weight, an evaluation is performed to check if this group can fit within the compute node. If the node has sufficient capacity for the neighbouring group, it is added to the sub-graph and the next highest weighted neighbour will be evaluated. But, in the event that the highest weight neighbour is not able to fit within the compute node, an additional fine-grained partitioning will be performed on this group. Partitioning a single group will be explained in more detail shortly. After performing the single group partitioning, we add the group to the sub-graph which reaches its capacity at this point and therefore is fully utilised.

Fine-grained Group Pair Partitioning. To resolve the issue of insufficient capacity to accommodate the group pair selected as the starting point, we partition this group pair into two smaller group pairs, thereby allowing a subset of the initial group pair to be assigned to the compute node. For instance, assume that the group pair denoted as (A, B), is unable to fit within the current compute node. Therefore, we have to partition the group pair, (A, B), into two smaller group pairs (A_1, B_1) and (A_2, B_2) such that (A_1, B_1) cann fit. The aim of partitioning (A, B) is to minimise the edge cuts between (A_1, B_1) and (A_2, B_2) while maximising the number of tasks in (A_1, B_1). To achieve this, the task pairs with the highest rate from (A, B), are repeatedly selected and assigned to (A_1, B_1) until the node's capacity is reached.

However, when selecting a task pair (t_i, t_j) with the highest data transfer rate from (A, B), three scenarios are possible. To keep track of which tasks have been selected from (A, B), selected tasks are marked as 'selected' in (A, B) when they are assigned to (A_1, B_1).

1. Both tasks, t_i and t_j, are new and have not been selected before. In this case, both tasks will be assigned to (A_1, B_1) if the sum of the load of t_i and t_j is less than or equal to compute node's capacity.
2. One of the tasks is not new and is already marked as selected in A or B. To simplify the explanation, we assume that t_i in task pair (t_i, t_j) is a task already marked as 'selected' in A and is not new. We first find all the task pairs, denoted as (t_k, t_j) from (A, B) where t_k in A is not marked as 'selected'. Then, among these task pairs, we pick the task pair with the highest rate that can fit in the compute node and assign it to (A_1, B_1). By doing this, (t_i, t_j) is also included in (A_1, B_1) due to full connectivity of two communicating groups. This has the benefit of assigning two new tasks to (A_1, B_1) at each step with the highest data transfer rate and therefore minimising the edge cuts between (A_1, B_1) and (A_2, B_2).
3. Both tasks have already been assigned to (A_1, B_1) and are marked as 'selected' in (A, B). In this case, no further processing is done and we move to the next task pair which has the highest data transfer rate.

If one group is smaller than the other, for example A is smaller than B, we cannot always find a task pair with two new tasks. In this case, we just assign the task pair with the highest data transfer rate, that can fit in the compute node, to (A, B_1). After repeatedly selecting the task pairs and reaching the compute node's capacity, all the unmarked tasks in B are assigned to B_2 which will be inspected for assignment to another compute node later by T3-Scheduler. The simplified graph is updated with the new vertices, edges and their weights every time a partitioning is performed.

Fine-grained Single Group Partitioning. When expanding the sub-graph, the situation can arise where an entire group, denoted as A, is unable to fit within the current compute node's remaining capacity, requiring A to be partitioned. The aim is to utilise the node by filling it with the most highly communicating tasks from A. At each step, the task with the highest data transfer rate from A, which is connected to the sub-graph within the compute node, is found and assigned to a smaller group, denoted as A_1, until the compute node is full. The selected task from A is marked as 'selected' in A after assignment to A_1. In the case that the selected task's load is higher than available capacity, the task with the next highest data transfer rate is inspected for assignment. This process is repeated until we find a task that can fit in the node. Otherwise, the group partitioning process is complete. The remaining tasks from A, which are not marked as selected, form a new group, denoted as A_2. Then, the simplified graph is updated with the new vertex, edges and their weights. The new group, A_2, has this chance to be placed in another compute node with the unassigned task groups in the simplified graph that it communicates with.

2.5   Second Level Scheduling

It is common in stream processing systems to have multiple tasks in a worker process which, in Java-based DSPSs such as Apache Storm, is a Java Virtual Machine (JVM). In such stream processing systems, where each compute node has multiple workers, T3-Scheduler needs to schedule the tasks within each node. Therefore, at the second level of scheduling, it is determined which tasks should be assigned to the same worker. Finding the number of workers per node is hard to know *a priori*, because it is dependent upon the number of tasks and tasks' load which varies between stream applications. In our simple heuristic, we set a threshold, T, for the maximum number of tasks per worker. For each node, we divide the number of tasks to be assigned to a compute node, denoted as t, by T to determine the required number of workers on that compute node, denoted as w, for the given application:

$$w = \left\lceil \frac{t}{T} \right\rceil \tag{1}$$

T balances the need for fewer tasks per worker, to tolerate failures better, and the reduced latency from inter-worker communication, where more tasks are assigned to each worker. The value of T is empirically determined, by observing which value gives stable performance results. After finding w, we further partition the sub-graphs, found by the first level of scheduling, into w parts using the graph partitioning tool METIS [3]. The partitions, found by METIS, are of roughly equal size which means each part may contain fewer than T tasks. The number of tasks will remain close to T, but will not exceed this threshold value. Each part is then assigned to a worker, where the most highly communicating tasks are grouped together, minimising inter-worker communication.

3   Evaluation

In this section, we first provide a brief overview of Apache Storm for the sake of completeness, then we provide the evaluation of T3-Scheduler which is implemented within the Storm framework and discuss our experimental results. A stream application in Storm is called a *topology*. There are two types of processing elements/components in Storm: *spouts* and *bolts*. A spout is the source of a data stream and emits data, while a bolt is the computational unit used to process the data, before emitting new data to the next bolt in the DAG. A stream is defined as an unbounded sequence of tuples where a tuple is a named list of values. Each component in Storm consists of a number of *executors* that can be run in parallel. In other words, each executor is an executing instance of the component's code that can be run in parallel with other executors of the same component. Each executor normally consists of one task. When a topology, consisting of spouts and bolts, is submitted to a Storm cluster, the tasks are grouped into a number of JVMs/workers. Each compute/worker node is configured with a number of slots/ports where each JVM is assigned to one slot.

We implement T3-Scheduler on Apache Storm 0.9.7, running on a heterogeneous Storm cluster, configured with one master node, one ZooKeeper node and eight worker nodes. Ubuntu 12.04 LTS is installed on each node inside a VirtualBox VM. We use VMs as they allow us to specify the hardware configuration, where four worker nodes have 4 cores, 4 GiB of RAM, using four slots per node, whereas the remaining worker nodes have 2 cores, 2 GiB of RAM, with two slots per node. Each node has a 2.7 GHz Intel Core i5-3330S processor and is connected to a 1 Gbps network. Although a heterogeneous environment typically refers to different models of hardware with different configurations, we argue that the same hardware, where not all resources are available, can also be considered a heterogeneous environment. In our experiments we control the amount of RAM and available CPU cores on the test machines.

We use the average throughput, defined as the average number of tuples executed in each bolt's task per 10 s period, as our performance metric. Each executor in all our topologies has only one task. We limit average CPU usage of each node to 80%, which prevents any node from becoming overloaded. T in Eq. 1 is set to 5. These values were empirically determined, by evaluating multiple configurations in which this configuration provided good stable performance. We compare our scheduler with the Aniello et al.'s 'Online scheduler' [4] (referred to as 'OLS'). Unlike many other adaptive Storm schedulers, the OLS implementation is publicly available, allowing for a fair comparison. Similar to our scheduler, OLS considers the communication pattern and is able to handle cluster heterogeneity which is another reason to compare T3-Scheduler with it. We use three micro-benchmark topologies and one real-world topology with real data for our evaluation. Each experimental topology is run ten times for 700 s, achieving consistent improvements for T3-Scheduler over OLS in the throughput across all runs. In the following, we describe details of each experiment and present a typical execution of each topology to demonstrate the results.

3.1 Micro-Benchmarks

To evaluate T3-Scheduler, we first perform our experiments using three micro-benchmarks that represent common shapes of a Storm topology and evaluate a different congestion pattern: linear, diamond and star. Linear is one of the most common types of topology, which consists of a single spout and multiple bolts, where tuples are passed from one component to the next. Diamond has one spout which emits tuples to multiple bolts. Each bolt then passes these tuples to a single sink bolt. Star has multiple spouts which emit tuples to one bolt. This bolt then emits the received tuples to multiple bolts, passing them along. We have based our micro-benchmark implementations on the designs originally presented in [12]. For our experiments, we configure the linear and diamond

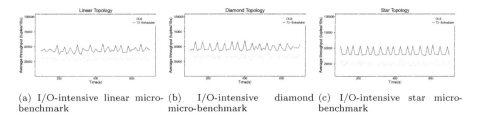

(a) I/O-intensive linear micro-benchmark
(b) I/O-intensive diamond micro-benchmark
(c) I/O-intensive star micro-benchmark

Fig. 1. Experimental results of I/O-intensive micro-benchmarks

micro-benchmark spouts and bolts to have four and eight tasks respectively. The star micro-benchmark is configured with two and eight tasks for the spout and bolts respectively. To evaluate T3-scheduler, we run each micro-benchmark in two different configurations: I/O-intensive and CPU-intensive, described as follows.

I/O-intensive. In this configuration, the throughput of the system is limited by the amount of communication between the nodes. We reduce the workload of each bolt by slowing the rate of the spout, so that each bolt has little processing to do, causing processing time to be limited by the network latency. The results for the I/O-intensive micro-benchmark execution for T3-Scheduler and OLS are presented in Figs. 1a, b, and c. As the results show, T3-Scheduler is able to achieve a higher average throughput of 45–72% for all of the micro-benchmarks than OLS. For instance, it can be seen in Fig. 1a that T3-Scheduler executes on average 45,000 tuples per 10 s in each bolt's task of the linear micro-benchmark, while OLS has a lower average throughput of 30,000. T3-Scheduler is able to increase the throughput by fully utilising the higher capacity nodes by assigning more communicating tasks to the same node. This allows it to use fewer total nodes—on average 2—for linear and star micro-benchmarks, and 3 nodes for diamond micro-benchmark, reducing inter-node communication. This is far fewer nodes than OLS, which uses all 8 nodes, leaving each node underutilised. T3-Scheduler further increases throughput by reducing inter-JVM communication, having on average 3 JVMs per node, calculated by Eq. 1. In comparison, OLS uses all 8 nodes where each available slot is assigned a JVM, increasing inter-JVM communication.

CPU-intensive. In this configuration, the throughput of the system is limited by the CPU utilisation of each node. We increase the workload of each bolt by supplying tuples at a faster rate, ensuring the bolts are fully loaded, resulting in a high CPU load. The results for the CPU-intensive micro-benchmark execution for the T3-Scheduler and OLS are shown in Figs. 2a, b, and c. As can be seen from the figures, T3-Scheduler outperforms OLS with higher throughput for the linear and star micro-benchmarks, and has similar throughput for the diamond micro-benchmark. The throughput for each of the micro-benchmarks is much

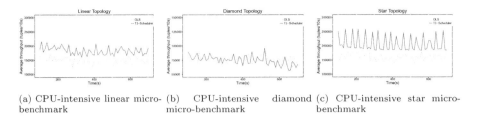

(a) CPU-intensive linear micro-benchmark   (b) CPU-intensive diamond micro-benchmark   (c) CPU-intensive star micro-benchmark

Fig. 2. Experimental results of CPU-intensive micro-benchmarks

higher than was previously seen for the I/O-intensive configuration, which is a result of a higher rate for the spouts. While this will place a greater load on the CPUs, T3-scheduler has an average throughput 20–28% higher than OLS for the linear and star micro-benchmarks. By placing more communicating tasks closer together, T3-Scheduler is able to fully utilise on average 4 of the higher capacity nodes, while OLS uses all 8 nodes of the cluster. Furthermore, T3-Scheduler decreases the inter-JVM communication, having on average 2 JVMs per compute node while OLS assigns one JVM to each slot. Both T3-Scheduler and OLS have similar throughput for the diamond micro-benchmark because of the greater number of tasks than were used by the linear and star micro-benchmarks, resulting in a higher CPU load. Despite having similar throughput, T3-Scheduler places more highly communicating tasks in each node, using an average of 6 nodes, where each node is fully utilised.

In summary, these results demonstrate the ability of T3-Scheduler to efficiently utilise each node by placing more communicating tasks closer together, improving overall throughput. In comparison, OLS tends to use all the nodes as a result of inspecting each task pair in isolation, which fails to see the whole communication pattern. Therefore communicating tasks end up in different nodes.

3.2 Real-World Topology

In this experiment, we use a real-world topology to evaluate T3-Scheduler. This topology is based on the first query of DEBS 2015 grand challenge.[1] The query is to find the top 10 most frequent routes of New York taxis for the last 30 min using the 2013 dataset. The layout of this topology has a linear shape with one spout and four bolts. The spout reads the records of each taxi trip from the dataset and sends the data to the PreProcess bolt with shuffle grouping. Then, the PreProcess bolt processes each trip record in order to find the start and end cell numbers based on longitude and latitude coordinates of the pickup and drop off locations. PreProcess bolt then emits the routes to Rolling Count bolt with shuffle grouping. This bolt counts the occurrence of each route using a rolling counter, implemented with a sliding window. The data is then passed to the Intermediate Rank bolt with fields grouping. This bolt has multiple tasks and is

---

[1] http://www.debs2015.org/call-grand-challenge.html.

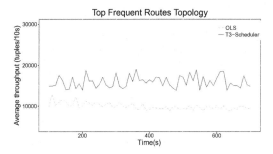

Fig. 3. Experimental results of top frequent routes topology

used to distribute the load coming from the Rolling Count bolt. Each task of the Intermediate Rank bolt finds 10 top frequent routes for a specified window. The Final Rank bolt has only one task, which aggregates the incoming intermediate rankings from the Intermediate Rank bolt with global grouping into a final rank. The numbers of tasks for Spout, PreProcess bolt, Rolling Count bolt, Intermediate Rank bolt and Final Rank bolt are 16, 16, 8, 4 and 1 respectively. We use a Redis server to store the trip records. We simulate a replay of the taxi data, by setting a simulation time that is a constant ratio with real time. This ratio is set so that 1 min is equal to 0.1 s of time in our experiment—thus the sliding window in Rolling Count bolt is 3 s.

Figure 3 shows the experimental results using T3-Scheduler and OLS. As it can be seen in the figure, OLS has an average throughput of 9,900 tuples per 10 s, while T3-Scheduler has a much higher average throughput of 15,800 tuples per 10 s. This represents a 60% improvement on average in throughput of T3-Scheduler over OLS. T3-Scheduler is able to fully utilise each node by putting more communicating tasks within each node, helping reduce the inter-node communication. This results T3-Scheduler using only 3 nodes on average, while OLS uses all 8 nodes. Additionally, T3-Scheduler is able to reduce inter-JVM communication by having 3 JVMs per node on average. In comparison, OLS has four JVMs on higher capacity nodes and 2 JVMs on the lower capacity ones, resulting in higher inter-JVM communication, contributing additional latency to processing, increasing the load on each node. In a system configuration that does not allow for node consolidation because it is already more heavily utilised, we would still gain in throughput over OLS as T3-Scheduler is better able to place highly communicating tasks closer together as a result of the overall view taken, whereas OLS will still suffer from the limitation of only evaluating individual task pairs in isolation. It can also be seen that this real-world topology has a lower throughput than the previous I/O-intensive micro-benchmarks. The lower throughput is the result of extra network latency for each task in the spout, as it has to pull data from Redis server instead of generating data in the spout.

In summary, our experimental results have shown that T3-scheduler is able to achieve a higher overall throughput for each of the micro-benchmarks and top frequent routes in a dataset of New York taxi trips. This is a result of T3-Scheduler making more efficient placement of tasks within the compute nodes, which leads to lower amounts of inter-node and intra-node communication. Our experimental results have shown that we consistently achieve 20–72% improvement over the OLS due to our improved task assignment. The fluctuations in throughput that can be seen in the experimental results is similar to the fluctuations seen in previous work [12]. From the detailed log files, there is no unexpected characteristics, so we are not concerned by this trend.

4   Related Work

Scheduling in data stream processing systems is similar to scheduling in distributed systems, however data locality is not an issue in stream processing systems. Generally, there are three main approaches to tackle the scheduling problem: Mathematical programming, graph theoretic and heuristics. [5] is an example of mathematical programming, which formulates the optimal scheduling based on integer linear programming approach, considering heterogeneity of computing and networking resources and finds the optimal solution for a small number of tasks. However, in this approach the resolution time for finding optimal scheduler grows exponentially as the problem size becomes larger. Adopting a graph theoretic approach, P-Scheduler [8] exploits graph partitioning algorithms to schedule the DAG on a homogeneous cluster. More commonly, heuristic algorithms are used which identify the communicating tasks which should be co-located in the system. Such an approach was used in [4] to put communicating tasks in the same compute node. Also, [7] inspects communicating groups of tasks instead of task pairs and has provided some inspiration for this paper. However, each pair is inspected in isolation and the connections between pairs is not considered which might results in spreading the pairs across the nodes. There exist some heuristic schedulers for distributed stream processing systems which fully utilise the nodes such as R-Storm [12] for homogeneous cluster and T-Storm [14] for a heterogeneous cluster. Additionally, there are different approaches to improve performance of a DSPS. For example, DRS [9] finds the optimised number of tasks for each operator, minimising the processing time for the input data. Elasticity on-demand approach, used in Stela [15], dynamically changes the resource allocation based on the load. Each of these algorithms are based upon varying sets of assumptions and use different optimisation techniques.

5   Conclusions and Future Work

T3-Scheduler utilises nodes effectively when they have different capacities, and puts as many communicating tasks together as possible on the same node. We evaluated T3-Scheduler using three micro-benchmarks and one real-world stream application. The experimental results showed that T3-Scheduler outperformed Aniello et al.'s state-of-the-art online scheduler significantly, improving throughput by 20–72% for the micro-benchmarks and 60% for a real-world application. As future work, we will evaluate T3-Scheduler on a larger cluster with a larger set of real-world applications. We will also continue work on run-time performance monitoring, investigating how workload characteristics change during execution and when rescheduling should be performed.

References

1. Apache Flink. https://flink.apache.org/
2. Apache Storm. https://storm.apache.org/
3. METIS. http://glaros.dtc.umn.edu/gkhome/metis/metis/overview
4. Aniello, L., Baldoni, R., Querzoni, L.: Adaptive online scheduling in Storm. In: Proceedings of the 7th ACM International Conference on Distributed Event-Based Systems, pp. 207–218 (2013)
5. Cardellini, V., Grassi, V., Lo Presti, F., Nardelli, M.: Optimal operator placement for distributed stream processing applications. In: Proceedings of the 10th ACM International Conference on Distributed and Event-Based Systems, pp. 69–80. ACM (2016)
6. Chakravarthy, S., Jiang, Q.: Stream Data Processing: A Quality of Service Perspective: Modeling, Scheduling, Load Shedding, and Complex Event Processing, vol. 36. Springer Science & Business Media, Berlin (2009). https://doi.org/10.1007/978-0-387-71003-7
7. Chatzistergiou, A., Viglas, S.D.: Fast heuristics for near-optimal task allocation in data stream processing over clusters. In: Proceedings of the 23rd ACM International Conference on Conference on Information and Knowledge Management, pp. 1579–1588. ACM (2014)
8. Eskandari, L., Huang, Z., Eyers, D.: P-scheduler: adaptive hierarchical scheduling in Apache Storm. In: Proceedings of the Australasian Computer Science Week Multiconference, p. 26. ACM (2016)
9. Fu, T.Z., Ding, J., Ma, R.T., Winslett, M., Yang, Y., Zhang, Z.: DRS: dynamic resource scheduling for real-time analytics over fast streams. In: Proceedings of the 35th International Conference on Distributed Computing Systems (ICDCS), pp. 411–420. IEEE (2015)
10. Gary, M.R., Johnson, D.S.: Computers and Intractability: A Guide to the Theory of NP-completeness. WH Freeman and Company, New York (1979)
11. Neumeyer, L., Robbins, B., Nair, A., Kesari, A.: S4: distributed stream computing platform. In: Proceedings of 2010 International Conference on Data Mining Workshops (ICDMW), pp. 170–177. IEEE (2010)
12. Peng, B., Hosseini, M., Hong, Z., Farivar, R., Campbell, R.: R-Storm: Resource-aware scheduling in Storm. In: Proceedings of the 16th Annual Middleware Conference, pp. 149–161. ACM (2015)
13. Shan, A.: Heterogeneous processing: a strategy for augmenting moore's law. Linux J. **2006**(142), 7 (2006)
14. Xu, J., Chen, Z., Tang, J., Su, S.: T-Storm: traffic-aware online scheduling in Storm. In: Proceedings of the 34th International Conference on Distributed Computing Systems (ICDCS), pp. 535–544. IEEE (2014)
15. Xu, L., Peng, B., Gupta, I.: Stela: enabling stream processing systems to scale-in and scale-out on-demand. In: Proceedings of 2016 IEEE International Conference on Cloud Engineering (IC2E), pp. 22–31. IEEE (2016)

Stateful Load Balancing for Parallel Stream Processing

Qingsong Guo[1](✉) and Yongluan Zhou[2]

[1] North University of China, Taiyuan, China
qingsongg@gmail.com
[2] University of Copenhagen, Copenhagen, Denmark
zhou@di.ku.dk

Abstract. Timely processing of streams in parallel requires dynamic load balancing to diminish skewness of data. In this paper we study this problem for stateful operators with key grouping for which the process of load balancing involves a lot of state movements. Consequently, load balancing is a bi-objective optimization problem, namely MINIMUM-COST-LOAD-BALANCE (MCLB). We address MCLB with two approximate algorithms by a certain relaxation of the objectives: (1) a greedy algorithm ELB performs load balancing eagerly but relaxes the objective of load imbalance to a range; and (2) a periodic algorithm CLB aims at reducing load imbalance via a greedy procedure of minimizing the covariance of substreams but ignores the objective of state movement by amortizing the overhead of it over a relative long period. We evaluate our approaches with both synthetic and real data. The results show that they can adapt effectively to load variations and improve latency efficiently comparing to the existing solutions whom ignored the overhead of state movement in stateful load balancing.

Keywords: Stream processing · Load balancing · State movement

1 Introduction

Timely processing of big streaming data on a cluster of commodity machines is the major concern for a *stream processing engines* (SPEs) like Storm [1]. Usually, a streaming computation is represented as an operator graph in which vertices stand for operators and an arc in the graph represents a data stream flowing between a pair of operators called *producer* and *consumer* respectively. To handle data deluge, a SPE exploits data parallelism that splits a stream into a number of disjoint substreams processed independently by a collection of parallel instances.

Process a stream in parallel relies on the grouping scheme for dispatching tuples to the instances of its consumer. Typically, there are two primitives of our interest: (1) *shuffle grouping* and (2) *key grouping* [10]. In shuffle grouping, tuples are randomly routed to downstream instances. It fits for stateless operators like

© Springer International Publishing AG, part of Springer Nature 2018
D. B. Heras and L. Bougé (Eds.): Euro-Par 2017 Workshops, LNCS 10659, pp. 80–93, 2018.
https://doi.org/10.1007/978-3-319-75178-8_7

map and *filter*, which are content-oblivious so that a tuple can be processed by any instances. In contrast, the key grouping partitions a stream into a number of substreams based on the key, i.e., a set of attributes, where tuples have equal values on key will be dispatched to the same instances. Stateful operators like **window-join** are content-sensitive since tuples with the same value should be processed by the same instance. Therefore, key grouping is preferable for stateful operators.

In this paper, we concern the problem of balancing load for stateful operators implementing key grouping. For a stateless operator with shuffle grouping, its load can be balanced evenly in a round-robin manner. However, it becomes much challenging in our context since the key grouping results in load imbalance. A substantial feature of stream processing is that data is in a state of ceaseless change [13,15,16]. Load variations like fluctuation of data rate and change in data distribution are ubiquitous, especially for such applications with their sources geographically located. If the load distribution is skewed on the partition key, the number of tuples handled by instances vary greatly. The computation will often be situated in an erratic state if we do not react to the imbalance, which is a disaster for processing latency if the state lasts for a long time.

Load balancing has received much attention in distributed stream processing [2,15,16]. Xing et al. [16] presented a correlation-based load distribution policy for a homogeneous shared nothing cluster. They focused on balancing load for a whole operator graph with an implicit assumption that every operator is not parallelized. In contrast, we focus on balancing load for a single operator with very high volume of load. In addition, load balancing has been also addressed for stateless operators with key grouping [10]. The impact of processing state has been widely studied in parallel stream processing [12,14], but it rarely brings about any attention to load balancing. In the presence of state, it involves a lot of state movements in load balancing because we have to change the allocations for many substreams. This problem is referred to as *stateful load balancing* and we formally define it as MINIMUM-COST-LOAD-BALANCE (MCLB). It associates two objectives: (1) minimize imbalance of all instances as much as possible; and (2) minimize the state movements as many as possible.

Unfortunately, the two objectives of MCLB can not be optimized consistently since they conflict with each other. Timely processing of data stream relies on efficient algorithms to address this dilemma. We propose two approximate algorithms for MCLB by relaxing the constraint on load imbalance: (1) ELB that balances the load eagerly, and thus has expensive cost of state movements; and (2) an algorithm CLB based on a procedure of minimizing correlations, that performs the load balancing periodically, where the cost for state movement is amortized and which is negligible when the period length is long enough. We evaluate the algorithms, with both synthetic streams and real datasets, and compare them with the exiting solutions. The experimental results justify the advantage of our solutions.

1.1   Related Work

Load balancing has received much attention in the last decade for its application in the peer-to-peer system [4] and cloud computing [11]. These approaches are static and hence are insufficient for a streaming scenario in which data is in ceaseless change [5]. Madsen et al. [8,9] recognized the problem of stateful load balancing while optimizing cluster utilization and minimizing latency for parallel stream processing. They modeled it as a Mixed-Integer Linear Program (MILP) problem and derive a solution with a MILP solver by incorporating the overhead of state movements into the constraints. In addition, there are three existing work that are analogous to our work [3,10,13].

Shah et al. [13] studied how to process a single continuous query operator on multiple shared-nothing machines. In this work, load imbalance is distinguished into *short-term imbalance* and *long-term imbalance*. Load balancing is in charge by an operator Flux that encapsulates adaptive partitioning and routing. To reduce the state movements, Flux sorts the sites in descending order of load and pairs them together, where load balance is realized by moving partitions around the sites in each pair. However, the parallelism in Flux is fixed and the cost for state movements has also not been quantified.

Nasir et al. [10] investigated the load balancing problem for stateless operators by applying the *"power of two choices"* approach. Their solution, namely Partial Key Grouping (PKG), improves the performance by mapping each key to two distinct substreams and forwarding each tuple to the less loaded of the two substreams. This approach can not be applied directly to stateful operator, because we need an extra operator to consolidate the partial results.

Gedik [3] proposed a partition scheme that is close to our solution. Stream is split with a partition function $\langle \mathcal{H}_t, \mathcal{H}_c \rangle$, which is a hybrid of consistent hash and explicit mapping, for multidimensional load balancing in stateful paralleliza-tion. This strategy can be applied for dynamic load balancing, but it has two drawbacks: (1) it has to reconstruct a new partition function after each process, which introduces new overhead for processing latency; and (2) it will result in expensive state migration since it uses a hash function to rebalance the load as we addressed.

2   Stateful Load Balancing

2.1   Problem Statement

A streaming computation is usually organized as an operator graph [1]. Each operator implements a bunch of predefined processing logic, such as *join, aggre-gate, filter*, or *user-defined functions*. A stream s can be written as an opera-tor pair (u_s, o_s), where u_s and o_s are the producer and consumer of it respec-tively. At runtime the consumer o is parallelized into a number of instances $\mathcal{I} = \{o^1, \ldots, o^n\}$, where $n \in \mathbb{N}^+$ is the parallelism. Stream s associates with a key k, the domain of the partition key k_u is split into p partitions with a hash function $\mathcal{H}(K_u) : \mathcal{D} \to [1 \ldots p]$, which separates s into non-overlapping substreams $\mathcal{S} = \{s^1, \ldots, s^p\}$, where $p \gg n$ and $p = \mathcal{O}(n)$. If o is stateful, then its processing state PS is also split into p partitions $ps = \{ps_1, ps_2, \ldots, ps_p\}$. A parallel processing of s is defined by the assignment $\mathcal{F} : \mathcal{S} \rightarrow \mathcal{I}$.

Stateful load balancing. For a stateful operator with key grouping, the number of tuples processed by each instance vary greatly if the distribution on the key is skewed. It is inevitable to balance load for instances. We focus on load balancing for a single operator o rather than the whole query graph. For convenience of discussion, we suppose that operator o has a unique input stream s. The assignment $\mathcal{F}$ changes at runtime so as to handle load variations. A state partition ps_i should be moved to another instance if the allocation of substream s^i has been changed. Therefore, the process of load balancing involves a lot of state movements and we call it as *stateful load balancing*.

2.2 Minimum Cost Load Balancing

Decision on load balancing relies on statistics about data rate, load distribution, and state distribution. Statistics are collected periodically over *statistic windows* of length Δ. We use a histogram $Y_t = (y_{1t}, y_{2t}, \ldots, y_{pt})^T$ to record the load distribution of $s_1 \ldots s_p$ in the t-th window, where y_{it}, $i = 1 \ldots p$, is the number of tuples of s_i arrived in this window. Other statistics about s like the mean $\bar{y}_t$ and the variance $var(Y_t)$ of Y_t can be derived accordingly. With Y_t and an assignment $\mathcal{F}_1$, we can measure the load imbalance and the number of state movements for the t-th statistic window.

Load imbalance. Encoding the assignment $\mathcal{F}_1$ as a matrix $\boldsymbol{A} = [a_{ij}]_{p \times n}$, where a_{ij} is a binary variable such that $a_{ij} = 1$ if substream s_i is assigned to instance o^j and $a_{ij} = 0$ otherwise. Since each substream only can be processed by an instance, we have $\sum_{j=1}^{n} a_{ij} = 1$. Let $L_t = (l_{1t}, l_{2t}, \ldots, l_{nt})^T$ be the *load vector* for instances $(o^1, \ldots, o^n)$ in the t-th window, then it is given by a linear transformation $L_t = \boldsymbol{A}^T Y_t$. If $\mathcal{F}_1$ is a balanced assignment, then $\boldsymbol{A}^T Y_t = \bar{\boldsymbol{l}}_t$, where $\bar{\boldsymbol{l}}_t = (\bar{l}_t, \bar{l}_t, \ldots, \bar{l}_t)^T$ and $\bar{l}_t = \frac{1}{n} \sum_{i=1}^{p} y_{it}$ is the *average load* in the t-th window.

Much work [13] defines the load imbalance in the t-th window as the difference between the maximum and the average load of instances, i.e., $\max_i(l_{it}) - \bar{l}_t$. But this value is insufficient to reflect the load distribution, which plays an essential role in changing the assignment. Alternatively, we use the *variance* of load vector $L_t = (l_{1t}, l_{2t}, \ldots, l_{nt})^T$ to measure the load imbalance in the t-th window. That is,

$$var(L_t) = \frac{1}{n} \sum_{i=1}^{n} (l_{it} - \bar{l}_t)^2, \tag{1}$$

where $L_t = \boldsymbol{A}^T Y_t$, and $\bar{l}_t$ is the mean of L_t, i.e., $\bar{l}_t = E(L_t) = \frac{1}{n} \sum_{i=1}^{n} l_{it}$.

State movement. Consider an adaptation and $\mathcal{F}_2$ is a new assignment. A state partition ps_i, $i = 1 \ldots p$, will be moved to another instance if the allocations given by two assignments are different, i.e., $\mathcal{F}_1(s_i) \neq \mathcal{F}_2(s_i)$. Let $\boldsymbol{x} = (x_1, \ldots, x_p)^T$ be a vector of binary variables, where $x_i = 1$ if $\mathcal{F}_1(s_i) \neq \mathcal{F}_2(s_i)$ and $x_i = 0$ otherwise. Let $\boldsymbol{d} = (d_1, \ldots, d_p)^T$ be the *state distribution* at present, where d_i is the number of tuples in ps_i. Then the number of state movements $\psi(\mathcal{F}_1, \mathcal{F}_2)$ in this load balancing is:

$$\psi(\mathcal{F}_1, \mathcal{F}_2) = \boldsymbol{x} \cdot \boldsymbol{d} = \sum_{i=1}^{p} x_i d_i \tag{2}$$

Given a set of substreams $\mathcal{S} = \{s_1, \ldots, s_p\}$ and a number of instances $\mathcal{I} = \{o^1, \ldots, o^n\}$, we consider a load balancing that replaces the current assignment $\mathcal{F}_1 : \mathcal{S} \rightarrow \mathcal{I}$ with a new one $\mathcal{F}_2$. The decision of load balancing must rely on statistics of historical data. Assuming we have a sequence of histograms $\boldsymbol{Y} = (Y_1, \ldots, Y_m)$, $m \in \mathbb{N}$, over the latest m statistic windows. We have a sequence of load vectors $\boldsymbol{L} = (L_1, \ldots, L_m)$, where the load vector L_j is given by $L_j = \boldsymbol{A}^T Y_j$. The overall imbalance over the statistic windows is $\hbar(\mathcal{F}_1) = \sum_{j=1}^{m} var(L_j)$. In addition, the cost of state movements of replacing $\mathcal{F}_1$ with $\mathcal{F}_2$ is given by Eq. 2, which quantifies the amount of communication required for approaching the load balancing. Therefore, the stateful load balancing is to compute an assignment that minimize both simultaneously. We denote this problem as MINIMUM-COST-LOAD-BALANCE (MCLB).

MCLB is a *bi-objective optimization* problem and it has been proved to be NP-hard. It is apparent that the two objectives conflict with each other: (1) to minimize $\psi(\mathcal{F}_1, \mathcal{F}_2)$, one hopes to change the assignment as less as possible; (2) to minimize $\hbar(\mathcal{F}_2)$ one needs more movements for which one can try more possible plans so as to balance the load. Therefore we cannot compute a feasible solution that minimizes both objectives simultaneously. Instead, we present two approximate algorithms for MCLB.

3   Eager Load Balancing

The *eager load balancing* (ELB) algorithm balances load in each statistic window and leverages heuristics to reduce state movements as many as possible. In ELB, the objective of minimizing load imbalance is relaxed to a range $[v, u]$, where v and u define the lower and upper bounds of load for each instance. For this relaxation, it is much easier to find a feasible assignment with less state movements. In addition some substreams are being hot spots at runtime, which have large volume of load and challenge load balancing. Consequently two heuristics are leveraged by ELB: (1) distribute the hot spots as evenly as possible; (2) fit the load of each instance into the range $[v, u]$ and make it as close as possible to $\frac{u+v}{2}$. Furthermore, we assume that the load for each substream in any window satisfy $y_{ik} \leq \frac{u-v}{2}$, which can be fulfilled by choosing a suitable value for p and a partition function.

Algorithm 1. Eager Load Balancing (ELB)

Input: The rurrent assignment $\mathcal{F}$, Histogram $Y_t = (y_{1t}, \ldots, y_{pt})^T$
Output: New assignment

1 Initialization: $OI \leftarrow \emptyset$, $UI \leftarrow \emptyset$, $R \leftarrow \emptyset$, $PQ \leftarrow \emptyset$;
2 /* Phase 1: preparing   */
3 $(l_{1t} \ldots l_{nt})^T \leftarrow AY_t$, $w \leftarrow \sum_{j=1}^{n} l_{jt}$;
4 $\pi \leftarrow \lceil \frac{2w}{u+v} \rceil$, $\bar{l}_t \leftarrow \frac{w}{\pi}$;
5 $o^1 \ldots o^n \leftarrow$ sort $\mathcal{I}$ in descending order of loads ;
6 **if** $\pi > n$ **then**
7 $\quad$ $o^{n+1} \ldots o^\pi \leftarrow$ initialize $\pi - n$ instances with load of 0;
8 $\quad$ $\mathcal{I} \leftarrow \mathcal{I} \cup \{o^{n+1}, \ldots, o^\pi\}$

9 **if** $\pi < n$ **then**
10 $\quad$ $R \leftarrow o^{\pi+1} \ldots o^n$;
11 $\quad$ $\mathcal{I} \leftarrow \mathcal{I} - R$;

12 $OI \leftarrow$ all overloaded instances with load larger than $\bar{l}_t$;
13 $UI \leftarrow \mathcal{I} - OI$;
14 /* Phase 2: identifying   */
15 **foreach** *instance* o^j *in* OI **do**
16 $\quad$ $\theta \leftarrow \min\{l_{jt} - \bar{l}_t, \frac{u-v}{2}\}$, $S_k \leftarrow$ the substreams of o^j ;
17 $\quad$ **while** $S_k \neq \emptyset$ **do**
18 $\quad\quad$ $s_i \leftarrow$ get the largest substream such that $y_{it} < \theta$;
19 $\quad\quad$ insert s_i into PQ;
20 $\quad\quad$ $l_{jt} \leftarrow l_{jt} - y_{it}$, $\theta \leftarrow \theta - y_{it}$;
21 $\quad\quad$ $S_k \leftarrow S_k - \{s_i\}$

22 **foreach** *substream* s_i *is assigned to an instance in* R **do**
23 $\quad$ insert s_i into PQ;

24 /* Phase 3: reassigning   */
25 **while** PQ *is not empty* **do**
26 $\quad$ $s_i \leftarrow$ peek the substream with the largest load from PQ ;
27 $\quad$ $o^j \leftarrow$ get the least-loaded instance from UI ;
28 $\quad$ $\mathcal{F}(s^i) \leftarrow o^j$, $l_{jt} \leftarrow l_{jt} + y_{it}$;
29 $\quad$ **if** $l_{jt} \geq \frac{u+v}{2}$ **then**
30 $\quad\quad$ $UI \leftarrow UI - \{o^j\}$, $OI \leftarrow OI + \{o^j\}$;

31 **return** $\mathcal{F}$;

As shown in Algorithm 1, ELB includes three phases. In the first phase, we first calculate the load vector $L_t = (l_{1t}, \ldots, l_{nt})$ with the latest histogram Y_t and the current assignment $\mathcal{F}_1$. Let w be the overall load, then the average load is $\bar{l} = \frac{w}{\pi}$, where $\pi = \lceil \frac{2w}{u+v} \rceil$. If $\pi > n$, then $\pi - n$ empty instances will be added into $\mathcal{I}$. If $\pi < n$, then $n - \pi$ instances should be removed from $\mathcal{I}$. To reduce state movements, we pick the $n - \pi$ least-loaded instances and keep them in a set R. The substreams assigned to instances in R should be reassigned to the instances in $\mathcal{I} - R$. All instances in $\mathcal{I}$ are sorted in a descending order of loads, and we use two sets OI and UI to keep track of the overloaded and underloaded instances respectively. The assignments for substreams are only allowed to changed from OI to UI, for which state movements reduce efficiently.

The second phase is to identify substreams that should be reassigned (Line 15–23). For an overloaded instance o^j, a substream can be removed from it has load at most $l_{jt} - \bar{l}_t$. Since load for each substream is under $\frac{u-v}{2}$, an identified substream must has load under the threshold $\theta = \min\{l_{jt} - \bar{l}_t, \frac{u-v}{2}\}$. Each time we identify the largest substream of load smaller than θ (Line 18–21) and insert it to the priority queue PQ. The value of θ and load for o^j should be updated thereafter and then the search repeats until no substream of o^j satisfying the condition (Line 17–21). The substreams assigned to o^j are also supposed to be sorted in a descending order of load, and hence the search completes in one traversal. Moreover, R is not empty if $\pi < n$, therefore the substreams assigned to the instances in R should be inserted in to PQ as well (Line 22–23).

In the last phase (Line 19–26), we assign the identified substreams to the underloaded instances in UI. The instances in UI are sorted in a descending order of load. The assignment completes by repeating the *first-fit procedure*, where each time we peek a substream s_i with the largest load from PQ and assign it to the least-loaded instance $o^j \in UI$ that can hold it. If o^j get overloaded, then it will be removed from UI and added into OI.

4   Correlation-Based Algorithm

In contrast to ELB, we present an algorithm that balances load for every m, $m > 1$, statistic windows. To reduce load imbalance, we compute an assignment that fits for a sequence of histograms $\mathbf{Y} = (Y_1, \ldots, Y_m)$ over m windows. The overhead of state movements is amortized over m windows and it is negligible if m is large enough. Therefore, we can ignore the overhead of state movement and only focus on minimizing the load imbalance.

We are given an assignment $\mathcal{F}$ and a sequence of load vectors $\mathbf{L} = \{L_1, \ldots, L_m\}$. Since $var(L_j) = \frac{1}{n} \sum_{i=1}^{n} l_{ij}^2 - \bar{l}_j^2$, the overall load imbalance can be written:

$$\sum_{j=1}^{m} var(L_j) = \sum_{j=1}^{m} \left(\frac{1}{n} \sum_{i=1}^{n} l_{ij}^2 - \bar{l}_j^2 \right) = \frac{1}{n} \sum_{j=1}^{m} \sum_{i=1}^{n} l_{ij}^2 - \sum_{j=1}^{m} \bar{l}_j^2 \tag{3}$$

Each substream s_i associates with a *load series* $X_i = (y_{i1}, \ldots, y_{im})$. X_i can be viewed as a discrete-time stochastic process $X_i = \{y_{it} : t \in \mathbb{N}^+\}$, where y_{it} is the number of tuples of s_i arrived in the t-th window. Let $S_i = \{s_1, \ldots, s_r\}$ be the substreams that is assigned to instance o^i ($1 \le i \le n$), then $\mathcal{S} = \cup_{i=1}^{n} S_i$ and $S_i \cap S_z = \emptyset$ if $i \ne z$. Let $N_i = X_1 + \cdots + X_r$ and $\eta_i = E(N_i) = \sum_{s_i \in S_i}^{|S_i|} E(X_i)$, then we have

$$\sum_{i=1}^{n} var(N_i) = \frac{1}{m} \sum_{i=1}^{n} \sum_{j=1}^{m} l_{ij}^2 - \sum_{i=1}^{n} \eta_i^2. \tag{4}$$

By some transformations of Eqs. (3) and (4), we can prove that $\min \sum_{j=1}^{m} var(L_j)$ is equivalent to $\min \sum_{i=1}^{n} var(N_i)$. In addition, by studying the variances $var(N_k) = var(X_1 + \cdots + X_r)$ and $var(X) = var(X_1 + \cdots + X_p)$, we have

$$var(X) - \sum_{k=1}^{n} var(N_k) = 2 \sum_{X_i \in S_k, X_j \in S_z, k \ne z} cov(X_i, X_j) \tag{5}$$

Algorithm 2. Correlation-based Load Balancing (CLB)

Input: Load series $\{X_1, \ldots, X_p\}$
Output: Assignment $\{S_1, \ldots, S_n\}$

1 Initialization: $S_1 \leftarrow \{s_1, \ldots, s_p\}$, $r \leftarrow 1$;
2 **foreach** *substream* s_i **do**
3 $\quad$ $\omega_i \leftarrow 0$;
4 $\quad$ **foreach** *substream* s_j *($j \neq i$)* **do**
5 $\quad\quad$ $cov(X_i, X_j) \leftarrow E[X_i X_j] - E[X_i]E[X_j]$;
6 $\quad\quad$ **if** $cov(X_i, X_k) \geq \theta$ **then**
7 $\quad\quad\quad$ $\omega_i \leftarrow \omega_i + cov(X_i, X_k)$;

8 **while** $r \leq n$ **do**
9 $\quad$ $s_k \leftarrow$ the substream with the maximum weight ω_k ;
10 $\quad$ $S_h \leftarrow$ get the set containing s_k ;
11 $\quad$ **foreach** *substream* s_i *of* S_h **do**
12 $\quad\quad$ **if** $cov(X_k, X_i) \leq \theta$ **then**
13 $\quad\quad\quad$ $S_h \leftarrow S_h - \{s_i\}$, $S_r \leftarrow S_r \cup \{s_i\}$;
14 $\quad\quad\quad$ $\omega_i \leftarrow 0$;
15 $\quad\quad\quad$ **foreach** *substream* $s_j \in S_h$ **do**
16 $\quad\quad\quad\quad$ $\omega_j \leftarrow \omega_j - cov(X_i, X_j)$
17 $\quad\quad\quad$ **foreach** *substream* $s_j \in S_r$ **do**
18 $\quad\quad\quad\quad$ $\omega_j \leftarrow \omega_j + cov(X_i, X_j)$

19 $\quad$ **if** $r < n$ **then**
20 $\quad\quad$ $r \leftarrow r + 1$;
21 $\quad\quad$ $S_r \leftarrow \emptyset$;

22 $\quad$ **else**
23 $\quad\quad$ **return**; // already n subsets

The right component $var(X) - \sum_{k=1}^{n} var(N_k)$ in Eq. (5) is denoted as *cross covariance*, which counts the covariances of substreams that fall into different subsets. Since $var(X)$ is a constant, minimizing $\hbar(\mathcal{F})$ is equivalent to finding a partition of $\mathcal{S}$ into subsets $S_1 \ldots S_n$ that maximize $var(X) - \sum_{k=1}^{n} var(N_k)$.

We construct a complete graph $G = (V, E)$ from the load series $X_1 \ldots X_p$, where a vertex $v_i \in V$ represents the load series X_i and the edge $e_{ij} \in E$ connecting v_i and v_j, $v_i, v_j \in V$, is assigned a weight $2cov(X_i, X_j)$. Let $n = 2$, then $\max[var(X) - \sum_{k=1}^{n} var(N_k)]$ is equivalent to computing the *Max-cut* of G. However, the *Max-cut* problem is NP-complete, and thus we present a greedy solution, as shown in Algorithm 2, in which each time we choose a substream s_k based on an alternative metric and split the set containing it to two subsets.

Given a threshold θ, $0 \leq \theta < 1$, and a substream $s_1 \in S$, we consider a split of the set S into two subsets S_1 and S_2, where S_1 keeps s_1 and any substream s_i such that $cov(X_1, X_i) \geq \theta$ and S_2 includes others otherwise, i.e., $S_1 = \{s_1\} \cup \{x_i | x_i \in S, cov(X_1, X_i) < \theta\}$ and $S_2 = S - S_1$. Let ω_1 be the contribution of o_1 to the cross covariance in this split, then $\omega_1 = \sum_{s_i \in S, i \neq 1} cov(X_1, X_i)$, if $cov(X_1, X_i) \geq \theta$. Calculation of the covariance matrix $\Sigma = [cov(X_i, X_j)]_{p \times p}$ is described by Line 2–7.

The set splitting proceeds in runs (Line 8–23). For each run we choose the substream with the largest contribution to perform a set splitting rather than maximizing the overall cross covariance, which is NP-complete as we showed earlier. Suppose that substream s_k has the largest weight in the current run, i.e., $s_k = \max\{w_i | s_i, i = 1 \ldots p\}$, then the set S_h containing it will be split into two subsets S_h and S_r, where S_r is an empty set and each substream s_i such that $cov(X_k, X_i) \geq \theta$ will be move to S_r from S_k. Since ω changes as set splitting, we should update its value for each substream of S_h and S_r to prepare the next run (Line 15–18). Repeat this procedure until n sets are created.

5   Evaluation

We evaluated our algorithms with three metrics: (1) *load imbalance var*(L_t), (2) *state movements*, and (3) *processing latency*. The processing latency measures the time for processing each tuple. Based on this measurements, we can also calculate the system throughput $1/avg$, where avg is the average processing latency for a stream of tuples. In the experiments, we compared *ELB* and *CLB* with two existing solutions:

PKG also implements the key grouping but it was designed for stateless LB [10]. **UHLB** balances load with a universal hash function rather than the key grouping in our context. It returns $h(t)$, where $h : [p] \rightarrow [n]$ is chosen at random from a family of 2-universal hash functions.

Datasets. Two types of datasets, both real and synthetic, are used in this evaluation.

Twitter stream. The real dataset consists of a collection of tweets extracted from an interval around 29 h: Feb 27 15:24:12—Feb 28 20:47:34, 2013. There are 10,637,691 tweets and about 13.9 GB in total. Each tweet is viewed as a tuple of JSON objects.

Synthetic stream. Two synthetic streams S1 and S2 are used to simulate the fluctuation of data rate and the change of data distribution respectively. S1 and S2 conform to a relational schema (ts, a_1, a_2), where ts is a Unix timestamp, a_1 is an integer falls into $[1, 100]$, and a_2 is a string of words. The field a_1 is designated as the partition key on which S1 and S2 have been partitioned into 100 substreams. The partition keys of S1 and S2 follow the Gaussian and Zipf distributions respectively, which are used to simulate various data skewness. The means for Gaussian and Zipf are set as the same.

In addition, a Poisson process is used to control the data rates of S1 and S2. In a Poisson process, tuples arrive sequentially and their inter-arrival times Z_i are exponentially distributed with a rate parameter $\lambda : Prob\{Z_m \leq \tau\} = 1 - e^{-\lambda\tau}$, where the parameter is $\lambda = 10000$.

5.1   Simulation Results

Experimental results are based on two hours simulation. In this experiment, we implement a simple topology, as shown in Fig. 1, where the operator u is

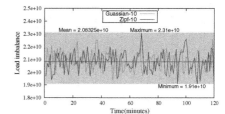

Fig. 1. A simple topology with 3 operators. The size of state of o is set to one tenth of the data rate, $\psi(o) = \frac{1}{10}r(o)$.

Fig. 2. Load imbalance with $\pi = 10$ and $1/f = 1$

responsible for generating tuples or read data from Amazon S3. The operator v serves as a sink for collecting the statistics for o. Operator o is used for evaluating the tested algorithms. The length of a statistic window is set to 1 min and thus we have 120 histograms $Y = (Y_1, \ldots, Y_{120})$ for each stream in total. To compare the load imbalance, the number of instances in the experiment is fixed.

Load imbalance with respect to data distribution—As we claimed earlier, load imbalance is mainly caused by skewness of data. Therefore, we use S1 and S2, have different distributions, to investigate the impact of data skewness. Since S1 and S2 follow the same traffic model, i.e., they have approximately the same data rates, the load imbalances are only determined by data skewness. Figure 2 shows the change of imbalance over time for CLB when we use 10 instances, i.e., $n = 10$. The results are similar for $n = 5$ and $n = 15$. The experiments on other algorithms also show similar features, and thus we just take CLB as an example.

Let Y_i and Y_i' be the histograms for the i-th statistic windows of S1 and S2 respectively, where Y_i satisfies the normal distribution and Y_i' satisfies the Zipf distribution. The variance of Y_i' is larger than that of Y_i, although Y_i' and Y_i have equal means. The imbalances over statistic windows are plotted in Fig. 2, in which the parallelism n is 10 and $1/f = 1$. We calculate the mean and standard deviation of the imbalances. As we expected, the mean of $var(L_i), i = 1 \ldots 120$, is 2.08983e+10, which is approximately equals to the mean of $var(L_i')$ (2.08325e+10). The standard deviations of $var(L_i)$ and $var(L_i')$ are 6.76016e+08 and 7.92797e+08 respectively. Therefore, the fluctuation of $var(L_i)$ is much severer than that of $var(L_i')$. This is confirmed by the plots in Fig. 2. The lines labeled "Gaussian-10" and "Zipf-10" in the figure capture the fluctuation of imbalances $var(L_i)$ and $var(L_i')$ of CLB on S1 and S2 respectively. The maximum and minimum imbalances occur in the line labeled "Zipf-10". The range between the maximum and minimum values on "Zipf-10" is colored with blue. By looking at the figure, all points of $var(L_i)$ falls into the range colored with blue and thus the change of $var(L_i)$ is much more moderate. This confirms that data skewness has significant impact to load imbalance.

Performance comparison of various algorithms—We used the real dataset to test the performance on load imbalance and state movements for each

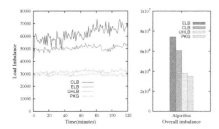
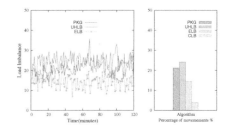

Fig. 3. Load imbalance over time.   **Fig. 4.** Percentage of state movements.

Table 1. Mean and standard deviation

$1/f$		CLB	ELB	PKG	UHLB
1	μ	–	5.1E+4	3.1E+4	2.9E+4
	δ	–	1806.8	1018.8	770.4
24	μ	6.1E+4	–	–	–
	δ	5133.7	–	–	–

Table 2. Processing latencies (ms)

Latency	CLB	ELB	PKG	UHLB
Max	1103.13	1109.51	1551.30	1505.13
Mean	0.76	0.73	0.92	1.01
Median	0.30	0.33	0.38	0.38
95%	1.12	0.68	1.70	1.89

algorithm. The results for $n = 10$ are plotted in Figs. 3 and 4. In general, as we expected, UHLB and PKG beat our algorithms on load imbalance, but they perform much worse on state movements. In terms of CLB, UHLB and PKG reduce imbalance by at least an order of magnitude. The reason is apparent that the primary objective of CLB is to minimize state movements rather than load imbalance.

We have calculated the standard deviation of the imbalance $var(L_t)$ for all algorithms. In the experiments, the frequency of load balancing is set to $1/f = 24$, i.e., there are 5 load balancing in total. Table 1 summarizes the mean μ and standard deviation δ of imbalance $var(L_t)$ of all algorithms. The average percentage of state movements for CLB is 48.4% when $1/f = 24$. The value drops to 1.6% when we amortize them over the statistic windows.

By looking at Fig. 3, we can observe that ELB outperforms CLB on load imbalance, which is determined by their optimization objective and hence justifies the assertion we addressed earlier. CLB aims at minimizing the overall load imbalance $\hbar(\boldsymbol{L})$ by greedily reducing the covariance. In contrast, ELB executes load balancing eagerly at each statistic window. Figure 4 shows the comparison of state movements. The left figure plots the percentage of movements for ELB, UHLB, and PKG. By looking at the figure, it is apparent ELB has far less state movement than UHLB and PKG. The average percentages of PKG, UHLB, and ELB are 21.2%, 24.2%, and 14.5% respectively. In the right figure, we compared the average percentages of PKG, UHLB, and ELB with the amortized percentage of CLB. As we expected the state movements of CLB is negligible comparing to the other three algorithms.

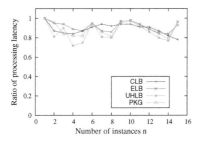
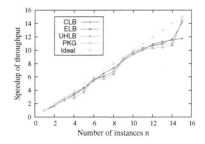

Fig. 5. Ratio of processing latency.   **Fig. 6.** Speedup of throughput.

5.2   Processing Latency

We implemented the algorithms in Enorm [6,7], which extends Apache Storm [1] by integrating the ability of dynamic reconfiguration at runtime [8]. The experiments were conducted on Amazon's EC2 with medium VM instances, where each has 1.7 GB of RAM, moderate IO performance and 1 EC2 compute unit. We evaluated the metric by explicitly scaling out an operator *WordCounter* that counts the occurrence for each word every 1 min over the Twitter stream. To exclude the interference from other factors, we fix the processing capacity of each VM to 1000 tuples/s. The data rate of Twitter stream starts at 1000 tuples/s and linearly grows to 16,000 tuples/s, and we add one more instances for the operator at a scale-out.

Processing latency with respect to data rate—Statistics of processing latency is illustrated in Table 2, where 95% is the 95-th percentile. By examining the 95-th percentile, we know that most tuples have processing latency less than 1.89 ms. In contrast, a small portion of tuples have very high latencies. It confirms that state movement indeed has significant impact to the processing latency of tuples. As we can see from the table, the maximum latency reaches up to 1.5 s. The processing latency is mainly due to stream buffering and replay. In the implementation of load balancing, we adopt a *pause-configuring-resume* procedure, and thus tuples from upstream operators will be buffered and then replayed to downstream after the completion of the process.

By comparing the mean of processing latency, we can assert that our algorithms outperform the existing solutions. In particular, CLB approaches the least reduction of 17% and ELB reduces the mean of processing latency up to 50%. To have better understanding of the processing latency, we calculated the ratio $\frac{\mu_1}{\mu_i}$, where μ_1 is the mean of processing latency of CLB when $n = 1$ and μ_2 is the mean of processing latency of any algorithm when $n = i$, $i = 1 \ldots 15$. Figure 5 plots the ratio by varying the number n of instances. It is apparent that UHLB and PKG fluctuate more severely than CLB and ELB.

Speedup of throughput—The speedup of throughput achieved by each algorithm is illustrated in Fig. 6. In the figure, the line labeled "Ideal" represents the theoretical speedup of scaling out the operator. The speedups for ELB and

CLB are approximately linear to the parallelism. In contrast, PKG and UHLB cannot approach linear speedups. The change of speedups for the latter two algorithms show interesting features. By looking at the figure, we can observe remarkable phase transition on the lines labeled "PKG" and "UHLB". The two lines can be divided into multiple stages, such as the ranges 3–5, 6–8, and 10–14. The speedup improves slightly in a stage, but it shows a sudden jump at the end of that stage. This phenomenon undoubtedly confirms the impact of load balancing. During the execution of a load balancing, the incoming tuples are temporarily buffered by the upstream operator. The buffered tuples would get congested if there are too many state movements involved in the load balancing. The upcoming tuples are delayed until the congested tuples have been processed and then we can observe a sudden jump of the speedup.

We also observe that the speedup of CLB gradually deviate from the "Ideal" line as we scale out the operator. As we can see from the figure, ELB, PKG and UHLB outperform CLB when $n = 15$. Since the execution of load balancing is infrequent, $1/f > 1$, for CLB, load imbalance cannot be removed in time. The overhead is too high for a single load balancing and this problem get worse when we have more instances. Consequently, the throughput declines seriously due to the load imbalance. It shows that the frequency f of load balancing is also very important to throughput. We have to carefully choose the value for f.

6   Conclusion

We have shown that load balancing for stateful stream processing is a bi-objective optimization problem. It is NP-hard and we proposed two approximate algorithms, ELB and CLB, in which the objectives of minimizing load imbalance and state movements are relaxed. The evaluation shows that our approaches outperform the existing solutions in processing latency and throughput even though them have higher load imbalance.

Acknowledgements. The author from North University of China is supported by NSFC No. 61602427 and NSF of Shanxi No. 201601D202037.

References

1. Apache Storm. http://storm.apache.org/
2. Abadi, D.J., Ahmad, Y., et al.: The design of the Borealis stream processing engine. In: CIDR 2005, Asilomar, CA, January 2005
3. Gedik, B.: Partitioning functions for stateful data parallelism in stream processing. VLDB J. **23**(4), 517–539 (2014)
4. Godfrey, B., Lakshminarayanan, K., Surana, S., Karp, R.M., Stoica, I.: Load balancing in dynamic structured P2P systems. In: INFOCOM 2004, Hong Kong, China, 7–11 March 2004
5. Kifer, D., Ben-David, S., Gehrke, J.: Detecting change in data streams. In: VLDB 2004, pp. 180–191. VLDB Endowment (2004)

6. Madsen, K.G.S., Thyssen, P., Zhou, Y.: Integrating fault-tolerance and elasticity in a distributed data stream processing system. In: SSDBM 2014. ACM, New York (2014)
7. Madsen, K.G.S., Zhou, Y.: Demo: elastic mapreduce-style processing of fast data. In: DEBS 2013, pp. 335–336 (2013)
8. Madsen, K.G.S., Zhou, Y., Cao, J.: Integrative dynamic reconfiguration in a parallel stream processing engine. CoRR abs/1602.03770 (2016)
9. Madsen, K.G.S., Zhou, Y., Cao, J.: Integrative dynamic reconfiguration in a parallel stream processing engine. In: 33rd IEEE International Conference on Data Engineering, ICDE 2017, San Diego, CA, USA, 19–22 April 2017, pp. 227–230 (2017)
10. Nasir, M.A.U., Morales, G.D.F., García-Soriano, D., Kourtellis, N., Serafini, M.: The power of both choices: practical load balancing for distributed stream processing engines. In: ICDE 2015, Seoul, South Korea, 13–17 April 2015, pp. 137–148 (2015)
11. Nuaimi, K.A., Mohamed, N., Nuaimi, M.A., Al-Jaroodi, J.: A survey of load balancing in cloud computing: challenges and algorithms. In: NCCA 2012, London, UK, 3–4 December 2012, pp. 137–142 (2012)
12. Schneider, S., Hirzel, M., Gedik, B., Wu, K.L.: Auto-parallelizing stateful distributed streaming applications. In: PACT 2012, pp. 53–64. ACM, New York (2012)
13. Shah, M.A., Chandrasekaran, S., Hellerstein, J.M., Ch, S., Franklin, M.J.: Flux: an adaptive partitioning operator for continuous query systems. In: ICDE 2002, pp. 25–36 (2002)
14. Wu, S., Kumar, V., Wu, K.L., Ooi, B.C.: Parallelizing stateful operators in a distributed stream processing system: how, should you and how much? In: DEBS 2012, pp. 278–289. ACM, New York (2012)
15. Xing, Y., Hwang, J.H., Çetintemel, U., Zdonik, S.: Providing resiliency to load variations in distributed stream processing. In: VLDB 2006, pp. 775–786. VLDB Endowment (2006)
16. Xing, Y., Zdonik, S., Hwang, J.H.: Dynamic load distribution in the borealis stream processor. In: ICDE 2005, pp. 791–802. IEEE Computer Society (2005)

Towards Memory-Optimal Schedules for SDF

Mitchell Jones[1], Julián Mestre[2,3], and Bernhard Scholz[2(✉)]

[1] Department of Computer Science, University of Illinois at Urbana-Champaign,
Champaign, USA
[2] School of Information Technologies, University of Sydney, Sydney, Australia
`Bernhard.Scholz@sydney.edu.au`
[3] Facebook, Menlo Park, USA

Abstract. The Synchronous Data Flow (SDF) programming model is an established programming paradigm for stream processing applications. SDF programs are expressed by actors and streams that establish communication among actors. Streams are implemented as FIFO buffers, and the size of the FIFO buffers depends on the steady-state schedule. Finding a steady-state schedule that minimizes the sizes of FIFO buffers, is of great importance to minimize the memory consumption. The state-of-the-art provides ad-hoc heuristics only, so finding memory-optimal steady-state schedules is still an open challenge.

In this work, we study three objective functions capturing the memory utilization of three different implementations of the FIFO buffers. We show that one objective is NP-hard to optimize, while the other two can be solved optimally in polynomial time. The algorithm for computing these optimal schedules is implementable as an online algorithm. We show the effectiveness of our new algorithm comparing it with the state-of-the-art heuristics. Our experiments show that for large synthetic instances, our algorithm generates schedules that use up to 8 times less memory.

Keywords: Synchronous Data Flow (SDF) · Scheduling
Optimality · FIFO-buffer

1 Introduction

Stream programming paradigm has its origins in the Kahn's processing model [5] and data-flow computing [3]. Stream programs are a natural fit for applications that process large unbounded regular sequences of data. There are many examples for established stream programming applications including digital signal processing, audio, video, graphics, networking and for big data.

Stream programs are expressed by a set of *actors* and a set of *data channels* between actors. Conceptually, actors are independent processing units with their own memory and program counters. An actor exchanges information with another actor via a data channel using tokens. The channels fully expose the dependencies between actors, and are directed: the *producer* is the actor at the

© Springer International Publishing AG, part of Springer Nature 2018
D. B. Heras and L. Bougé (Eds.): Euro-Par 2017 Workshops, LNCS 10659, pp. 94–105, 2018.
https://doi.org/10.1007/978-3-319-75178-8_8

source of a data channel, and the *consumer* is the actor at the destination of the data channel. The data channels are commonly implemented as FIFO buffers, and the size of the FIFO buffers depend on the point in time when actors are executed (also known as *fired*).

If the firing of actors is not coordinated, actors may starve or the memory of FIFO buffers may deplete. To overcome this problem, Synchronous Data Flow (SDF) Model was introduced [2] to bound the size of FIFO buffers and make computations of infinite streams of data deterministic and controllable. In the SDF model, the actor are constrained such that for each actor firing, only a fixed number of tokens are consumed and produced, respectively. For a well-formed SDF program, a finite periodic schedule can be constructed [2] that consists of a finite sequence of actor firings. The schedule can be computed a priori and invokes each actor of the stream graph at least once, and produces no net change in the system state after executing the schedule. I.e., the number of tokens in each data channel is the same before and after executing the schedule. Hence, a periodic schedule can be executed again and again for unbounded regular streams without starving actors and without exhausting memory. The state before and after the execution of a periodic schedule is known as a *steady-state*. Hence, the SDF model is a popular model for stream programming because the memory consumption of the data channels is known a prior at compile time. There are many different steady-state schedules for an SDF program, and the sizes of the FIFO buffers for channels depend on the chosen steady-state schedule. Finding a steady-state schedule that minimizes the sizes of FIFO buffers, is still an open research problem. The current state-of-the-art algorithms for finding steady-state schedules are ad-hoc heuristics only [2] that do not optimize for minimal memory. Hence, stream programs may not fully utilize caches and/or modern massively parallel architectures (e.g. GPGPUs) may need to utilize slower memory rather than fast memory. Hence, finding memory-optimal steady-state schedules is of importance for the SDF model.

Contributions: This work is of theoretic nature and explores the problem of finding memory optimal steady-state schedules in an algorithmic fashion. We anticipate large instances of SDF programs in near future that necessitates new algorithmic contributions for memory-optimal steady-state schedules. We provide three notions of memory optimality based on how FIFO buffers utilize memory. We show for each notion of optimality, algorithmic and complexity theoretic results. We also provide a synthetic set of experiments to show the effectiveness of our new algorithmic approach in comparison with the state-of-the-art algorithm for large instances.

2   Motivating Example

The data-flow model [3] represents a program as a *stream graph* $G = (V, E)$ whose vertices V are called *actors* and whose edges $E \subseteq V \times V$ are called *channels*. A channel $(u, v) \in E$ buffers data elements called *tokens*, which are passed from the output of actor u to the input of actor v. In Fig. 1(a) a stream

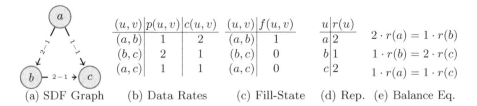

| (a) SDF Graph | (b) Data Rates | (c) Fill-State | (d) Rep. | (e) Balance Eq. |

Fig. 1. Example: stream graph consists of actors a, b, and c; channels are augmented with numbers of produced and consumed tokens for its adjacent actor when its fires. Fill-state, repetition for steady-state, and balance equation are given.

graph is depicted whose actors are a, b and c. The directed edges of the example graph represent channels that transport streams of tokens from the producing actor to the consuming actor. In the following we denote by n and m the number of actors and channels, respectively.

Synchronous dataflow [7] restricts the semantics of the dataflow model by fixing the number of consumed and produced tokens for a single firing of an actor. The number of consumed tokens for a single firing of actor v from an incoming channel $(u, v) \in E$ is given by function $c : E \to \mathbb{N}$. Function $p : E \to \mathbb{N}$ denotes the number of produced tokens for an outgoing channel of an actor. We also refer to the functions p and c as *data rates*. The data rates of our motivating example are shown in Fig. 1(b) and are also depicted as edge annotation in the graph in Fig. 1(a). A *schedule* $s = \langle u_1, \ldots \rangle \in V^*$ is a sequence of actors, where a given actor may occur several times. Each occurrence $u_i \in V$ in the schedule is called a *firing* of actor u_i. A firing of an actor modifies the state of the system by producing and consuming tokens from the channels adjacent to the actor. The *fill-state* of the system is the numbers of tokens on the channels between actor invocations that have been queued but have not been consumed yet. We will specify the fill-state of the system at a given point in time with a function $f : E \to \mathbb{N}$. The fill-state is an abstraction of the actual tokens that are stored on the channels. Let us assume that we have an initial fill-state as given in Fig. 1(c), which implies that there is a single token in channel (a, b) and there are no tokens on channel (b, c), and channel (a, c).

A *periodic schedule* has finite length, includes every actor of the stream graph at least once, and its execution produces no net change in the fill-state after executing the schedule. A periodic schedule may be computed a-priori [7], and executed ad-infinitum without exhausting memory[1]. We refer to the fill-state before and after the execution of a periodic schedule as *steady-state*. A periodic schedule s has a *repetition vector* $r : V \to \mathbb{N}$ that counts the occurrences of each actor in s. The *length* of s is given by $\sum_{u \in V} r(u)$. We denote with $\mathcal{S}$ the set of periodic schedules for a given stream graph instance. Periodic schedules are constrained by two factors. First, recall that every actor needs to be fired at

---

[1] Under the assumption that the memory consumption for a single actor invocation is bounded.

least once. For our example, actor a, b, and c must occur in schedule s. Second, in order to conserve the fill-state of the FIFO-buffers after the execution of the schedule, for each buffer the number of tokens put into the buffer must equal the number of tokens consumed from the buffer. These constraints give rise to the so-called *balance equations*:

$$p(u,v) \cdot r(u) = c(u,v) \cdot r(v) \qquad\qquad \forall\, (u,v) \in E \qquad (1)$$
$$r(u) > 0 \qquad\qquad \forall\, u \in V \qquad (2)$$

The balance equations of the example in Fig. 1 are given in the Fig. 1(e) with the additional constraint that $r(a) > 0$, $r(b) > 0$, and $r(c) > 0$ where $r(u)$ are the *repetitions* for actor u, i.e., there must be $r(u)$ occurrences of actor u in the schedule s. Finding the smallest integral repetitions for actors can be expressed as a problem of finding the smallest integral vector in the null-space of the *topological matrix* [7]. It is known that for connected stream graphs, an integral repetition vector satisfying Eqs. (1) and (2) exists if and only if the *topological matrix* of the stream graph has rank $n - 1$. The repetitions of the motivating example in Fig. 1(a) is shown in Fig. 1(d).

Algorithm 1. GREEDY$((V, E, p, c), t)$

---

1. $L \leftarrow \sum_{u \in V} r(u)$
2. let F be the set of fireable actors in V using fill-state t
3. let D be the set of deferrable actors in F
4. **for** $i = 1$ to L **do**
5.   **if** $F \setminus D \neq \varnothing$ **then**
6. $u \leftarrow$ an actor from $F \setminus D$
7.   **else**
8. $u \leftarrow$ an actor in F that increases total number of tokens the least
9.   add u to the schedule s
10. $r(u) \leftarrow r(u) - 1$
11.   invoke actor u
12.   update F and D // An actor u is not fireable if $r(u) < 1$.
13. **return** s

For the example, actor a is invoked twice since it produces only one token on the edge (a, b), but to fire b at least once it needs to consume two tokens on (a, b). Actor c is invoked twice because a is invoked twice, and c only consumes a single token for every token produced by a along the channel (a, c). No smaller repetition vector can be found. To find a schedule s, a greedy heuristic was devised by Battacharyya *et al.* [2] (cf. Sect. 3.3.2). The heuristic is outlined in Algorithm 1. The goal of GREEDY is to minimize the sum of the maximum number of tokens required for each channel over a periodic schedule. Given a graph G, and the initial delay t as part of the input, it returns a schedule s. Note that we say an actor v is *fireable*, if for every incoming edge (u, v), $f(u, v) \geq$

$c(u, v)$. An actor v is *deferrable* if it is fireable, and for at least one of its outgoing edges (v, u) (that is not a transitive edge[2]) it holds that $f(v, u) \geq c(v, u)$.

For our motivating example in Fig. 1(a), the greedy algorithm will fail to find the optimal periodic schedule. For the example we further assume, that we have an initial delay of one token on edge (a, b). To minimize the memory consumption the optimal periodic schedule to use is $s = \langle a, b, c, a, c \rangle$.

During the firing of these actors, we can keep track of the maximum number of tokens needed for each channel. For the edge (a, b), the initial fill-state $f(a, b)$ on the edge is 1. We first fire actor a, and thus the fill on the edge (a, b) is increased to 2. Similarly, the edge (a, c) is now storing a single token. Next, actor b is invoked, consuming two tokens from the channel (a, b) and producing two tokens on the channel (b, c). Actor c fires, which consumes one token from edge (b, c) and (a, c). At this point, the edge (a, b) has a fill of zero. In order to ensure this schedule is periodic, we must fire a again, producing a single token on both (a, b) and (a, c). We return back to our initial fill-state by firing c once more. Over this execution, we can see that the maximum number of tokens on the channels (a, b) and (b, c) is two, while the maximum number of tokens on the channel (a, c) is one. Summing this together, this schedule requires memory to store at most five tokens during this execution.

However, it is entirely possible that the greedy algorithm could choose the schedule $s' = \langle a, b, a, c, c \rangle$. By executing each actor in s' one-by-one, we can observe that the maximum number of tokens used by the channels (a, b), (b, c) and (a, c) is two. Thus enough memory will be needed to store six tokens, which is clearly suboptimal compared to the schedule s.

To see why this is the case, note that the difference between s and s' is the order of the 3rd and 4th actors a and c. After firing a and then b, both a and c are fireable but not deferrable. Notice that a is not deferrable, even though there is an outgoing edge that meets the consumption requirements ($f(a, c) \geq c(a, c)$), the edge (a, c) is a transitive edge. Since $f(a, b) \not\geq c(a, b)$ at this point in time, a does not meet the criteria to be marked as a deferrable actor. Thus, the greedy algorithm can choose to fire either actor a or c. The greedy algorithm could make the suboptimal choice to fire a again (Line 6 of Algorithm 1), instead of firing c, which would consume the single token on the channel (a, c). By choosing to fire a, the greedy algorithm produces a second token on the channel (a, c). This leads to the schedule s'.

3   Problem Statement

Stream programs admit an exponential number of periodic schedules. In fact, given a repetition vector r, any sequence of length $L = \sum_{u \in V} r(u)$ where actor u occurs $r(u)$ times is a periodic schedule. Therefore, the number of periodic schedules is given by $|\mathcal{S}| = \frac{L!}{\prod_{u \in V} r(u)!}$. Among these schedules some consume less

---

[2] We say that a directed edge (v, u) is a transitive edge in a graph $G = (V, E)$ if there exists a directed path from v to u in G using only the edges $E \setminus \{(v, u)\}$.

memory on their FIFO-buffers than others. How much memory a given schedule consumes will depend on the implementation details of the FIFO-buffers and on the evolution of the fill-state over the execution of the schedule.

Recall that the fill-state function keeps track of the number of tokens stored on each channel waiting to be consumed. Given the current fill-state of the system, it is possible to determine the fill-state after the execution of the particular actor. Therefore, given the initial fill-state, we can easily compute the fill-state after the i-th step of the schedule execution. The fill-state function $f_s^i : E \rightarrow \mathbb{N}$ defines the fill-state of channel (u, v) after the i-th execution step of schedule s and may be defined as $f_s^0(u, v) = t(u, v)$ for the first step, and

$$f_s^{i+1}(u, v) = \begin{cases} f_s^i(u, v) + p(u, v), & \text{if } u = s(i + 1), \\ f_s^i(u, v) - c(u, v), & \text{if } v = s(i + 1), \\ f_s^i(u, v), & \text{otherwise.} \end{cases}$$

where $t(u, v)$ is initial fill-state of (u, v) at the beginning of the execution of s.

A periodic schedule and an initial fill-state are said to be *admissible* if the schedule can be executed without ever running out of tokens on any channel.

Definition 1. *Finite periodic schedule s with initial fill-state t is admissible, if*

$$f_s^i(u, v) \geq 0, \qquad\qquad \forall (u, v) \in E,\ i \in \{0, \ldots, L\}$$
$$f_s^0(u, v) = f_s^L(u, v), \qquad\qquad \forall (u, v) \in E$$

It is worth noting that for each periodic schedule $s \in S$ there exists an initial fill-state that makes it admissible. Therefore, all we need is a method for deciding which periodic schedule to use.

We study three objective functions that capture the memory utilization of the system under different implementations of the FIFO buffers. In each case the goal is to compute an admissible schedule (s, t), the only difference is the objective being optimized:

(P1) The Min-Max-Max Problem:

$$\min_{(s,t)}\ \max_{0 \leq i \leq L}\ \max_{(u,v) \in E}\ f_s^i(u, v)$$

(P2) The Min-Sum-Max Problem:

$$\min_{(s,t)}\ \sum_{(u,v) \in E}\ \max_{0 \leq i \leq L}\ f_s^i(u, v)$$

(P3) The Min-Max-Sum Problem:

$$\min_{(s,t)}\ \max_{0 \leq i \leq L}\ \sum_{(u,v) \in E}\ f_s^i(u, v)$$

The objective **(P1)** minimizes the maximum buffer requirement across all buffers. This objective captures a simplistic implementation of FIFO buffers where space is allocated ahead of time and buffers have uniform length. The objective **(P2)** minimizes the sum of the maximum requirements. This objective captures a simple implementation of FIFO buffers where space is allocated ahead of time, but different buffers can differ in size. The objective **(P3)** minimizes the maximum combined size of all buffers at any point in time. This objective capture a more sophisticated implementation where buffer space can be acquired and released dynamically.

4   Scheduling to Minimize Memory Usage

In this section we consider the objectives defined in Sect. 3 under the assumption that the initial fill-state of each buffer can be set arbitrarily. In other words, given an instance (V, E, c, p), the goal is to compute a schedule s and an initial fill-state $t : E \to \mathbb{N}$ so that the schedule is admissible and one of the three objectives **(P1–P3)** is minimized.

Our algorithm for Min-Max-Max and Min-Sum-Max assumes the Balance Eqs. (1) and (2) for the instance are feasible and that we are given the smallest integral repetition vector r that the instance admits. In addition to the instance (V, E, p, c) the algorithm take as a parameter a permutation of the actors, we use $\pi : V \to [1, n]$ to the denote the position of each actor within this permutation.

First, the algorithm computes for each channel the appropriate initial fill-state that will ultimately make the schedule admissible. Second, each actor u is added to a priority queue with priority 0. The algorithm then enters an infinite loop where in each iteration we remove from the priority queue the actor u with the smallest key x (if there are several actors with the same key, we break ties using the permutation order), we invoke u, and re-insert u with priority $x + \frac{1}{r(u)}$. The pseudo-code of the procedure is given in Algorithm 2.

Notice that for each actor u, its priority becomes 1 after $r(u)$ invocations. Therefore, after $L = \sum_{u \in V} r(u)$ executions of the while loop every actor has priority 1. At this point in time, the schedule executed thus far is periodic. We call this periodic schedule, the canonical schedule induced by π and denote it by (s_π, t_π). Notice, however, that Algorithm 2 itself never ends. Indeed, after the L-th iteration the while loop goes on to repeat this periodic schedule ad-infinitum.

The proof of correctness hinges on the following observation on the minimum buffer size of a channel based on the data rates of its endpoints.

Lemma 1 ([2, Theorem 3.3]). *Let (u, v) be a channel. In any admissible schedule, the buffer for channel (u, v) has size at least $p(u, v) + c(u, v) - \gcd(p(u, v), c(u, v))$ at some point in time during the execution of the schedule.*

Proof. For sake of brevity, let us denote $p(u, v)$ with a, $c(u, v)$ with b, and $a + b - \gcd(a, b)$ with $\text{LB}(a, b)$. Let (s, t) be an admissible schedule. Since we are interested in deriving a lower bound on the buffer size for channel (u, v), we assume without loss of generality that this is the only channel in the graph.

If $a \mid b$ then the buffer size has to be at least $b = \text{LB}(a, b)$, so the lemma follows. Let us then assume from now on that $1 < a < b$ and that b is not a multiple of a; a symmetric argument can be used to handle the cases $b \mid a$ and $1 < b < a$.

Consider two executions of v in s. If we have two consecutive executions of v, or the schedule begins and ends with v, then the buffer size is at least $2b > \text{LB}(a, b)$. So let us assume this does not happen. We apply the following transformation to the schedule: If the schedule starts by executing v, then we fuse every execution of v with the execution of u that immediately follows it into a new actor v'; if the schedule starts by scheduling u, then we fuse every execution of v with the execution of u that immediately precedes it into a new actor v'. The result is a schedule for a new channel (u, v') with production rate a and consumption rate $b - a$. It is easy to check that if $\text{LB}(a, b - a)$ is a lower bound on the buffer size for the new channel, then $\text{LB}(a, b - a) + a$ is a lower bound on the buffer size for the original channel.

A simple proof by induction finishes the argument if $a \mid b$ then we are at the base of the inductive proof. Otherwise, the size of the buffer for the channel (u, v) must be at least

$$\begin{aligned} \text{LB}(a, b - a) + a &= a + b - a - \gcd(a, b - a) + a \\ &= a + b - \gcd(a, b - a) \\ &= a + b - \gcd(a, b), \end{aligned}$$

where the last equality follows by Euclid's algorithm.

Now that we have a lower bound on the size of each buffer, we will prove that these bounds are attained simultaneously by our algorithm.

Lemma 2. *For any permutation π, the schedule (s_π, t_π) is admissible and for each channel (u, v) the maximum size of the buffer during the execution of the schedule is $p(u, v) + c(u, v) - \gcd(p(u, v), c(u, v))$.*

Algorithm 2. CANONICAL$((V, E, p, c), \pi)$

---

1. **for** $(u, v) \in E$ **do**

2. $t_\pi(u, v) \leftarrow \begin{cases} c(u, v) - \gcd(p(u, v), c(u, v)) & \text{if } \pi(u) < \pi(v) \\ c(u, v) & \text{if } \pi(v) < \pi(u) \end{cases}$

3. let Q be an empty priority queue

4. **for** $u \in V$ **do**

5.   **insert** u with priority 0 into Q

6. **while** true **do**

7. $(u, x) \leftarrow$ **delete-min**(Q) // break ties using the π order

8.   execute actor u

9.   **insert** u with priority $x + \frac{1}{r(u)}$ into Q

Proof. We prove the bounds on the size of the buffer for a fixed, but arbitrary, channel (u, v). For sake of brevity, let us denote $p(u, v)$ with a and $c(u, v)$ with b. Recall that Balance Eq. (1) for channel (u, v) implies $\frac{r(u)}{r(v)} = \frac{b}{a}$.

First, consider the case $\pi(u) < \pi(v)$. Notice that the 1st execution of v is preceded by an execution of u. In general, the $k+1$st execution of v is preceded by

$$\left\lfloor \frac{k \frac{1}{r(v)}}{\frac{1}{r(u)}} \right\rfloor + 1 = \left\lfloor k \frac{r(u)}{r(v)} \right\rfloor = \left\lfloor \frac{kb}{a} \right\rfloor + 1$$

executions of u. Therefore, the fill-state of the channel after the $k+1$st execution of v is precisely

$$t_\pi(u, v) + a \left(\left\lfloor \frac{kb}{a} \right\rfloor + 1 \right) - (k+1)b.$$

Using the fact that $t_\pi(u, v) = b - \gcd(a, b)$ when $\pi(u) < \pi(v)$, we can show that the fill-state of the channel is always non-negative:

$$t_\pi(u, v) + a \left(\left\lfloor \frac{kb}{a} \right\rfloor + 1 \right) - (k+1)b =$$

$$= a \left(\left\lfloor \frac{kb}{a} \right\rfloor + 1 \right) - kb - \gcd(a, b) \geq \gcd(a, b) - \gcd(a, b) = 0,$$

where the inequality follows from the fact that $a \left(\left\lfloor \frac{kb}{a} \right\rfloor + 1 \right) - kb > 0$ and Bézout's Lemma [9].

On the other hand, just before before the $k+1$st execution of v, the fill-state of the buffer is

$$t_\pi(u, v) + a \left(\left\lfloor \frac{kb}{a} \right\rfloor + 1 \right) - kb.$$

Again, using the fact that $t_\pi(u, v) = b - \gcd(a, b)$ we get

$$t_\pi(u, v) + a \left(\left\lfloor \frac{kb}{a} \right\rfloor + 1 \right) - kb = a + b - \gcd(a, b) + a \left\lfloor \frac{kb}{a} \right\rfloor - kb \leq a + b - \gcd(a, b),$$

so the buffer size never exceeds $a + b - \gcd(a, b)$.

Now consider the case $\pi(v) < \pi(u)$. In this case the $i+1$st execution of v is preceded by $\lceil \frac{ib}{a} \rceil$ executions of u. A similar argument (but using the fact that $t_\pi(u, v) = b$ when $\pi(u) > \pi(v)$) shows that the schedule is admissible and that the maximum buffer size is $a + b - \gcd(a, b)$.

Combining the lower bound from Lemma 1 and the upper bound from Lemma 2 we get that every canonical schedule is an optimal solution for **(P1)** and **(P2)**. The following theorem summarizes the results in this section.

Theorem 1. *There is a polynomial time algorithm for computing an optimal periodic schedule for the objectives **(P1)** and **(P2)** with flexible initialization. Furthermore, the schedule can be computed online using $\Theta(n)$ space and $O(\log n)$ time per actor invocation.*

Proof. The optimality of the objectives **(P1)** and **(P2)** follows immediately from Lemmas 1 and 2. The complexity claims follow from using a priority queue implementation that uses $\Theta(n)$ space and performs `insert` and `delete-min` operations in $O(\log n)$ time.

We contrast our positive results from the previous section by showing that it is NP-hard to optimize the Min-Max-Sum (cf. **(P3)**).

Theorem 2. *It is NP-hard to optimize **(P3)** with flexible initialization.*

The theorem can be shown by reducing the Minimum Feedback Arc Set (MFAS) problem to our problem.

5   Experiments

With the advent of stream programming we anticipate large instances of stream programs. In the absence of large stream programs, we have generated complete, directed, acyclic graphs as a synthetic benchmark suite. We generated the graphs as follows: We start with a directed graph $G = (V, E)$ of n nodes, and number the vertices $v_1, v_2, \ldots v_n$. For each vertex $v_i \in V$, we select a random repetition value $r(v_i)$ uniformly at random from the range $\{1, \ldots, n\}$. We then iterate through every pair of vertices $v_i, v_j \in V$. If $i \neq j$ and $i < j$, we add the directed edge (v_i, v_j) to E, with $p(v_i, v_j) = \frac{r(v_j)}{\gcd(r(v_i), r(v_j))}$ and $c(v_i, v_j) = \frac{r(v_i)}{\gcd(r(v_i), r(v_j))}$. This generation template guarantees that a repetition vector exists, and the topological matrix of this directed, acyclic graph has rank $n - 1$.

Using this approach, we generated graphs of size $n = 10, 15, \ldots, 50$ and ran both algorithms. As before, we timed the execution of each algorithm, taking the average over twenty runs. The numerical results of these experiments are shown in Table 1 and are visualized in Fig. 2.

Table 1. Performance comparison on randomly generated instances.

Instance	CANONICAL			GREEDY	
$\|V\|$	**(P1)**	**(P2)**	Time (s)	**(P2)**	Time (s)
10	20	586	0.0030	1226	0.0097
15	28	1048	0.0047	2937	0.0362
20	32	2483	0.0081	7818	0.1124
25	48	6131	0.0143	30306	0.5421
30	60	9486	0.0188	47979	1.6658
35	70	16782	0.0291	68126	5.0272
40	80	22927	0.0352	149469	8.3609
45	84	29781	0.0454	244380	17.6809
50	100	46203	0.0567	347676	39.5296

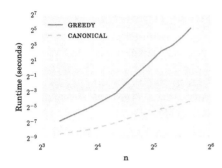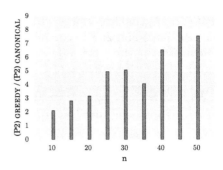

Fig. 2. Visualizing the performance on randomly generated instances.

Two observations stand out from Fig. 2. First, CANONICAL seems to be asymptotically faster GREEDY. We suspect that this is due to the fact that as the graph becomes denser, there will be many "fireable" actors in each iteration, leading GREEDY to spend nearly quadratic time per iteration, whereas CANONICAL, is guaranteed to spend at most logarithmic time. Second, GREEDY was never able to find an optimal schedule and the quality of the solutions it produced deteriorated as n grew.

These experiments strongly support the hypothesis that GREEDY is slower and produces worse schedules with respect to memory consumption when more actors become "fireable" at each iteration.

6 Related Work

Our work is closely connected to the greedy algorithm proposed in [2]. Their approach is based on a heuristic which keeps track of the set of "fireable" actors. Our algorithm is based on optimality theorems which produces both the optimal memory schedule and the required initial delay to achieve optimality. With a given initial delay, the NP-hard proof of the problem is given in [2]. The approach in [4] uses a model-checking method to find optimal schedules which requires a machinery which is outside of the complexity class P. There is a stream of literature on scheduling of SDF programs with model checking. Other approaches use time automata to solve the scheduling problem for SDF [1], and variations of the problem definition taking other metrics such as throughput into account [8]. There is also related work concerning to eliminate buffers via unrolling the finite periodic schedules [6].

7 Conclusion

In this work, we have studied three mathematical definitions of memory optimality based on how FIFO buffers utilize memory. We started by showing that two of these objectives can be solved in logarithmic worst-case time per actor invoked, and that the last objective is NP-hard. Experiments showed that our new algorithm drastically outperformed existing heuristics in both speed and the memory usage of schedules produced on dense instances.

Acknowledgements. This project has been partially supported by the Australian Research Council Discovery Project DP1096445. We would like to thank our reviewers for the insightful feedback, and Yousun Ko for her help with the experiments.

References

1. Ahmad, W., de Groote, R., Hölzenspies, P.K.F., Stoelinga, M., van de Pol, J.: Resource-constrained optimal scheduling of synchronous dataflow graphs via timed automata. In: Proceedings of the 2014 14th International Conference on Application of Concurrency to System Design, ACSD 2014, pp. 72–81. IEEE Computer Society, Washington, DC (2014). https://doi.org/10.1109/ACSD.2014.13
2. Battacharya, S.S., Murthy, P.K., Lee, E.A.: Software Synthesis from Dataflow Graphs. Kluwer Academic Publishers, Norwell (1996)
3. Dennis, J.B.: First version of a data flow procedure language. In: Robinet, B. (ed.) Programming Symposium. LNCS, vol. 19, pp. 362–376. Springer, Heidelberg (1974). https://doi.org/10.1007/3-540-06859-7_145
4. Geilen, M., Basten, T., Stuijk, S.: Minimising buffer requirements of synchronous dataflow graphs with model checking. In: Proceedings of the 42nd Annual Design Automation Conference, DAC 2005, pp. 819–824. ACM, New York (2005). https://doi.org/10.1145/1065579.1065796
5. Kahn, G.: The semantics of simple language for parallel programming. In: IFIP Congress, pp. 471–475 (1974)
6. Ko, Y., Burgstaller, B., Scholz, B.: LaminarIR: compile-time queues for structured streams. In: Proceedings of the 36th ACM SIGPLAN Conference on Programming Language Design and Implementation, PLDI 2015, pp. 121–130. ACM, New York (2015). https://doi.org/10.1145/2737924.2737994
7. Lee, E.A., Messerschmitt, D.G.: Synchronous data flow. Proc. IEEE **75**(9), 1235–1245 (1987)
8. Wiggers, M.H., Bekooij, M.J.G., Smit, G.J.M.: Buffer capacity computation for throughput-constrained modal task graphs. ACM Trans. Embed. Comput. Syst. **10**(2), 17:1–17:59 (2011). https://doi.org/10.1145/1880050.1880053
9. Wikipedia: Bézout's identity (2016). https://en.wikipedia.org/wiki/Bzout%27s_identity. Accessed 12 Aug 2016

Towards Hierarchical Autonomous Control for Elastic Data Stream Processing in the Fog

Valeria Cardellini(✉) ⬡, Francesco Lo Presti ⬡, Matteo Nardelli ⬡,
and Gabriele Russo Russo ⬡

Department of Civil Engineering and Computer Science Engineering,
University of Rome Tor Vergata, Rome, Italy
{cardellini,nardelli,russo.russo}@ing.uniroma2.it,
lopresti@info.uniroma2.it

Abstract. In the Big Data era, Data Stream Processing (DSP) applications should be capable to seamlessly process huge amount of data. Hence, they need to dynamically scale their execution on multiple computing nodes so to adjust to unpredictable data source rate. In this paper, we present a hierarchical and distributed architecture for the autonomous control of elastic DSP applications. It revolves around a two layered approach. At the lower level, distributed components issue requests for adapting the deployment of DSP operations as to adjust to changing workload conditions. At the higher level, a per-application centralized component works on a broader time scale; it oversees the application behavior and grants reconfigurations to control the application performance while limiting the negative effect of their enactment, i.e., application downtime. We have implemented the proposed solution in our distributed Storm prototype and evaluated its behavior adopting simple policies. The experimental results are promising and show that, even with simple policies, it is possible to limit the number of reconfigurations while at the same time guaranteeing an adequate level of application performance.

Keywords: Data Stream Processing · Self adaptive
Hierarchical control · MAPE loop

1 Introduction

Data Stream Processing (DSP) applications can continuously collect and process data generated by an increasing number of sensing devices, to timely extract valuable information in many application domains, including health-care, energy management, logistic, and transportation. These scenarios pose new challenges to DSP systems in terms of strict latency requirements in face of variable and high data volumes to process. To deal with operator overloading, a commonly adopted stream processing optimization is data parallelism, which consists in scaling-out or scaling-in the number of parallel instances for the operators, so that each instance can process a subset of the incoming data flow in parallel.

ⓒ Springer International Publishing AG, part of Springer Nature 2018
D. B. Heras and L. Bougé (Eds.): Euro-Par 2017 Workshops, LNCS 10659, pp. 106–117, 2018.
https://doi.org/10.1007/978-3-319-75178-8_9

Recently, since data sources are in general geographically distributed (e.g., in IoT scenarios), we also have witnessed a paradigm shift with the deployment and execution of DSP applications over distributed Cloud and Fog computing resources, which *de facto* bring applications closer to the data, rather than the other way around, to improve application latency and make better use of the ever increasing amount of resources at the network periphery. Nevertheless, this very idea makes it difficult to control DSP application performance. Most of the approaches proposed in the literature (as detailed below) have been designed for cluster environments with a centralized control component overlooking the DSP operations. These solutions typically do not scale well in a distributed environment given the spatial distribution, heterogeneity, and sheer size of the infrastructure itself. While scalable decentralized solutions have been proposed, e.g., [12], their inherent lack of coordination might result in frequent reconfigurations which negatively affect the application performance due to continuous system downtime.

In this paper, to take the best of the two worlds, we propose a hierarchical distributed approach to the autonomous control of elastic DSP applications in Fog-based environment. Our contributions are as follows. We present in Sect. 2 a hierarchical distributed architecture for the autonomous control of elasticity, named *Elastic and Distributed DSP Framework* (EDF). The control is organized according to the Monitor, Analyze, Plan and Execute (MAPE) reference model for self-adapting systems. Specifically, the proposed architecture relies on a high-level centralized MAPE-based *Application Manager* that coordinates the run-time adaptation of subordinated MAPE-based *Operators Managers*, which, in turn, locally control the adaptation of single DSP operators.

As a second contribution, we present in Sect. 3 a simple reference control strategy for each component, we name the *local* (for the Operator Managers) and *global* policy (for the Application Manager), respectively. The first monitors and analyzes the operator performance to determine whether it needs to be reconfigured by scaling the number of replicas or by migrating a replica. The global policy identifies the most effective reconfigurations proposed by the Operator Managers, accepting or declining the proposed reconfigurations in order to control their number, and hence the application downtime.

As a third contribution, we have implemented EDF on our extension [1,2] of Apache Storm and evaluated the proposed solution on our prototype. We implemented two simple policies: the local policy employs a threshold approach to request operator reconfigurations to the Application Manager; the global policy adopts a token bucket scheme to control the number of allowed reconfigurations in any control interval. As shown in Sect. 4, our results are promising and show the effectiveness of the proposed solution in achieving a good trade-off between application performance and reconfiguration cost.

Related Work. Run-time adaptation of DSP applications achieved through elastic data parallelism is attracting many research and industrial efforts. Most approaches that enable elasticity are often implicitly organized as self-adaptive systems based on the MAPE model. Some works, e.g., [4,6,7], exploit best-effort threshold-based policies based on the utilization of either the system nodes or the operator instances. The basic idea is that when the utilization exceeds the threshold, the replication degree of the involved operators is modified accordingly. Other works, e.g., [5,10,11,16], use more complex centralized policies to plan the scaling decisions. Lohrmann et al. [10] propose a strategy that enforces latency constraints by relying on a predictive latency model based on queueing theory. Stela [16] relies on throughput-based metric to identify those operators that need to be scaled-out/in. Heinze et al. [8] estimate latency spikes caused by operator reallocations through a model and use it to define a heuristic placement algorithm. In [1] we present a centralized optimization problem for the runtime elasticity management of DSP applications that minimizes migration costs while satisfying the application QoS requirements. Differently from the above works that present reactive scaling strategies, De Matteis and Mencagli [3] propose a proactive strategy that takes into account a limited future time horizon to choose the reconfigurations. However, all these works rely on a centralized planner for the run-time adaptation of DSP applications, that may suffer from network latencies in a geo-distributed operating environment. Mencagli [11] presents a game-theoretic approach where the control logic is distributed on each operator, but it is not integrated in a DSP system.

As regards the deployment of DSP applications in geo-distributed environments, we extended Apache Storm [2] with a self-adaptive and distributed placement heuristics [12], but it suffers from frequent and uncoordinated reconfigurations. SpanEdge [13] is implemented in Apache Storm, but it does not support operator migrations. Saurez et al. [14] propose a new Fog-specific programming model supporting the migration of application components.

2 System Architecture

2.1 Problem Definition

A DSP application can be regarded as directed acyclic graph (DAG), where data sources, operators, and sinks are connected by streams. An operator is a self-contained processing element that carries out a specific operation (e.g., filtering, POS-tagging), whereas a stream is an unbounded sequence of data (e.g., tuple). We distinguish between stateless and stateful operator whether the operator computes the output data using only the incoming data or also some internal state information, respectively. For the execution, multiple replicas can be used to run an operator, where each replica processes a subset of the incoming data flow. By partitioning the stream over multiple replicas, running on one or more computing nodes, the load per replica is reduced, which yields lower application latency. Since the load can vary over time, the number of replicas can change at run-time as to optimize some non-functional requirements. As infrastructure on which DSP applications are executed, we consider computing resources that are scattered in a geo-distributed environment as Fog computing.

For the execution, a DSP application needs to be deployed on computing resources, which will host and execute the operators. Since DSP applications are usually long-running, the operators can experience changing working conditions (e.g., fluctuations of the incoming workload, variations in the execution environment). To preserve the application performance within acceptable bounds, their deployment should be adapted at run-time, through migration and scaling operations. A *migration* moves an operator replica to another computing resource, so to balance resource utilization. A *scaling* operation changes the replication degree of an operator: a scale-out decision increases the number of replicas when the operator needs more computing resources, whereas a scale-in decreases the number of replicas when the operator under-uses its resources. The drawback of reconfigurations is that they cause application downtime; hence, if applied too often, they negatively impact the application performance.

Being in charge of the application execution, the DSP system (e.g., Storm) can control the application performance. To agree on satisfying execution conditions, the user and the DSP system provider stipulate a Service Level Agreement (SLA). We consider that the SLA specifies as Service Level Objective (SLO) the maximum acceptable response time R_{max}, that is the worst end-to-end delay from a data source to a data sink, and the maximum tolerable downtime during normal execution conditions. The latter indicates how often the application can be reconfigured when its response time is far from the critical value R_{max}.

2.2   Hierarchical Architecture

The MAPE loop represents a prominent and well-know reference model to organize the autonomous control of a software system, where four components (Monitor, Analyze, Plan, and Execute) are responsible for the primary functions of self-adaptation. When the controlled system is geo-distributed as in Fog computing, a MAPE loop where analysis and planning decisions are centralized on a single component may not be sufficient for effectively managing the adaptation, because of the network latencies among the system components. As described by Weyns et al. in [15], different patterns to design multiple MAPE loops have been used in practice by decentralizing the functions of self-adaption.

When studying the strategies for placing DSP applications in a geo-distributed environment, we observed that a fully decentralized approach as in [2], where a multiplicity of peer MAPE loops autonomously manages the operator placement, may negatively affect the application performance, because of too frequent and uncoordinated decisions. This situation can be exacerbated when scaling operator decisions are involved besides those regarding the operator placement.

To address such lack of coordination in the multiple MAPE loops, in this paper we present a hierarchical distributed architecture, named *Elastic and Distributed DSP Framework* (EDF), for the autonomous control of elastic DSP applications in a Fog environment. The proposed solution is organized according to the hierarchical pattern for decentralized control described in [15], where higher-level MAPE components control subordinate MAPE components. Specifically, our proposal revolves around a two layered approach with separation of

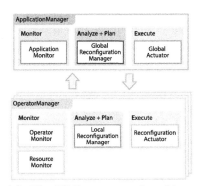

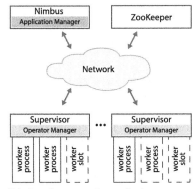

(a) The EDF conceptual architecture: hierarchical MAPE loops

(b) Implementation of the system architecture in Storm

Fig. 1. System architecture

concerns and time scale between layers. Figure 1a illustrates the conceptual architecture of EDF, highlighting the hierarchy of the multiple MAPE loops and the system components in charge of the MAPE loop phases.

At the lower level (i.e., at the per-operator grain) and a faster time scale, the *Operator Manager* is the distributed entity in charge of controlling the adaptation of a single DSP application operator/subset of the DSP application operators through a local MAPE loop. It monitors the system logical and physical components used by the operator(s) through the *Operator Monitor* and the *Resource Monitor*, and then, through the *Local Reconfiguration Manager*, it analyzes the monitored data and determines if and which local reconfiguration action (among operator scale-in, scale-out, or migration) is needed. When the Operator Manager determines that some adaptation should occur, it issues an operator adaptation request to the higher layer.

At the higher level (i.e., at the per-application grain) and a slower time scale, the *Application Manager* is the centralized entity that coordinates the adaptation of the overall DSP application through a global MAPE loop. By means of the *Application Monitor* it oversees the global application behavior. Then, through the *Global Reconfiguration Manager* it analyzes the monitored data and the reconfiguration requests received by the multiple Operator Managers, and decides which reconfigurations should be granted. These decisions are then communicated by the *Global Actuator* to each Operator Manager, which can, finally, execute the operator adaptation actions by means of the its local *Reconfiguration Actuator*.

The EDF architecture is general enough to not limit the specific internal policies and goals that can be designed for each component in the two layers. For example, the planning components can be either activated periodically or on event-basis, can rely on optimization problem formulation or heuristics with the goal to minimize the application response time, maximize its availability or a combination of the two. As a proof-of-concept of the proposed architecture, we present, in Sect. 3, simple heuristic adaptation policies whose overall adaptation goal is to preserve the application performance, avoiding unnecessary or too frequent reconfigurations which might result in excessive application downtime.

We have implemented the proposed EDF architecture in Apache Storm, an open source, real-time, and scalable DSP system. Figure 1b shows the high-level instantiation of the EDF components on the Storm architecture. Due to space limitations, we omit a description of the basic Storm architecture and refer the reader to Sect. 6 in [1], where we also describe how to support in Storm elasticity mechanisms, including the migration of stateful operators. To obtain monitoring information (including network latencies) we rely on Distributed Storm [2].

3   Multi-level Elasticity Policy

The proposed two-layered architecture for self-adaptive DSP elasticity control identifies the different macro-components (i.e., Application Manager and Operator Managers) that, by means of abstraction layers and separation of concerns, cooperate to adapt the deployment of DSP applications at run-time. By properly selecting each component internal policy, the proposed solution can address the needs of different execution contexts, which can comprise applications with different requirements, infrastructures with different computing resources, and different user preferences. For example, specific policies can execute the application by minimizing its response time, maximizing its availability, or limiting the adaptation efforts (i.e., executing the application in a best-effort manner). The Operator Manager works at the granularity of a single DSP operator and implements what we called a *local policy*. By monitoring and analyzing the performance of each operator replica, the local policy can plan a reconfiguration of number and location of the operator replicas. Specifically, by scaling the number of replicas, the operator exploits parallelism to quickly process its incoming data, whereas by migrating some of the operator replicas, the operator better distributes the incoming load among computing resources. The Operator Manager sends the planned reconfiguration to the Application Manager, which runs periodically and decides, according to its so called *global policy*, which reconfiguration should be enacted. The global policy works at the granularity of the whole application, thus it coordinates the reconfigurations so to limit them and avoid deployment oscillations, if needed. On the basis of the monitored application performance and the stipulated SLA, the global policy identifies the most effective reconfigurations proposed by the Operator Managers: it accepts or declines each reconfiguration with the aim to adapt the DSP application to changing working conditions while meeting the SLA.

3.1   Local Policy

The Operator Manager local policy implements the Analyze and Plan phases of the decentralized MAPE loop, which controls the execution of a single DSP operator. Running on a decentralized component, this policy has only a local view of the system, which results from the monitoring components (i.e., Operator Monitor and Resource Monitor). The local view consists of the status (i.e., resource utilization) of each operator replica and of a restricted suitable set of computing nodes (i.e., located in the neighborhood). By analyzing this information, the policy can plan a reconfiguration of the operator deployment, either by changing the number of replicas, or by migrating some of them. The proposed reconfiguration plan is then communicated to the centralized Application Manager which, based on all the Operator Manager's reconfiguration plans and the global policy, determines which plan can be executed and which not.

Reconfiguration Plan. A reconfiguration plan is expressed through the following information: *adaptation actions, reconfiguration gain,* and *reconfiguration cost*[1]. We consider two types of adaptation actions: replica migration and operator scaling. Actions can be of the form: "move replica α of *op* from r_i to r_j", "add a new replica to *op* on r_i", or "remove replica α of *op* from r_i", where *op* and r_i denote an operator and a computing resource, respectively. The *reconfiguration gain* is a function, adopted by every Operator Manager, which captures the benefits of the planned adaptation action. It can express, for instance, the reduction of the operator's processing latency, the reduction of monetary cost for running the operator, or the improvement of some utility function. In this paper, we assume a simple gain function that induces an order relation among the reconfiguration actions, namely `scale-out` > `migration` > `scale-in`. The *reconfiguration cost* expresses the cost of reconfiguring the system. In this paper, we express it in terms of application downtime. It results from the time required to add/remove an operator replica, to relocate the operator code, and to migrate its internal state (if any). We now discuss the two types of adaptation action.

Replica Migration. A computing resource can host replicas of one or more operators, which, in turn, are controlled by dedicated Operator Managers. When the computing resource becomes overloaded, the hosted replicas can experience a performance degradation. To overcome this issue, an Operator Manager proposes to move some of the operator replicas away from the resource.

We adopt a reactive and threshold-based policy in order to decide when and how to perform the migration. The local policy analyzes the monitoring data coming from the computing resources that host at least one operator replica. We denote with U_r the overall CPU utilization of the resource r. When U_r is above a critical value $U_{\max}$, the policy plans to migrate at most one operator replica to a new location. The latter is identified in two steps. First, the policy sorts the known neighbor resources according to their distance, measured in terms of network delay. Then, it selects the new location using a randomized approach: the closer the resource, the higher the probability of being selected. The policy checks if the new selected location has room to run the migrating replica; in negative case, a new resource is selected from the sorted list.

---

[1] For the sake of simplicity, we assume that the local policy proposes, for an operator, a single reconfiguration decision (i.e., migration, scaling) at a time.

Reconfiguration Cost. If the operator is stateless, the migration of a replica can be easily performed by terminating the replica on the old location, moving its code to the new location, and restarting it. On the other hand, if the operator is stateful, we also need to efficiently migrate its internal state, so to preserve the integrity and consistency of the outputted streams. Our migration protocol follows a pause-and-resume approach with the help of a data store as staging area for the replica internal state (details on our migration protocol in [1]).

Operator Scaling. When an operator replica receives an increasing workload, it can saturate the capacity of the hosting computing resource. To prevent the performance penalty associated to overloading, the Operator Manager proposes to add an additional replica and redistribute the incoming workload accordingly. Conversely, when the incoming workload decreases, the Operator Manager can reduce the number of replicas in order to decrease the number of allocated resources, and redistribute the workload among the remaining ones. Let us denote by S_α the resource utilization of the hosting resource by replica α, which measures the fraction of CPU time used by α. We adopt a simple threshold-based scale-out policy to each replica. When the utilization of α exceeds a usage threshold $S_{\text{s-out}} \in [0, 1]$ (i.e., $S_\alpha > S_{\text{s-out}}$), the Operator Manager proposes to add a new replica. Its placement is computed relying on the same strategy used for the replica migration. Conversely, the Operator Manager proposes a scale-in operation, which removes one of the running n replicas, when the sum of their utilization divided by $n-1$ is significantly below the usage threshold, i.e., when $\sum_{\alpha=1}^{n} S_\alpha/(n-1) < cS_{\text{s-out}}$, being $c < 1$. The replica to be removed is randomly chosen between the two replicas with the highest utilization.

Reconfiguration Cost: If the operator is stateless, a scaling operation implies only to start or stop a replica. Conversely, if the operator is stateful, we also need to reallocate its internal state among the new set of replicas. We assume that each replica can work on a well-defined state partition [5]. A scale-out operation redistributes equally the partitions among replicas, whereas a scale-in operation aggregates the partitions from the merged replicas.

3.2   Global Policy

The Application Manager global policy implements the Analyze and Plan steps of the centralized MAPE loop. Its main goal is to satisfy the DSP application SLA, while minimizing the allocated resources (or their cost). To this end, it monitors the application response time and analyzes its behavior with respect to the SLO specified in the SLA. In the planning phase, the policy determines which reconfiguration plans, proposed by the decentralized Operator Managers, should be enacted as to improve performance while controlling the number of application reconfigurations (which cause application downtime). In this paper, we consider a simple global policy scheme which is exemplified in Fig. 2. Time is divided in control intervals of fixed length T. During each interval, the global policy collects reconfiguration requests from the Operator Managers: these requests can take different forms, e.g., replica migrations (the continuous arrows in the

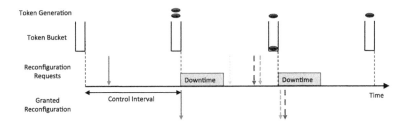

Fig. 2. Global policy behavior

figure), operator scale-out (the dotted arrow) and operator scale-in (the dashed arrow). At the end of each interval, the policy determines how many and which reconfigurations should be enacted by the Operators Managers. In order to control the number of reconfigurations, and hence the downtime, we adopt a simple token bucket scheme whereby each reconfiguration consumes a token. Tokens are generated at the end of each control interval T and are accumulated in a token bucket, which has a finite capacity (i.e., when the bucket is full, it cannot store any other token). The number of reconfigurations allowed at the end of each control interval is thus limited by the number of available tokens. If the number of requests is higher than the number of available tokens, the global policy has to identify the most valuable reconfigurations to accept. As simple scheme, the policy uses a greedy approach by prioritizing the requests according to the gain to cost ratio; the higher this index, the better the reconfiguration.

In the proposed scheme, a key role is played by the token generation rate. Ideally, when the application response time is well within the SLO (defined by $R_{\max}$), reconfigurations should be limited since performance is guaranteed and the possibly sub-optimal behavior is preferable to the downtime caused by reconfigurations. On the other hand, should the performance degrades, the system should be more prone to reconfigure itself. As such, the token generation frequency depends on how far is the response time from $R_{\max}$, with increasing token generation rates as performance gets close to $R_{\max}$.

4   Evaluation

We evaluate EDF equipped with the proposed proof-of-concept policies, using Apache Storm 0.9.3 on a cluster with 5 worker nodes and one further node to host Nimbus and ZooKeeper (details in [1]). Each node has a dual CPU Intel Xeon E5504 (8 cores at 2 GHz) with 16 GB of RAM.

The reference application solves a query of DEBS 2015 Grand Challenge [9], where data streams originated from the New York City taxis are processed to find the top-10 most frequent routes during the last 30 min. Figure 3 shows the application DAG. *Data source* reads the dataset from Redis; *parser* filters out irrelevant and invalid data. Then, *filterByCoordinates* forwards only the events related to a specific area to *computeRouteID*, which identifies the routes covered by taxis. So, *countByWindow* computes the route frequency in the last 30 min,

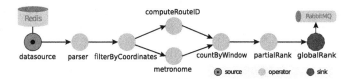

Fig. 3. Reference DSP application

supported by *metronome* that defines the passing of time. Finally, *partialRank* and *globalRank* compute the top-10 most frequent routes.

We feed the application with a sample dataset provided by DEBS, and process real data collected during 2 days. The taxi service utilization significantly changes during the day, thus the application input rate is variable as well. As regards the Operator Manager local policy, we set the scale-out and migration thresholds, U_{max} and $S_{s\text{-out}}$, to 0.7 and the scale-in parameter c to 0.75. Both OperatorManager and ApplicationManager run once every 30 s, respectively proposing and accepting/rejecting reconfigurations. We compare the baseline approach in which all reconfiguration requests are always accepted by the ApplicationManager to one in which the global policy in Sect. 3.2 is employed in order to determine which reconfigurations will be enacted. In particular, the token bucket stores at most 1 token at any time and the token generation rate is 1 per min only if the achieved application response time is above βR_{max}, where $\beta \in [0, 1]$, otherwise no token is generated. In these experiments we set $R_{max} = 200$ ms and vary β.

Figure 4a shows the application response time and number of replicas during the experiment when using the baseline approach. Since every reconfiguration proposed by any OperatorManager is accepted (like in a fully decentralized policy), the application is frequently reconfigured. As a consequence, the application is available only for 93.7% of the time. The measured response time shows many spikes, which are caused by tuples buffering during reconfiguration.

Figure 4b shows the application response time and number of operator replicas during the experiment using the full reconfiguration policy, with $\beta = 0.5$. As the response time frequently rises above $\beta R_{max} = 100$ ms, the number of granted reconfigurations is not significantly reduced with respect to the baseline approach in Fig. 4a (and so the application downtime). Nevertheless, we can observe that, by performing less reconfigurations, the total number of replicas is never reduced to 8, due to the lack of tokens and the low priority of the scale-in action.

Figure 4c shows the results when $\beta = 0.75$. As tokens are now generated in a more conservative manner (being $\beta R_{max} = 150$ ms), the number of reconfigurations is significantly reduced. In the initial part of the experiment, the input rate grows up to 300 tuples/s, resulting in high response time; therefore, EDF generates tokens for performing a migration and for increasing the total number of replicas to 10. Then, the application is stable until a new input peak (at around 4000 s), when a scale-in followed by a scale-out of the bottleneck operator are accepted. The application downtime is limited (only 1.7%), which is beneficial for response time, but it might lead to higher cost, having more active replicas.

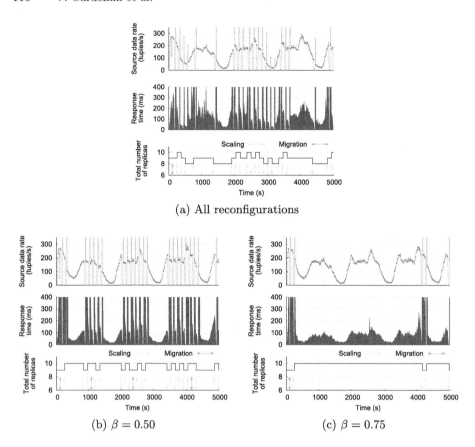

(a) All reconfigurations

(b) $\beta = 0.50$ (c) $\beta = 0.75$

Fig. 4. Response time and number of replicas using different policies for Application-Manager: in (a) accepting all the reconfiguration requests, in (b) and (c) generating a token only when response time is greater than $\beta R_{\max}$

5   Conclusions

In this paper, we presented Elastic and Distributed DSP Framework (EDF), a hierarchical autonomous control for elastic DSP applications. Designed according to the decentralized MAPE control pattern, our proposal revolves around a two layered approach with separation of concerns and time scale between layers. At the lower level, distributed components control the adaptation of DSP operators, so to improve their performance by means of scaling and migration actions. At the higher level, a per-application centralized component oversees the overall DSP application performance and coordinates its deployment by accepting or declining the proposed reconfiguration actions. Then, relying on an application that processes real-time data generated by taxis, we conducted an experimental evaluation. The results showed the effectiveness of our solution in achieving good trade-off in terms of application performance and number of application reconfigurations even adopting simple control policies. As future work, we will further investigate the hierarchical approach for adapting DSP applications over geo-distributed infrastructures. We plan to extend some of the existing distributed policies to make them more robust to oscillations, and to design hierarchical multi-time scale policies relying on optimization frameworks such as Markov Decision Processes and reinforcement learning.

References

1. Cardellini, V., Lo Presti, F., Nardelli, M., Russo Russo, G.: Optimal operator deployment and replication for elastic distributed data stream processing. Concurrency Comput.: Practice Exper. (2017). https://doi.org/10.1002/cpe.4334
2. Cardellini, V., Grassi, V., Lo Presti, F., Nardelli, M.: Distributed QoS-aware scheduling in Storm. In: Proceedings of ACM DEBS 2015, pp. 344–347 (2015)
3. De Matteis, T., Mencagli, G.: Elastic scaling for distributed latency-sensitive data stream operators. In: Proceedings of PDP 2017, pp. 61–68 (2017)
4. Fernandez, R.C., Migliavacca, M., Kalyvianaki, E., Pietzuch, P.: Integrating scale out and fault tolerance in stream processing using operator state management. In: Proceedings of ACM SIGMOD 2013, pp. 725–736 (2013)
5. Gedik, B., Schneider, S., Hirzel, M., Wu, K.L.: Elastic scaling for data stream processing. IEEE Trans. Parallel Distrib. Syst. **25**(6), 1447–1463 (2014)
6. Gulisano, V., Jiménez-Peris, R., Patiño Martínez, M., Soriente, C., Valduriez, P.: StreamCloud: an elastic and scalable data streaming system. IEEE Trans. Parallel Distrib. Syst. **23**(12), 2351–2365 (2012)
7. Heinze, T., Pappalardo, V., Jerzak, Z., Fetzer, C.: Auto-scaling techniques for elastic data stream processing. In: Proceedings of IEEE ICDEW 2014, pp. 296–302 (2014)
8. Heinze, T., Roediger, L., Meister, A., Ji, Y., et al.: Online parameter optimization for elastic data stream processing. In: Proceedings of ACM SoCC 2015, pp. 276–287 (2015)
9. Jerzak, Z., Ziekow, H.: The DEBS 2015 grand challenge. In: Proceedings of ACM DEBS 2015, pp. 266–268 (2015)
10. Lohrmann, B., Janacik, P., Kao, O.: Elastic stream processing with latency guarantees. In: Proceedings of IEEE ICDCS 2015, pp. 399–410 (2015)
11. Mencagli, G.: A game-theoretic approach for elastic distributed data stream processing. ACM Trans. Auton. Adapt. Syst. **11**(2), 13:1–13:34 (2016)
12. Pietzuch, P., Ledlie, J., Shneidman, J., Roussopoulos, M., et al.: Network-aware operator placement for stream-processing systems. In: Proceedings of IEEE ICDE 2006 (2006)
13. Sajjad, H.P., Danniswara, K., Al-Shishtawy, A., Vlassov, V.: Spanedge: towards unifying stream processing over central and near-the-edge data centers. In: Proceedings of 2016 IEEE/ACM Symposium on Edge Computing, pp. 168–178 (2016)
14. Saurez, E., Hong, K., Lillethun, D., Ramachandran, U., et al.: Incremental deployment and migration of geo-distributed situation awareness applications in the fog. In: Proceedings of ACM DEBS 2016, pp. 258–269 (2016)
15. Weyns, D., et al.: On patterns for decentralized control in self-adaptive systems. In: de Lemos, R., Giese, H., Müller, H.A., Shaw, M. (eds.) Software Engineering for Self-Adaptive Systems II. LNCS, vol. 7475, pp. 76–107. Springer, Heidelberg (2013). https://doi.org/10.1007/978-3-642-35813-5_4
16. Xu, L., Peng, B., Gupta, I.: Stela: enabling stream processing systems to scale-in and scale-out on-demand. In: Proceedings of IEEE IC2E 2016, pp. 22–31 (2016)

PiCo: A Novel Approach to Stream Data Analytics

Claudia Misale[1]([✉]), Maurizio Drocco[2], Guy Tremblay[3],
and Marco Aldinucci[2]([✉])

[1] Cognitive and Cloud, Data-Centric Solutions, IBM T.J. Watson Research Center,
Yorktown Heights, NY, USA
c.misale@ibm.com

[2] Computer Science Department, University of Torino, Torino, Italy
{drocco,aldinuc}@di.unito.it

[3] Dépt. d'Informatique, Université du Québec à Montréal, Montréal, QC, Canada
tremblay.guy@uqam.ca

Abstract. In this paper, we present a new C++ API with a fluent interface called PiCo (Pipeline Composition). PiCo's programming model aims at making easier the programming of data analytics applications while preserving or enhancing their performance. This is attained through three key design choices: (1) unifying batch and stream data access models, (2) decoupling processing from data layout, and (3) exploiting a stream-oriented, scalable, efficient C++11 runtime system. PiCo proposes a programming model based on pipelines and operators that are polymorphic with respect to data types in the sense that it is possible to re-use the same algorithms and pipelines on different data models (e.g., streams, lists, sets, etc.). Preliminary results show that PiCo can attain better performances in terms of execution times and hugely improve memory utilization when compared to Spark and Flink in both batch and stream processing.

1 Introduction

In the context of Big Data analytics, there is a series of tools aiming at simplifying programming applications to be executed on clusters. Although each tool claims to provide better programming, data and execution models—for which only informal (and often confusing) semantics are generally provided[1]—they all share some characteristics at different levels. From a high-level perspective, Big Data is about extracting knowledge from both structured and unstructured data. Extracting knowledge from Big Data requires tools satisfying strong requirements with respect to programmability and performance. The common aim of Big Data tools is to ensure ease of programming by providing a unique framework addressing both batch and stream processing. Even when they accomplish

---

[1] For instance, consider Spark's `dstream.foreachRDD`, which provides access to RDDs in a DStream, declared as immutable collections of objects, accessible only with collective operators.

D. B. Heras and L. Bougé (Eds.): Euro-Par 2017 Workshops, LNCS 10659, pp. 118–128, 2018.
https://doi.org/10.1007/978-3-319-75178-8_10

this task, they often lack of a clear semantics of their programming and execution model. For instance, users can be provided with two different data models for representing collections and streams, both supporting the same operations but often having different semantics. We advocate a new API with a fluent interface (with method chaining) [11], called PiCo (**Pi**peline **Co**mposition), designed over the presented layered Dataflow conceptual framework [13,14]. PiCo programming model aims at *easing the programming* and *enhancing the performance* of Analytics applications through three design choices: (1) unifying batch and stream data access models, (2) decoupling processing from data layout, and (3) exploiting a stream-oriented, scalable, efficient C++11 run-time system.

These design choices move further the level of abstraction in the programming and execution model achieved in mainstream approaches for Big Data analytics. For instance, Spark [18], Storm [15], Flink [10], and Google Dataflow [1] typically force the specialization of the algorithm to match the data access and layout. Specifically, data transformation functions (called *operators* in PiCo) exhibit different functional types when accessing data in different ways.

For this reason, the source code must often be revised when switching from one data model to the next. Some of them, such as the Spark framework, provide the runtime with a module to convert streams into micro-batches (Spark Streaming, a library running on Spark core), but still different code needs to be written at the user-level. The Kappa architecture advocates the opposite approach, i.e., to "streamize" batch processing, but the streamizing proxy has to be coded. As for the Lambda architecture, it requires the implementation of both a batch-oriented and a stream-oriented algorithm, which means coding and maintaining two codebases.

PiCo fully decouples algorithm design from data model and layout. Code is designed in a fully functional style by composing stateless *operators*. As we discuss in the present paper, all PiCo operators are polymorphic with respect to data types. This makes it possible to (1) re-use the same algorithms and pipelines on different data models (e.g., streams, lists, sets, etc.); (2) reuse the same operators in different contexts, and (3) update operators without affecting the calling context, i.e., the previous and following stages in the pipeline. Note that in other mainstream frameworks, such as Spark, the update of a pipeline by changing a transformation with another may not be trivial, since this may require the development of input and output proxies to adapt the new transformation for the calling context. Moreover, PiCo relies on FastFlow [3,4,9], a parallel programming framework designed to support streaming applications on cache-coherent multicore platforms.

2   Related Work

In this section, we provide background related to Big Data analytics tools from a stream processing perspective. Apache Spark design is intended to address iterative computations by reusing the working dataset by keeping it in memory [18–20]. For this reason, Spark represents a landmark in Big Data tools history, having a strong success in the community. The overall framework and parallel computing model of Spark is similar to MapReduce, while the innovation is in the data model, represented by the *Resilient Distributed Dataset* (RDD). An RDD is a read-only collection of objects partitioned across a cluster of computers that can be operated on in parallel. A Spark program can be characterized by the two kinds of operations applicable to RDDs: *transformations* and *actions*. Those transformations and actions compose the directed acyclic graph (DAG) representing the application. For stream processing, Spark implements an extension through the Spark Streaming module, providing a high-level abstraction called *discretized stream* or *DStream* [20]. Such streams represent results in continuous sequences of RDDs of the same type, called *micro-batches*. Operations over DStreams are "forwarded" to each RDD in the DStream, thus the semantics of operations over streams is defined in terms of batch processing according to the simple translation $\mathsf{op}(a) = [\mathsf{op}(a_1), \mathsf{op}(a_2), \ldots]$, where $[\cdot]$ refers to a possibly unbounded ordered sequence, $a = [a_1, a_2, \ldots]$ is a DStream, and each item a_i is a micro-batch of type RDD. All RDDs in a DStream are processed in order, whereas data items inside an RDD are processed in parallel without any ordering guarantees.

Formerly known as Stratosphere [5], *Apache Flink* [7] focuses on stream programming. The abstraction used is the *DataStream*, which is a representation of a stream as a single object. Operations are composed (i.e., pipelined) by calling operators on DataStream objects. Flink also provides the *DataSet* type for batch applications, that identifies a single immutable multiset—a stream of one element. A Flink program, either for stream or batch processing, is a term from an algebra of operators over DataStreams or DataSets, respectively. Flink, differently from Spark, is a stream processing framework, meaning that both batch and stream processing are based on a streaming runtime. It can be considered one of the more advanced stream processors as many of its core features were already considered in the initial design [7].

Apache Storm is a framework targeting only stream processing [15–17]. It is perhaps the first widely used large-scale stream processing framework in the open source world. Storm's programming model is based on three key notions: *Spouts*, *Bolts*, and *Topologies*. A Spout is a source of a stream, that is (typically) connected to a data source or that can generate its own stream. A Bolt is a processing element, so it processes any number of input streams and produces any number of new output streams. A topology is a composition of Spout and Bolts.

Google Dataflow SDK [1] is part of the Google Cloud Platform [12]. Here, the term "Dataflow" is used by reference to the "Dataflow model", to describe the processing and programming model of the Cloud Platform. This framework aims at providing a unified model for stream, batch, and micro-batch processing. The base entity is the *Pipeline*, representing a data processing job consisting of a set of operations that can read a source of input data, transform that data, and write out the resulting output. The data model in Google Dataflow is represented by *PCollection*s, representing a potentially large, immutable bag of elements, that can be either bounded or unbounded. The bounded (or unbounded) nature of a PCollection affects how Dataflow processes the data. Bounded PCollections can be processed using batch jobs, that might read the entire data set once and perform processing in a finite job. Unbounded PCollections must be processed using streaming jobs, as the entire collection may never be available for processing at any one time and they can be grouped by using windowing to create logical windows of finite size.

Thrill [6] is a prototype of a general purpose big data batch processing framework with a dataflow style programming interface implemented in C++ and exploiting template meta-programming. Thrill's data model is the *Distributed Immutable Array* (DIA), an array of items distributed over the cluster, to which no direct access to elements is permitted—i.e., it is only possible to apply operations to the array as a whole. A DIA remains an abstract entity flowing between two concrete DIA operations, allowing to apply optimizations such as pipelining or chaining, combining the logic of one or more functions into a single one (called pipeline). A consequence of using C++ is that memory has to be managed explicitly, although memory management in modern C++11 has been considerably simplified—for instance, Thrill uses reference counting extensively. Thrill provides a SPMD (Single Program, Multiple Data) execution model, similar to MPI, where the same program is run on different machines.

3   PiCo Programming Model

In this section, we present the PiCo C++ API, consisting of two main categories of elements: Pipelines and Operators—PiCo's formal semantics is described in [8]. Note that the design of the Operators API is based on inheritance, following faithfully PiCo's grammar specification [8]—even though the use of template programming without inheritance might have slightly improved the runtime performance. Thus, the implementation makes use of dynamic polymorphism when building the semantics DAG, where virtual member functions are invoked to determine the kind of Operator currently processed.

3.1   Pipe and Operators

A C++ PiCo program is a set of operator objects composed into a `Pipe` object, processing bounded or unbounded data.

A Pipeline can be: 1. created as the empty `Pipe` (default constructor); 2. created as a `Pipe` consisting of a single operator; 3. modified by adding an operator, through the `add` function; 4. modified by appending other `Pipe`s, through the `to` functions; 5. merged with another `Pipe`, through the `merge` function; 6. paired with another `Pipe` by means of a binary operator, through the `pair` function.

Operators can be unary or binary. `UnaryOperator` is the base class representing PiCo unary operators, those with no more than one input and/or output collection. For instance, a `Map` object takes a C++ callable value (i.e., a kernel)

```
1    typedef KeyValue<std::string, int> KV;
2
3    static auto tokenizer = [](std::string& in,FlatMapCollector<KV>& collector) {
4      std::istringstream f(in);
5      std::string s;
6      while (std::getline(f, s, ' ')) {
7        collector.add(KV(s,1));
8      }
9    };
10
11   int main(int argc, char** argv) {
12     // Parse command line
13     parse_PiCo_args(argc, argv);
14
15     // Define a generic word-count pipeline
16     Pipe countWords;
17     countWords
18       .add(FlatMap<std::string, std::string>(tokenizer))
19       .add(Map<std::string, KV>([&](std::string in) { return KV(in,1); } ))
20       .add(PReduce<KV>([&](KV v1, KV v2) { return v1+v2; } ));
21
22     // Define I/O operators from/to file
23     ReadFromFile reader();
24     WriteToDisk<KV> writer([&](KV in) {
25       return in.to_string();
26     });
27
28     // Compose the pipeline
29     Pipe p2;
30     p2
31       .add(reader)
32       .to(countWords) // append to...
33       .add(writer);
34
35     // Execute the pipeline
36     p2.run();
37
38     return 0;
39   }
```

Listing 1.1. Word count example in PiCo.

as parameter and represents a PiCo operator map, which processes a collection by applying the kernel to each item. Also, ReadFromFile is a sub-class of UnaryOperator and represents PiCo operators that produce a (bounded) unordered collection of lines, read from an input text file.

BinaryOperator is the base class representing operators with two input collections and one output collection. For instance, a BinaryMap object represents a PiCo operator b-map that processes pairs of elements coming from two different input collections and produces a single output for each pair. A BinaryMap object is passed as parameter to Pipeline objects built by calling the pair member function.

Listing 1.1 shows a complete example for our Word Count benchmark.

4   Anatomy of a PiCo Application

When the run() member function is called on a pipeline p1, the semantics dataflow is processed to create the parallel execution dataflow. This latter graph represents the application in terms of processing elements (i.e., actors) connected by data channels (i.e., edges), where operators can be replicated to express data parallelism. We implemented this intermediate representation directly in Fast-Flow by using nodes, farms and pipelines patterns.

The creation of the parallel execution dataflow is straightforward. Having an empty ff_pipeline picoDAG that will be executed, we then start visiting the first node of the semantics dataflow, which can be an input or an entry point node. On the basis of its role, a new ff_node or ff_farm is instantiated and added to picoDAG.

The semantics DAG is recursively visited and the following operations are performed: 1. A single ff_node is added in case of input/output operators; 2. The corresponding ff_farm is added in case of operators different from I/O operators; 3. If an entry point is encountered, a new ff_farm is created and added to picoDAG: (a) a new ff_pipeline is created for each entry point's adjacent node; (b) these ff_pipelines are built with new ff_nodes created by recursively visiting the input Pipe's graph, until reaching the last node of each Pipe visited.

At the end, the resulting picoDAG is thus a composition of ff_pipelines and ff_farms.

4.1   FastFlow Network Execution

In this section, we describe the execution of the picoDAG pipeline, starting from a brief summary of the FastFlow runtime.

From the orchestration viewpoint, the process model to be employed is based on the Communicating Sequential Processes (CSP)[2] model, where processes (i.e., ff_nodes) are named and the data paths between processes are explicitly identified (which is thus different from the Actor model). The abstract units of communication and synchronization are known as *channels* and represent a stream of data exchanged between two processes. Each ff_node is a C++ class entering an infinite loop through its svc() (*service*) member function where: 1. it gets a task from input channel; 2. it executes business code on the task; 3. it puts a task into the output channel. Representing communication and synchronization by a channel ensures that synchronization is tied to communication and allows layers of abstraction at higher levels to compose parallel programs where synchronization is implicit. Patterns to build a graph of ff_nodes, such as farms, are defined in the *core patterns* level of the FastFlow stack. Since the graph of ff_nodes is a streaming network, any FastFlow graph is built using two streaming patterns (farm and pipeline) and one pattern-modifier (loopback, to build

---

[2] The CSP model describes a systems in terms of component processes operating independently, which interact with each other through message-passing communication.

cyclic networks). As an example, we highlight the key steps during the execution of the FastFlow network of processes for a simple PiCo application with three operators: Read from File, Map, and Write to Disk. The first node is the Read from File (Rff), which reads lines from a file that are then forwarded to their following node of the pipeline. Tokens are sent out at microbatch granularity (in this case, a microbatch is a fixed size array of lines read from the input file). Since also a fixed size dataset is streamized, the Rff node reads the text file and sends out microbatches until the EOF is reached. The next stage of `Rff`s is the Emitter of the `map` farm, which processes stream of microbatches. Each worker of the `map ff_farm` processes the received microbatch by applying the user-defined function. Then each worker allocates a new microbatch to store the result of the user-defined function, and then deletes the received microbatch. The new microbatch is forwarded to the next node. The general behavior of a worker during its `svc()` call is that it deletes each input microbatch (allocated by the Emitter) after it has been processed and the results of the kernel function (applied to all elements of the microbatch) are stored into a new microbatch. When the Collector receives *PICO_EOS* tokens from all workers—a token specifying that the stream is finished and that there are no more tokens to process (i.e., end of file or socket closed)—it then forwards the token to the next stage, namely the Write to Disk (Wtd) node. This last node is a single sequential `ff_node`—input and output processing nodes are always sequential—writing the received data to a specified file. When the Wtd node receives *PICO_EOS*, the file is closed and the computation terminates.

5   Experiments

We compare PiCo to Flink v1.2.0 and Spark v2.1.0, focusing on expressiveness of the programming model and on performances in shared memory. We tested PiCo with both batch and stream applications. A first set of experiments were made of the following two applications: word count and stock market analysis.

Word count is considered as the "Hello, World!" of Big Data analytics, typically an example of batch processing. The input is a text file, which is first split into lines. Then, each line is tokenized into a sequence of words: this is implemented using `flatmap`, as each line may contain varying numbers of words. Each of these words from the input file are processed by a `map` operator that produces a key-value pair $\langle w, 1 \rangle$ for each word w. After all words have been processed, the pairs are grouped by the word from each pair, and then the values (i.e., the 1s) are reduced by a sum. The final result is a single pair for each word, where the value represents the number of occurrences of the word in the text. (See also Listing 1.1.) As for the stock market analysis, it implements the "Stock Pricing" program computing a price for each option read from a text file. Each line is parsed to extract stock names followed by stock option data. A `map` operator then computes prices by means of the Black & Scholes algorithm for each option and, finally, a reducer extracts the maximum price for each stock name.

The architecture used for experiments is the Occam Supercomputer (Open Computing Cluster for Advanced data Manipulation) [2], designed and managed by the University of Torino and the National Institute for Nuclear Physics. We used one node having the following characteristics. At hardware side: 4x Intel® Xeon® Processor E7-4830 v3 12 core/2.1 GHz, 768 GB/1666 MHz (48 × 16 GB) DDR4 RAM, 1x SSD 800 GB + 1x HDD 2 TB/7200 rpm, InfiniBand 56 GB + 2x Ethernet 10 GB. At software side: Linux CentOS v7.3 with Linux kernel 3.10, gcc v4.8.5 compiler (PiCo has been compiled with O3 optimization flag), and OpenJDK Server v1.8 Java runtime.

5.1   Batch Applications

The size of the input file for the Word Count application is 600 MB. It is a text file containing random words taken from a dictionary of 1K words. In the Word Count pipeline, PiCo instantiates a total of 5 fixed threads (corresponding to sequential operators), plus the main thread, plus a user-defined number of workers for the `flatmap` operator. To exploit at most 48 physical cores, we can run at most 42 worker threads. We provide a comparison on minimum execution time obtained by each tool as the average of 20 runs for each application. For the Stock Pricing application, the size of the input file is 10 MB.

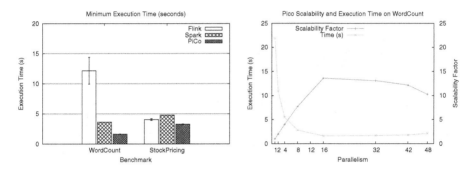

Fig. 1. (Left) Comparison of best execution times for Word Count and Stock Pricing obtained by Spark, Flink, and Pico. (Right) Scalability and execution time for Word Count in PiCo.

Figure 1 (left) shows that PiCo obtains the best execution times when compared to Spark and Flink, for both the Word Count and Stock Pricing applications. Figure 1 (right) shows scalability and execution times for the Word Count application: each value represents the average of 20 runs for each number of workers, the microbatch size is 512, and the thread pinning strategy is physical cores first.

5.2   Stream Applications

In this set of experiments, we compare PiCo to Flink and Spark when executing a stream application, the Stock Pricing one. The application is similar to the one from the batch experiment, except we added two additional option pricing algorithms—Binomial Tree and Explicit Finite Difference—and the data comes from a socket, not from a text file.

In the Stock Pricing pipeline, PiCo first instantiates 6 threads corresponding to sequential operators, such as read from socket and write to standard output, plus Emitter and Collector threads for `map` and `p-reduce` operators. Then, there is the main thread, and then k (a user-specified number) workers for the `map` and k for the `w-p-reduce` operators. With 16 workers for the `map` and 16 workers `w-p-reduce` operator mapped on physical cores, PiCo obtains the best average execution time of 7.348 s and a scalability factor of 14.87. We compared PiCo to Flink and Spark on the Stock Pricing streaming application. The window is count-based (or tumbling) and has size 8 in Flink and PiCo. For stream processing, Spark implements an extension through the Spark Streaming module, providing a high-level abstraction called *discretized stream* or *DStream*. Such streams represent results in continuous sequences of RDDs of the same type, called *micro-batches*. Operations over DStreams are "forwarded" to each RDD in the DStream, thus the semantics of operations over streams is defined in terms of batch processing. All RDDs in a DStream are processed in order, whereas data items inside an RDD are processed in parallel without any ordering guarantees. Hence, Spark implements its stream processing runtime over the batch processing one, thus exploiting the BSP runtime on stream microbatches, without providing a concrete form of pipelining and reducing the real-time processing feature.

Table 1 presents the best execution times obtained by each tool, showing that PiCo obtains the best execution time and with a higher scalability compared to other tools, with a scalability of 14.87 in PiCo while 9.21 for Flink and 2.24 for Spark. Let us stress that the comparison with Spark is not completely fair since windowing is not performed in a count-based fashion. Table 1 also shows that PiCo processes more than 1.3M stock options per second, outperforming Flink and Spark, as they processes approx. 400K and 200K stock options per second respectively.

Table 1. Flink, Spark and PiCo performance on Stream Stock Pricing. The execution time is the best average on 20 runs, For the same configuration, also the scalability (against Parallelism 1) and the sustained throughput are reported.

Throughput values for 10M stock options				
	Execution time (s)	Parallelism	Throughput (stocks/s)	Scalability
Flink	24.78	16	403476.35	9.21
Spark	42.22	16	236875.81	2.24
PiCo	7.35	16	1360806.94	14.87

6 Conclusions

In this paper, we presented PiCo, a new C++ API with a fluent interface for data analytics pipelines.

One key feature of PiCo is that the data model is hidden to the programmer, thus making it possible to create a model that is *polymorphic* with respect to the data model as well as to the processing model (i.e., stream or batch processing). This make it possible to (1) re-use the same algorithms and pipelines on different data models (e.g., stream, lists, sets, etc.); (2) reuse the same operators in different contexts, and (3) update operators without affecting the calling context. These aspects are fundamental to PiCo, differentiating it from other frameworks exposing different data types to be used in the same application, forcing the user to re-think the whole application when moving from one operation to another.

We compared PiCo to Flink and Spark, focusing on expressiveness of the programming model and on performances in shared memory. The current (preliminary) experiments were performed on shared memory only. By comparing execution times in both batch and stream applications, PiCo attained the best execution time when compared to two state-of-the-art frameworks, Spark and Flink. However, an aspect not mentioned above is that those experiments showed high dynamic allocation contention in input generation nodes, thus limiting PiCo scalability, a problem that will be addressed in future work. Also, results for stream processing showed that PiCo processes more than 1.3M stock options per second, outperforming Flink and Spark, that process about 400K and 200K stock options per second respectively.

Acknowledgements. This work has been partially supported by the OptiBike experiment of the EU-H2020-IA "Fortissimo2" project (no. 680481), the EU-H2020-RIA "Rephrase" project (no. 644235), the EU-H2020-RIA "Toreador" project (no. 688797), and the 2015-2016 IBM Ph.D. Scholarship program.

References

1. Akidau, T., Bradshaw, R., Chambers, C., Chernyak, S., Fernàndez-Moctezuma, R.J., Lax, R., McVeety, S., Mills, D., Perry, F., Schmidt, E., Whittle, S.: The dataflow model: a practical approach to balancing correctness, latency, and cost in massive-scale, unbounded, out-of-order data processing. Proc. VLDB Endow. **8**, 1792–1803 (2015)
2. Aldinucci, M., Bagnasco, S., Lusso, S., Pasteris, P., Rabellino, S.: The open computing cluster for advanced data manipulation (OCCAM). In: Journal of Physics: Conference Series 898 (CHEP 2016), San Francisco, USA (2017)
3. Aldinucci, M., Danelutto, M., Kilpatrick, P., Torquati, M.: Fastflow: high-level and efficient streaming on multi-core. In: Pllana, S., Xhafa, F. (eds.) Programming Multi-core and Many-core Computing Systems, Parallel and Distributed Computing, Chap. 13. Wiley (2017)
4. Aldinucci, M., Danelutto, M., Meneghin, M., Torquati, M., Kilpatrick, P.: Efficient streaming applications on multi-core with FastFlow: the biosequence alignment test-bed. Advances in Parallel Computing, vol. 19. Elsevier (2010)

5. Alexandrov, A., Bergmann, R., Ewen, S., Freytag, J.-C., Hueske, F., Heise, A., Kao, O., Leich, M., Leser, U., Markl, V., Naumann, F., Peters, M., Rheinländer, A., Sax, M.J., Schelter, S., Höger, M., Tzoumas, K., Warneke, D.: The stratosphere platform for big data analytics. VLDB J. **23**(6), 939–964 (2014)
6. Bingmann, T., Axtmann, M., Jöbstl, E., Lamm, S., Nguyen, H.C., Noe, A., Schlag, S., Stumpp, M., Sturm, T., Sanders, P.: Thrill: high-performance algorithmic distributed batch data processing with C++. CoRR, abs/1608.05634 (2016)
7. Carbone, P., Fóra, G., Ewen, S., Haridi, S., Tzoumas, K.: Lightweight asynchronous snapshots for distributed dataflows. CoRR, abs/1506.08603 (2015)
8. Drocco, M., Misale, C., Tremblay, G., Aldinucci, M.: A formal semantics for data analytics pipelines, May 2017. https://arxiv.org/abs/1705.01629
9. Fastflow website. http://mc-fastflow.sourceforge.net/. Accessed 2017
10. Flink. Apache Flink website. https://flink.apache.org/. Accessed 2017
11. Fowler, M.: Domain-Specific Languages. Addison-Wesley, Boston (2011)
12. Google Cloud Dataflow. https://cloud.google.com/dataflow/. Accessed 2017
13. Misale, C.: PiCo: a domain-specific language for data analytics pipelines. Ph.D. thesis, Computer Science Department, University of Torino, May 2017
14. Misale, C., Drocco, M., Aldinucci, M., Tremblay, G.: A comparison of big data frameworks on a layered dataflow model. Parallel Process. Lett. **27**(01), 1740003 (2017)
15. Nasir, M.A.U., Morales, G.D.F., García-Soriano, D., Kourtellis, N., Serafini, M.: The power of both choices: practical load balancing for distributed stream processing engines. CoRR, abs/1504.00788 (2015)
16. Storm. Apache Storm website. http://storm.apache.org/. Accessed 2017
17. Toshniwal, A., Taneja, S., Shukla, A., Ramasamy, K., Patel, J.M., Kulkarni, S., Jackson, J., Gade, K., Fu, M., Donham, J., Bhagat, N., Mittal, S., Ryaboy, D.: Storm@twitter. In: Proceedings of the 2014 ACM SIGMOD International Conference on Management of Data, SIGMOD 2014, pp. 147–156. ACM, New York (2014)
18. Zaharia, M., Chowdhury, M., Das, T., Dave, A., Ma, J., McCauley, M., Franklin, M.J., Shenker, S., Stoica, I.: Resilient distributed datasets: a fault-tolerant abstraction for in-memory cluster computing. In: Proceedings of the 9th USENIX Conference on Networked Systems Design and Implementation, NSDI 2012. USENIX, Berkeley (2012)
19. Zaharia, M., Chowdhury, M., Franklin, M.J., Shenker, S., Stoica, I.: Spark: cluster computing with working sets. In: Proceedings of the 2nd USENIX Conference on Hot Topics in Cloud Computing, HotCloud 2010, p. 10. USENIX Association, Berkeley (2010)
20. Zaharia, M., Das, T., Li, H., Hunter, T., Shenker, S., Stoica, I.: Discretized streams: fault-tolerant streaming computation at scale. In: Proceedings of the 24th ACM Symposium on Operating Systems Principles, SOSP, pp. 423–438. ACM, New York (2013)

Viper: Communication-Layer Determinism and Scaling in Low-Latency Stream Processing

Ivan Walulya$^{(\boxtimes)}$, Yiannis Nikolakopoulos, Vincenzo Gulisano(iD),
Marina Papatriantafilou(iD), and Philippas Tsigas(iD)

Chalmers University of Technology, Gothenburg, Sweden
{walulya,ioaniko,vinmas,ptrianta,tsigas}@chalmers.se

Abstract. Stream Processing Engines (SPEs) process continuous streams of data and produce up-to-date results in a real-time fashion, typically through one-at-a-time tuple analysis. When looking into the vital SPE processing properties required from applications, determinism has a strong position besides scalability in throughput and low processing latency. SPEs scale in throughput and latency by relying on shared-nothing parallelism, deploying multiple copies of each operator to which tuples are distributed based on the semantics of the operator. The coordination of the asynchronous analysis of parallel operators required to enforce determinism is then carried out by additional dedicated sorting operators. In this work we shift such costly coordination to the communication layer of the SPE. Specifically, we extend earlier work on shared-memory implementations of deterministic operators and provide a communication module (Viper) which can be integrated in the SPE communication layer. Using Apache Storm and the Linear Road benchmark, we show the benefits that can be achieved by our approach in terms of throughput and energy efficiency of SPEs implementing one-at-a-time analysis.

Keywords: Data streaming · Low-latency
Shared-nothing and shared-memory parallelism
Stream processing engines

1 Introduction

Data streaming emerged to meet the stringent demands of massive on-line data analysis in a variety of contexts, such as cloud and edge-computing architectures. Stream Processing Engines (SPEs) allow programmers to formulate continuous queries, defined as Directed Acyclic Graphs of interconnected operators, that process incoming data producing results on a continuous fashion. Examples of such Stream Processing Engines include StreamCloud [12], Apache Storm [26], Apache Flink [10] and Saber [19].

Parallelism is key for modern hardware to achieve *high-throughput* and *low latency* in SPEs processing increasingly large data volumes in evolving cyber-physical infrastructures [16]. The importance of scaling in throughput and keeping low-latency processing in SPEs is clear, manifested also by work in elasticity

© Springer International Publishing AG, part of Springer Nature 2018
D. B. Heras and L. Bougé (Eds.): Euro-Par 2017 Workshops, LNCS 10659, pp. 129–140, 2018.
https://doi.org/10.1007/978-3-319-75178-8_11

of parallelism, e.g. [9,12]. With parallelization, though, careful orchestration of operators' execution is required to preserve *determinism*. An operator's implementation is *deterministic* if, given the same sequences of input tuples, the same sequence of output tuples is produced independently of the tuples' inter-arrival times or the degree of parallelism of the operator [14,15].

The guarantee of determinism in SPEs, under concurrent execution of parallel operators, relies on dedicated sorting operators that are either added to continuous queries by dedicated query compilers [12] or in SPEs such as Apache Storm [26], or are left to the application developers to place them within their streaming applications. Minimizing the computational overhead introduced by such dedicated operators (we refer to this as *operator-layer* determinism) is nevertheless challenging, especially for one-at-a-time, fine-grained low latency tuple processing. We address the issue of guaranteeing determinism in a modular, automated and efficient way. We start from the observation that, commonly in SPEs, each physical stream is piped from a producer (e.g., an incoming link from a sensor, or an outgoing link of an operator instance) to its consumer (another operator instance), without coordination or sharing state. Sharing and synchronizing efficiently in an automated way is the challenging key to provide a transparent determinism method to application developers, alleviating them from the responsibility of developing custom solutions and proof argumentation as required.

ScaleGate [15] is a data structure introduced for aggregate and join operators to guarantee determinism in a customized way. The work in this paper builds upon it and provides the following contributions: (i) It modularly shifts the procedure of guaranteeing determinism, from the operator-layer to the *communication layer* of an SPE, thus relieving application developers from the burden of devising application-dependent methods. (ii) It designs and implements a module, called *Viper*, which can be transparently integrated in an SPE communication layer. Building on ScaleGate, it lifts the data-structure's context into the communication layer of an SPE architecture. From ScaleGate to Viper, the novelty is on the transparency provided to the application developer in efficiently guaranteeing determinism. (iii) It integrates the module in Apache Storm (as a representative example of SPEs) and demonstrates via an extensive evaluation the feasibility of the idea of modularly providing determinism, while caring for efficiency in parallelism. The experimental evaluation of the proposed methodology used the Linear Road benchmark and shows the throughput as well as energy efficiency benefits, the latter being important with respect to sustainability of the evolution of processing infrastructures for cyberphysical systems.

The rest of the paper is organized as follows. We present preliminary concepts in Sect. 2. We describe our proposal for distinguishing the operator layer and communication layer in an SPE and discuss the advantages of doing that, we also introduce the Viper module, in Sect. 3. We evaluate the benefits of the Viper module in Sect. 4. Discuss related work and conclude in Sects. 5 and 6.

2   System Model

A stream is defined as an unbounded sequence of tuples $t_0, t_1, \ldots$ sharing the same schema composed of attributes $\langle ts, A_1, \ldots, A_n \rangle$. Given a tuple t, $t.ts$ represents its creation timestamp while $A_1, \ldots, A_n$ are application-related attributes.

Continuous queries (or simply queries in the remainder) are defined as DAGs of *operators* that consume and produce tuples. Operators are distinguished into *stateless* or *stateful*, depending on whether they keep any state that evolves with the tuples being processed. Stateless operators include Map (to alter the schema of tuples) and Filter (to discard or route tuples). Stateful operators include Aggregate (to compute aggregation functions such as sum or average over tuples) and Join (to match tuples coming from multiple streams). Due to the unbounded nature of streams, stateful operations are computed over *sliding windows*. Following the data streaming literature (e.g., [5,12,18]), we assume that streams fed by each data source contain timestamp-sorted tuples.

The performance of an operator depends on its *cost* and *selectivity*. That is, the average time needed to process an input tuple and (optionally) produce any resulting output tuple and the average number of output tuples produced upon the processing of one input tuple (e.g., an operator with selectivity 0.5 will produce, on average, one output tuple each time it processes two input tuples).

To illustrate the aforementioned terms and notions, Fig. 1A presents a sample streaming query from the Linear Road benchmark [4]. In this example, position reports are forwarded by vehicles traveling on a highway. The query checks if the report refers to a vehicle entering, leaving or changing a segment. In the affirmative case, it updates the number of vehicles and the tolls of the involved segments. Finally, it notifies the interested vehicles. The schema of each stream is presented on top of the operators. Aggregate A1 enriches each position report with the previous segment observed for the same vehicle. Subsequently, Filter F discards reports referring to vehicles that have not changed segment. Aggregate A2 updates the count for each segment. Finally, Map M computes the toll for a segment based on the number of vehicles in it and notifies vehicles.

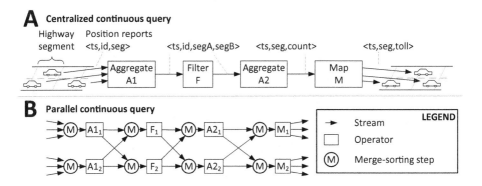

Fig. 1. Sample centralized and parallel query (Linear Road benchmark [4]).

2.1   Parallel and Deterministic Execution of Queries

A parallel version of a query, e.g. Fig. 1, is desirable to cope with large and fluctuating volume of tuples. Deterministic execution ensures that the results produced by the parallel query are exactly the same produced by its centralized counterpart. As explained in [12,13], determinism is enforced if the processing of each operator composing the query is deterministic. For an operator's processing to be deterministic, special merge-sorting steps[1] are defined before each operator *instance*, as shown in Fig. 1B, presenting a parallel version of the centralized query with two instances for each operator. The M steps merge-sort deterministically the incoming timestamp-sorted input streams of an operator instance into a single timestamp-sorted stream of tuples, allowing the operator instance's execution to be deterministic independently of the arrival interleaving of its input streams [12] by forwarding tuples when the latter are *ready*. Formally:

Definition 1 (ready tuple [14,15]). *Let t_i^j be the i-th tuple from timestamp-sorted stream S_j. t_i^j is **ready** to be processed if $t_i^j.ts \leq merge_{ts}$, where $merge_{ts} = min_k\{t_l^k.ts\}$ is the minimum timestamp among the timestamps in the set of tuples comprising the latest received tuples t_l^k from each timestamp-sorted stream S_k.*

2.2   Performance Metrics

We consider metrics that are commonly used to assess the performance of a streaming framework (from individual operators to queries or SPEs as a whole). More concretely, we take into account *throughput* and *latency* [12,15], as well as *energy consumption* [3]. Throughput, commonly measured in tuples per second (t/s), represents the maximum rate at which tuples can be fed to the operators composing a given query. Latency, commonly measured in milliseconds, represents the interleaving time between the forwarding of an output tuple and the timestamp carried by the latest input tuple contributing to it. For the energy consumption, we utilize RAPL energy counters [8] to measure power consumption in Watts and take the average over the counter samples during an execution.

3   From Operator- to Communication-Layer Determinism

As we explained in Sect. 1, determinism is typically enforced by SPEs at the operator layer. That is, the merge-sorting required to enforce determinism (cf. Sect. 2) is run by dedicated operators that are deployed together with the operators defined by the application programmer. Alternatively, as we propose and explain in this section, determinism can be achieved by the communication layer of an SPE, used for buffering operators' input and output tuples.

---

[1] We use the term steps rather than operators because, as shown in the following sections, merge-sorting and routing can be both assigned to dedicated operators or integrated in the communication layer of an SPE.

To introduce *layering* for SPE functionality provisioning, without loss of generality, we consider in the following the node shown in Fig. 2. The node depicts the operators F, $A2$ and M of Fig. 1B. Our discussion holds independently of whether other operators are deployed within the SPE running the query and of whether more than two instances are defined for each operator.

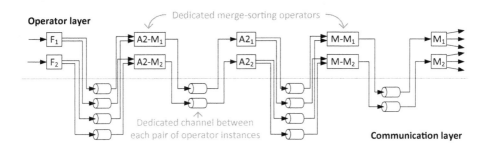

Fig. 2. Parallel query run by an SPE with operator-layer determinism.

3.1   Overheads of Operator-Layer Determinism

The deployment of dedicated merge-sorting operators in-between the query's operators results in an increase of the number of threads in SPEs such as Storm [26] or Flink [10] or in scheduling overheads for SPEs with schedulers ordering operators' execution [1,2,12], thus degrading throughput and increasing energy consumption. A lower throughput and a higher latency are also expected because of the increased number of operator instances and number of queues each tuple traverses. Using our example to provide an intuitive reasoning for the above claim, let us observe that each tuple traverses four queues and three operator instances from operator F to operator M (Fig. 2).

Moreover, merge-sorting operators might become the processing bottleneck. The maximum throughput of an operator instance can be observed as long as its preceding operators are not under-provisioned. That is, as long as the cost of its preceding merge-sorting operator is not a bottleneck. Unfortunately, the latter's cost (which is in the best case logarithmic in the number of input streams [15]) might be comparable to or higher than the query's operators. It should also be observed that, opting for a higher degree of parallelism when an operator cannot cope with its input rate might have a relapse on the throughput and latency of its downstream merge-sorting operator instances (which will have to merge-sort a higher number of input streams). For example in Fig. 2, suppose the processing cost of operator instances $A2_1, A2_2$ is higher than the cost of merge-sorting for operator instances $A2\text{-}M_1$, $A2\text{-}M_2$. The degree of parallelism for operator $A2$ could be increased to e.g. four instances. By doing this, each of the four instances of operator $A2\text{-}M$ would then be responsible for the merge-sorting of half of the input tuples. Nevertheless, each instance of the merge-sorting operator preceding operator M would now observe a higher cost for the merge-sorting of its input tuples (coming from four rather than two input streams). Hence, increasing the degree of parallelism for $A2$ could overload the merge-sorting of tuples feed to M, thus decreasing, rather than increasing, the overall throughput of the query.

3.2 Benefits of Communication-Layer Determinism

The aim of communication-layer determinism is to avoid the deployment of merge-sorting operators in between each operator and its upstream peer instances. As shown in Fig. 3, this allows for the instances of operator F to be directly connected to those of operator $A2$. Since the merge-sorting would still need to be run to enforce determinism, a requirement of communication-layer determinism is to leverage threads that are already deployed by the SPE and share such operations rather than assigning them to a dedicated one, as this would in turn result in the previously discussed overheads. As discussed in [15], shared-memory merge-sorting can be carried out by multiple threads in a scalable fashion when the cost and the relapse that merge-sorting itself introduces is minimized by avoiding coarse-grained locking mechanisms.

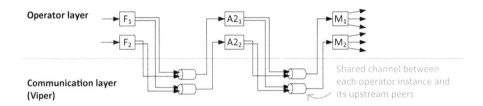

Fig. 3. Parallel query run by an SPE with communication-layer determinism.

3.3 The Viper Module

The Viper module allows for communication-layer determinism and provides an API defined by three main methods (Table 1). A channel is maintained at the Viper for any set of source operator instances $S_1, \ldots, S_m$ feeding a reader operator instance R (we use the term channel to refer to the data object used by a set of operator instances to share information, such an object can be a queue or another object). The channel, in our scheme, is either a thread-safe concurrent queue (when exactly one source S_1 and the reader R are connected) or a Scale-Gate [15] object (when at least two source operators S_1, S_2 and the reader R are connected). Method add allows tuples from different sources to be merge-sorted into a single list, assuming that each source delivers tuples in non-decreasing timestamp order. Method getReady allows the list to be read in timestamp order by the reader guaranteeing that only *ready* tuples (cf. Definition 1) will be delivered. In this work, we extend the original ScaleGate proposing and integrating a flow-control approach using special watermark tuples [17] internally in the data structure. Such tuples are added periodically by the sources and allow the readers to acknowledge the consumption rate to the sources, through a handshake mechanism, so that the latter can limit injection rate for slow readers.

With Viper, the merge-sorting cost is efficiently shared by the threads assigned to the instances of a parallel operator feeding the same downstream operator instance, thanks to its scalable probabilistically logarithmic lock-free implementation [15], which minimizes the necessary synchronization overheads [6].

Table 1. API of the Viper module

Method	Description
`void register(channel, sources, reader)`	Register a new *channel*, specifying its *sources* and the *reader* retrieving the timestamp-sorted stream of ready tuples
`void add(channel, sourceID, tuple)`	Add a *tuple* from a given *sourceID* to the specified *channel*
`tuple getReady(channel, readerID)`	Retrieve next ready *tuple* (if any) for the given *readerID* from the specified *channel*

4   Evaluation

To quantify the benefits of communication-layer determinism over operator-layer determinism, we integrated the Viper module in Apache Storm [26], studying its performance in terms of throughput (t/s), latency (ms) and energy consumption (mJ/t). In the following, we refer to operator-layer determinism as *OL* and communication-layer determinism as *CL*. We conducted our experiments on a dual-socket Intel Xeon E5-2687W 3.4 GHz server, with 8 cores per socket (yielding a total of 16 cores, 32 threads) and 64 GB of RAM. The server runs Scientific Linux 6.5 (5) based on the Red Hat Enterprise Linux operating systems. We used *likwid* [20] to read out RAPL Energy counters for the power metrics presented in our evaluation. All experiments have been run using Storm version 0.9.7 and OpenJDK Java version 1.8.0_91. The ScaleGate implementation is the one available at [23]. For channels accessed by a single source and reader (cf. Sect. 3), the Viper module relies on Java's `ConcurrentLinkedQueue`.

The evaluation runs the *Linear Road benchmark* [4], an established benchmark to study SPEs' performance that simulates vehicular traffic on a number of linear expressways, each composed of predefined *segments*. *Position reports* are forwarded every 30 s and carry the vehicle's *position* and *speed*. Vehicles are charged with a variable toll based on the traffic congestion level and the presence of *accidents*. The generated data is continuously processed to (i) detect possible accidents and (ii) compute tolls and notify vehicles. We provide the evaluation results for both a stateless (pos_rep) and a stateful (new_seg) operator of the benchmark. Operator pos_rep forwards an incoming tuple if it is a position report. Its selectivity is 0.99. Operator new_seg checks whether a vehicle is entering a new segment. Its selectivity is 0.34.

To study the performance of an operator, we start by deploying one instance of such operator together with one data injector and one sink. The injector is in charge of forwarding input tuples while maintaining the throughput statistics (per-second averages). The sink is in charge of maintaining latency statistics (per-second averages). This initial deployment allows us to measure the performance of the operator's centralized execution. The performance of its parallel counterpart depends on its parallelism degree (i.e., its number of parallel instances) and the parallelism degree of its upstream operator (i.e., the overhead introduced by deterministically merge-sorting the streams of the parallel upstream operator), as discussed in Sect. 3. For this reason, we increase the number of instances both for the injector and the operator to 2, 4 and 6 (i.e., we deploy 1 injector and 1, 2, 4 and 6 parallel operator instances, 2 parallel injectors and 1, 2, 4 and 6 parallel operator instances, . . .) for a total of 16 configurations for each operator. The number of parallel sink instances deployed in each experiment is equal to the number of parallel instances of the operator in order for the former not to constitute a bottleneck. With OL-determinism provisioning, a merge-sorting operator is deployed for each instance of the operator if two or more injectors are deployed. Similarly, a merge-sorting operator is deployed before each instance of the sink if two or more parallel operator instances are deployed (no extra merge-sorting operators are needed for CL-determinism provisioning, using the Viper module). The highest degree of parallelism for the injector and operator is chosen so that the overall number of threads for both OL and CL that process and forward tuples is in the same order as the number of logical threads provided by the server.

For each configuration, we measure throughput as the number of tuples generated over each 5 s period and report the average throughput per second. The experiments are repeated 5 times; the reported values are averages over the runs of the same configuration.

4.1   Operator pos_rep

Figure 4a presents the performance results for the pos_rep operator for CL (left column) and OL (right column). Each sub-graph contains 4 lines, for 1, 2, 4 and 6 injectors, respectively. The upper sub-graphs present the throughput for the increasing number of instances of the parallel pos_rep operator. The middle sub-graphs present the latency while the lower ones present the energy consumption.

Given that operator pos_rep has a very high selectivity, almost each input tuple results in an output tuple. Since the operator is also a light stateless filtering operator, the cycles spent by it communicating (i.e., receiving and forwarding tuples) are higher than those spent processing tuples. Looking at the throughput performance of OL when one single injector is deployed, we can observe a stable throughput lower than 600,000 t/s. For the increasing number of operator instances, the latency increases to 600 ms (because the same output rate is shared by an increasing number of threads, thus resulting in longer times for output tuples to become *ready*) while the energy consumption stabilizes around 100 W. A similar behavior can be observed for a single injector

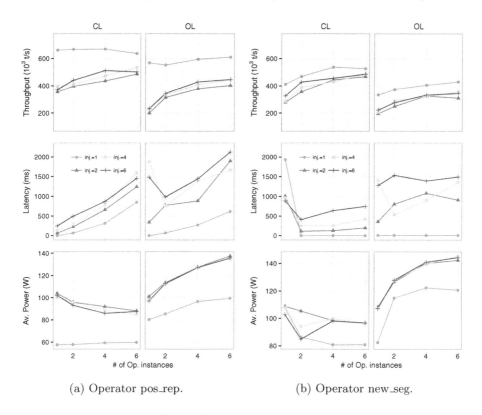

(a) Operator pos_rep.   (b) Operator new_seg.

Fig. 4. Performance evaluation.

for CL, with a higher throughput that stabilizes at 650,000 t/s and a latency that also increases (to ~800 ms). However, the energy consumption decreases to 60 W, 60% of that observed for OL, due of the channel shared by Viper between operator instances.

A different behavior can be observed for OL and CL when an increasing number of injectors is deployed. As shown in the figure, despite the lower throughput, due to the sorting overhead introduced to enforce determinism, CL results in a throughput growing over 500,000 t/s while OL stabilizes around 400,000 t/s. While still incurring in similar latency (lower in this case for CL than OL), OL's energy consumption grows up to 140 W while CL's achieves a consumption of 90 W due to the shared sorting work performed by the threads already deployed.

4.2   Operator new_seg

Using the same sub-graphs of Fig. 4a, b presents the performance results for OL and CL and operator new_seg. Differently for the stateless operator pos_rep, the stateful operator new_seg is characterized by a lower selectivity. This implies that, for the same input rate, the latter results in a lower output stream rate.

Given also its stateful nature, it results in an higher number of cycles spent processing rather receiving and forwarding tuples. As shown in Fig. 4b, the throughput achieved by CL is always higher than that of OL while observing a lower latency, both for the increasing number of injectors and the increasing number of operators. Also for this operator, CL achieves a throughput that is of approximately 100,000 t/s higher than that of OL. Finally, CL also results in lower power consumption, which does not exceed 100 W. On the other hand, OL's consumption grows to more than 140 W.

4.3   Power Consumption

Modern architectures deploy dynamic frequency scaling or CPU throttling where processors in idle state run at low frequency to conserve power and scale up the frequency on-demand. We observe in Fig. 4, that OL dissipates on average more power than CL. This is a result of differences in the number of threads utilized during a computation. With increasing number of execution threads, more cores are activated at high frequency which ultimately increases the power.

5   Related Work

Parallel execution of streaming operators has been first discussed by Flux [25] and implemented in StreamCloud [12,13]. The latter provided dedicated merge-sorting operators (added to queries by a dedicated compiler) to enforce deterministic execution at the operator layer, incurring the limitations discussed in Sect. 3. The techniques in [12,13,25] are now found in widely-adopted SPEs.

The communication-layer determinism we introduce in this paper is motivated by the increasing research interest in shared-memory parallelism. The most relevant advances, nonetheless, have so far been only tailored to Aggregates [14,24] and Joins [11,15,21,27]. The principles of the ScaleGate data object [23] have been proposed in [7] and leveraged in shared-memory parallelism for streaming aggregation [14] and joining [15]. In relation with our work, papers such as [3,22] discuss and provide evidence of the importance of careful design decisions for the internal communication mechanisms of SPEs. Differently from this work, nonetheless, optimizations focus on the reduction of unnecessary copies of tuples for the Borealis SPE in [3] (not considering determinism) and in a batching mechanism (complementary to the mechanism we propose) for Apache Storm.

6   Conclusions

Motivated by the observation that deterministic execution of streaming operators requires expensive synchronization to merge-sort streams from multiple operator instances (or data sources), we studied the limitations of operator-layer parallelism and how these can be overcome by communication-layer parallelism. Reducing the communication and synchronization costs among operator instances running within an SPE is a key factor in boosting its scale up potential.

In this paper, we propose a module, which we call Viper, that encapsulates and reduces the aforementioned costs, enabling for deterministic execution to be provided in a transparent way by the communication layer of an SPE. We provide evidence that such a module can be leveraged by SPEs, by integrating it into Apache Storm, which is a representative SPE of one-at-a-time analysis paradigm, for ultra-low latency processing. Our evaluation shows that the throughput of parallel operators interconnected with the Viper module increases by up to 70% and results in half of the energy consumption.

Acknowledgments. This work was supported by the Swedish Foundation for Strategic Research under the project "Future factories in the cloud (FiC)", grant number GMT14-0032 and the Swedish Research Council (Vetenskapsrådet) projects "HARE: Self-deploying and Adaptive Data Streaming Analytics in Fog Architectures" Contract nr. 2016-03800 and "Models and Techniques for Energy-Efficient Concurrent Data Access Designs" Contract nr. 2016-05360.

References

1. Abadi, D.J., Ahmad, Y., Balazinska, M., Cetintemel, U., Cherniack, M., Hwang, J.-H., Lindner, W., Maskey, A., Rasin, A., Ryvkina, E., et al.: The design of the borealis stream processing engine. In: CIDR, vol. 5, pp. 277–289 (2005)
2. Abadi, D.J., Carney, D., Çetintemel, U., Cherniack, M., Convey, C., Lee, S., Stonebraker, M., Tatbul, N., Zdonik, S.: Aurora: a new model and architecture for data stream management. VLDB J. Int. J. Very Large Data Bases **12**(2), 120–139 (2003)
3. Akram, S., Marazakis, M., Bilas, A.: Understanding and improving the cost of scaling distributed event processing. In: Proceedings of the 6th ACM International Conference on Distributed Event-Based Systems, pp. 290–301. ACM (2012)
4. Arasu, A., Cherniack, M., Galvez, E., Maier, D., Maskey, A.S., Ryvkina, E., Stonebraker, M., Tibbetts, R.: Linear road: a stream data management benchmark. In: Proceedings of the Thirtieth International Conference on Very Large Data Bases, vol. 30, pp. 480–491. VLDB Endowment (2004)
5. Balazinska, M., Balakrishnan, H., Madden, S.R., Stonebraker, M.: Fault-tolerance in the Borealis distributed stream processing system. In: ACM TODS (2008)
6. Cederman, D., Chatterjee, B., Nguyen, N., Nikolakopoulos, Y., Papatriantafilou, M., Tsigas, P.: A study of the behavior of synchronization methods in commonly used languages and systems. In: 2013 IEEE 27th International Symposium on Parallel and Distributed Processing (IPDPS), pp. 1309–1320. IEEE (2013)
7. Cederman, D., Gulisano, V., Nikolakopoulos, Y., Papatriantafilou, M., Tsigas, P.: Brief announcement: concurrent data structures for efficient streaming aggregation. In: Proceedings of the 26th ACM Symposium on Parallelism in Algorithms and Architectures, SPAA 2014, pp. 76–78. ACM (2014)
8. David, H., Gorbatov, E., Hanebutte, U.R., Khanna, R., Le, C.: RAPL: memory power estimation and capping. In: Proceedings of the 16th ACM/IEEE International Symposium on Low Power Electronics and Design, ISLPED 2010, pp. 189–194. ACM, New York (2010)
9. De Matteis, T., Mencagli, G.: Keep calm and react with foresight: strategies for low-latency and energy-efficient elastic data stream processing. In: Proceedings of the 21st ACM SIGPLAN Symposium on Principles and Practice of Parallel Programming, PPoPP 2016, pp. 13:1–13:12. ACM, New York (2016)

10. Apache Flink. https://flink.apache.org/
11. Gedik, B., Bordawekar, R.R., Philip, S.Y.: CellJoin: a parallel stream join operator for the cell processor. VLDB J. **18**(2), 501–519 (2009)
12. Gulisano, V.: StreamCloud: an elastic parallel-distributed stream processing engine. Ph.D. thesis, Universidad Politécnica de Madrid (2012)
13. Gulisano, V., Jimenez-Peris, R., Patino-Martinez, M., Valduriez, P.: StreamCloud: a large scale data streaming system. In: 2010 IEEE 30th International Conference on Distributed Computing Systems (ICDCS), pp. 126–137. IEEE (2010)
14. Gulisano, V., Nikolakopoulos, Y., Cederman, D., Papatriantafilou, M., Tsigas, P.: Efficient data streaming multiway aggregation through concurrent algorithmic designs and new abstract data types. CoRR, abs/1606.04746 (2016)
15. Gulisano, V., Nikolakopoulos, Y., Papatriantafilou, M., Tsigas, P.: ScaleJoin: a deterministic, disjoint-parallel and skew-resilient stream join. IEEE Trans. Big Data (99) (2016)
16. Gulisano, V., Nikolakopoulos, Y., Walulya, I., Papatriantafilou, M., Tsigas, P.: Deterministic real-time analytics of geospatial data streams through ScaleGate objects. In: Proceedings of the 9th ACM International Conference on Distributed Event-Based Systems, DEBS 2015, pp. 316–317. ACM, New York (2015)
17. Johnson, T., Muthukrishnan, S., Shkapenyuk, V., Spatscheck, O.: A heartbeat mechanism and its application in gigascope. In: Proceedings of the 31st International Conference on Very Large Data Bases, VLDB 2005, pp. 1079–1088. VLDB Endowment (2005)
18. Kalyvianaki, E., Fiscato, M., Salonidis, T., Pietzuch, P.: THEMIS: fairness in federated stream processing under overload. In: Proceedings of the 2016 International Conference on Management of Data, pp. 541–553. ACM (2016)
19. Koliousis, A., Weidlich, M., Castro Fernandez, R., Wolf, A.L., Costa, P., Pietzuch, P.: SABER: window-based hybrid stream processing for heterogeneous architectures. In: Proceedings of the 2016 International Conference on Management of Data, pp. 555–569. ACM (2016)
20. LIKWID: Performance measurement and benchmark suite. https://github.com/RRZE-HPC/likwid
21. Roy, P., Teubner, J., Gemulla, R.: Low-latency handshake join. Proc. VLDB Endow. **7**(9), 709–720 (2014)
22. Sax, M.J., Castellanos, M., Chen, Q., Hsu, M.: Aeolus: an optimizer for distributed intra-node-parallel streaming systems. In: 2013 IEEE 29th International Conference on Data Engineering (ICDE), pp. 1280–1283. IEEE (2013)
23. ScaleGate. https://github.com/dcs-chalmers/scalegate
24. Schneidert, S., Andrade, H., Gedik, B., Wu, K.-L., Nikolopoulos, D.S.: Evaluation of streaming aggregation on parallel hardware architectures. In: Proceedings of the Fourth ACM International Conference on Distributed Event-Based Systems, pp. 248–257. ACM (2010)
25. Shah, M.A., Hellerstein, J.M., Chandrasekaran, S., Franklin, M.J.: Flux: an adaptive partitioning operator for continuous query systems. In: Proceedings of the 19th International Conference on Data Engineering, pp. 25–36. IEEE (2003)
26. Apache Storm. http://storm.apache.org/
27. Teubner, J., Mueller, R.: How soccer players would do stream joins. In: Proceedings of the 2011 ACM SIGMOD International Conference on Management of Data (2011)

Scalability and State: A Critical Assessment of Throughput Obtainable on Big Data Streaming Frameworks for Applications With and Without State Information

Shinhyung Yang, Yonguk Jeong, ChangWan Hong, Hyunje Jun,
and Bernd Burgstaller$^{(\boxtimes)}$

Department of Computer Science, Yonsei University, Seoul, Korea
{shinhyung.yang,bburg}@yonsei.ac.kr

Abstract. Emerging Big Data streaming applications are facing unbounded (infinite) data sets at a scale of millions of events per second. The information captured in a single event, e.g., GPS position information of mobile phone users, loses value (perishes) over time and requires sub-second latency responses. Conventional Cloud-based batch-processing platforms are inadequate to meet these constraints.

Existing streaming engines exhibit low throughput and are thus equally ill-suited for emerging Big Data streaming applications. To validate this claim, we evaluated the Yahoo streaming benchmark and our own real-time trend detector on three state-of-the-art streaming engines: Apache Storm, Apache Flink and Spark Streaming. We adapted the Kieker dynamic profiling framework to gather accurate profiling information on the throughput and CPU utilization exhibited by the two benchmarks on the Google Compute Engine.

To estimate the performance overhead incurred by current streaming engines, we re-implemented our Java-based trend detector as a multi-threaded, shared-memory application in C++. The achieved throughput of 3.2 million events per second on a stand-alone 2 CPU (44 cores) Intel Xeon E5-2699 v4 server is 44 times higher than the maximum throughput achieved with the Apache Storm version of the trend detector deployed on 30 virtual machines (nodes) in the Cloud. Our experiment suggests vertical scaling as a viable alternative to horizontal scaling, especially if shared state has to be maintained in a streaming application. For reproducibility, we have open-sourced our framework configurations on GitHub [1].

1 Introduction

The increasing demand for Big Data streaming has become prevalent in Cloud-based applications where data streams are characterized by sub-second latency, high density at high velocity, statefulness and near real-time response requirements. Social interactions from existing services such as Twitter and Facebook, real-time click-streams from e-commerce Cloud platforms and GPS position information from mobile applications qualify as such data. Traditionally,

© Springer International Publishing AG, part of Springer Nature 2018
D. B. Heras and L. Bougé (Eds.): Euro-Par 2017 Workshops, LNCS 10659, pp. 141–152, 2018.
https://doi.org/10.1007/978-3-319-75178-8_12

MapReduce-based batch processing was applied with Big Data streaming applications. In pursuit of programming abstractions tailored specifically for streaming applications, and to support sub-second event response times, the Aurora and Apache Storm Big Data streaming platforms rapidly became popular for businesses and with the academic community.

Today's prominent Big Data streaming engines are programmed in Java, Scala or related programming languages targeting the Java virtual machine (JVM). The hardware abstraction provided by the JVM facilitates deployment in the Cloud. Users are provided with high-level programming primitives to compose streaming applications as a set of nodes (actors) connected by FIFO data channels. The resulting stream-graph topologies can then be readily deployed on the underlying, Cloud-based streaming engine. It is the sole responsibility of the underlying streaming engine to orchestrate a given stream graph topology on a set of Cloud nodes. The programmer is only required to provide high-level configuration parameters such as the number of nodes or virtual machines (VMs).

To assess the efficiency of streaming applications on current state-of-the-art streaming engines, and to determine the cost of the provided programming abstractions, this paper makes the following contributions.

1. We created a Java-based trend detection benchmark for Wikipedia user clickstreams. This benchmark was implemented for the Apache Storm and Flink streaming engines. We employed the Yahoo streaming benchmark [10] as our second real-world streaming benchmark.
2. We adopted the Kieker dynamic profiling framework [5] for Spark Streaming and the Apache Storm and Flink streaming engines. To the best of our knowledge, this is the first detailed evaluation of the throughput and CPU utilization of two real-world benchmarks on the before-mentioned streaming engines run on the Google Compute Engine. From our measurements we conclude that CPU resources are under-utilized with current Big Data streaming engines.
3. We re-implemented our Java-based trend detector as a multi-threaded application in C++. Through manual performance optimizations such as the adoption of lock-free data-structures, it was possible to maintain shared state and raise the throughput by a factor of 44x to 3.2 million events per second on a stand-alone shared-memory multicore server. From this result two conclusions can be drawn: (1) the cost of current stream programming abstractions is non-negligible, and (2) vertical scaling on a multi-CPU, multicore computer benefits from the high bandwidth of chip interconnects and can thus be preferable to (pre-mature) horizontal scaling.

The remainder of this paper is structured as follows. In Sect. 2, we present the constituents of the Yahoo benchmark and how the Kieker framework was incorporated to obtain dynamic profiling information. Section 3 introduces our trend detector for the streaming APIs and the low-level C++ version. We present our experimental evaluation in Sect. 4, discuss the related work in Sect. 5 and draw our conclusions in Sect. 6.

2   Yahoo Streaming Benchmark

The purpose of the Yahoo streaming benchmark [10] is to determine the performance of three state-of-the-art Big Data streaming engines: Apache Storm, Apache Flink, and Apache Spark Streaming. The benchmark constitutes a Cloud-deployment of an advertising analytics pipeline. Events arrive through Kafka, the JSON format is deserialized, and events are filtered, projected and joined. Windowed counts of events per campaign are stored in the Redis in-memory database. The Yahoo streaming benchmark consists of three Cloud components: (1) the Kafka distributed data queue, (2) the analytics pipeline expressed for one of the three before-mentioned streaming engines, and (3) the Redis in-memory database.

The Yahoo streaming benchmark as provided on GitHub [10] is configured to run on a single (Cloud) node. It was a non-trivial, time-consuming process to adapt this single-node configuration to multiple nodes. To obtain detailed dynamic profiling information, we incorporated the Kieker dynamic profiling framework as a system daemon on each Cloud node. We developed the system daemon to automatically launch at each boot and it starts to sample per-core CPU utilization every 500 ms. Sampled data is stored locally on each Cloud node and from this raw data we analyze performance of Cloud streaming applications. To make our results reproducible, we have open-sourced these configurations on GitHub [1].

2.1   Kafka Distributed Streaming Queue

Apache Kafka 0.8.2 is deployed as the default data queue with the benchmark. Kafka is a subscription-based distributed streaming queue platform. Data generators written in the Clojure programming language subscribe to the Kafka platform as producers. A streaming application will subscribe to the Kafka platform as a consumer. Kafka works as a Cloud-based global data-queue which hides underlying details and only exposes a few interfaces to producers and consumers. The queue is constructed as a Kafka cluster which consists of one or more Kafka broker servers. In this benchmark, we deploy a Kafka cluster of five Kafka broker servers where each broker server occupies an entire Cloud node.

2.2   Anatomy of Streaming Engines

Streaming engines are the major targets in this streaming benchmark. Because of the high arrival rate of tuples from Kafka at the streaming engine, the throughput of the Yahoo streaming benchmark is solely constrained by the throughput of the streaming engine itself. The streaming engines compared in this experiment are Apache Storm version 0.9.7, Spark Streaming version 1.6.2, and Apache Flink version 1.1.3. With the Storm configuration, Storm Nimbus does bookkeeping and the orchestration of the entire platform. More than one Storm supervisor instance is assigned to a Nimbus instance and runs a subset of the target stream topology. Similarly, the Flink platform is operated by two types of managers,

Job Managers and Task Managers. A Job Manager is responsible for allocating subsets of the target stream topology to Task Manager entities. Apache Spark Streaming is an additional layer built upon the Apache Spark platform. This enables stream processing using traditional batch processing of Apache Spark. A Spark cluster is managed by the Spark Master. A Spark Master may have multiple Spark Slaves. Each Slave instance may be assigned to execute a subset of the target stream application.

3   Trend Detector

Trend detection is a popular technique employed with real-world enterprises to discover user trends on Cloud services such as social media, e-commerce and search engines. It is important to note that user-generated data streams have to be analyzed by the Cloud streaming environment. Therefore, trend detection has to be implemented and operated in a Cloud environment using streaming operators.

Monitoring an incoming data stream of user-generated keywords, a trend detection algorithm analyzes the stream to detect irregularities in the occurrences of registered keywords over the most recent consecutive time-windows. Each and every uniquely distinguished keyword is given its own timebucket to store and update a series of occurrences and they are constantly evaluated to list the most trending keyword(s) in the system.

3.1   Java Trend Detector

We implemented a trend detector in Java for the Storm streaming engine. Based on the original approach from Twitter's trend detection [4], our implementation incorporates the point-by-point Poisson model. This Poisson model is employed to explicitly distinguish locally irregular occurrences of a particular keyword within the target time-series, where the overall count of the keyword is insignificant. The point-by-point model is especially applicable to find trending keywords from a small set of data. We improved this model by introducing a parallel reduction algorithm. With our approach, we employ trend-detection actors and aggregator actors as depicted in Fig. 1. They constitute n layers of actors such that 2^n trend-detection actors receive data streams from spout s_0. This layer of trend-detection actors is followed by $n - 1$ levels of aggregators. Level k consists of 2^{n-k-1} aggregators, where k indicates the position of the aggregators in the topology.

In this parallel reduction, each trend-detection actor evaluates the trendiness of incoming keywords with its own set of timebuckets of unique keywords. That is, for a single stream of keywords that are equally distributed into 2^n trend-detection actors, there will be 2^n parallel evaluations of trendiness on local sets of timebuckets. This strategy was necessary in two aspects: first, in a Big Data streaming application, there is no guarantee on how many "sibling" instances of an actor exist in the stream graph topology. No exchange of information is

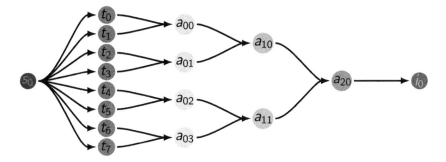

Fig. 1. Our Java-based trend-detector's topology of 3 layers. The topology is dynamically created at the beginning of the run-time with given number of layers for speculative parallel reduction.

allowed between actors except for the FIFO data channels connecting producers to consumers. Thus in such stream graph topologies it is not possible to share a single global set of timebuckets across all actors (actors cannot have shared state). Therefore each trend-detection actor is designed to keep its own set of timebuckets and evaluate it separately. Secondly, by parallel reduction, multiple actors can jointly conduct the evaluation.

The trend detection layer is followed by layers of aggregator actors. An aggregator actor accepts a tuple which contains a keyword and its trendiness from a pair of preceding trend-detection actors or aggregator actors. An aggregator determines a keyword of the highest trendiness from its local list. With the Java trend detector, the last layer consists of a single aggregator actor. The resulting keyword from this actor is considered as the most trending keyword.

In our design of the Java trend detector, actors have local state only. Thus trend detection is based on local decisions and hence semantically incorrect and speculative. (I.e., the parallel trend detector may not always compute exactly the same trends as the underlying sequential solution. Nevertheless, differences materialize only under certain adversary cases of event-distributions, which are outside of the scope of this paper.)

3.2   C++ Trend Detector

Our goal for the C++ version of the trend detector is to fully utilize the underlying hardware of a single multicore node, while focusing on creating a semantically correct, non-speculative trend detector. In conducting an evaluation of the C++ trend detector, we assumed that all keyword tuples arrive in the right order between preceding and succeeding tuples in terms of creation time. That is because, if a tuple arrives too early or too late, it won't be placed in the right time window on which trend detection is performed.

As depicted in Fig. 2, one datagenerator is employed per CPU. The program targets a server with two Xeon E5-2699 v4 CPUs, where one CPU consists of

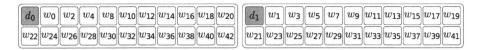

Fig. 2. Thread-to-core allocation of the C++ trend detector on a server with two Xeon E5-2699 v4 CPUs. One datagenerator $d_{[01]}$ is assigned per CPU; the remaining cores are filled with worker threads w_*.

22 cores. Our design of the C++ trend detector leverages information about the hardware architecture. To prevent the OS from moving threads between cores, we pinned one datagenerator thread onto the first core of each CPU and the other cores are pinned with worker threads. (Pinning was done with the LIKWID-pin utility [8], which manipulates the CPU affinity of a program's threads.) At the worker thread creation stage, allocation of multiple worker threads will take turn between the two CPUs. The worker threads pinned onto the same CPU receive tuples in a round-robin fashion from the datagenerator inhabiting the same CPU through a dedicated queue.

To maximize throughput, we utilize B-Queues [9] as the system-level streaming queues between a datagenerator and its workers. A B-Queue is a lock-free single-producer, single-consumer queue, and we use one dedicated B-Queue from a datagenerator to each of its connected workers. We unrolled the innermost loop of the C++ datagenerator such that tuples are entered into each queue once per iteration.

Once a worker receives a keyword, it looks up the corresponding, dedicated timebucket for this keyword in a global hashmap. Then the keyword's timestamp of its creation time is inserted into the timebucket and the keyword's trendiness is evaluated periodically. The evaluated trendiness is then inserted into the global trending list and the most trending keyword at the current time is determined from the list. The global hashmap is a highly-contended shared data-structure causing serialization from lock contention. We overcame this problem by introducing a global lock-free hashtable [7].

3.3   An Example Data Set

As an example data set which qualifies as Big Data, we chose a snapshot of Wikipedia's traffic from the Amazon web services public data set page [2]. This data set contains 150 GB of hourly page traffic statistics collected from January 1, 2011 to March 31, 2011. This data set was employed for benchmarking both the Java and the C++ trend detector.

4   Experimental Results

In this paper, we ran three benchmarks. One is our C++ trend detector which was evaluated on a CentOS 7 server machine consisting of two Xeon E5-2699 v4 CPUs with 512 GB of RAM. The other two are Big Data streaming applications—the

Yahoo streaming benchmark and our Java trend detector (the counterpart of the C++ trend detector). To evaluate them correctly we referred to Yahoo's Cloud setup [3]. First, we configured 30 hypervised machines on the Google Compute Engine. In this setup, one hypervised machine has 16 virtual CPUs (vCPUs) with 24 GB of RAM. Each vCPU is a hyperthreaded core of an Intel Xeon processor running at 2.50 GHz. Nineteen hypervised machines are dedicated to "infrastructure" purposes: three Zookeeper nodes, one Redis in-memory database instance, five Kafka brokers constituting one Kafka cluster, and 10 Kafka producer nodes which feed tuple streams into the Kafka cluster. Eleven hypervised machines are dedicated to the actual application running on the streaming engine under evaluation. One coordinator is needed to manage an entire streaming engine and its workers. Thus we are left with 10 workers which run the streaming application itself.

We measured the CPU utilization of our Big Data streaming benchmarks using the Kieker dynamic profiling framework. We configured the Kieker framework's periodic sampler facility to measure per-core CPU utilization of 11 streaming engine nodes every 500 ms during the execution of the benchmark to sample at the double frequency of per-second sampling rate according to the Nyquist-Shannon sampling theorem. Measurements from the 16 vCPUs of a single hypervised machine node are averaged to denote per-node and per-second CPU utilization during the period of the benchmark execution. From this refinement we produced two graphs: Average (AVG) and Coefficient of Variation (CV) graphs. Each AVG graph shows per-node CPU utilization of hypervised machines which run the streaming engine. Each CV graph shows the degree of sparseness among per-second utilization of each hypervised machine.

To determine the efficiency of each streaming engine's orchestration of worker nodes, we generated a diagram where the actor allocation across the 10 worker nodes is depicted. Each hypervised machine is depicted in a unique color and all actor instances are included, to provide the complete picture of how a streaming engine orchestrated actor instances across hypervised machine nodes. Due to substantial differences with the programming interface, we did not produce actor orchestration diagrams for the Spark streaming engine.

4.1   Yahoo Streaming Benchmark

Big Data streaming engines require complicated Cloud configurations in which multiple hypervised machines collaborate to run different types of software components which have dependencies to other components. In this benchmark, the infrastructure consists of Zookeepers, Redis database nodes, the Kafka cluster, Kafka producers, and streaming engines. Thirty hypervised machines are required to execute a streaming application.

In Fig. 3c and e, CPUs are under-utilized. Most of the worker nodes are only utilizing 10% or less of their CPU resources. Although Flink has one outlier node depicted in green, its top CPU utilization is only 40%. On the other hand, Fig. 3a shows higher CPU utilization. Five worker nodes are utilizing more than 75% of their CPU resource. It is more clearly depicted in Fig. 4a. With the Storm

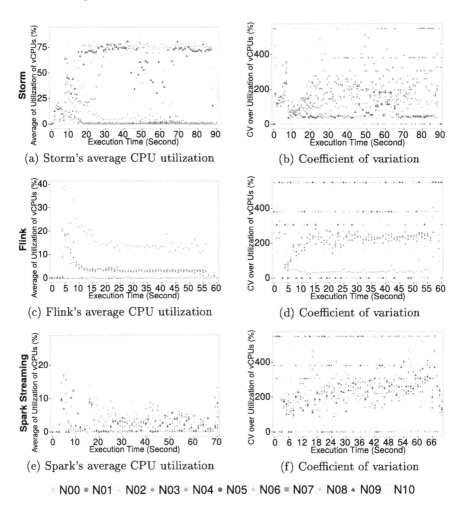

(a) Storm's average CPU utilization

(b) Coefficient of variation

(c) Flink's average CPU utilization

(d) Coefficient of variation

(e) Spark's average CPU utilization

(f) Coefficient of variation

N00 • N01   N02 ◆ N03   N04 • N05   N06 ▪ N07   N08 ▲ N09   N10

Fig. 3. CPU utilization of Big Data streaming engines with the Yahoo streaming benchmark

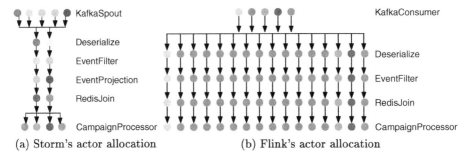

(a) Storm's actor allocation

(b) Flink's actor allocation

Fig. 4. Stream graph topology and actor distribution for the experiment from Fig. 3 (employing the same color code)

configuration, all participating worker nodes are allocated with actor instances of the target topology. This is different from Flink's actor distribution diagram in Fig. 4b. Flink actors are only partly distributed on five worker nodes. Compared to Storm, this orchestration does not seem efficient. However, Flink in fact achieved higher throughput than Storm. The throughput of the Yahoo streaming benchmark with Flink is 282 141 tuples per second whereas Storm only achieved 24 703 tuples per second. In terms of throughput, Flink's orchestration works better, however the problem still remains that it did not utilize five worker nodes at all. In the evaluation of Cloud applications, this is clearly inefficient because energy resources to run worker nodes are wasted.

4.2   Trend Detector

In comparing the Java trend detector to the C++ trend detector, two key factors are to be considered: First, the Java trend detector runs on a Big Data streaming platform, which means there will be multiple worker nodes participating in an execution of the application. Second, by necessity of the streaming engine programming abstractions, the actors of the Java trend detector are restricted to local state only. In particular, each trend-detection actor has its own actor-local set of timebuckets, and the aggregator actors do not share global state. Local state reduces the communication overhead compared to a shared, global (distributed) store of timebuckets. Nevertheless—as pointed out before—this performance advantage comes at the cost of analysis precision.

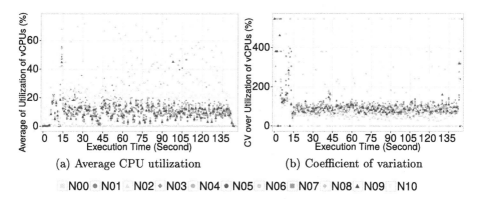

(a) Average CPU utilization   (b) Coefficient of variation

N00   N01   N02   N03   N04   N05   N06   N07   N08   N09   N10

Fig. 5. CPU utilization characteristics of the Java-based trend detector

To benchmark the Java trend detector, we adopted the Cloud setup that we employed with the Yahoo streaming benchmark. Although Flink's throughput was higher than Storm's in our experiment with the Yahoo streaming benchmark, we chose Storm due to its prevalence in industry. Therefore Storm's programming interface was used to implement our Java trend detector. Because our implementation is based on Storm APIs, we ran the benchmark on Storm only.

In the benchmark result of Fig. 5, under-utilization of CPUs is also shown with the Java trend detector's average utilization (see Fig. 5a). Except for a few nodes that reach just under 80%, most nodes stay below 20% average CPU utilization. In Fig. 5b, abundant sparseness of CPU utilization is depicted. Only two nodes are utilized more, and those are at 80%. In the CV diagram, one node, i.e., "▲", performs well in terms of consistently utilizing CPU resources. The Java trend detector's highest throughput is 72 499 tuples per second.

The C++ trend detector was evaluated on a stand-alone Intel Xeon E5-2699 v4 system. The throughput of our shared-memory stateful C++ trend detector implementation is 3 217 432 tuples per second. It can be evaluated in two ways: first, even though we chose to use a global timebucket hashtable, because the hashtable is designed lock-free, it avoids cache coherence overhead from locking. This way, we achieved correct semantics with state information shared by all worker threads. Second, we showed that a single C++ trend detector on a single machine can obtain higher throughput than its Java-based Cloud counterpart.

To determine the maximum possible throughput in terms of tuples emitted by the datagenerators, we removed all worker threads except one consumer per queue which had the sole purpose of emptying its queue. This configuration achieved 309 360 800 tuples per second.

The shared-memory trend detector shows that it is possible to reduce energy consumption and increase the performance over current Cloud streaming engines. However, the C++ programming interface is not as easy as developing streaming applications with Cloud streaming frameworks. Big Data stream programming interfaces are easier for beginners than C++ programming. Developing efficient C++ multi-threaded applications requires careful, manual hand-tuning and optimizations to detect and remove performance bottlenecks.

In conclusion, our experiment shows that the raw performance of sending tuples across processes is two orders of magnitude higher than the performance of a carefully hand-tuned, multi-threaded C++ streaming application. And the performance of this C++ streaming application is 44x times higher than what can be achieved with current state-of-the-art of Cloud streaming frameworks.

In terms of programming effort, the C++ version required the 3-week attention of a multicore programming expert, whereas the Java version of our trend detector was created by a group of software capstone students new to stream programming—in about the same amount of time.

5   Related Work

In [3], Chintapalli et al. introduce the Yahoo streaming benchmark and its purpose to measure the latency for a complete processing of a tuple at different Kafka emission rates. Although three streaming engines, namely Apache Spark streaming, Apache Storm and Apache Flink were compared in the paper, because of architecture and language differences, Spark streaming was evaluated differently with regard to micro-batching intervals. Although the micro-batching interval does affect the result, Spark streaming was the slowest with Flink being as the 2nd-slowest of the three. It is important to note that our measurement of throughput is different from what its authors intended to measure with the same framework. Chintapalli et al. measured the up-to-date latency at each stage of tuple process completion. Contrary, in our benchmark, we measured the throughput of tuples at the source-node of a streaming application.

In [4], the principles of trend detection are explained. Three popular models are explained with the point-by-point Poisson model being the simplest but the most effective for a small set of time series. With large-enough sets of time series, the authors recommend the cycle-corrected Poisson model, which will increase the precision of the algorithm. Lastly, a data-driven method is introduced for its stableness and adaptability. In our Java trend detector and the C++ trend detector, we adapted the point-by-point Poisson model.

In [6], McSherry et al. propose a new paradigm in evaluating the performance of distributed data processing systems (aka Big Data processing systems). The authors take examples of parallelized algorithms that scale well compared to other algorithms, while in fact, the performance of the compared algorithm is better. They point out the importance of better (highly-optimized) baselines. If the baseline single-threaded algorithm is of low performance, a parallelized algorithm will inevitably perform better than this baseline, even if it is only parallelizing the overhead contained in the baseline. They suggest to improve the baseline with better algorithms. The paper's idea aligns well with our introduction of the C++ trend detector. Our Java trend detector and other streaming applications that scale well within Big Data platforms should be re-evaluated in terms of energy-efficiency and throughput, because we have shown that our stateful C++ trend detector showed the highest throughput over the other benchmarks, although it runs on a single machine.

6   Conclusions

We have shown that existing Big Data streaming platforms exhibit low throughput and inefficient utilization of the underlying Cloud infrastructure. Measurement data was obtained for the Yahoo streaming benchmark and our real-time trend detectors with the help of the Kieker dynamic profiling framework. Our stateful C++ trend detector uses vertical scaling on a shared-memory multicore server. It outperformed its Cloud-based counterparts by 44 times higher throughput. For reproducibility, we have open-sourced our streaming framework configurations on GitHub [1].

Acknowledgements. Research supported by the Next-Generation Information Computing Development Program through the National Research Foundation of Korea (NRF), funded by the Ministry of Science, ICT & Future Planning under grant NRF2015M3C4A7065522.

References

1. Yang, S.: Cloud framework configurations for the Yahoo and the real-time trend-detector benchmarks. https://github.com/shinhyungyang/cloud-ready. Created 13 Feb 2017
2. Wikipedia page traffic statistic v3. https://aws.amazon.com/datasets/wikipedia-page-traffic-statistic-v3/. Accessed 13 Feb 2017
3. Chintapalli, S., Dagit, D., Evans, B., Farivar, R., Graves, T., Holderbaugh, M., Liu, Z., Nusbaum, K., Patil, K., Peng, B.J., Poulos, P.: Benchmarking streaming computation engines: Storm, Flink and Spark streaming. In: 2016 IEEE International Parallel and Distributed Processing Symposium Workshops, pp. 1789–1792, May 2016
4. Hendrickson, S., Kolb, J., Lehman, B., Montague, J.: Trend detection in social data. https://github.com/jeffakolb/Gnip-Trend-Detection/raw/master/paper/trends.pdf. Accessed 13 Feb 2017
5. van Hoorn, A., Waller, J., Hasselbring, W.: Kieker: a framework for application performance monitoring and dynamic software analysis. In: Proceedings of 3rd ACM/SPEC International Conference on Performance Engineering, ICPE 2012, pp. 247–248. ACM, New York (2012)
6. McSherry, F., Isard, M., Murray, D.G.: Scalability! But at what cost? In: Proceedings of 15th USENIX Conference on Hot Topics in Operating Systems, p. 14, May 2015
7. Preshing, J.: The world's simplest lock-free hash table. http://preshing.com/20130605/the-worlds-simplest-lock-free-hash-table/. Accessed 13 Feb 2017
8. Treibig, J., Hager, G., Wellein, G.: LIKWID: a lightweight performance-oriented tool suite for x86 multicore environments. In: Proceedings of First International Workshop on Parallel Software Tools and Tool Infrastructures, PSTI 2010, San Diego, CA (2010)
9. Wang, J., Zhang, K., Tang, X., Hua, B.: B-queue: efficient and practical queuing for fast core-to-core communication. Int. J. Parallel Prog. **41**(1), 137–159 (2013)
10. Yahoo Inc.: Yahoo streaming benchmarks GitHub page. https://github.com/yahoo/streaming-benchmarks. Accessed 13 Feb 2017

COLOC – Workshop on Data Locality

Open Workshop on Data Locality (COLOC)

Workshop Description

A well-known handicap for HPC applications running on modern highly parallelized and heterogeneous HPC platforms is that an increasing amount of time is spent in communication and data transfers; thus, it is necessary to design, implement and validate new approaches to optimize process placement and data locality management. COLOC is a forum for exposing contribution from HPC application developers interested in exploring new ways to optimize their code, HPC centers and clusters managers to enhance cluster usage and application efficiency, Academics and researchers in scientific computing.

The different areas or research interest include, but are not limited to:

- Modeling node topology.
- Modeling network and communication.
- Performance analysis of applications to understand affinity.
- Affinity metrics.
- Runtime support for extracting affinity from application.
- Code analysis in order to understand communication pattern.
- Algorithm to improve locality.
- Language, abstraction and compiler support for data locality.
- Data structure and library support to better manage memory access.
- Runtime-system and dynamic locality management.
- System-scale locality optimization.
- Validating locality optimization at thread or process level.
- Memory management.
- Locality management in large-scale applications.

We have received six submissions and we have accepted four. Three of them are published in this proceedings. The workshop also featured an invited talk from Rosa Badia (BSC, Spain) on *Managing data locality for convergence HPC/Big Data.*

Program Chairs

Emmanuel Jeannot	Inria France
François Verbeck	Atos/Bull, France

Program Committee

Erik Abenius	Efield, Sweden
George Bosilca	UTK, USA
Matthias Diener	Univ. of Illinois at Urbana-Champaign, USA

Anshu Dubey	Argonne Natl Lab, USA
Karl Fuerlinger	LMU, München, Germany
Yiannis Georgiou	ATOS BULL, France
Brice Goglin	Inria, France
Aleksandar Ilic	INESC-ID/IST, Univ. de Lisboa, Portugal
Vitus Leung	Sandia National Laboratories, USA
Hatem Ltaief	KAUST, Saudi Arabia
Allen Malony	University of Oregon, USA
Farouk Mansouri	Inria, France
Naoya Maruyama	Riken, Japan
Lawrence Mitchell	Imperial College, UK
Hartmut Mix	Technische Universität Dresden, Germany
Marc Perache	CEA, France
Eric Petit	Intel, France
Didem Unat	Koç University, Turkey

Netloc: A Tool for Topology-Aware Process Mapping

Cyril Bordage, Clément Foyer, and Brice Goglin[(✉)]

Inria Bordeaux, Sud-Ouest, LaBRI, University of Bordeaux, Bordeaux, France
{cyril.bordage,clement.foyer,brice.goglin}@inria.fr

Abstract. Interconnection networks in parallel platforms can be made of thousands of nodes and hundreds of switches. The communication cost between tasks of a parallel application varies significantly with their actual location in such platforms. Topology-aware process mapping consists in matching the application communication pattern with the network topology to improve the communication cost by placing related tasks close on the hardware.

We show that our Netloc tool for gathering network topology in a generic way can be combined with the state-of-the-art Scotch partitioner for computing topology-aware MPI process placement. Our experiments with a stencil application on a fat-tree machine show that we are able to significantly improve the runtime in the vast majority of cases.

Keywords: Topology-aware mapping · Network topology
Process placement · MPI

1 Introduction

Parallel platforms are increasingly complex. They feature deep memory hierarchies as well as multi-level interconnection networks that cause locality to severely impact application performance. Topology-aware process placement is a widely used optimization technique for improving the overall application time by reducing communication overheads. It requires knowledge of the hardware organization, of the application needs, and algorithmics to make them match.

The internals of nodes are nowadays well modeled thanks to software tools such as hwloc [5]. However, there is still a need for a generic way to model networks and map processes to different compute nodes. We present in this paper the implementation of topology-aware process placement using the Netloc tool and the Scotch graph partitioner.

2 Generic Network Topology Discovery

On the road to exascale, parallel platforms are growing. Computing nodes now contain tens of cores. There is also an increasing number of nodes interconnected

© Springer International Publishing AG, part of Springer Nature 2018
D. B. Heras and L. Bougé (Eds.): Euro-Par 2017 Workshops, LNCS 10659, pp. 157–166, 2018.
https://doi.org/10.1007/978-3-319-75178-8_13

with various network technologies and fabric topologies, such as InfiniBand or Intel Omni-Path fat-trees, or Cray Aries dragonfly. Understanding the organization of these networks is required for administration, debugging, and performance optimization.

The topology inside nodes is well understood problem. It was solved by using software such as hwloc [5] which builds a hierarchical model of each host by organizing processors, cores, caches, NUMA nodes and hardware threads as a tree. Although this strategy is only a structural model of the hardware without performance information such as physical distances between components, it still provides valuable information for describing hardware affinities and easing locality-aware task placement [8,9,11].

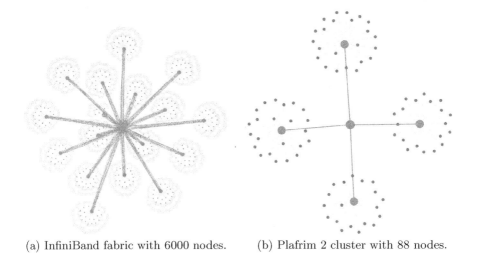

(a) InfiniBand fabric with 6000 nodes.   (b) Plafrim 2 cluster with 88 nodes.

Fig. 1. Network topologies of two machines. Nodes in red and switches in grey. (Color figure online)

On the network side, each technology has its own custom command-line administration tools (`ibnetdiscover`, `opareport`, `xtprocadmin`, *etc.*) with different outputs or even different notions of nodes, ports and links. Some technology-specific tools have been proposed [12] for exposing the network topology in a convenient manner. However, they cannot be extended to other technologies because of these different management tools, query APIs, and fabric topologies.

The Netloc project was designed to manage network topologies in a generic manner [6]. It uses hardware-specific tools to discover the entire fabric topology (nodes, switches, and links) and exposes it to HPC applications and runtimes through an abstracted API. This enables visualization of the topology as depicted on Fig. 1. However, Netloc was mostly developed for improving the performance of applications by taking the network locality into account in HPC runtimes. Possible optimizations include selecting the best route between peers or building neighborhoods for mapping hierarchical algorithms to the hierarchy of nodes and switches. We discuss in the next sections the use of Netloc for topology-aware process placement.

3 Topology-Aware Mapping in Fat-Trees

In an MPI application, the communication cost between two ranks depends on where the processes are mapped on the machine. If a task sends a message to a task on the same processor, it will be faster than if they are on two different nodes connected to different switches. Hence, it is important to consider the topology of the machine when placing tasks on a parallel platform. In order to reduce the communication time, it seems obvious to map processes on close cores if they communicate a lot. Some applications may also have been optimized for other criteria (e.g. placing specific tasks near GPUs or I/Os), which can fortunately usually be combined with our policy.

The vast majority of message-passing applications can potentially benefit from communication-aware task placement. This has been the subject of several research projects [7,8,12]. Nevertheless, none of these approaches provide state-of-the-art network topology discovery tools that can be used on a variety of hardware, neither state-of-the-art graph partitioning techniques for computing a good mapping. We propose in this paper to combine Netloc and Scotch to address this problem.

3.1 Scotch

Scotch [10] is a widely-used library for graph partitioning and mapping. It can operate on very large graphs (up to billions of vertices) using thousands of cores in parallel.

In our work, we use Scotch *Graphs* to model applications (communication patterns) and Scotch *Architecture Graphs* to represent platforms. Scotch can deal with random architectures but works best with regular structures such as fat-trees, torus, meshes, hypercubes, etc. Scotch is also able to deal with partial architectures, i.e. a restriction of a regular architecture, for instance to represent the subset of cluster nodes that were actually allocated by the resource manager.

3.2 Using Scotch from Netloc

The whole topology of a machine is given by the network topology but also by the node topology. The latter is generally a tree as depicted in the example in Fig. 2.

Consequently, the whole topology of a platform interconnected through a fat-tree fabric is a tree as shown in Fig. 3. Thus, we only need to give the right tree to Scotch.

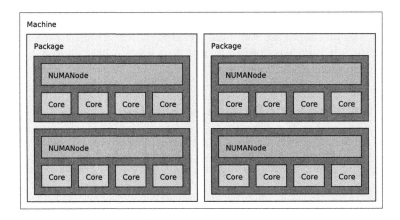

Fig. 2. Example of the topology of a node, given by hwloc.

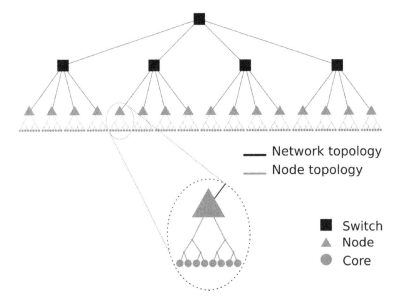

Fig. 3. Example of a fat-tree with node topologies nodes.

The architecture graph needed by Scotch to compute the mapping is then created from Netloc by exporting the network topology as well as the node topology provided by hwloc into the Scotch format. Moreover, Netloc is able to find the currently allocated resources and export them into a Scotch partial architecture.

We have integrated a tool in Netloc that builds a Scotch architecture representing the topology of the machine and uses Scotch to generate a good process mapping. Then, it converts the mapping returned by Scotch into a rank file for MPI. Thus, if a user provides a communication matrix between the MPI ranks, we can give him a rank file that will be used to launch the MPI application in a topology-aware-optimized way. Instead of manually building a communication matrix, the user can generate it using existing monitoring tools [4].

4   Evaluation

To see the relevance of our topology-aware mapping, we have conducted tests and compared our mapping to the default mapping of MPI that is round-robin.

4.1   Setup

The experiments were carried out using Plafrim 2, an 88 node machine with a fat-tree network, as shown in Fig. 1b. It is an InfiniBand QDR fat-tree network made of four leaf switches with 22 nodes each. There are 2 spine switches although they were combined into a single virtual switch on the figure. Each node contains two Intel Xeon E5-2680 v3 processor (24 cores total, split in 4 NUMA nodes with 6 cores each).

The tested application was miniGhost [3], a miniapp doing stencil computations. It allows to set a lot of different parameters that will change the communication pattern.

We use Open MPI with monitoring [4] to build our communication matrices. Each value in the matrices corresponds to the volume of communication between a pair of ranks during the overall execution.

4.2   Results

We have run miniGhost with more than 300 parameter sets to see the influence of our mapping in different configurations. We have changed grid sizes, stencil patterns, schemes of communication, number of variables, *etc.* The gain is measured when using the mapping given by Netloc with Scotch compared to the default mapping of the MPI implementation. To summarize the gains and make that more readable, we have computed the percentage of test cases that have a gain at least greater than a specific value. These results are presented in Fig. 4.

In 92.5% of the test cases, our mapping is at least as good as round-robin mapping. It means that we lose performance in only 7.5% of the cases. The largest loss is 3.6%. It can be due, for instance, to cache pollution from more shared memory communication. Our mapping shows a gain at least equal to 10.1% for 50% of the tested cases, at least 20% for 24.9% of the cases, and at least 30% for 5.7% of cases. The maximum gain is 33.6%.

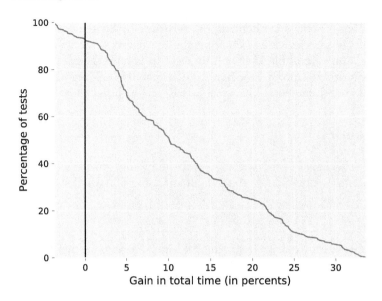

Fig. 4. Percentages of test cases with gain greater than x-value.

5   Mapping on Complex Topologies

As we use Scotch to do the mapping, the architecture of the machine must be a topology handled by Scotch. Scotch can handle a lot of different structures, as shown in Sect. 3.1. Nevertheless, the whole topology must be a single topology and not an aggregation of different kinds. However, as we saw in Fig. 3, the whole topology is composed of the network topology and the node topologies. Since the node topology is generally a tree, to have a topology handled by Scotch, it imposes to the network topology to be a fat-tree.

To tackle this problem, we propose a method to handle architectures composed of different topologies.

5.1   Expression of the Topology

The mapping is done on the cores allocated by the resource manager. Therefore, to build the mapping, we need to get only the part of the topology with the current resources. Thus, our description of the topology will contain the lists of available nodes. For that we chose a hierarchical format, with one line for one level of the global topology:

```
<type> <number of dimensions> <dimension1 size> <dimension1 speed>
... <dimensionD size> <dimensionD speed> <number of nodes> <node1
index>...<nodeN index>
```

The field called type designates the type of topology. For now, it can only be tree or torus. With that we can handle fat-trees and Cray XE [2]. However, we will extend it with composition of simple topologies such as `alltoall` or `ring` to handle more topologies like, for instance, Dragonfly with Cray XC [1]. The node indices represent the available elements in the topology. The index is a way to identify the position of the element in the topology. Moreover, if the line describes a compute node, we prefix it with:

node <hostname>

To make it clearer, we consider an example with a 3D torus of size 4 for each dimension. On each point of the torus, we have a router that connects 6 other routers (two neighbors in each dimension) and 4 local nodes together. This topology is quite similar to Cray XE but with 4 nodes in a router instead of 2. A node contains two processors split in 2 NUMA nodes with 4 cores each.

Assuming the resource manager gives us 3 nodes, two on the same router and the third on another one, this network topology is represented in Fig. 5.

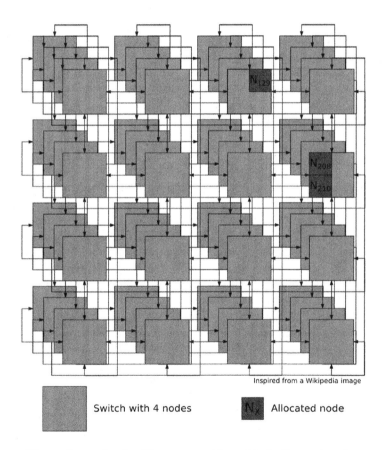

Fig. 5. Example of a 3D torus machine with 3 allocated nodes.

This topology will be described by the following lines:

```
torus 3 4 1600 4 1600 4 1600 2 32 52
tree 1 4 800 1 0
node n129 tree 4 2 80 2 40 4 20 2 10 -1
tree 1 4 800 2 0 1
node n208 tree 4 2 80 2 40 4 20 2 10 -1
node n210 tree 4 2 80 2 40 4 20 2 10 -1
```

The first line (`torus`) indicates the 3D torus with 4 nodes in each dimension. 32 and 52 indicate the indices of the two used routers in our allocation.

Each line starting with `tree` describes what is connected to each coordinate of the torus. Since we have a router with 4 nodes, it is modeled as a tree with 4 leaves. For the first occurrence of the `tree` line we have 1 0 to indicate that we have a single node on this router at the index 0. For the other occurrence, 2 0 1 shows that the router has two nodes of indices 0 and 1.

The lines beginning with `node` give us the hostname of the nodes followed by their structures that are trees with 4 levels: 2 processors, with 2 NUMA nodes each, 4 cores each. The value −1 is to avoid putting the complete list of the cores, it simply means that the node is fully available.

The values 10, 20, 40, 80, 800 and 1600 represent the costs of communication of their corresponding links.

5.2   Handling Hierarchical Topology

There are two ways to process complex topologies. The first strategy that we propose is to compute the mapping recursively. We do not create the general graph of the platform but rather keep the information that it is composed of a torus of trees on our example. First, we compute a mapping for the top topology. Usually this is network fabric. On our example, this step consists in mapping processes to routers on the torus (torus partitioning). Then, we recursively compute the mapping inside sub-topologies. In our example, this consists in considering all ranks selected for a router actually mapping them to individual cores on nodes connected to that router (tree partitioning). This approach has the advantage of using optimized partitioning technique for each step since both torus and trees are regular and well-known Scotch architectures.

Unfortunately, it is not possible in Scotch to put weight on nodes on the predefined architectures and it can lead to unbalanced mapping. In our torus example, if you use this technique without any weight on the routers, both routers will have the same amount of processes when the one with only one node needs one third of the processes, not half.

The other strategy is not concerned with this issue. The principle is to describe the entire topology, including switches, torus, routers, nodes and cores as a single graph. Scotch can handle such graphs using the *deco* architecture but it is more complex to compute than for regular topologies such as fat-trees or torus. Nonetheless, the time of computation is very low, since the complexity depends only on the number of used cores, and the quality of the mapping is preserved.

6   Conclusion

We showed how to perform a topology-aware mapping using state-of-the-art topology discovery and graph partioning tools, Netloc with Scotch, and a communication matrix. Tests on a stencil application showed the relevance of this approach on this kind of applications since we are able to significantly decrease the runtime in the vast majority of cases.

We are now running more tests with different applications and network technologies to further show the genericity and usefulness of our proposal. As we have proven the utility of our model, we are extending Netloc to handle more process placement algorithms. In the meantime, the user can get the discovered topology by exporting into a Scotch architecture and converting it into his desired format.

Our implementation is freely available in the current Netloc development code that can be found in the hwloc git repository at https://github.com/open-mpi/hwloc. It will be officially released in the upcoming hwloc 2.0 release in the next months.

Acknowledgements. Experiments presented in this paper were carried out using the PLAFRIM experimental testbed, being developed under the Inria PlaFRIM development action with support from Bordeaux INP, LABRI and IMB and other entities: Conseil Régional d'Aquitaine, Université de Bordeaux and CNRS and ANR in accordance to the Programme d'Investissements d'Avenir (see https://www.plafrim.fr/).

This work is partially funded under the ITEA3 COLOC project #13024.

References

1. Alverson, B., Froese, E., Kaplan, L., Roweth, D.: Cray XC series network. White Paper WP-Aries01-1112, Cray Inc. (2012)
2. Alverson, R., Roweth, D., Kaplan, L.: The Gemini system interconnect. In: 2010 18th IEEE Symposium on High Performance Interconnects, pp. 83–87, August 2010
3. Barrett, R.F., Vaughan, C.T., Heroux, M.A.: MiniGhost: a miniapp for exploring boundary exchange strategies using stencil computations in scientific parallel computing. Technical report SAND 5294832, Sandia National Laboratories (2011)
4. Bosilca, G., Foyer, C., Jeannot, E., Mercier, G., Papauré, G.: Online dynamic monitoring of MPI communications. In: Rivera, F.F., Pena, T.F., Cabaleiro, J.C. (eds.) Euro-Par 2017. LNCS, vol. 10417, pp. 49–62. Springer, Cham (2017). https://doi.org/10.1007/978-3-319-64203-1_4. Extended version in https://hal.inria.fr/hal-01485243
5. Broquedis, F., Clet-Ortega, J., Moreaud, S., Furmento, N., Goglin, B., Mercier, G., Thibault, S., Namyst, R.: hwloc: A generic framework for managing hardware affinities in HPC applications. In: Proceedings of 18th Euromicro International Conference on Parallel, Distributed and Network-Based Processing (PDP 2010), pp. 180–186. IEEE Computer Society Press, Pisa, Italia, February 2010. http://hal.inria.fr/inria-00429889
6. Goglin, B., Hursey, J., Squyres, J.M.: netloc: towards a comprehensive view of the HPC system topology. In: Proceedings of 5th International Workshop on Parallel Software Tools and Tool Infrastructures (PSTI 2014), held in conjunction with ICPP-2014, Minneapolis, MN, pp. 216–225, September 2014. http://hal.inria.fr/hal-01010599

7. Hoefler, T., Snir, M.: Generic topology mapping strategies for large-scale parallel architectures. In: Proceedings of 2011 ACM International Conference on Supercomputing (ICS 2011), pp. 75–85. ACM, June 2011

8. Jeannot, E., Mercier, G., Tessier, F.: Process placement in multicore clusters: algorithmic issues and practical techniques. IEEE Trans. Parallel Distrib. Syst. **25**(4), 993–1002 (2014)

9. Li, S., Hoefler, T., Snir, M.: NUMA-aware shared-memory collective communication for MPI. In: Proceedings of 22nd International Symposium on High-Performance Parallel and Distributed Computing, HPDC 2013, pp. 85–96. ACM (2013)

10. Pellegrini, F., Roman, J.: Scotch: a software package for static mapping by dual recursive bipartitioning of process and architecture graphs. In: Liddell, H., Colbrook, A., Hertzberger, B., Sloot, P. (eds.) HPCN-Europe 1996. LNCS, vol. 1067, pp. 493–498. Springer, Heidelberg (1996). https://doi.org/10.1007/3-540-61142-8_588

11. Solernou, A., Thiyagalingam, J., Duta, M.C., Trefethen, A.E.: The effect of topology-aware process and thread placement on performance and energy. In: Kunkel, J.M., Ludwig, T., Meuer, H.W. (eds.) ISC 2013. LNCS, vol. 7905, pp. 357–371. Springer, Heidelberg (2013). https://doi.org/10.1007/978-3-642-38750-0_27

12. Subramoni, H., Potluri, S., Kandalla, K., Barth, B., Vienne, J., Keasler, J., Tomko, K., Schulz, K., Moody, A., Panda, D.K.: Design of a scalable InfiniBand topology service to enable network-topology-aware placement of processes. In: Proceedings of 2012 ACM/IEEE Conference on Supercomputing, Salt Lake City, UT, November 2012

Runtime Support for Distributed Dynamic Locality

Tobias Fuchs[(⊠)] and Karl Fürlinger

MNM-Team, Computer Science Department, Ludwig-Maximilians-Universität (LMU)
München, Oettingenstr. 67, 80538 Munich, Germany
{tobias.fuchs,karl.fuerlinger}@nm.ifi.lmu.de

Abstract. Single node hardware design is shifting to a heterogeneous nature and many of today's largest HPC systems are clusters that combine heterogeneous compute device architectures. The need for new programming abstractions in the advancements to the Exascale era has been widely recognized and variants of the Partitioned Global Address Space (PGAS) programming model are discussed as a promising approach in this respect. In this work, we present a graph-based approach to provide runtime support for dynamic, distributed hardware locality, specifically considering heterogeneous systems and asymmetric, deep memory hierarchies. Our reference implementation *dyloc* leverages hwloc to provide high-level operations on logical hardware topology based on user-specified predicates such as filter- and group transformations and locality-aware partitioning. To facilitate integration in existing applications, we discuss adapters to maintain compatibility with the established hwloc API.

1 Introduction

The cost of accessing data in Exascale systems is expected to be the dominant factor in terms of execution time and energy consumption [11]. To minimize data movement, programming systems must therefore shift from a compute-centric to a more data-centric focus.

The Partitioned Global Address Space (*PGAS*) model is particularly suitable for programming abstractions for data locality [3] but differentiates only between local and remote data access in its conventional form. This two-level abstraction lacks the expressiveness to model locality of increasingly deep and heterogeneous machine hierarchies. To facilitate *plasticity*, the capability of software to adapt to the underlying hardware architecture and available resources, programmers must be provided with fine-grained control of data placement in the hardware topology. The 2014 PADAL report [11] summarizes a wish list on programming environment features to facilitate this task. This work is motivated by two wish list items in particular:

- Flexible, memory-agnostic mappings of abstract processes to given physical architectures

© Springer International Publishing AG, part of Springer Nature 2018
D. B. Heras and L. Bougé (Eds.): Euro-Par 2017 Workshops, LNCS 10659, pp. 167–178, 2018.
https://doi.org/10.1007/978-3-319-75178-8_14

– Concise interfaces for hardware models that adjust the level of detail to the requested accuracy.

This work introduces an abstraction of dynamic distributed locality with specific support for deep asymmetric memory hierarchies of heterogeneous systems which typically do not exhibit an unambiguous tree structure. In this context, *dynamic locality* refers to the capability to create logical representations of physical hardware components from run-time specified, imperative and declarative constraints. Application-specific predicates can be applied as distance- and affinity metrics to define measures of locality. Our approach employs a graph-based internal representation of hierarchical locality domains. Its interface allows to request light-weight views which represent the complex locality graph as a well-defined, consolidated hierarchy.

The remainder of this paper is structured as follows: After a brief review of related work, we illustrate the need for dynamic hardware locality support using requirements identified in the DASH library. Section 4 introduces the concept of a graph-based locality topology and general considerations for implementation. Addressing dynamic characteristics, Sect. 4 outlines fundamental operations on locality hierarchies and selected semantic details. To substantiate our conceptual findings, we introduce our reference implementation 'dyloc' and explain how it achieves interoperability with hwloc in Sect. 5. Finally, the benefit of the presented techniques is evaluated in a use case on SuperMIC, a representative heterogeneous Ivy Bridge/Xeon Phi system.

2 Related Work

Hierarchical locality is incorporated in numerous approaches to facilitate programmability of the memory hierarchy. Most dynamic schemes are restricted two levels in the machine hierarchy.

In X10, memory and execution space is composed of places, and tasks execute at specific places. Remote data can only be accessed by spawning a task at the target place. Chapel has a similar concept of locales.

The task model implemented in Sequoia [1] does not consider hardware capacity for task decomposition and communication is limited to parameter exchange between adjacent parent and child tasks.

Hierarchical Place Trees (HPT) [12] extend the models of Sequoia and X10 and increase flexibility of task communication and instantiation. Some fundamental concepts of HPT like hierarchical array views have been adopted in DASH. The HPT programming model is substantially task-parallel, however, and based on task queues assigned to places. HPTs model only static intra-node locality collected at startup.

All abstractions of hierarchical locality in related work model the machine hierarchy as a tree structure, including the de-facto standard *hwloc*. However, shortcomings of trees for modeling modern heterogeneous architectures are known [8] while hierarchical graphs have been shown to be more practicable to represent locality and hardware capacity in task models [9].

Notably, the authors of hwloc explain that graph data structures are used in the network topology component *netloc* as a tree-based model was too strict and inconvenient [7]. We believe that this reasoning also applies to node-level hardware. Regarding current trends in HPC hardware configurations, we observed that interdependent characteristics of horizontal and vertical locality in heterogeneous systems cannot be sufficiently and unambiguously represented in a single, conventional tree. This is already evident for recent architectures with cores connected in grid- and ring bus topologies.

More important, heterogeneous hosts require communication schemes and virtual process topologies that are specific to hardware configuration and the algorithm scenario. This involves concepts of vertical and horizontal locality that are not based on latency and throughput as distance measure. For example in a typical accelerator-offloading algorithm with a final reduction phase, processes first consider physical distance and horizontal locality. For communication in the reduction phase, distance is measured based on PCI interface affinity to optimize for vertical locality.

Still, formal considerations cannot disprove the practical benefit of tree data structures as a commonly understood mental model for algorithms and application development. We therefore came to the conclusion that two models of hardware locality are required: an internal *physical* model representing the machine architecture in a detailed, immutable graph and *logical* views resulting from projections of the physical model to a simplified tree structure.

3   Background and Motivation

The concepts discussed in the following sections evolved from specific requirements of DASH, a C++ template library for distributed containers and algorithms in Partitioned Global Address Space. While the concepts and methods presented in this work do not depend on a specific programming model, terminology and basic assumptions regarding domain decomposition and process topology have been inherited from DASH. In this section, these are briefly discussed as motivating use cases for dynamic hardware locality (Fig. 1).

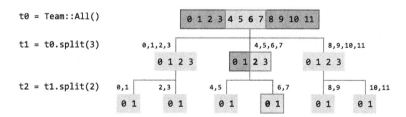

Fig. 1. Team hierarchy created from two balanced splits: numbers in boxes indicate unit ranks relative to the current team, with corresponding global ranks above

Virtual Process Topology: DASH Teams. In the DASH execution model, individual computation entities are called *units*, a generic name chosen because terms such as process or thread have a specific connotation that might be misleading for some runtime system concepts. In the MPI-based implementation of the DASH runtime, a unit corresponds to an MPI rank.

Units are organized in hierarchical *teams* to represent the logical structure of algorithms and machines in a program [10]. On initialization of the DASH runtime, all units are assigned to the predefined team instance ALL. New teams can be only created by specifying a subset of a parent team in a `split` operation. Splitting a team creates an additional level in the team hierarchy [6].

In the basic variant of the team split operation, units are evenly partitioned in a specified number of child teams of balanced size. A balanced split does not respect hardware locality but has low complexity and no communication overhead. It is therefore preferable for teams in flat memory hierarchy segments. On systems with asymmetric or deep memory hierarchies, it is highly desirable to split a team such that locality of units within every child team is optimized. A locality-aware split at node level could group units by affinity to the same NUMA domain, for example.

Organizing units by locality requires means to query their affinity in the hardware topology. Resolving NUMA domains from given process IDs can be reliably realized using hwloc. When collaboration schemes are to be optimized for a specific communication bus, especially with grid- and ring topologies, concepts of affinity and distance soon depend on higher-order predicates and differ from the textbook intuition of memory hierarchies.

This does not refer to experimental, exotic architecture designs but already applies to systems actively used at the time of this writing. Figure 2 shows the physical structure of a SuperMIC system at host level and its common logical interpretation. Note that core affinity to PCI interconnect can be obtained, for example by traversing hwloc topology data, but is typically not exploited in applications due to the lack of a locality information system that allows to express high-level, declarative views.

Adaptive Unit-Level Parallelism. Node-level work loads of nearly all distributed algorithms can be optimized using unit-level parallelization like multithreading or SIMD operations. The available parallelization techniques and their suitable configuration depend on the unit's placement in the process- and hardware topology. As this can only be determined during execution, this again requires runtime support for dynamic hardware locality that allows to query available *capacities* of locality domains – such as cache sizes, bus capacity, and the number of available cores – depending on the current team configuration.

Domain Decomposition: DASH Patterns. The Pattern concept in DASH [5] allows user-specified data distributions similar to Chapel's domain maps [2]. As only specific combinations of algorithms and data distribution schemes maintain data locality, hardware topology and algorithm design are

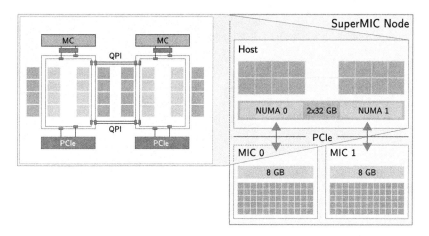

Fig. 2. Hardware locality of a single SuperMIC compute node with host-level physical architecture to the left and corresponding logical locality domains including two MIC coprocessors to the right.

tightly coupled. Benefits of topology-aware selection of algorithms and patterns for multidimensional arrays have been shown in previous work [4].

4   Locality Domain Hierarchies

An hwloc distance matrix allows to express a single valid representation of hardware locality of non-hierarchical topologies. However, it is restricted to latency and throughput as distance measures. A distance matrix can express the effects of grouping and view operations but does not support high-level queries and has to be recalculated for every modification of the topology view. In this section, we present the *Locality Domain Hierarchy* (LDH) model which extends the hwloc topology model by additional properties and operations to represent locality topology as dynamic graph.

In more formal terms, we model hardware locality as directed, acyclic, multi-indexed multigraph. In this, nodes represent *Locality Domains* that refer to any physical or logical component of a distributed system with memory or computation capacities, corresponding to *places* in X10 or Chapel's *locales*. Edges in the graph are directed and denote one of the following relationships:

Containment indicating that the target domain is logically or physically contained in the source domain

Alias source and target domains are only logically separated and refer to the same physical domain; this is relevant when searching for a shortest path, for example

Leader the source domain is restricted to communication with the target domain.

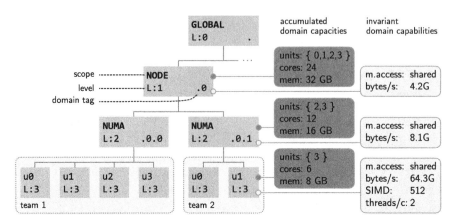

Fig. 3. Domain nodes in a locality hierarchy with domain attributes in dynamically accumulated capacities and invariant capabilities

Figure 3 outlines components of the locality domain concept in a simplified example. A locality hierarchy is specific to a team and only contains domains that are populated by the team's units. At initialization, the runtime initializes the default team ALL as root of the team hierarchy with all units and associates the team with the global locality graph containing all domains of the machine topology.

Leaf nodes in the locality hierarchy are *units*, the lowest addressable domain category. A single unit has affinity to a specific physical core but may utilize multiple cores or shared memory segments exclusively. Domain capacities such as cores and shared memory are equally shared by the domain's units if not specified otherwise. In the example illustrated in Fig. 3, two units assigned to a NUMA domain of 12 cores each utilize 6 cores.

When a team is split, its locality graph is partitioned among child teams such that a single partition is coherent and only contains domains with at least one leaf occupied by a unit in the child team. This greatly simplifies implementation of locality-aware algorithms as any visible locality domain is guaranteed to be accessible by some unit in the current team configuration.

4.1   Domain Attributes and Properties

The topological characteristics of a domain's corresponding physical component are expressed as three correlated yet independent attributes:

scope category of physical or logical component represented by the domain object such as "socket" or "L3D cache"

level number of logical indirections between the locality domain and the hierarchy root; not necessarily related to distance

domain_tag the domain's hierarchical path from the root domain, consisting of relative subdomain offsets separated by a dot character.

Domain tags serve as unique identifiers and allow to locate domains without searching the hierarchy. For any set of domains, the longest common prefix of their domain tags identifies their lowest common ancestor, for example. Apart from these attributes, a domain is associated with two *property maps*:

Capabilities invariant hardware locality properties that do not depend on the locality graph's structure, like the number of threads per core, cache sizes, or SIMD width.

Capacities derivative properties that might become invalid when the graph structure is modified, like L3 cache size available per unit.

Dynamic locality support requires means to specify transformations on the physical topology graph as *views*. Views realize a projection but must not actually modify the original graph data. Invariant properties are therefore stored separately and assigned to domains by reference only. A view only contains a shallow copy of the graph data structure and only the capacities of domains included in the view.

4.2   Operations on Locality Domains

A specific domain node can be queried by their unique *domain tag* or unit. Conceptually, locality hierarchy model is a directed, multi-relational graph so any operation expressed in path algebra for multi-relational graphs is conceptually feasible and highly expressive, but overly complex. For the use cases we identified in applications so far, it is sufficient to provide the operations with semantics listed in Fig. 4, apart from unsurprising operations for node traversal and lookup by identifier. These can be applied to any domain in a locality hierarchy, including its root domain to include the entire topology.

```
domain_at(d, u)                        -> t    get tag of domain assigned to unit u
domain_find_if(d, pred)                -> t[]  get tags of domains satisfying predicate
domain_copy(d)                         -> d'   create a copy of domain d

domain_select(d, domain_tags[])  -> d'   remove all but the specified subdomains
domain_exclude(d, domain_tags[]) -> d'   remove specified subdomains
domain_group(d, domain_tags[])   -> d'   separate subdomains into group domain
```

Fig. 4. Fundamental operations in the locality domain concept on a locality domain hierarchy d. Modifying operations return the result of their operation as locality domain view d'.

Operations for selection and exclusion are applied to subdomains recursively. The runtime interface can define complex high-level functions based on combinations of these fundamental operations. To restrict a virtual topology to a single NUMA affinity, for example:

```
numa_tags := domain_find_if(topo, (d | d.scope = NUMA))
numa_topo := domain_select(topo, numa_tags[1])
```

The domain_group operation combines an arbitrary set of domains in a logical group. This is useful in various situations, especially when specific units are assigned to special roles, often depending on a phase in an algorithm. For example, Intel suggests the *leader role* communication pattern[1] for applications running MPI processes on Xeon Phi accelerator modules where communication between MPI ranks on host and accelerator is restricted in the reduction phase to a single, dedicated process on either side.

As groups are virtual, their level is identical to the original LCA of the grouped domains and their communication cost is 0. Like any other modification of a locality graph's structure, adding domain groups does not affect measures distance or communication cost as a logical rearrangement has, of course, no effect on physical connectivity. Figure 5 illustrates the steps of the domain grouping algorithm.

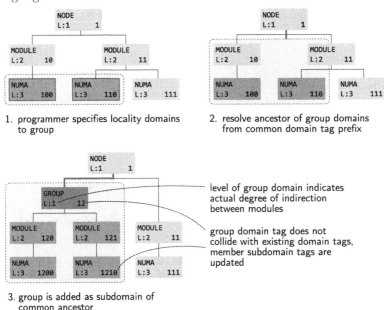

Fig. 5. Simplified illustration of the domain grouping algorithm. Domains 100 and 110 in NUMA scope are separated into a group. To preserve the original topology structure, the group includes their parent domains up to the lowest common ancestor with domain 121 as alias of domain 11.

4.3   Specifying Distance and Affinity Metrics

Any bidirectional connection between a domain and its adjacent subdomains in the locality hierarchy model represents a physical bus exhibiting characteristic communication overhead such as a cache crossbar or a network interconnect.

---

[1] https://software.intel.com/sites/default/files/managed/09/07/xeon-phi-coprocessor-system-software-developers-guide.pdf.

Therefore, a cost function $cost(d)$ can be specified for any domain d to specify communication cost of the medium connecting its immediate subdomains. This allows to define a measure of locality for a pair of domains (d_a, d_b) as the cumulative cost of the shortest path connection, restricted to domains below their lowest common ancestor (LCA). A domain has minimal distance 0 to itself.

Heterogeneous hosts require communication schemes and virtual process topologies that are specific to hardware configuration and the algorithm scenario. In a typical accelerator offload algorithm with a final reduction phase, processes first consider physical distance and horizontal locality. For communication in the reduction phase, distance is measured based on PCI interface affinity to optimize for vertical locality.

5   The dyloc Library

Initial concepts of the dyloc library have been implemented for locality discovery in the DASH runtime. In this, hardware locality information from hwloc, PAPI, libnuma, and LIKWID has been combined into a unified data structure that allowed to query locality information by process ID or affinity.

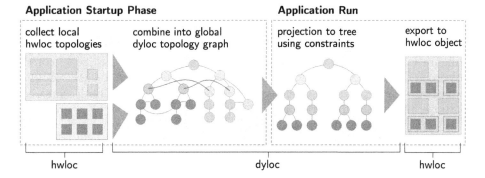

Fig. 6. Using dyloc as intermediate process in locality discovery.

This query interface proved to be useful for static load balancing on heterogeneous systems like SuperMIC and was recently made available as the standalone library $dyloc^2$. Figure 7 outlines the structure of its dependencies and interfaces, with APIs provided for C and C++.

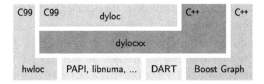

Fig. 7. Dependencies and interfaces of the dyloc/dylocxx library

---

[2] https://github.com/dash-project/dyloc.

The boost graph library[3] offers an ideal abstraction for high-level operations on locality domain graphs. These are exposed in the C++ developer API and may be modified by user-specified extensions. The boost graph concepts specify separate storage of node properties and the graph structure. This satisfies the requirements of the domain topology data structure as introduced in Sect. 4 where domain capabilities are independent from the topology structure. As a consequence, consolidated views on a locality graph do not require deep copies of domain nodes. Only their accumulative capacities have to be recalculated.

We consider compatibility to existing concepts in the hwloc API a critical requirement and therefore ensured, to the best of our knowledge and understanding, that configurations of dyloc's graph-based locality model can be projected to a well-defined hierarchy and exported to hwloc data structures.

A possible scenario is illustrated in Fig. 6. Topology data provided by hwloc for separate nodes are combined into a unified dyloc locality graph that supports high-level operations. Queries and transformations on the graph return a light-weight view that can be converted to a hwloc topology and then used in applications instead of topology objects obtained from hwloc directly.

6   Proof of Concept: Work Balancing Min_element on SuperMIC

The SuperMIC system[4] consists of 32 compute nodes with identical hardware configuration of two NUMA domains, each containing an Ivy Bridge (8 cores) host processor and a Xeon Phi "Knights Corner" coprocessors (Intel MIC 5110P) as illustrated in Fig. 2. This system configuration is an example of both increased depth of the machine hierarchy and heterogeneous node-level architecture.

```
1   TeamLocality        tloc(dash::Team::All());
2   LocBalancedPattern  pattern(NELEM, tloc);
3   dash::Array<T>       array(pattern);
4   GlobIt min_element(GlobIt first, GlobIt last) {
5     auto uloc      = UnitLocality(myid());
6     auto nthreads = uloc.num_threads();
7     #pragma omp parallel for num_threads(nthreads)
8     { /* ... find local result ... */ }
9     dash::barrier();
10    // broadcast local result:
11    auto leader    = uloc.at_scope(scope::MODULE)
12                     .unit_ids()[0];
13    if (leader == myid())
14       ...
15  }
```

Listing 1.1. Pseudo code of the modified min_element algorithm

To substantiate how asymmetric, heterogeneous system configurations introduce a new dimension to otherwise trivial algorithms, we briefly discuss the implementation of the min_element algorithm in DASH. Its original variant is implemented as follows: domain decomposition divides the element range into contiguous blocks of identical size. All units then run a thread-parallel scan on

---

[3] http://www.boost.org/doc/libs/1_64_0/libs/graph/doc/index.html.
[4] https://www.lrz.de/services/compute/supermuc/supermic.

their local block for a local minimum and enter a collective barrier once it has been found. Once all units completed their local work load, local results are reduced to the global minimum. For portable work load balancing on heterogeneous systems, the employed domain decomposition must dynamically adapt to the unit's available locality domain-capacities and -capabilities:

Capacities: total memory capacity on MIC modules is 8 GB for 60 cores, significantly less than 64 GB for 32 cores on host level

Capabilities: MIC cores have a base clock frequency of 1.1 GHz and 4 SMT threads, with 2.8 GHz and 2 SMT threads on host level (Fig. 8).

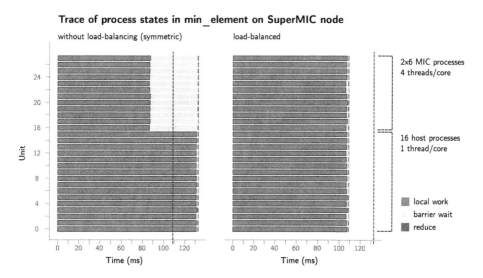

Fig. 8. Trace of process activities in the min_element algorithm exposing the effect of load balancing based on dynamic hardware locality

Listing 1.1 contains the abbreviated modified implementation of the min_element scenario utilizing the runtime support proposed in this work. The full implementation is available in the DASH source distribution[5].

7 Conclusion and Future Work

Even with the improvements to the *min_element* algorithm explained in Sect. 6, the implementation is not fully portable, yet: the load factor to adjust for the differing elements/ms has been determined in auto tuning. In future work, we will extend the locality hierarchy model by means to register progress in local work loads to allow self-adaptation of algorithms depending on load imbalance measured for specified sections.

---

[5] https://github.com/dash-project/dash/blob/development/dash/examples/bench.08.min-element/main.cpp.

Acknowledgements. This work was partially supported by the German Research Foundation (DFG) by the German Priority Programme 1648 Software for Exascale Computing (SPPEXA) and by the German Federal Ministry of Education and Research (BMBF) through the MEPHISTO project, grant agreement 01IH16006B.

References

1. Bauer, M., Clark, J., Schkufza, E., Aiken, A.: Programming the memory hierarchy revisited: supporting irregular parallelism in Sequoia. ACM SIGPLAN Not. **46**(8), 13–24 (2011)
2. Chamberlain, B.L., Deitz, S.J., Iten, D., Choi, S.-E.: User-defined distributions and layouts in Chapel: philosophy and framework. In: Proceedings of 2nd USENIX Conference on Hot Topics in Parallelism, p. 12. USENIX Association (2010)
3. Da Costa, G., Fahringer, T., Gallego, J.A.R., Grasso, I., Hristov, A., Karatza, H., Lastovetsky, A., Marozzo, F., Petcu, D., Stavrinides, G., et al.: Exascale machines require new programming paradigms and runtimes. Supercomput. Front. Innov. **2**(2), 6–27 (2015)
4. Fuchs, T., Fürlinger, K.: A multi-dimensional distributed array abstraction for PGAS. In: Proceedings of 18th IEEE International Conference on High Performance Computing and Communications (HPCC 2016), Sydney, Australia, pp. 1061–1068, December 2016
5. Fuchs, T., Fürlinger, K.: Expressing and exploiting multi-dimensional locality in DASH. In: Bungartz, H.-J., Neumann, P., Nagel, W.E. (eds.) Software for Exascale Computing - SPPEXA 2013-2015. LNCSE, vol. 113, pp. 341–359. Springer, Cham (2016). https://doi.org/10.1007/978-3-319-40528-5_15
6. Fürlinger, K., Fuchs, T., Kowalewski, R.: DASH: a C++ PGAS library for distributed data structures and parallel algorithms. In: Proceedings of 18th IEEE International Conference on High Performance Computing and Communications (HPCC 2016), Sydney, Australia, pp. 983–990, December 2016
7. Goglin, B.: Managing the topology of heterogeneous cluster nodes with hardware locality (hwloc). In: International Conference on High Performance Computing & Simulation (HPCS 2014), July 2014, Bologna, Italy. IEEE (2014)
8. Goglin, B.: Exposing the locality of heterogeneous memory architectures to HPC applications. In: 1st ACM International Symposium on Memory Systems (MEMSYS 2016). ACM (2016)
9. Hajiaghayi, M., Johnson, T., Khani, M.R., Saha, B.: Hierarchical graph partitioning. In: Proceedings of 26th ACM Symposium on Parallelism in Algorithms and Architectures, pp. 51–60. ACM (2014)
10. Kamil, A.A., Yelick, K.A.: Hierarchical additions to the SPMD programming model. Technical report UCB/EECS-2012-20, EECS Department, University of California, Berkeley, February 2012
11. Tate, A., Kamil, A., Dubey, A., Größlinger, A., Chamberlain, B., Goglin, B., Edwards, C., Newburn, C.J., Padua, D., Unat, D., et al.: Programming abstractions for data locality. Research report, PADAL Workshop 2014, 28–29 April, Swiss National Supercomputing Center (CSCS), Lugano, Switzerland, November 2014
12. Yan, Y., Zhao, J., Guo, Y., Sarkar, V.: Hierarchical place trees: a portable abstraction for task parallelism and data movement. In: Gao, G.R., Pollock, L.L., Cavazos, J., Li, X. (eds.) LCPC 2009. LNCS, vol. 5898, pp. 172–187. Springer, Heidelberg (2010). https://doi.org/10.1007/978-3-642-13374-9_12

Large-Scale Experiment for Topology-Aware Resource Management

Yiannis Georgiou[1], Guillaume Mercier[2(✉)], and Adèle Villiermet[3]

[1] Atos–Bull, Grenoble, France
`yiannis.georgiou@atos.net`
[2] Bordeaux INP, Talence, France
`guillaume.mercier@bordeaux-inp.fr`
[3] Inria Bordeaux Sud-Ouest, Talence, France
`adele.villiermet@inria.fr`

Abstract. A Resource and Job Management System (RJMS) is a crucial system software part of the HPC stack. It is responsible for efficiently delivering computing power to applications in supercomputing environments and its main intelligence relies on resource selection techniques to find the most adapted resources to schedule the users' jobs. In [8], we introduced a new topology-aware resource selection algorithm to determine the best choice among the available nodes of the platform based on their position in the network and on application behaviour (expressed as a communication matrix). We did integrate this algorithm as a plugin in SLURM and validated it with several optimization schemes by making comparisons with the default SLURM algorithm. This paper presents further experiments with regard to this selection process.

Keywords: Resource management · Job allocation
Topology-aware placement · Scheduling · SLURM

1 Introduction

Computer science is more than ever a cornerstone of scientific development, as more and more scientific fields resort to simulations in order to help refine the theories or conduct experiments that cannot be carried out in reality because of their scale or their prohibitive cost. Currently, such computing power can be delivered only by parallel architectures. However, harnessing the power of a large parallel computer is no easy task, because of several factors. It features most of the time a huge amount of computing nodes, and this scale has to be taken into account when developing applications. Then, the nodes architecture has become more and more complex, as the number of cores per node is in constant increase from one generation of CPU to the next. One way of dealing with this complexity would be to take into account the application behavior (e.g. its communication pattern, or its memory access pattern) and to deploy it on the computer accordingly by mapping processes to cores depending on their affinity [9]. However,

© Springer International Publishing AG, part of Springer Nature 2018
D. B. Heras and L. Bougé (Eds.): Euro-Par 2017 Workshops, LNCS 10659, pp. 179–186, 2018.
https://doi.org/10.1007/978-3-319-75178-8_15

since a parallel machine can be very large, it is often shared by many users running their applications at the same time. In such a case, an application execution will depend on a nodes allocation that has been determined by the Resources and Jobs Management System (RJMS). Most of the time, a RJMS works in a best-effort fashion, which can lead to suboptimal allocations. As a consequence, we did investigate in [8] the idea of taking into account an application behaviour directly in the RJMS, in its process of allocation and reservation of computing resources (nodes). We carried out experimental validation on small scales and did conduct simulations for larger scales. In this paper, we shall present larger experiments (not simulations) to confirm our simulations results. This paper is organized as follows: Sect. 2 gives an overview of the context and background of this work. It introduces the software elements leveraged by this work before giving some technical insights about the integration of TREEMATCH into SLURM. Then Sect. 3 shows and explains the results obtained. We discuss the comparison between simulation and emulation in Sect. 4 while some related works are listed in Sect. 5. Finally, Sect. 6 concludes this paper.

2   Context and Background

A substantial part of this work deals with the integration of a new resource allocation and reservation policy within the SLURM [14] RJMS. This policy takes into consideration application behaviour and a matching between the needed resources and the behaviour is determined, thanks to a dedicated algorithm called TreeMatch [10]. We now describe both software elements in this section.

2.1   SLURM

Simple Linux Utility Resource Management (a.k.a SLURM) is a RJMS used and deployed on a large number of parallel machines.

Its resource selection process takes place as part of the global job scheduling procedure. In particular, this procedure makes use of the `plugin/select`, which is responsible for allocating the computing resources to the jobs. There are various resource selection plugins in SLURM that can take into account the specificities of the underlying platforms' architecture such as `linear` and `cons_res`. The `select/cons_res` plugin is ideal for multicore and manycore architectures where nodes are viewed as a collection of consumable resources (such as cores and memory). In this plugin, nodes can be used exclusively or in a shared mode where a job may allocate its own resources differently than the other jobs sharing the same node [1].

2.2   TreeMatch

TREEMATCH [10], is a library for performing process placement based on the topology of the underlying machine and the behaviour of the application. This behaviour can be expressed in several ways: communication scheme, memory accesses pattern, etc. As for the target architectures, TREEMATCH is able to deal with multicore, shared memory machines as well as distributed memory machines. It computes a permutation of the processes to the processors/cores in order to minimize some cost function (e.g. communication costs). To be more specific, it takes as input a tree topology (where the leaves stand for computing resources and internal nodes correspond to switches or cache levels) and a matrix describing the affinity graph between processes. Such a matrix can be obtained using an application monitoring tool [2]. A hierarchy is extracted from this graph that matches the topology tree hierarchy. The outcome is therefore a mapping of the processes onto the underlying computing resources. The objective function optimized by TREEMATCH is the Hop-Byte [15], that is, the number of hops weighted by the communication cost: Hop-Byte$(\sigma) = \sum_{1 \leq i < j \leq n} \omega(i,j) \times d(\sigma(i), \sigma(j))$, where n is the number of processes to map, σ is the process permutation produced by TREEMATCH (process i is mapped on computing resource $\sigma(i)$), $A = (\omega_{i,j})$ $1 \leq i \leq n$, $1 \leq j \leq n$ is the affinity matrix between these entities and hence $\omega(i,j)$ is the amount of data exchanged between process i and process j and $d(p_1, p_2)$ is the distance, in number of hops, between computing resources p_1 and p_2. An important feature of TREEMATCH lies in its ability to take *constraints* into account. When not all leaves are available for mapping (because some of them are already used by other applications as it is the case in this paper), there is a possibility to restrict the leaves onto which processes can be mapped so that only a subset of nodes is used for the mapping.

2.3 TreeMatch Integration Within SLURM

We have implemented a new selection option for the SLURM cons_res plugin. In this case the regular best-fit algorithm used for nodes selection is replaced by our TREEMATCH variant. To this end, we need to provide three pieces of information: the job affinity matrix, the hardware topology but also the constraints due to other jobs allocations. The communication matrix is provided at job submission time through a distribution option available in the srun command. As for the global cluster topology, it is provided to the controller by a new parameter in a SLURM configuration file. Whenever a job allocation is computed, this topology is completed by the constraints information. These constraints are provided by the nodes and cores bitmaps used by the SLURM controller to describe the cluster utilization. TREEMATCH then utilizes all these pieces of information to compute the allocation of resources tailored for the submitted job. However, as the TREEMATCH overhead increases with the size of the hardware topology (in terms of nodes count), we improve the computation time by restricting the search in a fitting subtree in the global architecture.

3 Experimental Validation

We presented some preliminary results in [8] that we completed with new experiments described in this section. We carried out experiments on a larger scale than previously and we also make comparisons between these real-world results and the simulations of large-scale experiments shown in [8] to demonstrate the accuracy of the simulator used in our work. Our experiments have been carried out on the Edel cluster from the Grid'5000 Grenoble site. Edel is composed of 72 nodes featuring 2 Intel Xeon E5520 CPUs (2.27 GHz, 4 cores/CPU) and 24 GB of memory. We use the Edel cluster to emulate Curie (a TGCC cluster with 5040 nodes and 80640 cores[1]) using an SLURM internal emulation technique called `multiple-slurmd` initially described and used in [6]. We base our experiments on a Curie workload trace taken from the Parallel Workload Archive[2]. Two sets of jobs are considered: the first one fills the cluster, and the jobs belonging to this set are always scheduled using SLURM in order to have the same starting point for all the experiments. The second set, called the *workload*, is the one we actually use to compare the different strategies. All the measurements are done through the SLURM login system which gives us workload traces similar to the ones obtained from Curie. Finally, we need to provide each job with a communication matrix in order to use TREEMATCH. For these experiments we use randomly generated matrices featuring various sparsity rates. Since we do not know the real nature of the jobs executed on Curie, creating random matrices is acceptable as the only available data from the original workload is a job duration. However, in a real setting, we will need the user to provide the communication matrix of its application. This can be done through monitoring in the MPI library with [2]. Moreover, in the real case, it may happen that not every application can provide their communication matrix. We have studied this in simulation in [7] and show that the whole system can benefit from this approach even though only a fraction of the applications provide their communication matrix.

We made comparisons between three cases: the classical topology-aware SLURM selection mechanism (SLURM), the same mechanism but using TREEMATCH for process placement after the allocation process and just before the execution starts (TM-A) and last when TREEMATCH is used both for the allocation process *and* for the process placement using the subtree technique to reduce the overhead (TM-Isub).

Three metrics have been used in this performance assessment: two of them regard the whole workload while the last one concerns each individual job:

- *makespan* measures the time taken between the submission of the first job and the completion of the last job of the *workload*.
- *utilization* represents the ratio between the CPUs used and the total number of CPUs in the cluster during the execution of the *workload*.
- *job flowtime (or turnaround time)* represents the time taken between the submission and the completion of a given job.

In our previous work, the *workload* comprised about 60 jobs. In this paper we used a much larger *workload* of 1500 jobs. To keep jobs duration reasonable

---

[1] http://www-hpc.cea.fr/en/complexe/tgcc-curie.htm.

[2] http://www.cs.huji.ac.il/labs/parallel/workload/.

Com	SLURM	TM-A	TM-Isub
50%	51002	38252	37230
33%	50997	45897	41817

(a) Makespan

Com	SLURM	TM-A	TM-Isub
50%	34%	44%	46%
33%	34%	38%	42%

(b) Utilization

Fig. 1. Workload metrics for various strategies and different amounts of communication ratio. Emulation of the Curie cluster with the Edel cluster (Grid'5000)

we decreased their runtime by a 50% factor. This reduction factor impacts the flowtime and was used to keep our experiments under the 48 h time limit for each case. Figure 1 describes the results obtained for this workload and two different communication ratios of the jobs. The communication represents the ratio between the communication time over the whole runtime of the application. These ratios are fixed to 33% and 50% to illustrate the case of a communication bound application (50% of communication ratio) and more compute-bound cases (1/3 of communication time). However, as they are not an input of the algorithm, we will not need to measure it in a real setting. Here, we use these ratios to see their impact on the performance of the algorithm. Figure 1a shows that using TREEMATCH to reorder the process ranks of the jobs reduces the makespan, but using it inside SLURM to allocate nodes decreases it even more. We can also see that the larger the communication ratio, the greater the gain. This is an expected outcome, as TREEMATCH reduces the communication times. Figure 1b also shows that for the same submission workload, TREEMATCH improved the resource utilization.

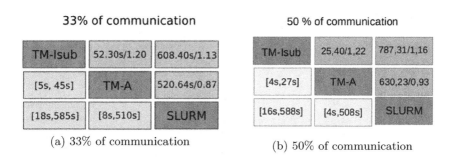

(a) 33% of communication

(b) 50% of communication

Fig. 2. Statistical comparison of selection methods: flow time. Emulation of the Curie cluster with the Edel cluster (Grid'5000)

In Fig. 2, we use paired comparisons between different strategies for jobs flowtime. In this case, we considered job-wise metrics, as we want to understand if, when we average all the jobs, a strategy turns out to be better than another. Each strategy is displayed on the diagonal. On the upper right, we have the average difference between the strategy on the column and the one on the row and the geometric mean of the ratios. For instance, we see that on average the job flowtime is 608.40 s faster with TM-Isub than with SLURM and the average ratio is 1.13. On the lower left part, we plot the 90% confidence interval of the corresponding mean. The interpretation is the following: if the interval is positive, then the strategy on the row is better than the strategy on the column with a 90% confidence. In this case, the corresponding mean is highlighted in green. If the interval is negative, the strategy on the line is better than the one on row and the corresponding mean is highlighted in red. Otherwise, we cannot statistically conclude with a 90% confidence on which strategy is the best and we do not highlight the corresponding mean. For example, we can see that using TREEMATCH in SLURM is better than not using it.

4   Comparison Between Simulation and Emulation

As explained in the previous section, we have emulated the SLURM execution of the Curie machine using the Edel cluster of Grid'5000. As a matter of fact, it is not possible to experiment new scheduling strategies for a batch scheduler on a production machine. As the SLURM engine is unmodified, this emulator is, in any cases, very close to the real behavior of SLURM. On the other hand in [7,8], we have used a simulator to perform extensive tests on different settings. Here, we present early results to validate the simulator using emulation measurements. In Fig. 3 we present the comparison between the simulation and the emulation flowtime for the 1500 jobs used in experiments of the previous sections. Measuring the average flowtime is very important as this metric assesses each job independently and is less affected by the last submitted job than the makespan.

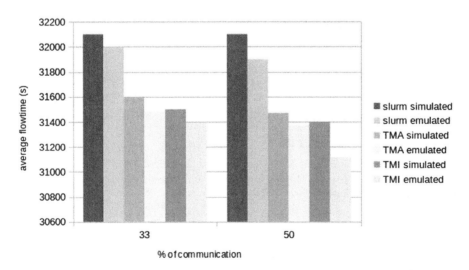

Fig. 3. Comparison of the emulated flowtime vs. the simulated one for 1500 jobs of the Curie trace. Remark that the Y-axis does not start at 0.

We plot the results for the different strategies (plain SLURM, TREEMATCH after (TMA) or TREEMATCH inside SLURM (TMI)). We see that the simulator keeps the order of the emulator concerning this metric: in both cases, TMI is better than TMA that is better than plain SLURM. Moreover, we see that simulation results are very close to emulation results (be aware that the y-axis does not start at 0). In all cases, the simulator has at least 6% of accuracy.

Having a simulator that is very close to the emulator is very important. This justifies the use of simulations and hence saves a lot of experimental time and allows for testing many different settings.

5   Related Works

Many RJMS take advantage of the hardware topology to provide compact and contiguous allocations (SLURM [14], PBS Pro [12], Grid Engine [11], and LSF [13] or Fujitsu [5]) so as to reduce the communication costs during the application execution (switches that are the deeper in the topology tree are supposed to be cheaper communication-wise than upper ones). Some other RJMS offer task placement options that can enforce a clever placement of the application processes. It is the case of Torque [4] which proposes a NUMA-aware job task placement. OAR [3] uses a flexible hierarchical representation of resources which offers the possibility to place the application processes upon the memory/cores hierarchy within the computing node. However, to the best of our knowledge there is no work that considers the application communication pattern to optimize the HPC resource selection and mapping.

6   Conclusion and Future Work

Job scheduling plays a crucial role in a cluster administration and utilization, enabling both a better response time and a better resource usage. In this paper, we have presented the results of large-scale experiments using our allocation policy that allocates and maps at the same time application processes onto the computing resources, based on the behaviour (a communication matrix in our case) of the considered application. This strategy has been implemented in SLURM. We have tested this strategy on emulation and compared it with the standard SLURM topology-aware policy and the method consisting in mapping processes after the allocation is determined.

Results show that our solution yields better makespan, flowtime and utilization compared to these approaches and especially to the standard SLURM policy, which is what we had shown through simulation only in our previous work.

To get further insights we plan to compare these large-scale experiments with the results obtained through simulation in more details.

Acknowledgments. Experiments presented in this paper were carried out using the Grid'5000 testbed (see https://www.grid5000.fr). Part of this work is also supported by the ANR MOEBUS project ANR-13-INFR-0001 and by the ITEA3 COLOC project #13024.

References

1. Balle, S.M., Palermo, D.J.: Enhancing an open source resource manager with multi-core/multi-threaded support. In: Frachtenberg, E., Schwiegelshohn, U. (eds.) JSSPP 2007. LNCS, vol. 4942, pp. 37–50. Springer, Heidelberg (2008). https://doi.org/10.1007/978-3-540-78699-3_3

2. Bosilca, G., Foyer, C., Jeannot, E., Mercier, G., Papaure, G.: Online dynamic monitoring of MPI communication. In: 23rd International European Conference on Parallel and Distributed Computing (EuroPar), p. 12. Santiago de Compostella, August 2017. Extended Verion: https://hal.inria.fr/hal-01485243

3. Capit, N., Da Costa, G., Georgiou, Y., Huard, G., Martin, C., Mounié, G., Neyron, P., Richard, O.: A batch scheduler with high level components. In: Cluster Computing and Grid 2005 (CCGrid 2005). IEEE, Cardiff (2005). https://hal.archives-ouvertes.fr/hal-00005106

4. Adaptive Computing: Torque Resource Manager. http://docs.adaptivecomputing.com/torque/6-0-0/Content/topics/torque/2-jobs/monitoringJobs.htm

5. Fujitsu: Interconnect Topology-Aware Resource Assignment. http://www.fujitsu.com/global/Images/technical-computing-suite-bp-sc12.pdf

6. Georgiou, Y., Hautreux, M.: Evaluating scalability and efficiency of the resource and job management system on large HPC clusters. In: Cirne, W., Desai, N., Frachtenberg, E., Schwiegelshohn, U. (eds.) JSSPP 2012. LNCS, vol. 7698, pp. 134–156. Springer, Heidelberg (2013). https://doi.org/10.1007/978-3-642-35867-8_8

7. Georgiou, Y., Jeannot, E., Mercier, G., Villiermet, A.: Topology-aware job mapping. Int. J. High Perform. Comput. Appl. **32**(1), 14–27 (2018)

8. Georgiou, Y., Jeannot, E., Mercier, G., Villiermet, A.: Topology-aware resource management for HPC applications. In: Proceedings of 18th International Conference on Distributed Computing and Networking, Hyderabad, India, 5–7 January 2017, p. 17. ACM, Hyderabad, January 2017

9. Jeannot, E., Mercier, G.: Near-optimal placement of MPI processes on hierarchical NUMA architectures. In: D'Ambra, P., Guarracino, M., Talia, D. (eds.) Euro-Par 2010. LNCS, vol. 6272, pp. 199–210. Springer, Heidelberg (2010). https://doi.org/10.1007/978-3-642-15291-7_20

10. Jeannot, E., Mercier, G., Tessier, F.: Process placement in multicore clusters: algorithmic issues and practical techniques. IEEE Trans. Parallel Distrib. Syst. **25**(4), 993–1002 (2014). https://doi.org/10.1109/TPDS.2013.104

11. Oracle: Grid Engine. https://blogs.oracle.com/templedf/entry/topology_aware_scheduling

12. PBSWorks: PBS. http://www.pbsworks.com/PBSProduct.aspx?n=PBS-Professional&c=Overview-and-Capabilities

13. Smith, C., McMillan, B., Lumb, I.: Topology aware scheduling in the LSF distributed resource manager. In: Proceedings of Cray User Group Meeting (2001)

14. Yoo, A.B., Jette, M.A., Grondona, M.: SLURM: simple Linux utility for resource management. In: Feitelson, D., Rudolph, L., Schwiegelshohn, U. (eds.) JSSPP 2003. LNCS, vol. 2862, pp. 44–60. Springer, Heidelberg (2003). https://doi.org/10.1007/10968987_3

15. Yu, H., Chung, I.H., Moreira, J.: Topology mapping for Blue Gene/L supercomputer. In: Supercomputing 2006. ACM, New York (2006). https://doi.org/10.1145/1188455.1188576

Euro-EDUPAR – European Workshop on Parallel and Distributed Computing Education for Undergraduate Students

Workshop on Parallel and Distributed Computing Education for Undergraduate Students (Euro-EDUPAR)

Workshop Description

Parallel and Distributed Computing (PDC) is omnipresent. It is in all the computational environments, from mobile devices and laptops to clusters, data centers and super-computers. It becomes now vital to train new generations of scientists and engineers in the use of these environments: PDC-related topics must be incorporated in Computer Science (CS) and Computer Engineering (CE) programs. In 2010, the IEEE Computer Society Technical Committee on Parallel Processing launched the Curriculum Initiative on Parallel and Distributed Computing, with Core Topics for Undergraduates, and in 2011 started the workshop EduPar. Motivated by differences in education in different parts of the world, Euro-EDUPAR aims to analyze PDC Education in a European context.

The 3rd European Workshop on Parallel and Distributed Computing Education for Undergraduate Students (Euro-EDUPAR) invited unpublished manuscripts on topics pertaining to the teaching of PDC-related topics in the CS and CE curriculum as well as in Computational Science with PDC or HPC concepts, with emphasis on European undergraduate teaching.

Ten papers were submitted and, following a review of each paper by four members of the Program Committee, seven papers were accepted for presentation. The final program also featured: (i) a keynote presentation from Peter Rodgers on Resource-Oriented Computing; (ii) two invited talks, from Domingo Giménez on using parallel programming contests for teaching and Sushil Prasad on the NSF/TCPP curriculum initiative for CS undergraduates; (iii) a panel where Sheikh Ghafoor, Domingo Giménez, Sushil Prasad and Peter Rodgers debated the question of how to evaluate the success of curriculum changes in Parallel and Distributed Computing, eloquently moderated by Arny Rosenberg. Overall, the workshop generated good interest and was held in a pleasant environment thanks to the support of the Euro-Par 2017 organizers.

Steering Committee

Henri E. Bal	Vrije Universiteit, The Netherlands
Alexey Lastovetsky	University College Dublin, Ireland
Christian Lengauer	University of Passau, Germany
Pierre Manneback	University of Mons, Belgium
Sushil K. Prasad	Georgia State University, USA
Yves Robert (Chair)	École Normale Supérieure de Lyon, France
Arnold L. Rosenberg	Northeastern University, USA
Rizos Sakellariou	University of Manchester, UK

Cristina Silvano	Politecnico di Milano, Italy
Paul G. Spirakis	University of Liverpool, UK
Denis Trystram	Grenoble Institute of Technology, France
Mateo Valero	Barcelona Supercomputing Center, Spain
Vladimir Voevodin	Moscow State University, Russia

General Co-chairs

Sushil K. Prasad	Georgia State University, USA
Yves Robert	École Normale Supérieure de Lyon, France
Arnold L. Rosenberg	Northeastern University, USA

Program Chair

Rizos Sakellariou	University of Manchester, UK

Program Committee

Marco Aldinucci	University of Torino, Italy
Jorge G. Barbosa	University of Porto, Portugal
Pascal Bouvry	University of Luxembourg, Luxembourg
Marian Bubak	AGH Krakow, Poland and University of Amsterdam, The Netherlands
Alex Delis	University of Athens, Greece
Efstratios Gallopoulos	University of Patras, Greece
Chryssis Georgiou	University of Cyprus, Cyprus
Domingo Giménez	University of Murcia, Spain
Sergei Gorlatch	University of Muenster, Germany
Thilo Kielmann	Vrije Universiteit Amsterdam, The Netherlands
Alexey Lastovetsky	University College Dublin, Ireland
Tomàs Margalef	Autonomous University of Barcelona, Spain
Svetozar Margenov	Bulgarian Academy of Sciences, Bulgaria
Milan D. Mihajlović	University of Manchester, UK
Marcin Paprzycki	Polish Academy of Sciences, Poland
Dana Petcu	West University of Timisoara, Romania
Gudula Rünger	TU Chemnitz, Germany

Jesper Larsson Träff   TU Wien, Austria
Philippas Tsigas   Chalmers University, Sweden
Juan Touriño   University of A Coruña, Spain
Vladimir Voevodin   Moscow State University, Russia
David Walker   Cardiff University, UK

SCoPE@Scuola: (In)-formative Paths on Topics Related with High Performance, Parallel and Distributed Computing

Giovanni Battista Barone[1], Vania Boccia[2], Davide Bottalico[1], and Luisa Carracciuolo[3(✉)]

[1] University of Naples Federico II, Naples, Italy
[2] Liceo Classico e Scientifico "R. Cartesio", Giugliano, Naples, Italy
[3] Italian National Research Council, Naples, Italy
luisa.carracciuolo@cnr.it

Abstract. The SCoPE@Scuola initiative was born with the aim to inspire curiosity in high school students about High Performance Computing (HPC) and Parallel and Distributed Computing (PDC). The HPC/PDC world could be an interesting matter for students because is a necessary tool to solve challenging problems in science and technology and it provides context where a plenty of knowledge acquired at school can find a real application. In fact, the themes related to HPC/PDC involve a large range of knowledge and skills: from mathematical modelling of problems to algorithm design, from software implementation to design and management of complex computer systems. The initiative, begun at the end of 2014, involved several schools in the Naples (Italy) district, and has also been used for work-based learning activities and projects aimed to avoid students "dropouts". The results collected during all the last years make us hopeful that such initiative could be useful both to increment students awareness about the utility in the real world of all the knowledge acquired at school and to help them in their future educational and/or working choices.

Keywords: Education · Scientific computing
Parallel and Distributed Computing

1 Introduction

As expected by *"Recommendation of the European Parliament and of the Council on key competences for lifelong learning"* [16], nowadays students need to be oriented toward an active participation in building their knowledge with the aim to acquire some key competences (e.g. skills in math, science and technology).

Teachers and students have to build together a path which, starting from the acquisition of specific disciplinary skills and passing through the ability to transfer them into different contexts/fields, finally reaches the target of building a knowledge able to support students as active and responsible citizens during

© Springer International Publishing AG, part of Springer Nature 2018
D. B. Heras and L. Bougé (Eds.): Euro-Par 2017 Workshops, LNCS 10659, pp. 191–202, 2018.
https://doi.org/10.1007/978-3-319-75178-8_16

their life. Along this path the teachers have to play the role of a guide for students with the aim to increase their awareness and motivation.

The SCoPE@Scuola initiative was created by the Management and Support Team (the authors of this work) of the SCoPE data center at the University of Naples Federico II. We intended to offer to secondary school students the chance to acquire a wider vision on how the use of IT systems allows the solution of challenging problems and the advancement of knowledge in various fields of academic and industrial research.

The SCoPE datacenter [14] is an example of computing resources integrated in international distributed computing infrastructures and usable in various research contexts. The chance to present SCoPE, and all the issues related both to High Performance Computing (HPC) and to Parallel and Distributed Computing (PDC) (outside the academic research environment) represents two significant opportunities for students and teachers: (1) to *"touch"* modern and advanced technologies outside the school context and (2) to develop the "Computational Thinking" attitude [35] by mean of glance on the real world complexity.

The initiative, conceived and designed during 2013, started at the end of 2014 with the involvement of the first "pilot" schools. The related activities include some seminars and different kinds of laboratory experiences. The feedback from students (to date about 400) and their teachers is continuing to confirm the interest in the initiative, as it provides young students with new skills spendable in the short/medium terms (e.g. during stages and final high school exam) and, in the long term, by helping them in their future choice for university courses and job. In fact, the topics associated with HPC/PDC involve a large amount of knowledge areas and skills (from mathematical modelling of problems to algorithm design, from software implementation to design and management of complex computer systems) and can be interdisciplinarily linked to various disciplines at school (from Mathematics to Informatics, from Physics and Earth Science to Biology and Geography).

This work is organised as follows: in Sect. 2 we describe how the initiative fits into the context of the HPC/PDC education, in Sect. 3 we describe the initiative and give details about all the involved *"actors"* and their *"modus operandi"*, in Sect. 4 we give details on how the initiative has been perceived from the students, in Sect. 5 we explain why the initiative can be considered the starting point for work-based learning activities and in Sect. 6 we summarise the contents of the work giving some details about our future activities.

2   Related Works

Much is being done in the international context to strengthen the chance for students to access curricula or contents related with themes of Parallel and Distributed Computing [6]. However, at the moment, in Italy it seems difficult enough to introduce such contents into the school curricula. Nevertheless, in a few years all students will live and work in a world where problems that mankind will have to solve will be more and more complex and will be faced only with the massive amount of computing power made available by the achieved goal of the *Exascale Computing Project* [10].

The approaches used and the contributions given to initiate students to the HPC/PDC world are many and various: some people have developed tools to help the teaching of parallel programming (i.e., see [25, 27, 29]), others built experiences on how to iniziate students to parallel programming by using and comparing different paradigms and technologies (i.e., see [4, 21, 23, 33]); some people realized experiences and programs to initiate students in the building-up and management of supercomputing systems (i.e., see [22, 30]), others used science demands to motivate the need for the computational simulation (and its related tools) to solve problems of the present (i.e., [28, 31, 36]).

In this scenario, SCoPE@Scuola is a framework where activities concerning almost all of the above-mentioned themes can be carried out. Such activities can be chosen by the schools that intend to adhere to the initiative on the basis of their needs. Up to now, SCoPE@Scuola doesn't want to be the context where all the above topics are deeply acquired but it intends to play a role in the approach described in [34]: to realize a sort of *"HPC/PDC Immunization"* by giving school students small doses of HPC/PDC themes to help them to feel familiar and therefore not hostile to HPC/PDC world.

3   The Initiative and Its *"Actors"*

Too often, the so-called *"digital natives"* are unaware of the real potential of the many IT resources they access to via the Internet (such as search engines, shared storage spaces, social networks, etc.): few of them wonder what's behind everything they use daily. Even less of them are able to realize how IT resources can be used in finding solutions for problems of everyday's life (such as weather forecasts, mapping and geo localization systems, traceability and security of bank transactions, air traffic logistics management, etc. - i.e., [19, 20]).

So, the ideators of SCoPE@Scuola initiative some years ago wondered about the way to motivate young people in studying and in being awareness about technology usage: we were confident that telling students about the HPC/PDC world (the world where we enthusiastically work) could be a way. We have also been driven by the conviction that the HPC/PDC world could be an interesting matter for school students because (1) it is a necessary tool to solve present challenging problems both in science and technology, (2) it involves a large amount of knowledge and skills in an interdisciplinary context, (3) its topics can be linked, using an interdisciplinary approach, to various disciplines at school. We contestually decided to address the initiative to students (and teachers) that are attending (are teaching) the last years of high school and whose studies (teaching) are related with STEM Education [7].

SCoPE@Scuola, inspired by the ancient Chinese saying *"I hear and I forget. I see and I remember. I do and I understand"*, is a "place" conceived both for information and for real training activities: the informative part of this initiative provides two seminars and a guided tour at the SCoPE datacenter, while the training activities include laboratory experiences focused on technological/scientific topics related to HPC/PDC. The SCoPE@Scuola's implementation protocol (see Subsect. 3.1) outlines all the steps of the interaction between the School Teachers Group and the Academic Team. The activities related with the experiences to be carried out in laboratories are part of the SCoPE@Scuola's portfolio (see Subsect. 3.2).

3.1   SCoPE@Scuola: The Implementation Protocol

During the year 2013, when the initiative was conceived and designed, we worked to identify the set of contents and procedures that represents the SCoPE@Scuola "modus operandi" and constitutes the so called "implementation protocol" of the initiative [18]. The protocol provides the following steps:

Introduction phase

- *The first meeting*: The SCoPE@Scuola team meets school teachers and discuss about a possible set of laboratory activities identifying curricola subjects that might benefit from the experience.
- *The second meeting*: The SCoPE@Scuola team goes to school to meet students and to hold a first seminar on the history of supercomputers and on the role of scientific computing in complex problems solution.

Design phase

- *The third meeting*: The SCoPE@Scuola team and school teachers define together the content and calendar of the laboratory activities.

Realization phase

- *The fourth meeting*: Students and their teachers attend a descriptive seminar on the SCoPE infrastructure and carry out the guided tour to the SCoPE datacenter.
- *The following meetings*: The SCoPE@Scuola team prepares/integrates the material for the laboratory. Students attend the laboratory activities related to the HPC/PDC themes.

The initiative promoters expect to have a quite varied audience for school curricula and students maturity, so in concert with the teachers, they attempt to develop activities with frequent references to what students acquire at school (where possible). All the activity's remaining part, that cannot be referred to curricola, is made enough easy to be understood by students.

Infact, the objective of the initiative is not to make the students able to master complex contents (e.g. advanced mathematical tools) but to help young minds in appreciating the role of each components of science and technology for the solution of complex problems. In particular, we want put a strong emphasis on the role of mathematics as a useful tool because it is perceived by most students as difficult and useless.

3.2   The Portfolio of the Activities

The portfolio for laboratory activities consists of a set of macro assets that allow to explore all the aspects of designing, managing and using computing infrastructures: from the realization of *"homemade"* (or *"schoolmade"*) parallel computer prototypes up to the process that, from the mathematical formalization of the problem, leads to the *"parallel"* software for the "in silico" solution of the problem itself [24]. The portfolio currently includes the following macro assets:

1. *The "Problem solving steps in Scientific Computation" - From problem to software, passing through mathematical and numerical modeling*: How to use the computer to simulate and/or describe physical and natural phenomena (e.g. the simulation of the Tsunami trend).
2. *When HPC becomes necessary because the problem is "too big"*: Implementation of simple parallel algorithms (i.e. the computation of the sum of n numbers, the computation of BLAS operations [3], etc.) and "performance" evaluation of the implemented software when the problem size varies.
3. *A parallel computer "within everyone's reach"*: the realization of a Beowulf cluster [32] - From the installation of the operating system to the benchmarks execution to evaluate the implemented system performance.
4. *Infrastructures and Platforms for Big Data*: Introduction to "Big Data" [26] theme and practice in using Apache Hadoop [8], and related tools (i.e., Apache Hive [9]), to manage and use large amount of data.

Each group of students can be involved in laboratory activities related with one or more themes in one of the above described assets. As described in Subsect. 3.1, all the aspects related with the activities to be performed, are discussed with the student's teachers during the first two phases of the initiative.

Such decision-making process can not ignore issues related to the students knowledge and to the curricula offered in the different schools in order to better choose both the level of in-depth approach to some themes (e.g. the mathematical tools used to describe physical phenomena) and the type of activities (technology- or science- oriented).

3.3   The First Involved Schools: The "Pilot" Schools

In September 2014, after a year of reflection and design, the activity of the SCoPE@Scuola initiative was launched (through the participation at conferences, the production of leaflets and the sending of emails to the School Executives of the High Schools of Naples district). After about a month, a dozen schools had shown interest for the initiative. Among them, three schools decided to join: the **Polo Tecnico "E. Fermi - C.E. Gadda"**, the **Istituto Statale di Istruzione Superiore "A. Serra"** and the **Istituto Tecnico Industriale "A. Righi"**. In the following years, also the **Istituto Tecnico Industriale "A. Volta"** began to participate to the initiative. With all of the above listed schools the collaboration still goes on enriching itself with new contents.

All the above schools have Computer Science curricula of good quality, but very poor was the amount of HPC/PDC-related contents presented in such curricula (just some experiences related with the implementation of *"naif"* parallel algorithms). To date, the total number of students and teachers involved was about 400. All the students attended to the informative sections of the initiative (the seminars on the history of supercomputers and on the SCoPE infrastructure, the guided tour to the SCoPE data center).

Some students (about 40), and their teachers, of the **The Polo Tecnico "E. Fermi - C.E. Gadda"** and the **The Istituto Statale di Istruzione Superiore "A. Serra"** attended to laboratory activities included in the second asset of the portfolio (i.e. 2-*When HPC becomes necessary because the problem is* "too big"). The activities concerned the implementation, execution and performance analysis of simple parallel codes (e.g. the sum of n numbers) on different hardware platforms (multi-core and multi-node architectures). The activities were partially prepared at school. During these activities (of about 5 h), the students used a small set of computational resources of the SCoPE data center: a cluster of 8 nodes with 8 core per node and Infiniband connectivity.

Some students (about 50), and their teachers, of the **The Istituto Tecnico Industriale "A. Righi"** and the **Istituto Tecnico Industriale "A. Volta"** attended to laboratory activities included in the third asset of the portfolio (i.e. 3-*A parallel computer "within everyone's reach"*). The activities concerned the "construction" of a Beowulf cluster for parallel computation. For each school, the activities were carried out in different meetings (3 meetings of about 4 h) during which the following topics were dealt with: the Linux operating system installation and configuration, the network cabling and configuration, the installation and configuration of the Resource Management System, the installation and configuration of software library for Message Passing paradigm (MPI) [13], the execution of parallel software based on the MPI paradigm used to test the developed cluster. The students, during these activities, used *off-the-shelf* hardware (PCs end SOHO network switches) and open-source software as the Torque Resource Management System [15] and the OpenMPI library [1].

During the last school year, the following activities are ongoing with the students of the **Istituto Tecnico Industriale "A. Volta"** and of the **Istituto Statale di Istruzione Superiore "A. Serra"**:

– from the fourth asset of portfolio (i.e. 4-*Infrastructures and Platforms for Big Data*): Introduction to the Big Data theme and practice in using Apache Hadoop and Apache Hive to manage and use large structured databases (about 30 students are involved in about 10 h of activities). The students used a small Hadoop-based infrastructure: a set of 5 * (HDFS DataNode + Yarn NodeManager) services configured on off-the-shelf hardware.
– from the first asset of portfolio (i.e. 1-*The "Problem solving steps in Scientific Computation"*): Seminar on the Problem Solving steps in Tsunami case study and practice in executing basic linear algebra operations using software computational environment as Matlab/Octave [11,12] (about 15 students are involved in about 10 h of activities).

4   Results

At the end of the first year of activity, we have summarised the results of the initiative using data collected through an online survey submitted to participants in anonymous form. The results obtained, and related with about 100 survey completed responses, can be classified in terms of: (1) satisfaction of the initiative, (2) impact of the initiative on awareness of utility, use and structure of supercomputing systems, (3) impact of the initiative on choices related with remodulation of the own training path.

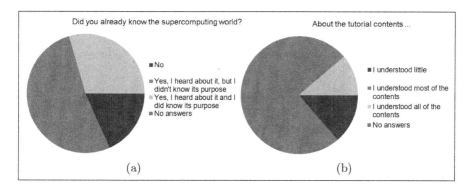

Fig. 1. The previous knowledge of the HPC/PDC world (a) - The level of tutorial comprehension (b)

From the students answers emerges:

- the lack of awareness of the HPC/PDC world before participating in the initiative: only a few students responded that they knew usefulness of the HPC/PDC world before their participation (see Fig. 1(a));
- that the contents presented during the seminars was considered by the students quite understandable (see Fig. 1(b));
- that the contents presented during the tutorial and preferred by the students are related with the most technological and practical aspects: much appreciated was in fact the visit to the SCoPE datacenter and the laboratory activity (see Fig. 2);
- the students said they were significantly interested in the possibility to continue to explore the issues addressed during the initiative. The most preferred topics are related with Computer Science (Computational Science is almost neglected) (see Figs. 3 and 4).

Our survey ended with a question about students desire to take a training/work experience in an environment where issues related to the HPC/PDC world could be tackled: even in this case, the interest expressed by the students was high. Students who have expressed their interest in this kind of experience have also answered the question *"Would you like to be part of the SCoPE data center management team? To deal with what?"*. Here are the students's answers that we prefered:

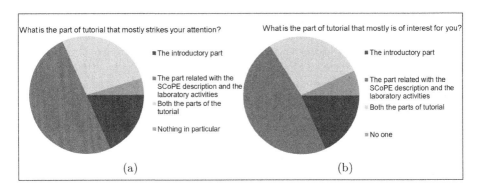

Fig. 2. The part of tutorial that mostly strikes the attention (a) - The part of tutorial that mostly is of interest (b)

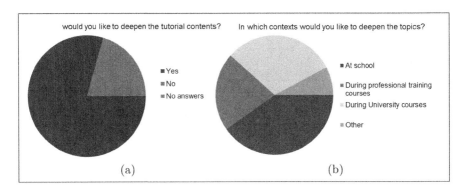

Fig. 3. Level of interest in deepening the contents (a) - Where to deepen the contents (b)

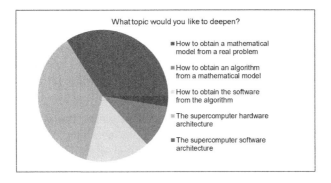

Fig. 4. Interest in deepening the contents: some details

- "... to divulge knowledge on supercomputers, I would like to help other people know about this world ..."
- "... I would like to be able to deepen all the supercomputing system issues with skilled people because I believe that such people have a lot to teach me ..."

Students also appreciated the initiative because such experience brought them closer to the university environment in a not formal context, allowing them to do (with absolute freedom) any useful questions to satisfy both curiosity on the university context and to ask for information useful to define their future training and working path.

The above-described results merely give an idea on how the students perceived the informative part of the initiative and they confirmed that issues related to HPC/PDC might be of interest to high school students. However, as the initiative is consolidating, we are thinking about the methods to use to evaluate how all the proposed contents have actually been acquired by students. This is a necessary step to remodel both the contents and the modalities by which these are presented also in order to make them not just a one-time extracurricular experience but also an integral part of existing curricula.

5   Other Offered Opportunities

"... The dissemination of high quality work-based learning forms is at the heart of the most recent European education and training guidelines and is one of the pillars of the Europe 2020 strategy for smart, sustainable, inclusive growth ..." [17]

In addition, the Italian Law 107 of July 13, 2015, reiterates the importance of work-based learning - in a mode called "Alternanza Scuola-Lavoro (aSL)" - including through internships and quality apprenticeships. The same law enables these activities to be carried out outside the industrial companies in the strict sense provided that the host institutions are able to fulfill the aims of the aSL initiative [2]:

- "to implement educational and learning methods which systematically combine classroom training with practical experience";
- "to enrich the training at school by skills that can also be spent on the labour market";
- "to foster the orientation of young people to enhance their personal vocations, interests and individual learning styles".

The SCoPE@Scuola initiative can be characterised as a suitable context for the aSL activities for students. Therefore, one of the pilot schools decided to start aSL path in the SCoPE@Scuola context to teach students, on the job, how "to configure and to manage a simple system for parallel computing".

With some schools, SCoPE@Scuola was involved in projects aimed to avoid students "dropouts" (e.g., see the "Scuola Viva" Project [5] funded by Campania Italian region). In such context SCoPE@Scuola performed activities which aims was: (1) to introduce, or to get stronger, students to the *"Computational thinking"* and to the *"coding"* action, (2) to explain how such skills can be used to *"ask"* things with computational capacity to perform useful actions (*"smart object programming"*).

6   Conclusions and Future Work

SCoPE@Scuola is a one-time extracurricular experience in a not formal academic context that provides us the chance to try *"to infect"* some young minds with the virus of passion for HPC/PDC world: the students and the teachers could together know a world that is still too hidden.

Students seem to appreciate all of the content exhibited during meetings, mostly those related with the technological and practical aspects: the structure of computing systems and how to handle and maintain them. They also appreciated the need for parallel computation as the only tool to solve *"the very large"* problems. There is a lot of work to foster knowledge and appreciation of the scientific computation and computational simulation, especially respect to mathematical modelling and numerical aspects, as indispensable tools for solving current and frontier problems. SCoPE@Scuola hopes to have soon an effective role in fostering students appreciation for the themes related with Computational Science.

The main difficulty faced by students is due to the construction of a *"forma mentis"* capable of identifying and integrating different knowledge and skills to solve concrete and complex problems. Often the students have shown that they possess knowledge and skills but they ignore how to spent them in complex and interdisciplinary contexts far from the school ones. SCoPE@Scuola wanted, by a little experience on the field, to provide students and their teachers, a glance on

> *how to solve a (very large) problem by means of powerful computer, using an interdisciplinary approach, in an interdisciplinary context.*

We hope that this glance on the complexity (made of more simple and interconnected pieces) can be effective in generating in many young people what Wing calls *"an attitude"* [35]: knowing how to look at problems using the *"best"* perspective in formulating solutions that are useful also to the others.

References

1. A High Performance Message Passing Library. https://www.open-mpi.org/. Accessed 06 Oct 2017
2. Attivitá di alternanza Scuola-Lavoro - guida operativa per la scuola. https://labuonascuola.gov.it/area/a/25282/. Accessed 06 Oct 2017
3. BLAS (Basic Linear Algebra Subprograms). http://www.netlib.org/blas/. Accessed 06 Oct 2017
4. HPC Wire: Intel Brings Parallel Computing to High School. https://www.hpcwire.com/2009/07/30/intel_brings_parallel_computing_to_high_school/. Accessed 06 Oct 2017

5. Il Programma "SCUOLA VIVA". http://www.fse.regione.campania.it/scuola-viva. Accessed 06 Oct 2017
6. NSF/IEEE-TCPP Curriculum Initiative on Parallel and Distributed Computing - Core Topics for Undergraduate. https://grid.cs.gsu.edu/~tcpp/curriculum/. Accessed 06 Oct 2017
7. Science, Technology, Engineering and Math: Education for Global Leadership. https://www.ed.gov/stem. Accessed 06 Oct 2017
8. The Apache Hadoop Project. http://hadoop.apache.org/. Accessed 06 Oct 2017
9. The Apache Hive data warehouse software. http://hive.apache.org/. Accessed 06 Oct 2017
10. The Exascale Computing Project. https://exascaleproject.org/. Accessed 06 Oct 2017
11. The GNU Octave Software. https://www.gnu.org/software/octave/. Accessed 06 Oct 2017
12. The MATLAB Software. https://www.mathworks.com/products/matlab.html. Accessed 06 Oct 2017
13. The Message Passing Interface (MPI) Standard. http://www.mcs.anl.gov/research/projects/mpi/. Accessed 06 Oct 2017
14. The SCoPE PON Project and the SCoPE data center. http://www.scope.unina.it. Accessed 06 Oct 2017
15. TORQUE Resource Manager. http://www.adaptivecomputing.com/products/open-source/torque/. Accessed 06 Oct 2017
16. Recommendation of the European Parliament and of the Council on key competences for lifelong learning (2006/962/EC), December 2006. http://eur-lex.europa.eu/legal-content/EN/TXT/HTML/?uri=CELEX:32006H0962. Accessed 06 Oct 2017
17. Communication from the Commission Europe 2020: A strategy for smart, sustainable and inclusive growth, March 2010. http://eur-lex.europa.eu/LexUriServ/LexUriServ.do?uri=COM:2010:2020:FIN:EN:PDF. Accessed 06 Oct 2017
18. Barone, G.B., Boccia, V., Bottalico, D., Campagna, R., Carracciuolo, L.: SCoPE@Scuola: percorsi (in)formativi sulle tematiche del supercalcolo. In: Atti della Conferenza DIDAMATICA 2016 - Innovazione: sfida comune di scuola, universitá, ricerca e impresa. Associazione Italiana per l'Informatica ed il Calcolo Automatico (AICA), Milano, Italia (2016)
19. Carracciuolo, L., Casaburi, D., D'Amore, L., D'Avino, G., Maffettone, P., Murli, A.: Computational simulations of 3D large-scale time-dependent viscoelastic flows in high performance computing environment. J. Nonnewton. Fluid Mech. **166**(23–24), 1382–1395 (2011)
20. Carracciuolo, L., D'Amore, L., Murli, A.: Towards a parallel component for imaging in PETSc programming environment: a case study in 3-D echocardiography. Parallel Comput. **32**(1), 67–83 (2006)
21. Cesar, E., Cortés, A., Espinosa, A., Margalef, T., Moure, J.C., Sikora, A., Suppi, R.: Teaching parallel programming in interdisciplinary studies. In: Hunold, S., et al. (eds.) Euro-Par 2015. LNCS, vol. 9523, pp. 66–77. Springer, Cham (2015). https://doi.org/10.1007/978-3-319-27308-2_6
22. Connor, C., Bonnie, A., Grider, G., Jacobson, A.: Next generation HPC workforce development: the computer system, cluster, and networking summer institute. In: 2016 Workshop on Education for High-Performance Computing (EduHPC), pp. 32–39, November 2016
23. Eijkhout, V.: Teaching MPI from mental models. In: 2016 Workshop on Education for High-Performance Computing (EduHPC), pp. 14–18, November 2016

24. Gallopoulos, E., Sameh, A.: CSE: content and product. IEEE Comput. Sci. Eng. **4**(2), 39–43 (1997)
25. Gardner, W.B., Carter, J.D.: Using the pilot library to teach message-passing programming. In: 2014 Workshop on Education for High Performance Computing, pp. 1–8, November 2014
26. Mayer-Schonberger, V., Cukier, K.: Big Data: A Revolution That Will Transform How We Live, Work, and Think. Houghton Mifflin Harcourt, Boston (2013)
27. Nowicki, M., Marchwiany, M., Szpindler, M., Bała, P.: On-line service for teaching parallel programming. In: Hunold, S., et al. (eds.) Euro-Par 2015. LNCS, vol. 9523, pp. 78–89. Springer, Cham (2015). https://doi.org/10.1007/978-3-319-27308-2_7
28. Rostami, M.A., Bücker, H.M.: An educational module illustrating how sparse matrix-vector multiplication on parallel processors connects to graph partitioning. In: Hunold, S., et al. (eds.) Euro-Par 2015. LNCS, vol. 9523, pp. 135–146. Springer, Cham (2015). https://doi.org/10.1007/978-3-319-27308-2_12
29. Schlarb, M., Hundt, C., Schmidt, B.: SAUCE: a web-based automated assessment tool for teaching parallel programming. In: Hunold, S., et al. (eds.) Euro-Par 2015. LNCS, vol. 9523, pp. 54–65. Springer, Cham (2015). https://doi.org/10.1007/978-3-319-27308-2_5
30. Slezak, D.F., Turjanski, P.G., Montaldo, D., Mocskos, E.E.: Hands-on experience in HPC with secondary school students. IEEE Trans. Educ. **53**(1), 128–135 (2010)
31. Sozykin, A., Chernoskutov, M., Koshelev, A., Zverev, V., Ushenin, K., Solovyova, O.: Teaching heart modeling and simulation on parallel computing systems. In: Hunold, S., et al. (eds.) Euro-Par 2015. LNCS, vol. 9523, pp. 102–113. Springer, Cham (2015). https://doi.org/10.1007/978-3-319-27308-2_9
32. Sterling, T., Becker, D.J., Savarese, D., Dorband, J.E., Ranawake, U.A., Packer, C.V.: Beowulf: a parallel workstation for scientific computation. In: Proceedings of the 24th International Conference on Parallel Processing, pp. 11–14. CRC Press (1995)
33. Torbert, S., Vishkin, U., Tzur, R., Ellison, D.J.: Is teaching parallel algorithmic thinking to high school students possible?: one teacher's experience. In: Proceedings of the 41st ACM Technical Symposium on Computer Science Education, SIGCSE 2010, pp. 290–294. ACM, New York (2010)
34. Valentine, D.: HPC/PDC immunization in the introductory computer science sequence. In: 2014 Workshop on Education for High Performance Computing, pp. 9–14, November 2014
35. Wing, J.M.: Computational thinking. Commun. ACM **49**(3), 33–35 (2006)
36. Zarestky, J., Bangerth, W.: Teaching high performance computing: lessons from a flipped classroom, project-based course on finite element methods. In: 2014 Workshop on Education for High Performance Computing, pp. 34–41, November 2014

A Set of Patterns for Concurrent and Parallel Programming Teaching

Manuel I. Capel[1], Antonio J. Tomeu[2], and Alberto G. Salguero[2(✉)]

[1] College of Informatics and Telecommunications, University of Granada,
18017 Granada, Spain
manuelcapel@ugr.es
[2] College of Engineering, University of Cádiz, 11519 Cádiz, Spain
{antonio.tomeu,alberto.salguero}@uca.es

Abstract. The use of key parallel-programming patterns has proved to be extremely helpful for mastering difficult concurrent and parallel programming concepts and the associated syntactical constructs. The method suggested here consists of a substantial change of more traditional teaching and learning approaches to teach programming. According to our approach, students are first introduced to concurrency problems through a selected set of preliminar program code-patterns. Each pattern also has a series of tests with selected samples to enable students to discover the most common cases that cause problems and then the solutions to be applied. In addition, this paper presents the results obtained from an informal assessment realized by the students of a course on concurrent and real-time programming that belongs to the computer engineering (CE) degree. The obtained results show that students feel now to be more actively involved in lectures, practical lessons, and thus students make better use of their time and gain a better understanding of concurrency topics that would not have been considered possible before the proposed method was implemented at our University.

Keywords: Parallel design patterns · Teaching innovation
Blended learning · ICT integration lecturing model
Concurrent programming · Parallel programming · Virtual Campus

1 Introduction

An effective teaching and learning in Concurrent and Parallel Programming (CPP) cannot be only based on theoretical lectures on process management and their concurrency, but on how to program with specific syntactical constructs included in concurrent programming languages and libraries. Currently, it is of paramount importance to include practical education on programming techniques that can provide scalability, speedup and performance to programs for today's multi and many-core processors.

To learn many different parallel patterns and syntactical constructs in CPP is by no means an easy task for students, and thus they tend to avoid taking

© Springer International Publishing AG, part of Springer Nature 2018
D. B. Heras and L. Bougé (Eds.): Euro-Par 2017 Workshops, LNCS 10659, pp. 203–215, 2018.
https://doi.org/10.1007/978-3-319-75178-8_17

the courses on the subject or postpone for as long as possible. Current CSE University Curricula [16], however, recognize the importance of teaching such subjects early in CS or SE curricula, which would enable future IT professionals to exploit the parallel potential that multiprocessors now offer.

The use of patterns to teach parallelism is in line with new didactics for teaching CPP [2,6,16]. The GoF catalog [4] proposes a comprehensive set of design patterns in the domain of simple object-oriented software design. Our intention is for the parallel *programming* pattern (henceforth referred to simply as *pattern*) to resemble the *parallel design* pattern [12] by describing solutions to recurrent problems in the domain of parallel and distributed software systems.

However, there are several drawbacks to conduct teaching and learning based on patterns: lack of interoperability, since some patterns are highly dependent on the platform or memory models (STM, volatile, immortal, etc.); scalability issues, especially if big data structures need to be mapped onto multicore and many-core processor architectures; impossibility of quality and performance testing, as long as for checking patterns it is necessary to simulate the execution context of each used pattern within a program code that needs to be verified.

We dealt with these issues by defining a selected set of patterns for obtaining optimal scalable parallel software code. Our approach is based on a new method that involves *blended learning* [7], i.e., students can check/compile/run codes generated from this set of key patterns. The student's work is supervised and evaluated by teachers aided by the Virtual Campus (Moodle supported) platform at our University. Students can therefore import program code into the programming language environment that they know and start working with the proposed pattern in order to produce correct program code. Each learning session is completed with a series of exercises to reinforce the students understanding of each pattern introduced.

The paper concludes with an evaluation of the satisfaction degree of students on the pilot course on concurrency, parallelism and real-time programming that we taught over the last three years. As result of the teaching experience, our model has been suggested for application to other courses on programming by the officers in charge of educational issues at the University of Cádiz, and is in process of implementation as a Massive Open Online Course (MOOC).

The paper is organized as follows: Sect. 2 examines the didactical objectives of the course; Sect. 3 details the suggested teaching model and its development in practical tasks and student assignments; Sect. 4 describes the most important patterns in the set selected for the study; Sect. 5 details how the experiment was evaluated and results analyzed; and finally, Sect. 6 outlines the conclusions reached and future work to be developed.

2   Course on Concurrent, Parallel and Real-Time Programming

The teaching and learning objectives of the experiment outlined in this article aim not only to generally improve the quality of the theory content of lessons but also to increase student involvement in classes through a more practical ICT integration in classical theory content teaching, which includes the core concepts:

1. Fundamental concurrent programming concepts: mutual exclusion, race conditions, synchronization, concurrent systems properties (15%).
2. Mutual exclusion: algorithms for shared memory multiprocessors (20%).
3. Monitors: Hoare's model, signal semantics, concurrent property verification (safety, liveness and fairness) (20%).
4. Message passing and distributed parallel programs: RPC and RMI models, MPI, rendez-vous (15%).
5. Real-time systems: periodic task scheduling based on static priority assignment, scheduling tests, priority inversion anomaly, aperiodic and sporadic task scheduling (30%).

Table 1. Lecture hours and a selected set of patterns from the last course

Course topics	%	Hours (lectures + lab)	No. of patterns used	Pattern names
Fundamentals	15	4.5 + 6	2	Thread creation(*), race-condition
Mutual exclusion	20	6 + 8	2	Lamport's protocol(*), Peterson's algorithm
Monitors	20	6 + 8	2	Readers/writers, passing the baton
Message passing	15	4.5 + 6	4	Rendez-vous, broadcast, geometric parallelism, tumor growth
Real-time systems	30	9 + 2	2	Observer, priority ceiling
Total	100	30 + 30	12	-

Table 1 shows the number of lecture hours allocated to each course topic, the number of patterns typically used to teach each one and a possible selection of patterns that covers all the important concepts of the course. Topics taught on previous courses and reexamined on this one are labelled with an (*).

As with any lecture on general computer programming techniques, we are particularly concerned that the content taught on CPP courses is both clear and *conceptually significant*. We agree with other authors [5] that the use of programming patterns, together with a documentary base of code samples, improves comprehension of the material taught. These patterns must be easily available to students in lectures [14,15].

By compiling and executing the program code arising from the application of one of these patterns once it has been presented by the teacher, students become more actively involved and participate more in lessons [9], and therefore they are following a *blended learning* method that is identified as the most successful for teaching programming contents effectively [7]. There has been, consequently, a significant increase of the time that students spent in the practical work done in our course [11].

3   Teaching Model for Concurrent Programming

In a previous paper [1], we proposed a new concurrent program development process, which students undertake to complete the assignments during the lectures. Students are involved in the initial program design although they are not required to design it from scratch. An initial design was validated by teachers and the students are provided with pre-selected input data to check their implementations (following the above development process). With this work students are ready to apply programming patterns to specific applications.

In our approach, students' assignments comprise the following parts:

1. a set of active components or *processes*.
2. a concurrent ADT or *shared resource*.
3. a localized communication structure.

Students have to develop a solution that uses these elements particularized for each exercise. Communication and synchronization between processes is only carried out through this *shared resource*.

3.1   Predicative Specification Model

The students must develop a formal specification (*pre-*, *post-*, *invariant*) of the initial shared resource design and its operations. We use a specification language that admits a first-order logic semantics as in Logic of Programs [10] but we decided to keep a similar style of specifications to a single-assignment procedural language. The language also includes Z-like mathematical annotations for easy specification of data structures and this facilitates translation into an OO programming language.

Formal resource specification consists of three sections:

1. the declaration of the resource's operations,
2. the definition of the correct states of the resource as a type invariant (*Semantics Domain* section) and
3. the specification of the behavior of operations as pre- and post-conditions (`CPre` and `CPost` annotations).

Pre-, post-conditions and type or class invariants are part of the *design by contract* software construction method [13].

3.2   Validation and Code Generation

First, a model checker can be used to check that the invariant is not violated as Fig. 1 shows. TLC [8] model checker is given to validate the entire `System`. The logic of the processes is encoded into TLA+ and combined with the resource specification so as to explore the interleavings that the real system can afford. By considering this validation scenario, stronger invariants can therefore be proved. Figure 1 points out that a *test generation* tool can be used for testing a large set of traces that explore all the system states up to a given depth. A typical tester executes between 500 and 1,000 different traces of the system to be checked. By exploring traces it is also possible to locally detect any malfunction of flawed parts of the system. Students can use testers to discover what is wrong with their implementations.

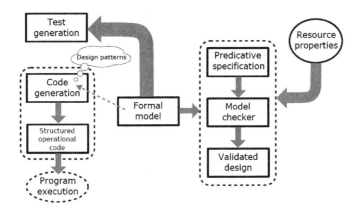

Fig. 1. Suggested development of the teaching model

Students are then instructed to deliver a code snippet that implements the concurrent shared resource behavior. The programming work done by the students has to prove the correct use of the parallel and concurrent constructs taught during the course and it is graded as the 50% of the assignment. By doing so, a set of design patterns are used to transform the formal model of a resource specification into C++11 or Java code. This transformation is susceptible of being automated for specific cases. Concurrent properties (safety, fairness, etc.) must have been assured through correct synchronization programming. Different synchronization idioms are suggested for programming thread interaction (*notify–notifyAll*, *locks* and *conditions*, *MPI operations*, etc.) to students to implement the required code.

4   Set of Selected Patterns

Since our *programming patterns* are aimed at the coding level and, unlike *algorithmic skeletons* or *structured parallel patterns* [3], they do not hide concurrent instructions or synchronization operations. The connection topology or low-level dependencies are not hidden either in the parallel algorithms used.

The main role of a parallel design pattern is to find solutions for different aspects that must be addressed when designing a parallel application or algorithm, i.e., to be capable of finding concurrency, and then to determine a suitable algorithm structure and to define its supporting structure (data, communications, user-interface). Finally, the implementation mechanism must be described.

In order to give a general overview of our teaching method, we present here only three of the patterns included in the set of Table 1 and the rest of those can be found in the prior publication [1].

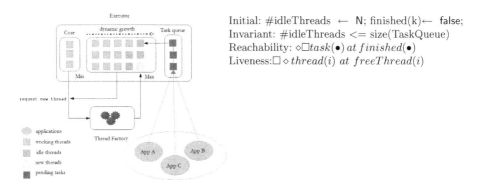

Initial: #idleThreads ← N; finished(k)← false;
Invariant: #idleThreads <= size(TaskQueue)
Reachability: ◇□$task(\bullet)$ at $finished(\bullet)$
Liveness:□◇$thread(i)$ at $freeThread(i)$

Fig. 2. Shared resource model for the executor pattern

4.1   Thread Creation: Executor Pattern

In this pattern tasks can be considered as logical units of work and threads are a mechanism by which tasks can run asynchronously. A graphical high-level model of the pattern is shown in Fig. 2.

When students attend first courses on concurrent and parallel programming, they program by assigning a thread per task, or sequentially executing all the applications's tasks on a single thread. Assigning one thread per task is a bad solution that might lead to poorly performant implementations, and a sequential approach yields extremely bad application responsiveness. We propose to our students to learn and use a high-level pattern for obtaining performance for thread creation and launching in concurrent applications.

The *executor* pattern can be seen as a variant of the *producer-consumer* concurrency paradigm. Application activities that submit tasks to the *executor* monitor have a *producer*-behavior and the executor's threads that pick up from the queue and execute tasks have a *consumer*-behavior. The fundamental idea that supports the executor pattern is to set up an adjustable number of threads that sit idle, waiting for any pending work on the task queue that they can perform.

Predicative Specification of the Executor Pattern. The resource's operations are `executeTask()`, `freeThread()` and `nextTask()` and must be defined in the context of a monitor to synchronize the concurrent access to resource `TaskQueue` list. The correct states of the resource are defined as the invariant in the Semantics Domain section of Fig. 3, i.e., the number of pre-created threads cannot exceed the maximum number of tasks waiting on the queue.

The behavior of the operations above is expressed in the form of pre- and post-conditions (CPre and CPost annotations). When an application has a task to execute, it calls the method executeTask(i), which inserts the task into the TaskQueue list and informs the executor's thread-pool that there is a new executable task. One of the idle threads calls nextTask() and starts executing the returned task; when the execution of the *task-i* finishes, the program calls freeThread(i) method and goes back to waiting for the next task to perform.

After doing the shared resource specification, the student must choose the correct concurrent language *idioms*, i.e., *notify()*, *locks*, *conditions*, etc. in order to correctly synchronize operations on the *TaskQueue* shared resource and this part of the exercise will then be completed.

```
TaskQueueExecutor
Operations
   executeTask(processId == i)
   freeThread(processId == i)
   nextTask():processId == i
Semantics   Domain:
   Type: TaskQueue(0..N-1) == seq N, processId: 0..N-1
   Invariant: #idleThreads <= size(TaskQueue);
   CPre: size(TaskQueue) > 0 and #idleThreads > 0;
   int nextTask(){} //operation
   CPost: size(TaskQueue) == size(TaskQueue)@pre - 1;

   CPre: #idleThreads >0 and size(TaskQueue) >= 0;
   void executeTask(i){}  //operation
   CPost: size(TaskQueue) == size(TaskQueue)@pre + 1;

   CPre: size(TaskQueue) >= 0 and #idleThreads > 0;
   void freeThread(i){} //operation
   CPost: #idleThreads >= 0 and
        #idleThreads == #idleThreads@pre - 1
```

Fig. 3. TaskQueue-monitor specification for the executor

4.2   Monitors: Readers and Writers Protocol

The problem of readers and writers is one of the classic problems in concurrent programming (Fig. 4). There is a shared resource that two types of processes try to access: the *readers* access the resource to obtain information, but do not modify it; the *writers* modify the shared resource when they get access to it. Because the readers do not modify the shared resource, multiple readers may be accessing it at the same time. However, no other process can access the shared resource while a writer is already in.

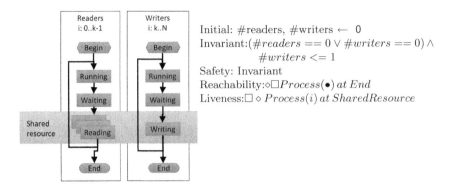

Initial: #readers, #writers ← 0
Invariant:$(\#readers == 0 \vee \#writers == 0) \wedge$
$\#writers <= 1$
Safety: Invariant
Reachability:$\diamond\square Process(\bullet)\,at\,End$
Liveness:$\square\diamond Process(i)\,at\,SharedResource$

Fig. 4. Shared resource monitor pattern for reader/writer access

Predicative Specification Model. The problem begins from a situation where there are no processes accessing to the shared resource. When a process tries to access it, it must first check that there are no processes of the other type already accessing to the resource, i.e., the condition $\#readers ==$ $0 \vee \#writers == 0$ is satisfied. In any case, there can be only one writer accessing to the resource at the same time, i.e., the condition: $\#writers <= 1$ has to be part the invariant.

When processes of both types are trying to access the shared resource it is necessary to decide which of them can access it. The readers-writers problem can be solved by giving readers or writers higher priority to access the resource. In case of prioritizing readers, only when there are no other readers trying to access the shared resource, the lock of writers is released. On the other hand, if writers are prioritized, it will be the writers which will unlock the readers when there are no other writers trying to access the shared resource, as Fig. 5 shows.

```
SharedResource
Operations
  void* read(void* p)
  void* writer(void *p)
Semantics   Domain:
    Type: SharedResource == SQL_Type, readerId: 0..N-1,
        writerId: 0..M-1
    Invariant: (#readers==0 or #writers==0) and #writers <= 1;

    CPre: #writers == 0 and #attending_writers == 0;
    void* read(void* p){} //operation
    CPost: #readers == #readers@pre + 1;

    CPre: #writers == 0 and #readers == 0;
    void* write(void* p){}  //operation
    CPost: #writers == 1;
```

Fig. 5. SQL-SharedResource specification with priority to writers

Obviously, a third possibility consists of not giving priority to any of these process categories. The semaphore-based solution to the readers/writers problem with equal priorities is a little brain teaser. The students are asked to solve the equal priorities problem in order to motivate the students to follow our systematic scheme (based on *shared resource* formal specification) to find a correct solution by themselves (Fig. 5).

The correct solution to the readers/writers problem with equal priority includes many aspects of the versions with priorities, but also the need for a second level of synchronization. Before allowing a process to check the processes that are already accessing to the shared resource, a stage must be added to determine the order in which the processes have to proceed. With this problem the students learn to design multi-level synchronization protocols by using shared variables.

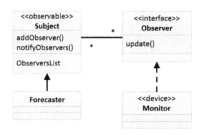

Invariant: $queue.q \mathrel{!=} null \land queue.q.size() = m$
$\quad$ *if m items were added* $\land queue.q[i] = k_i$
$\quad$ *where k_i is the i-th item added*
Safety: Invariant
Liveness: $\Box \Diamond Subject(i).notifyObservers()$
Guarantee: $\Box(Subject(i) \ at \ notifiable\_state \land$
$\quad Observer(\bullet).notify() \rightarrow \Diamond update())$

Fig. 6. ObserversList data structure for the *Observer* pattern

4.3   Real-Time Systems Design: The Observer Pattern

The standard Observer pattern was considered during the course to introduce real-time programming to students. Observer pattern serves to map Subject to Observer entity-roles in algorithms and applications. The objective of the pattern is to keep consistency between the state of the object with the Subject role and the state(s) of the object(s) with Observer roles.

Predicative Specification Model. Each Subject entity of the application maintains a set of references to the observers attached to it. Each Subject has a ObserverList queue as its representation type, which defines attach() and detach() methods for adding and deleting observers, respectively, to that observers-list. Subject entities will provide a notify() method as well, which has to be immediately invoked whenever the subject's state experiences a change. A call to notify() method of the Subject must guarantee that the method update() is invoked on each of the observers in the list. A call to an observer's update() method changes the observers state to make it consistent with the new Subject state.

When the Subject's `notify()` is called, it is compulsory, according to the standard specification in Fig. 7, that the `update()` method is invoked on each attached observer, which updates the `observer` state and propagates the call to its successor on the `ObserverList` queue. Therefore, the `notify()` call needs only invoke `update()` on the first observer in the chain.

```
ObserverList
bool[N] notified=false; //N observers attached to Subject
Operations
  attach(ObserverId == i)
  detach(ObserverId == i)
  notify(): {true, false}
Semantics   Domain:
  Type: ObserverList(0..N-1) == seq N, ObserverId:0..N-1
  Invariant: #observers >= size(ObserverList);
  CPre: size(ObserverList) >= 0 and  #observers > 0;
  void attach(i){}
  CPost: size(ObserverList) == size(ObserverList)@pre + 1;

  CPre: #observers >= 0 and size(ObserverList) > 0;
  void detach(i){}
  CPost:  size(ObserverList) == size(ObserverList)@pre - 1;

  CPre: size(ObserverList) > 0 and #observers > 0;
  boolean notify(i){}
  CPost: notified(i) == true

  Guarantee: forall k:0..N-1: notified(k) == true;
```

Fig. 7. `ObserversList` and `Subject` operations specification for the Observer pattern

5   Assessment of the Teaching Experience

Learning concurrency in undergraduate courses is generally difficult for students, because of the complexity and depth of the set of concepts that they must master during the course. The main objective of the study proposed here has been to facilitate the work of the students. For this, we have chosen to conduct a teaching approach based on demonstrative teaching that uses patterns as the conceptual guide to ease the communication between teacher and class. In this way, the student got a pattern that allows her to take in new concepts in concurrent programming when these concepts are presented anew by the teacher.

The patterns we have been used to develop this study were carefully chosen to illustrate key aspects of concurrent/parallel programming, e.g., *driver-implementer* patterns allow the programmer to delegate the entire responsibility of tasks management to an *executor*, which also takes in any future asynchronous computation of those tasks; the *executor* is therefore a complex design pattern, but at the same time it can be considered of enormous usefulness when it is well understood. Another pattern introduced here amounts to the synchronization of simultaneous accesses to a shared resource by tasks of *reader* and *writer* type. This is another situation that must be frequently tackled by programmers, and because of that we have included a specific pattern in the demostrative set that reflects such synchronization between reader and writer threads.

We assessed how the model improves the final results obtained by the students on the subject on completing our course. We also noticed more active participation of students during lecture-oriented lessons. Additionally, working time spent in the classroom became actually fun and optimized, and the breadth and depth of the contents covered increased too.

5.1   Evaluation of the Study Results

To evaluate the results obtained from the course teaching experience, we ellaborated a survey form that included four dimensions to be evaluated by the students:

(a) The concepts introduced in lectures were better apprehended through the models provided by our set of *parallel patterns*.
(b) The number of exercises was adquate.
(c) The time required to complete the assigned exercises was sufficient.
(d) The students were satisfied with this approach to the teaching of concurrency and parallelism.

All the four study dimensions were evaluated with a score between 1 (completely disagree) and 5 (completely agree) with the inclusion of an additional value (0) for when the student does not want to answer. The survey was made available to a sample of n = 67 students at the end of the semester. The results obtained are illustrated in Fig. 8. It is observed that the students significantly improved their understanding of the concepts explained in the theoretical classes, the number of programming exercises developed in the laboratories and their

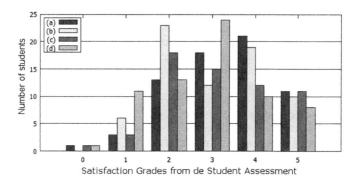

Fig. 8. Students' assesment

weekly work assignments were considered as *adequate*, they had enough time to finish the assignments and exercices, and thus the satisfaction level with the pattern-based concurrency/parallelism model was generally high or very high among the students.

6   Conclusions and Future Work

The outcome of the ICT-based experiment has been a noticeable improvement in the grades obtained by the students in the final examination of the subject. This ICT-based interactive teaching approach can easily be applied to other courses in many different areas beyond the sphere of normal university courses. Teaching projects such as MOOC could immediately benefit from our approach on many of their engineering courses since in these cases our method would only require a simple adaptation of specific course contents.

In the long term, we intend to develop a pattern-based CPP teaching tool in the Cloud which would facilitate systematic learning for any student or person interested and which would enable the method and techniques discussed in this paper to be implemented. Our future work is focused on extending the set of patterns proposed here, developing a course (MOOC) with exercises in several programming languages, such as Java, C++ and MPI. We will include new programming languages that are of interest for industry in the future.

References

1. Capel, M.I., Tomeu, A.J., Salguero, A.G.: Teaching concurrent and parallel programming by patterns: an interactive ICT approach. J. Parallel Distrib. Comput. **105**, 42–52 (2017)
2. Carro, M., Herranz, A., Mario, J.: A model-driven approach to teaching concurrency. ACM Trans. Comput. Educ. **13**(1), 1–19 (2013)
3. Cole, M.: Algorithmic Skeletons: Structured Management of Parallel Computation. ACM/MIT Press, New York/Cambridge (1991)
4. Gamma, E., Helm, R., Johnson, R., Vlissides, J.: Design Patterns: Elements of Object-Oriented Software. Addison-Wesley, Reading (1994)
5. Goetz, B., Peierls, T., Bloch, J., Bowbeer, J., Holmes, D., Lea, D.: Java Concurrency in Practice. Addison-Wesley, Reading (2006)
6. Grossman, D., Anderson, R.E.: Introducing parallelism and concurrency in the data structures course. In: Proceedings of the 43rd ACM Technical Symposium on Computer Science and Education (SIGCSE 2012), pp. 505–510. ACM, New York (2012)
7. Hadjerrouit, S.: Towards a blended learning model for teaching and learning computer programming: a case of study. Inf. Educ. **7**(2), 181–210 (2008)
8. Joshi, R., Lamport, L., et al.: Checking Cache-Coherence Protocols with TLA+. https://www.microsoft.com/pubs/65162/fmsd.pdf. Accessed Sept 2016
9. Law, K., Lee, V., Yu, Y.: Learning motivation in e-learning facilitated computer programming courses. Comput. Educ. **55**(1), 218–228 (2010)
10. Manzano, M.: Extensions of First Order Logic. Cambridge University Press, Cambridge (1996)

11. Marowka, A.: Think parallel: teaching parallel programming today. IEEE Distrib. Syst. Online **9**(8), 1–8 (2008). Article no. 0808-o8002
12. Mattson, T., Sanders, B., Massingill, B.: Patterns for Parallel Programming. Addison-Wesley, Reading (2004)
13. Mitchell, R., McKim, J.: Design by Contract, by Example. Addison-Wesley, Reading (2002)
14. Mohorovicic, S., Tijan, E.: New technologies in teaching university level programming. In MIPRO, 2010 Proceedings of the 33rd International Convention, Opatija, Croacia, pp. 1024–1028 (2010)
15. Papp-Varga, Z., Szlavi, P., Zsako, L.: ICT teaching methods-programming languages. In: Annales Mathematicae et Informaticae, vol. 35, pp. 163–172 (2008)
16. Saraswat, V.A., Bruce, K.: Curricula in concurrency and parallelism. In: Proceedings of the ACM International Conference Companion on Object Oriented Programming Systems Languages and Applications Companion (SPLASH 2010), pp. 281–282. ACM, New York (2010)

Integrating Parallel Computing in Introductory Programming Classes: An Experience and Lessons Learned

Sheikh Ghafoor[✉], David W. Brown, and Mike Rogers

Department of Computer Science, Tennessee Tech University, Cookeville, USA
{sghafoor, dwbrown, mrogers}@tntech.edu

Abstract. Parallel and distributed computing (PDC) has become ubiquitous to the extent that even common users depend on parallel programming. This points to the need for every programmer to understand how parallelism and distributed programming affect problem solving, teaching only traditional sequential programming is no longer sufficient. To address the rapidly widening gap between emerging highly-parallel computer architectures and the sequential programming approach taught in traditional CS/CE courses, the Computer Science Department at Tennessee Technological University has integrated PDC into their introductory programming course sequence. This paper presents our implementation efforts, experience and lessons learned, as well as preliminary evaluation results.

Keywords: Parallel and distributed computing · Introductory programming Undergraduate education

1 Introduction

The widespread deployments of multicore and GPU based computing systems in recent years have changed the computing landscape. Parallel and Distributed Computing (PDC) now permeates almost all computing activities. The pervasiveness of multicore computing devices is making even common users dependent on PDC techniques. The ever-increasing use of web-based services and emerging applications, such as mobile applications, cloud computing, big data analytics, and the Internet of Things (IoT), has made high performance computing common. Therefore, the most effective programmers understand how parallelism and distributed programming affect problem solving. Acquiring only traditional sequential programming skills is no longer sufficient, even for basic programmers. These changes emphasize the need for providing a broad-based skill set in PDC technology at various levels in Computer Science (CS) and Computer Engineering (CE) programs, as well as related computational disciplines. However, the rapid changes in hardware platforms, devices, languages and supporting programming environments continue to challenge educators in ascertaining appropriate content for curriculum and how to effectively teach that material.

The computer science education community now recognizes that integrating PDC concepts in undergraduate curriculums is vital to comprehensive CS/CE education.

© Springer International Publishing AG, part of Springer Nature 2018
D. B. Heras and L. Bougé (Eds.): Euro-Par 2017 Workshops, LNCS 10659, pp. 216–226, 2018.
https://doi.org/10.1007/978-3-319-75178-8_18

The TCPP curriculum report [1] has identified core and elective PDC topics that a student graduating with a Bachelor's degree in CS or CE is expected to have covered. Furthermore, PDC has been designated as a new 'required knowledge' unit in the ACM/IEEE-CS Curricula 2013 [2]. However, most undergraduate CS/CE/Engineering programs still do not teach PDC concepts, and such programs typically train students to think and program exclusively in a sequential manner. Although some CS/CE programs offer PDC courses as an upper division elective, very few introduce PDC early, in the introductory programming classes (CS1 and CS2). The gap is rapidly widening between the emerging parallel computing architectures and the sequential computing approach taught in traditional undergraduate curriculums. There are currently three thousand and eleven (3011) 4-year universities in the United States [3] and most of them offer an undergraduate degree program in CS and/or CE. In addition, one thousand, eight hundred and ninety one (1891) two year community colleges offer CS/CE pre-university coursework [3]. However, while no statistics are available on how many institutions are teaching PDC concepts at the undergraduate level, the authors conservatively estimate this number at no more than 300. This estimation is based on grants sponsored by the National Science Foundation, "early adaptor" mini-grants awarded by the CDER Center [4], and faculty development workshops conducted by CS in Parallel [1].

This paper presents the PDC topics and related hands on exercises that have been integrated in traditional CS0, CS1 and CS2 classes taught in the Computer Science Department at Tennessee Technological University (TTU). The paper further describes our experiences and lessons learned from this PDC integration effort.

2   Related Works

Researchers are actively seeking methodologies and tools for introducing PDC into introductory CS courses. In [5], the authors present their effort to implement parallelism in first and second year CS courses. The authors found that students can learn the material and enjoyed the experience. However, in [6], the author suggests that CS2 is the natural place to introduce parallelism, and the author uses minimalistic parallel programming patterns, called patternlets, to teach the student in CS2.

Some researchers have focused on teaching PDC topics to students in upper division courses. For example, Geist et al. [7] describes a course for seniors and first year graduates that covers a real-world problem. Similarly, Lupo et al. [8] focusses on real world experiences with students working in teams. The authors state that eight of the ten learning objectives were met, and that the students enjoyed the real-world experience.

Researchers have also attempted to integrate PDC throughout the curriculum. Burtscher et al. [9] taught PDC in several lower division courses and a senior capstone course. The authors show encouraging empirical results that they achieve their goals in terms of student outcomes, engagement, and interest. Graham [10] used various software models and programming options to teach PDC at various levels of the curriculum. The author also states the students show interest in the topics, but that PDC must be introduced early for the concepts to take root. Neelima and Li [11] present their experiences in introducing PDC topics over 6 academic years. The authors state that the PDC topics were well received by the students. Many students implemented successful projects, and some participated in conferences. Brown, Shoop [12, 13] and Adams [14] argue that PDC concepts should be taught at all undergraduate levels. They have developed a community of PDC educators available at CSinParallel.org [1].

Foley and Hursey [15] state that complex and unfamiliar parallel computing environments, or PCEs, present a barrier to students. The authors present a web portal, called OnRamp, which allows students to interactively explore PDC concepts.

The CDER Center [4] is an NSF supported center for PDC Curriculum and educational resources development. Project personnel chair PDC educational conferences such as EduPar and EduHPC, as well as workshops. Additionally, the CDER Center provides competitive grants for early adopters of PDC in CS courses. The center also provides a book [16] for introducing concurrency in undergraduate courses and provides downloadable and searchable courseware.

3 PDC Implementation

3.1 CS Curriculum at TTU

TTU is a medium sized, accredited public university with an enrollment of approximately twelve thousand students. The Computer Science department has approximately four hundred undergraduate majors and offers BS, MS, and Ph.D. degrees in Computer Science. The introductory courses offered as part of this degree are *Introduction to Problem Solving and Computer Programming (CS1)*, *Data Structures and Algorithms (CS2)*, and *Object Oriented Programming and Design (CS3)*. Multiple sections of these introductory courses are offered each semester; usually the different sections of these courses are taught independently by different instructors. To address the high DFW rates in the 1st and 2nd programming classes, a required *Principles of Computing (CS0)* class was added to the curriculum in fall 2013. The students in these courses are usually first or second semester freshmen and are placed in CS0/CS1 according to their math aptitude scores. If the students are able to enroll in calculus, they are allowed to take CS0 and CS1 concurrently. In addition, CE students are required to take CS1 and CS2 but are exempted from CS0. For the majority of students involved, these courses represent their first real exposure to programming.

In addition to the introductory level coursework, required upper division courses are typically offered once each school year. Our required upper division courses for the traditional CS degree include *Assembly Language Programming, Operating Systems, Computer Networks, Computer Architecture, Database Systems*, and a two-semester capstone *Software Engineering* series.

Beginning in fall 2015, we began introducing parallel concepts into some sections of our CS0, CS1 and CS2 curriculum. One to two days of lecture per semester have been dedicated to introducing why PDC programming is necessary, parallel architecture, basic concepts and how PDC programming differs from sequential coding. Examples are provided to the student outlining parallelism, distributed computing, race conditions and concurrency. In the weeks following these lectures, hands on PDC exercises are introduced into the attached lab portion of the class, or as homework, that highlight a particular attribute of PDC development.

Following the idea of exposing the students "early and often" to the concepts of PDC, each class introduces topics that build upon previous coursework. To accomplish this, we introduce similar concepts in CS0, CS1 and CS2 but at different levels of depth. This model allows the students to practice one facet of PDC in a manner that does not lead to confusion over the complex details of any advanced techniques. Each lab exercise or homework assignment takes as part of the study is worth 8-10% of the final grade in the lab course. The following sections briefly describe the implementation in each class with concise descriptions of the hands on exercises. One of the exercises is described in greater detail for the better understanding of our reader.

3.1.1 Principles of Computing (CS0)
The concepts introduced in the CS0 lecture include *serial computing*, *parallel computing*, *concurrency*, *race condition* and *speed-up*, and the need for parallel computing. We used SNAP [17] to implement the in class examples highlighting these topics. Using animated sprites, provided in SNAP, to represent which components of the application are computing and which ones are not. To highlight the benefits of parallelism, the students are shows two lists of random numbers and the instructor will work them through a sort done in parallel. The instructor can spawn the final merge step for this application in parallel or sequentially after the parallel sort to show that synchronization is needed to overcome the race condition. The module focuses on visualization and examples of parallelism, and does *not* include coding parallel algorithms. Once the students have been exposed to the concepts, a hands on exercise allows the students to run the sort over data collections and time their results to demonstrate *speed-up*.

3.1.2 Introduction to Problem Solving and Computer Programming (CS1)
The objective in the CS1 parallel introduction is to introduce the students to basic OpenMP coding, the *fork-join* model of parallel processing, as well as have the student become more familiar with the ideas of *shared* v. *distributed memory*, *designing parallel programs* and the differences between *concurrency* and *parallelism*. In addition, the topics covered in CS0 are restated since that course is not a requirement for all students.

Two modules have been created for use in the CS1 laboratory course. The first is a simple demonstration of fork-join summation and allows the students to create a basic parallel program and observe the speed-up PDC allows. The second more complex module walks the students through the manipulation in parallel of arrays for the means of image manipulation. Both modules help reinforce the concepts covered in the main lecture.

Parallel Sum for CS1: The parallel sum lab is designed to introduce students to the fork-join model of parallel programming. The lab begins by introducing the concepts and reasoning behind PDC programming and explaining the expected results of the experiment. The students are instructed to create a program which will create a large array, at least 1 million elements, of randomly generated integers. A function is created to process the array, adding all the elements in a standard sequential manner. A separate function is created to perform the same process but utilize fork – join through OpenMP. A timer function placed in the program allows the users to accurately determine how long each function took to arrive at the answer. The students run the program multiple times using each of the two functions and are able to see the time savings adding simple parallel code can have on their programs performance.

Parallel Image Processing for CS1: The lab describes image flipping and gray-scaling with an example, shown in Fig. 1. In particular, images are represented as colored dots, known as pixels, on the monitor screen. The color of the pixel is represented as a mixture of intensities of the colors red, green and blue. Each intensity is characterized by an 8-bit number in the range from 0 to 255. For example, the value (0, 0, 0) represents the color black, the values (255, 0, 0) represents red, and the values (255, 255, 0) represent yellow. We call these intensities, the colors RGB (or red, green, blue) values.

a)   Color original image   b) Gray-scaled and flipped image

Fig. 1. Flipping and gray-scaling an image (Color figure online)

Gray-scaling an image represented as a series of RGB values is easy. Different methods exist, but an effective method is called the *luminosity method*. In this method, if you are given the ith pixel, you gray-scale that pixel with the following formula:

$$gray\_value[i] = 0.21 * pixel[i].red + 0.72 * pixel[i].green + 0.07 * pixel[i].blue \quad (1)$$

Then, for each i, set the red, green and blue component of *pixel*[i] to *gray_value* [i] to gray-scale the image. Flipping an image is accomplished by flipping the first pixel with the last pixel, the second pixel with the second-to-last pixel, and so on. The lab then describes how an image can be flipped and gray-scaled in parallel. An image has both a height and a width. The array of color values represents rows of pixels, where each row is a line of pixels that would appear across the screen. The size of each line of pixels is equal to the image's width, and the number of lines is equal to the images height. When writing a parallel application, the programmer must first determine how to divide the problem among the available processors. Dividing the problem requires determining (1) how much of the problem each processor should compute, and (2) determining where, in the input data, the processor should begin and end its computations. In general, when dividing the rows among processors, the programmer should divide the work equally. So, if the image consists of *n* rows, and there are *p* processors available, then each processor should get roughly *n/p* rows.

A natural division for an image is to divide the image into chunks, where each chunk consists of a number of rows of pixels. Then, each processor computes its assigned chunk. So, if the given machine has four processors and the image file is eight pixels square, each processor would compute two rows. Processor 1 would compute the first two rows, starting at index 0 and finishing with index 15, processor 2 would start at index 16 and process through index 31, and so on.

Next, the lab describes the tools needed to edit and compile a parallel program, and includes a link to download code for loading and saving images in the simple PMM format, as well as a description of the PPM libraries API. The lab also describes pseudocode gray-scaling and flipping before finally explaining how OpenMP can make writing parallel programs easier. In fact, when using OpenMP, writing code to parallelize simple loops, such as the ones in this lab, becomes trivial.

3.1.3   Data Structures and Algorithms (CS2)

The objective in the CS2 parallel introduction is to reinforce the material the students had covered in CS1 while expanding their ability to learn and think in parallel, as well as how to design programs to effectively take advantage of the speed increases PDC provides. As with CS1, multiple modules exist to reinforce the instruction provided in the course lecture sections. The first allows the students to again observe speed-up of parallel programming by implementing a parallelized bubble sort. The second works with image modification, but this time utilizing *pipelining* and the *producer-consumer* model of parallelization.

Simple Bubble Sort with Merge for CS2: Even though the student should have covered sorting before attempting this lab, the module gives a brief description of Bubble Sort with examples for review. The lab exercise then describes a simple method for parallelizing the sort using domain decomposition. The computation occurs in two phases, the first of which divides the work equally among the available processors. A second phase occurs after all of the processors are finished with the initial sort, because sorting the pieces of the array does not result in a completely sorted array. In this step, the master must merge sorted pieces to produce a completely sorted result. However, the second phase must be done in serial using a single processor.

Parallel Image Processing for CS2: The CS2 image processing lab is similar to the CS1 image processing lab but follows the producer-consumer paradigm. This module does not apply gray-scaling in parallel followed by flipping in parallel, but instead the lab describes the image processing concept of pipelining filters as shown in. By utilizing a pipeline and the producer-consumer model, the students are able to gray-scale the image and flip the pixels in the same loop. In other words, once the gray-scale filter has been applied to a single row, that row can be enqueued to the flip filter while the gray-scale filter moves to the next row (Fig. 2).

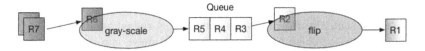

Fig. 2. Implementing a pipeline with a queue

4 Evaluation

We assessed how our integration efforts affected our students' ability to think effectively using parallel concepts and the knowledge gained in PDC topics. As part of this assessment, we have conducted subjective and objective evaluations of the knowledge transfer. The objective evaluations were accomplished through quizzes, lab assignments, and homework, which is reflected in the course grade. The subjective evaluation was achieved through pre and post surveys designed to gather the students' self-evaluation of their understanding of PDC concepts. We assessed the self-evaluations on a five point Likert scale to subjectively gauge their understanding of the concepts taught during the coursework.

Results for this study were gathered from students in multiple sections of CS0, CS1 and CS2 courses over three semesters; fall 2015, spring 2016 and spring 2017. Due to time constraints with the existing curriculum and faculty capabilities this was a very sporadically applied implementation, which is something that we hope to address in the future. The class sizes for the courses under study have varied during the implementation of this study, see Table 1, but while the lecture size has fluctuated greatly, the associated lab sections have stayed around a 40 student enrollment on average.

Table 1. Enrollment in courses

Course/semester	Section	Lecture size	Laboratory size
CS0 FA15	001	44	N/A
	002	43	N/A
CS1 SP16	002	60	51
CS2 SP16	001	37	39
	002	54	49
CS1 SP17	001	103	36
	002	103	34
	003	103	36
	004	91	25

Grades for the PDC module assignments followed the general template for laboratory work in the CS1/CS2 computer classes at TTU. If the assignment is complete and on time, the user is given full credit, work with errors are reduced in score either by 25% or 50% depending on the severity of the errors present. Regardless of errors, as long as work is submitted the student scores a 25%. Based on this scale, the classes we observed have performed below average on the PDC lab. The 2016 CS1 averaged a 67.9% on the PDC lab and those same students finished the semester with an average lab grade of 78.4%. Meanwhile, the 2017 students averaged a 72.6% on the PDC lab and finished the semester with an 80.9% average in the course. This is to be expected considering the overall lack of experience and limited time the professors were able to spend covering the PDC material prior to the work being accomplished.

Figures 3 through 5 show the results of the students' self-evaluation of their understanding of PDC concepts. These evaluations were done using a 5-point Likert scale (1 – none to 5 – a great deal). From these evaluations we can see that race conditions appear to be one of the hardest PDC topics to understand for CS0 and CS1. We can also see that the number of responses of 'None at All' and 'Little' decrease

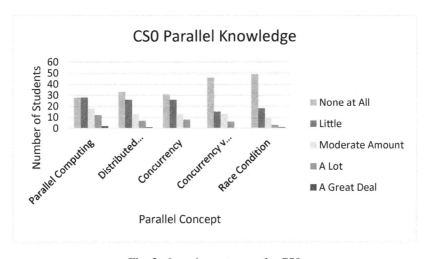

Fig. 3. Learning outcomes for CS0

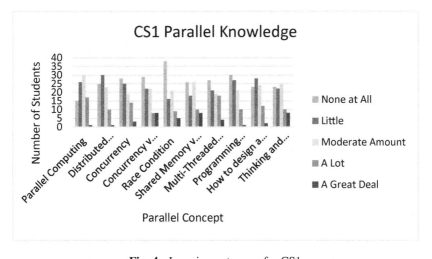

Fig. 4. Learning outcomes for CS1

from CS0 to CS1, we can also see the responses for 'A Lot' and 'A Great Deal' increase between CS1 and CS2 (Fig. 4). While our implementation was sporadic, these changes are to be expected as the students' aptitude and exposure to programming has increased (Fig. 5).

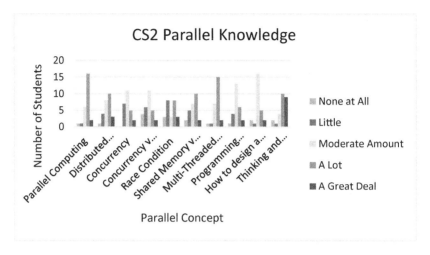

Fig. 5. Learning outcomes for CS2

5 Conclusion

Over the past two years, we have attempted to introduce PDC concepts into multiple sections of the CS0, CS1 and CS2 coursework at TTU. These implementations, limited though they may be, have been somewhat successful and point to several promising outcomes moving forward. The biggest challenge we faced was the time constraints that were placed upon us due to the nature of these courses and the amount of material already present in their curriculum. This challenge made implementation of the necessary PDC material very difficult. Despite this, the subjective analysis of the results from the implementation show that the students can learn this material at this point in their academic careers and it is feasible to introduce these concepts in early classes.

A second lesson we learned is that students tended to learn more from doing the PDC labs and homework rather than just listening to the lectures. Part of this is the trial and error learning that occurred as the users attempted to solve the problems presented, but also that we waited too long into the semester to begin talking about the concepts. In CS1, the PDC lab was the 10th out of 13 labs, and we feel that if we could introduce the concepts sooner in the semester before the students had started tuning out the lectures, we would be more successful in imparting the necessary skills.

A third lesson is we need to formalize the introduction. The work we accomplished was only possible in a rather scattershot manner and instead we will work with the entire faculty teaching the CS0, CS1 and CS2 courses to develop lesson plans that will fit into their existing coursework and allow us to test the early and often paradigm over the course of several semesters to ensure the knowledge retention. For this to work will require coordination between all members of faculty responsible for teaching these courses and buy in to support the introduction of these topics.

Though we have not tested the theory yet, we believe including unplugged activities that demonstrate parallel concepts away from the computer will be beneficial and should be included in future implementations. We would also like to include concepts of distributed computing in future research, possibly adding them to web based activities in CS0 or coding assignments in CS2. Regardless, we still believe the topics introduced should be presented in small, bite size doses because of variations in student preparedness at this early point in their careers.

References

1. Parallel computing in the computer science curriculum. http://csinparallel.org/index.html. Accessed 11 Jan 2017
2. ACM. Computer Science 2013: Curriculum Guidelines for Undergraduate Programs in Computer Science. http://www.acm.org/education/CS2013-final-report.pdf. Accessed 11 Jan 2017
3. Digest of Education Statistics (2015). https://nces.ed.gov/programs/digest/d15/tables/dt15_317.10.asp?current=yes. Accessed 16 Jan 2017
4. Prasad, S.K., Gupta, A., Rosenberg, A., Sussman, A., Weems, C.: CDER Center – NSF/IEEE-TCPP Curriculum Initiative
5. Ko, Y., Burgstaller, B., Scholz, B.: Parallel from the beginning: the case for multicore programming in the computer science undergraduate curriculum. In: Proceeding of the 44th ACM Technical Symposium on Computer Science Education. ACM (2013)
6. Adams, J.C.: Injecting parallel computing into CS2. In: Proceedings of the 45th ACM technical symposium on Computer science education. ACM (2014)
7. Geist, R., Levine, J.A., Westall, J.: A problem-based learning approach to GPU computing. In: Proceedings of the Workshop on Education for High-Performance Computing. ACM (2015)
8. Lupo, C., Wood, Z.J., Victorino, C.: Cross teaching parallelism and ray tracing: a project-based approach to teaching applied parallel computing. In: Proceedings of the 43rd ACM Technical Symposium on Computer Science Education. ACM (2012)
9. Burtscher, M., et al.: A module-based approach to adopting the 2013 ACM curricular recommendations on parallel computing. In: Proceedings of the 46th ACM Technical Symposium on Computer Science Education. ACM (2015)
10. Graham, J.R.: Integrating parallel programming techniques into traditional computer science curricula. ACM SIGCSE Bull. **39**(4), 75–78 (2007)
11. Neelima, B., Li, J.: Introducing high performance computing concepts into engineering undergraduate curriculum: a success story. In: Proceedings of the Workshop on Education for High-Performance Computing. ACM (2015)
12. Brown, R., Shoop, E.: CSinParallel and synergy for rapid incremental addition of PDC into CS curricula. In: 2012 IEEE 26th International Parallel and Distributed Processing Symposium Workshops and Ph.D. Forum (IPDPSW). IEEE (2012)

13. Brown, R., Shoop, E.: Modules in community: injecting more parallelism into computer science curricula. In: Proceedings of the 42nd ACM Technical Symposium on Computer Science Education. ACM (2011)
14. Adams, J., Brown, R., Shoop, E.: Patterns and exemplars: compelling strategies for teaching parallel and distributed computing to CS undergraduates. In: 2013 IEEE 27th International Parallel and Distributed Processing Symposium Workshops and Ph.D. Forum (IPDPSW). IEEE (2013)
15. Foley, S.S., Hursey, J.: OnRamp to parallel and distributed computing. In: Proceedings of the Workshop on Education for High-Performance Computing. ACM (2015)
16. Prasad, S.K., et al.: Topics in Parallel and Distributed Computing: Introducing Concurrency in Undergraduate Courses. Morgan Kaufmann, Burlington (2015)
17. Harvey, B., et al.: Snap!(build your own blocks). In: Proceedings of the 45th ACM Technical Symposium on Computer Science Education. ACM (2014)

Revisiting Flynn's Classification: The Portfolio Approach

Yanik Ngoko[1(✉)] and Denis Trystram[2]

[1] Qarnot Computing, 92120 Montrouge, France
`yanik.ngoko@qarnot-computing.com`
[2] Univ. Grenoble-Alpes, Inria, CNRS, Grenoble INP, LIG, Grenoble, France

Abstract. Today, we are reaching the limits of Moore's law: the progress of parallel components does not grow exponentially as it did continuously during the last decades. This is somehow a paradox since the computing platforms are always more powerful. It simply tells us that the efficiency of parallel programs is becoming less obvious.

If we want to continue to solve hard computational problems, the only way is to change the way problems are solved. In this work, we propose to investigate how algorithms portfolio may be a direction to solve hard and large problems. It is also the occasion for us to revisit the well-known Flynn's classification and clarifying the *MISD* (Multiple Instructions Single Data) class which was never really well-understood.

Keywords: Flynn's taxonomy · Algorithm portfolio
Cooperative parallelism

1 Motivation

As we are currently witnessing the end of Moore's law, interrogations are raised on our capacity in solving challenging computational problems in a reasonable amount of time [16]. This could appear as a vain debate since a wide range of problems are efficiently addressed by today's computer technologies. However, such an argument is questionable since it neglects the fact that the usefulness of Computer Science in various scientific domains is constantly growing; as a consequence, the set of new and challenging computational problems becomes broader every day (for instance Molecular Dynamics codes include now sophisticated visualization modules, multi-scale physical models through coupling classical n-body with chemistry or quantum physics, interactive processing, etc.). In addition, computer history gives us many examples of various technologies, that, because they led to a major increase in computing power, supported *new revolutions.* In other words: developing more powerful platforms creates always more needs.

For continuing to speedup the resolution of challenging computational applications, two classes of approaches are generally proposed. The former class deals

© Springer International Publishing AG, part of Springer Nature 2018
D. B. Heras and L. Bougé (Eds.): Euro-Par 2017 Workshops, LNCS 10659, pp. 227–239, 2018.
https://doi.org/10.1007/978-3-319-75178-8_19

with *alternative machines and/or computing models* in which fundamental concepts of current machines are replaced by other mechanisms (like when Von Neumann architectures moved to RISC, superscalar or VLIW [13]). Examples of such alternatives include quantum computers, dataflow or neural networks-based machines. In the second class, the idea is to enrich current computing models with new features in order to continuing to scale. Here, a good illustration is given by multicore architectures: Since the technology is not yet able to build more powerful processors, several cores are gathered into the same board to obtain more power.

In this paper, we propose to concentrate on the second class of the previous proposals. In particular, we are convinced that there is a *neglected model of parallelism*, suggested in the Flynn's classification, that can break the limits observed in the resolution of several hard computational problems.

Parallel processing is usually presented late in the french academic curricula (it is only rarely addressed at an undergraduate level). The obvious consequence is that the students are educated in *thinking sequential*. Teaching some basic principles in an historical perspective is a good way to prepare the student minds to the unknown concepts of parallelism. The neglected model of parallelism, discussed in this paper, is easy to deploy on a cluster or multicore system. It is also a good illustration of concurrent programming and synchronization of parallel processes.

1.1   A New Look at the Old Time

Historically, Flynn's taxonomy [7] served as a clear construct to think parallelism. He introduced a classification in the way the french savants of the Lumière in the XVIII-th century did in the *Encyclopedia* [5] with their effort to classify and organize the scientific knowledge. This taxonomy proposed two concepts for building parallel *organizations*[1]: the stream of instructions and the stream of data. Depending on the multiplicity of these streams, Flynn proposed to define all possible combinations of instructions/data, leading to four classes of organizations: starting from the classical Von Neumann's processor SISD (Single Instruction Single Data), SIMD (Single Instruction Multiple Data), MISD (Multiple Instructions Single Data) and MIMD (Multiple Instructions Multiple Data). In his original work [7], Flynn also discussed the *effectiveness* of the various organizations. That is, he located existing computer technologies in his taxonomy and defined the fundamental problems raised by each organization.

Flynn's taxonomy conceptualized the parallelism at the level of machine instructions. This conceptualization inspired other models, where the control of parallelism is put at a higher level or layer[2]. Thus, in considering the applica-

---

[1] Flynn introduced his taxonomy with the notion of 'organization'. But, in his latter work [8], he also used the term of 'parallel machine architectures'. Our position is that an organization is a generic concept that could or not be realized with a computer architecture.

[2] In this paper, we assume common layered computer architectures: hardware, operating system and applications.

tion level, the SPMD (Single Program Multiple Data) [4] and MPMD (Multiple Program Multiple Data) models were introduced.

Regarding MISD organizations, Flynn concluded to their *little interest* [8]. This opinion is still shared today by most parallel computing experts and students; beyond the model of systolic arrays (which may be debatable [13]) or replication systems, the community considers that there are only few examples where MISD architecture could be of interest.

This work goes in the direction of putting emphasis on MISD organizations. With the end of Moore's law, we are convinced that the increase of parallelism in large scale parallel platforms is becoming the most serious issue for building powerful machines. To fully benefit from the whole parallelism and in particular to reach significant speedups, *MISD models could be the key*. The model we propose to consider is the discrete resource sharing model (DRSM) [1]. This abstract model and its practical counterpart (algorithm portfolio) is the missing brick in Flynn's classification. It is detailed in the next section.

1.2   Informal Presentation of the Discrete Resource Sharing Model

We consider in this work the discrete resource sharing model (DRSM) where the control of parallelism is done at the application level. We consider a set of parallel algorithms (denoted by $\mathcal{A}$) solving the same problem, these algorithms provide the exact solution (but it is also possible to consider that they provide an approximation of the optimal for optimization problems). Let us assume a parallel platform composed of homogeneous computing units, which consist of processors, cores or virtual machines. Each algorithm can run on a part or the whole set of the computing units, with its own execution time (which may differ from an algorithm to another). DRSM defines a concurrent run of several algorithms in $\mathcal{A}$ where each computing unit is assigned to at most one algorithm. In the execution, any instance of the problem is processed concurrently by some algorithms in $\mathcal{A}$, depending on the computing units that execute each algorithm. The concurrent runs are stopped as soon as one algorithm finds a solution. The link between DRSM and MISD (or MPMD) organizations is natural if we consider that the algorithms with at most one computing unit are streams of *instructions* that operate on the data of the problem instance to solve.

1.3   Contributions and Content

With DRSM the resolution of a computational problem (denoted by Π) is formulated as a cooperative execution of multiple algorithms that concurrently solve the same instances of Π. To demonstrate the interest in thinking parallelism under this vision, this paper has been organized in three parts: Firstly, we propose a formal model for building cooperative executions of algorithms in DRSM (Sect. 3). Our model assumes a statistical (context-aware) modeling of the instances of Π. The main challenge here is to decide on the best allocation of computing units to parallel algorithms. In the second part (Sect. 4), we analyze the runtime gains using DRSM when applied to the resolution of the classical

SAT decision problem. The analysis is based on a performance evaluation that uses data from the SAT competition[3]. Finally, Sect. 5 discusses some perspectives opened by DRSM in the development of parallel processing systems and machines.

It is worth noting that DRSM was already considered in our prior work [1,2], we are going one step further here. In this previous work, we introduced the discrete Resource Sharing Scheduling Problem (DRSSP) for deciding on the resource allocation in DRSM. This paper introduces new variants of the initial formulation, more suitable to special resource allocation situations that depend on both machine architectures and algorithms (namely, portfolio of teams, equal sharing portfolio and QoS portfolio that are detailed in Sect. 3). Moreover, in comparison to our past work, we provide a better proof-of-concept of the runtime gain induced by DRSM on the SAT problem. Indeed, whereas our past evaluations [1,2], assumed a known theoretical model for the speedup of SAT solvers, the experiments proposed here do not rely on such assumption.

2   Related Works

As already mentioned, Flynn's work inspired further parallel computing taxonomies, which can be ranged into the two following categories.

- The first one corresponds to studies that extent Flynn's classification. For instance, putting the parallelism control at the application level instead of at the hardware. This is the case of the well-known SPMD and MPMD classes where programs generalize instructions. This is also the case while considering the memory pattern accesses in MIMD machines with shared-memory, distributed-memories, uniform and non-uniform memory accesses (UMA and NUMA) [12].
- The second category of works proposed alternative taxonomies, that use other foundations to distinguish between parallel machines. In this spirit, Feng [6] introduced a taxonomy where machines are distinguished depending on the number of bits processed in parallel in a word. Despite its interest, this proposition never had the impact of Flynn's taxonomy. One of its recurring criticism is that it does not make a clear distinction between pipelining and parallelism [10]. Another alternative taxonomy was proposed by Händler [10] where the parallel machines are categorized depending on their number of control units, the number of arithmetic and logical units and the number of elementary logic circuits. With this model, Handler classified several actual computer machines. However, as recognized by the author him-self, one of its limitation is that it is specifically related to a given Von Neumann architecture. This differs from Flynn's taxonomy that is formulated over a more abstract model that could or not be realized by a Von Neumann model.

---

[3] http://www.satcompetition.org/.

The work proposed in this paper is related to *algorithm portfolio*. Indeed, DRSM was inspired by the concept of algorithm portfolio introduced by Huberman et al. [11] for the resolution of hard computational problems. The original motivation for algorithm portfolio can be summarized as follows: hard computational problems are often solved with heuristics based on randomization. Usually, for the same problem, there exist several randomized heuristics that can be used. However, the quality of the result will certainly differ and, despite randomization, their runtime could remain expensive. The question then is to know how to use these heuristics to solve the problem. For this purpose, Huberman et al. proposed to take example of practices developed in Finance to minimize the risks in investments. Indeed, given an initial capital that could be invested on several assets, financial agents generally prefer to distribute the capital between the assets, instead on investing only on a unique asset. In considering the various assets as randomized heuristics, Huberman proposed to solve hard computational problems in launching several randomized heuristics that each solves the problem. As soon as a heuristic finds a solution, the execution is interrupted.

Huberman promoted an economic approach whose idea is to *invest* on several algorithms to solve a computational problem. A critical question is to determine *how and what to invest* on each heuristic in order to ensure an economy of time. In their introductory paper, Huberman et al. discussed about investments done on fractions of processor clock cycles. For instance, given two heuristics h_1 and h_2 and a CPU, one can run h_2 every two clock cycles (attributed to the portfolio of algorithms) and h_1 the remaining cycles. Such a proposition however supposes that the execution can be controlled at the clock cycles level, which might be challenging with parallel randomized heuristics in a multiprocessor context. Some other authors proposed to define the execution of the algorithm portfolio based on time slots (time sharing) [14] or on the number of CPUs or cores (resource sharing) [2]. The interest in these latter models is that we can control the execution at the application level. For instance, in time sharing, an internal counter can be used for aggregating the cumulative running times allocated to each individual heuristic. In this paper, we will mainly focus on the resource sharing model that we introduced in our prior work [2]. Nonetheless, let us observe that our contribution can be extended to other algorithm portfolio models.

3   The Discrete Resource Sharing Model

We formally define a DRSM by a triple $\Gamma = (\mathcal{A}, \mu, S)$ where $\mathcal{A}$ is an ordered set of parallel algorithms, $\mu \in \mathbb{N}^+$ is the number of parallel computing units to use and $S = [s_1, \ldots, s_k]$ $(k = |\mathcal{A}|)$, where $s_i \in \{0, \ldots \mu\}$, defines a resource allocation of algorithms in $\mathcal{A}$ to the computing units. In this definition, the ith algorithm A_i of $\mathcal{A}$ is associated with s_i, the number of computing units allocated to the algorithm. We must also have $\sum_{i=1}^{k} s_i \leq \mu$ at any time slot.

Γ is associated with a halting condition expressed by the *economic gain* targeted in the execution. In this paper, we will focus on the economy of *time*.

Thus, $(\mathcal{A}, \mu, S)$ implies that on each problem instance I_j, each algorithm A_i runs on I_j using s_i computing units until one algorithm finds a solution.

This definition is restricted to the homogeneous setting where the computing units typically correspond to identical CPUs, cores, etc. The halting condition was targeted to the economy of time, however, other objectives are possible. For instance, distributed computing systems are nowadays associated with a pricing model in which users pay depending on the CPU time, memory size or any other feature that they consumed. In such a context, the halting condition can be defined as follows: stop when the execution price exceeds a given threshold[4]. Such a criteria is in particular meaningful if the execution of the algorithms in $\mathcal{A}$, generates local solutions (e.g. local search or anytime algorithms). As already mentioned, an important question in DRSM is to determine the s_i. We propose an adequate basic formulation model for this purpose in the next section and we give some examples of its variants.

3.1   The Discrete Resource Sharing Problem (DRSSP)

Base Formulation. To decide on the resource sharing, we propose to consider a context in which a computational problem Π is *represented* by a finite set of n instances $\mathcal{I}$. Each instance I_j has an *individual representativity*, modeled as weight $w_j \in [0, 1]$. We assume that the running times $C(A_i, I_j, s_i), j = 1 \ldots n$ spent by A_i to process I_j with s_i computing units is known *a priori*. The objective within DRSSP is to choose the vector S that will lead to the minimization of $\sum_{j=1}^{n} w_j.\mathcal{C}(S, I_j)$ where

$$\mathcal{C}(S, I_j) = \min_{A_i \in \mathcal{A}} C(A_i, I_j, s_i)$$

One can consider the representativity of an instance I as an estimation of the probability that the instance we want to solve (at any given date) is I or has a runtime close to the one of I. In this case, the optimization function in the above definition can also be associated with the average case complexity. Indeed, as defined, this function proposes to minimize the average runtime in the processing of $\mathcal{I}$. Another objective function is to consider the worst case complexity or energy minimization. In the former case, the objective will then be to minimize $\max_{I_j} \mathcal{C}(S, I_j)$.

We introduced this base formulation (without weights) in our prior work [1]. For a hard combinatorial problem like the classical satisfiability problem SAT [9], $\mathcal{I}$ could be chosen as one or a union of benchmarks of Π. We also assume that each instance I_j is associated with a weight $w_j \in [0, 1]$. We introduced the weights for taking into account the individual representativity of some instances. For instance, the NP-completeness proofs of problems is usually based on worst-case analysis on some specific classes of instances. As a result, the benchmarks for NP-complete problems often distinguish between instances that are *really*

---

[4] Such values are often formulated under the umbrella term of *capping conditions*.

hard or easy to solve[5]. Thus, if a user aims at solving more *hard* instances than easy ones, he/she can adjust the weights accordingly. Weights can also be used to set preference on algorithms. Indeed, one algorithm may be preferred to the others since it provides faster solutions. In this case, it is worth to introduce a weight to put emphasis on some algorithms. We recommend by default to consider the uniform distribution ($w_j = \frac{1}{n}$) (for instance in Finance, this latter setting corresponds to the situation of an equal weighted portfolio).

DRSSP proposes an explicit cost function for the portfolio execution time expressed by the individual runtime of algorithms. It is important to notice that this formulation does not consider the runtime overhead induced by the concurrent run of the algorithms. Let us now derive several variants showing how to adapt the basic formulation to concrete examples.

Portfolio of Teams. The first example is to build portfolio of algorithm portfolios. Such a situation can be motivated as follows: Let us assume that the computing platform consists in 16 cores, belonging to 2 identical CPUs (8 cores per CPU). Let us assume that A_1 is run on 8 cores. According to the formulation of Sect. 3.1, we should expect the same running time from A_1 whether it is deployed only on one CPU or if we use cores of both CPUs. Unfortunately, this is not realistic if we consider communication costs[6]. For a more realistic portfolio formulation, it is possible to avoid the combination of algorithms deployed on distinct CPUs. A portfolio of teams could be used for this purpose where the algorithms are grouped in teams, associated with a DRSM defined over a subset of resources. In the case of two teams whose resource sharing are defined by $Q = [q_1, \ldots, q_k]$ and $R = [r_1, \ldots r_k]$ s.t $\sum_{i=1}^{k} q_i \leq 8$ and $\sum_{i=1}^{k} r_i \leq 8$, the runtime of the portfolio on I_j is $\min\{\mathcal{C}(Q, I_j), \mathcal{C}(R, I_j)\}$.

Equal Sharing Portfolio. The second example is when DRSSP serves to build DRSMs that consist of the execution of several sequential algorithms (called the equal sharing portfolio). This variant allows to derive simply parallel algorithms from sequential ones. It has been used in several winner solvers of the SAT competition. We formally define it as follows: A resource allocation corresponds to a vector $S = [s_1, \ldots, s_k]$ where $s_i \in \{0, 1\}$ and $\sum_{i=1}^{k} s_i \leq \mu$. The DRSSP question is then to find an allocation that leads to the minimization of $\sum_{j=1}^{n} w_j.\mathcal{C}(S, I_j)$.

It is important to notice that in the case where $\mu > k$, the question is straightforward and the optimal solution is vector $S = [1, 1, \ldots, 1]$. If instead, $k < \mu$, then we have at least $\binom{\mu}{k}$ potential portfolio executions.

As already said, the equal sharing portfolio captures the situation where a portfolio is built in combining sequential algorithms. Consider a cluster of identical CPUs on which can be run the sequential algorithms A_i. The equal sharing portfolio remains interesting even in the case of parallel algorithms. Indeed, to build the optimal solution in the base DRSSP formulation, we need a cost estimation $C(A_i, I_j, s_i)$ for each algorithm, instance and number of processors. In

---

[5] See satcompetition.org for SAT.

[6] Most multicore systems are based on a NUMA architecture.

order to avoid the big overhead spent to collect these values, one could instead only consider for each algorithm A_i a single number of processors s_i^* on which the instances are evaluated. Thus, we would have to consider a formulation close to the equal sharing portfolio: each algorithm A_i runs on s_i^* processors and $\sum_{i=1}^{k} s_i^* \leq \mu$.

Portfolio with Quality of Service. The last DRSSP variant we present is the case where the algorithms A_i are heuristics solving an optimization problem (like Traveling Salesman Problem). In this case, each instance I_j and algorithm A_i could be associated with an *instance performance guarantee* $\rho_{i,j}$, defined as the fraction between the tour length found by A_i and the one of a lower bound on the problem. The shorter $\rho_{i,j}$, the better the solution found by A_i. Now, in considering the above DRSSP formulations, on the instance I_u, the algorithm A_l that causes the interruption of the portfolio could be the one for which $\rho_{i,u}$ is maximal, $1 \leq i \leq k$. This means that the results returned by a DRSM generated from DRSSP could be the ones whose quality are the worst, regarding the instance performance guarantee. Thus, an important question is how to extend DRSSP for the optimization of the quality of results. A simple solution is to change the halting condition. For instance, we can consider that the execution of the portfolio is interrupted when k' algorithms $(1 < k' \leq k)$ found a solution. The best of the k' results is the solution of the portfolio.

From our prior work, it is easy to establish that the all the described DRSSP variants remain NP-hard. Thus, an interesting question is the one of building efficient heuristics for their resolution. However, this will not be discussed in this paper. Instead, we will propose in the next section a performance evaluation whose goal is to demonstrate the interest in building DRSM (based on DRSSP) on the SAT problem.

4   Application to SAT

We propose to illustrate the power of the portfolio approach on two series of experiments. Each series considers a particular scenario for creating a parallel solver for the resolution of the SAT problem. The first one is the base parallel portfolio, the second one is the equal sharing portfolio.

In the first experiments, we consider the construction of a portfolio of solvers built in combining several parallel SAT solvers in a multicore context. The portfolio of solvers was built with the running time distribution of 6 existing parallel SAT solvers. In the objective function, we assumed uniform weights. The resource sharing problem to solve in this series is a base DRSSP in which the running times are only defined for solvers that are run on 1, 8 and 32 cores. These running times come from a public database of SAT solvers[7]. We distinguish two cases in these experiments. In the first case, we simulate a portfolio with the 6 parallel solvers and 300 instances. The results obtained here clearly show that there is

---

[7] http://www.cril.univ-artois.fr/~hoessen/penelope.html.

a dominant solver. We then did another simulation where the dominant solver was excluded. In both cases, we compared the running time of the portfolio of solvers versus the time of the best parallel solver on 32 cores.

The experimental results are depicted in Fig. 1. These experiments raised several conclusions. The first lesson learned is that we can effectively benefit from parallelism in combining several sequential SAT solvers according to a resource sharing obtained in solving a DRSSP instance. The second lesson is that we are able to build a portfolio of solvers that outperforms existing parallel algorithms. Indeed, from Fig. 1, one can notice that on 32 cores, the optimal portfolio was better than the best parallel algorithm available for this number of cores. The third lesson is that the greater the number of resources, the better the portfolio.

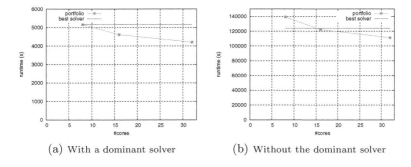

(a) With a dominant solver   (b) Without the dominant solver

Fig. 1. Runtime of the base parallel portfolio

Table 1. Experimental plan for the second series

Competitions	#solvers	#SAT instances	Cutoff time (s)
Random SAT + UNSAT session	14	150	5000 s
Hard certified UNSAT session	9	150	5000 s
Application certified UNSAT session	11	150	5000 s

In the second series of experiments, we consider a portfolio of solvers built in combining sequential solvers, according to DRSSP. The resource sharing problem we have to solve in this setting corresponds to an Equal Sharing portfolio, with uniform weights, presented in the previous section. We measured the runtime gain induced by the portfolio of solvers (over the best sequential one) and the number of SAT instances that were solved. Indeed, as the resolution of some SAT instances may be highly time consuming, we introduced in practice a maximal cutoff time. Thus, if the solver answers before the cutoff time, then we know whether the SAT instance is satisfiable or not. Otherwise, we conclude that the solver was not able to provide an answer. In these experiments, the

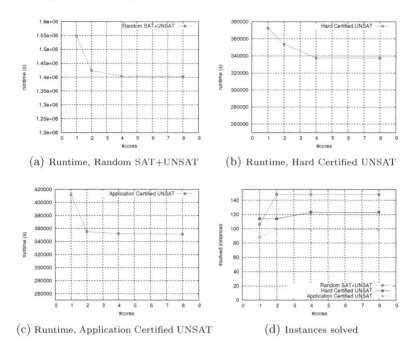

(a) Runtime, Random SAT+UNSAT   (b) Runtime, Hard Certified UNSAT

(c) Runtime, Application Certified UNSAT   (d) Instances solved

Fig. 2. Experimental evaluation

Equal Sharing portfolio problem with the running times data issued from 3 sessions of the 2013 SAT competition[8]. The chosen sessions names are: (1) Core solvers, Sequential, Random SAT+UNSAT (Random, SAT+UNSAT session), (2) Core solvers, Sequential, Hard-combinatorial certified UNSAT (Hard Certified UNSAT session), (3) Core solvers, Sequential, Application certified UNSAT (Application Certified UNSAT session). The data of our experimental plan are summarized in Table 1.

Figure 2 depicts the running time of the built portfolio and the number of instances we were able to solve. As one can notice, we can clearly benefit from parallelism in combining several sequential algorithms. In addition, we were also able to increase the number of SAT instances in the built portfolio. The speedup gain we observed in these experiments was not linear and did not change significantly between 4 and 8 cores. These results clearly show a *leadership phenomenon* that can be observed in team sports: a subgroup gives the whole team a boost. Here, there is a subset of *complementary solvers* that dominates the others. To improve the speedup, one should define another leadership by considering a more diversified basis of sequential SAT solvers.

Both experiments assess the approach proposed in this paper: algorithms portfolio can be used to design efficient SAT solvers better than usual approaches. We hope that the readers are convinced by the proof of concept. However, as the

---

[8] http://satcompetition.org/edacc/SATCompetition2013/.

previous results are limited to focused examples and are based on simulations, an effective implementation on a more systematic and larger campaign would be important to consolidate these results.

5   Discussion

With DRSSP, the parallel execution is decided on the basis of a statistical model that is contextualized to the execution environment in which the algorithms are run. Thus, while classical parallel processing models only focus on the way the concurrency is formulated (threads, processes, fork-join, SPMD, etc.), DRSSP goes further in introducing an optimization model that defines the optimal parallel execution. There are several advantages of such a model, in particular for the users who do not have to choose the adequate algorithm for solving (optimally or not) their instances. Another advantage is on the flexibility in the objectives (for instance, we can optimize the parallel execution on energy consumption, by redefining DRSSP with this new target).

The experimental results obtained on the two case-studies of SAT confirm the interest in building algorithm portfolio. They not only provide a concrete application for the MISD class, but they also open new research directions for the design of parallel algorithms. One of the most important direction consists in building a library for automating the design of algorithms portfolio, according to the theoretical models discussed in this paper. In our viewpoint, such a library could be based on a generative programming model similar to the one we have in the implementation of remote procedure calls [15]. At the beginning, a user describes the input of the portfolio of algorithms to be constructed. This description is done according to a language model proposed by the library. Then, an optimization engine (included into the library) generates the optimal DRSM and returns it to the user. Finally, the user can launch the generated program. The importance of this research direction is that it can lead to an implementation that will have an impact, comparable to the one that PVM/MPI have had in the promotion of the SPMD model.

To end this discussion, let us come back to the Flynn's classification. A contribution of this paper was to show that in considering the control of the parallelism at the application layer, the (extended) MISD class is efficient for the resolution of hard combinatorial problems and could even outperform parallel programs built upon other Flynn's classes. This efficiency was emphasized in considering the DRSM model. An important question is then to translate this model (DRSM) at the operating system and hardware levels. We will not discuss what can be done at the hardware level, but at the level of operating system, we do believe that it makes sense to introduce a new type of process group [3] that supports a time/resource, aware of the concept of portfolio. Roughly speaking, in an operating system, a process group refers to a collection of one or several processes. In a process group that is DRSM aware, one could balance the time slots allocated to each process, according to a resource sharing specified at the user level. The automatic interruption of all processes of the group is initiated as soon as one process finds a solution. The execution such a process group must also try to isolate as much as possible the different processes. This is important to guarantee that the resource allocation is respected. Finally, the group can also be improved in order to handle various halting conditions.

6   Conclusion

The end of the Moore's law is a great opportunity for the renewal of "parallel thinking" and the design of parallel systems. The thesis of this paper is that historically, there was a neglected model of parallelism (MISD) that deserves to be invested; in particular, we propose an extended MISD model where parallelism is formulated as a cooperation of concurrent algorithms solving the same problem. The proposed concurrency model is associated with an optimization model that defines optimal parallel executions. Our paper showed how we can build efficient parallel algorithms according to this model at the application layer. The portfolio approach is easily accessible and it allows to introduce fundamental concepts of parallelism like concurrency and synchronization. As showed in this paper, the approach puts a new light on the Flynn' classification and the formulation of optimal parallel algorithms. For these reasons, we do believe that the notion deserves to be taught in undergraduate classes on concurrent programming, synchronization, and models for parallelism.

References

1. Bougeret, M., Dutot, P., Goldman, A., Ngoko, Y., Trystram, D.: Combining multiple heuristics on discrete resources. In: 23rd IEEE International Symposium on Parallel and Distributed Processing, IPDPS 2009, Rome, Italy, 23–29 May 2009, pp. 1–8. IEEE (2009)
2. Bougeret, M., Dutot, P., Goldman, A., Ngoko, Y., Trystram, D.: Approximating the discrete resource sharing scheduling problem. Int. J. Found. Comput. Sci. **22**(3), 639–656 (2011)
3. Bovet, D., Cesati, M.: Understanding the Linux Kernel. Oreilly & Associates Inc., Sebastopol (2005)
4. Darema, F., George, D., Norton, V., Pfister, G.: A single-program-multiple-data computational model for EPEX/FORTRAN. Parallel Comput. **7**(1), 11–24 (1988)
5. Diderot, D., le Rond d'Alembert, J., (eds.): Encyclopédie, ou dictionnaire raisonné des sciences, des arts et des métiers. André le Breton, Michel-Antoine David, Laurent Durand and Antoine-Claude Briasson, France (1751–1766)
6. Feng, T.Y.: Some characteristics of associative parallel processing. In: Proceedings of the 1972 Sagamore Computing Conference, pp. 5–16 (1972)
7. Flynn, M.J.: Some computer organizations and their effectiveness. IEEE Trans. Comput. **21**(9), 948–960 (1972)
8. Flynn, M.J., Rudd, K.W.: Parallel architectures. ACM Comput. Surv. **28**(1), 67–70 (1996)
9. Garey, M.R., Johnson, D.S.: Computers and Intractability: A Guide to the Theory of NP-Completeness. W.H. Freeman & Co., New York (1979)

10. Händler, W.: The impact of classification schemes on computer architecture. In: Agrawal, D.P. (ed.) Advanced Computer Architecture, pp. 3–11. IEEE Computer Society Press, Los Alamitos (1986)
11. Huberman, B.A., Lukose, R.M., Hogg, T.: An economics approach to hard computational problems. Science **275**(5296), 51–54 (1997)
12. Lameter, C.: Numa (non-uniform memory access): an overview. Queue **11**(7), 40:40–40:51 (2013)
13. Null, L., Lobur, J.: Essentials of Computer Organization and Architecture, 3rd edn. Jones and Bartlett Publishers, Inc., USA (2010)
14. Streeter, M.J., Golovin, D., Smith, S.F.: Combining multiple heuristics online. In: Proceedings of the Twenty-Second AAAI Conference on Artificial Intelligence, 22–26 July 2007, Vancouver, British Columbia, Canada, pp. 1197–1203 (2007)
15. Thurlow, R.: RPC: remote procedure call protocol specification version 2. Technical report, Sun Microsystems (2009)
16. Vardi, M.Y.: Moore's law and the sand-heap paradox. Commun. ACM **57**(5), 5 (2014)

Experience with Teaching PDC Topics into Babeş-Bolyai University's CS Courses

Virginia Niculescu$^{(\boxtimes)}$ and Darius Bufnea

Faculty of Mathematics and Computer Science, Babeş-Bolyai University,
Cluj-Napoca, Romania
{vniculescu,bufny}@cs.ubbcluj.ro

Abstract. In this paper, we present an analysis of the outcomes of teaching Parallel and Distributed Computing within the Faculty of Mathematics and Computer Science from Babeş-Bolyai University of Cluj-Napoca. The analysis considers the level of interest of students for different topics as being determinant in achieving the learning outcomes. Our experiences have been greatly influenced by the specific context defined by the fact that the majority of the students are already enrolled into a software company either as interns in an internship program or as employees. The level of interest of students for a specific topic is also determined by the development of the IT industry in the region. The learning activity is in general influenced by this specific context, and a new, high demanding topic as Parallel and Distributed Computing is even more influenced, when is to be taught to the undergraduate level. This analysis further leads to a more general analysis on the appropriateness of introducing PDC topics, or other relatively advanced topics, to all undergraduate students in CS, or to consider newly defined educational degrees.

Keywords: Parallel and distributed programming · Curricula
Courses · Undergraduate · IT industry · Workforce

1 Introduction

Recent years have brought an explosive growth in multiprocessor computing, including multi-core processors and distributed data centers. The mass marketing of multi-cores and general-purpose graphics processing units induces the possibility for common users to rely on its effectiveness. This enforces the software developers to efficiently use it, and also to contribute to the technology development.

As a consequence, there is a clear need for undergraduate computer science education to be aware of the role that parallel and distributed computing technologies play in the computing landscape.

The ACM/IEEE Curricula 2013 Report [1] and the NSF/IEEE-TCPP Curriculum Initiative on Parallel and Distributed Computing [7], argue that the undergraduate computer science programs should include topics in parallel and

© Springer International Publishing AG, part of Springer Nature 2018
D. B. Heras and L. Bougé (Eds.): Euro-Par 2017 Workshops, LNCS 10659, pp. 240–251, 2018.
https://doi.org/10.1007/978-3-319-75178-8_20

distributed computing (PDC). This approach implies important changes and their impact should be carefully analyzed.

Babeş-Bolyai University is a top university in Romania, being also one of the oldest universities in the country. At the same time, it is a dynamic and constructive institution well integrated into society and oriented towards the future. The Faculty of Mathematics and Computer Science follows the Bologna system of study. In the last decade the number of students attending Computer Science has continuously increased, exceeding in 2016–2017 academic year 2600 students enrolled in undergraduate, graduate and doctoral programmes.

Parallel and distributed computing topics have been studied at our faculty especially at master level programs, but still there were some modules related to concurrency, multi-threading and client-server application, RPC, RMI included into the syllabi of some undergraduate courses. Since spreading PDC concepts across several courses encounters difficulties, which has been also emphasised in [4,5], in 2015 a dedicated compulsory course *Parallel and Distributed Programming* has been introduced for students in the third year of study. Before this, it was also an elective course *Paradigms and Techniques of Parallel Programming* that aimed to introduce the main concepts and paradigms of parallel programming; the syllabus changes for this course addresses more advanced topics.

In 2014 a master program with the title *High Performance Computing and Big Data Analytics* has been included into academic program of our faculty. This offers to students the possibility of acquisition of theoretical, applicative and practical knowledge in high performance computing, big data analytics, and on using HPC in data analysis.

In terms of PDC infrastructure, the university owns a hybrid (High Performance Computing + Cloud Computing) cluster, acquired in 2015, capable of reaching 40 Tflops in Rmax (sustained) and 62 Tflops in Rpeak (theoretical). The HPC component has 68 nodes with a total of 1360 physical computing cores overall. Also, 6 nodes are hosting an additional Intel Phi coprocessor, while 12 others are equipped with 2 Nvidia Tesla K40 GPU each.

This paper intends to present the evolution of courses that include modules from the topic of PDC. Also a broad analysis of the outcomes of these teaching subjects in correlation to the level of interest of the students for them is presented.

The next section presents the existing courses, and modules, and Sect. 3 describes the particular context of our region that has an important influence on the level of interest of the students for different subjects. Section 4 shows the analysis results and their correlation, and the final conclusions are presented in Sect. 5.

2   The Subject of Analysis

As in other reports on various curricula, we will use Bloom's classification [2] (B class) considering also a correlation to ACM level of mastery. So, we will use the following classes:

- K = Know the term (⇔ Familiarity)
- C = Comprehend so as to paraphrase/illustrate (⇔ Usage)
- A = Apply it in some way (requires operational command) (⇔ Assessment)
- N = Not in Core, but can be in an elective course

The courses from the undergraduate curriculum that address Parallel and Distributed Computing topics are presented in Table 1. The number of students enrolled is about 180 for a compulsory course and varies between 30 and 70 for an elective one.

Table 1. Undergraduate courses addressing PDC topics

Course name	Semester of study	ECTS	Hours per week (course, seminar, lab)
Operating Systems (OS)	2	5	2,1,2
Advanced Programming Methods (APM)	3	6	2,2,2
Computer Networks (CN)	3	6	2,0,2
Systems for Design and Implementation (SDI)	4	6	2,1,1
Parallel and Distributed Programming (PDP)	5	6	2,1,2
Paradigms and Techniques of Parallel Programming (elective) (PTPP)	6	7	2,0,1

At the master level there are other courses related to PDC from which we may mention the following: 'Formal Models of Concurrency', 'Operating Systems for Parallel and Distributed Architectures', 'Models in Parallel Programming', 'Functional Parallel Programming for Big Data Analytics', 'Workflow Systems', 'Grid, Cluster and Cloud Computing', 'Algorithms, Models, and Concepts in Distributed Systems', 'GPU and Distributed Architecture Computing'. Most of these courses are part of the *High Performance Computing and Big Data Analytics* or *Distributed Systems in Internet* graduate programmes' curriculum.

The next two tables emphasis (to a great extent but not completely) the PDC topics discussed in these courses. Table 2 presents some general topics with the focus on concepts, and Table 3 shows the topics for which concrete implementations are analysed.

A certain topic could be introduced in a certain course where the corresponding learning outcome belongs to (K) or (C) in Bloom's classification, and then it is discussed to a following course where the learning outcomes are moved to a more advanced level by Bloom's classification. So, for example, the semaphore concept is first introduced at *Operating Systems* course considering an outcome

Table 2. General conceptual topics. The table emphasizes the main concepts associated to the corresponding courses were they are discussed.

Topic	B class	Courses
SISD/SIMD/ SPMD/ MIMD	K	PDP, PTPP
Computation decomposition strategies	C	PDP, PTPP
Data Distribution	C	PDP, PTPP
Functional Decomposition	C	PDP, PTPP
PCAM methodology	K	PTPP
Synchronisation Concepts	C	OS, PDP, PTPP
processes, pipe, fifo	C	OS
critical section, race condition	C	OS, PDP, PTPP
mutex, semaphore, monitor	C	OS, PDP, PTPP
barriers, conditional variable	C	PDP, PTPP
deadlock, livelock	C	OS, PDP, PTPP
starvation, fairness	K	OS, PDP
Tasks and threads	C	APM, CN, PDP, PTPP
Non-determinism	C	PDP, PTPP
Performance metrics	C	PDP, PTPP
Speedup, Efficiency, Cost	C	PDP, PTPP
IsoEfficiency	K	PTPP
PRAM	C	PDP, PTPP
Brent Theorem	K	PTPP
Dependencies	A	PDP, PTPP
Task graphs	K	PDP, PTPP
Divide & conquer (parallel aspects)	A	PDP, PTPP
Recursion (parallel aspects)	C	PDP, PTPP
Master-slave	A	CN, PDP
Pipeline (parallel aspects)	A	PDP, PTPP
Scalability	K	PDP, PTPP
Granularity	K	PDP, PTPP

of class (K), and then is discussed again at *Parallel and Distributed Programming* course where a more deeply understanding is provided and also it is used in the context of the current implementations in Java or C#.

Examples of parallel algorithms are given especially at the *Paradigms and Techniques of Parallel Programming* course. In the curriculum there is a course of *Data Structures and Algorithms* – DSA, but at the moment the possible parallelization of the algorithms is not treated there. The parallelization techniques are introduced at PDP course, and then they are detailed at PTPP course. Still, time-complexity and space-complexity issues for sequential algorithms are analysed at DSA, and so when the parallel programs performance metrics are introduced we may start from some already introduced concepts.

Table 3. Specific topics ⇒ implementation oriented.

Topic	B class	Exemplification	Courses
Shared memory	A	Java, C/C++, C#	OS, PDP
Thread/Task spawning	A	Java, C/C++, C#	OS, APM, SDI, CN, PDP
Executors,Threads pools	A	Java	APM, PDP, PTPP
Work stealing	K	Java	PTPP
Synchronisation tools	A		OS, PDP, PTPP
mutex, semaphore	A	Java, C/C++, C#	OS, PDP, PTPP
barriers, conditional variable	A	Java, C	PDP, PTPP
Asynchrony	A		PDP, PTPP
Futures/promises/Async tasks	A	Java, C++	PDP, PTPP
Streams	A	Java	PDP, PTPP
Parallel loop	A	C/C++,OpenMP	PDP, PTPP
Hybrid	C	CUDA/C++	PDP, PTPP
Distributed memory	C		PDP, PTPP
Message passing	C	MPI, C/C++	PDP, PTPP
Broadcast, Scatter/Gather	C	MPI, C/C++	PDP, PTPP
Client Server	A	C/C++, Java, C#	SDI, CN, PDP
RPC, RMI	A	Java, C#	SDI
P2P	K		PDP

3   The Context of the Analysis

Cluj-Napoca is now the most important educational and economic center in Transylvania and the second largest in Romania after Bucharest and it has a long standing tradition in IT development - the beginnings of the computer sciences in Cluj are situated around the years 1960. According to a recent study, done by iTech Transilvania Cluster, Cluj has the highest density of IT employees in Romania, 1 in 25 employees working in this industry [10]. A decade ago, when most of the IT companies were founded, the main activity of Romanian software industry was outsourcing. On the long run this had scalability issues since the number of potential new employees, although raising, couldn't satisfy the increasing market demand. Another important factor was that man-day rates in neighbor countries were very competitive. What tip the balance in favor of Romanian IT specialists is that half of them are software developers and that almost 90% of them speak English. The economic factor also had an important influence in this together with the focus on education proven by students' results in Informatics and Math Olympiads or software competitions over the years [6].

Outsourcing is still the main activity but the current trends are moving towards innovation (startups or developing of own products) and providing high level roles (such as solution architects, business analysts or project managers) and business knowledge to clients in order to achieve added value for the constantly increased rates.

There are some IT companies in the region that are starting to work with big data analytics, but to the best of our knowledge, there is no one involved in software development that implies scientific computation.

The cooperation between students and companies starts usually with an internship program (required by the academic curriculum), which is followed by real employment before graduation. So, when we discuss the impact of some changes in the academic curriculum, we have to consider the fact that the feedback that we obtain from students, includes also, indirectly, a feedback from industry.

There is a known gap between academic world and the industry. The industry is productivity oriented with some expense in the software quality. Consolidated frameworks, libraries and APIs are frequently used in the development, alongside development tools that are required in a productive environment.

This is why there are companies that can afford to hire students even from their first years of study, and encourage them for early employment with the promise that they will learn "all they have to know" at the workplace. Of course their perspective is on the present day, without considering the future. This comes with the drawback that students focus less on obtaining general knowledge in computer science and they start learning/using only specific fields of computer science (databases, user interface development, etc.). Often enough students that are not yet employed are reluctant to learn things that wouldn't help them during an internship or a job interview.

The development is very often based on *"applying patterns..."* but the meaning of the term – pattern, in this context, is not the same with the one used in [3], where it is used to emphasise the situation when a design pattern (a well defined solution) is used in a new context in a creative way. Here, we have to understand that the software is built using specific framework and technologies by composing components based on some specific recipes. So, many times the developers build the software by using some tools and without a deep understanding of what they are really doing. The leading questions are: *"how to do"*, *"what to apply"* and not *"why"*, or *"what is hidden behind"*.

It is important to say that the described situation has a large spreading, but it is not generalized. Not all companies adopt this kind of development, but there is a large majority that has an important influence.

The university purpose is to prepare the young minds for whatever is out there in the industry without limiting the knowledge to a specific area. The graduates need to acquire enough information from all the fields in such a way that they can face the industry switches without too much effort, having the basics in place.

4   The Analysis

In order to move from "traditional" development to distributed development, the students need to possess the most basic knowledge of development. It is always easier to 'build' on top of something that has solid ground. The challenges that come from the current industry context (students start focusing on employment rather than finalising their studies) trigger different approaches regarding teaching techniques:

- Before moving to a topic that requires specific background, we need to validate that students have this background; this comes with the drawback that some of the students that already have the background cannot move faster to the specific distributed programming topics, and they become distrustful.
- Some of the important courses have been condensed or made elective in order to accommodate the students needs to have the bare minimum knowledge for employment.

In our study we went from the premise that the success of introducing new topics in the curriculum, and consequently achieving the desired learning outcomes, depends in a great measure on the level of interest of the students in that topic. In the context described in the previous section, we are aware that the level of interest of the students for one topic and another depend very much if they are working for a company or not, and when they have started to do this.

So, the first steps of our investigation was to find out the level of interest of students for the topics specified in Tables 1 and 2. For each topic they have been asked to choose a value between 1 and 5 (1 represents the lowest level of interest and 5 represents the highest level of interest). The students of the second and third year of study have been asked to participate in our analysis. The results are reflected in Tables 4 and 5.

The differences between the two categories are given by the fact that the students of the second year haven't studied yet some of the questionnaire included topics, but also by the distribution of their employment per year of study:

- 10% students of the first year of study,
- 25% students of the second year of study,
- 60% students of the third year of study,
- 75% students at the end of the third year.

(The students have a mandatory internship of 3 weeks between the 2nd and the 3rd year, and this is the moment when almost all get hired.)

Parallel programming is not easy if we have to control threads/processes executions, synchronization, communication, etc. As the level of abstraction is increasing, the things could become simpler, but an associated performance degradation could appear, too [8]. So, we may work with frameworks and libraries that make the parallel programming easier and probably more attractive for students. On the other hand, this way the main concurrency issues will not be well understood. Also, in contexts where the performance is a critical issue, the ability to work only with high level frameworks would not be enough.

There is a large interest from students to learn APIs and tools that implicitly use parallelization without the explicit control from the programmers (Java parallel streams, Scala parallel collection, OpenMP). This approach has the advantage of offering a simple and rapid development and also offers a high degree

Table 4. Level of interest for general conceptual topics.

Topic	Level of interest 2nd year	Level of interest 3rd year
SISD/SIMD/ SPMD/ MIMD	1	1.87
Computation decomposition strategies	1	4.5
Data Distribution	1.37	3
Functional Decomposition	1	3.12
PCAM methodology	1	3.25
Synchronisation Concepts	2.56	3.75
processes, pipe, fifo	3.75	3
critical section, race condition	1.5	3.25
mutex, semaphore, monitor	2.25	3.18
barriers, conditional variable	1.62	3.25
deadlock, livelock	3	4.37
starvation, fairness	1	3
Tasks and threads	3.75	4.5
Non-determinism	1.31	3.87
Performance metrics	2.87	3.12
Speedup, Efficiency, Cost	3.06	4.25
IsoEfficiency	1.25	1.75
PRAM	1	2
Brent Theorem	1	1.75
Dependencies	2.37	3
Task graphs	1.62	1.87
Divide & conquer (parallel aspects)	3.68	2.75
Recursion (parallel aspects)	3.81	2.62
Master-slave	1.5	4.25
Pipeline (parallel aspects)	3	3.37
Scalability	2.06	3
Granularity	1.37	2

of confidence in the correctness of the resulted code. It is known that parallel programming is sensitive to hidden errors that are very difficult to detect and hence to debug. On the other hand the programmers are limited to the defined constructions, and also cannot control very well the level of performance.

The analysis includes also the results obtained by the students for the tests and assignments of the curriculum required course *Parallel and Distributed Programming*. The evaluation for this course has been based on the followings tests and assignments:

1. Practical works/assignments (relative short problems that should have been implemented using discussed strategies and technologies);
2. Multithreading practical test (a problem of medium complexity that had to be solved using threads – explicit thread creation);
3. MPI practical test (a simple problem that had to be solved using MPI);
4. Theoretical test (written exam).

Table 5. Level of interest for the specific topics.

Topic	Exemplification	Level of interest -2nd year	Level of interest -3rd year
Shared memory	Java, C/C++, C#	2.12	3.62
Thread/Task spawning	Java, C/C++, C#	2.93	4.12
Executors,Threads pools	Java, C#	2.31	4.5
Work stealing	Java(ForkJoin)	1.37	4
Synchronisation tools			
mutex, semaphore	Java, C/C++, C#	2.75	3.75
barriers, cond.variable	Java, C/C++	2.25	3.25
Asynchrony			
Futures/promises		1.5	4.12
Async tasks	Java, C++	3	3.12
Streams	Java	2.06	4.25
Parallel loop	C/C++,OpenMP	3.25	3.75
Hybrid	CUDA/C++	2.25	2
Distributed memory			
Message passing	MPI, C/C++	2	2.12
Broadcast, Scatter/Gather		3.25	2
Client Server	C/C++, Java, C#	4.25	4
RPC, RMI		3.68	2.75
P2P		1.75	2.75

The corresponding results for these evaluations are presented in Fig. 1. Practical works included:

– some multithreading examples in C/C++, Java, and C#,
– examples that use OpenMP,
– a very simple CUDA example,
– a client-server application that also includes asynchronous tasks, and
– a simple MPI example.

The students had to solved them independently, at home, and then present them to the instructors.

The practical tests assume solving a given problem in a given period of time, on the students' laptops – if they chosen this way; computers from the faculty laboratories could also be used.

From these results, we may consider that MPI programming have been proved difficult for students. A deeper analysis emphasizes that, in fact, the interest of the students in learning MPI was low.

The students are much more confronted to using multithreading programming, for different types of applications, and this leads to a much better knowledge acquisition. This includes working with threads directly or using APIs such as: OpenMP or Java Streams.

The theoretical evaluation shows the fact that even students initially declare that they have certain interest in studying concepts, still either because they

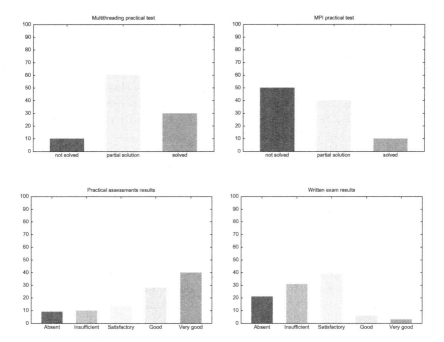

Fig. 1. Evaluation results.

don't have enough time (being involved in others activities as working for companies) or because they looses their ability for theoretical approaches, the results are not very good.

Since the students are soon to be enrolled in productive activities, they are much oriented on practical skills. Hence, the results obtained for practical works in correspondence with the results of the theoretical test confirm this situation.

For the elective course *Paradigms and techniques of parallel programming* (PTPP) the students have been allowed to choose a paradigm and a technology for solving a problem in a parallel way. This problem could have been chosen from a list of proposed problems, but the students also had the possibility to propose new ones. From the 35 students that attended this course in the current academic year (2016–2017), only one has chosen MPI as a programming model. All the others chosen to go on the multithreading paradigm and to use different implementation languages (Java – 23, C# – 5, C++ – 4, Scala –2). The project also required to do a written documentation that includes design pattern oriented analysis of the design decisions, theoretical performance evaluation and results of a set of the empirical testing.

At this elective course, some techniques of algorithm parallelization are discussed, and some concrete examples for well know problems are analyzed (sorting, searching, matrix multiplication algorithms, ...). Even if the level of interest for these was not formally evaluated, we may say that the students consider them interesting. These techniques have been used in a certain measure by the students in the development of their projects.

Even for this elective course, which is chosen by the students that have an increased interest in parallel programming, the students' choices are influenced by the mainstream technologies and their abilities in working in a specific programming language. These abilities are on their turn influenced by their personal experience, which is, in a vast majority of cases, driven by their employers and industry demands, not by the academic environment.

We have also received some informal feedback from direct discussions with the students that emphasizes the fact that an orientation on distributed aspects of programming is considered by them much useful than an orientation on parallelization techniques and tools.

5   Conclusions

The main conclusion of our experience with teaching PDC topics is that even if they are very necessary and important to be studied, due to the last development of systems architectures and of the associated programming, it is also very important to take into consideration the latest approaches and paradigms applied in the IT industry. The need for high productivity induces some changes in the way the programming activity and software systems construction are developed. All these lead to a new category of software developers which are not supposed to understand all the components that they usually assemble. An adapted and simplified curriculum could be in this case specified. In such a curriculum some PDC topics should be included, but in a pragmatic, usage-oriented way – how to use parallel programming frameworks/libraries, etc.

Also, there are some topics – as MPI – that have a great importance for the well understanding of some basic concepts of Parallel and Distributed Programming, but they are not yet very much used in the industry. This leads to a low level of interest for this topic from the undergraduate students.

Also, the acquisition of the theoretical concepts and general principles is not very good, since our students are now, very much oriented on achieving practical abilities.

Master students that choose a specialization that includes High Performance Computing, have of course, a much higher degree of interest and opening to fields as Scientific Computation, Models of Computation, or Correctness and Formal Methods.

The premise of our study was that the success of introducing new topics in the undergraduate curriculum, and most importantly achieving the desired learning outcomes, depend in a great measure on the level of interest of the students in that topic. This premise proved to be correct.

On the other hand, the level of interest on different topics of Parallel and Distributed Computing depends very much on the students' levels. The distinction between undergraduate and master students is very clear, but between undergraduates we may emphasise at least two classes of interest.

A solution could be based on moving more topics on the elective courses. Another, more complex solution, would involved also other Computer Science fields and introducing a new defined educational degree. A proposal that comes from the Cluj Innovation City Project - a project of the Cluj IT Cluster [11] - is to develop *Vocational Studies*. The proposal claims that this way an important part of the IT industry employees could come directly from an IT related vocational curriculum, and this would reduce part of the pressure on the employment market, but most importantly would engage young people into the industry in their early twenties. (The drawbacks of this proposal have not been studied, yet.)

There is an important trend in the software development in using Parallel and Distributed Computing and, at the same time, in using more efficiently the present hardware resources. There is also a wide acceptance that "Parallelism is the future of programming". Still, we may paraphrase the title of the paper of Domenico Talia: "Parallel computation still not ready for the mainstream" [9] and say: "Mainstream still not ready for [all kind of] Parallel Computation".

References

1. ACM/IEEE-CS Joint Task Force on Computing Curricula: Computer Science Curricula 2013. Technical report, ACM Press and IEEE Computer Society Press, December 2013. https://dx.doi.org/10.1145/2534860
2. Bloom, B.S., Engelhart, M.D., Furst, E.J., Hill, W.H., Krathwohl, D.R.: Taxonomy of Educational Objectives: The Classification of Educational Goals. Handbook I: Cognitive Domain. David McKay Company, New York (1956)
3. Gamma, E., Helm, R., Johnson, R., Vlissides, J.: Design Patterns: Elements of Reusable Object-Oriented Software. Addison-Wesley Longman Publishing Co. Inc., Boston (1994)
4. John, D.J., Thomas, S.J.: Parallel and distributed computing across the computer science curriculum. In: IEEE International Parallel and Distributed Processing Symposium Workshops (IPDPSW) (2014)
5. Lu, G., Xu, J., Liu, J., Dai, B., Gui, S., Zhan, S.: Integrating parallel and distributed computing topics into an undergraduate CS curriculum at UESTC. In: IEEE International Parallel and Distributed Processing Symposium Workshop (IPDPSW) (2015)
6. Martin, B.: The Silicon Valley of Transylvania, April 2016. https://techcrunch.com/2016/04/06/the-silicon-valley-of-transylvania/. Accessed 10 May 2017
7. Prasad, S.K., et al.: NSF/IEEE-TCPP curriculum on parallel and distributed computing - core topics for undergraduates - version I (2012). http://cs.gsu.edu/~tcpp/curriculum/. Accessed 10 May 2017
8. Skillicorn, D.B., Talia, D.: Models and languages for parallel computation. ACM Comput. Surv. **30**(2), 123–169 (1998)
9. Talia, D.: Parallel computation still not ready for the mainstream. Commun. ACM **40**(7), 98–99 (1997)
10. ARIES Transilvania: iTech Transilvania cluster study by ARIES. http://itech.aries-transilvania.ro/. Accessed 10 May 2017
11. Cluj IT Cluster: Cluj Innovaton City. http://www.clujit.ro/236/cluj-innovaton-city/. Accessed 10 May 2017

Cellular ANTomata: A Tool for Early PDC Education

Arnold L. Rosenberg[✉]

Computer and Information Science, Northeastern University,
Boston, MA 02115, USA
rsnbrg@cs.umass.edu

Abstract. The thesis of this essay is that the *Cellular ANTomaton* (CAnt) computational model—obtained by deploying a team of mobile finite-state machines (the model's "Ants") upon a *cellular automaton* (CA)—can be a highly effective platform for introducing early undergraduate students to a broad range of concepts relating to *parallel and distributed computing* (*PDC*). CAnts permit many sophisticated PDC concepts to be taught within a unified, perspicuous model and then experimented with using the many easily accessed systems for simulating CAs and CAnts. Space restrictions limit us to supporting the thesis via only three important PDC concepts: synchronization, (algorithmic) scalability, and leader election (symmetry breaking). Having a single versatile pedagogical platform facilitates the goal of endowing *all* undergraduate students with a level of computational literacy adequate for success in an era characterized increasingly by ubiquitous parallel and/or distributed computing devices.

Keywords: Cellular automata and ANTomata
Teaching PDC to early undergrads

1 Introduction

1.1 Our Overall Goal

A. Computational literacy for all. The current era is characterized by ubiquitous computational devices. As such devices proliferate, they also become more sophisticated, containing multiple processors and/or cores. Indeed, we employ *parallel and distributed computing* (*PDC*) when we drive cars, use household appliances, go shopping, ... It is now widely recognized (cf. [15]) that *all* undergraduate students—all the more so those who aspire to a career in a computation-related field—must achieve a level of computational literacy adequate to succeed in our computing-rich society—and such literacy must encompass PDC and its enabling technologies. The thesis of this essay is that the *Cellular ANTomaton* (CAnt) computation model [18]—obtained by deploying a team of mobile finite-state machines (the model's "Ants") atop a *cellular automaton* (CA)—has traits that recommend it as a conceptual platform for introducing early undergraduate

© Springer International Publishing AG, part of Springer Nature 2018
D. B. Heras and L. Bougé (Eds.): Euro-Par 2017 Workshops, LNCS 10659, pp. 252–265, 2018.
https://doi.org/10.1007/978-3-319-75178-8_21

students to a broad range of sophisticated notions relating to *PDC*. We support this thesis by discussing three sophisticated PDC concepts that CANTs render accessible to early students. With more space, we could easily expand this list.

Benefit #1 of CANT-based Pedagogy. CANTs *provide a single perspicuous platform for many core PDC concepts. Thereby, students need not master a range of platforms as they strive to master a variety of core concepts.*

B. What is computational literacy? We define "computational literacy" via three main features. For a *core concept* as defined in, e.g., [15], we expect a student to provide a:

1. *precise definition*—to a degree of rigor commensurate with the student's level;
2. *rudimentary implementation*—on a "reasonably simplified" computing platform;
3. *rudimentary analysis of an implementation on a "reasonably simplified" platform.*

"Reasonable simplifications" include, e.g., assuming that a key constant is a power of 2 or a perfect square or assuming that CANTs' constituent agents[1] act (perfectly) synchronously, rather than only approximately synchronously (cf. [5, 22]).

1.2   Illustrating CANT-Pedagogy via Some "Core" Concepts

A. The illustrative core concepts. We defend our pedagogical thesis by discussing "reasonably simplified" versions of three core PDC concepts. We chose these concepts because they invoke different strengths and features of the CANT model.

1. *Synchronization.* The *Firing Squad Synchronization Protocol (FSSP)*—see [8,13]—allows the agents of arbitrarily large CANTs to initiate a process at the same step. A "reasonably simplified" FSSP should be accessible to early students.
   Enrichment opportunity #1. *A more advanced discussion could also address synchronicity—how to control* clock skew [5, 22] *so that agents in neighboring cells "hear" temporally proximate clock signals almost simultaneously.*
2. *Scalability.* For many problems, one can craft a single algorithm that works on CANTs having arbitrarily many agents.
3. *Symmetry breaking (leader election).* Initiating concurrent procedures is more challenging for *distributed* agents than for *parallel* ones. CANTs admit a simple, efficient "leader-election" protocol for their (distributed) Ants.

With more space we could easily expand this list. As but two examples, the mesh structure underlying CAs and CANTs provides access to the following important topics. (*a*) The observation that many genres of computation can

---

[1] "Agents" comprise the *parallel* FSMs within a CA $\mathcal{C}$ and the *distributed* Ants atop $\mathcal{C}$.

be orchestrated as waves of data that pass though an array of identical computing agents spawned the elegant notion of *systolic array*: a highly structured form of *data flow* [11]. This topic has since advanced along several fronts [1,16]. (*b*) The advent of *massively* parallel computers via fragile VLSI-based technology heightened awareness of the importance of *fault tolerance*. Elegant and effective schemes have been developed for tolerating both faults and failures in mesh-based systems; cf. [7,10]. The details within the five just-cited sources are too sophisticated for beginning students, but the underlying ideas are readily accessible.

B. Our goal. We strive to help instructors appeal to a range of students, from the nonspecialist to the aspiring professional, as they teach our illustrative PDC-related concepts.

- Striving to serve the entire target range of students, we discuss *synchronization* in Sect. 3 via a verbally described synchronization algorithm, together with a small simulation of the algorithm and a simplified timing analysis.
- We discuss *scalability* in Sect. 4 via two examples. One is treated via an elementary verbally described algorithm. The other accompanies a verbally described algorithm with a program in pseudo-code and a proof of validity.
- We discuss *symmetry breaking/leader election* in Sect. 5 via a verbally described algorithm accompanied by a proof of validity and timing analysis.

1.3 Platforms for Implementing PDC Concepts

Implementing concepts helps students assimilate often-subtle details. The following tools provide quite distinct "programming" styles for simulating CANTs.

- *NETLOGO* [14] employs a rather general agent-based approach.
- *CARPET* [21] specifies Agents via *case-statement* programs.
- *MATLAB*® processes array-structured data using declarative programming.

Additionally, certain *systolic* computations can be specified perspicuously; cf. [1,16].

Benefit #2 of CANT-based Pedagogy. *Several well-developed tools enable students to craft implementations of core concepts and experiment with them.*

1.4 A (Very) Brief History of CAs and CANTs

CAs have been studied since at least the 1960s [13] and continue to be of interest to this day [6,8]. They provide an attractive alternative to other formal models of computers [23], combining mathematical simplicity with levels of efficiency that make them feasible candidates for many real computational tasks. Indeed, CAs are remarkably efficient for a broad range of tasks that require the tight coordination of many simple agents [2,3,8,13]. In [2], CAs implement an ant-inspired clustering algorithm; in [3], they support an ant-inspired algorithm for a genre of flow problem. In [12], a CA-like model greedily pre-plans a route for a single robot to a single goal, by having the goal broadcast its position. Several recent CA-based robotics-motivated studies appear in [20]. CANTs are introduced in [18], and algorithms are developed for some robotics-inspired problems. In contrast to CANTs, the models in the preceding sources support algorithms that are: • fully synchronous (there is a single clock that is "heard" by all agents); • centrally controlled (there is a central planner); • not scalable (the central planner knows and exploits the size of the system). Some models are centrally programmable, using systems such as CARPET [21]; their global name spaces preclude scalability. CAs have also been used for rather general suites of parallel-computing applications in [21] and related sources. Algorithms for (bio-inspired) pattern matching appear in [9] for one-dimensional CAs and in [19] for (two-dimensional) CANTs.

2   A Technical Introduction to CAs and CANTs

2.1   Overview of the Models

A *cellular automaton* (CA) is obtained by placing a copy of a single *finite-state machine* (*FSM*) at each cell of a *square mesh*. A *Cellular ANTomaton* (CANT) is obtained by deploying a team of mobile FSMs (*Ants*) atop a CA, at most one Ant per cell. Each FSM communicates at each step with the FSMs within cells that are adjacent along the eight compass directions ($E, SE, S, SW, W, NW, N, NE$); it also communicates with an Ant that resides in its cell. Ants communicate with their host FSM and with any Ants that reside in adjacent cells. FSMs detect when the mesh-cell they reside in is on an edge or at a corner; thereby, a CANT can ensure that Ants never "fall off" the mesh. The preceding informal definition will suffice for many styles of early introductory course. For other styles, one could add detail and formalism, as found in, e.g., [17,18].

Enrichment Opportunity #2. *One can distinguish Ants as physical devices (say, robots) or as virtual algorithmic devices (which can simplify subprocessing). In the former case, one could discuss inter-cellular message-transmission speeds: the electronic propagation of signals vs. the electro-mechanical movement of Ants.*

2.2   Pedagogically Useful Details

A. (Orthant) Meshes. We enable teaching opportunities by building the world of CAs and CANTs atop the (infinite) 2-*dimensional orthant mesh*[2], whose *cells* are labeled by all nonnegative integer-pairs, $\{\langle i, j \rangle \mid i, j \geq 0\}$. Each mesh-cell $\langle i, j \rangle$ has ≤ 8 types of *neighbors* (or, *adjacencies*), corresponding to the 8 compass directions; see Fig. 1(left).

---

[2] Our 2-*dimensional* (orthant) mesh is easily restricted to one dimension or extended to three.

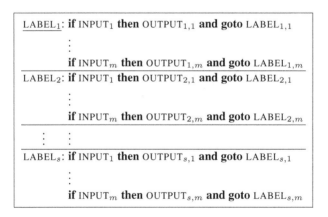

Fig. 1. A "prefix" of: (left) a mesh $\mathcal{M}_n$; (center) a cellular automaton [CA] whose cells contain copies of an FSM F; (right) a Cellular ANTomaton [CAnt] with three Ants.

B. Finite-State Machines. As their name suggests, finite-state machines (*FSMs*) were historically viewed as abstract machines (such as, say, elevators) whose behavior could be described and analyzed by characterizing "states" in which all "interesting" actions occurred. Myriad texts (e.g., [17]) adopt this view of FSMs. When teaching introductory computer science courses, though, students may be more receptive to viewing (and experimenting with) FSMs specified as *programs of case statements*, of the form indicated in Fig. 2.[3] One can simulate the operation of the FSM specified by such a program by iteratively cycling through the specified conditions until one finds one that applies.

LABEL$_1$: **if** INPUT$_1$ **then** OUTPUT$_{1,1}$ **and goto** LABEL$_{1,1}$

   $\vdots$

   if INPUT$_m$ **then** OUTPUT$_{1,m}$ **and goto** LABEL$_{1,m}$

LABEL$_2$: **if** INPUT$_1$ **then** OUTPUT$_{2,1}$ **and goto** LABEL$_{2,1}$

   $\vdots$

   if INPUT$_m$ **then** OUTPUT$_{2,m}$ **and goto** LABEL$_{2,m}$

 $\vdots$ $\vdots$

LABEL$_s$: **if** INPUT$_1$ **then** OUTPUT$_{s,1}$ **and goto** LABEL$_{s,1}$

   $\vdots$

   if INPUT$_m$ **then** OUTPUT$_{s,m}$ **and goto** LABEL$_{s,m}$

Fig. 2. A finite-state machine (FSM) F specified via a program of case statements.

C. CAs and CANTs. One turns a mesh $\mathcal{M}$ into a CA $\mathcal{C}$ as follows.

- • Populate $\mathcal{M}$'s cells with copies of a single FSM F, one per cell (Fig. 1 (center)); we refer to the FSM at cell $\langle i, j \rangle$ as $\mathsf{F}^{\langle i,j \rangle}$.
  • Endow FSMs with bidirectional communication channels to FSMs in neighboring cells and to resident Ants (when they exist).

---

[3] The CARPET programming environment [21] employs a similar programming style.

- • Deploy $c \geq 0$ Ants on $\mathcal{M}$, at most one Ant per cell.
  - • Endow each Ant $\mathcal{A}$ with bidirectional communication channels to Ants in neighboring cells and to the FSM in the cell that $\mathcal{A}$ is standing on.
- Endow FSMs and Ants with sensors: FSMs sense a resident Ant; FSMs and Ants sense mesh-edges, obstacles, and goal-objects (when relevant).

At each step: each copy of F polls the states of FSMs in neighboring cells and of any Ant that resides on F's cell; each Ant $\mathcal{A}$ polls the state of the FSM in its current cell plus the states of Ants on neighboring cells. Based on these polls, FSMs and Ants performs actions such as sending signals (an FSM may, e.g., tell its resident Ant to move). FSMs and Ants then change state—and the cycle repeats.

3   Synchronization

Synchronization in parallel/distributed systems seems at first blush to be an advanced topic that requires substantial background. In fact, for CAs and CANTs, the topic can be taught with varying levels of rigor to students having varying levels of preparation.

3.1   FSSP: The Firing Squad Synchronization Problem

We describe an algorithm for synchronizing Agents within CANTs, in a way that can "unfold" through a series of courses in the CS/CE curriculum, from a CS0-type course (e.g., "Computer Literacy") through a course in algorithm design/analysis.

- The motivation for and definition of the colorfully named *Firing Squad Synchronization Problem* (*FSSP*, for short) should be accessible to students even in a CS0-level course. This can whet students' appetites for more advanced courses by exposing them to a problem that is both interesting and non-"programmy."
- The solution to the FSSP sketched here should be accessible to students in any course that introduces recursion (as an algorithmic control structure). Students can observe a sophisticated recursion within a "reasonably simplified" framework, solving a problem that some students will initially doubt can even be solved.
- Our "simplified" analysis of the FSSP should be accessible to students whose algorithmic preparation includes the Master Theorem for Linear Recurrences [4].

The FSSP can be specified informally as follows. Start with n identical autonomous Agents standing (*physically or logically*) contiguously along row 0 of a mesh. Each Agent can communicate *only* with its immediate neighbors. (The two end Agents have one neighbor each; all others have two neighbors, one on each side.) The initially *dormant* Agents must enter an *active* state *at the exact same step* when told to do so by the leftmost ("leader") Agent. The Agents' only tool for accomplishing the task is their limited ability to intercommunicate.

Solutions to the *one-dimensional* FSSP (the version just described) have been known since at least 1962 [13]. Easily, any solution requires at least $2n - 2$ steps, just so a message can reach the farthest Agent and this Agent can respond to the leader. *There exist solutions that use only this number of steps—in fact, using only 1-bit inter-Agent messages* [8]. Surprisingly, any solution to the one-dimensional FSSP can be converted to a solution for any k-dimensional FSSP *that operates in exactly the same number of steps.* (**Note:** *This is actually a readily accessible exercise for even early students.*)

3.2   A Simplified Solution to the FSSP

We sketch a recursive algorithm for the FSSP that operates in roughly $3n$ steps instead of the optimal $2n - 2$ steps. We then provide a "simplified" analysis that avoids floors and ceilings. This algorithm and analysis should be accessible to students at many levels. Beginning students should "get the basic idea"; students who have the basics of recursion and linear recurrences should understand the "simplified" details; really clever students should be able to build on this setting to obtain an improved solution.

A. A simple recursive solution. The solution has each Agent send messages of two types to its neighbors. These messages do not individually instigate actions; it is the *co-arrival* of messages of distinct types that triggers actions, as will become clear. Our verbal sketch ignores certain details that complicate the "end game" of the FSSP; these details do appear (beginning at step 15) in our illustration of the process in Fig. 3.

1. The initial stage. The leader Agent, ([▢] in the figure) initiates the process by sending two messages, m_1 (● in the figure) and m_2 (○ in the figure), to its eastward neighbor. Message m_1 is sent immediately; message m_2 is sent at step 3.

   – Message m_1 travels at the rate of one Agent per step. It is relayed from each receiving Agent to its eastward neighbor until it reaches the end of the line of Agents, at which point it begins to travel westward at the same rate. (On this return trip, each receiving Agent relays m_1 to its westward neighbor.)
   – Message m_2 travels at the rate of one Agent every third step. It also is relayed from each receiving Agent to its eastward neighbor.

At some point, messages m_1 and m_2 meet, i.e., arrive simultaneously, at some Agent $\mathcal{A}_i$. At this point, $\mathcal{A}_i$ becomes a *subleader* (□ in the figure).

2. The inductive stage. Every newly anointed subleader recursively initiates the described process simultaneously and independently into the half-line of Agents to its left and into the half-line of Agents to its right. During these recursive invocations: (*a*) references to "left" and "right" are adjusted in the obvious way; (*b*) a (sub)leader encountered by a message in transit plays the same role as an end of the line.

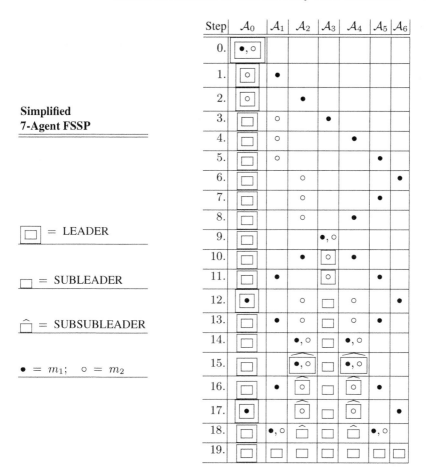

Fig. 3. The FSP synchronization protocol illustrated for seven Agents

3. **Terminating the process.** The process terminates when an Agent learns that both of its neighbors are subleaders—which will occur at the same step for all Agents. Figure 3 illustrates the sketched procedure for seven Agents. Note in Fig. 3 that the detailed algorithm suffers additional complication during the "end game" of a synchronization, to accommodate the (unknown) number n. To wit, from step 15 in the figure onward, we employ *sub-subleaders* ($\widehat{\square}$ in the figure) to prevent a subleader from activating too soon. Note also that the rightmost Agent (A_6 in the figure) acts differently from other Agents. This does not mean that A_6 differs structurally, only that the absence of a righthand neighbor modifies its behavior—specifically, with respect to termination.

B. Analyzing the recursion. We verify that the process terminates for all Agents at the same step by showing that messages m_1 and m_2 meet during the initial stage at the midpoint of the line of Agents. (The analysis then recurses down to quarter-points, eighth-points, etc.) To see this: Say that m_1 and m_2 meet when t steps have passed since the initiation of the process. Ignoring floors and ceilings, during this time:

(a) message m_2 travels $t/3$ steps eastward;

(b) message m_1 travels n steps eastward then $x = t - n$ steps westward.

Clearly, m_2 has traveled from the leader to $\mathcal{A}_{t/3}$, while m_1 has traveled from the leader to $\mathcal{A}_{n-x}$, where $n - x = 2n - t$. But m_1 and m_2 *meet* at this time, so $t/3 = 2n - t$ or, equivalently, $t = \frac{3}{2}n$. This analysis verifies the algorithm's validity and also allows us to estimate the number of steps, $T(n)$ needed to synchronize n Agents:

$$T(n) \;=\; \frac{3}{2}n + T\left(\frac{1}{2}n\right) \;=\; \frac{3}{2}\left(1 + \frac{1}{2} + \frac{1}{4} + \cdots\right)n \;=\; 3n - \frac{3}{2}.$$

Our recursive procedure thus allows the n Agents to synchronize within $3n$ steps.

4   (Algorithmic) Scalability in CANTS

Our algorithm for the FSSP never refers to the number of Agents being synchronized; instead it uses the positions of the "leader" and the rightmost Agent as the delimiters of the messages that enable the synchronization. It is this feature—the fact that *a single algorithm works for* CANTs *of arbitrary sizes*—that we identify as *(algorithmic) scalability*. Of course, there are other valuable notions of scalability in PDC, but ours has advantages: (a) It requires no background beyond basic definitions. (b) It can be accessible to beginning students. (c) It can engage the students by requiring some thought to achieve. We present two computational problems that illustrate these advantages.

4.1   Example #1: Scalably Creating Square Meshes from Orthant Meshes

"Natural" computational problems for a CANT $\mathcal{C}$ usually operate within a *(finite) square* mesh, rather than the semi-infinite orthant mesh. For many such problems—specifically those that supply an input to $\mathcal{C}$ in the form of a length-n pattern $\sigma_0 \cdots \sigma_{n-1}$ left-justified along mesh-row 0—the following simple—and *scalable*—process converts the orthant mesh to a square mesh that is "natural" for the problem. See Fig. 4.

1. Simultaneously (via an FSP-synch, i.e., a synchronization using the FSSP):

   (a) $\mathcal{A}^{\langle 0,0 \rangle}$ sends a southeasterly signal, which is propagated toward the southeast, i.e., toward cell $\langle n-1, n-1 \rangle$;

   (b) $\mathcal{A}^{\langle 0,n-1 \rangle}$—which knows its identity because its easterly neighbor contains no σ-symbol—sends a signal that is propagated southward (toward $\langle n-1, n-1 \rangle$).

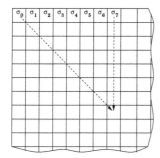 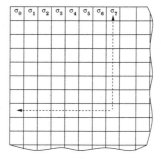

Fig. 4. Using an input pattern to delimit a square mesh from an orthant mesh: (left) measuring the square; (right) establishing the square mesh's eastern and southern boundaries.

> Because CANTs operate synchronously (one of our "reasonable simplifications"), the signals from $\mathcal{A}^{\langle 0,0 \rangle}$ and $\mathcal{A}^{\langle 0,n-1 \rangle}$ arrive simultaneously at $\langle n-1, n-1 \rangle$.

2. When $\mathcal{A}^{\langle n-1,n-1 \rangle}$ receives the signals from $\mathcal{A}^{\langle 0,0 \rangle}$ and $\mathcal{A}^{\langle 0,n-1 \rangle}$, it simultaneously:

   (a) sends a message YOU ARE A BOTTOM CELL westward;
   (b) sends a message YOU ARE A RIGHT-EDGE CELL northward;
   (c) initiates an FSP-synch among all cells to its northwest.

After this $O(n)$-step process:

   – the cells $\{\langle i,j \rangle \mid 0 \leq i,j \leq n-1\}$, the copies of $\mathcal{A}$ within these cells, and the Ants residing on these cells can function as an $n \times n$ CANT $\mathcal{C}_n$;
   – the cells $\{\langle i,j \rangle \mid [0 \leq i \leq n-1], [j = n-1]\}$ function as the "right edge" of $\mathcal{C}_n$;
   – the cells $\{\langle i,j \rangle \mid [i = n-1], [0 \leq j \leq n-1]\}$ function as the "bottom row" of $\mathcal{C}_n$.

4.2   A Scalable Pattern-Reversing CANT

The *Pattern-Reversal Problem* on an $n \times n$ mesh begins with an n-symbol input pattern $\Pi = \sigma_0 \cdots \sigma_{n-1}$ along row 0. The challenge is to design a CANT $\mathcal{C}$ that copies Π along row $n-1$ *in reversed order*. Our CANT $\mathcal{C}$ employs n identical *virtual* Ants, $\mathcal{A}_0, \ldots, \mathcal{A}_{n-1}$, with each $\mathcal{A}_k$ deployed initially on cell $\langle 0,k \rangle$. Figure 5 sketches a program that is shared by all Ants $\mathcal{A}$. The sketch is easily expanded to a formal program as in Fig. 2—*that nowhere mentions the length n of pattern Π*.

Figure 6 depicts the n-step (not counting the initiating FSP-synch) "multi-trajectory" for $\mathcal{C}$ mandated by the program of Fig. 5. To validate $\mathcal{C}$'s solution, focus on an Ant $\mathcal{A}_r$ that begins at a cell $\langle 0,r \rangle$. When $\mathcal{A}_r$ takes a *southwesterly* (resp., *southeasterly*) step, this adds $\langle +1,-1 \rangle$ (resp., $\langle +1,+1 \rangle$) to $\mathcal{A}_r$'s current cell's coordinates. It follows that, under the dogleg patterns of Fig. 6, $\mathcal{A}_r$'s trajectory consists of:

At each step:	
Case	**Action**
$\mathcal{A}$ on $\mathcal{M}_n$'s left edge	- delays one step
	- then moves symbol one cell *southeastward*
$\mathcal{A}$ moving southeastward	continues toward $\mathcal{M}_n$'s bottom edge
$\mathcal{A}$ on $\mathcal{M}_n$'s bottom edge	deposits its symbol and **halts**
Otherwise	$\mathcal{A}$ moves symbol one cell southwestward

Fig. 5. A sketch of a program for one of $\mathcal{C}$'s (identical) pattern-reversing Ants $\mathcal{A}$, as it: (1) *picks up* the symbol in its initial cell c; (2) *conveys* the symbol, via a SW-then-SE path, to c's "mirror" bottom-edge cell $\overline{c}$; (3) *deposits* the conveyed symbol in cell $\overline{c}$; (4) *halts*.

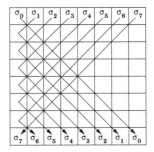

Fig. 6. CANT $\mathcal{C}$'s trajectory as it copies the pattern along row 0 *in reversed order* along row $n-1$.

1. an r-step *southwesterly* walk from cell $\langle 0, r \rangle$ to cell $\langle r, 0 \rangle$;
2. an $(n-r-1)$-step *southeasterly* walk from cell $\langle r, 0 \rangle$ to cell $\langle n-1, n-r-1 \rangle$.

The fact that cell $\langle n-1, n-r-1 \rangle$ is the "mirror image" along row $n-1$ of cell $\langle 0, r \rangle$ completes the validation.

5   Leader Election/Symmetry Breaking

A central challenge in distributed computing is coordinating the actions of identical autonomous agents. An important approach to meeting this challenge is to "elect" one of the agents as a "leader," thereby "breaking" the "symmetry" caused by agents' being indistinguishable. Many leader-election protocols have been invented, all requiring algorithmic sophistication. When the distributed agents are Ants within a CANT $\mathcal{C}$, the underlying CA affords us a rather simple, efficient leader-election protocol. In particular, $\mathcal{C}$ selects as the "leader" the unique Ant (if any exist!) that is "closest" to the origin Agent, $\mathcal{A}^{\langle 0,0 \rangle}$, in the following sense. For each Ant $\mathcal{A}$, we count the number of cells $\mathcal{A}$ needs to traverse in order to reach $\mathcal{A}^{\langle 0,0 \rangle}$ via a path of northward moves (toward row 0) followed by a path of westward moves (toward column 0), *under a regimen that gives a westward moving Ant priority over northward moving one*. (The latter clause resolves ties when two Ants compete to enter the same row-0 cell.)

5.1   The Leader-Election Process

(a) $\mathcal{A}^{\langle 0,0 \rangle}$ initiates the process by simultaneously sending two messages:

1. an FSP-synch to start the process for any Ants that exist within $\mathcal{M}_n$;
2. an eastward-bound message, NO ANT YET.
    - This message is relayed along row 0 up to $\mathcal{M}_n$'s eastern edge, whence it is bounced back toward $\mathcal{A}^{\langle 0,0 \rangle}$.
    - If the message reaches an Agent $\mathcal{A}$ that knows of an Ant—from receiving Ant-related messages—then $\mathcal{A}$ "swallows" this message by not relaying it.
   Note that if $\mathcal{A}^{\langle 0,0 \rangle}$ receives the bounced-back message, *and* it has not received an Ant-related message, then it knows that no Ant resides on $\mathcal{M}_n$.

(b) When "activated" (via the FSP-synch), each cell that contains an Ant sends the message I HAVE AN ANT northward, toward row 0.
(c) While a row-0 Agent $\mathcal{A}^{\langle 0,k \rangle}$ is *active:*

- The *first time* it receives the message I HAVE AN ANT from its southern neighbor, $\mathcal{A}^{\langle 1,k \rangle}$, it sends the message ANT IN MY COLUMN westward, toward cell $\langle 0,0 \rangle$.
- If it receives the message ANT IN MY COLUMN from its eastern neighbor, $\mathcal{A}^{\langle 0,k+1 \rangle}$, then it relays that message westward, toward cell $\langle 0,0 \rangle$.

In both cases, $\mathcal{A}^{\langle 0,k \rangle}$ *then becomes inactive.*
(d) While a row-0 Agent $\mathcal{A}^{\langle 0,k \rangle}$ is *inactive,* it ignores all messages from its eastern and southern neighbors.
(e) $\mathcal{A}^{\langle 0,0 \rangle}$ learns about the presence or absence of Ants in one of three ways.

- If $\mathcal{A}^{\langle 0,0 \rangle}$ receives the message NO ANT YET from its eastern neighbor, $\mathcal{A}^{\langle 0,1 \rangle}$, then it knows that no Ant resides on $\mathcal{M}_n$.
   In response, $\mathcal{A}^{\langle 0,0 \rangle}$ broadcasts NO ANTS FOUND eastward and southward.
- • If the first message that $\mathcal{A}^{\langle 0,0 \rangle}$ receives is I HAVE AN ANT from its southern neighbor, $\mathcal{A}^{\langle 1,0 \rangle}$, then a leader-Ant has been discovered.
   • The first time $\mathcal{A}^{\langle 0,0 \rangle}$ receives ANT IN MY COLUMN from its eastern neighbor, $\mathcal{A}^{\langle 0,1 \rangle}$, it knows that a leader-Ant has been discovered.

When either occurs, $\mathcal{A}^{\langle 0,0 \rangle}$ broadcasts LEADER ANT FOUND eastward and southward. It also transmits YOU ARE THE LEADER in the direction from which it received the Ant-related message. This "congratulatory message" is relayed back to the originating Ant by intermediate Agents.

   In parallel with its broadcast, $\mathcal{A}^{\langle 0,0 \rangle}$ initiates an FSP-synch to terminate the procedure.
(f) When row-0 Agent $\mathcal{A}^{\langle 0,k \rangle}$ receives LEADER ANT FOUND from its western neighbor, $\mathcal{A}^{\langle 0,k-1 \rangle}$, it relays the message eastward to $\mathcal{A}^{\langle 0,k+1 \rangle}$ and southward to $\mathcal{A}^{\langle 1,k \rangle}$.

5.2 Analyzing the Leader-Election Process

A. Validation. The correctness of the process follows from the observations that: (a) If there is an Ant upon $\mathcal{M}_n$, then $\mathcal{A}^{\langle 0,0 \rangle}$ receives precisely one message I HAVE AN ANT—and that comes from an Ant that is closest to $\mathcal{A}^{\langle 0,0 \rangle}$. Competing messages are swallowed by intervening Agents. The message NO ANT YET tells $\mathcal{A}^{\langle 0,0 \rangle}$ there is no resident Ant. Thus, the leader-election process always halts, with a closest leader Ant if one exists.

B. Timing. The leader-election process completes within $4n$ steps on an $n \times n$ CANT:

- $\exists$ *Ant on* $\mathcal{M}_n$. Then $\mathcal{A}^{\langle 0,0 \rangle}$ receives the message I HAVE AN ANT within $2n$ steps.
- $\nexists$ *Ant on* $\mathcal{M}_n$. Then $\mathcal{A}^{\langle 0,0 \rangle}$ receives the message NO ANT YET within $2n$ steps.

Within an additional $2n$ steps, $\mathcal{A}^{\langle 0,0 \rangle}$ initiates an FSP-synch that both terminates the process and announces either the election of a leader or the absence of an Ant. In parallel, $\mathcal{A}^{\langle 0,0 \rangle}$ sends a "congratulatory message" to the new leader.

6 Conclusion

Many PDC-related concepts that are quite sophisticated in general settings have rather simple versions within the Cellular ANTomaton (CANT) model. An instructor can use CANTs to gently introduce such problems to students who have only basic knowledge about topics such as linear recurrences, asymptotics, and Agents. When a student encounters the sophisticated versions of the problems later, s/he has intuitions from the CANT-based simplifications. Additionally, these intuitions can be strengthened using the many convenient tools such as *NETLOGO* [14], *CARPET* [21] and *MATLAB*®. It would be exciting to try this approach with a range of classes, beginning even with CS0.

References

1. Avis, D., Bremmer, D., Deza, A. (eds.): Polyhedral computation. In: CRM Proceedings and Lecture Notes, vol. 48. American Mathematical Society (2009)
2. Chen, L., Xu, X., Chen, Y., He, P.: A novel ant clustering algorithm based on cellular automata. In: IEEE/WIC/ACM International Conference, Intelligent Agent Technology (2004)
3. Chowdhury, D., Guttal, V., Nishinari, K., Schadschneider, A.: A cellular-automata model of flow in ant trails: non-monotonic variation of speed with density. J. Phys. A: Math. Gen. **35**, L573–L577 (2002)
4. Cormen, T.H., Leiserson, C.E., Rivest, R.L., Stein, C.: Introduction to Algorithms, 2nd edn. MIT Press, Cambridge (1999)
5. Fisher, A.L., Kung, H.T.: Synchronizing large VLSI processor arrays. IEEE Trans. Comput. **C-34**, 734–740 (1985)

6. Goles, E., Martinez, S. (eds.): Cellular Automata and Complex Systems. Kluwer, Norwell (1999)

7. Greene, J.W., El Gamal, A.: Configuration of VLSI arrays in the presence of defects. J. ACM **31**, 694–717 (1984)

8. Gruska, J., La Torre, S., Parente, M.: Optimal time and communication solutions of firing squad synchronization problems on square arrays, toruses and rings. In: Calude, C.S., Calude, E., Dinneen, M.J. (eds.) DLT 2004. LNCS, vol. 3340, pp. 200–211. Springer, Heidelberg (2004). https://doi.org/10.1007/978-3-540-30550-7_17

9. Laurio, K., Linaker, F., Narayanan, A.: Regular biosequence pattern matching with cellular automata. Inf. Sci. **146**(1–4), 89–101 (2002)

10. Leighton, F.T., Leiserson, C.E.: Wafer-scale integration of systolic arrays. IEEE Trans. Comput. **C-34**, 448–461 (1985)

11. Leiserson, C.E.: Systolic and semisystolic design. In: IEEE International Conference on Computer Design, pp. 627–630 (1983)

12. Marchese, F.: Cellular automata in robot path planning. In: EUROBOT, pp. 116–125 (1996)

13. Moore, E.F: The firing squad synchronization problem. In: Moore, E.F. (ed.) Sequential Machines, Selected Papers, pp. 213–214. Addison-Wesley, Boston (1962)

14. https://ccl.northwestern.edu/netlogo/

15. Prasad, S.K., Gupta, A., Kant, K., Lumsdaine, A., Padua, D., Robert, Y., Rosenberg, A.L., Sussman, A., Weems, C.: Literacy for all in parallel and distributed computing: guidelines for an undergraduate core curriculum. CSI J. Comput. **1**(2), 10:81–10:95 (2012)

16. Quinton, P.: Automatic synthesis of systolic arrays from uniform recurrence equations. In: 11th IEEE International Symposium on Computer Architecture, pp. 208–214 (1984)

17. Rosenberg, A.L.: The Pillars of Computation Theory: State, Encoding Nondeterminism. Universitext Series. Springer, New York (2009). https://doi.org/10.1007/978-0-387-09639-1

18. Rosenberg, A.L.: Cellular ANTomata. Adv. Complex Syst. **15**(6) (2012)

19. Rosenberg, A.L.: Bio-inspired pattern processing by cellular ANTomata. J. Cell. Automata **13**(1–2), 53–80 (2018)

20. Sirakoulis, G.C., Adamatzky, A. (eds.): Robots and Lattice Automata. ECC, vol. 13. Springer, Cham (2015). https://doi.org/10.1007/978-3-319-10924-4

21. Spezzano, G., Talia, D.: The CARPET programming environment for solving scientific problems on parallel computers. Parallel Distrib. Comput. Practices **1**, 49–61 (1998)

22. Williams, T.: Clock skew and other myths. In: IEEE International Symposium on Asynchronous Circuits and Systems (2003)

23. Wolfram, S. (ed.): Theory and Application of Cellular Automata. Addison-Wesley, Boston (1986)

Teaching Software Transactional Memory in Concurrency Courses with Clojure and Java

Antonio J. Tomeu[1]($\boxtimes$), Alberto G. Salguero[1]($\boxtimes$), and Manuel I. Capel[2]

[1] Dpto. de Ingeniería Informática, Universidad de Cadiz,
11519 Puerto Real, Spain
{antonio.tomeu,alberto.salguero}@uca.es
[2] College of Informatics and Telecommunications,
University of Granada, 18071 Granada, Spain
manuelcapel@ugr.es

Abstract. In the field of concurrency and parallelism, it is known that the use of lock-based synchronization mechanisms limits the programming efficiency of concurrent applications and reveals problems in thread synchronization. Software Transactional Memory (STM) is a consolidated concurrency control mechanism that may be considered as an alternative to lock-based constructs for programming critical software, although STM is still not fully accepted as a programming model for the industry. It is our opinion that STM programming must be more emphasized in undergraduate courses on concurrency and parallelism. In this paper we propose an academic experience regarding the introduction of STM programming in concurrency courses by using the Clojure language as the common vehicle for teaching Concurrent Programming. Java, the most popular and extended programming language for teaching concurrency, becomes a second language in our course, and thus our students can take advantage of Clojure API which is defined in Java in order to simplify the development of programming, lectures and assignments.

Keywords: Clojure · Concurrency · Java · Locks · Mutual exclusion
Threads · Transactions · Software Transactional Memory · Performance

1 Introduction

At moment, programming with locks at different abstraction levels is the dominant programming paradigm to teach how to program thread synchronization in concurrency courses. There is an ample range of concurrent constructs for programming concurrent applications; from the simple, standard locks or semaphores to the most sophisticated syntactical constructs such as monitors, they all offer good performance and a relative ease of use when it comes to program concurrent applications. However, all these syntactical mechanisms suffer from the lack of verifiability and reliability. Therefore, sometimes is difficult to obtain solutions applicable to concurrent programs that guarantee safety and

© Springer International Publishing AG, part of Springer Nature 2018
D. B. Heras and L. Bougé (Eds.): Euro-Par 2017 Workshops, LNCS 10659, pp. 266–277, 2018.
https://doi.org/10.1007/978-3-319-75178-8_22

liveness properties even when using formal techniques. The probability of a program code produced with non-verified synchronization mechanisms to crash or yield a deadlock situation is not negligible. However, if we analyze popular concurrent/parallel programming languages such as Java or C ++, we find that any specific API for managing concurrent tasks usually offer a wide variety of lock-based synchronization tools, being only a few of them based on STM. In particular, the last revision of Java [9] does not include native STM, whereas the C++14 [11] revision does as an "experimental feature". If we analyze the situation in concurrency courses, the situation is very similar. Information about STM programming model is mentioned superficially in concurrency courses. It is pointed out that, although STM programming is a mature model commonly used in research, it is still not used for commercial exploitation of parallel/-concurrent software development [3,16]. Moreover, recent curriculum guides [5], [17] that outline courses on concurrency do not pay special attention to that topic or include STM contents in course programs. This paper shows the results obtained from a study of teaching improvement in Concurrent and Real Time Programming course, which was carried out at the University of Cadiz (Spain) during one semester. The main objectives of the study have been:

(a) To introduce the STM model to students, as a viable alternative to the blocking thread model (thread synchronization based on locks) along with the model advantages and disadvantages.
(b) To provide the students with the necessary skills to allow the development of concurrent programs that include transactions for shared data access by Clojure's concurrent threads.
(c) To use Clojure as a programming language on top of Java for transactional programming in a multi-core environment, and thus to allow the students to develop programming solutions by programming Clojure's transactions.
(d) To show the students that both paradigms are not mutually exclusive but complementary.

The paper is organized as follows: Sect. 2 briefly describes the academic context of the study. Section 3 introduces the STM programming "paradigm" and how is presented to the students. Section 4 shows the way STM that uses Clojure is taught and Sect. 5 does the same with Java on Clojure. Section 6 gives further details on how the experiment was developed by the students and evaluated to check the performance of STM-based w.r.t. the solutions based on the classic blocking thread model. Section 7 outlines the conclusions reached and the future work to be developed.

2   Academic Context

The reported study was developed in the third semester of the CSE curriculum at the University of Cádiz (UCA), Spain, in an undergraduate course. A total amount of $n = 199$ students were enrolled in the course "Concurrent and Real Time Programming", which was divided into two groups for theoretical lectures and eight groups for practical work in the labs in this study. The semester lasted fifteen weeks (60 h per student with 4 h of teaching per week: 2 h of lectures and 2 of practical work. The course structure and contents, according to the current recommendation guides [5,17], were the next ones:

1. Fundamental concepts of concurrent programming: race conditions, mutual exclusion, synchronization, and properties of concurrent systems (15%).
2. Mutual exclusion: algorithms for shared memory multiprocessors, semaphores and **software transactional memory**[1]. (20%).
3. Monitors: Hoare's monitor model, signaling semantics, verification of concurrency properties (security and liveness) (20%).
4. Message passing and distributed programs: RPC and RMI models, MPI, rendez-vous (15%).
5. Real-time systems: periodic tasks scheduling based on static priority assignment, scheduling tests, priority inversion anomaly and sporadic task scheduling (30%).

The distribution of course topics within the 60 h of teaching (lectures + lab) was the following one: fundamentals (4.5+6), mutual exclusion (6+8), monitors (6+8), message passing (4.5+6) and real-time systems (9+2). 30 h of lab work were spent to teach theoretical contents with the help of Java code-snippets, which were taught according to a weekly schedule proposed by teachers. A total of 3 h were spent to carry out the experiment regarding learning mutual exclusion conditions and solutions, which were distributed following the next format: one hour for a theoretical seminar on STM fundamental concepts and two hours for practical work at the laboratory, where the students can experiment with the STM Clojure and Java code-templates provided by teachers. The course development has been supported by a Moodle virtual platform, which provided students: previous readings to each lecture, the slides shown in classroom, and all the code samples used in the exercises proposed to the students during the semester.

3   Software Transactional Memory

It is well known that common synchronization techniques in concurrent programming suffer from several drawbacks, i.e., if these techniques are not used properly, or we forget to do a good lock release check control, the changes performed by one thread in the program may not be visible to the other threads. In spite of all that have been written about how to avoid these problems [12], [7], and the numerous formal techniques that have been proposed recently, concurrency control remains a complex issue in general. Not all people are able to produce valid code (free from race conditions, threads starvation and livelock).

---

[1] The transactional memory was introduced by us in this section during the academic year 2016–2017 to carry out the study.

The STM paradigm can change now the previous situation, i.e., it becomes feasible to program safe and fair concurrent code by everybody, by introducing the concept of transaction, which can be defined as a region of code that is executed atomically, consistently and in isolation with respect to other program regions. When two threads try to access the same data, the transaction manager is activated to resolve the conflict, without resorting to explicitly use blocks in the code. When a transaction is in progress, the transaction is completed and the changes are written into memory if there is no conflict with other threads/transactions. However, as soon as the transaction handler finds that one transaction has progressed beyond a certain point that makes the current transaction unsafe by compromising the data consistency, it undoes the changes and tries again.

When STM is used, the concurrent readings are done without any problems, and without the presence of contention. With the STM model, conflicts only occur when a thread is writing to shared data; in that case, the transaction manager records the program state, so that all previous work done by the thread can be *rolled-back* and then the thread retries until the transaction can be successfully completed; this occurs when the threads that are modifying data finish to do so and validate those changes in memory (*commit*). The STM model is very suitable when considering critical sections with many readings and occasional writings, where we can expect little containment [13]. By contrast, the blocking model degrades the performance in this case, since it implements a pessimistic control of the concurrency, eliminating the parallelism within the critical sections. At this point, we consider the need to choose an implementation of STM to work with our students. Compatibility with the Java language was fundamental, as the students had developed all their practical assignments in Java in other courses of the curriculum. There are multiple STM implementations for Java [1,7,10,14,15,20]. We did not choose any of them, because they are too complex for the objectives we set for the teaching of STM. Instead, we chose to use Clojure functional language, which is interpreted by the JVM, and yields compatibility between both languages/APIs, which was very useful for us.

4   Teaching STM with Clojure

In Clojure, the STM separates the identity of an object from its state [18]. Clojure is a functional language where the states never change, as they are immutable by definition. The changes are produced in identity of the object, which is actually the visible information for the threads. Values are only immutable within the scope of a Clojure transaction. By design, the identities are the mutable part, and therefore it is not possible to inconsistently change the states. Any attempt to change the identity of an object outside of a transaction is considered illegal in Clojure, and thus an exception is thrown if that situation arises.

Since there are no locks, concurrency is improved in comparison to the thread blocking model [2,6]. Correct understanding of this separation between identity and state is crucial for the students to internalize the operation of the STM in

Clojure. It is also explained to the students that the STM model works as long as its implementation can guarantee that threads always get a consistent view of the world during the program execution. This is true with Clojure, so we do not have to worry about checking it, which is an advantage for newcomers to the STM world. The transaction manager, which supports STM, is responsible for doing it for us. Teaching the Clojure transactional control to our students was not an issue, since we used a set of Clojure code patterns, as the one shown below. In that code our students can visualize how to perform the identity change that we want to achieve by wrapping it in a transaction ((`dosync...`)). Clojure implementation of STM guarantees that any transaction execution is atomic, isolated and consistent. We also specially insisted on the similarities and differences that the pattern presents with respect to the classic blocking thread synchronization pattern with locks.

```
1  ;; how to use transactions in Clojure
2  ;; now, the shared data...
3  (def n (ref 0))
4  (println "n is: " @value)
5  ;; doing the transaction...
6  (dosync
7    (ref-set n 1))
8  (println "n is: " @value)
```

A thread's transaction is only completed if there is no conflict with another running threads/transactions at the moment, and the changes are written to memory (*commit*). If some conflict is detected by the transaction handler, as result of multiple threads concurrently accessing[2] to the shared data, the transaction handler pauses the contending threads, undoes the transaction (*roll-back*) and starts them again. Therefore, blocking situations among threads cannot arise with Clojure transactions, though there is obviously a price to pay for that, i.e., transactions require an extra processing time [4] compared with thread synchronization based on locks. As one part of the correct understanding and basic use of Clojure transactions, there were foreseen practical work assignments at the laboratory that included the following actions: the elaboration of a multi-threaded application for the concurrent access to the variable **n** as in the previous code, and the elaboration and analysis of a number of critical sections following the previous model.

5   Teaching STM with Java over Clojure

Once the theoretical and practical concepts to develop secure transactions with Clojure have been presented to students, we have extended our experience to the field of Java language, which was used during all the practical lessons conducted at the laboratory during the semester. To develop the analysis of the STM behavior in the Java language, we began to familiarize the students with the transactional pattern that had to be used, which is shown below,

---

[2] Students were asked, within the corresponding assignment, to do just that.

```
1  myThread h = (myThread) Thread.currentThread();
2  while (true) {
3    t.beginTransaction();
4    ... // do critical section
5    if (t.commitTransaction()) {
6    break;
7  }
8  }
```

The code illustrates how the general transaction pattern in Java surrounds and protects the access to the shared data in a transaction, within which the threads remains until the transaction ends up and the writing of data in memory is successfully validated. The pattern shows to the students the transaction execution continuity, by following a continuous iterative form while the transaction needs to perform, and without the presence of locks. When this pattern was correctly understood by our students, we went on to develop two Java STM experiments in Clojure with the students, (1) concurrent multi-thread access to a shared variable using a standard race condition, and (2) concurrent access to a bank account abstraction[3]. Below we show the control of a race condition with transactions. The control of the bank account is very similar, and is not shown for reasons of space. The code provided to our students for solving a standard race condition was as it follows,

```
1  import clojure.lang.Ref;
2  import clojure.lang.LockingTransaction;
3  import java.util.concurrent.Callable;
4
5  public class Counter {
6    final private Ref count;
7
8    public Counter(final int valInic) throws Exception {
9      count = new Ref(valInic);
10   }
11
12   public int getCount() { return (Integer) count.deref(); }
13
14   public void inc() throws Exception {
15     LockingTransaction.runInTransaction(new Callable<Integer>() {
16       public Integer call() {
17         int countNow = (Integer) count.deref();
18         count.set(countNow+1);
19         return (Integer) count.deref();
20
21       }
22     });
23   }
24
```

[3] All code shown in the rest of the document is available at the following URL: https://antoniotomeu.wixsite.com/atomeu/stmjavaonclojure.

```
25   public void dec() throws Exception {
26     LockingTransaction.runInTransaction(new Callable<Integer>() {
27       public Integer call()   {
28
29           int countNow = (Integer) count.deref();
30           count.set(countNow−1);
31           return (Integer) count.deref();
32
33       }
34     });
35   }
36
37 }
```

The support for STM programming that Clojure offers to its users is imported in lines 1 and 2 into the Java code. Line 6 declares the shared resource with the implicit separation of the identity and the state that Clojure offers. The `Counter` class shows an API with three methods. The first one is an observer that allows the client to obtain the value of `count`. The other two methods are modifiers that increase or decrease the value of `count`. Please, notice that `count` is a counter with the initial value 0 set by the class constructor. The `inc ()` method increments the value of `count`, which is value referenced, and thus it is firstly necessary to dereference it, i.e., we have to follow the reference to obtain its value (line 17). Line 18 increments the counter value by means of an auxiliary variable, and sets the reference to that new value by using `count.set(CountNow + 1)`. Since the program uses Clojure to support transactions the code that is executed inside the transaction must implement the interface `Callable`, which models the asynchronous execution in Java. This is not a problem, since the students acquired familiarity with this interface from previous practical assignments. The entire code of the method is programmed within only one transaction defined in line number 15 and supported by Clojure. The referred transaction includes the entire code of the method with the appropriate syntax delimiter, which is written as:

```
1    LockingTransaction.runInTransaction{
2        //critical section
3    }
```

It was crucial for our students to understand that this delimiter encompasses the persistent looping behavior shown above and that the transaction is continuously running until it is capable of validating data writing into memory. If several threads make a call to the `inc ()` or `dec ()` methods, the Clojure transaction handler makes sure that the modification process is performed properly so that the final value of `count` is consistent. Within the practical assignment that the students had to develop, an exercise was included to develop a Java program that activates multiple threads against an object of the class `Counter`. Half of the threads must invoke the `inc()` method in a `for` loop and the remainder must invoke the `dec()` method. To finish this experiment, students must check that the resulting final value was 0. An example of that program, which we developed, is contained in `userCounter.java` and can be downloaded and tested from the given `url`.

6   Performance Analysis

We also wanted to offer to our students a benchmark for the comparison of the performance between the transactional and the standard thread blocking model. To do this, we developed an experiment, during practical work on transactional memory in the lab, consisting on defining a fine-grain standard critical section code region (`n++`), and to write code for threads that concurrently accessed to it. We have used different control techniques with locks [8] to achieve secure access to the critical section region. More specifically, the access to the region was controlled using `synchronized` methods; versions using the standard API for concurrency, i.e., the `AtomicInteger`, `ReentrantLock` and `Semaphore` classes, included in the high-level API for concurrency control, were also developed; all of those primitives were already known by the students. Finally, we have written a version that wraps the critical region within a transaction written in Java by means of the Clojure API. In addition, we have written an alternative version in Clojure without the Java API, which supports access to the critical data section through its native STM.

Using this code, and the Java previously described models, we proposed two additional experiments to our students for conducting performance measurement:

(a) Basic load experiment: in this experiment the students had to measure the time required to execute a protected critical region that was defined either by using the standard synchronization control techniques of the Java language, or by using STM in Java by means the Clojure language.

(b) High load experiment: in this experiment the students must perform a temporal analysis by using multiple threads which contend to access to a shared resource during a high number of iterations (2×10^6).

Below we describe with more detail the experiments that our students developed under our direction.

6.1   Basic Load Experiment

An elementary critical section with a single write operation was used, and the time required to execute that operation under all typologies of the blocking model and under the STM in Java through Clojure were measured[4]. The students were

---

[4] Time were measured using the `nanoTime()` method of Java `System` class. This implies that it is a time that only and exclusively makes sense in the realm of the virtual machine, and has no relation whatsoever was the time provided by the system clock. However, Clojure, like Java itself, executes *bytecodes* on the JVM, which gives consistency to the results.

required to complete a tabular questionnaire with these times as part of their practical assignment in order to make them aware of the actual time cost of each control technique.

The table, once completed, should show to students how executing a single transaction to provide a safe access to a shared resource nearly doubles the execution time needed by a slower lock-based access in regular Java code. This can happen even in a scenario without multiple threads in execution. Of course, students checked through this exercise that the use of transactions of Clojure was a good election in a situation that requires few accesses to shared resources. However, when the number of accesses to shared resources is high, it is necessary to evaluate the performance of using STM with Clojure in Java.

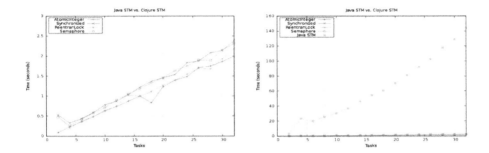

Fig. 1. Java synchronization vs. Java-STM

6.2   High Load Experiment

In this scenario, students were required to run each test program with an increasing number of threads, from 2 to 32. Half of the threads had to increase the counter, and the rest had to decrease it. In all cases the threads had to be launched using a fixed-size executor. A condition had to be entered in all programs for waiting the executor to run all threads, followed by a control printout of the value of the shared variable, which should always be 0 in our case. Each thread made a total of 2×10^6 iterations. The students were then required to develop the measurements for the scenario described, and to draw the curves $Time = F(threads)$. To do this, we made available the required *GnuPlot scripts* to the students through the virtual platform of the course. We also provided our own curves as a working guide, indicating the parameters that supported our own experiment: Intel (R) Core i5-4440 CPU @ 3.10 GHz processor, with 4 physical cores without *hyper-threading*, using Fedora 22 as the Linux platform. The version used for the JDK was 1.8.0_54, and version 1.8.0 was used for Clojure. The results of our test, were given as a guide to the students, are shown in Figs. 1 and 2.

The Fig. 1 (left) illustrates the behavior of standard synchronization techniques in Java, and has no further interest. The Fig. 1 (right) shows the comparative performance of standard Java synchronization techniques compared with

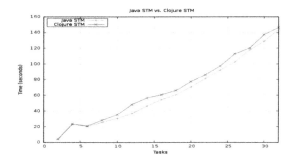

Fig. 2. Java-STM vs. Clojure-STM

STM with Clojure in Java. We can appreciate that the performance of this particular implementation of the STM is bad for tasks that try to frequently access the shared resource, since the necessary roll-backs are very expensive overhead [10]. Finally, the Fig. 2 compares the usage of STM in both languages (Clojure and plain Java). Even in this case, in which we compare a native Clojure implementation of STM with the Java implementation of the STM, we see how Java always behaves better in the range of tasks analyzed, which cannot be considered as a surprise, because Clojure is a pure interpreted functional language.

It is necessary to clarify, however, that the behavior we have shown here corresponds to the analysis of really extreme scenarios, where the typology of the developed threads is very specific, and always use the critical section to perform data writing. It is important to persuade the students to analyze and decide on these aspects by their own [19].

7   Experience Results and Conclusions

To measure the results of the experiment, we asked our students to respond a survey ($n = 124$), where the answers range from 1 (completely disagree) to 5 (fully agree). The value 0 was used when the student did not respond to an item. The items selected were:

(a) I have understood the concept of transaction as an alternative to the use of blocking techniques based on locks.
(b) I have learned how to use transactions with Clojure to protect concurrent access to shared data.
(c) I have learned how to use transactions with Java to protect concurrent access to shared data.
(d) I have understood the advantages and disadvantages of using STM.

The results of the survey are shown in Fig. 3, which shows that the results of the experiment were satisfactory, and that students finally reach an adequate level of understanding of the concept of transactional memory presented, both theoretical and practical.

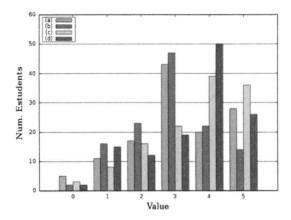

Fig. 3. Valuation survey

From the experiment results evaluation, we decided to keep on teaching the STM as part of the concurrent programming education programme in future editions of the course, and perhaps to slightly extend the time planned for this topic within the course schedule. We also believe that it could be of great interest for other courses on concurrency the development of a similar experience with other programming languages such as Akka, Scala or perhaps C++ if it finally includes transactional memory in the corresponding API.

References

1. Brevnov, E., Dolgov, Y., Kuznetsov, B., Yhershov, D., Shakin, V., Chen, D., Menon, V., Srinivas, S.: Practical experiences with Java software transactional memory. In: The 13th ACM SIGPLAN Symposium on Principles and Practice of Parallel Programming (2008)
2. Carlstrom, B., Chung, J., Chafi, H., McDonald, A., Minh, C., Hammond, L., Kozyrakis, K., Olukotun, K.: Executing Java programs with transactional memory. Sci. Comput. Program. **63**, 111–129 (2006)
3. Cascaval, C., Blundell, C., Michael, M., Cain, H., Wu, P., Chiras, S., Chaterjee, S.: Software transactional memory: why is it only a research toy. Commun. ACM **51**(11) (2008). https://doi.org/10.1145/1400214.1400228
4. Clarke, F., Ekeland, I., Pedrero, M., Gutierrez, E., Romero, S., Plata, O.: Improving transactional memory performance for irregular applications. Procedia Comput. Sci. **51**, 2714–2718 (2015)
5. The Joint Task Force on Computing Curricula, Association for Computing Machinery (ACM) and IEEE Computer Society. Computer Science Curricula 2013 Curriculum Guidelines for Undergraduate Degree Programs in Computer Science. https://www.acm.org/education/CS2013-final-report.pdf. Accessed 27 Mar 2017
6. Dias, R., Vale, T., Lourenço, J.: Efficient support for in-place metadata in Java software transactional memory. Concurr. Comput. Pract. Exp. **25**, 2394–2411 (2013). https://doi.org/10.1002/cpe.3098. Wiley Online Library

7. Diegues, N., Fernandes, S., Cachopo, J.: Parallel nesting in a lock-free multi-version software transactional memory. Technical report RT/2/2012 (2012). http://algos. inesc-id.pt/~jpa/InscI/poisson/varwwwhtml/portal/ficheiros/publicacoes/7621. pdf. Accessed 20 Mar 2017

8. Fernández, J.: Java 7 Concurrency CookBook. Packt Publishing, Birmingham (2012)

9. Gosling, J., Joy, B., Steele, G., Bracha, G., Buckley, A.: The Java Language Specification. Java SE, 8 edn (2015). https://docs.oracle.com/javase/specs/jls/se8/jls8. pdf. Accessed 15 Feb 2017

10. Herlihy, M., Luchangco, V., Moir, M.: A flexible framework for implementing software transactional memory. http://citeseerx.ist.psu.edu/viewdoc/download? doi=10.1.1.394.9533&rep=rep1&type=pdf. Accessed 20 Mar 2017

11. ISO: Working Draft, Standard for Programming Language C++ (2016). http:// open-std.org/JTC1/SC22/WG21/docs/papers/2016/n4618.pdf. Accessed 16 Feb 2017

12. Malde, K.: Can software transactional memory make concurrent programs simple and safe? http://cs.brown.edu/~mph/HerlihyLM06/dstm2.pdf. Accessed 20 Mar 2017

13. Mizuno, K., Nakaike, T., Nakatani, T.: Reducing rollbacks of transactional memory using ordered shared locks. In: Sips, H., Epema, D., Lin, H.-X. (eds.) Euro-Par 2009. LNCS, vol. 5704, pp. 704–715. Springer, Heidelberg (2009). https://doi.org/ 10.1007/978-3-642-03869-3_66

14. Mohamedin, M., Ravindran, B., Palmieri, R.: ByteSTM: Virtual Machine-level Java Software Transactional Memory. http://www.ssrg.ece.vt.edu/papers/ coordination_15_CR.pdf. Accessed 20 Mar 2017

15. Nakaike, T., Odaira, R., Nakatani, T., Michael, M.: Real Java applications in software transactional memory. In: IEEE International Symposium on Workload Characterization (2010). https://doi.org/10.1109/IISWC.2010.5654431

16. Pankratius, V., Adl-Tatabai, A.: Software engineering with transactional memory versus locks in practice. Theory Comput. Syst. **55**(3), 555–590 (2013). https://doi. org/10.1007/s00224-013-9452-5

17. Prasad, S.K., et al.: NSF/IEEE-TCPP curriculum initiative on parallel and distributed computing - core topics for undergraduates. https://grid.cs.gsu. edu/~tcpp/curriculum/?q=system/files/NSF-TCPP-curriculum-version1.pdf. Accessed 20 Mar 2017

18. Subramanian, V.: Programming Concurrency on the JVM: Masterig Synchronization, STMA, and Actors. The Pragmatic Bookshelf, Dallas (2011)

19. Yamada, Y., Iwasaki, H., Ugawa, T.: SAW: Java synchronization selection from lock or software transactional memory. In: Proceeding of IEEE 17th International Conference on Parallel and Distributed Systems, pp. 104–111 (2011)

20. Ziarek, L., Welc, A., Adl-Tatabati, A., Menon, V., Shpeisman, T., Jagannathan, S.: A uniform transactional execution environment for Java. https://www.cs.purdue. edu/homes/suresh/papers/ecoop08.pdf. Accessed 20 Mar 2017

F2C-DP – Workshop on Fog-to-Cloud Distributed Processing

Workshop on Fog-to-Cloud Distributed Processing (F2C-DP)

Workshop Description

Future service execution in different domains (e.g. smart cities, e-health, smart transportation, etc.), will rely on a large and highly heterogeneous set of distributed devices, located from the edge to the cloud, empowering the development of innovative services. In such envisioned scenario, the main objective for the workshop was to set the ground for researchers, scientists and members of the industrial community to interact each other, fueling new discussions in the emerging area coming out when shifting distributed services execution towards the edge. Analyzing the way existing programming models and distributed processing strategies may support such a scenario and to what extent these solutions should be extended or just replaced, is also fundamental to support the expected evolution in edge computing.

The workshop aimed at bringing together the community of researchers interested in new applications, architectures, programming models, applications and systems based on these computing environments. The workshop was organized with the support of the mF2C, a H2020 funded project.

This was the first edition of the workshop, that took place in Santiago de Compostela, Spain, in conjuction with the Euro-Par annual series of international conferences. The workshop format included a keynote speaker, technical presentations and a panel. The workshop was attended by around 20 people.

The workshop received eight submissions, and each of them was reviewed at least three times. The program committee took into account the relevance of the papers to the workshop, the technical merit, the potential impact, and the originality and novelty. From these submissions, and taking into account the reviews, six papers were selected for presentation in the workshop (75% acceptance ratio). The papers focused on different aspects of the fog to cloud computing platforms: application requirements and specifications, architecture, programming models, and deployment with containers.

The workshop included also a keynote presentation and a panel that discussed technology and business challenges posed by the fog to cloud paradigm.

We would like to thank the Euro-Par organizers for their support in the organization, specially to the Euro-Par workshop chairs, Dora Blanco and Luc Bougé. We would like also to thank John Kennedy (Intel) for his keynote presentation and Christian Perez (INRIA) for his participation in the panel, as well as to all the programm committee members.

Organizing Committee

Rosa M. Badia	Barcelona Supercomputing Center, Spain
Xavier Masip	Universitat Politècnica de Catalunya, Spain
Ana Juan Ferrer	ATOS Research, Spain

Program Committee

Eva Marn	Universitat Politècnica de Catalunya, Spain
Toni Cortés	Barcelona Supercomputing Center, Spain
Francisco Carpio	Technical University of Braunschweig, Germany
Jens Jensen	Sciences and Technology Facilities Council, UK
John Kennedy	Intel, Ireland
Alec Leckey	Intel, Ireland
Anna Queralt	Barcelona Supercomputing Center, Spain
Matija Cankar	XLAB, Slovenia
Antonio Salis	Tiscali, Italy
Jorge Ejarque	Barcelona Supercomputing Center, Spain
Daniele Lezzi	Barcelona Supercomputing Center, Spain
Vitor Barbosa	Universitat Politècnica de Catalunya, Spain

Benefits of a Coordinated Fog-to-Cloud Resources Management Strategy on a Smart City Scenario

Andrea Bartolí[1]([⊠]), Francisco Hernández[1], Laura Val[1], Jose Gorchs[1],
Xavi Masip-Bruin[2] [ID], Eva Marín-Tordera[2], Jordi Garcia[2], Ana Juan[3],
and Admela Jukan[4]

[1] Worldsensing Group, London 9-10 Carlos Place, Mayfair,
London W1K 3AT, UK
{abartoli,fhernandez,lval,jgorchs}@worldsensing.com
[2] Advanced Network Architectures Lab (CRAAX), UPC,
Neapolis Building, Vilanova i la Geltrú, Spain
{xmasip,eva,jordig}@ac.upc.edu
[3] ATOS Research & Innovation, Pere IV, Barcelona, Spain
ana.juanf@atos.net
[4] Technische Universität of Braunschweig,
Hans-Sommer St, 66, Brunswick, Germany
a.jukan@tu-bs.de

Abstract. The advent of fog computing devices as computing paradigm enriching traditional cloud computing applications, paves the way to deploy innovative services, typically not completely appropriate and well supported by cloud computing technology. For example, fog computing is highly suitable for services requiring high constraints on delay, such as dependable services in the e-health arena or tracking strategies in manufacturing processes. Recently, some initiatives have focussed on putting together fog and cloud computing to make the best out of utilizing both, such as the reference architecture by the OpenFog consortium or the Fog-to-Cloud (F2C) concept. However, such a scenario requires a novel management strategy taking over the foreseen specific demands. In this paper, we argue the benefits of a F2C architecture on a particular application to be deployed on a smart city or smart environment scenario.

Keywords: Cloud computing · Fog computing · F2C computing
Coordinated management

1 Introduction

Several efforts have been done recently analyzing the complex scenario brought by putting together cloud and fog resources, such as Fog-to-Cloud (F2C) [1] or the recent OpenFog reference architecture [2], growing from a logical evolution in the cloud arena as shown in Fig. 1.

© Springer International Publishing AG, part of Springer Nature 2018
D. B. Heras and L. Bougé (Eds.): Euro-Par 2017 Workshops, LNCS 10659, pp. 283–291, 2018.
https://doi.org/10.1007/978-3-319-75178-8_23

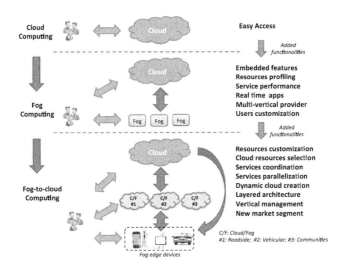

Fig. 1. Cloud evolution towards fog-to-cloud computing (from [1])

The main rationale for this scenario boils down to using resources best suiting expected services demands, be it at the cloud or at the fog, to support services execution and related quality (QoS). Indeed, the advent of fog computing [3] has paved the way to introduce novel concepts that are undoubtedly impacting on services performance in typical smart environment. Particularly relevant are the effects on reducing latency, improving security and limiting the traffic to be sent throughout the core network to reach out the cloud. When fog and cloud are put together, a new scenario is envisioned, setting a stack of resources (Fig. 2), where the resources must be managed in a coordinated fashion to facilitate an optimal match between technology capacities and services needs/ demands.

Moreover, such a coordinated management layer may also set the roots for new services execution strategies based on sub-services decomposition, aggregation and parallelization techniques. The effects of such an innovative strategy will have a large impact on the development of new business models, novel market opportunities and unquestionably new avenues for research; for example, devices naming, services allocation or resources categorization, etc. It is worth noticing that the fog scenario is strongly aligned to consider edge devices, what usually strongly links to mobility aspects. Mobility indeed brings undesired constraints on resources management, such as volatility and availability, what when added to the devices heterogeneity sets a very complex scenario.

In this context, the mF2C project [4], which is an EU Research and Innovation action funded by the Horizon 2020 program, aims to design, implement and validate novel management architecture and methodology for achieving the F2C paradigm. Within this initiative, the demonstration part is supported by the deployment of the mF2C project's outcomes into three different use cases; each use case will bring a different set of characteristics where the mF2C paradigm is expected to show its main capabilities and benefits. This paper is intended to overview the main characteristics for one of the proposed mF2C use cases as well as to envision the benefits brought by

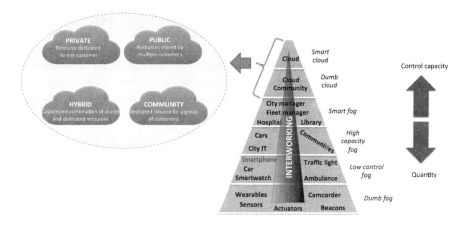

Fig. 2. The stack of resources architecture envisioned in F2C

considering a successful deployment of the mF2C management solution within the selected experimentations. In a nutshell, the proposed use case focuses on a scenario of emergency management enriched with mF2C innovation to provide added value for the smart city ecosystem: customers, companies, governments, citizens, etc.

The paper is structured as follows. Section 2, briefly introduces the mF2C architecture. Section 3 draws the proposed scenario and Sect. 4 identifies main expected benefits. Finally, Sect. 5 concludes the paper.

2   Preliminary mF2C Architecture

In general, the main deployment for the mF2C vision and architecture will turn into management agents, which will be deployed on a device to be mF2C-capable. The strategy to define how devices joint mF2C, are discovered and identified, clustered and categorized, etc. is still under research. However, a preliminary version of the main building blocks of the mF2C architecture is shown in Fig. 3. The tentative architecture considers three main blocks which work together to allocate the different expected control and management functionalities. Notably, the main blocks are called:

- Controller: Includes the set of control and management functions, distributed in various architectural entities.
- Gearbox: Includes the set of policies, strategies, configurations, etc., enriching mF2C, and paving the way to adopting novel strategies, such as service orchestration, runtime systems, etc.
- Interfaces: Different interfaces are envisioned to guarantee internal and external openness.

More in detail, the proposed set of control and management blocks include:

2.1   Controller Block

This block splits into three main components, resources, services and user, putting all together the set of expected functionalities to deploy the whole Controller Block. They include aspects yet under active research, such as semantic adaptation, resource management (monitoring discovering, virtualization, etc.), security and privacy, etc. It is worth noticing that the dynamicity inherent to F2C resources, the heterogeneity foresaw for the devices and systems comprising mF2C as well as the business relationship to be established among resources providers makes these aspects very challenging. Moreover, the matching between resources available and services demands is also posing several challenges; for example, in resources/services taxonomy, categorization, mapping and final allocation, considering active policies on resources provisioning while always providing the expected quality (QoS) as defined in the Service Level Agreement (SLA) set with the final user to run the expected service. The proposed taxonomy should be dynamic enough to accommodate future developments. When required, the service can be decomposed (atomized) into sub-services, turning into a set of *atomic* services (sub-services), commonly requiring fewer resources and facilitating new approaches, such as parallel execution. The set of sub-services may be preconfigured and stored in a repository. Challenging issues in this area include: (i) to find the appropriate place to locate the service decomposition, (ii) to minimize the computing load while keeping fast reaction time, (iii) to define what extent these functions must be associated to the aggregation points, (iv) to define the graph rules including not only the sub-services but also their dependencies and strategies for sub-services search, etc.

Finally, considering security, mF2C must benefit from the user-specific context information to tailor service execution to the specific user demands. To that end, a comprehensive set of functionalities must be defined, including but not limited to

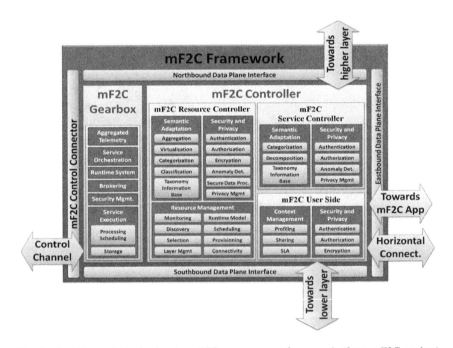

Fig. 3. Architectural blocks for the mF2C management framework (from mF2C project)

authentication, privacy, location, profiling, agreement policies, etc. (i.e., User and Context Functions). All these functionalities must meet the business policies in place to guarantee real mF2C deployment.

2.2   Gearbox Block

The set of preliminary components defined to build the Gearbox block focus on two main components: monitoring and service orchestration. The first is required to inform decision making systems such as service orchestration; it should be dynamically configurable, and support derived or aggregated metrics at the edge for maximum scalability of the overall solution. The second is responsible for allocating services to the best suitable resources; the optimal allocation will depend on many factors, such as historical analysis, real-time resources configuration, QoS, etc.

2.3   Interfaces

Different interfaces are envisioned to ease the mF2C interconnectivity and interoperation. The whole system must support a northbound and southbound interface to vertically facilitate connection within the F2C architecture. The Eastbound interface enables multi-cloud/fog communication within the same layer and the westbound interface is envisioned for control functionalities.

3   The Smart City Scenario

Worldsensing will take advantage of mF2C project by implementing secure and powerful specific IoT services based on a prolific relation between end-devices and a central platform. This SME is interested in both the scalable and flexible approach brought by the mF2C resources management and its suitability to deploy services out of a data-center, and therefore move the computation close to the origin of data. The synergies and the knowledge obtained in the proposed use case will enable more ambitious developments to thus allow the access to wider markets that are not currently explored by Worldsensing due to the limited availability of cost-effective technology in this context. In this section, we will present Worldsensing group and its use case within mF2C.

3.1   Worldsensing Group

Within the mF2C project, one of the use cases is brought by Worldsensing group. Worldsensing was founded in 2008 and currently employs more than 60 people in Barcelona and London premises. It enjoys exponentially growing sales worldwide: it concluded its Serie-A investment in early 2013; in 2016, it received a Serie-B inversion from international parties; and, in 2017, it is currently focusing on a novel round of Serie-C investment. The great grow of Worldsensing group is depending on its main expertise: the company provides high-quality sensing and machine-to-machine technologies and services to specific industry verticals. It has two product portfolios: one being Smart Traffic solutions for Smart Cities, and the other being Heavy-Industry Monitoring solutions. As for smart traffic, it counts on its own smart parking product and a journey-time monitoring solution through its acquisition of smart traffic giant Bitcarrier. As for heavy-industry monitoring, it instruments critical infrastructures such as buildings, bridges, tunnels, ports, wells, etc. and offers seismic monitoring capabilities for engineering, oil/gas/water acquisition and CO_2-sequestration purposes.

Worldsensing is currently market leader in most of above M2M/IoT industry monitoring markets. It has won numerous prizes and awards, has enjoyed vast press coverage by the WSJ and the BBC, has shaped many IoT/M2M standards, and has driven the R&D developments in Europe through the participation of numerous FP7 and H2020 projects.

3.2   Emergency Situation Management in a Smart City (ESM)

Continuing into this century, society has supported a movement of people from rural areas to cities. Nowadays, more people live in urban environments than in rural ones. It is estimated that this process will not stop and within 20 years the urban population will be around 5 billion. The big challenges for the whole society will be related to resource management in these overcrowded environments. Worldsensing works in the development of a model for smart cities and its products intend to solve current and future problems related to the use of innovative technology to challenge emergency management.

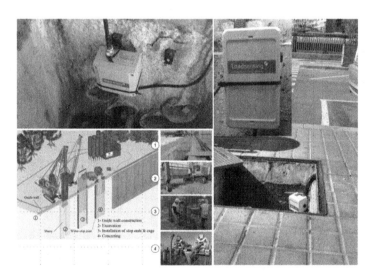

Fig. 4. WOS IoT industrial device

The proposed "Emergency Situation Management" use case within mF2C project aims to validate a novel and innovative hybrid architecture that serves (i) to analyse flows of people and infrastructure state in order to provide useful information to private customers and authorities, (ii) to detect a possible emergency in real-time, and (iii) to decrease the necessary resources in terms of energy, latency, etc. to respond to specific situations in accordance with the applications requirements.

The proposed use case is based on the implementation of distributed elements of capturing signals and data (Worldsensing IoT device, see Fig. 4) as well as a centralized asset management system to integrate heterogeneous industrial-related information in a flexible and efficient cloud platform (Worldsensing asset management platform, see Fig. 5). The mF2C paradigm should suggest policies to manage the aforementioned hybrid architecture where services and decisions have to be taken in real-time for improving the performance of today industrial systems.

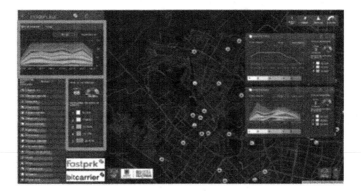

Fig. 5. WOS asset management platform

Normally, the information captured by today IT (Information Technology) and OT (Operational Technology) devices is stored and processed in a cloud computing system to present such information to the end user. Occasionally, in case of emergency situations, the information captured by the devices is processed through FOG devices to optimise the Quality of Service (QoS) factors. In mF2C project, a complete approach where asset management and control data are considered in the same solution suite.

The proposed use case is subdivided into 3 phases: (i) To assess the performance of a central industrial management system in terms of key parameters in normal operations: latency, reliability, data elaboration, etc. (Cloud Computing assessment); (ii) To assess the performance of monitoring devices considering specific requirements when emergency situation are detected, i.e. an accident (Fog computing assessment); and (iii) To assess the mF2C solution, where a hybrid framework guarantees high Fog and Cloud computing performance, both during ordinary operation and emergency management situation. The results have to be at least similar to point 1 and 2 where the centralized and distributed problems are solved in isolated fashion (mF2C model assessment).

Finally, Fig. 6 shows the technological perspective deployed in the use case. This last figure shows the different components provided by Worldsensing and mF2C consortium as well as its location in the proposed Smart City scenario.

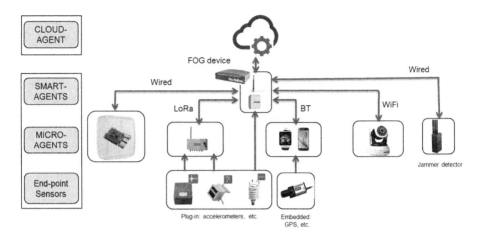

Fig. 6. Technologies deployment in the smart city scenario

4   Potential Impact Brought by mF2C

The Smart City use case aims to integrate industrial solutions to provide advanced and more efficient services to both end-users and decision makers. The introduction of mF2C paradigm within the Smart City ecosystem will provide more scalable and secure commercial solutions. Indeed, the mF2C implementation will enable progressive scaling of the infrastructure complexity and can absorb the increasing needs of computational demand (such as due to big data). This is very relevant, considering market opportunities and business forecast in Smart Cities and IoT. The developed management system will facilitate scaling and lowering infrastructure cost, especially for the envisioned smaller-scale deployments that today are too expensive due to the need for over-dimensioned dedicated infrastructure. The mF2C solution will also enable the introduction of new computing paradigms, including edge-technology computing approach, where computation is moved close to the "edges" of the Internet to reduce risks of failure and delay, and improve reliability in the sense that data is not lost while the edge device is temporarily disconnected. This approach will enable cities to install fog computing infrastructure locally and enable new real-time services. More concretely the mF2C benefits in the context of managing Emergency Situations in smart cities may be summarized as:

- Increasing service reliability by 30% and Quality of service (QoS) by 10%
- Decreasing delays by 30%
- Decreasing operational costs (OPEX) by 10%.

Worldsensing will take advantage of the mF2C framework to build secure and powerful specific IoT services based on a prolific relation between end-devices and central platform. The synergies and the funding obtained in the project will enable more ambitious developments which will permit to access to wider markets that are not touched currently due to the limited availability of suitable platforms. The issues addressed in this project will be of great importance to improve energy-efficiency, robustness, ease-of-use and security required for meeting the needs of the World-sensing's roadmap towards deploying applications in urban and industrial scenarios. In particular, mF2C achievements will allow us to design new IoT services, therefore, creating new and strengthening considerably existing business lines.

5   Conclusions

In this paper, we describe the main impact brought by deploying a coordinated management strategy for a scenario combining fog and cloud resources, on a specific service addressing the management of emergency situations in a smart city. The presented benefits do not only focus on the specific service itself, but also put the focus on the impact it may have on a well-established company deploying such a service. Thus, the main objective of the paper does not deal with conceptually deploying architecture to support such a management, what is briefly introduced in the paper, but on highlighting the benefits brought by such a deployment. Certainly, the proposed scenario is just one vertical showing the foreseen benefits, and many others are also envisioned, such as on the e-health area or in smart transportation.

Acknowledgements. This work is supported by the H2020 mF2C project (730929). For UPC authors is also supported by the Spanish Ministry of Economy and Competitiveness and by the European Regional Development Fund under contract TEC2015-66220-R (MINECO/FEDER).

References

1. Masip, X., Marín, E., Jukan, A., Ren, G.J., Tashakor, G.: Foggy clouds and cloudy fogs: a real need for coordinated management of fog-to-cloud (F2C) computing systems. IEEE Wirel. Commun. Mag. **23**, 120–128 (2016)
2. Openfog reference architecture. https://www.openfogconsortium.org/ra/
3. Bonomi, F., Milito, R., Natarajan, P., Zhu, J.: Fog computing: a platform for internet of things and analytics. In: Bessis, N., Dobre, C. (eds.) Big Data and Internet of Things: A Roadmap for Smart Environments. SCI, vol. 546, pp. 169–186. Springer, Cham (2014). https://doi.org/10.1007/978-3-319-05029-4_7
4. mF2C project. http://www.mf2c-project.eu

Fog and Cloud in the Transportation, Marine and eHealth Domains

Matija Cankar[1(✉)], Eneko Olivares Gorriti[2], Matevž Markovič[1], and Flavio Fuart[1]

[1] XLAB d.o.o., Pot za Brdom 100, 1000 Ljubljana, Slovenia
`matija.cankar@xlab.si`
[2] Department of Communications, Universitat Politècnica de València, Camino de Vera, s/n, 46022 Valencia, Spain

Abstract. Amazing things have been achieved in a wide range of application domains by exploiting a multitude of small connected devices, defined as the Internet of Things. Managing of these devices and their resources is a task for the underlying Fog technology that enables building of smart and efficient applications. Currently, the Fog is not implemented to the extent that we can submit application requirements to a Fog provider, select returned resources and deploy an application on them. A widely adopted workaround is to deploy Cloud applications that exploit the functionality of IoT and Fog devices. Although Clouds provide virtually unlimited computation power, they could present a bottleneck and unnecessary communication overhead when a huge number of devices needs to be controlled, read or written to. Therefore, it is reasonable to formulate use cases that will exploit the Edge and Fog functionality and define a set of basic requirements for Fog providers.

Keywords: Cloud computing · Fog · Edge · Internet of Things
Fog to cloud

1 Introduction

Small and powerful computing devices have reached a production price low enough to become affordable, thus also to be attached and used on things (sensors, actuators) in different domains. Formation of the so-called Internet of Things (IoT) [1] produces a huge amount of new computing power, new capabilities and different innovative ways of employing computers and things. The management of new IoT capabilities has become a hot topic in the field of Computer Science, which is also evident from numerous current initiatives [2].

On the other side, we have a mature technology of Cloud computing that brought infrastructure provisioning, leasing and management to a new level. It has become a synonym for infrastructure provision to users and stakeholders that need to run their services. IoT-enabled devices that share data over the Internet probably, at some point, access resources that are stored or processed on a Cloud-powered infrastructure.

© Springer International Publishing AG, part of Springer Nature 2018
D. B. Heras and L. Bougé (Eds.): Euro-Par 2017 Workshops, LNCS 10659, pp. 292–303, 2018.
https://doi.org/10.1007/978-3-319-75178-8_24

IoT-based applications require reliable technology for data processing. Cloud computing is currently the preferred approach due its maturity and scaling capabilities, as they allow services to grow and shrink in-line with demands. Cloud owners and users have the ability to choose from a large portfolio of high-quality tools for managing IaaS from centralized data centres [3,4]. Unfortunately, these tools are currently not capable of managing IoT or Edge infrastructure. Therefore, both domains are not reaching optimal resource utilization levels. With the new Fog paradigm [5,6], new concepts of service infrastructure will arise combining the lease of Fog and Cloud resources. Efficient resource management of Fog and Cloud resources is the main topic of the mF2C project [7].

In this paper, we first introduce the enabling technologies and explain the Fog and Cloud application concept, as embodied in the mF2C project, and lay the groundwork for its usage in conjunction with above-mentioned candidate IoT domains. Then we present challenges and fields of interest through use cases in candidate IoT domains that could benefit the most from the mF2C approach. Through analysis of these use cases, we have found out that the underlying requirement for our new platform is that it should be more distributed and less dependent on the Cloud. We further describe the concrete benefits of applying the Fog and Cloud application context to the presented use-cases. Most notably, we describe the Smart Boat use case that is based on Sentinel IoT devices. In this use case, the focus is on minimizing the communication between IoT devices and Cloud, as well as on encouraging autonomous collaboration of multiple Sentinel devices, demonstrating benefits and compliance with the Fog to Cloud architecture.

2   Fog and Cloud

The Cloud application concept is well known and widely accepted in the industrial and academic fields, while the Fog concepts, which enable Cloud functionality available on the Edge [5], only recently began to properly evolve as first applicable architectures have become available, e.g. Open Fog Consortium recently made its architecture publicly available [8]. Because the Fog approach is still in early stages of development, current applications for IoT devices mainly follow the client-web server approach with limited scalability as it allows Cloud-based orchestration only. This concept prevents powerful Edge devices, like gateways and end-devices, to efficiently share resources in a complex application data processing work-flow. As one might deduce from the application domains introduced in the following sections, a better way of understanding and utilizing the underlying technology is required to enable efficient deployment and management of next-generation Fog and Cloud applications. The mF2C project [7,9] initiative will provide a multi-layer platform with strong focus on the use of devices on the Edge. The list of improvements that mF2C brings into the Cloud and IoT area is large, therefore we shall, for the purpose of this article, limit ourselves to the following few:

Efficient processing. Processing raw data near the source, while storing into the Clouds only filtered and cleaned data, contributes to *offloading Cloud resources, saving the bandwidth* and *removing single points of failure.*

Security and privacy. Processing data near the source allows removing sensible data before its transfer into the Cloud. This improves security while minimizing the attack surface. Moreover, the mF2C consortium will focus on developing tools and libraries for secure IoT communication, such as anonymous authentication [16].

Advanced orchestration. Improving resource usage on Edge devices opens a new dimension of scaling and contributes to application orchestration. The mF2C goal is to provide the foundation of intelligent data processing, which could be moved from Fog to Cloud or vice-versa, depending on current availability of resources.

Autonomous behaviour. Giving more knowledge and processing power to Edge devices will make the system more resilient, self-healing and capable of solving issues faster and autonomously at the Edge.

Fig. 1. The conceptual schema of mF2C platform and domain devices.

From the architectural perspective, mF2C would like to employ the power of Fog resources and provide seamless integration with Cloud infrastructure management. The basic concept and mF2C layers are presented in Fig. 1. These layers are:

Cloud layer. The multi-Cloud resources from multiple private or public Cloud providers.

Fog layer. The Fog layer includes everything between Cloud and IoT devices. The list includes gateways and smart agents that are capable of: providing processing or storage resources to applications, managing the application work-flow execution or handling application requests.

IoT layer. Beside resources from Cloud and everything down to the Edge, the Fog as a whole, is not complete and useful without sensors and domain-specific devices that are connected to the Edge. These resources are mainly sensors, actuators and devices that interact with the application resources or notification endpoints, such as smartphones, smart watches, etc.

Each individual layer can have more complex hierarchy of devices (sub-layers) that provide all required resources to the application. The functionality contributed by the Cloud, Fog and IoT resources will be shared to the application through the mF2C framework, which will develop mechanisms to discover and manage the resources.

The main goal of mF2C is to provide a framework that will allow development and seamless deployment of Fog applications on the presented architecture. Furthermore, the mF2C platform will follow the same multi-tenancy principles and provide the ability to share, use and buy Fog resources in the same way as it can be done in the Cloud. In this way, mF2C brings the Fog closer to the users, makes it more accessible to the stakeholders and provides a strong resource backbone for the future IoT applications. Users and stakeholders will benefit from employing the mF2C concepts on IoT domains, resulting in more efficient and safer applications.

3   Challenges and Fields of Interest for Fog to Cloud

IoT devices are on the rise and scientists, as well as business developers, are daily finding new ways of their usage. Their attempts to create the most optimal software and hardware solutions encounter many obstacles and challenges, which will be tackled one by one and solved in the future when Fog will be mature and fully-operable tool. Our research brings on a plate few projects and use-cases that generate challenges and drive the Fog-to-Cloud research. The first step in building a Fog-to-Cloud framework is the provision of interoperability among components and protocols. The second step is the inspection of best possible use-cases to demonstrate the benefits of the new functionalities that will be reached through Fog-to-Cloud. In this section, we first focus on the interoperability approach defined by INTER-IoT project and afterwards we present the hottest application domains, populated with IoT devices that most eagerly strive for new improvements in the IoT/Cloud management fields - Transport, Health and Marine.

3.1   Cross-Layer IoT Platforms Interoperability

A growing number of heterogeneous IoT architectures, standards and solutions across all application domains in the past few years have been driven by advances in the underlying technology. This has resulted in isolated solutions at all levels that are, although efficient for a specific application, isolated from the rest of the IoT ecosystem. Bridging this gap is difficult because there is no emerging standard that would be embraced by the majority of solution providers. To allow cross-platform and cross-domain interoperability, the INTER-IoT project [12] is aiming at the design, implementation and experimentation of an open cross-layer framework and associated methodologies to provide voluntary interoperability among heterogeneous Internet of Things (IoT) platforms. It will allow the development of smart and efficient applications, atop of different heterogeneous IoT platforms, spanning single and/or multiple application domains. The two application domains and use cases addressed in the project, in which the IoT interoperability framework will be applied, are m-health and port transportation and logistics.

Interoperability is implemented at all architectural levels:

– Device level interoperability supports seamless inclusion of novel IoT devices and their inter-operation with already existing, even heterogeneous ones,
– Networking level interoperability supports smart objects mobility and information routing. This will allow design and implementation of fully connected ecosystems,
– Middleware level allows seamless service discovery and management system for smart objects and their basic services,
– Application service level enables reuse and exchange (import/export) of heterogeneous services between different IoT platforms,
– Data and semantics level allows common interpretation of data and information based on a globally shared ontology in order to achieve semantic interoperability between heterogeneous data sources.

In the context of Cloud and Fog computing, components developed at device and middleware levels could be leveraged by novel Cloud to Fog approaches. In the context of IoT middleware interoperability, bridging among different platforms (e.g. FIWARE [13], OM2M [14], universAAL [15]) may be achieved through Cloud deployment of the INTER-IoT Inter-middleware component. On the other hand, a more federated architecture may be appropriate for settings where bridging is needed towards the Edge in order to take into account performance, computing complexity and privacy requirements. Although modular in design, this interoperability layer would need a robust system to manage Cloud/Fog deployments.

Interoperability at device level is achieved through the Device-to-Gateway communication pattern. This pattern is commonly used when less widely available radio technologies are needed, especially in the case of interoperability between legacy non-IP-based devices.

IoT gateways have evolved beyond the sole role of ensuring networking operations. Nowadays they are providing more advanced functionalities that have to be shifted to the Edge of the network so that they are closer to the devices. Those advanced functionalities (more storage, simple rule engines, advanced API access, etc.) that need more computing power than constrained devices can provide, can be implemented through Fog Computing.

Shifting Cloud Computing to the Edge of the network in the case of IoT gateways implies virtualization of those gateway functionalities that need more computing power. INTER-IoT solves this by creating a dual physical/virtual gateway, where the physical gateway only performs network-level operations. Its virtual counterpart is located in the Fog, where all other functions are performed. A fast, secure and robust network link is created between the physical and virtual part, so that there is no data loss and the physical-virtual gateway is perceived as a single advanced IoT gateway.

The mapping of INTER-IoT Inter-Layer interoperability components to the mF2C conceptual architecture would facilitate their deployment and management. The Cloud layer, would still remain the most capable storage and processing backbone, hosting the Inter-Layer application and Inter-Layer middleware components. In specific cases, the middleware component would be deployed at the Edge level. At Fog layer, the virtualized gateway would provide necessary computing power to its physical counterpart at IoT layer.

3.2 Intelligent Transport Systems

Intelligent transportation systems (ITS) form a complex and dynamic environment that combines a huge amount of devices, each of which has its own logistic purpose. Most important of all ITS devices are road vehicles, which have a great information sharing potential. These are employing next generation (5G) communication systems to collaborate, reach consensus in road usage and contribute to safer and faster transport of goods and people. Even though vehicle to vehicle (V2V) and vehicle to infrastructure (V2I) communications are already well defined and known, their exploitation is still in its infancy. Nowadays all collaborative decisions and majority of communication is driven through the Cloud.

One such project that works within the scope of ITS is TIMON [11], an EU project initiative, which aims at delivering a framework of services to all users of the transport ecosystem – drivers, vulnerable road users and businesses. TIMON services will be structured in five key areas, namely Driver assistance services, Services for vulnerable road users, Multi-modal dynamic commuter service, Enhanced real-time traffic API and TIMON collaborative ecosystem. A detailed presentation of TIMON architecture is presented in Fig. 2.

TIMON services will gather data from Open Data sources, mobile devices, roadside units (RSU), vehicle on-board units (OBU) and process the data in the Cloud to provide routing services and hazard warnings to the users. A small fraction of communication will go directly between the devices through V2V or V2I communication, but when devices are not in the range of a direct wireless connection, the communication will go through geo-messaging servers. Geo-messaging

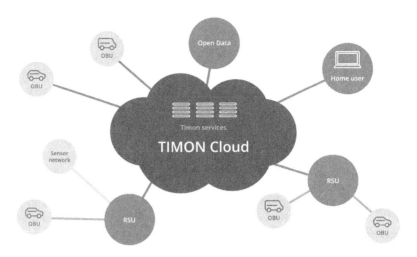

Fig. 2. TIMON Cloud architecture

servers are deployed in the Cloud and take care of location-based warning messages. One of the major reasons to use Cloud services is that the technology is mature enough to provide a required level of privacy, as well as trust, and is easily accessible to the stakeholders (municipalities) that do not need to buy and maintain the server infrastructure.

The TIMON Cloud together with OBU and RSU is a valuable manifestation of a large dynamic Fog to Cloud system. Therefore we have a large expectations from the TIMON results and their requirements which will help us in understanding the dynamic Fog applications. The TIMON example can be perfectly mapped onto the mF2C conceptual architecture. The TIMON Cloud, which is in Cloud layer, remains to be the most capable storage and processing backbone, but it produces high latency as it is not close to the Edge. The majority of on-board units (OBU) and roadside units (RSU) primarily become IoT layer devices for sensing and notification endpoints. The Fog layer devices, which are gateways or smart agents, become powerful hubs between the Cloud and other Fog devices. Note that this powerful device could be also the RSU which provides the resources to OBU which share the resources with other OBU.

3.3   Ambient Assisted Living (AAL) and Homecare

Ambient Assisted Living (AAL) is a term that describes the way we make lives of elderly people, who want to live independently for as long as possible, easier and more manageable through the use of technology. It embraces the ambient intelligence paradigm, which seeks empowerment of elderlies' capabilities by the means of digital environments, built upon the IoT model. These environments are sensitive, adaptive and responsive to human needs. In other words, it enhances person's independence, lowers the cost of health-care and lessens the burden upon the caretakers by employing both wearable and ambient devices (such as ambient temperature sensors, sensors for gas leaks, GPS locators) and integrates them into a RPM (Remote Patient Monitoring) system. The RPM system monitors and records everyday life activities, it enables quick detection and response to problematic situations, as well as remote communication. It enables caregivers to remotely access data on elder's level of activity and medical condition and thus also to assess whether treatment needs to be changed, whether the elder complies with the care plan, as well as to contact them when in need. However, the RPM system can also act on the data independently, calling emergency in case of fall or injury, or when a presence of a poisonous gas is detected within the elder's home environment. A possible upgrade to this operation of AAL could be the introduction of artificial learning, which would enable the system to recognize correlations of the present situation with the past negative situations and to warn the elder about that.

The operation of mobile and wearable sensors in the context of AAL is divided into a three-tier Body Area Network (BAN). BAN includes Intra-BAN (which consists of devices in close proximity to elder's body), Inter-BAN (which consists of devices that communicate directly with the devices within Intra-BAN) and Beyond-BAN (all other devices, including the internet). In general, smart objects that form the AAL can either be active (local decision making is possible with them) or passive (they just store data).

The aim of the Ambient Assisted Living Health Platform (AALHP) project is to integrate already existing and compatible smart house installations into a home-care product, which will build upon the already existing health-care platforms. The Fig. 3 presents AALHP that will use data both from the environment (from ambient devices) and from the devices, worn by the user (wearables), most notable of which will be the wrist watch or wrist ring, worn by the elder, and his or her smartphone. It will integrate and analyse this data, and then act upon the results, either through smart home devices or through notifying the elder or some other authorized entity. Analysed data will be available to all parties, who have an appropriate level of access to elder's Personal Health Record (for example, the elder's physician and relatives). AALHP will also predict likely outcomes of the present condition, based on past cases, and act accordingly (for example, by advising the elder to act differently in a particular situation, or overriding smart home appliance's operation).

The AALHP approach is an example of an application domain that could greatly benefit from novel Fog-to-Cloud (F2C) approaches, as it defines specific technical, legal and ethical requirements. On the technical side, its complex event processing (CEP) and analytics could be pushed to the Edge. Edge processing should also allow for opportunistic clustering of devices (e.g. a physician examining the patient at home, a person entering her car and devices connecting to the car's system, temporary usage of medical devices for a specific therapy, etc.). The mapping of AALHP on the mF2C architecture is straightforward, with the High Performance Analytics (HPA) residing in the Cloud layer and the IoT Concentrator module at Fog layer, where basic CEP is performed in order to detect key event to be transmitted to the Cloud.

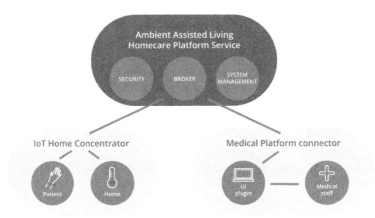

Fig. 3. The schematic architecture of the AALHP.

Moreover, on the non-technical side, performing part of the processing at the Edge would implicitly solve privacy concerns (privacy by design, privacy preserving analytics). Specific solutions may be proposed for consent management in specific conditions, where consent could be waived in emergency situations and additional information forwarded from Edge to Cloud services or ad-hoc device clustering allowed.

3.4   Marine Ecosystem

In the marine domain, there is a lot of interest for the use of IoT devices on boats, especially for monitoring and control of the vessel. The main reason is to have a total overview over the location of your fleet, as well as to detect malfunctions or dangerous situations. The basic portfolio of marine IoT solutions functions includes GPS tracking, beige water monitoring, battery monitoring and battery drain alarm, door hatch alarm and anchor alarm.

Sentinel Boat monitor device [10] covers all above-mentioned functions. It also has additional sensors (such as an accelerometer) and the ability to connect additional Bluetooth Low Energy (BLE) sensors. These further expand the functionality to, for example, capturing weather data and motion detection. In order to satisfy the interest of larger stakeholders, such as insurance companies, the next generation of Boat monitoring devices will implement video and voice capturing capabilities. The capacity of collected data on the boat presents a huge issue for Marine IoT systems that generally have intermittent communication or expensive bandwidth connection to the Internet and consequently to the Cloud. Vessels are frequently out of WiFi or 3G/4G coverage, which means that data processing should be done locally. In this aspect, the target platform for future IoT applications should be more distributed and less Cloud dependent.

A new Smart Boat solution has been designed that introduces the middle layer between Cloud and IoT devices and provides a possibility to offload the

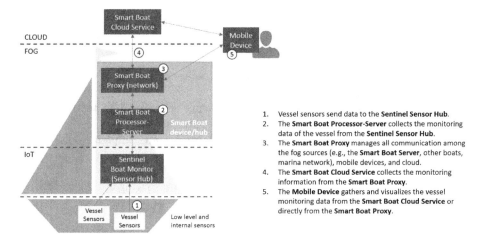

Fig. 4. The architecture of the Smart Boat use-case based on Sentinel Devices.

processing locally or nearby devices. Figure 4 presents the Smart Boat process-ing and networking piece in the Fog/Edge layer that covers efficient processing and communication, while Cloud layer and IoT layer remains the same that they were before. The new architecture design is ready for new marine IoT applica-tions and ensures the compatibility with the new modern Marine IoT standards and protocols, e.g. open source universal marine data exchange format called Signal K[1].

The proposed architectural expansion tends to be an improvement that will be employed in many areas where the management of IoT devices through the Cloud will be too difficult or network consuming. Note that the Fig. 4 explains only the most basic workflow of the application, which connects the sensors to the Cloud. The Smart Boat devices, i.e. Smart Boat Proxy, are equipped with multiple connectivity options, as WiFi, BLE, 3G/4G and LoRa. As such, the Fog devices on the boat are able to form ad-hoc networks with other boats or marinas if possible and share its processing and networking resources when required by applications and services.

The mapping of Smart Boat use case onto the proposed mF2C architecture is quite straightforward, as can be seen in Fig. 4. The Sentinel Boat Monitor sensor hub presents an IoT layer and the Cloud application will reside in the Cloud layer. The Fog layer is reserved for a Smart Boat processing and networking devices capable of locally processing or storing the requests from IoT or Cloud layer. Note that not every boat would have a powerful smart agent or Edge device, therefore it is necessary to provide a possibility to share those resources to Sentinel devices in the vicinity when the boats are close together anchored in a bay or waiting in the harbour. To make this vision a reality, the smart boat team expects from mF2C to provide a platform that will actively monitor

---

[1] http://signalk.org/.

the availability of the resources and move the data and processing to the most efficient resources at the moment. Moreover, the proposed Smart Boat use-case will become the test bed to four security related scenarios will be demonstrated:

Continuous Boat Monitoring will include secure collection of data from the boats to the Cloud and vice versa.

Anomaly detection will focus on secure sharing of sensor data to the nearby boats and detecting if one boat sensors measures are off.

On-line Docking and Anchoring reservation is an implementation of complex mechanisms for the docking and anchorage permissions, based on anonymous proof of the payment.

Data plan sharing secure manifestation of data plan sharing among the group of boats, based on fair exchange of goods.

The proposed scenarios cover the most important topics of the secure IoT, Fog and Cloud communication and thus present a perfect environment for testing the mF2C platform. In the Smart Boat use case the focus will be on minimizing the communication between IoT devices and Cloud, and encouragement for collaboration between multiple autonomous smart boat devices in order to get them to share their resources for communication (as data plans) or processing power (improving the weather predictions from the data gathered by single or multiple smart boat devices).

4   Conclusion and Contribution

This paper presents the needs for the next generation of resource provision concepts that take into account sharing and managing the resources on the Edge of the networks. First, the paper describes the concept of Fog-to-Cloud approach which is the topic of the ongoing mF2C project and presents the proposed three layer architecture. Within the concept presentation, the main improvements of current technology state were selected and explained. Further, the main concerns from the use-cases covering three domains of IoT applications are explained. With the concrete examples, the basic requirements for the future IoT applications were described. Alongside the mapping of the applications from the use cases to the proposed mF2C architecture is described and the most important contributions to each IoT domain was elaborated.

The contribution of the work is in the selection of the representative use-cases from which the core lessons will be learned, which will drive the work on the mF2C project. For example, the ITS use-case presented through the TIMON project is currently based on the resources that have wide availability to the stakeholders. With a good promotion of Fog to Cloud and supporting multi-tenancy, new business opportunities will arise for the public resource providers. This will be an important milestone for applications that require Fog to Cloud capabilities and needed to be deployed on a large and scalable infrastructure. The main improvement of TIMON using the Fog to Cloud would be in lowering latencies, while the number and location of running geo-messaging servers required for local and near-real time notifications could be determined on current demand. The placement and density of geo-messaging servers would reflect the density and activeness of IoT devices in the fog. Similar improvements are applicable also in Ambient Assisted Living and Cross-layer IoT platforms interoperability use-cases.

The future work includes a detailed inspection of the presented use-cases, scenarios, its implementation and provide an mF2C platform that supports these use cases. The experiences from the use cases will help to design an appropriate building blocks of mF2C platform and demonstrate its potential with the representative applications deployed on Smart Boat use-case.

Acknowledgements. This work is supported by the European Union through the Horizon 2020 research and innovation program under grants 730929 (mF2C), 636220 (TIMON) and 687283 (Inter-IoT). AALHP is co-financed by the Republic of Slovenia and the European Union from the European Regional Development Fund.

References

1. Gubbi, J., et al.: Internet of Things (IoT): a vision, architectural elements, and future directions. Future Gener. Comput. Syst. **29**(7), 1645–1660 (2013)
2. IoT-epi. http://iot-epi.eu/projects/
3. ManageIQ. http://www.manageiq.org/
4. OpenStack. http://www.openstack.org/
5. Vaquero, L.M., Rodero-Merino, L.: Finding your way in the fog: towards a comprehensive definition of fog computing. SIGCOMM Comput. Commun. Rev. **44**(5), 27–32 (2014)
6. Yi, S., Li, C., Li, Q.: A survey of fog computing: concepts, applications and issues. In: Proceedings of the 2015 Workshop on Mobile Big Data (Mobidata 2015), pp. 37–42. ACM, New York (2015)
7. mF2C. http://www.mf2c-project.eu
8. Open Fog consortium. https://www.openfogconsortium.org/ra/
9. H2020 mF2C. http://cordis.europa.eu/project/rcn/206164_en.html
10. Sentinel. http://www.sentinel.hr
11. TIMON. http://www.timon-project.eu
12. INTER-IoT. http://www.inter-iot-project.eu/
13. FIWARE. https://www.fiware.org/
14. OM2M. http://www.eclipse.org/om2m/
15. universAAL. http://www.universaal.info/
16. EMMY - Library for zero-knowledge proofs. https://github.com/xlab-si/emmy

Scalable Linux Container Provisioning in Fog and Edge Computing Platforms

Michele Gazzetti[1(⊠)], Andrea Reale[1], Kostas Katrinis[1], and Antonio Corradi[2]

[1] IBM Research, Dublin, Ireland
michele.gazzetti1@ibm.com
[2] Department of Computer Science and Engineering,
University of Bologna, Bologna, Italy

Abstract. The tremendous increase in the number of mobile devices and the proliferation of all kinds of new types of sensors is creating new value opportunities by analyzing, developing insights from, and actuating upon large volumes of data streams generated at the edge of the network. While general purpose processing required to unleash this value is abundant in Cloud datacenters, bringing raw IoT data streams to the Cloud poses critical challenges, including: (i) regulatory constraints related to data sensitivity, (ii) significant bandwidth costs and (iii) latency barriers inhibiting near-real-time applications. Edge Computing aspires to extend the traditional cloud model to the "edge of the network", to deliver low-latency, bandwidth-efficiencies and controlled privacy. For all the commonalities between the two models, transitioning the provisioning and orchestration of a distributed analytics platform from Cloud to Edge is not trivial. The two models present totally different cost structures such as price of bandwidth, data communication latency, power density and availability. In this paper, we address the challenge associated with transitioning scalable provisioning from Cloud to distributed Edge platforms. We identify current scalability challenges in Linux container provisioning at the Edge; we propose a novel peer-to-peer model taking on them; we present a prototype of this model designed for and tested on real Edge testbeds, and we report a scalability evaluation on a scale-out virtualized platform. Our results demonstrate significant savings in terms of provisioning latency and bandwidth utilization.

1 Introduction

The number of devices connected to the Internet has registered a steady increment, and the 6 billion things connected today define an ecosystem of objects called "Internet of Things" (IoT). An increasing number of industries is betting on IoT as a way to boost efficiency and explore new business models through better real-time insights on their processes. While various new paradigms are emerging to support and make this vision a reality, Edge Computing, which enables the placement of services directly at the edge of the network, is a very promising one. Edge Computing augments the traditional cloud model, by allowing to create new latency/privacy sensitive services and, at the same time, lowers

© Springer International Publishing AG, part of Springer Nature 2018
D. B. Heras and L. Bougé (Eds.): Euro-Par 2017 Workshops, LNCS 10659, pp. 304–315, 2018.
https://doi.org/10.1007/978-3-319-75178-8_25

operational costs by reducing communication between devices and remote backends. Following well consolidated industrial practices adopted in Cloud computing, virtualization approaches based, for example, on hypervisor-governed virtual machines [11] and Linux containers [12], have been proposed as the execution environment of choice for Edge computing answering the common requirements of resource isolation and dependency management.

Still, the new paradigm does not come without new challenges, including scalable distribution and update of applications across large Edge/IoT deployments. In this paper, we attempt to address this challenge in an Edge computing environment employing Linux containers as application distribution and execution unit. In Sect. 2, we introduce a baseline (best-practice to date) method to deploy Linux containers on the Edge and discuss its scalability challenges. To overcome them, we present in this paper a distributed streamed deployment approach. Our method leverages the inherent layered structure of container images and filesystems to develop a peer-to-peer provisioning protocol that improves latency at scale, while conserving on Edge-Cloud bandwidth costs.

We have implemented our approach on target edge devices (NVidia Tegra, ARMv7 Raspberry Pi) as a proof of viability. To showcase the promise of the approach at scale, we have used the device-based results to calibrate Virtual Machines (VMs) executing Edge device operating system and applications. We obtained results on up to 21 Edge nodes running on this virtual environment, showing an up to 3 times improvement in container provisioning time within each locality and up to 10 times reduction of Edge-Cloud bandwidth utilization, when compared to provisioning a locality from a single centralized container image registry.

2   Motivation: Naive Edge Container Provisioning

The Edge computing model we assume in this paper is the following. As shown in Fig. 1, Edge devices are grouped in "localities". Nodes within a locality are horizontally interconnected at lower latency and cost of bandwidth, when compared to the network link used for Edge-Cloud communication. We assume Edge nodes to be executing on embedded/microserver devices, running a general purpose operating system. Without loss of approach applicability to other operating systems and virtualization approaches - as long as a layered structuring of deployment images can be inferred - we focus our presented work to devices using Linux and Docker containers as the runtime for Edge applications.

Docker [1] defines a container as a runtime instance of a Docker image. An image is an ordered collection of changes compared to the initial filesystem representing the base of the image. We can think of an image as a set of layers stacked on top of each other to form the container filesystem. To facilitate image sharing and streamlining of container provisioning, Docker provides a dedicated image repository and server called Registry. The Registry is a stateless, highly scalable server side application that stores Docker images and responds to requests for deployment from remote nodes. This component of the architecture is usually running within a (Cloud) datacenter, receives pull requests and responds with the requested image. As part of this deployment procedure, the layers comprising an image are combined into a single archive binary file and then transmitted to the host where the container image is instantiated.

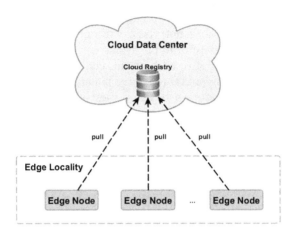

Fig. 1. Edge computing model with nodes in each locality pulling container images from a centralized Docker Registry

Applying the above baseline best practice approach ("naïve") for container provisioning at the Edge leads to multiple pull requests coming from different nodes of the same locality. This is inefficient in terms of cost of bandwidth, as it entails avoidable exchange of redundant data for the same location. Moreover, this approach can lead to increased load at the Registry and thus decreased service quality, to the extent that the Registry itself could rapidly become a bottleneck. The latter effect can specifically occur when a large number of edge nodes concurrently issue download requests for an image, for example, when updated image versions become available. One solution that can limit the load on the registry is clustering or geo-distribution, which though again clearly raises the cost of the service.

The graph presented in Fig. 2 provides a visual representation of the problem, showing the time to deploy a container image of 500 MB on a varying number of concurrently provisioned edge nodes. The concurrent scenario represents the worst-case in terms of provisioning overhead, for reasons outlined above. The data represented in the graph is derived assuming 200 Mb/s bandwidth between the Cloud Registry and the Edge locality and Edge nodes with 100 Mb/s network interfaces. Figure 2 shows that the time taken to deploy a new container image in a locality increases linearly: while a single node requires only 40 s to pull the image, provisioning 10 nodes saturates the available Edge-Cloud bandwidth. In case of 1000 nodes, provisioning takes more than 5 h.

Mirroring the remote Registry within each locality would help improving the scalability of the solution and reduce provisioning latency; however, such an

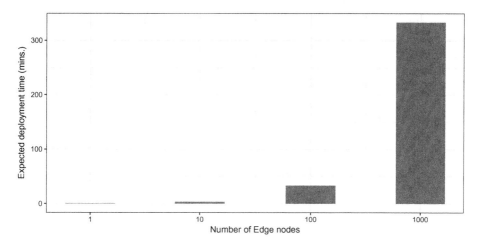

Fig. 2. Estimated time to fully provision a locality with a container image of 500 MB as the number of Edge nodes in the locality increases.

approach would suffer from following shortcomings: (a) cost of bandwidth would still be very high, due to continuous syncing between edge and cloud registries, especially if there is a large set of discrete images deployed in a locality and (b) the typically limited processing capability and storage capacity of Edge devices would be an important limiting factor for them to act as local Registries, given the average size of container images and the potential size in terms of devices of a locality. Beyond the technical challenges, there are also business barriers in following such an approach, since, in some deployments, the Edge premise may not be under the control of the Registry/Cloud providers.

3   Streamed Container Deployment

To overcome the complexity of distributing the image within a locality without creating bottlenecks, we propose a paradigm shift toward a novel peer-to-peer provisioning approach where nodes in a locality co-operate to accelerate provisioning. We call this approach "Streamed Deployment" (SD). Figure 3 shows the block diagram of the components involved in our streamed deployment approach. To provision an image within a locality, one of the Edge nodes is elected as entry point to the Edge-Cloud network. This node (termed "Gateway") interacts with the remote Cloud infrastructure, pulls the image on behalf of the entire locality and provides information regarding the status of the nodes within it. Within the Gateway, the Gateway Manager (GM) dynamically manages the formation of a peer-to-peer distribution graph within the locality. This includes the dynamic repair of the distribution topology in the case of node timeouts (due to, e.g., failures or in case of mobile nodes exiting a locality). The coordination between the various nodes within the locality occurs via a Message Broker (MB, in our case realized through a stock MQTT broker), a PUB/SUB broker capable of decoupling sender and receiver through asynchronous messaging. Last, each edge node carries an implementation of a Stream Manager (SM), an agent that implements the real-time container image streaming protocol on top of the formed peer-to-peer distribution graph. Also, the SM interacts with the Docker daemon on each node to import received image layers to the local image store that each Docker Edge instance maintains.

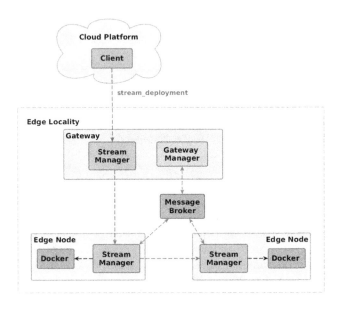

Fig. 3. Architecture of our Streamed Deployment implementation.

Figure 4 provides a more comprehensive representation of the interactions performed during the deployment. There are three actors involved in the depicted workflow: the formerly described Gateway Manager of the locality, the Stream Managers of each Edge node being provisioned (only one instance of the SM is shown for brevity), and the client initiating the deployment. Typically, the client would be situated in a remote location relative to Edge localities, e.g., within an Edge orchestration entity running in the Cloud as part of an integrated IoT platform solution. In this case, the client contacts the edge Gateway to request the deployment of a new container image including ancillary information of the image that needs to be deployed (image identifier and composing layers). The SM on the Gateway responds with an ID that uniquely identifies the deployment procedure and the list of layers to be pulled. If a subset of the requested layers is already present within the locality, the SM requests to pull only the differences between the received list of deployment layers and the ones that are already stored in the locality. After this handshaking phase succeeds, the GM establishes the peer-to-peer distribution topology within the locality describing the communication chains among Edge nodes. Depending on different optimization objectives, different algorithms can be used to build this tree. As this aspect is not central to our method, and for reasons of space, we do not discuss it further in this paper, but we refer the interested reader to the many existing solutions described in the literature [7,8,10]. Finally, the differential container image is streamed through the distribution topology to the edge nodes within the locality, thus getting all nodes eventually provisioned.

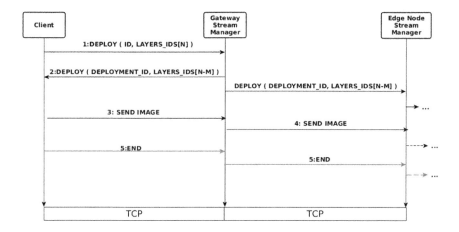

Fig. 4. Workflow of a Streamed Deployment within an edge locality

We now elaborate on the streamed forwarding procedure that implements our approach. The procedure is implemented within the Stream Manager, implemented as an application server running on each Edge node and serving deployment requests coming from peers. The algorithm executed by the SM is summarized in the pseudocode listing of Algorithm 1. The algorithm is executed by the Gateway in response to client deployment requests and, symmetrically, by Edge nodes in response to subsequent requests by peer nodes.

Upon its submission, the deployment request is first handled by the Gateway. After constructing a distribution topology (line 2), it extracts information about the layered image to deploy from the request (line 3). This information is used to compute the difference between the set of layers in the image to deploy and the layers already available within the locality (lines 4–6); the result is sent back to the client which will start streaming only missing layers.

The rest of the algorithm is executed simultaneously and identically by the Gateway and all the other Edge peers in the locality. Following the distribution topology computed (Gateway) or received (Edge device), each peer receives from its "parent" in the topology the missing layers and concurrently streams them to its "children" peers (lines 11–15). Our implementation is based on an in-memory Pipe data structure to which image data can be streamed in and out concurrently. The Pipe abstraction takes care of establishing and keeping connectivity with one peer's children (we used TCP connections for that) and of asynchronously saving the received image on secondary storage. Once the full content of the image is received, the SM instruct the local Docker daemon to import the image from disk (line 15).

Algorithm 1. Forwarding Mechanism

---

input: *parent, deploymentRequest*

1   **if** *isNodeGateway*() **then**
2   *distrTopology* ←computeTopology ();
3   *layers* ←getLayers (*deploymentRequest*);
4   *installedLayers* ←getInstalledLayers ();
5   *commonLayers* ←intersection (*layers, installedLayers*);
6   *layersToDeploy* ←difference (*layers, commonLayers*);
7   send (*parent, layersToDeploy*);
8   **else**
9   *distrTopology* ←getTopology (*deploymentRequest*);
10   **end**
11 *children* ←getReceivers (*distrTopology*);
12 *pipe* ← createPipe ();
13 startReader (*parent, pipe*);
14 startWriter (*children, pipe*);
15 importImage ();

---

4   Evaluation Results

To prove the feasibility of our approach, we developed a prototype implementation of the Streamed Deployment architecture and implementing logic, as shown in Fig. 3 and outlined in the previous section. We deployed the prototype on representative Edge/microserver boards, specifically on an NVidia Tegra TK1 development board (acting as locality Gateway) and a Raspberry-Pi 2 board (acting as Edge node), and successfully tested the prototype, demonstrating correct and efficient chained deployment from a centralized Docker registry.

To evaluate the proposed solution at higher, more realistic, scale, we created a virtual Edge locality leveraging a set of virtual machines (VMs) running on a fully dedicated Openstack [4] private Cloud hosted at IBM Research. Our deployment consists of one VM acting as Gateway and a variable number of VMs acting as Edge nodes. The resulting testbed features a cluster of 11 bare-metal servers and up to 22 VMs running on these servers. We provisioned each VM with 2 virtual CPUs, and 2 GiBytes of DRAM. We also limited the network interface throughput of each VM to 100 Mbit/s, so as to emulate the nominal bandwidth available on typical edge nodes. In order to make it easier to reason about the collected the results, our Streamed Deployment experiments assume a linear distribution tree, where each node has one parent and one child only.

To demonstrate the improvement in terms of deployment latency within a locality, we executed a set of experiments where all nodes within the locality are concurrently deploying a specified container image. For that, we chose to deploy a popular media server image, namely the Plex Media Server [5] - the back-end media server component of Plex. This image was chosen because representative (especially in size) of a large class of multimedia applications that might be running on an Edge locality. In each experiment execution, we vary the number of nodes in the locality from 1 up to 21 nodes. With this configuration, we made two groups of experiments, using either the Streamed Deployment (SD) approach or the baseline approach outlined in Sect. 2.

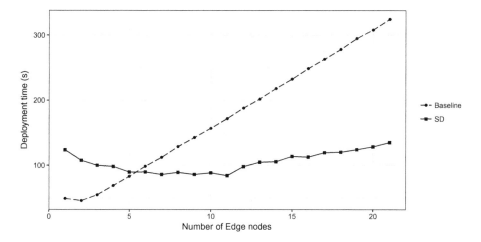

Fig. 5. Time taken to deploy a Plex Docker container within a locality with an increasing number of edge nodes

Figure 5 reports the results of the time taken to deploy a Docker container within a locality using the two approaches, versus an increasing number of Edge nodes. We observe that in a locality with less than five nodes, the baseline approach (centralized Docker Registry) provides faster deployments compared to the proposed solution, because of the co-ordination overhead in the Streamed Deployment. However, as the locality size increases, our approach yields faster deployments compared to the baseline. At the largest scale tested (21 nodes), our approach is 3 times faster compared to the baseline. While continuing the evaluation to larger locality sizes is part of our on-going work, we don't have a reason to expect that the shown trends will change: while the naive registry baseline has a steep linear scaling pattern, our approach exhibits a much more gradual linear increase pattern, fit for much larger scale localities.

In addition to provisioning latency, another important factor in Edge Computing deployments is bandwidth utilization. Figure 6 reports the network throughput time-series on the downstream direction of the Edge-Cloud link. The Edge Gateway pulls the image from the registry only once for the entire locality. Therefore, the amount of data that needs to be sent to the locality does not

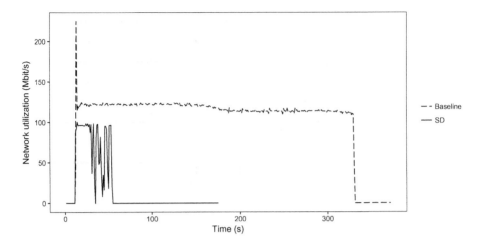

Fig. 6. Bandwidth utilization during container deployment on the Edge-Cloud link.

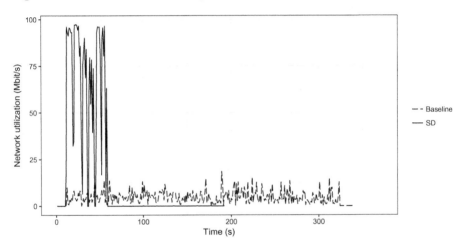

Fig. 7. Bandwidth utilization on one edge node within the locality during container deployment.

increase with the number of nodes, resulting in reduced bandwidth utilization in both size and time. The same cannot be said for the baseline approach: as the Docker Registry is the only image provider for the 21 nodes, there is a lengthy and steady utilization of the Edge-Cloud link, until the separate deployment on each locality node completes.

Although Edge-Cloud bandwidth is, in general, the most expensive network resource, making efficient use of local bandwidth might also be critical, especially in scenarios where local connectivity is also being used for application traffic (e.g., real time data-communication among Edge nodes). We evaluated how the Streamed Deployment uses this resource and we show the results in Fig. 7, which depicts the network utilization of an Edge node while receiving an image as a time-series. The graph clearly highlights how, in the baseline approach, the local link is underutilized during image deployment, due to the bottleneck effect of the Edge-Cloud link being shared among all the local nodes (21 in our experiment). On the contrary, Streamed Deployment makes full use of the 100 MBit/s local link, leading to faster deployment and, in general, to better network utilization.

5   Related Work

While commercial and enterprise deployment of Internet of Things is a reality, to date the vast majority of roll-outs has either employed very thin general purpose computing on the edge (e.g. filtering/aggregation/sampling of sensor time-series) or highly specialized - both software- and hardware-wise - processing that is monolithically designed and usually tied to a specific solution (e.g. signal processing for speech recognition [9]). There are several standardization efforts aspiring to develop consensus on an edge/fog computing reference architecture [3] and its constituent layers [2]; also, ample research efforts have experimented with various challenges, among others node roles and node architecture [6,14,15], end-user value exploration [13] and customized storage/data models [16].

As the field of general purpose distributed, potentially multi-tenant, computing and analytics at the edge of the Internet of Things is only nascent, the vast amount of prior art has focused on architectural exploration, with no special focus on addressing provisioning and infrastructure/platfrom management challenges, more so from the perspective of massive scalability. Pahl and Lee [12] have discussed the fitness of Linux containers as the execution unit in edge deployments versus hypervisor-based virtualization; major advantages of containers are typically their lightweight footprint, performance and native support for microservices. Early results presented by the Superfluid Cloud [11] indicated that customization of virtual machines resp. hypervisors (Xen) can yield provisioning latency results at large scale that are comparable to those of LXC containers. It must be noted though that these results have been obtained on a mid-range datacenter-grade server (64-core x86-64 with 128 GB DRAM) and it remains to be seen how the two technologies compare against each other in terms of provisioning/footprint, when tested on low-power microservers and embedded devices. The latter are typically much more highly candidate to host edge/fog computing nodes in large-scale, distributed deployments. For the same reason, it is impractical to put the findings of [11] in perspective to our findings, as this paper has focused its value on addressing Xen virtualization optimizations for edge computing purposes. Instead, we focus on provisioning techniques of stock Linux containers, whereby we evaluate our approach in a full-fledged distributed setting, incorporating edge-cloud bandwidth and latency, compute/memory/storage capabilities that are representative of an edge gateway/node (microserver) and a remote centralized image repository.

6 Conclusions

Container-based virtualization techniques are being commonly accepted as a solution to support packaging, deployment and execution of applications on Edge/Fog computing deployments. In this paper, we have discussed the challenges in provisioning containerized applications to large numbers of Edge nodes, especially in terms of scalability of deployment latency and bandwidth utilization. We have shown that baseline/standard methods for container provisioning directly derived from Cloud best-practices are not suitable to be used unmodified in Edge scenarios, where bandwidth can be limited and more expensive (e.g., if based on cellular connectivity).

We have therefore presented the design and prototype implementation of a novel approach that addresses these problems, called Streamed Deployment. Based on a simple peer-to-peer data distribution model, our approach distributes the cost of container image provisioning across all the interested nodes within an Edge locality. Our evaluation on a scale-out testbed shows that Streamed Deployment provides up to a threefold deployment speed-up and a tenfold reduction on the utilization of the expensive Edge-to-Cloud network link.

While our solution improves provisioning speed and cost, it also creates new complexities and challenges if considering aspects like security and high-availability. Future work will investigate solutions to guarantee secure authentication and data exchange between all the involved actors, and protocols to guarantee deployment success despite dynamic topology reconfigurations and failures. Furthermore, we are extending our evaluation results to more realistic environments where edge devices are distributed across multiple locations. We also plan to evaluate the impact of different levels of Registry replication on system performance and reliability. These additional experimental results will provide a better understanding of the overall performance of the two approaches, especially for scenarios featuring a large number of devices.

References

1. Docker. https://www.docker.com/
2. Open edge computing. http://openedgecomputing.org
3. Open fog consortium. https://www.openfogconsortium.org
4. Openstack open source cloud computing software. http://www.openstack.org
5. Plex media server. https://github.com/greensheep/plex-server-docker-rpi
6. Chandra, A., Weissman, J., Heintz, B.: Decentralized edge clouds. IEEE Internet Comput. **17**(5), 70–73 (2013)
7. Chen, K., Nahrstedt, K.: Effective location-guided tree construction algorithms for small group multicast in MANET. In: Proceedings of Twenty-First Annual Joint Conference of the IEEE Computer and Communications Societies, vol. 3, pp. 1180–1189 (2002)
8. Hosseini, M., Ahmed, D.T., Shirmohammadi, S., Georganas, N.D.: A survey of application-layer multicast protocols. IEEE Commun. Surv. Tutor. **9**(3), 58–74 (2007)

9. Jones, A., Benton, M.: Amazon Echo: A Simple User Guide to Amazon Echo and Essential Hacking Guide, vol. 6. CreateSpace Independent Publishing Platform, USA (2016)

10. Kim, M.S., Lam, S.S., Lee, D.Y.: Optimal distribution tree for internet streaming media. In: Proceedings of 23rd International Conference on Distributed Computing Systems, pp. 116–125, May 2003

11. Manco, F., Martins, J., Yasukata, K., Mendes, J., Kuenzer, S., Huici, F.: The case for the superfluid cloud. In: Proceedings of the 7th USENIX Conference on Hot Topics in Cloud Computing, HotCloud 2015, p. 7. USENIX Association, Berkeley (2015)

12. Pahl, C., Lee, B.: Containers and clusters for edge cloud architectures - a technology review. In: 3rd International Conference on Future Internet of Things and Cloud, pp. 379–386, August 2015

13. Satyanarayanan, M., Bahl, P., Caceres, R., Davies, N.: The case for VM-based cloudlets in mobile computing. IEEE Pervasive Comput. **8**(4), 14–23 (2009)

14. Tong, L., Li, Y., Gao, W.: A hierarchical edge cloud architecture for mobile computing. In: IEEE INFOCOM 2016 - The 35th Annual IEEE International Conference on Computer Communications, pp. 1–9. IEEE, April 2016

15. Zachariah, T., Klugman, N., Campbell, B., Adkins, J., Jackson, N., Dutta, P.: The internet of things has a gateway problem. In: Proceedings of the 16th International Workshop on Mobile Computing Systems and Applications - HotMobile 2015, pp. 27–32. ACM Press, New York (2015)

16. Zhang, B., Mor, N., Kolb, J., Chan, D.S., Lutz, K., Allman, E., Wawrzynek, J., Lee, E., Kubiatowicz, J.: The Cloud is Not Enough: Saving IoT From The Cloud (2015)

A Hash-Based Naming Strategy for the Fog-to-Cloud Computing Paradigm

Alejandro Gómez-Cárdenas$^{(\boxtimes)}$, Xavi Masip-Bruin,
Eva Marín-Tordera, Sarang Kahvazadeh, and Jordi Garcia

Advanced Network Architectures Lab (CRAAX),
Universitat Politècnica de Catalunya (UPC), Barcelona, Spain
{alejandg,xmasip,eva,skahvaza,jordig}@ac.upc.edu

Abstract. The growth of the Internet connected devices population has fuelled the emergence of new distributed computer paradigms; one of these paradigms is the so-called Fog-to-Cloud (F2C) computing, where resources (compute, storage, data) are distributed in a hierarchical fashion between the edge and the core of the network. This new paradigm has brought new research challenges, such as the need for a novel framework intended to controlling and, more in general, facilitating the interaction among the heterogeneous devices conforming the environment at the edge of the network and the available resources at cloud. A key feature that this framework should meet is the capability of uniquely and unequivocally identify the connected devices. In this paper a hash-based naming strategy suitable to be used in the F2C environment is presented. The proposed naming method is based on three main components: certification, hashing and identification. This research is an ongoing work, thus, the steps to follow since a device connects to the F2C network until it receives a name are described and the major challenges that must be solved are analyzed.

Keywords: Naming · Identification · Fog-to-Cloud · Internet of Things

1 Introduction

In simple words, the Internet of Things (IoT) is a communication paradigm where all kind of everyday objects are capable to connect to the Internet network with different purposes. This paradigm allows the creation of a range of new services and applications in diverse areas like smart homes, buildings and cities, eHealth, vehicular networks, wearables, monitoring and surveillance, etcetera. It is estimated that by 2020 the worldwide population of Internet connected objects will reach 50 billions [1].

Taking advantage of the large number of devices with network connectivity and in consideration of the expected growth, new computer paradigms have emerged, one of them is the Fog-to-Cloud (F2C) computing.

F2C is a collaborative and distributed compute model where resources (like storage, compute or data) are located in a hierarchical fashion not only at the core of the network but also at the edge [2]. In many cases, the resources conforming the F2C at the edge of the network are supplied by the end users, thus, users can not only access to the service provider or third parties resources but also share their own resources.

© Springer International Publishing AG, part of Springer Nature 2018
D. B. Heras and L. Bougé (Eds.): Euro-Par 2017 Workshops, LNCS 10659, pp. 316–324, 2018.
https://doi.org/10.1007/978-3-319-75178-8_26

Being a hierarchical model, the resources are deployed in a bottom-up fashion, usually with the most constrained devices in the lower layer (very basic sensors and actuators) and in the top of the hierarchy a virtually unlimited resource data center: the cloud.

Many research efforts are focused in the design of a suitable F2C architecture [3] for managing the distributed storage, compute, data, control and networking functions.

A key functionality that any F2C architecture must meet is the capability to identify uniquely and unequivocally every device connected to the F2C network, thus, the adoption of a naming strategy is required.

The list of available naming schemes is not short [4, 5] and ranges from the use of existing services like the Domain Name Service (DNS) to the redesign of the computer networks as are known nowadays to a not host-based-centric network. The problem with those naming schemes is that most of them doesn't meet the inherent F2C requirements (such as interoperability, mobility, uniqueness and scalability) or the effort to implement them is far beyond the scheme itself.

Regardless the application specific requirements, according with [6] a good naming service should meet the three characteristics described in the "Zooko's Triangle": decentralization, human-meaningful names and secure mapping of names. These three design goals are represented as a side of the triangle and each side represents a design tradeoff, so according with the original author, it isn't possible to have the three characteristics at the same time.

In this paper a new distributed hash-based naming strategy that meets the afore-mentioned F2C requirements is presented. The proposed strategy is based in three support modules which are: certification, hashing and identification.

The remainder of this paper is organized as follow: In Sect. 2 the hashing technique is discussed and similar works are reviewed. In Sect. 3 the proposed hash-based naming strategy and its support modules are explained in detail. In Sect. 4 the key advantages of the proposal are studied. Finally, in Sect. 5 the research conclusions are exposed.

2   State of the Art

In this section the hash functions and its properties are briefly described, also an example of a hash string value is shown and three distinct works where authors have used a hash-based method for naming entities (virtual or physical) are analyzed.

2.1   Background

The hashing is a cryptographic technique widely used to map a data block of variable size to a fixed-length output. It means that it does not matter whether the input is 1 byte or 1 terabyte, the output will be a string with a predefined size length. In [7] the hash technique is described in function of its main properties, which are:

- Variable input size. In the hash function $h(x)$ where x is the input, the size of x does not matter at all.

- Fixed length output. As said before, the output size isn't in function of the input size.
- Compute facility. It is relatively easy to compute h(x) for any given x.
- One-way. For any given y, it is computationally infeasible to find x such that h (x) = y, what means that it cannot be "unhashed".
- Collision resistance. It is computationally infeasible to find y != x such that h (x) = h(y). It means that two different inputs always produce two different outputs and vice versa, two different outputs always belong to two different inputs.

There are many algorithms designed to implement the hash function, the most popular are briefly reviewed in [8]. In the United States as well as much of the world, the MD5 and SHA algorithms are the most widely used [7], nevertheless any other algorithm that fulfill the listed properties is suitable for generating hash values.

In order to illustrate better the properties of the hash function three examples are presented below (Table 1). In the examples, the SHA-1 algorithm is used to hash three different strings.

Table 1. Hash transformation examples using the SHA-1 algorithm.

First example	
Input	Hello
Hash value	f7ff9e8b7bb2e09b70935a5d785e0cc5d9d0abf0
Second example	
Input	hello
Hash value	aaf4c61ddcc5e8a2dabede0f3b482cd9aea9434d
Third example	
Input	Hello World! This is a test
Hash value	cf3491c6524b19f1965b112c37e5360e6920a136

The input in every example is different. While in the first two examples the inputs difference is very subtle (only changes the first letter, from capital "H" to "h"), in the third example the input is not a word but a phrase. In the three cases the hash value output always is a totally different 160-bits string.

The hashing is a destructive process, what means that there is not a way to return to the original input starting from the hash output value.

2.2 Related Work

Some researchers have found in the properties of the hash function an opportunity for the creation of new naming schemes. In [9] the authors review extensively the use of the hash function for naming objects. They claim that in order to avoid collisions the SHA-256 algorithm must be implemented. However, in constrained environments or in scenarios where a higher collision probability can be tolerated, the system administrator can opt for using a truncated version of the hash function output. In no case they recommend the use of names with less than 100-bits; they assert that in those scenarios the collision resistance property cannot be guaranteed.

In the previously cited publication the authors use the SHA-256 algorithm to include a hash string as a segment in Universal Resource Locators (URL). With the purpose of standardize the uses of hash outputs in URLs, they specify a new URI scheme and a way to map these to URL's, however, their proposed method lacks of a clear hash input proposal. Although they mention that public keys are a good hash function input candidate, they let the users to choose the input value, so in scenarios where the user not only select an inappropriate input but also decide to use the truncated hash function output, the collision probability could be very high.

In [10] a hybrid naming scheme for vehicular content centric networks is presented. In the proposal the authors divide the content name (CN) into three parts: the scheme, the prefix and the hash. The first part is the naming scheme identifier that is used to represent CN. This field can take two different values in function of the used protocol.

The prefix is the hierarchical part of the name scheme and is used to identify the content originating node that is a vehicle and the content itself in a human-readable format. The distinct parts of the prefix are separated by a slash ("/") and the firsts four fields are reserved for the publisher vehicle's information. The rest of the hierarchical section signifies the information about the digital content (e.g. text, video, image, or any other digital content).

Finally, the hash section of the CN corresponds to the full or truncated hash value generated using the digital content, the content attributes or the public key of the information related to it.

According with the authors, the last field is used to uniquely identify the content item. Nevertheless, in a scenario in which two or more vehicles are sharing distinct contents but with the same attributes, if the hash function input are those attributes, the probability of having duplicated records making reference to different contents will be high. The solution to this problem could be to increase the number of attributes in the prefix section, but this decision will impact the lookup throughput, what in content centric networks is critical.

Another similar work is the presented in [11]. In their work the authors does not propose a naming strategy but a name resolution scheme consisting of two parts: name mapping and name resolution.

Basically, what they do is to use a hash function to translate the heterogeneous device name to a fixed-length string, hiding like this the original name from the outside Internet for security and privacy reasons.

In the name mapping the object name is received and translated to a 160-bits string using the SHA-1 hash function algorithm. A notable drawback that this strategy presents is that to be recognized by the system the user has to hash the object name and register the resulted string to the resolution system in advance. This could be a tedious task for users owning multiple devices.

Another weak point of this strategy is that two devices with the same name will have exactly the same hash output value and as result, duplicate register may exist in the resolution adopted scheme (DNS or DHT).

3   Proposed Naming Strategy

In this section the naming strategy is presented. The proposed scheme consists of three main components: a certification, a hash function and the identification module. The technique described in the next lines aims to be a part of the resource management functions (Fig. 1) in a F2C environment.

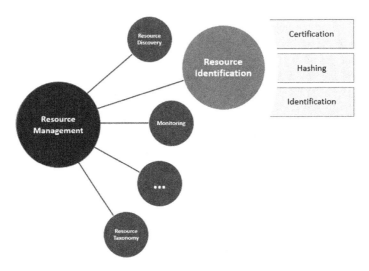

Fig. 1. Resource identification strategy for the F2C architecture.

3.1   Certification

The certification is the very first step that users must complete to have their device(s) connected to the F2C network. In this phase the users register his personal information in the system to get a secret key.

This registration process must to be done once per entity (person, institution or company) regardless the number of devices the entity wants to use in the F2C ecosystem. For example, if a government department needs to deploy thousands of devices through a specific area in the city, the institution only have to register once to get the secret key. This process is shown in the Fig. 2.

The implementation of this first phase will bring new challenges that must to be solved. The major challenges are related with the system security. There is a lot of attacks that the system must not only to resist but also to detect.

In the certification phase as well as in the other two components of the identification strategy to provide a secure communication channel that discard the risk of interception is a crucial requirement.

Apart from security, other considerations must to be taken into account in the certification, for example, due the key assignation will be a distributed process, a mechanism to disallow secret key overlapping will be necessary. Also, the system must to be able to suspend, revoke and update the user secret key.

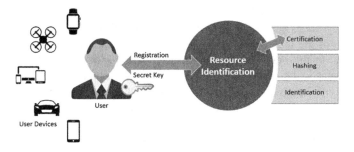

Fig. 2. Certification phase in the Resource identification strategy

3.2 Hash Function

Being the module that stores the naming scheme, the hash function is the core of the identification strategy. This function is the responsible of transforming the device identification input into a hash string.

The device identification input is composed by two concatenated string. The first string is the user secret key obtained during the registration phase while the other is an "optional" user string (Fig. 3).

Fig. 3. Hash function process.

Due the purpose of the second part of the string is to differentiate among the user devices, it will be optional only in those cases where the user owns or wants to use only one of his devices in the F2C network, otherwise it will be a mandatory field.

In [12] the author explains that it is nearly impossible to have one global naming convention mainly because industries have been using their own proprietary naming conventions for long time and migrating to a different naming convention will impact their infrastructure considerably. Nevertheless, this method does not force the users to abandon their own internal naming convention. In the second part of the string the user can use whatever value they want regardless the length.

Continuing with the previous government department example, let's assume that for internal reasons the institution uses a hierarchical naming convention that includes the city, a code area where the device is located and at the end a consecutive number. The internal records will look something like this: LA347-01, LA347-02, LA347-XX. The adoption of this or any other naming scheme won't affect the string conversion process.

Once the user identification string has been transformed into the final hash value it is stored in key nodes across the F2C network using Distributed Hash Tables (DHT). A full backup of the records always is kept in a cloud data server.

As well as in the previous step, the hash function module also have some challenges that must to be addressed. One of the biggest challenges is the need of an incentive that encourage users to keep using exactly the same string in both sides of the hash input. This is particularly important for the implementation of long term identification mechanisms and other historical functions because as was shown in Table 1, the minimum change in the input string will change dramatically the device identifier/name.

3.3   Identification

The last step in the proposed strategy is to look up for the hash value of the device in the DHT, it is the identification.

In this point there could be three distinct scenarios:

- The device is new in the system. When a device connects for the very first time to the F2C network the look up in the DHT won't find any coincidence. In that case, the system should register the device and perform other assistant tasks (e.g. device characterization) in order to recognize it in future interactions. The device will be registered in the DHT closer to the device physical location and after x seconds, this and other new records will be propagated to the upper F2C nodes in a hierarchical fashion, until the record(s) reach the cloud where will be stored for a long term.
- The device is connected to the F2C network in a known location. The DHT will store for a predefined period of time a cache with all the devices that have been connected in the last x days, so when a device reconnects to the same F2C node, it will recognize the device without going to an upper level to look up for the device

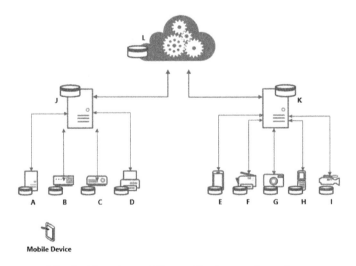

Fig. 4. Three layered Fog-to-Cloud network topology.

information. In this process the network hierarchy will be leveraged. When a device is connected to a different but still close node from the habitual one, it won't have to go to cloud to have the device information; going to one layer higher will be enough (Fig. 4).

- The device is connected in a distinct location than the habitual. Let's assume a three layered F2C network; if the device is connected in a distant location and there is not information available in the same layer or even in the next upper layer, there is still the cloud database, what in terms of costs will be cheaper that characterize again the device.

In the Fig. 4 the "mobile device" uses to connect to the F2C network through the nodes "A" and "B", so every time it connects using one of those nodes the system automatically detects and retrieves all the device information. In the case that the node connects for the first time or after a long time to the F2C using the node "C" where there is not information available about this device, the system will search in the next upper layer for information about it. In the node "J" a copy of all the device information is kept and updated for the nodes "A" and "B".

Now, let's consider that the "mobile device" moved to the area of the aggregator node "H" and connects to the system using that node. Being the first time in this zone there is not information available about the device, neither at the node "H" nor at the next layer (node "K"), however, the node "J", aggregator of the nodes "A", "B", "C" and "D" registered the device in the cloud database so there is information about it that the node "K" can access anytime and thus, the node "H".

In this third step the main two problems that may arise are a poor throughput in the lookup process and a high network overhead caused by the mobile devices. Nevertheless, if suitable policies are applied these two problems can be overcome.

4   Proposal Advantages

The key advantages of the proposed naming strategy are the capability of assign worldwide unique names to the devices connected to the F2C network. In the case of two or more F2C providers sharing the certification and hashing modules, the device not only will use the same secret key to be identified but also it will keep the name regardless the system provider.

The use of the Distributed Hash Tables will facilitate the implementation of new functionalities in the system, such as a trust system, where the devices can get a classification in function of its availability, uptime, and other parameters. Other function that the historical information stored in the DHTs will allow to implement in the platform is a predictive resource utilization/available system without expose the device specs or location.

Finally, if the hash function is implemented correctly, the possibility of a duplicated name will be minimal, what means that the proposed strategy is secure.

5   Conclusions

In this research work an integral hash-based naming strategy suitable for the Fog-to-Cloud environment was proposed. The strategy is conformed for three main modules: certification, hashing and identification. The proposal meets the F2C requirements, such as mobility, scalability, security, privacy and uniqueness.

Even when the proposed naming strategy presents important advantages in comparison with other naming strategies and schemes there are still open challenges that must to be addressed. Those challenges include the need of provide a secure channel for the communications among edge devices and F2C nodes, a mechanism that disallow the secure key overlapping, the DHT lookup throughput, etcetera.

In order to solve the mentioned issues more research effort in every component of the proposed method is needed, so the future work will be focused in overcome the existing challenges.

Acknowledgement. This work is supported by the H2020 mF2C project (730929), as well as by the Spanish Ministry of Economy and Competitiveness and by the European Regional Development Fund under contract TEC2015-66220-R (MINECO/FEDER).

References

1. Datta, S.K., Da Costa, R.P.F., Bonnet, C.: Resource discovery in Internet of Things: current trends and future standardization aspects. In: 2015 IEEE 2nd World Forum on Internet of Things (WF-IoT), pp. 542–547 (2015)
2. Masip-Bruin, X., Marín-Tordera, E., Tashakor, G., et al.: Foggy clouds and cloudy fogs: a real need for coordinated management of fog-to-cloud computing systems. IEEE Wirel. Commun. **23**, 120–128 (2016). https://doi.org/10.1109/MWC.2016.7721750
3. OpenFog Consortium: OpenFog Reference Architecture for Fog Computing (2017)
4. European Research Cluster on the Internet of Things: EU-China Joint White Paper on Internet-of-Things Identification (2014)
5. Li, Y., Jain, R.: Naming in the Internet of Things (2013)
6. Webster, C.: WebNS: model for a peer-to-peer name service. Monash University (2011)
7. Easttom, C.: Modern Cryptography: Applied Mathematics for Encryption and Information Security. McGraw-Hill Education, New York (2015)
8. Kumar Raghuvanshi, K., Khurana, P., Bindal, P.: Study and comparative analysis of different hash algorithm. JECAS **3** (2014)
9. Farrell, S., Dannewitz., C, Ohlman, B., et al.: Naming Things with Hashes (2013). https://doi.org/10.17487/rfc6920
10. Bouk, S.H., Ahmed, S.H., Kim, D.: Hierarchical and hash based naming with Compact Trie name management scheme for Vehicular Content Centric Networks. Comput. Commun. **71**, 73–83 (2015). https://doi.org/10.1016/j.comcom.2015.09.014
11. Yan, Z., Kong, N., Tian, Y., Park, Y.J.: A universal object name resolution scheme for IoT. In: 2013 IEEE International Conference on Green Computing and Communications and IEEE Internet of Things and IEEE Cyber, Physical and Social Computing, pp. 1120–1124 (2013)
12. Balakrichenan, S.: Why DNS should be the naming service for Internet of Things? (2016)

An Architecture for Programming Distributed Applications on Fog to Cloud Systems

Francesc Lordan[1,2]([envelope]) [ORCID], Daniele Lezzi[1] [ORCID], Jorge Ejarque[1] [ORCID], and Rosa M. Badia[1,3] [ORCID]

[1] Department of Computer Sciences, Barcelona Supercomputing Center (BSC), Barcelona, Spain
{francesc.lordan,daniele.lezzi,jorge.ejarque,rosa.m.badia}@bsc.es
[2] Department of Computer Architecture, Universitat Politècnica de Catalunya (UPC), Barcelona, Spain
[3] Artificial Intelligence Research Institute, Spanish National Research Council (CSIC), Barcelona, Spain

Abstract. This paper presents a framework to develop and execute applications in distributed and highly dynamic computing systems composed of cloud resources and fog devices such as mobile phones, cloudlets, and micro-clouds. The work builds on the COMPSs programming framework, which includes a programming model and a runtime already validated in HPC and cloud environments for the transparent execution of parallel applications. As part of the proposed contribution, COMPSs has been enhanced to support the execution of applications on mobile platforms that offer GPUs and CPUs. The scheduling component of COMPSs is under design to be able to offload the computation to other fog devices in the same level of the hierarchy and to cloud resources when more computational power is required. The framework has been tested executing a sample application on a mobile phone offloading task to a laptop and a private cloud.

Keywords: Distributed computing · Mobile computing
Fog computing · Programming model · Computation offloading
Fault tolerance · Security

1 Introduction

The traditional cloud computing model, based on a centralized control of computing and data resources, does not provide the proper support to the requirements of big data applications that produce and consume volumes of data through IoT devices, fast mobile networks, AI applications, etc. Fog computing has emerged as a complementary solution to overcome the issues related to real time processing, security, latency and transparent management of a decentralized, heterogeneous and dynamic set of resources.

This paper proposes a Fog-to-Cloud (F2C) ready programming framework to develop applications that involve the use of traditional cloud systems, smart end-user devices, and IoT sensors. The framework transparently offloads parts of the

© Springer International Publishing AG, part of Springer Nature 2018
D. B. Heras and L. Bougé (Eds.): Euro-Par 2017 Workshops, LNCS 10659, pp. 325–337, 2018.
https://doi.org/10.1007/978-3-319-75178-8_27

computation to fog and cloud resources and optimizes the execution considering time, energy consumption and monetary cost. The proposed solution builds on COMPSs [8], a programming model for distributed computing and its associated run-time. On the one hand, COMPSs distributes the computational load of the application transparently to the user and exploits its inherent parallelism and the heterogeneity of the underlying infrastructure. On the other hand, it also handles the distribution of data to provide a seamless offloading and schedules the data processing in larger nodes considering its locality to optimize the execution. COMPSs applications are completely agnostic to the underlying infrastructure and their code runs, with no changes, in all the backends supported by the runtime: HPC systems and private and public cloud. Recently, COMPSs has been integrated with container solutions based on Docker [9] and Mesos [1]. To support the execution of COMPSs applications from mobile devices, the runtime has been refactored to include the support to Android devices and to improve the data management via a Peer-to-Peer (P2P) mechanism. These new features are basic pillars to develop the proposed framework.

A key feature of COMPSs is the ability to distribute the tasks that compose the application on the available nodes of the computing platform. In the case of traditional cloud environments, the decision where to execute a task considers historical data of previous executions and the locality of the data to process. Moreover, the cloud gives the illusion of having access to infinite computing resources; COMPSs can instantiate additional VMs on cloud providers from a settable list. In contexts more dynamic than traditional cloud computing, such as the ones considered in this work, resources might spontaneously disappear from the pool. Handling this volatility is an additional requirement either for data management and proper work balancing between fog nodes. Another relevant issue addressed in the proposed framework is the security since usually edge devices are located in non-controlled environments.

The paper is structured as follows: Sect. 2 includes an overview of the related work in the field of F2C computing framework; Sect. 3 describes the architecture of the proposed solution while Sect. 4 provides the details of how the COMPSs framework has been extended to support F2C environments. Section 5 presents the results of the tests and Sect. 6 concludes the paper and provides ideas for future work.

2   Related Work

Application partitioning, task scheduling, and offloading mechanisms are all problems widely explored in the field of distributed computing. The main differences between previous work on cloud computing and mobile computing are due to issues related to the high mobility of the device, the limited availability of energy of the devices and the impact of the network (latency, monetary cost, bandwidth) on the performance of the entire framework. This analysis of the related work in the field of fog to cloud computing, takes into account capabilities such as how to fragment the applications in order to offload the parts of the computation to the resources, the scheduling model and the management of parallelism.

CloneCloud [4] offers the developer a thread level granularity mechanism. The strong point of CloneCloud is its partitioning mechanism that combines a static analysis of the code with a dynamic profiling of the application to pick the optimal migration and re-integration points. When a thread reaches a migration point, it suspends, and its state (including virtual state, program counter, registers, and stack) is shipped to a synchronized clone. When the migrated thread reaches a re-integration point, it is similarly suspended and shipped back to the mobile device. The drawback of this system is that it still requires the developer to manage threads and application parallelism. Cuckoo [6] hides the partitioning problem by exploiting the service component of Android operating systems. During the build process, the stubs generated to access service components are replaced by invocations to the Cuckoo framework that decides, at runtime, whether to run the service on the local device or a remote implementation. Since the framework only replaces calls, all the parallelism must be managed by the programmer on the service invocations. ThinkAir [7] provides a mechanism to automatically parallelize the execution of an offloaded method considering intervals of input variables. The main drawback of ThinkAir is that the offloading mechanism works synchronously: the executing thread is suspended until the method invocation is performed and its result collected. Thus, any subsequent method invocation is not executed until previous ones are executed even when they could run concurrently. Mobile Fog [5] is a high level programming model for the future Internet applications that are geospatially distributed, large-scale, and latency-sensitive. The goal is to allow applications to dynamically scale based on their workload using ondemand resources in the fog and in the cloud. In Mobile Fog, an application consists of distributed Mobile Fog processes that are mapped onto distributed computing instances in the fog and cloud, as well as various edge devices. Mobile Fog API is not hiding the distribution of the infrastructure to the application, requiring a large programming effort to the application developer.

3   Architecture Overview

Figure 1 depicts the layered-based architecture of a Fog-to-Cloud platform where the proposed framework can be instantiated; the architecture is designed following the OpenFog Reference Architecture [3]. The lowest layer represents the low processing capability devices, such as sensors or embedded devices that produce data, while the middle layer contains fog devices that have more processing power (as a smartphone or a tablet) and are able to deploy and orchestrate the execution of a distributed application using other fog devices as workers (fog-to-fog). Clouds are at the top layer, hosting services for the control of the entire stack or used for the execution of computing intensive applications started both from the same layer and from a fog device. It is worth noting, indeed, that the framework can be used to instantiate applications on smart devices on the fog

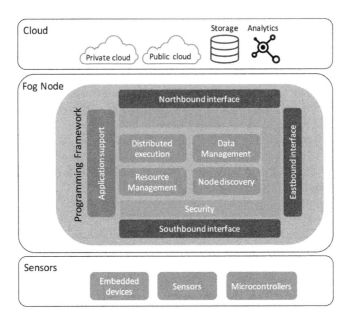

Fig. 1. F2C architecture

layer and to offload part of the computation to the cloud (fog-to-cloud) or use the fog devices as workers for a cloud application.

The main contribution of this work is represented as a programming component in the Fog Node together with the capabilities it offers and the interfaces needed to interact with other elements of the platform. The application support has to be implemented through a high level programming model that enables the development of applications to be executed in distributed, heterogeneous, volatile, data and processing infrastructures. However, these complex infrastructures will remain hidden to the application in such a way that the application can focus on the logic. The aim of this programming model is to keep the code almost untouched avoiding the need for APIs to implement the required functionalities. The application interacts with a runtime that takes care of the coordination of the distributed execution of the applications in a parallel way when possible. The interaction with different computing backends is delegated to a specific component for resource management. Data management is required to let the runtime access to the data produced on the working nodes as well as to synchronize the information on data location in order to proper schedule the tasks on the nodes. The Node Discovery component enables resource discovery and registration. For example, an IoT device coming online "close" to the coordination node can notify its availability to the controller and then this information has to come to the node. Security is a transversal issue common to all the components that have to fulfill a common base set of security and privacy requirements in an environment by nature unsecure and dynamic. Interfaces are needed to ensure communication between nodes and realizes the data channels. Eastbound interface connects the runtime with other nodes in the same level and allows the sharing of data; Northbound allows to implement the connection with cloud nodes while Southbound interface realizes the connection between a fog node and a sensor or from a cloud application down to the Fog layer.

4   Programming Framework Overview

COMP Superscalar (COMPSs) is a programming model that aims to ease the development of parallel applications to run atop distributed infrastructures. For that purpose, it offers a sequential, infrastructure-agnostic way of programming that abstracts coders from the parallelization and distribution concerns. COMPSs considers applications as composites of invocations to pieces of software encapsulated as methods called Core Elements (CE). To manage the parallelism inherent in the application, the framework instruments the application and replaces CE invocations by calls to a runtime system to execute them atop the infrastructure. Also, accesses to data generated on remote nodes need to synchronize their value before being used. The following subsections introduce the programming model and the architecture of the runtime system, highlighting those aspects relevant to support executions on Fog-to-Cloud environments.

4.1   Programming Model

For developing applications, programmers write their code in a sequential fashion with no references to any COMPSs-specific API or the underlying infrastructure. At execution time, calls to CE methods are transparently replaced by asynchronous tasks whose execution is to be orchestrated by the runtime system. To select which methods become a CE developers define an interface, called Core Element Interface (CEI), where they declare those methods along with some meta-data in the form of annotations. To pick a method as a CE, the programmer annotates the method declaration on the CEI with *@Method* indicating the class containing the method implementation. The code snippet in Fig. 2 contains a simple COMPSs application example. Figure 2(a) shows the sequential code of the application which runs N simulations and selects the best one. As shown in the CEI presented in Fig. 2(b), only two methods are chosen as CE: simulate and getBest. For the runtime system to determine the dependencies between CE invocations, developers specify how each CE operates on the accessed data (its parameters) by adding (*@Parameter*) annotations indicating the parameter type and directionality (in, out, in-out).

4.2   Runtime Library

The main purpose of the runtime toolkit is to orchestrate the execution of CE invocations (tasks) fully exploiting the available computing resources (local devices or remote nodes) guaranteeing the sequential consistency. Applications

```
public Sim checkSimulation(int N) {
    Sim best = null;
    for (int i=0; i < N; i++) {
        Sim s = new Sim(...);
        s.simulate();
        best = Sim.getBest(best, s);
    }
    return best;
}
```

(a) Application main code

```
public interface SampleCEI {
    @Method(declaringClass="Sim")
    void simulate();

    @Method(declaringClass = "Sim")
    Sim getBest(
        @Parameter(direction = IN)
        Sim s1,
        @Parameter(direction = IN)
        Sim s2
    );
}
```

(b) Core Element Interface

Fig. 2. Sample application code written in Java

share computing resources and, potentially, data values; therefore, the runtime library is twofold. The front-end of the runtime, instantiated in every application, manages the private aspects of the applications: monitors accesses to private pieces of data, such as objects, and detects the CE invocations. The back-end manages all the aspects that the application can share from computing resources (CPU, GPU, nearby nodes or VM instances on the cloud) to data (currently only files, but we envisage to manage accesses to databases and Content Providers). Since all front-ends contact the same instance of the back-end, it is deployed as an Android service running in an independent process. Figure 3 contains a detailed diagram of the runtime architecture.

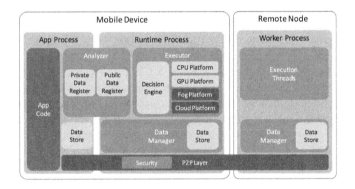

Fig. 3. Runtime system architecture

To monitor the data accessed from each task and the data dependences among task, the runtime processes the parameters of each task upon its detection on the *Analyzer* component. The *Private* and *Public Data Registers*, respectively located on the front-end and back-end of the runtime, record the accessed data values and assign a unique identifier for each version of the value. Once all the accessed values are registered, the *Analyzer* submits the task to the *Executor*, the component of the runtime that manages the resources.

To decide which resources host the execution of a task, the runtime is based on the concept of *Computing Platform*: a logical grouping of computing resources capable of running tasks. The decision is made on the *Decision Engine (DE)*, which is agnostic to the actual computing devices supporting the platform and the details to interact with them. The *DE* requests to each of the available platforms –configured by the user beforehand– a forecast of the expected end time, energy consumption and economic cost of the execution. According to a configurable heuristic, the *DE* picks the best platform to run the task and requests its execution; the selected platform is responsible for monitoring the data dependencies of the task and scheduling the execution of the task on its resources. Currently, there exist three different implementations of *Computing Platform* according to the nature of the computing devices composing it. *CPU Platform* manages the execution of tasks implemented as regular Android methods on the multiple cores of the mobile device CPU. *GPU Platform* executes tasks implemented as OpenCL code on the embedded GPU. Finally, the third implementation, *Remote Platform*, offloads the execution of methods to remote resources. For the runtime to properly exploit Fog-Cloud environments, users can instantiate four platforms: a *CPU Platform*, a *GPU Platform* and two *Remote Platforms*: the *Fog Platform* encapsulating the low-latency remote resources (West-bound) and the *Cloud Platform* representing those VM instances deployed on Cloud Providers (North-bound).

For sharing data across platforms, the runtime hosts a data repository: the *Data Manager (DM)*. Through a publish-subscribe mechanism, the *DM* asynchronously provides information and values of the accessed datums using the unique IDs assigned by the *Analyzer*. Computing Platforms lean on the *DM* for monitoring the data dependencies. When the *Executor* designates a platform to run a task, the platform subscribes for the existence of all the input datums; upon the publication of the creation of any of them, the *DM* forwards the notification to the platform. Once the platform realizes that all of them exist, it plans the execution of the task on its resources and queries the *DM* for the value of each datum. At the end of the task execution, the platform publishes the existence of the output datums and stores their value on the *DM*.

To uncharge the mobile device from the computational load of orchestrating the remote resources, Remote Platforms organize them as a peer-to-peer network. Each node of the network runs a worker process persistently listening to the network for task submissions; these processes are able to autonomously handle the execution of the task on the local computing devices. To ease the management of data dependencies, worker nodes subscribe for and publish information and values of the datums accessed by the tasks on the *DM*, whose content –either information or values– is consistently distributed across the whole infrastructure. The local instance of the *DM* is responsible for fetching the value from any hosting remote node.

The following subsections delve into detail in other features of the runtime specially significant for F2C environments: security on network communications and network-disruption tolerance.

Securing Communications. Data used on Fog applications is likely to be privacy-sensitive (pictures, videos, geolocation, etc.) and networks interconnecting the mobile device with other resources –either on the same layer or the Cloud – tend towards untrustworthiness.

To protect applications from eavesdroppers, the runtime has a security mechanism that provides communications with confidentiality, integrity and authentication. For its implementation the runtime leverages on the Generic Security Services API (GSSAPI) [2], an IETF standard API to access security services, so developers create secure applications while avoiding security-vendor lock-in.

Besides defining a common interface, GSSAPI also settles an operating model where both ends negotiate a secure context – authenticate themselves and agree on the mechanisms for data ciphering and integrity – before transferring any information. Upon the establishment of the context, GSSAPI processes (wraps) the messages and opaques their content returning token thats can be securely shipped to the other end. Although GSSAPI defines the format of the exchanged tokens and its content – actually, the security framework does –, it does not establish nor provide any transmission mechanism. Therefore, applications invoke GSSAPI to wrap a value and obtain a token to ship to the other end. Upon the reception of a token, the receiver invokes GSSAPI to unwrap the token and obtain the original content of the message. In our case, COMPSs uses the Java NIO library to transfer tokens over TCP sockets.

Although GSSAPI provides the infrastructure with an interoperable approach to secure communications, currently there is no generic mechanism to get the required credentials from the Authentication Server automatically. Application users need to manually set up the Authentication Infrastructure and authenticate all the nodes to obtain their credential beforehand. However, we consider this to be the foundational stone to build a platform with Authentication, Authorization and Accounting based on Federated Identity and Single Sign-On. Our ultimate goal is to build a global service where local institutions offer nearby computing resources (Fog nodes) where to offload computation securely from mobile devices belonging to users from other organizations within their federation. Using the same credential, users could always turn to VM instances deployed on the Cloud to obtain additional computing power.

Network Disruption Tolerance. A consequence of the high mobility of Fog devices is instability on the network conditions. Fog devices are likely to face Wi-Fi network handovers, changing the used network interface between Wi-Fi and mobile data, switching to different mobile network protocols (GPRS, EDGE, UMTS, HSPA, LTE, etc.) and eventually the device can disconnect from the network. Controlling all the possibilities is main challenge to tackle not only for Fog Computing but also for IoT and MANET frameworks.

As a first approach to solve the problem, we focused on the device running the application (master) and considered a network disruption that isolates it while the rest of the infrastructure stays up and online. Eventually, the device might reconnect to the same network recovering access to the same pool of workers, but using a different IP address.

To tolerate short, sporadic network disruptions, the master sends a message to every worker node upon the reconnection indicating its new address. Upon its reception, worker nodes update every reference to the master node with the new IP and re-start any interrupted transaction – transfer of a value or submission of internal COMPSs command.

On long-lasting disruptions, worker nodes should keep progressing on the computation despite the isolation. In the case of reconnection, workers autonomy reduces the impact of the network failure on the performance of the application. Upon the broadcast reconnection notification, *DM* instances synchronize their content, thereby all the components of the infrastructure become aware of the progress done by the other part.

On the other end, the master device should produce the expected result even if the network connection is never re-established. Therefore, the master may need to run all the pending tasks, even those already offloaded. Probably, some input values for a pending task are the output of an offloaded one and they are not likely to be on the master; hence, the value must be computed locally by running the producing task. This mechanism results in a backtracking process that only stops when all the input data required by a task exists in the device. So the runtime can go back in the execution, it keeps track of all the detected tasks and builds a data-dependency graph. Tasks can not be removed from the graph until the master never needs to re-execute them again – i.e., all its output values have a replica on the master or neither the main application nor any task use them.

Upon the detection of a network breakdown, the *Executor* prioritizes the execution of the not offloaded tasks whose input values are already on the mobile. When there are not enough tasks to use all the computing devices within the mobile, the *Executor* picks one of the not offloaded tasks and triggers the backtracking process to generate the missing input values for the task. Finally, once all the not offloaded tasks have started their execution, it runs pending offloaded tasks (if necessary, re-computing the input data values).

To prevent this backtracking process from re-running tasks already executed on the workers, the runtime transfers the output values back to the mobile to establish checkpoints. To avoid transferring every remotely generated value, the runtime picks some strategic values splitting the graph – currently, fixed-size partitions according to the chronological order of task generation – and analyzing each partition for all the output values of the block that succeeding partitions might use. The master fetches these values upon their creation; once the master has all the output values from a block, it removes the whole block from the graph.

5   Experiments

As a proof of concept that validates the feasibility of the described architecture and the proper behavior of the runtime system, we have ported the HeatSweeper application and executed it on a smartphone that offloads parts of the computation to nearby and remote devices. The following subsections introduce the application, describe the testbed used to conduct the tests, and present the obtained results in terms of execution time and energy consumption.

5.1   Application: HeatSweeper

HeatSweeper is an application to find the optimal placement of 1-to-N heat sources on the surface of a solid body to reduce the time to heat up its whole surface to a certain temperature. Its algorithm consists on an intensive search looking for the best combination of 1-to-N locations for the heat sources, and relies on two different solvers to simulate the heat diffusion based on the Jacobi (used on the tests) and Gauss-Seidel equations.

On the COMPSs version, the application defines two CEs. *Simulate* encapsulates within a task the simulation of the heat transfer over a surface for a specific combination of locations and generates a report summarizing the simulation. In a second phase, the application compares all the simulation reports to select the best combination. To compare two reports the application defines the second CE: *getBest*. On the conducted tests, the application considers 25 different spots of the surface where to locate the heat sources; simulations stop after 10,000 steps if the surface has not reached the desired temperature before. With this configuration, the application generates 325 *simulate* tasks and 323 *getBest*.

5.2   Testbed

HeatSweeper runs on a OnePlus One (OPO) smartphone, equipped with a Krait 400 quad-core processor at 2.5 GHz and 3 GB of RAM memory. As mentioned above, the defined tests consider two different infrastructures where to offload task. For the fog case, the smartphone offloads the computation to a laptop equipped with an Intel i7-2760QM quad-core processor at 2.40 GhZ and 8 GB of RAM memory. The mobile device connects to the laptop via an 802.11g wireless network. On the Cloud scenario, the phone uses as surrogates up to eight quad-core VM instances deployed on an OpenNebula cloud. The physical nodes supporting the Cloud have six-core Intel Xeon X5650 at 2.67 GHz processors and 24 GB of memory each. Cloud nodes are interconnected through a Gigabit Ethernet network, while the connection between the mobile device and the surrogates goes through the Internet and has an 85.5 ms RTT.

5.3   Results

Measurements of the elapsed time to execute a *simulate* task highlight the performance differences among the devices composing the infrastructure. Running a task on the smartphone takes around 288 s. When the screen of the device is Off, Android reduces the frequency of the processor to a 10% of its regular value. This increases the execution time to 6,794 s; however, it also reduces the power consumption of the processor from 1.4 W to 0.16 W. Executing the same simulation on the laptop and on a Cloud instance takes 16 and 29 s, respectively. The execution time of running a *getBest* task is negligible. Overall, running the application on the phone – with its screen on – takes 99,641 s (more than 27 h), and it forces the smartphone to stay plugged in and drawning power.

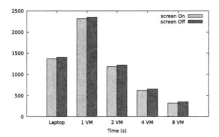 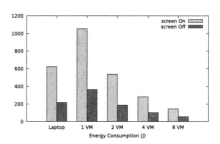

Fig. 4. Elapsed time and energy consumption of executing HeatSweeper according to the surrogate platform

Charts in Fig. 4 illustrate the elapsed time and the energy consumption measured when executing HeatSweeper in the different platforms. Offloading parts of the computation to resources with higher computing capabilities allows a significant reduction of either the execution time and the energy consumed by the smartphone. The laptop is the most powerful resource, and offloading tasks to it reduces the execution time to 1368 s. Although the execution using a single VM instance achieves a worse execution time than the laptop, the cloud provides the runtime with higher amount of resources. The more VMs the application uses, the lower the execution time is; using all eight instances, the application only takes 321 s to finish. Obviously, offloading tasks saves to the master the energy spend on the processor to compute them; however, keeping the mobile on and transferring data through the network maintains part of this consumption. For the 8-VM case, the smartphone consumes up to 146 J. The screen of the devices is responsible for a significant part of this energy; with the screen Off, the application reaches a consumption of less than 55 J. The impact of switching the screen Off on the execution time is not significant. The frequency reduction only affects to the communications and task management performed by the runtime; it does not affect the actual computation of the tasks since remote resources keep their performance.

6   Conclusions and Future Work

This paper presents the preliminary design of an architecture for a programming framework that enables distributed computing on Fog-to-Cloud environments. The baseline of this architecture is COMPSs, a programming tool that has been successfully applied to port applications and parallelize their execution on clusters, grids and clouds. The COMPSs runtime, as explained in this work, has been extended to be executed on Android devices equipped with CPUs and GPUs and to offload tasks to clouds backends or other fog devices available in the same network. An important improvement and contribution is the design of a new distributed data management mechanism that allows to efficiently share information about data across the different platforms. A checkpointing strategy has been also implemented to make the runtime resilient to network fluctuations and disruptions, allowing to resume the computation after a working node failure. Finally, security mechanisms have been added to secure the communications between the main runtime process and the worker nodes. The results of the tests demonstrate that the refactoring and extensions to the runtime, do not affect the performance of the execution when offloading the tasks to remote nodes.

Future work includes several optimizations as the implementation of a distributed scheduling policy, the improvements on the security mechanisms in order to add authentication at application level, extensions to the resource management to allow elasticity on the Cloud and to use dynamically appearing resources as workers.

Acknowledgment. This work is partly supported by the Spanish Ministry of Science and Technology through project TIN2015-65316-P and grant BES-2013-067167, by the Generalitat de Catalunya under contracts 2014-SGR-1051 and 2014-SGR-1272, and by the European Union through the Horizon 2020 research and innovation programme under grant 730929 (mF2C Project).

References

1. Apache Mesos: http://mesos.apache.org/. Accessed 12 May 2017
2. Linn, J.: Generic security service application program interface version 2, update 1. Internet Requests for Comments, RFC 2743. RFC Editor, January 2000. ISSN 2070-1721
3. OpenFog Reference Architecture. https://www.openfogconsortium.org. Accessed 12 May 2017
4. Chun, B.G., Ihm, S., Maniatis, P., Naik, M., Patti, A.: Clonecloud: elastic execution between mobile device and cloud. In: Proceedings of the Sixth Conference on Computer Systems, EuroSys 2011, pp. 301–314. ACM, New York (2011). https://doi.org/10.1145/1966445.1966473
5. Hong, K., Lillethun, D., Ramachandran, U., Ottenwälder, B., Koldehofe, B.: Mobile fog: a programming model for large-scale applications on the internet of things. In: Proceedings of the Second ACM SIGCOMM Workshop on Mobile Cloud Computing, MCC 2013, pp. 15–20. ACM, New York (2013). https://doi.org/10.1145/2491266.2491270
6. Kemp, R., Palmer, N., Kielmann, T., Bal, H.: Cuckoo: a computation offloading framework for smartphones. In: Gris, M., Yang, G. (eds.) MobiCASE 2010. LNICST, vol. 76, pp. 59–79. Springer, Heidelberg (2012). https://doi.org/10.1007/978-3-642-29336-8_4

7. Kosta, S., Aucinas, A., Hui, P., Mortier, R., Zhang, X.: Thinkair: dynamic resource allocation and parallel execution in the cloud for mobile code offloading. In: 2012 Proceedings IEEE INFOCOM, pp. 945–953, March 2012. https://doi.org/10.1109/INFCOM.2012.6195845

8. Lordan, F., Tejedor, E., Ejarque, J., Rafanell, R., Alvarez, J., Marozzo, F., Lezzi, D., Sirvent, R., Talia, D., Badia, R.M.: Servicess: an interoperable programming framework for the cloud. J. Grid Comput. **12**(1), 67–91 (2014). https://doi.org/10.1007/s10723-013-9272-5

9. Merkel, D.: Docker: lightweight linux containers for consistent development and deployment. Linux J. **2014**(239), 2 (2014)

Making Use of a Smart Fog Hub to Develop New Services in Airports

Antonio Salis$^{(\boxtimes)}$ and Glauco Mancini

Engineering Sardegna Srl, Loc. Sa Illetta, SS195 km 2,3, 09123 Cagliari, Italy
{antonio.salis,glauco.mancini}@eng.it

Abstract. The EC H2020 mF2C Project aims at developing a software framework that enables the orchestration of resources and communication at Fog level, as an extension of Cloud Computing and interacting with the IoT. In order to show the project functionalities and added-values three real world Use Cases have been chosen. This paper introduces the mF2C Use case 3: Smart Fog Hub Service (SFHS), in the context of an airport, with the objective of proving that great potential value and different business opportunities can be created in physical environments with a great concentration of smart objects, to showcase the wide range of scenarios on which mF2C can impact, validate the project in industrial events and determine a massive interest of relevant stakeholders.

Keywords: Cloud computing · Fog Computing · Fog-to-cloud
Distributed systems · IoT · B2B · Airports

1 Introduction

More than 8 billion connected devices will be in use worldwide in 2017, up 31% from 2016 [1]. The forecasts of the world's largest research institutes agree to over 20 billion of IoT by 2020 with a growth of 140% in just three years. In 2017 more than 4 billion passengers will concentrate in the airports with an average of two connected devices for each passenger [2]. Current technology infrastructures and architectures have not been designed to process in real time the great amount of information data that is being made available from such a number of devices with a so high concentration. As one of the first technical response to such technological challenges Fog Computing is emerging as an architectural model that places itself between the Cloud and the IoT, expanding Cloud Computing and Services to the IoT objects.

This paper is structured as follows. Section 2, introduces the Fog Computing concept and how a Fog layer can address some of the challenges of connecting the IoT to the cloud. Section 3 draws the proposed use case in the airport and Sect. 4 identifies main expected benefits. Finally, Sect. 5 concludes the paper.

© Springer International Publishing AG, part of Springer Nature 2018
D. B. Heras and L. Bougé (Eds.): Euro-Par 2017 Workshops, LNCS 10659, pp. 338–347, 2018.
https://doi.org/10.1007/978-3-319-75178-8_28

2 The Fog Computing Scenario

The Internet of Things (IoT) is the set of objects within electronic devices, sensors and actuators that are widely diffused and capable of communicating with the Internet and other devices through communication protocols that do not request human intervention. By way of example, we can mention:

- Web-cameras (for surveillance, traffic detection, pollution, etc.);
- Appliances (refrigerators, washing machines, kettles, etc.), door openers or shutter controllers;
- Lifts and other smart building equipment;
- Various avionics devices such as flight recorders;
- Card readers or RFID (for logistic applications);
- Biomedical appliances and sensors;
- Meters, thermostats, digital regulators for electricity, gas, water, heat;
- Wearable devices such as bracelets and watches.
- Environmental and territorial sensors (light and humidity sensors, air quality and parking sensors, etc.)

The amount of such objects grows at dizzying rates, and the volumes, variety and speed of the data they produce also grow considerably. According to McKinsey [5], by 2020 some predictions suggest over 20 billion edge devices are to be connected collecting more than 1 trillion GB of data. The information that is made available therefore constitutes a Big Data generator of great potential value.

To take advantage of the quantity and variety of such data and generate value and services from them, the most immediate approach was to connect the IoT directly with the Cloud. Cloud service providers (Amazon AWS, Google Compute Engine, Microsoft Azure) today enable customers to quickly deploy a myriad of private and corporate services to be a competitive alternative to buying and maintaining their own infrastructure.

Although this may in some cases be feasible, a more careful analysis has immediately underlined that the direct "Cloudification" of IoT is generally problematic since the approach of transferring all data from the device to the datacenter generates considerable latency and a large computational load and storage at non-negligible economic costs. There are also regulatory constraints that limit the use of personal data in the cloud and infrastructure complications such as the use of dedicated communication gateways between the IoT and the cloud.

In summary, the "Cloudification" of IoT makes an unwise use of the precious and expensive resources of the Cloud computing system, namely the transmission capacity, data storage and processing capabilities. There are also a large number of services that require a nearly instant response to the reception of IoT data and this is not compatible with the ability to transfer and process the huge amount of data of IoT devices in the cloud.

A first technical response to these issues has been given by Cisco introducing the Fog Computing concept as an architectural model that, between the Cloud and the IoT, extends Cloud Computing and Services to IoT objects to the ends of the network [3]. In the same way as Cloud, Fog provides data, computing, storage, and end-user application services, but supports a dense geographic distribution, aimed at approaching IoT devices and providing support for object mobility. In this way the Fog reduces latency in services, which in the case of critical services can be decisive, by improving their Quality and Overall Experience of End Users.

The great interest in this new Fog architecture has given place to the establishment of the Open Fog Consortium [4] consisting of research and industry giants such as ARM, Cisco, Dell, Intel, Microsoft, Princeton University, which recently released the first Reference Architecture. Fog Computing is defined as a horizontal-level system architecture that deploys more computing, storage, control, and networking functions closer to end-users in the continuum from cloud computing to IoT objects.

The architecture expects that deployments can reside on multiple layers, while retaining all the benefits of cloud computing, such as containerization, virtualization, orchestration, and resource-efficient management. Processes are moved by the cloud to the edges of the network, near the IoT sensors and actuators, on elements called Fog Nodes, consisting of autonomous processing, storage and IP communications. These computing elements can be deployed anywhere, such along a railway, lighting poles or a car, or can be capable of acting in mobility.

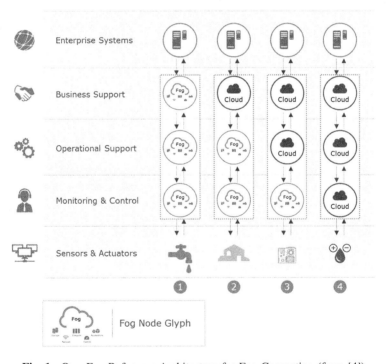

Fig. 1. OpenFog Reference Architecture for Fog Computing (from [4])

The peculiarities of OpenFog's architectures are to enable cloud-to-cloud and cloud-to-fog interfaces and communication flows and thus offer, with respect to other approaches, particular advantages represented by the SCALE acronym:

- Security: data generated by IoT devices must be protected both in transfers and in storage to ensure secure and trusted transactions; The integrity and availability of infrastructure and data should not be questioned;
- Cognition: awareness of end-user and surrounding environment goals; It also has the ability to adapt connections and computing resources even in the unavailability of some of them, so that architecture is autonomous and adaptive, starting with objects at the extremes of the network;
- Agility: rapid innovation and scalability within a common infrastructure where choosing the most suitable node depends on various factors such as the speed of decision making required; So, for example, for instant responses, the node may be at the generating device, while for other cases it may be transferred to a fog layer or cloud;
- Latency: real-time processing and cyber-physical control systems, data analysis is done close to the device that generated it for immediate response;
- Efficiency: dynamic, commonly used local resources not utilized by participating end-user devices, for orchestrated and optimized computational resources.

Applications will need to be redesigned, starting with the gathering of elementary information from sensors, for a new distribution of functions, previously thought only for the cloud, and now placed between Cloud and Fog levels in the environment. The most critical response time data will be processed in the first fog layer, while less critical data may be transferred to higher aggregation layers for analysis and treatment. The less critical data will then be brought to the cloud for historical analysis, big data analytics, and long-term storage.

The Fog Computing model is not a compulsory choice in all situations. Various scenarios can be better managed with just Cloud Computing, but many other scenarios will be better implemented with fog extensions. Cloud backend remains a key part of architecture even with the introduction of Fog Computing layers. Deploying tasks between Fog and Cloud depends on specific applications; it can be originally planned, but also dynamically adapted to the status of key resources such as processing load, communication link saturation, storage capacity, security threats detected, unavailability of resources, batteries consumption, cost targets, etc.

Recent business research, remarkably by McKinsey [5] examined the economic impact that IoT based applications can bring by analyzing the potential benefits, including productivity improvements, time savings, improved asset utilization, as well as the value coming from reduced diseases, accidents, and deaths. The outcome focused on the importance on the analysis of applications in the context of settings, the physical environments where these systems are deployed. The most relevant findings include how much IoT value is being created in business-to-business vs. consumer markets, and which players in the value chain will capture the most value from IoT applications. To name the most relevant we mention:

- Interoperability among IoT systems plays a major role, most of the expected value to be unlocked requires multiple IoT systems to work together, then to integrate and analyze data from various IoT systems;
- Most of IoT data generated is merely collected but not stored nor used, so the potential value contained in these data is not exploited. So there is a key source of big data that can be leveraged to capture value, and open data, to be used in several scenarios;
- B2B applications of IoT have greater economic potential than consumer applications. While consumer uses of IoT have obtained a lot of attention and show a tremendous potential for creating value, there is even greater potential value from IoT use in business-to-business applications. A great deal of additional value can be created when consumer IoT systems, such as connected consumer health-care products are linked to B2B systems, such as services provided by health-care providers and payers. This happens more frequently in environments with high concentration of IoT devices.

Consequently typical scenarios to be considered with particular attention are:

- smart IoT objects in mobility (cars, ships, drones, airplanes, smartphones)
- the directions on which smart objects move (roads, railways, nautical routes, airways)
- aggregation points for smart objects (ports, airports, railway/metro/bus stations, malls, parking areas, factories, hospitals, schools/universities, building/houses)

The adoption of the Fog offers the following benefits:

- a globally distributed network improves fault tolerance and resilience, minimizing downtime,
- better interconnection and balancing of processing loads,
- better system scalability also guaranteed by virtualized and containerized systems,
- better use of the network bandwidth, reducing transfers and avoiding congestion and bottlenecks,
- a reduction in latency will also result in better service quality,
- optimizing operating costs by streamlining the use of processing, storage, and network resources,
- more efficient security by encoding data to the source and reducing transfers, thus reducing risk exposure,
- better flexibility and agility of business models.

3   The Smart Fog-Hub Service (SFHS)

The EC Horizon 2020 program has recently funded a new research initiative (mF2C) bringing together relevant industry and academic players in the cloud arena, aimed at designing an open, secure, decentralized, multi-stakeholder management framework for F2C computing, including novel programming models, privacy and security, data storage techniques, service creation, brokerage solutions, SLA policies, and resource orchestration methods [6].

There is an increasing demand in evaluating and identifying new market sectors and opportunities, and interest at the IoT evolution as a potential arena where current Cloud offering could be enriched and differentiated. In this perspective a relevant focus in setting up hubs in public environments (e.g. airports, train stations, hospitals, malls and related parking areas) is suggested, capable of tracking the presence of people and other objects in the field, and developing value added services on top for proximity marketing, prediction of path/behavior of consumers, and taking real time decisions.

The foreseen hubs could be adapted to be used as a planning tool for determining the number and distribution of people that use, or can potentially use various services like public transport, etc. This kind of hub can be easily considered as a fog device that should embed cloud connectivity to either process large amount of data or request extra-data – perhaps data coming from other fogs nearby.

As an additional opportunity to be evaluated, different fogs located in near sites (e.g. airport, train/main bus/harbor station) could interact sharing data and customer behavior gathered to improve the effectiveness of marketing proposals, given that the identity of objects/customers is protected.

This scenario has been named as the Smart Fog-Hub Service (SFHS). The use case is experimental and extends the concept of a "cloud hub" to a new concept of "fog hub", driven by real market needs. In this scenario Tiscali believes that value is generated at the business services level, particularly in spaces with recurring concentrations of people and objects that can communicate and interact. Tiscali is interested in setting up Fog Hubs in such scenarios to interact with all the objects within the scope of coverage.

Tiscali believes that the IoT will be driven by business market instead of consumer market, and that SFHS would be the best way to aggregate business users, design new business scenarios and create value. There is no doubt that the capacities provided by

Fig. 2. Airport scenario

mF2C will enable the distribution of the processing of data, reducing traffic load between cloud & hub and latency in interactive services.

The envisioned Smart Fog-Hub Service should be set up in public crowded environments, so a preliminary version will be tested within the Tiscali Campus in Cagliari, and a final version will be deployed at the Cagliari Elmas airport. With this approach the whole infrastructure will be tested and validated in a real scenario with possibility for Tiscali to exploit the marketing potential of the developed services.

In the specific context of airports there are a growing number of objects that are related to passengers and partners, or people that work in this environment. The field include check-in area, security control area, and departure gates. Check-in and departure gates host several shops and other frequented places. The foreseen services, provided through a web portal, are oriented to track and engage all people in the field offering information, suggestions on the best way to use available services, e.g. suggest the moment for shorter waiting times in Security Control to departing people, to move close to the gate or notify the final call, or recommend relevant proposals and offerings in shops close to the user (proximity marketing). All these suggestions can be refined according to behavior and choices done by passengers.

The technological scenario will include the following elements:

- **Edge sensors**, which can include smartphones, laptops, tablets, any other IoT device with Wifi connection; most of them will be data generators, some could have some computing power and potentially could offer/share data and eventually also computing resources
- **Edge Fog**, which is basically composed by the Fog-Hub, that will perform the role of data collector, power provider for the fog layer processing and will consist of the following features:
  - a computing element that has relevant computing power to run the defined applications, analytics and management functions/tools,
  - Wifi AP to collect data from the perceived objects within the covered field,
  - enough local storage to retain local and temporary processed data,
  - fast link interface with the cloud,
  - (optional) Bluetooth LE beacons could be added, where the edge fog component would run the management functions
- **Link connection** between Edge Fog and Cloud,
- **Cloud**, connected to the Edge Fog, which will be based on an OpenStack instance that will provide scalable computing power for massive data processing.

The resulting infrastructure will be based on standard components and protocols and will be sized according to the data volumes, and open to use different devices that will be made available by the Project partners.

The data collected by the edge devices include some device specific and personal data, detailed tracking position and preferences according to the portal navigation, and different paths followed. This data has to be protected in the communication between fog and the edge.

The additional workload on the networking elements will be managed with SDN/NFV to provide bandwidth optimization and low latency, while from a security and privacy perspective Fog and Cloud should be able to use different policies, with

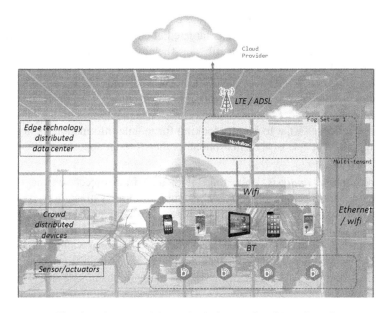

Fig. 3. Airport mF2C topological scenario of Use Case 3

anonymization of data when requested. The edge fog element will be configured with some resiliency capabilities, at least for stored data and fast reboot/recovery.

In this scenario the described Fog-Hub cannot be a "cloud hub" because the amount of data to be processed and managed would exceed the network capabilities, so part of the computation should be spent at Fog level, thus this hub could be better named the **Fog enabling Hub for ISPs,** namely **Smart Fog-Hub Service**.

4 Benefits

With this kind of fog hubs, proximity marketing and social aggregation would be enabled, with the possibility to collect a lot of information on objects moving within the covered environment, offering connections, customized advertising and interactive applications giving the connected users the chance to share or offer some resources. This could require new billing/revenue sharing models and tools that also take into account the correct use of users' personal information.

These are some of the Expected Benefits:

Proximity marketing and enhanced user engagement, the strict interaction of a huge amount of users enables a much more effective, customized offering and advertising, differentiating between B2B and B2C customers, based on user preferences and behavior, with the chance to determine the effectiveness of the proposition in terms of purchasing products/services. A continuous refinement in the proposition can be applied in terms of geo-fencing with a predefined set of boundaries, the recipient of the message can receive real value as well as a mere communication. It can be possible to organize customized promotional initiatives, ex ante or ex post with respect to the presence in the area. Prepare campaigns targeted at categorized users, e.g. workers in the airport, because they have been identified as such by people who are always passing between eight and nine o'clock. Of course, respecting privacy laws.

According to recent report from the Politecnico di Milano [7], 80% of users (chosen by those who usually browse the Internet) declare that online is the first source to look for information on a product or service to buy, 77% compare prices on the Internet, and a user in three chooses what to buy by looking for mobile information, typically from their smartphone. The use of the smartphone is therefore an appealing opportunity to engage customers.

Data collection and analysis, collecting lot of data from objects on the move can enable running advanced machine learning algorithms to extract user profiles and demands, but also trace trends or identify new required services. Most IoT data are not currently used nor stored [5]; the current use is mostly limited to address anomaly detection and real-time control, so a great deal of additional value remains to be captured, by using more data, as well as deploying more sophisticated applications such as analyzing workflows to optimize operating efficiency. Some Descriptive Analytics, what's happened, to Predictive Analytics, what will happen, to Prescriptive Analytics, what can be done, can drive the Analytics on the data and generate value.

Related to the Multi SHFS (airport, train station, bus station, etc.), it will be possible to answer several questions like: what are the most popular areas? Where does the user stop the most? What are the average times of stay in the area?

Social integration, offering connections and interactive applications provides a way for connected users to share or offer some resources, under user defined access rules.

New revenue models, sharing users' resources may drive new billing models and SLA policies not only between users and traditional providers but also among users themselves. Business-to-Business (B2B) applications can create more value than pure consumer applications and new business models for user and companies are emerging. The Internet of Things will enable—and in some cases force—new business models. The new "as-a-service" approach can give the supplier of services a more intimate tie with customers that competitors would find difficult to disrupt. The IoT will speed up this evolution path because IoT produces huge quantities of a type of asset that can be sold or exchanged: the data. The ability to identify facts and hidden relations in the data available to organizations not only allows the optimization of processes and increasing competitiveness, but also can open new opportunities for value creation. Data monetization is the process of generating new revenues through the sale or exchange of data in the possession of the organization and through the exploitation of these for the generation of new products and services.

Improved data Privacy and security, management of user personal data is done at edge level, separated from the cloud, encryption of storage and anonymization techniques are applied before moving data to the cloud, thus reducing the risk of disclosure on data, and preserving the confidentiality of data owners.

Optimized use of Resources and Service in the Airport field, the engagement and continuous tracking of people moving in the airport allows the proposition of suggestions oriented to an optimal use of available resources, services and an improved and pleasant quality of experience for passengers and partners. At the same time all dealers and service providers in the airport site will be facilitated in their marketing proposals and offering, by using the (anonymized) data collected by all people in the field.

5   Conclusions

This paper begins highlighting the Fog Computing concept as an architectural model that gives a better answer to the "Cloudification" approach. Fog computing, making the glue between the Cloud and the IoT, extends Cloud Computing and Services to IoT objects to the ends of the network.

Then an evaluation of current business trends on IoT was developed noting the importance of the physical environments where such systems are deployed, and spotted that a relevant IoT value is expected to be created in business-to-business vs. consumer markets, and which players in the value chain will capture the most value from IoT applications. This happens mostly in environments with high concentrations of IoT devices.

The experimental Use Case on Smart Fog Hub Service (SFHS) has been described, detailing the main objectives of exploring and analyzing proximity marketing and new revenue models through data collection and advanced analytics, and foreseeing new business models. Notably the data processing has to be distributed between cloud and fog layers because the amount of data to be managed can exceed network, storage and computing capabilities at the fog layer.

Finally the paper introduces the main expected benefits. Proximity marketing and social aggregation would be enabled, giving way the collection of relevant of information on objects moving within the covered environment, offering connections, customized advertising and interactive applications giving the chance to connected users to share or offer some resources, under controlled policies on users' personal information.

Acknowledgments.   This work is supported by the H2020 mF2C project (730929).

References

1. Gartner Press Release, (Egham, UK) (2017). http://www.gartner.com/newsroom/id/3598917
2. IATA, IATA Forecasts Passenger Demand to Double Over 20 Years, (Geneva, CH) (2016). http://www.iata.org/pressroom/pr/Pages/2016-10-18-02.aspx
3. Bonomi, F., et al.: Fog computing and its role in the internet of things. In: Proceedings of the First Edition of the MCC Workshop on Mobile Cloud Computing (Helsinki, Finland) (2012)
4. Open Fog Consortium, "OpenFog Reference Architecture for Fog Computing". https://www.openfogconsortium.org/ra/
5. McKinsey Global Institute, "The Internet of Things: mapping the value" (2015)
6. ICT-06-2016 RIA 730929 - mF2C Proposal-SEP-210346729, mF2C project. http://www.mf2c-project.eu
7. Politecnico di Milano: Mobile B2C Strategy, (Milan, Italy) (2017)

HeteroPar – Workshop on Algorithms, Models and Tools for Parallel Computing on Heterogeneous Platforms

Workshop on Algorithms, Models and Tools for Parallel Computing on Heterogeneous Platforms (HeteroPar)

Workshop Description

HeteroPar is a forum for researchers working on algorithms, programming languages, tools, and theoretical models aimed at efficiently solving problems on heterogeneous platforms. Heterogeneity is emerging as one of the most profound and challenging characteristics of today's parallel environments. From the macro level, where networks of distributed computers, composed by diverse node architectures, are interconnected with potentially heterogeneous networks, to the micro level, where deeper memory hierarchies and various accelerator architectures are increasingly common, the impact of heterogeneity on all computing tasks is increasing rapidly. Traditional parallel algorithms, programming environments and tools, designed for legacy homogeneous multiprocessors, will at best achieve a small fraction of the efficiency and the potential performance that we should expect from parallel computing in tomorrow's highly diversified and mixed environments. New ideas, innovative algorithms, and specialized programming environments and tools are needed to efficiently use these new and multifarious parallel architectures.

The fifteenth International Workshop on Algorithms, Models and Tools for Parallel Computing on Heterogeneous Platforms (HeteroPar'2017) was held in Santiago de Compostela, Spain. For the ninth time, this workshop was organized in conjunction with the Euro-Par annual international conference. The format of the workshop includes a keynote, followed by technical presentations. The workshop was well-attended with around 35 attendees.

In this edition, we have received 26 papers, from 13 countries. After a thorough peer-reviewing process, 10 papers were selected for presentation at the workshop. The review process focused on the quality of the papers, their innovative ideas and their applicability to heterogeneous architectures. Papers were accepted after a discussion and agreement among reviewers. As a consequence, the quality and the relevance of the selected papers was high, reflected also in a low acceptance rate of 38%. The accepted papers represent an interesting mix of topics, addressing modern SIMD architectures, CPU-GPU systems, compiler techniques towards GPU performance, software-Distributed Shared Memory, benchmarking, large scale graph processing, workflow and chain of tasks scheduling, and resource aware execution of multiprocessor tasks, exhibiting the diversity and growth of the heterogeneous computing field.

At last, I would like to thank to all authors, to the HeteroPar Steering Committee and the HeteroPar 2017 Program Committee, who made the workshop possible. I would like to thank Y. Srikant, Daniel Pérez and Maciej Malawski for chairing the sessions. I would also like to thank Euro-Par for hosting our community, and the Euro-Par workshop chairs Dora B. Heras and Luc Bougé for their help and support.

Steering Committee

Domingo Giménez	University of Murcia, Spain
Alexey Kalinov	Cadence Design Systems, Russia
Alexey Lastovetsky	University College Dublin, Ireland
Yves Robert	Ecole Normale Supérieure de Lyon, France
Leonel Sousa	INESC-ID/IST, Univ. de Lisboa, Portugal
Denis Trystram	University Grenoble-Alpes, France

Program Chair

Jorge Barbosa	LIACC & Universidade do Porto, Portugal

Program Committee

Alberto Proenca	Universidade do Minho, Portugal
Rizos Sakellariou	University of Manchester, UK
Hamid Arabnejad	Dublin City University (DCU), Ireland
Gabriel Falcao	Universidade de Coimbra, Portugal
Jianbin Fang	National University of Defense Technology, China
Giorgio Lucarelli	INRIA Grenoble Rhône-Alpes, France
Louis-Claude Canon	Université de Franche-Comté, France
Shuichi Ichikawa	Toyohashi University of Technology, Japan
Aleksandar Ilic	INESC-ID/IST, Portugal
Aurelien Bouteiller	University of Tennessee Knoxville, USA
Hatem Ltaief	KAUST, Saudi Arabia
Erik Saule	University of North Carolina at Charlotte, USA
Cristina Boeres	Universidade Federal Fluminense, Brasil
Ravindranath Manumachu	University College Dublin, Ireland
Helen Karatza	Aristotle University of Thessaloniki, Greece
Matei Ripeanu	The University of British Columbia, Canada
Dana Petcu	West University of Timisoara, Romania
Emmanuel Jeannot	Inria, France
Francisco D. Igual	Universidad Complutense de Madrid, Spain
Loris Marchal	CNRS, France
Jing Gong	KTH Royal Institute of Technology, Sweden
Klavdiya Bochenina	ITMO University, Russia
Pedro Tomás	INESC-ID, Instituto Superior Técnico
Rafael Mayo Gual	University Jaume I, Spain
Oliver Sinnen	DECE, The University of Auckland
Pierre Manneback	University of Mons, Belgium

Thomas Rauber	University Bayreuth, Germany
Olivier Beaumont	INRIA Bordeaux Sud-Ouest, France
Frédéric Suter	IN2P3 Computing Center, France
Enrique S. Quintana-Ortí	Universidad Jaume I, Spain
Antonio J. Peña	Barcelona Supercomputing Center, Spain

Approximation Algorithm for Scheduling a Chain of Tasks on Heterogeneous Systems

Massinissa Ait Aba[1](✉), Lilia Zaourar[1], and Alix Munier[2]

[1] CEA, LIST, Computing and Design Environment Laboratory,
91191 Gif sur Yvette Cedex, France
Massinissa.aitaba@cea.fr
[2] LIP6-UPMC, 4 place Jussieu, 75005 Paris, France

Abstract. This paper presents an efficient approximation algorithm to solve the task scheduling problem on heterogeneous platform for the particular case of the linear chain of tasks. The objective is to minimize both the total execution time (makespan) and the total energy consumed by the system. For this purpose, we introduce a constraint on the energy consumption during execution. Our goal is to provides an algorithm with a performance guarantee. Two algorithms have been proposed; the first provides an optimal solution for preemptive scheduling. This solution is then used in the second algorithm to provide an approximate solution for non-preemptive scheduling. Numerical evaluations demonstrate that the proposed algorithm achieves a close-to-optimal performance compared to exact solution obtained by *CPLEX* for small instances. For large instances, *CPLEX* is struggling to provide a feasible solution, whereas our approach takes less than a second to produce a solution for an instance of 10000 tasks.

Keywords: Linear chain of tasks · Makespan · Energy
Approximation algorithm

1 Introduction

Today, our daily life requires massive calculations on different computing systems (desktop, data centers) to perform various needs such as physical simulations or google searches. In order to improve the performance of these systems while keeping their energy consumption reasonable, heterogeneous system has merged. This heterogeneous architecture combines both processing elements (such as CPUs, GPUs), and reconfigurable logic (FPGAs).

However, taking advantage of such heterogeneous systems requires efficient use of resources to make profit from the performance of each part for application execution. Thus efficient scheduling of task's applications is difficult problem often faced by designers and engineers using these complex systems. In fact, with the complexity of applications and architectures, it becomes increasingly difficult

© Springer International Publishing AG, part of Springer Nature 2018
D. B. Heras and L. Bougé (Eds.): Euro-Par 2017 Workshops, LNCS 10659, pp. 353–365, 2018.
https://doi.org/10.1007/978-3-319-75178-8_29

to distribute the tasks application effectively. More than a simple load balancing problem, heterogeneity leads to consider efficient scheduling techniques to take account of the different resources specificities. The objective of this work is to determine an efficient scheduling of a parallel application on a heterogeneous resources system in order to minimize both the total execution time (makespan) and the energy consumption. For this purpose, we introduce a constraint on the total energy consumed by the system. We consider in this work, a chain of tasks and communication delay. We conducted this research using the fully heterogeneous micro-server system Christmann RECS©|BOX [3]. The rest of the paper is organized as follows. Section 2 discusses some previous efforts in scheduling parallel application on heterogeneous systems, with a focus on makespan and energy minimization. Section 3 presents a detailed description of the mathematical model proposed. In Sect. 4, we present an optimal algorithm for a chain of preemptive task. In Sect. 5 we describe the proposed algorithm for non-preemptive scheduling and approximation ratio we obtain. Section 6 shows some preliminary numerical results. The paper ends with a conclusion in Sect. 7.

2   Related Work

Due to its key importance on performance, the task scheduling problem on heterogeneous platform has been extensively studied and numerous methods have been reported in the literature. They proposed various models and techniques such as dynamical voltage scaling (DVS), list algorithms and genetic heuristics to optimize essentially two main objectives: makespan and energy consumption. Xie et al. [12], demonstrate that minimizing schedule length of a DAG-based parallel application with energy consumption constraint on heterogeneous distributed systems is a nondeterministic polynomial-hard optimization problem. They decompose the problem in two sub-problems beginning by treating the problem of the energy constraint. At each task assignment phase, the energy consumption constraint of the application can always be satisfied by supposing that the unassigned tasks are assigned to the processor with the minimum energy consumption. Then, they proceed to the minimization of makespan, assigning tasks to processors using the earliest finish time (EFT).

Authors in [13], considered the objective of maximizing the probability of completing tasks before a deadline D and to satisfy an energy constraint with execution times and stochastic communications delays. Zhang et al. [15] have treated the problem of robustness under energy constraint. The aim is to maximize system reliability by repairing runtime errors caused by various reasons such as hardware flaws and program bugs while maintaining the energy constraint. Authors in [16] began by giving an IP (Integer Programming) formulation of the problem, then a three-phase algorithm is proposed using the Dynamic Power Management (DPM) and DVS techniques. Several heuristics (iterative, Greedy, random, ...) are proposed in [8] for the problem of scheduling on heterogeneous processors that can change their frequencies among a set of possible values. The objective is to minimize the temperature more than performance and energy of the system. A three-phase list algorithm is proposed by Fard et al. [2]. They began by analyzing and classifying the different objectives and their impacts on the optimization process. The objective is to find a solution that minimizes up to four objectives (energy, makespan, reliability, economic cost).

Many works have also been done using genetic algorithms. Authors in [5], proposed the ECS heuristic (Energy Concious Heuristic) which is used in [7] to form a hybrid approach with the multi-objective genetic algorithm. This app-roach provides a set of Pareto solutions. More recently in [14], authors proposed a new genetic algorithm to study both objectives at once. Authors in [9–11] also use game theory strategies to prove the existence of Nash equilibrium and find a Pareto point.

However, all the aforementioned works did not consider approximation tech-niques. To the best of our knowledge, we propose the first algorithm with a guarantee of performance. Our model is inspired by [1], where authors seek to minimize the energy consumed during execution by imposing a Deadline D on completion time. In addition, we consider in this work communication cost between tasks and processing elements. Preliminary results on modeling appli-cations and heterogeneous platforms have been presented in [6], we focus in this work on tasks chain to determine a performance guarantee algorithm.

3   Model

This study considers a fully connected heterogeneous multiprocessor platform in which M is a set of m heterogeneous processing elements (GPU, CPU, FPGA...) noted PE. Each element $PE_k \in M$ is characterized by its execution frequency $f_j \geqslant 1$, $j = \overline{1..m}$. The processing elements are sorted by increasing order of their frequencies ($f_1 \leqslant f_2 \leqslant \ldots \leqslant f_m$). An application A of n tasks is modeled using a DAG graph $G(V, E, w)$. V represents set of nodes in G, and each node $v_i \in V$ represents a task t_i which is characterized by its weight w_i, $i = \overline{1..n}$. We note by W the total sum of the weights $W = \sum_{i=1}^{n} w_i$. E is set of communication edges. Each edge $e_{i,j} \in E$ represents a precedence constraint between two tasks t_i and t_j and refers to the volume of communication from t_i to t_j denoted by $Ct_{i,j}$ if they are not assigned to the same processing element. Communication cost between each pair of processing elements (PE_k, PE_l) is denoted by $Cm_{k,l}$ with $Cm_{k,l} \geqslant Max_i\ execut_{i,k}, \forall i \in \{1, 2, \ldots, n\}$ and $\forall k, l \in \{1, 2, \ldots, m\}$ as in [6].

A task t_i can be executed only after the execution of all its predecessors. We do not allow duplication of tasks or preemption. A task can be executed by all processing units. Execution of task t_i on PE_k generates execution time equal to $execut_{i,k} = \frac{w_i}{f_k}$ and power $p_{i,k} = w_i * f_k^2$. We denote by E the allowed quantity of energy consumed during the execution. E represents in our case an energy bound that should not be exceeded during the execution.

We focus this work to a chain of tasks. Our problem can be modeled by mixed integer quadratic constrained program (P). The first constraint simply expresses that each task must be executed only once and on a single processing element. Constraint (2) keeps energy consumption during execution less than

E. The third constraint describes that the task t_{i+1} must be carried out after the starting time of the task t_i $(i = \overline{1..n-1})$ plus the execution time of t_i. The communication cost $(Ct_{i,i+1} + Cm_{j1,j2})$ is added if both tasks are executed on two different processing elements $(PE_{j1}$ and $PE_{j2})$ s.t $x_{i,j1} = 1$ and $x_{i+1,j2} = 1$.

$$x_{i,j} = \begin{cases} 1 \text{ if task } t_i \text{ is placed on the processing element} PE_j, i = \overline{1..n}, \ j = \overline{1..m} \\ 0 \text{ otherwise} \end{cases}$$

$start_i = $ the starting time of the task $t_i, i = \overline{1..n}$.

$$(P) \begin{cases} \sum_{j=1}^{m} x_{i,j} = 1, \forall i = \overline{1..n} & (1) \\ \sum_{i=1}^{h} \sum_{j=1}^{m} x_{i,j} * p_{i,j} \leq E & (2) \\ start_i + x_{i,j_1} * execut_{i,j_1} + x_{i,j_1} * x_{i+1,j_2}(Ct_{i,i+1} + Cm_{j_1,j_2}) \leq start_{i+1} & (3) \\ \quad \forall j_1 = \overline{1..m}, \quad \forall j_2 = \overline{1..m} \quad \forall i = \overline{1..n-1} \quad j_1 \neq j_2 \\ Z(min) = start_n + \sum_{j=1}^{m} x_{n,j} * execut_{n,j} \end{cases}$$

4 Optimal Scheduling Algorithm for a Chain of Preemptive Tasks

In this section we propose an algorithm to find the optimal solution of the preemptive scheduling without communication cost for a chain of n tasks on a set of m processing elements.

Lemma 1. *The set of schedules that saturate energy constraint is dominant.*

Proof. Let $\widehat{C}_{max}$ be the makespan of a solution such that $\widehat{C}_{max} = \frac{P_1}{f_1} + \frac{P_2}{f_2} + \ldots + \frac{P_m}{f_m}$, $P_i \geq 0$ is the quantity of work put on the processing element PE_i, $i = \overline{1..m}$. $\sum_{i=1}^{m} P_i = W$. We assume that $\sum_{j=1}^{m} P_j * f_j^2 < E$. We construct another solution such that: $l = max\{j \in \{1..m\}, \sum_{i=1}^{j} P_i f_m^2 + \sum_{i=j+1}^{m} P_i f_i^2 < E\}$ and $P_1' = 0$, $P_2' = 0, \ldots, P_l' = 0, P_{l+1}' = \frac{E - \sum_{j=1}^{l+1} P_j f_m^2 - \sum_{j=l+2}^{m} P_j f_j^2}{f_{l+1}^2 - f_m^2}$, $P_{l+2}' = P_{l+2}, \ldots, P_m' = P_m + \sum_{j=1}^{l} P_j + (P_{l+1} - P_{l+1}')$. We obtain a new solution $\widehat{C}_{max}' = \sum_{j=1}^{m} \frac{P_j'}{f_j}$ with $\sum_{j=1}^{m} P_j' f_j^2 = E$. $\widehat{C}_{max}' = \sum_{j=1}^{m} \frac{P_j'}{f_j} = \frac{P_{l+1}'}{f_{l+1}} + \sum_{j=l+2}^{m} \frac{P_j}{f_j} + \frac{\sum_{j=1}^{l} P_j + (P_{l+1} - P_{l+1}')}{f_m}$. Since $f_m > f_j$, $j = \overline{1..l+1}$, induces $\frac{P_{l+1}'}{f_{l+1}} + \frac{(P_{l+1} - P_{l+1}')}{f_m} \leq \frac{P_{l+1}}{f_{l+1}}$ and $\frac{\sum_{j=1}^{l} P_j}{f_m} \leq \sum_{j=1}^{l} \frac{P_j}{f_j}$. Then, we obtain $\sum_{j=1}^{m} \frac{P_j'}{f_j} \leq \sum_{j=1}^{m} \frac{P_j}{f_j}$. Finally, $\widehat{C}_{max}' \leq \widehat{C}_{max}$. □

Theorem 1. *The following Algorithm 1 gives the optimal solution for preemptive scheduling without communication cost with a complexity of $\theta(m)$.*

We start by finding the fastest processing element PE_j, on which we can perform all the tasks. Then we look for the weight of tasks that can be put on the next processing element (PE_{j+1}) in order to saturate the energy constraint. We denote by W_j the quantity of work put on the processing element PE_j, W_{j+1}

on PE_{j+1}. The best solution is obtained when the energy constraint is saturated s.t $W_j f_j^2 + W_{j+1} f_{j+1}^2 = E$ with $W_j + W_{j+1} = W$. The solution of the system of two equations with two unknowns is $W_j = \frac{E - W * f_{j+1}^2}{f_j^2 - f_{j+1}^2}$ and $W_{j+1} = W - W_j$. This keeps the realizability of the solution: $E - W * f_{j+1}^2 \leqslant 0$ because $W * f_{j+1}^2 \geqslant E$ and $f_j^2 - f_{j+1}^2 < 0$ because $f_j < f_{j+1}$. Then $W \geqslant W_j > 0$ induces $W_{j+1} \geqslant 0$.

Algorithm 1. Preemptive scheduling (PS).

Data: Set of processing elements $M = \{PE_j, j = 1..m\}$ with $f_1 \leqslant f_2 \leqslant \ldots \leqslant f_m$, weights of the tasks $w_1, w_2, \ldots, w_n$, E.
Result: Optimal preemptive scheduling.
begin

    $W = \sum_{i=1}^{n} w_i$; $j = max\{l \in \{1..m\}, W * f_l^2 \leqslant E\}$
    if $W * f_j^2 < E$ **then**

        $W_j = \frac{E - W * f_{j+1}^2}{f_j^2 - f_{j+1}^2}$
        $W_{j+1} = W - W_j$

    else

        $W_j = W$, $W_{j+1} = 0$

    $k = max\{p \in \{1..n\}, \sum_{i=1}^{p} w_i < W_j\}$; $w'_{k+1} = W_j - \sum_{i=1}^{k} w_i$
    Put $t_1...t_k$ and a part w'_{k+1} of t_{k+1} on PE_j
    Put $t_{k+2}...t_n$ and the rest $(w_{k+1} - w'_{k+1})$ of t_{k+1} on PE_{j+1}

We show in the following that Algorithm 1 gives an optimal solution. Let $\widehat{C}_{max}$ be the makespan of the solution obtained by the Algorithm 1: $\widehat{C}_{max} = \frac{W_j}{f_j} + \frac{W_{j+1}}{f_{j+1}}$ due to the precedence constraint. Let $C'_{max} = \frac{P_1}{f_1} + \frac{P_2}{f_2} + \ldots + \frac{P_k}{f_k}$ be another solution on a set of $k > 2$ processing elements, $\sum_{i=1}^{k} P_i = W$. We distinguish three possible cases. The first case corresponds to all frequencies are lower than f_j s.t $f_1 \leqslant f_2 \leqslant \ldots \leqslant f_k \leqslant f_j$. Hence, $\frac{1}{f_i} \geqslant \frac{1}{f_j}$ induces $\frac{P_i}{f_i} \geqslant \frac{P_i}{f_j}$, $\forall i = \overline{1..k}$. Follows $\sum_{i=1}^{k} \frac{P_i}{f_i} \geqslant \frac{\sum_{i=1}^{k} P_i}{f_j} = \frac{W}{f_j}$. Finally, since $f_j < f_{j+1}$ induces $\sum_{i=1}^{k} \frac{P_i}{f_i} \geqslant \frac{W}{f_j} \geqslant \frac{W_j}{f_j} + \frac{W_{j+1}}{f_{j+1}}$. Then, $C'_{max} \geqslant \widehat{C}_{max}$.
The second case corresponds to all frequencies are greater than f_{j+1} such that $f_{j+1} \leqslant f_1 \leqslant f_2 \leqslant \ldots \leqslant f_k$. Hence, $\sum_{i=1}^{k} P_i * f_i^2 \geqslant \sum_{i=1}^{k} P_i * f_{j+1}^2 = W * f_{j+1}^2 > E$. The last case corresponds to $f_1 \leqslant \ldots \leqslant f_j < f_{j+1} \leqslant \ldots \leqslant f_k$. To study this case, we start with the following Lemma 2.

Lemma 2. *Let A, B, C be three positive integers such as $1 \leq A < B < C$ and W_1, W_2 be two non negative integers such as $W_1 + W_2 = W$. If $W_1 * A^2 + W_2 * C^2 = W * B^2$ then $\frac{W_1}{A} + \frac{W_2}{C} > \frac{W}{B}$.*

Proof. By replacing W_2 by $(W - W_1)$ in $W_1 * A^2 + W_2 * C^2 = W * B^2$, we obtain $W_1 = W(\frac{C^2 - B^2}{C^2 - A^2})$. Then, by replacing W_1 by $(W - W_2)$ we obtain $W_2 = W(\frac{B^2 - A^2}{C^2 - A^2})$. Follows, $\frac{W_1}{A} + \frac{W_2}{C} = \frac{W(C^2 - B^2)}{A(C^2 - A^2)} + \frac{W(B^2 - A^2)}{C(C^2 - A^2)}$.

Let $\Delta = \frac{W_1}{A} + \frac{W_2}{C} - \frac{W}{B}$, we prove in the following that $\Delta > 0$.

$\Delta = \frac{W(C^2 - B^2)}{A(C^2 - A^2)} + \frac{W(B^2 - A^2)}{C(C^2 - A^2)} - \frac{W}{B} = \frac{W}{C^2 - A^2}\left(\frac{C^2 - B^2}{A} + \frac{B^2 - A^2}{C} - \frac{(C^2 - A^2)}{B}\right)$.

We set $X = \frac{B}{A}$ and $Y = \frac{C}{A}$. Observe that $X > 1$ and $Y > X$. Follows:

$\Delta = \frac{W}{Y^2 A^2 - A^2}\left(\frac{Y^2 A^2 - X^2 A^2}{A} + \frac{X^2 A^2 - A^2}{YA} - \frac{(Y^2 A^2 - A^2)}{XA}\right)$.

$\Delta = \frac{W}{Y^2 A - A}\left(\frac{XY^3 - X^3 Y + X^3 - X - Y^3 + Y}{XY}\right) = \frac{W}{Y^2 A - A}\left(\frac{-(X-1)(Y-1)(X-Y)(X+Y+1)}{XY}\right)$.

Since $X > Y > 1$ we have $(Y - 1) > 0$, $(X - 1) > 0$ and $(X - Y) < 0$.

Therefore $\frac{-(X-1)(Y-1)(X-Y)(X+Y+1)}{XY} > 0$. Furthermore, $\frac{W}{Y^2 A - A} > 0$ because

$Y > 1$. Finally, $\Delta > 0$ induces $\frac{W_1}{A} + \frac{W_2}{C} > \frac{W}{B}$.   □

Proposition 1. If $\sum_{i=1}^{k} P_i * f_i^2 = W_j * f_j^2 + W_{j+1} * f_{j+1}^2$ and $\sum_{i=1}^{k} P_i = W_j + W_{j+1}$, then $\sum_{i=1}^{k} \frac{P_i}{f_i} > \frac{W_j}{f_j} + \frac{W_{j+1}}{f_{j+1}}$.

Proof. Let φ be a sequence of real such as $\varphi_1 = f_1$ and $\varphi_i = \sqrt{\frac{\sum_{\alpha=1}^{i-1} P_\alpha * \varphi_{i-1}^2 + P_i * f_i^2}{\sum_{\alpha=1}^{i} P_\alpha}}$,

for $i = \overline{2..j}$. This sequence guarantees that $\varphi_{i-1} < \varphi_i < f_i$, $\forall\, i = \overline{2..j}$. Indeed, since $\varphi_1 = f_1$, $\varphi_2^2 = \frac{P_1 * \varphi_1^2 + P_2 * f_2^2}{P_1 + P_2} > \frac{P_1 * f_1^2 + P_2 * f_1^2}{P_1 + P_2} = f_1^2$.

Furthermore, $\frac{P_1 * f_1^2 + P_2 * f_2^2}{P_1 + P_2} < \frac{P_1 * f_2^2 + P_2 * f_2^2}{P_1 + P_2} < f_2^2$ induces $\varphi_1 < \varphi_2 < f_2$.

We assume that this is true for $i = j - 1$ i.e. $\varphi_{j-2} < \varphi_{j-1} < f_{j-1}$.

$\varphi_j^2 = \frac{\sum_{\alpha=1}^{j-1} P_\alpha * \varphi_{j-1}^2 + P_j * f_j^2}{\sum_{\alpha=1}^{j} P_\alpha} < \frac{\sum_{\alpha=1}^{j-1} P_\alpha * f_{j-1}^2 + P_j * f_j^2}{\sum_{\alpha=1}^{j} P_\alpha} < \frac{\sum_{\alpha=1}^{j-1} P_\alpha * f_j^2 + P_j * f_j^2}{\sum_{\alpha=1}^{j} P_\alpha} = f_j^2$.

$\varphi_j^2 = \frac{\sum_{\alpha=1}^{j-1} P_\alpha * \varphi_{j-1}^2 + P_j * f_j^2}{\sum_{\alpha=1}^{j} P_\alpha} > \frac{\sum_{\alpha=1}^{j-1} P_\alpha * \varphi_{j-1}^2 + P_j * \varphi_j^2}{\sum_{\alpha=1}^{j} P_\alpha}$ induces $\varphi_j^2 > \varphi_{j-1}^2$.

Finally, $\varphi_{j-1} < \varphi_j < f_j$. By recurrence, we deduce that $\varphi_{i-1} < \varphi_i < f_i$.

From Lemma 2 we have:

$\frac{P_1}{f_1} + \frac{P_2}{f_2} > \frac{P_1 + P_2}{\varphi_2}, \frac{P_1 + P_2}{\varphi_2} + \frac{P_3}{f_3} > \frac{\sum_{i=1}^{3} P_i}{\varphi_3}$ and then, $\forall\, l \in \{1..j\}$ $\frac{\sum_{i=1}^{l-1} P_i}{\varphi_{l-1}} + \frac{P_l}{f_l} > \frac{\sum_{i=1}^{l} P_i}{\varphi_l}$. Follows, $\sum_{i=1}^{j} \frac{P_i}{f_i} > \frac{\sum_{i=1}^{j} P_i}{\varphi_j}$.

Let another sequence of real ϕ such as $\phi_k = f_k$ and $\phi_i = \sqrt{\frac{\sum_{\alpha=i+1}^{k} P_\alpha * \phi_{i+1}^2 + P_i * f_i^2}{\sum_{\alpha=i}^{k} P_\alpha}}$ for $i \in \{j+1..k-1\}$. In the same way, we get $f_i < \phi_i < \phi_{i+1}$, $\forall\, i \in \{j+1..k-1\}$.

And from Lemma 2, we obtain $\sum_{i=j+1}^{k} \frac{P_i}{f_i} > + \frac{\sum_{i=j+1}^{k} P_i}{\phi_{j+1}}$.

It result that $\sum_{i=1}^{k} \frac{P_i}{f_i} > \frac{\sum_{i=1}^{j} P_i}{\varphi_j} + \frac{\sum_{i=j+1}^{k} P_i}{\phi_{j+1}}$.

In order to apply once again Lemma 2, we have to decompose $\sum_{i=1}^{j} P_i$ and $\sum_{i=j+1}^{k} P_i$ into 4 values $W_{L1}, W_{L2}, W_{R1}, W_{R2}$ such that:

$$\begin{cases} W_{L1} + W_{L2} = \sum_{i=1}^{j} P_i \\ W_{R1} + W_{R2} = \sum_{i=j+1}^{k} P_i \\ W_{L1} + W_{R1} = W_j \\ W_{L2} + W_{R2} = W_{j+1} \\ W_{L1} * \varphi_j^2 + W_{R1} * \phi_{j+1}^2 = W_j * f_j^2 \\ W_{L2} * \varphi_j^2 + W_{R2} * \phi_{j+1}^2 = W_{j+1} * f_{j+1}^2 \end{cases} \implies \begin{cases} W_{L1} = W_j * \frac{(\phi_{j+1}^2 - f_j^2)}{(\phi_{j+1}^2 - \varphi_j^2)} \\ W_{L2} = W_{j+1} * \frac{(\phi_{j+1}^2 - f_{j+1}^2)}{(\phi_{j+1}^2 - \varphi_j^2)} \\ W_{R1} = W_j * \frac{(f_j^2 - \varphi_j^2)}{(\phi_{j+1}^2 - \varphi_j^2)} \\ W_{R2} = W_{j+1} * \frac{(f_{j+1}^2 - \varphi_j^2)}{(\phi_{j+1}^2 - \varphi_j^2)} \end{cases}$$

This part of proof is illustrated by Fig. 1. Observe that the result values are all

positive. From Lemma 2, we obtain $\frac{W_{L1}}{\varphi_j} + \frac{W_{R1}}{\phi_{j+1}} > \frac{W_j}{f_j}$ and $\frac{W_{L2}}{\varphi_j} + \frac{W_{R2}}{\phi_{j+1}} > \frac{W_{j+1}}{f_{j+1}}$.
Hence $\frac{W_L}{\varphi_j} + \frac{W_R}{\phi_{j+1}} = \frac{W_{L1}}{\varphi_j} + \frac{W_{R1}}{\phi_{j+1}} + \frac{W_{L2}}{\varphi_j} + \frac{W_{R2}}{\phi_{j+1}} > \frac{W_1}{f_j} + \frac{W_2}{f_{j+1}}$.
Follows, $\sum_{i=1}^{k} \frac{P_i}{f_i} > \frac{W_j}{f_j} + \frac{W_{j+1}}{f_{j+1}}$. $\qquad\qquad\square$

Now, from Proposition 1, $\widehat{C}'_{max} = \sum_{i=1}^{k} \frac{P_i}{f_i} > \widehat{C}_{max} = \frac{W_j}{f_j} + \frac{W_{j+1}}{f_{j+1}}$.

Remark 1. The proof remains valid if $\sum_{i=1}^{k} P_i * f_i^2 \leqslant W_j * f_j^2 + W_{j+1} * f_{j+1}^2$. Indeed, from Lemma 1, we can construct another solution with $P'_1, P'_2, \ldots, P'_k$ such as $\sum_{i=1}^{k} P'_i = \sum_{i=1}^{k} P_i$ and $\sum_{i=1}^{k} P'_i * f_i^2 = W_j * f_j^2 + W_{j+1} * f_{j+1}^2$. Hence, we obtain $\frac{W_j}{f_j} + \frac{W_{j+1}}{f_{j+1}} < \sum_{i=1}^{k} \frac{P'_i}{f_i} < \sum_{i=1}^{k} \frac{P_i}{f_i}$.

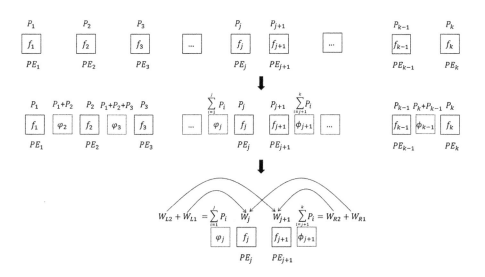

Fig. 1. Resume of the first part of the proof.

5 An Approximation Scheduling Algorithm for Chain of Non-preemptive Tasks with Communication Costs

We assume here a communication cost $Cm_{j,j+1}$ between PE_j and PE_{j+1} and communication cost $Ct_{i,i+1}$ between each pair of tasks t_i and t_{i+1} with $2 * min_i\, Ct_{i,i+1} \geqslant max_j\, Ct_{j,j+1}, \forall\, i,j \in \{1..n-1\}$. We do not allow preemption of tasks and we transform the previous solution of preemptive scheduling, using the processing elements PE_j and PE_{j+1} only.

Proposition 2. *If only two processing elements PE_j and PE_{j+1} are available, the schedules with only one communication between them are dominant.*

Proof. Let $\{t_{k+2}\ldots t_n\}$ be the set of uncut tasks of the preemptive solution on PE_{j+1} and S_1 the sum of their weights. Let C_{max1} the makespan of a feasible solution obtained by processing tasks $\{t_1\ldots t_{k+1}\}$ on PE_j and $\{t_{k+2}\ldots t_n\}$ on PE_{j+1}. By contradiction, let suppose that there exists a feasible solution with at least two displacements such as $S_1 \leqslant S_2$, where S_2 is the sum of the tasks weights on PE_{j+1} with this solution, let C_{max2} be its makespan. We prove that $C_{max2} \geqslant C_{max1}$. Since the second solution is feasible, $S2 \leqslant W_{j+1}$. By the previous algorithm, $W_{j+1} \leqslant S_1+w_{k+1} \leqslant S_1+\max w_i$ with $i \in \{1\ldots n\}$, and thus $S_2 \leqslant S_1 + \text{Max } w_i, i = \overline{1..n}$. $C_{max1} = \frac{W-S_1}{f_j} + \frac{S_1}{f_{j+1}} + Cm_{j,j+1} + Ct_{k+1,k+2}$ and $C_{max2} \geqslant \frac{W-S_2}{f_j} + \frac{S_2}{f_{j+1}} + 2*Cm_{j,j+1} + 2*\min Ct_{i,i+1}, i \in \{1\ldots n-1\}$. Follows, $C_{max2} - C_{max1} = \frac{S_2-S_1}{f_{j+1}} - \frac{S_2-S_1}{f_j} + Cm_{j,j+1} + 2*\min Ct_{i,i+1} - Ct_{k+1,k+2}$. Since $\frac{S_2-S_1}{f_{j+1}} \geqslant 0$ and $2*\min Ct_{i,i+1} - Ct_{k+1,k+2} \geqslant 0, \forall i = \overline{1..n-1}$, induce $C_{max2} - C_{max1} \geqslant Cm_{j,j+1} - \frac{S_2-S_1}{f_j}$. Finally, $Cm_{j,j+1} - \frac{S_2-S_1}{f_j} \geqslant Cm_{j,j+1} - \frac{\text{Max } w_i}{f_j}$, $i = \overline{1..n}$. According to the hypothesis, $Cm_{j,j+1} - \text{Max } \frac{w_i}{f_j} \geqslant 0, \forall i = \overline{1..n}$. Therefore $C_{max2} - C_{max1} \geqslant 0 \implies C_{max2} \geqslant C_{max1}$.   □

Theorem 2. *The following Algorithm 2 provides a solution for non-preemptive scheduling starting from the preemptive scheduling solution obtained by Algorithm 1 with a complexity of $\theta(n+m)$.*

The two variables α and β are used to determine the assignment of tasks. In the case $W_{j+1} = 0$, we put all the tasks on PE_j. Otherwise, let $Cost_1(v)$ be the cost of executing the first tasks (t_1 to t_v) on PE_j with $\sum_{i=1}^{v} w_i \geqslant W_j$, then the rest on PE_{j+1}. $Cost_1(v) = \{Ct_{v,v+1} + \frac{\sum_{i=1}^{v} w_i}{f_j} + \frac{\sum_{i=v+1}^{n} w_i}{f_{j+1}} + Cm_{j,j+1}\}$. Let $Cost_2(v)$ be the cost of executing the first tasks (t_1 to t_v) on PE_{j+1}, then the rest on PE_j with $\sum_{i=v+1}^{n} w_i \geqslant W_j$. $Cost_2(v) = \{Ct_{v,v+1} + \frac{\sum_{i=1}^{v} w_i}{f_{j+1}} + \frac{\sum_{i=v+1}^{n} w_i}{f_j} + Cm_{j,j+1}\}$.
We start by finding the tasks v_1 and v_2 that give the best respective scheduling makespan ($Cost_1$) and ($Cost_2$), and keeping the best one. Finally, we check if the cost generated by using both processing elements PE_j and PE_{j+1} is less than the scheduling makespan obtained by performing all tasks on PE_j.

Example 1. Consider the task graph given by Figure 2. It contains ten task nodes ($n = 10$) labeled from t_1 to t_{10} with two additional nodes S and E (beginning and end of the application). The edges are labeled with the communication cost between tasks. The nodes are labeled with the weight of each task.
Consider a heterogeneous platform with 3 processing elements, their frequencies are given in Table 1. The communication cost between processing elements are given in Table 2. The maximum energy consumption is $E = 1350$.
The application of preemptive scheduling Algorithm 2 gives $PE_j = PE_2$ and $PE_{j+1} = PE_3$ with $W_2 = 0,5625$ and $W_3 = 37,4375$. Since $W_3 > 0$, we obtain $Cost_1 = Ct_{1,2} + \frac{w_1}{f_2} + \frac{\sum_{i=2}^{10} w_i}{f_3} + Cm_{2,3} = 17, v_1 = 1. Cost_2 = Ct_{7,8} + \frac{\sum_{i=1}^{7} w_i}{f_2} + \frac{\sum_{i=8}^{10} w_i}{f_3} + Cm_{2,3} = 19, v_2 = 7. Cost_1 < Cost_2$, induces $Cost = Cost_1 = 17$, $\beta = 1$ and $\alpha = 1$. Finally, $\frac{W}{f_2} = \frac{38}{2} = 19 > Cost$. We put the task t_1 on the

---

Algorithm 2. Non-Preemptive Scheduling (NPS).

Data: Weights of the tasks $w_1, w_2, \ldots, w_n$. Communication costs between tasks $Ct_{i,i+1}$, $i \in \{1..n-1\}$.

Result: Approximate solution $\widehat{C}_{max}$ for non preemptive scheduling.

begin

    Find PE_j, PE_{j+1} and W_j, W_{j+1} with preemptive scheduling algorithm

    if $W_j = W$ **then**

        $\lfloor$ $\beta = n$, $\alpha = 1$

    else

        $Cost_1 = min\{Cost_1(v), v \in \{1..n-1\}, \sum_{i=1}^{v} w_i \geqslant W_j\}$; let

        $v_1 \in \{1..n-1\}$ such that $Cost_{v_1} = Cost_1$

        $Cost_2 = min\{Cost_2(v), v \in \{1..n-1\}, \sum_{i=v_2+1}^{n} w_i \geqslant W_j\}$; let

        $v_2 \in \{1..n-1\}$ such that $Cost_{v_2} = Cost_2$

        if $Cost_1 < Cost_2$ **then**

            $\lfloor$ $Cost = Cost_1$, $\beta = v_1$, $\alpha = 1$

        else

            $\lfloor$ $Cost = Cost_2$, $\beta = n$, $\alpha = v_2 + 1$

        if $Cost > \frac{W}{f_j}$ **then**

            $\lfloor$ $Cost = \frac{W}{f_j}$, $\beta = n$, $\alpha = 1$

    Put tasks between t_α and t_β on the processing element PE_j

    Order the rest on the processing element PE_{j+1}, $\widehat{C}_{max} = Cost$

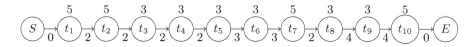

Fig. 2. Task chain graph.

Table 1. Frequencies of processing elements.

PE_j	PE_1	PE_2	PE_3
f_j	1	2	6

Table 2. Communication cost between processing elements.

PE_j	PE_1	PE_2	PE_3
PE_1	0	7	6
PE_2	7	0	7
PE_3	6	7	0

processing element PE_2 and tasks t_2 to t_{10} on PE_3. $\widehat{C}_{max} = Cost = 17$. For this instance, our approach gives the optimal solution.

Proposition 3. *Let $C_{max}^\star$ be the optimal solution for non-preemptive scheduling and $\widehat{C}_{max}$ the solution obtained by Algorithm 2, then $\frac{\widehat{C}_{max}}{C_{max}^\star} \leqslant \frac{W}{W_j + \frac{f_j W_{j+1}}{f_{j+1}}}$.*

Proof. The optimal solution C'_{max} of the preemptive scheduling is given by $C'_{max} = \frac{W_j}{f_j} + \frac{W_{j+1}}{f_{j+1}}$. In the worst case for our algorithm, all tasks are executed on the processing element f_j, thus we get $\widehat{C}_{max} \leqslant \frac{W}{f_j}$. Follows $\frac{\widehat{C}_{max}}{C'_{max}} \leqslant \frac{\frac{W}{f_j}}{\frac{W_j}{f_j} + \frac{W_{j+1}}{f_{j+1}}} \leqslant \frac{W}{W_j + \frac{f_j W_{j+1}}{f_{j+1}}}$. By optimality of Algorithm 1, $C'_{max} \leqslant C^\star_{max}$ induces $\frac{\widehat{C}_{max}}{C^\star_{max}} \leqslant \frac{\widehat{C}_{max}}{C'_{max}}$, then $\frac{\widehat{C}_{max}}{C^\star_{max}} \leqslant \frac{W}{W_j + \frac{f_j W_{j+1}}{f_{j+1}}}$. $\qquad\square$

Remark 2. This ratio is reached, let consider an instance which generates $W_{j+1} = 0$ and $W_j = W$ for the preemptive solution, then, $1 \leqslant \frac{\widehat{C}_{max}}{C^\star_{max}} \leqslant \frac{W}{W_j + \frac{f_j W_{j+1}}{f_{j+1}}} = \frac{W}{W} = 1$. So, we obtain the optimal solution, $\widehat{C}_{max} = C^\star_{max}$.

Remark 3. Since $\frac{f_j}{f_{j+1}} < 1$, $\frac{W}{W_j + \frac{f_j W_{j+1}}{f_{j+1}}} < \frac{W}{\frac{f_j}{f_{j+1}}(W_j + W_{j+1})} = \frac{f_{j+1}}{f_j}$, and finally, $\frac{\widehat{C}_{max}}{C^\star_{max}} < \frac{f_{j+1}}{f_j}$.

6   Experimental Results

In order to measure the efficiency of our algorithm, we performed several tests on randomly generated instances with different dimensions. For this purpose, we developed a random instances generator in $C++$ adjustable with several parameters.

General settings are number of tasks n and processing elements m. We denote by *test_n_m* instance defined by these two parameters. The weights of the tasks are generated randomly over an interval $[w_{min}, w_{max}]$. The frequencies of the processing elements are randomly generated over an interval $[f_{min}, f_{max}]$ while ensuring the heterogeneity of the system by generating different values. The communication costs between tasks are generated randomly over an interval $[Ct_{min}, Ct_{max}]$ and between processing elements over an interval $[Cm_{min}, Cm_{max}]$ in accordance with the hypothesis described in Sect. 3. The bound E is randomly generated with respect to $W * f_1^2 < E < W * f_m^2$.

Our proposed Algorithm 2 were implemented in $C++$. The exact solution is obtained by solving the model (P) with *CPLEX* 12.5.0 [4] and the OPL script language. The following Table 3 shows the results of tests on different instance sizes. We have generated 30 instances for the first four rows (from instance *test_8_3* to *test_20_4*) and then one instance for the others due to the large running time on *CPLEX*.

The *PS* (Preemptive Scheduling) columns present the makespan average solution obtained by the Algorithm 1. The *NPS* (Non-Preemptive Scheduling) columns present the makespan average solution obtained by the Algorithm 2 and its average execution time. The *CPLEX* columns present the average makespan solution of the resolution of the model (P) with *CPLEX* and the average computation cost required as well as the optimality of the solutions. Finally, the columns GAP_1 and GAP_2 present the average ratio between the solution obtained by $Bound_1 = CPLEX$ solution and $Bound_2 = $ Preemtive solution with NPS solutions which is calculated as follow:

$$GAP_i = \frac{\text{Heuristic Solution} - Bound_i}{Bound_i} * 100, i \in \{1, 2\}.$$

Since the execution time of a quadratic model is generally too large, we have therefore limited the running time for *CPLEX* to 60 min. In Table 3, we can notice that for most of the instances with less than 30 tasks, our algorithm gives an optimal solution with smaller running time than *CPLEX*. Moreover, for larger instances, *CPLEX* takes much longer to find a solution, whereas *NPS* gives a solution in less than one second for an instance with 10000 tasks.

Table 3. Evaluation of the NPS heuristic compared to *CPLEX*.

Instances	*PS*	*NPS*		*CPLEX*			*Gap₁*	*Gap₂*
		Sol	Time	Sol	Time	Opt		
test_8_3	15.03	19.89	0.0004 s	19.89	0.76 s	X	0%	31.14%
test_12_3	24.82	32.55	0.0005 s	32.55	2.17 s	X	0%	15.80%
test_15_4	29.87	34.59	0.0005 s	34.58	6.46 s	X	0.02%	21.91%
test_20_4	27.51	33.54	0.0007 s	33.54	8 min 3 s	X	0%	2.25%
test_30_6	24.84	25.40	0.001 s	25.40	35 min	X	0%	7.02%
test_50_6	40.27	43.10	0.01 s	102.24	60 min	/	−57.84%	8.03%
test_100_9	53.78	55.39	0.02 s	843.48	60 min	/	−93.43%	2.99%
test_200_9	123.21	128.92	0.03 s	1929.20	60 min	/	−93.31%	4.63%
test_500_11	207.44	217.52	0.05 s	3587.39	60 min	/	−93.93%	4.85%
test_10000_11	4814.62	4828.06	0.5 s	/	60 min	/	/	0.27%

7   Conclusion and Future Work

This paper presents an efficient approximation algorithm to solve the task scheduling problem on heterogeneous platform for the particular case of linear chain of tasks. Our objective is to minimize both the total execution time (makespan) and the energy consumption by imposing a constraint on the total energy consumed by the system. This work has shown that finding an efficient scheduling is not easy. Tests on large instances close to reality shows the limits of solving the problem with a solver such as *CPLEX*.

The main contribution of this work is to give an algorithm which provides a solution with small running time, and also guarantee the quality of the solution obtained compared to the optimal solution. The ratio obtained depends on the frequencies of two successive processing elements PE_j and PE_{j+1} used in preemptive scheduling. The performance ratio of our algorithm is bounded by $\frac{f_{j+1}}{f_j}$. As part of the future, we will focus on the extension to more general classes of graphs to handle real application.

References

1. Aupy, G., Benoit, A., Dufossé, F., Robert, Y.: Reclaiming the energy of a schedule: models and algorithms. Concur. Comput.: Pract. Exp. **25**(11), 1505–1523 (2013)
2. Fard, H.M., Prodan, R., Barrionuevo, J.J.D., Fahringer, T.: A multi-objective approach for workflow scheduling in heterogeneous environments. In: Proceedings of the 2012 12th IEEE/ACM International Symposium on Cluster, Cloud and Grid Computing (CCGRID 2012), pp. 300–309. IEEE Computer Society (2012)
3. Griessl, R., Peykanu, M., Hagemeyer, J., Porrmann, M., Krupop, S., Kosmann, L., Knocke, P., Kierzynka, M., Oleksiak, A., et al.: FPGA-accelerated heterogeneous hyperscale server architecture for next-generation compute clusters (2015)
4. IBM: IBM ILOG CPLEX V12.5 user's manual for CPLEX (2013). http://www.ibm.com
5. Lee, Y.C., Zomaya, A.Y.: Minimizing energy consumption for precedence-constrained applications using dynamic voltage scaling. In: 9th IEEE/ACM International Symposium on Cluster Computing and the Grid, CCGRID 2009, pp. 92–99. IEEE (2009)
6. Zaourar, L., Ait Aba, M., Briand, D., Philippe, J.M.: Modeling of applications and hardware to explore task mapping and scheduling strategies on a heterogeneous micro-server system (2017, to appear in IPDPSW)
7. Mezmaz, M., Melab, N., Kessaci, Y., Lee, Y.C., Talbi, E.G., Zomaya, A.Y., Tuyttens, D.: A parallel bi-objective hybrid metaheuristic for energy-aware scheduling for cloud computing systems. J. Parallel Distrib. Comput. **71**(11), 1497–1508 (2011)
8. Sheikh, H.F., Ahmad, I.: Efficient heuristics for joint optimization of performance, energy, and temperature in allocating tasks to multi-core processors. In: 2014 International Green Computing Conference (IGCC), pp. 1–8. IEEE (2014)
9. Tarplee, K.M., Friese, R., Maciejewski, A.A., Siegel, H.J.: Efficient and scalable pareto front generation for energy and makespan in heterogeneous computing systems. In: Fidanova, S. (ed.) Recent Advances in Computational Optimization. SCI, vol. 580, pp. 161–180. Springer, Cham (2015). https://doi.org/10.1007/978-3-319-12631-9_10
10. Tarplee, K.M., Friese, R., Maciejewski, A.A., Siegel, H.J., Chong, E.K.: Energy and makespan tradeoffs in heterogeneous computing systems using efficient linear programming techniques. IEEE Trans. Parallel Distrib. Syst. **27**(6), 1633–1646 (2016)
11. Vasquez Perez, O.C.: Ordonnancement de tâches pour concilier la minimisation de la consommation d'énergie avec la qualité de service: optimisation et théorie des jeux. Ph.D. thesis, Paris 6 (2014)
12. Xie, G., Xiao, X., Li, R., Li, K.: Schedule length minimization of parallel applications with energy consumption constraints using heuristics on heterogeneous distributed systems. Concurr. Comput.: Pract. Exp. (2016)
13. Young, B.D., Pasricha, S., Maciejewski, A.A., Siegel, H.J., Smith, J.T.: Heterogeneous makespan and energy-constrained DAG scheduling. In: Proceedings of the 2013 Workshop on Energy Efficient High Performance Parallel and Distributed Computing, pp. 3–12. ACM (2013)
14. Zhang, L., Li, K., Li, C., Li, K.: Bi-objective workflow scheduling of the energy consumption and reliability in heterogeneous computing systems. Inf. Sci. **379**, 241–256 (2017)

15. Zhang, L., Li, K., Xu, Y., Mei, J., Zhang, F., Li, K.: Maximizing reliability with energy conservation for parallel task scheduling in a heterogeneous cluster. Inf. Sci. **319**, 113–131 (2015)
16. Zhong, X., Xu, C.Z.: Energy-aware modeling and scheduling for dynamic voltage scaling with statistical real-time guarantee. IEEE Trans. Comput. **56**(3), 358–372 (2007)

Software-Distributed Shared Memory
over Heterogeneous Micro-server Architecture

Loïc Cudennec[(✉)]

CEA, LIST, Saclay, France
`loic.cudennec@cea.fr`

Abstract. Nowadays, the design of computing architectures not only targets computing performances but also the energy power savings. Low-power computing units, such as ARM and FPGA-based nodes, are now being integrated together with high-end processors and GPGPU accelerators into computing clusters. One example is the micro-server architecture that consists of a backbone onto which it is possible to plug computing nodes. These nodes can host high-end and low-end CPUs, GPUs, FPGAs and multi-purpose accelerators such as manycores, building up a real heterogeneous platform. In this context, there is no hardware to federate memories, and the programmability of such architectures suddenly relies on the developer experience to manage data location and task communications. The purpose of this paper is to evaluate the possibility of bringing back the convenient shared-memory programming model by deploying a software-distributed shared memory among heterogeneous computing nodes. We describe how we have built such a system over a message-passing runtime. Experimentations have been conducted using a parallel image processing application over an homogeneous cluster and an heterogeneous micro-server.

Keywords: S-DSM · Data coherence · Heterogeneous computing

1 Introduction

Heterogeneity is slowly entering high-performance computing. After a decade figuring out how to cope with mixed CPU and GPU nodes for performance at both the hardware and software levels, new requirements now concern the limitation of the power consumption. Low-power CPUs (ARM) and accelerators (manycore, FPGAs) are joining the computing resource list. These resources can run regular tasks in a massively parallel way, while keeping the electricity bill reasonable. Micro-servers have been developed in this direction. They offer a communication and power supply backbone onto which it is possible to plug heterogeneous computing and data storage nodes. These nodes can host regular CPU such as Intel i7, clusters of ARM Cortex (more popular in smartphones than in HPC) and Xilinx/Altera FPGAs to deploy specific IPs. But the micro-server architecture comes with a price: it escalates the problem of managing the heterogeneity of resources. Current approaches include hybrid programming such

© Springer International Publishing AG, part of Springer Nature 2018
D. B. Heras and L. Bougé (Eds.): Euro-Par 2017 Workshops, LNCS 10659, pp. 366–377, 2018.
https://doi.org/10.1007/978-3-319-75178-8_30

as MPI/OpenMP (message passing between nodes and parallel programming within nodes) and task-based models such as OpenCL, StarPu and OmpSs that encapsulate the user code into a specific framework (kernels, tasks, dataflow). These systems have been ported to different processor architectures, even on FPGAs for OpenCL, addressing the heterogeneity of the platforms. Unified distributed memory systems can be built on top of heterogeneous platforms using, for example, cluster implementations of OpenMP and PGAS implementations (provided it does not rely on hardware mechanisms such as RDMA). In this work, we explore the possibility of deploying a full software-distributed shared memory system to allow MPMD programming on micro-servers (a distributed architecture with heterogeneous nodes). This is quite new for such systems, for two reasons: First, there is a lack of specification and formalization against hardware shared memory, and also because of a potential scaling problem. Second, software shared memory, while being famous with computing grid and peer-to-peer systems, is seen as a performance killer at the processor scale. We think that micro-servers are standing somewhere in-between: from the multi-processors they inherit the fast-communication links and from the computing grids, they inherit the heterogeneity, the dynamicity of resources and a bit of scaling issues. In this work, we propose an hybrid approach where data coherency is managed by software between nodes and by regular hardware within the nodes. We have designed and implemented a full software-distributed shared memory (S-DSM) on top of a message passing runtime. This S-DSM has been deployed over the RECS3 heterogeneous micro-server, running a parallel image processing application. Results show the intricacies between the design of the user application, the data coherence protocol and the S-DSM topology and mapping. The paper is organized as follows: Sect. 2 describes some micro-server architectures and the way they are used. Section 3 presents the S-DSM. Section 4 describes the experiments on both homogeneous and heterogeneous architectures. Section 5 gives some references on previous works. Finally, Sect. 6 concludes this paper and brings new perspectives.

2   Micro-servers and Heterogeneous Computing

Micro-servers such as HP Moonshot [1] and Christmann RECS [7,10] are modular architectures that can be adapted to a particular application domain. As illustrated by Fig. 1, a chassis provides power supply, cooling systems, as well as a backplane that hosts several integrated networks (management, computing...) and a set of slots to plug computing boards (also called servers). These computing boards share the same interface and form factor (for example COM Express). However, the inner design is quite free, which is source of heterogeneity with important unbalance in computing performance and communication speed. Such architecture is known to reduce power consumption, save space and avoid cable spaghetti. Data management depends on the configuration of the micro-server: we assume that there is at least one CPU per node that is able to run a full operating system and locally store data, either on physical memory

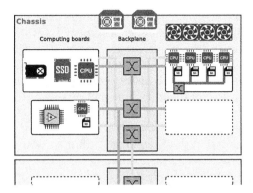

Fig. 1. Micro-server hosting nodes with CPU, low-power CPU, GPU and FPGA.

or on disk (SSD, SD card). On this type of distributed architecture, data are usually managed using message passing or remote accesses that do not take into account the heterogeneity of the storage medium. Furthermore, the user is in charge of the localization and the transfer of data. We think that there is room for some improvements in data management over such platforms. S-DSM can be used to transparently federate memories of the computing boards and offer an abstraction of the storage at the global scale. However, as far as we know, S-DSM are mainly designed for homogeneous platforms (except for the communications when deploying over NUMA architectures), and they have not been deployed over micro-servers. In this work we deploy an in-house S-DSM over a micro-server. We analyze what are the limitations of the approach and propose some improvements for future S-DSM deployments.

3   Software-Distributed Shared Memory

The Software-Distributed Shared Memory (S-DSM) interfaces user applications relying on the shared memory programming model to a given hardware architecture in which physical memories can be distributed. With this system, the application is written as a set of threads/tasks from which it is possible to allocate and access shared data (close to the *Posix* and *shmem* models). To perform such accesses we have defined an API inspired by the entry consistency model [5]. Portion of codes that access a shared data are protected between *acquire* and *release* instructions applied to the data. There are two *acquire* instructions to discriminate a shared access against an exclusive access (multiple readers, single writer). The API also provides *rendez-vous* and other synchronization primitives. The logical organization of the S-DSM follows a client-server model. A client runs the user code, as well as some S-DSM code (mainly hidden behind the *malloc, acquire* and *release* instructions). The server only runs S-DSM code and is used to manage metadata and store data. Each client is attached to at least one server. The resulting topology can be compared to the super-peer topology found in large distributed systems. *Chunks* are the atomic piece of data managed by the S-DSM. The size of the chunk can be set by the application. Whenever a data is allocated in the shared memory, if the size is larger than the chunk size, then it will allocate more than one chunk. The memory space allocated on the client is always a contiguous space on which it is possible to use pointer arithmetic. However, on the server side, the chunks are managed independently and can be spread among the servers in any order. *Chunks* can be compared to pages in operating systems and so-called *chunks* in peer-to-peer systems. Each *chunk* is under the control of a data coherence protocol. The S-DSM allows several coherence protocols to run concurrently, but not for the same chunks. The coherence protocol is in charge of the localization and the transfer of the chunk. Each protocol implements the actions to execute whenever *acquire* and *release* instructions are called on the client side, and it also implements a distributed automata for the servers. The home-based MESI protocol [8] is an example of a widely-used cache coherence protocol for multi-core processors. *Home-based* means that the management of each chunk, including metadata, is the responsibility of one server called *home-node*. The home-node does not necessarily store the data. Home-nodes are usually assigned to chunks using a round-robin arrangement. MESI is one of the protocols that has been implemented in the S-DSM. In this paper we only refer to this protocol. We have implemented an ANSI C version of such a S-DSM using the OpenMPI message passing runtime. There is a weak dependence on OpenMPI as it only uses *send* and *receive* primitives (no collective functions for example), and it is quite straightforward to switch to another MP middleware. However, the MPI runtime is convenient because it handles the deployment and the bootstrap of tasks and can be installed in many Linux distributions, which is a serious argument when deploying on an heterogeneous platform. The implementation of the S-DSM is roughly $12k$ lines of code, including data coherence protocols.

4 Experiments with an Image Processing Application

The S-DSM has been deployed over two testbeds: an homogeneous cluster of desktop computers and a heterogeneous micro-server. Descriptions of testbeds are given in Fig. 2. The purpose of these experiments is to highlight the behavior of the S-DSM runtime and the home-based MESI coherence protocol. This is why some choices regarding the S-DSM setup such as the granularity of the data and the topology are more set to stress the system rather than to get performance. All experiments use the exact same S-DSM and application codes, and the same input data. Only the description of the topology and the placement of tasks (MPI *rankfile*) differ.

4.1 Parallel Eager-Scheduled Convolution Application

The convolution application is an image processing application that calculates for each pixel of the input image a new value based on the surrounding pixels

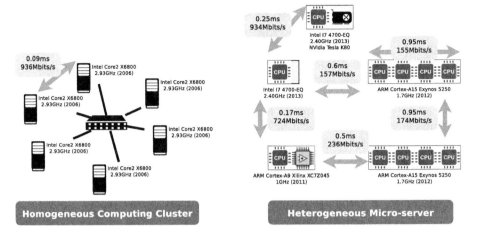

Fig. 2. Testbeds used for the experimentations: an homogeneous cluster of desktop computers and an heterogeneous Christmann RECS 3 Antares Box Microserver. Latencies are given by *Ping* and throughputs by *Iperf*. If not specified, we assume roughly the same performances as similar links.

(stencil) multiplied by some coefficients (kernel). For example, some stencil and kernel combinations can be used for edge detection. A parallel version of the code is straightforward and, because each pixel can be processed independently (the result does not depend on other results), there is no constraint on granularity: pixels, lines or macro blocks can be processed concurrently. We have implemented this algorithm using an eager scheduling strategy on top of the S-DSM. The eager strategy works as follows: a set of jobs is shared between tasks. Each task concurrently iterates on the next available job. Tasks that are running faster will process more jobs. This is an interesting property for running a parallel application onto heterogeneous resources: if the jobs are equally splitted between tasks then the tasks that are running on the most powerful resources will have to wait for the weakest one. Instead, eager scheduling allows load balancing and makes resources busy at -almost- all time. We have set the granularity of the parallel computation to the image line size and we use the same size for the S-DSM chunk size. Therefore, the input and output images (as well as the intermediate representation - this is a 2-step algorithm with a convolution followed by a normalization) are represented by a set of chunks, one chunk per line. A job consists of processing one line. The concurrency comes from the convolution kernel size that requires to read three contiguous lines to process the central line and a possible overlapping with other tasks. Shared data also include the available jobs vector and the current max pixel value found while applying the convolution, and used for normalization. All shared data are accessed under the control of the home-based MESI protocol. Experimentations are based on the same code, using a 3.7 MB 2560 × 1440 grayscale image as input. This image size is large enough to get tangible results on the behavior of the application, and the granularity is small enough to stress the S-DSM and see what are the bottlenecks (in fact the granularity is far too small to get any speedup and most of the time is spent into S-DSM mechanisms and communications). In the experiments, the amount of messages received by the main memory server, including the S-DSM bootstrap and the consistency protocol goes from 30000 to 112000 messages in a single run, which explains the poor performances. The application is composed of 3 main roles: at least one memory server, one and only one i/o task that copies the image from disk into the memory, waits for the end of calculation, and copies back the result from memory to disk, and at least one processing task. This makes possible to deploy different topologies of the same application. The minimal topology being one memory, one i/o and one processing task. This latter topology is used to bench the different CPUs of the testbeds with the following results: 1.4 s for i7-5600U, 2 s for i7-4700EQ, 3.2 s for Core2-X6800, 7.6 s for Cortex-A15 and 35.7 s for Cortex-A9. All processing times are *real* values given by the Unix *time* command and therefore include the OpenMPI runtime bootstrap, the S-DSM bootstrap and the disk accesses to the input and output files. The important gap between the Intel i7-5600U and the ARM Cortex-A9 is also explained by the disk technology: a SSD for the i7 and a SD card for the Cortex-A9. In that context, deploying a S-DSM over heterogeneous nodes can be used to pin i/o tasks onto nodes with high-speed disks and keep all data in memory otherwise.

4.2 Homogeneous Cluster Architecture

Before deploying the S-DSM onto the RECS3 micro-server, we use a homogeneous computing cluster with different application topologies. The goal is to observe the performance variations and determine if it comes from the S-DSM implementation or from the heterogeneity of the resources. Figure 3 shows the processing times for two topologies running on 6 nodes. Topology A is made of two memory clusters, three processing tasks in each memory cluster and one i/o in one memory cluster. Topology B is a single memory cluster hosting six processing tasks and the i/o task. A runs almost 4 times slower than B: adding a memory server brings complexity in the data management: more control and

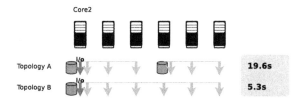

Fig. 3. Processing time on the cluster using different S-DSM topologies. The light-green cylinders represent memory servers and the arrows represent the clients. Orange clients are input/output tasks while blue clients are processing tasks. The horizontal blue lines define the memory clusters (to what server is connected each client). (Color figure online)

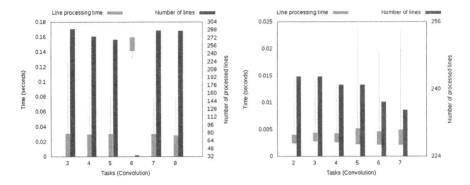

Fig. 4. Left: topology A. Memory servers are collocated with tasks 3 and 6. The i/o task is collocated with task 3. Right: topology B. The memory server and the i/o task are collocated with task 2.

data messages, as well as one additional MPI process that does not contribute to the job. The benefit of adding a new cache does not hide this overhead. Left Fig. 4 gives the minimum, maximum and standard deviation of the line processing time, as well as the number of processed lines for each computing task of topology A. Task 6 is performing badly, because of the activity of the collocated memory server. Despite a collocated memory server, task 3 has no performance drop because it directly benefits from the local cache that has been filled by the collocated i/o task. Right Fig. 4 presents the same metrics for topology B in which it appears that performances are now inline with the homogeneous cluster architecture. One conclusion at this step of experimentation is that the application topology must be tightly chosen according to the application behavior and the underlying hardware. In this particular scenario, adding a zealous cache is not an option.

4.3 Heterogeneous Micro-server Architecture

In this set of experiments we deploy the application onto the RECS3 micro-server as presented in Fig. 2, except that we use only one i7 node out of the two. We deploy four different topologies, as presented in Fig. 5. In topology C, Cortex-A9 (the weakest node regarding computing power) is discarded. We take the results as reference to study the influence of this particular node in the other topologies. Top-left of Fig. 6 shows the performance of each computing task. Despite the heterogeneity of the hardware, all tasks achieve quite similar performances. The MESI data coherence protocol implementation is designed for homogeneous architectures, in which distributed roles share the same duty. Metadata management is spread across the i7 and Cortex nodes and one access to shared data on the i7 can trigger some requests to a Cortex node in charge of the data, and vice-versa. In this experiment the processing time of a line is mainly spent in getting access to the data. And this time has to be paid by all tasks, whatever the resource they are running on. Topology D collocates a memory server and a processing task on the Cortex-A9. While it adds a new

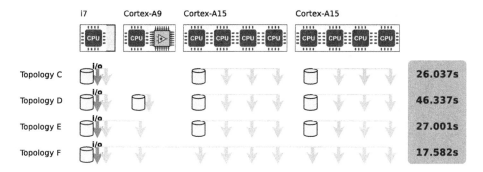

Fig. 5. Processing time on the RECS3 micro-server using different S-DSM topologies.

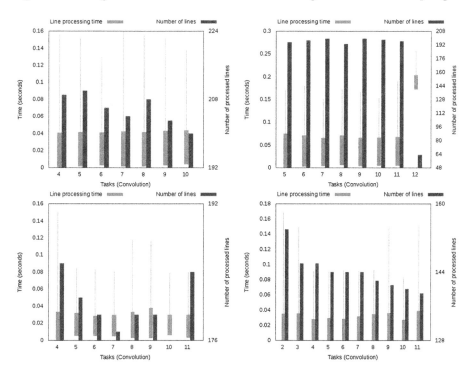

Fig. 6. Top-left: topology C. Task 4 is running on the i7 processor, tasks 5 to 10 on Cortex-A15 processors. Top-right: topology D. Task 5 is running on the i7 processor, tasks 6 to 11 on Cortex-A15 processors and task 12 on Cortex-A9. Bottom-left: topology E. Task 4 is running on the i7 processor, tasks 5 to 10 on Cortex-A15 processors and task 11 on Cortex-A9. Bottom-right: topology F. Task 2 is running on the i7 processor, tasks 6 to 10 on Cortex-A15 processors and task 11 on Cortex-A9.

worker to the application, it also adds a new server that will be responsible of managing some metadata. This is probably too much to handle for such CPU, as shown by top-right Fig. 6: the overall computing time is almost twice the time than without Cortex-A9 and task 12 runs slower than the other.

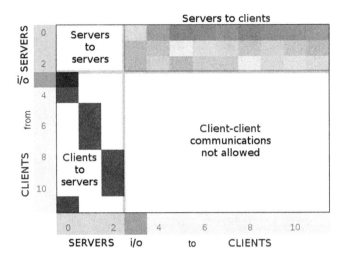

Fig. 7. Topology E. Communication heatmap. Each cell represents the cumulative size of messages that have been sent *from* tasks indexed vertically, *to* tasks indexed horizontally. Tasks 0 to 2 are memory servers. Task 3 is the i/o client. Tasks 4 to 11 are processing tasks. Values are normalized to grayscale, darker is bigger.

With topology E, the memory server is removed from Cortex-A9 and the remaining processing task (still running on Cortex-A9) is attached to the memory server located on the i7 node. This is the best scenario for Cortex-A9 because (1) it interacts directly with the memory server running on the most powerful resource and (2) the network connectivity is far better than with the Cortex-A15 nodes (0.17 ms, 724 Mbits/s versus 0.5 ms, 236 Mbits/s). The overall computing time is quite comparable with the C scenario: running a memory server on the Cortex-A9 was a terrible choice. Bottom-left Fig. 6 reveals that task 11 located on Cortex-A9 performs as good as tasks located on Cortex-A15 and has even be able to take more jobs than the other. The communication heatmap for topology E is given in Fig. 7. Communications between servers are quite light and mainly consist of a large number of very small control messages. This would be quite different in the case of a cache cooperative protocol. Communications from clients to servers strictly follow the topology description: a client only sends messages to the memory server it is attached to. The important traffic corresponds to messages for updating chunks on the server after completing jobs. Servers to clients communications consist of a mix of control and data messages. It shows that the memory server 0 located on the i7 node has sent more data to the clients than the two other servers located on the Cortex-A15 nodes. Finally, clients to clients communications are not allowed in this protocol (this optimization is not implemented at this time). Topology F is made of one memory server located on the i7 node and ten processing tasks (one per CPU). As for topology B this strategy gives better performance, but the improvement over topology C is not that important than with the homogeneous testbed. Bottom-right Fig. 6

shows that all processing tasks are now performing at the same speed, hiding the resource computing power they are running on.

4.4   Discussions

The S-DSM runtime has a major influence on the performance map of the application: we have shown that running over an heterogeneous architecture can lead to a global overhead in which computing tasks deployed on the most powerful processors cannot perform better than tasks deployed on weaker processors. This is mainly due to the home-based MESI coherence protocol implementation that equally balances the metadata management on memory servers. In this context, there is a performance fall when clients access shared data that are managed by a server running on a weak resource. And this is the case with the convolution application in which the management of lines is spread among the memory servers and the number of shared accesses is the same for all lines. Therefore, data coherence protocols should be designed with the possibility to adapt the metadata management load depending on the resource performances (computing power and network). In this direction, we can propose the dissociation of the data management (metadata) and the cache system. For example, in this paper experiments, the whole metadata management could be handled by the most powerful node while several data-only caches could be spread among other nodes. Another aspect is the importance of the placement (and possibly the routing) of the data coherence protocol roles onto the resources. A key aspect is the collocation of roles (and user tasks) that need to extensively communicate. In most of the message passing runtime implementations, such communications are locally optimized. Placement should be planned using offline static analysis and/or using dynamic mechanisms. In this paper we have proposed arbitrary topologies. We think that a more automated approach should be used, possibly with the help of operational research algorithms. Finally, one of the main purpose of the micro-server architecture is to offer computing power with interesting performance per watt compared to regular computing clusters. Some topologies might not be adapted to reach the best execution time, but could provide interesting properties regarding energy consumption. And in some scenarios the energy consumption might be a more valuable metric.

5   Related Works

Software-Distributed Shared Memory has become popular in the late eighties [11] with the introduction of systems for computing clusters [2,3,5,6], followed by systems for computing grids [4,12] and many-core processors [14]. These S-DSM are designed for a particular architecture and reasonably expect the same performance from the physical resources. Deploying S-DSM over heterogeneous systems has been studied in 1992 with Mermaid [15] and Jade [13] running on SPARC, DEC and DASH-based machines. With Mermaid, the authors focus on the problem of data conversion between processors. While both systems are undoubtedly a demonstration of a S-DSM running over an heterogeneous architecture, the conclusions only highlight the functional side of the approach. Later on, with the Asymmetric-DSM [9], the authors propose a data coherence protocol that is specific to asymmetric links between host CPU and accelerators. The work presented in this paper not only demonstrates the possibility of deploying a S-DSM over a state-of-the-art micro-server architecture. It also focuses on the intricacies between the S-DSM runtime, the data coherence protocol and the application behavior.

6   Conclusion

Low-power architectures are now entering high-performance computing systems. Micro-servers are one example of such integration, with a potentially high level of heterogeneity between computing nodes. Message passing and dataflow are natural programming paradigms that come into mind in order to exploit the architecture. We think that shared memory can also helps by providing a convenient abstraction layer between the application and the data storage systems. In this paper we have shown that a software-distributed shared memory can also be deployed on micro-servers. It also shows that the price to pay is a tight study of the S-DSM core functions, choosing or adapting the right data coherence protocol and profiling the application regarding shared data accesses.

Acknowledgments. This work received support from the H2020-ICT-2015 European Project M2DC - Modular Microserver Datacentre - under Grant Agreement number 688201.

References

1. HPE Serveur Moonshot: Hewlet Packard Entreprise. https://www.hpe.com/us/en/servers/moonshot.html
2. Amza, C., Cox, A.L., Dwarkadas, S., Keleher, P., Lu, H., Rajamony, R., Yu, W., Zwaenepoel, W.: TreadMarks: shared memory computing on networks of workstations. IEEE Comput. **29**(2), 18–28 (1996)
3. Antoniu, G., Bougé, L.: DSM-PM2: a portable implementation platform for multithreaded DSM consistency protocols. In: Mueller, F. (ed.) HIPS 2001. LNCS, vol. 2026, pp. 55–70. Springer, Heidelberg (2001). https://doi.org/10.1007/3-540-45401-2_5
4. Antoniu, G., Bougé, L., Jan, M.: JuxMem: an adaptive supportive platform for data-sharing on the grid. Scalable Comput.: Pract. Exp. (SCPE) **6**(3), 45–55 (2005)
5. Bershad, B.N., Zekauskas, M.J., Sawdon, W.A.: The midway distributed shared memory system. In: Proceedings of the 38th IEEE International Computer Conference (COMPCON Spring 1993), Los Alamitos, CA, pp. 528–537, February 1993
6. Carter, J.B., Bennett, J.K., Zwaenepoel, W.: Implementation and performance of Munin. In: 13th ACM Symposium on Operating Systems Principles (SOSP), Pacific Grove, CA, pp. 152–164, October 1991

7. Cecowski, M., Agosta, G., Oleksiak, A., Kierzynka, M., vor dem Berge, M., Christmann, W., Krupop, S., Porrmann, M., Hagemeyer, J., Griessl, R., Peykanu, M., Tigges, L., Rosinger, S., Schlitt, D., Pieper, C., Brandolese, C., Fornaciari, W., Pelosi, G., Plestenjak, R., Cinkelj, J., Cudennec, L., Goubier, T., Philippe, J.M., Janssen, U., Adeniyi-Jones, C.: The M2DC project: modular microserver datacentre. In: 2016 Euromicro Conference on Digital System Design (DSD), pp. 68–74, August 2016

8. Culler, D., Singh, J., Gupta, A.: Parallel Computer Architecture: A Hardware/Software Approach. The Morgan Kaufmann Series in Computer Architecture and Design. Morgan Kaufmann, Burlington (1998)

9. Gelado, I., Stone, J.E., Cabezas, J., Patel, S., Navarro, N., Hwu, W.W.: An asymmetric distributed shared memory model for heterogeneous parallel systems. In: Proceedings of the Fifteenth Edition of ASPLOS on Architectural Support for Programming Languages and Operating Systems, ASPLOS XV, pp. 347–358. ACM, New York (2010)

10. Griessl, R., Peykanu, M., Hagemeyer, J., Porrmann, M., Krupop, S., vor dem Berge, M., Kiesel, T., Christmann, W.: A scalable server architecture for next-generation heterogeneous compute clusters. In: 2014 12th IEEE International Conference on Embedded and Ubiquitous Computing, pp. 146–153, August 2014

11. Li, K.: IVY: a shared virtual memory system for parallel computing. In: Proceedings of the 1988 International Conference on Parallel Processing, pp. 94–101. University Park, PA, USA, August 1988

12. Nicolae, B., Antoniu, G., Bougé, L., Moise, D., Carpen-Amarie, A.: BlobSeer: next-generation data management for large scale infrastructures. J. Parallel Distrib. Comput. **71**, 169–184 (2011)

13. Rinard, M.C., Scales, D.J., Lam, M.S.: Heterogeneous parallel programming in Jade. In: Proceedings Supercomputing 1992, pp. 245–256, November 1992

14. Ross, J.A., Richie, D.A.: Implementing OpenSHMEM for the adapteva epiphany RISC array processor. Procedia Comput. Sci. **80**, 2353–2356 (2016). International Conference on Computational Science 2016, ICCS 2016, 6–8 June 2016, San Diego, California, USA

15. Zhou, S., Stumm, M., Li, K., Wortman, D.: Heterogeneous distributed shared memory. IEEE Trans. Parallel Distrib. Syst. **3**(5), 540–554 (1992)

A High-Throughput Kalman Filter for Modern SIMD Architectures

Daniel Hugo Cámpora Pérez[1,2]([✉]) [iD], Omar Awile[1] [iD], and Cédric Potterat[3]

[1] CERN, CH-1211 Geneva 23, Geneva, Switzerland
dcampora@cern.ch
[2] Universidad de Sevilla, C/San Fernando, 4, 41004 Sevilla, Spain
[3] Universidade Federal do Rio de Janeiro (UFRJ),
Caixa Postal 68528, Rio de Janeiro 21941-972, Brazil

Abstract. The Kalman filter is a critical component of the reconstruction process of subatomic particle collision in high-energy physics detectors. At the LHCb detector in the Large Hadron Collider this reconstruction must be performed at an average rate of 30 million times per second. As a consequence of the ever-increasing collision rate and upcoming detector upgrades, the data rate that needs to be processed in real time is expected to increase by a factor of 40 in the next five years. In order to keep pace, processing and filtering software must take advantage of latest developments in hardware technology.

In this paper we present a cross-architecture SIMD parallel algorithm and implementation of a low-rank Kalman filter. We integrate our implementation in production code and validate the numerical results in the context of physics reconstruction. We also compare its throughput across modern multi- and many-core architectures.

Using our Kalman filter implementation we are able to achieve a sustained throughput of 75 million particle hit reconstructions per second on an Intel Xeon Phi Knights Landing platform, a factor 6.81 over the current production implementation running on a two-socket Haswell system. Additionally we show that under the constraints of our Kalman filter formulation we efficiently use the available hardware resources.

Our implementation will allow us to better sustain the required throughput of the detector in the coming years and scale to future hardware architectures. Additionally our work enables the evaluation of other computing platforms for future hardware upgrades.

Keywords: Kalman filter · Data-intensive parallel algorithms
Numerical methods

1 Introduction

The LHCb detector at CERN will be upgraded in 2020 [1] to acquire data at an estimated rate of 30 MHz, requiring to process a data throughput of 40 Tbit/s. At the same time the first stage of filtering in the Data Acquisition process, also

© Springer International Publishing AG, part of Springer Nature 2018
D. B. Heras and L. Bougé (Eds.): Euro-Par 2017 Workshops, LNCS 10659, pp. 378–389, 2018.
https://doi.org/10.1007/978-3-319-75178-8_31

known as hardware level trigger, will be discontinued in favor of a full software trigger [2]. Consequently the throughput that the software level trigger will need to sustain in order to maintain a steady triggering rate will dramatically increase, due to both the increase in rate of events processed in software, and the influx of larger events.

To be able to cope with the increased data rate, several hardware architectures are currently under consideration. While the current LHCb software trigger farm is composed solely of Intel Xeon processors, in the last few years many High Performance Computing sites are adopting other alternative hardware architectures, such as ARM 64, IBM Power X, FPGAs, or manycore architectures such as GPGPUs or Intel Xeon Phi. This has raised the question within the High Energy Physics community whether these architectures are also suitable for performing the software trigger in a sustainable way. To answer this question, performance, economical, power consumption and software maintainability aspects need to be taken into account.

In this work we will consider the Kalman filter component used in the LHCb software framework. The Kalman filter is a linear quadratic estimator, first introduced by Kálmán in 1960 [3], that has been extensively used to estimate trajectories in various systems [4,5]. In its discrete implementation [6], it consists in a *predict* stage where the state of the system is projected according to a given model, and an *update* stage where the state is adjusted taking into account a measurement. In particular we consider here a filter that is low-rank.

In LHCb the Kalman filter is applied to estimate particle trajectories (*tracks*) as they travel through the particle detector [7]. Tens of millions of collisions per second occur in the detector, each requiring tens of thousands of filter computations. The Kalman filter is therefore the single largest time contributor in the LHCb software chain, taking about 60% of the first stage software trigger reconstruction time.

According to Amdahl's law [8], the achievable performance gain of an algorithm is bounded by its parallelizable portion. Due to the nature of the LHCb experiment, many particles travel through the detector simultaneously and independently. Hence, the Kalman filter is considered a petascale embarrassingly parallel problem in this context. Here we present a hardware architecture independent Kalman filter algorithm and implementation, *Cross Kalman*[1] extending beyond previously presented results [9].

In contrast to the work by Cerati et al. [10], we do not use our Kalman filter for track finding, but instead, we filter fully built tracks. That allows us to take into account the number of tracks and nodes when envisioning a scheduling strategy. Resulting in an effective use of the SIMD capabilities of the processors under study.

We explore performance gains over the current LHCb particle reconstruction software [11], and compare the speedup obtained over a variety of architectures. Additionally, we validate our implementation and integrate it back in the LHCb reconstruction framework, observing a performance gain on existing hardware.

---

[1] https://gitlab.cern.ch/dcampora/cross_kalman.

2   Cross Kalman

In LHCb track reconstruction a particle trajectory consists of *signal nodes* originating from detector signals. Additionally, virtual *reference nodes* are placed in large trajectory sections that have no detector signals. As opposed to signal nodes, reference nodes trigger a prediction with no update in the Kalman filter. Reference nodes improve trajectory prediction, at the cost of introducing additional complexity in the algorithm.

For a given particle trajectory, the Kalman filter is applied twice: First, a fit in the forward direction, positive in the Z axis, is followed by a fit in the backward direction, processing the nodes in reverse order. Afterwards, a smoothed state is calculated averaging both states. This introduces a dependency between the stages with little room for parallelization. However, a particle collision generates many independent particles that can be reconstructed at the same time, allowing us to envision a horizontally parallel scheme.

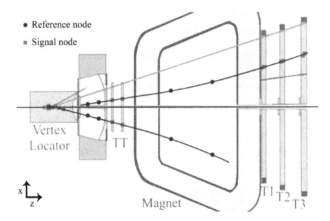

Fig. 1. Schematic of two particles (blue) traversing LHCb subdetectors. A particle collision is indicated by the two red arrows meeting in the center of the *Vertex Locator* subdetector. Particles produced from the collision traverse tracking subdetectors; here the Vertex Locator, TT and T1, T2 and T3 stations are depicted. A magnet bends the trajectory of produced particles according to their momentum and charge. (Color figure online)

For either direction, the first encountered signal node does not have any preceding signal data. *Reference parameters* according to their position are generated and fed onto those nodes, and the prediction is applied to these parameters. Figure 1 shows two particles traversing the LHCb detector with various nodes. When performing the forward fit, the top particle carries out three predictions from reference parameters before doing the first update. From that point on, all states are predicted from previous states, however only signal nodes trigger an update. The particle at the bottom performs a single prediction from reference parameters, given the first node is a signal node. Finally, when doing the backward fit, a similar procedure follows: The bottom particle requires three predictions before the first update while the top particle requires one.

Furthermore, given a node, the resulting state is calculated as the average between its forward updated state and its backward predicted state. However, if the node has no preceding signal node in one of the directions, the smoother copies the updated state of the other direction.

Given this problem formulation, we describe the design of our algorithm in the following parts: the control flow, the data structures and an efficient implementation for performing the math computations.

2.1 Control Flow

Since the control path of processing a particle trajectory diverges depending on the nature of its nodes, we have divided each particle trajectory in three stages: pre, main and post. pre is the forward trajectory from the first node until a signal node is encountered, inclusive. Similarly, post is the backward trajectory from the last node until a signal node is encountered, inclusive. Finally, main includes the remaining nodes. The forward fit processing logic differs between pre and main, while for the backward fit processing logic differs between post and main.

In order to fully exploit the capabilities of SIMD architectures, we employ a static scheduler that assigns node calculations to SIMD lanes. Since the execution of nodes from different particles is independent, we execute them in a horizontally parallel scheme. In order to minimize branches and guarantee instruction locality, we generate three such schedulers, one for each stage.

The amount of nodes processable at a time depends directly on the SIMD width of the processor. Hence our scheduler accepts a configurable vector width. It is also able to detect at compile time the supported vector width of the platform. There are no restrictions on the width of the lane, allowing this design to also target manycore architectures, where wider vector units are available.

More formally, given m particle trajectories with n_i nodes each and k processors, we want to assign nodes to processors minimizing the number of compute iterations. This problem is a variant of the number partitioning problem NPP [12], which is known to be NP-complete. Our scheduling algorithm orders the trajectories in descending order of nodes, and assigns nodes to processors following a Decreasing-Time Algorithm (DTA).

The same scheduler can be used for the forward fit, the backward fit, and the smoother. The forward and backward dependencies between node calculations are naturally resolved by traversing the scheduler in the respective direction. All tracks are processed on each stage prior to processing the next one. The smoother pre and post stages are processed after completion of the backward fit.

In our implementation we place particular emphasis on avoiding as much as possible memory copy operations and exploiting memory locality. We reuse data structures throughout the scheduler iterations replacing only necessary data portions when required to do so. Additionally, the data structures must be aligned and refer relatively to the same nodes in order for the smoother to be able to produce an average state from the previously calculated forward and backward states. Using our scheduler this requirement is trivially met.

2.2   Data Structures

The algorithm's main data structure is composed of three parts. A hardware-specific data backend stores data contiguously and aligned to the required SIMD width, and provides chunks of requested data agnostic to their contents. In order to avoid a performance impact of memory allocations of big chunks of contiguous space, data backends are created on demand and can store a configurable number of elements. Iterators point to the data backends and are configured with a structure size. We provide forward and reverse iterators in order to traverse the data as required.

We use Arrays of Structures of Arrays (AOSOA) as data views over the data backends. This kind of data structures benefit from locality when accessing any of their elements, and have been shown to work well with SIMD processors [13]. Further locality is preserved by storing these structures next to each other contiguously.

2.3   Efficient Vector Implementation

We have implemented the core routines of the fit and smoother algorithms using manual vectorization with the help of vector intrinsics libraries. An iterative fine-grained optimization has been carried out, testing several formulations, unrolling loops, inlining functions, changing compiler options and reordering code. Also, we have implemented the arithmetic backend with several libraries in our synthetic benchmark *Cross Kalman Mathtest*[2], namely the vectorization libraries VCL [14], UMESIMD [15], and the language extensions OpenCL and CUDA. Our implementations can efficiently target any sort of SIMD paradigm. Furthermore, a scalar implementation is provided as fall back. It allows to process single tracks, and it can run on architectures not supporting vectorization.

3   Results

We ran the experiments in this section under the conditions shown in Table 1.

Figure 2 shows the cross-architecture speedup. The leftmost bar shows the performance of the scalar implementation of the fit, obtained from the timings reported by the framework. Our Cross Kalman implementation outperforms the scalar implementation on the same hardware platform by a factor

---

[2] https://gitlab.cern.ch/dcampora/cross_kalman_mathtest.

Table 1. Run conditions.

The program was compiled with gcc 6.2.0, with options `-O2 -march=native`
Turbo Boost was on, where applicable
KNL was using quadrant and flat memory mode, and pinned against the MCDRAM
One process was spawned per Non-Uniform Memory Access (NUMA) domain, with as many TBB threads as logical cores in domain and pinned to its memory
Ran 500 000 events, each event is a Threading Building Blocks (TBB) task
Used Monte Carlo events from the LHCb Upgrade
Results are validated against expected result from original algorithm
Results were obtained using double precision
The figure of merit is the average throughput #fits/time

of 3.03x. ThunderX shows the poorest performance of the architectures under study. Even though a speedup of 1.75x over the scalar implementation on E5-2630 v3 is observed, this is only due to optimizations in the software. When both architectures run Cross Kalman, the E5-2630 v3 outperforms ThunderX by 1.73x. This is likely due to a comparatively lower peak DRAM bandwidth and peak floating point performance on ThunderX. The peak value is observed on a quad-socket high-end Intel Haswell system. This is, however, also the most expensive of the tested systems. It is interesting to note that Intel Xeon Phi outperforms our dual-socket Broadwell system, rendering it the most competitive from a price/throughput standpoint.

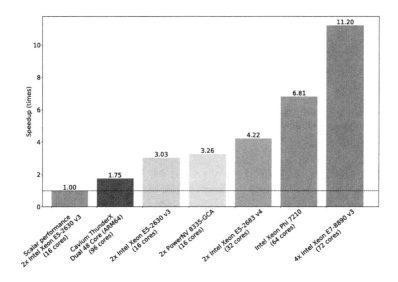

Fig. 2. Performance of Cross Kalman against the scalar implementation of the fit across several architectures.

A throughput scalability plot for all architectures is shown in Fig. 3a. The processor that shows less performance degradation up to using all of its cores is ThunderX. On the IBM Power8 architecture we are able to scale linearly while no Simultaneous MultiThreads (SMTs) are being used. Using 2 SMTs per processor, a performance improvement of 32% is observed. Moving from 2 to 4, a further 15% is gained, while moving from 4 to 8 no performance benefit is observed. On the Intel architectures we observe an almost linear scaling until we reach the limit of physical cores. The Intel Xeon Phi processor shows a 27% gain from using 2 HyperThreads, and a further 9% from using 4. We do not obtain any gain from HyperThreads on other Intel processors, which we attribute to the higher bandwidth of MCDRAM on Intel Xeon Phi.

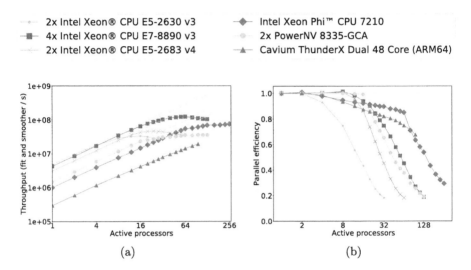

Fig. 3. (a) Throughput of Cross Kalman across various architectures. For each architecture, an increasing number of processors is enabled. Additional SMTs are only used on high core counts. (b) Parallel efficiency against active processors. The PowerNV processors shows no performance degradation using all its physical cores. In contrast, Xeon Phi shows a parallel efficiency of 85% (64 processors), ThunderX 68% (96 processors), E5-2630 v3 43% (16 processors), E7-8890 v3 40% (72 processors) and E5-2683 v4 45% (32 processors).

Figure 3b shows a parallel efficiency graph. All Xeon processors diverge from perfect scaling before the other processors under study. Xeon Phi and ThunderX show performance gains using all of their available processors, with a speedup of 74.98x and 64.88x respectively. For PowerNV, its optimal configuration is reached when configured with 96 processors (24.44x), where the performance flattens out. As expected on all tested hardware platforms, parallel efficiency is significantly degraded when using SMT. PowerNV shows a parallel efficiency of 1.0 until it starts using additional SMTs. We observe a similarly abrupt decrease in parallel efficiency in Xeon Phi when using additional HTs. The Xeon processors efficiency drop even without HTs. With all their physical cores active, we see 40–45% efficiency, which could be due to the memory requirements of the application.

Figure 4 shows the throughput of the fit and smoother as the vector width is increased. In order to obtain the results of these figures, we used our synthetic benchmark, that allows us to execute the bulk of the computation of the application in a portable and generic way. The tests were compiled against the UMESIMD library. The scalar performance of the application is very poor in this setting, because scalar data is emulated in the UMESIMD library by a vector of width one. The smoother application scales slightly better than the fit, which we believe is due to its higher arithmetic intensity. We observe the same scaling for single and double precision, as is depicted by the two gray scaling lines being very close to each other. Single precision produces a deviation from the expected results in 1% of the experiments.

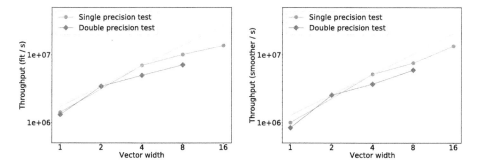

Fig. 4. Throughput of program as vector width increases, for single and double precision, under Intel Xeon Phi 7210. Left: fit throughput. Right: smoother throughput. We observe a scaled throughput for 128-bit vectors between single precision (width 4) and double precision (width 2). The smoother scales better than the fit for wider vector units, due to its higher arithmetic intensity.

Figure 5 shows a Roofline plot [16] for the fit and smoother processes. We ran for the Roofline benchmarks both the fit and smoother with 10 000 000 experiments. A high number of experiments is required in order to avoid data being cached from its generation to its execution, which would affect the arithmetic intensity of the application. This effect does not carry over to the full Cross Kalman code. The arithmetic intensity of the fit process is at about 0.5 FLOP/Byte, while the smoother is arithmetically more intensive at around 0.8 FLOP/Byte. Both fit and smoother performances are in the arithmetic-intensity regime limited by memory bandwidth and not peak floating point performance. However, our measurements show that we currently do not attain peak performance.

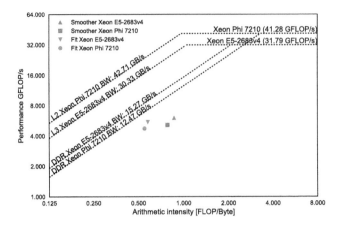

Fig. 5. Roofline model of Broadwell E5-2683v4 and Xeon Phi 7210 platforms. The performance of Cross Kalman Mathtest for the fit and smoother is shown for both platforms.

4   Validation

We have developed a module that implements the Cross Kalman filter inside the LHCb execution chain, named *TrackVectorFitter* (TVF). This module is already available to LHCb users and serves as the foundation for the numerical results described in this section. We have validated the physics performance of TVF against the original implementation under the current LHCb run conditions, and also under the foreseen conditions of the upgrade.

The LHCb experiment uses Monte Carlo simulation to generate validation data sets. Particle collisions and their interaction with the detector are simulated. This simulation generates a data set that can be processed by the LHCb reconstruction software. Finally the reconstructed particles are compared to the Monte Carlo generated ground truth.

Track reconstruction validation is done using three metrics [17]. The *reconstruction efficiency* compares the reconstructed tracks to the expected tracks reported by the Monte Carlo truth. The *clone rate* reports how many track equivalent track pairs were found. The *ghost rate* reports how many tracks were reconstructed with nodes belonging to different particles or noise. Finally, tracks are categorized by their physical properties and category statistics are compared to statistics from the ground truth.

Comparing the Cross Kalman implementation TVF to the original track filter TMF we observe an identical reconstruction efficiency, clone rate and ghost rate under all tested scenarios. While the reconstruction of the track itself does not depend on the fit, the final track χ^2 is used in the different categories as a track quality cutoff. Hence, the identical reconstruction efficiency between the two algorithms validates TVF for its physical properties.

We have checked the performance of TVF against TMF under various scenarios. Table 2 shows comparative execution times for LHCb nightly tests. These tests are representative of the conditions under which the LHCb reconstruction runs in the production environment.

Table 2. LHCb test times in seconds, run in various conditions. All tests are run on a single core of an Intel Xeon E5-2650 v3. All timings refer to the algorithm *TrackBest-TrackCreator*, configured with different filter settings. TMF is the original filter implementation. Internally, it executes a vertically vectorized code optimized for AVX on this setup. TVF refers to our implementation, compiled with either the SSE2 extension (default setting for x86_64) or AVX2+FMA. The *overall reconstruction speedup* refers to the entire reconstruction time of the test, compared between TMF and TVF AVX2+FMA.

Test name	TMF (AVX)	TVF SSE2	TVF AVX2+FMA	Overall reconstruction speedup
Magup2016	13.518	12.817	11.504	1.09x
Baseline-upgrade	93.713	93.839	91.014	1.03x
Sim08	8.307	8.134	7.986	1.02x

We observe a varying performance depending on the test under execution. Magup2016 shows gains of up to 9% in the overall reconstruction time, whereas baseline-upgrade and sim08 gains in TVF do not seem to impact much the overall performance. In the case of baseline-upgrade, we believe this is due to the configuration of such test. It uses a *full geometry* setting in its current form, which dominates the time distribution of the fit. We expect its performance to improve in the future.

5   Conclusions and Outlook

In this work we have presented Cross Kalman, an algorithm that is able to efficiently perform low-rank Kalman filters. Cross Kalman is particularly optimized for the LHCb particle tracking use case, but the presented algorithms and data structures can be applied to other situations where a large number of low-rank Kalman filters are used. Using this algorithm we were able to obtain up to 3x speedup over the previous scalar solution on the same hardware platform. Our implementation is flexible enough to accommodate for any kind of SIMD architecture and we have tested it a wide array of architectures. The choice of the Decreasing-Time Algorithm as a scheduling algorithm should be revisited, and we intend to explore other heuristics in the future. Our data structures allow us to efficiently perform the Kalman filter and smoother of many independent particles in parallel. Given the specific nature of our problem instances, it may be possible to reuse data structures across different particle trajectories, and further decrease the memory footprint of our application. In addition, we have showed that single precision performance scales similarly to its double precision counterpart.

An in-depth analysis of the precision requirements and numerical stability of the algorithm, taking into account also the possibility of alternative mathematical formulations, should be carried out. We expect that moving to single-precision and thus doubling the arithmetic intensity of our algorithms will significantly improve performance. Our software is validated and has been integrated in the LHCb codebase under the name TrackVectorFitter, making the overall reconstruction up to 9% faster for certain datasets.

We have verified that our implementation is able to scale to full hardware nodes and is able to adapt to the architectures under study. As expected enabling SMT does not yield further performance improvements with the notable exception of Intel Xeon Phi, which could be due to its higher memory throughput. However, other algorithms used in the LHCb software framework need to be adapted to make the most out of manycore architecture before a more definite answer can be given to the suitability of manycore hardware platforms such as Intel Xeon Phi for LHCb's software framework.

Given the arithmetical intensity of our formulation, our application utilizes efficiently the processors under study. We intend to port our software to GPU accelerators and further analyze our software scalability. We will continue to track the performance of modern hardware architectures and adapt our software to it, and observe the evolution of the different platforms.

Acknowledgements. The authors would like to thank the High-Throughput Computing Collaboration at CERN openlab for fruitful discussions through the process of designing and writing the presented software, and early access to Intel hardware. Thanks to F. Lemaitre for his contribution of the vectorized transposition code, and to O. Bouizi and S. Harald for the low-level code discussions and for providing early results and insight on the Xeon Phi architecture. In addition, thanks to W. Hulsbergen and R. Aaij for the mathematical discussions and data structure design. Finally, thanks to N. Neufeld and A. Riscos Núñez for their guidance and support.

References

1. The LHCb Collaboration: framework TDR for the LHCb upgrade: technical design report. Technical report CERN-LHCC-2012-007. LHCb-TDR-12, April 2012. https://cds.cern.ch/record/1443882
2. The LHCb Collaboration: LHCb trigger and online upgrade technical design report. Technical report CERN-LHCC-2014-016. LHCB-TDR-016, May 2014. https://cds.cern.ch/record/1701361
3. Kalman, R.E.: A new approach to linear filtering and prediction problems. J. Basic Eng. **82**(1), 35–45 (1960). https://doi.org/10.1115/1.3662552
4. Mcgee, L.A., Schmidt, S.F.: Discovery of the Kalman filter as a practical tool for aerospace and industry. Technical report, November 1985. https://ntrs.nasa.gov/search.jsp?R=19860003843
5. Houtekamer, P.L., Mitchell, H.L.: Data assimilation using an ensemble Kalman filter technique. Mon. Weather Rev. **126**(3), 796–811 (1998). http://journals.ametsoc.org/doi/abs/10.1175/1520-0493%281998%29126%3C0796%3ADAUAEK%3E2.0.CO%3B2

6. Welch, G., Bishop, G.: An introduction to the Kalman filter. Technical report, Chapel Hill, NC, USA (1995)
7. Hulsbergen, W.: The global covariance matrix of tracks fitted with a Kalman filter and an application in detector alignment. Nucl. Instrum. Methods Phys. Res. Sec. A: Accel. Spectrom. Detect. Assoc. Equip. **600**(2), 471–477 (2009). http://www.sciencedirect.com/science/article/pii/S0168900208017567
8. Amdahl, G.M.: Validity of the single processor approach to achieving large scale computing capabilities. In: Proceedings of the 18–20 April 1967, Spring Joint Computer Conference, pp. 483–485. AFIPS 1967 (Spring). ACM, New York (1967). http://doi.acm.org/10.1145/1465482.1465560
9. Cámpora Pérez, D.H.: LHCb Kalman filter cross-architecture studies (2016)
10. Cerati, G., Elmer, P., Lantz, S., McDermott, K., Riley, D., Tadel, M., Wittich, P., Würthwein, F., Yagil, A.: Kalman filter tracking on parallel architectures. J. Phy. Conf. Series **664**(7), 072008 (2015). http://stacks.iop.org/1742-6596/664/i=7/a=072008
11. Aaij, R., Fontana, M., Le Gac, R., Zacharjasz, E.A., Schwemmer, R., Fitzpatrick, C., Albrecht, J., Grillo, L., Szumlak, T., Yin, H., Couturier, B., Stahl, S., Williams, M.R.J., Vries, D., Andreas, J., Seyfert, P., Wanczyk, J., Esen, S., Neufeld, N., Hasse, C., Vesterinen, M.A., Nikodem, T., Quagliani, R., Polci, F., Dziurda, A., Jones, C.R., Matev, R., De Cian, M., Del Buono, L.: Upgrade trigger: biannual performance update. Technical report, February 2017. https://cds.cern.ch/record/2244312
12. Mertens, S.: The easiest hard problem: number partitioning, October 2003. arXiv:cond-mat/0310317
13. Gou, C., Kuzmanov, G., Gaydadjiev, G.N.: SAMS multi-layout memory: providing multiple views of data to boost SIMD performance. In: Proceedings of the 24th ACM International Conference on Supercomputing, pp. 179–188. ICS 2010. ACM, New York (2010). http://doi.acm.org/10.1145/1810085.1810111
14. Fog, A.: VCL C++ vector class library (2012). http://www.agner.org/optimize
15. Karpiński, P., McDonald, J.: A high-performance portable abstract interface for explicit SIMD vectorization. In: Proceedings of the 8th International Workshop on Programming Models and Applications for Multicores and Manycores, PMAM 2017, pp. 21–28. ACM, New York (2017). http://doi.acm.org/10.1145/3026937.3026939
16. Williams, S., Waterman, A., Patterson, D.: Roofline: an insightful visual performance model for multicore architectures. Commun. ACM **52**(4), 65 (2009)
17. Schiller, M.: Track reconstruction and prompt K_S^0 production at the LHCb experiment. Dissertation, University of Heidelberg (2011)

Resource Contention Aware Execution of Multiprocessor Tasks on Heterogeneous Platforms

Robert Dietze[✉], Michael Hofmann, and Gudula Rünger

Department of Computer Science, Chemnitz University of Technology,
Chemnitz, Germany
{dirob,mhofma,ruenger}@cs.tu-chemnitz.de

Abstract. In high performance computing (HPC), the tasks of complex applications have to be assigned to the compute nodes of heterogeneous HPC platforms in such a way that the total execution time is minimized. Common approaches, such as task scheduling methods, usually base their decisions on task runtimes that are predicted by cost models. A high accuracy and reliability of these models is crucial for achieving low execution times for all tasks. The individual runtimes of concurrently executed tasks are often affected by contention for hardware resources, such as communication networks, the main memory, or hard disks. However, existing cost models usually ignore the effects of resource contention, thus leading to large deviations between predicted and measured runtimes. In this article, we present a resource contention aware cost model for the execution of multiprocessor tasks on heterogeneous platforms. The integration of the proposed model into two task scheduling methods is described. The cost model is validated in isolation as well as within the utilized scheduling methods. Performance results with different benchmark tasks and with tasks of a complex simulation application are shown to demonstrate the performance improvements achieved by taking the effects of resource contention into account.

Keywords: Resource contention · Multiprocessor tasks
Heterogeneous platforms · Scheduling methods
Distributed simulations

1 Introduction

Reducing the overall execution time of compute-intensive applications is a major concern in high performance computing (HPC). The efficient utilization of the available HPC resources represents a key aspect for achieving such reductions of execution times. Complex applications in the area of scientific and engineering simulations usually consist of separated tasks that can be distributed among the compute nodes of a HPC platform. Thus, the goal is to find a distribution that minimizes the execution time of the whole application. This problem is usually

© Springer International Publishing AG, part of Springer Nature 2018
D. B. Heras and L. Bougé (Eds.): Euro-Par 2017 Workshops, LNCS 10659, pp. 390–402, 2018.
https://doi.org/10.1007/978-3-319-75178-8_32

solved by applying task scheduling methods. Sequential tasks are assigned to exactly one processor of a compute node. Multiprocessor tasks can be executed in parallel itself to reduce their individual execution times by using more than one processor. Thus, for distributing multiprocessor tasks on HPC platforms, not only the particular compute node but also the number of processors to be used on this node has to be determined for each task. The resulting distribution problem becomes increasingly complex, thus requiring dedicated scheduling methods.

Task scheduling methods usually base their decisions for distributing the tasks on predictions of the execution times of the tasks. These predictions can be determined with cost models that model the specific execution times of the tasks on the hardware platform to be utilized. For multiprocessor tasks, the cost model also has to include the number of processors employed. Thus, cost models from parallel computing, such as PRAM [9], BSP [11], or LogP [4], might be used. However, since these models abstract from many details of the compute systems, there can be large differences between modeled and measured execution times. These differences lead to improper decisions for scheduling the single tasks and, thus, might deteriorate the overall execution time of all tasks. Keeping these difference as small as possible is therefore an important goal for achieving an efficient execution of multiprocessor tasks on HPC platforms.

Heterogeneous platforms consist of a variety of compute nodes with different computational properties. Existing cost models for heterogeneous platforms take these properties into account, for example, by including different computational speeds of compute nodes. However, the influence of tasks on each other when being executed concurrently on the same node is currently not included in these models. For example, tasks that are executed concurrently on different processors of a compute node can utilize the same hardware resources (e. g., communication network, main memory, or hard disk). The access to these hardware resources has to be shared and might increase execution times due to *resource contention*.

In this article, we present a resource contention aware cost model for the execution of multiprocessor tasks on heterogeneous platforms. The proposed model considers the effects of resource contention, especially due to hard disk and main memory accesses. The integration of the cost model into two scheduling methods for multiprocessor tasks is described. Experiments with different types of tasks on a heterogeneous compute cluster are performed. This includes benchmark tasks with intensive hard disk and main memory accesses. Simulation tasks of a complex application for optimizing lightweight structures are used to represent tasks with accesses to various hardware resources.

The rest of the article is organized as follows: Sect. 2 discusses related work. Section 3 defines a scheduling problem for multiprocessor tasks and describes the modeling of the task execution times. Section 4 presents a resource contention aware cost model for multiprocessor tasks on heterogeneous platforms. Section 5 describes the integration of the cost model into different task scheduling methods. Section 6 presents experimental results and Sect. 7 concludes the article.

2   Related Work

Resource contention is mainly considered in the area of thread scheduling for operating systems [14]. Contention for accessing the main memory is integrated into the scheduling, for example, based on memory request rates [12] or cache miss rates [8]. The measured rates are used to prioritize or group applications to achieve a balanced utilization of memory resources. The measurement approach might also be used to estimate the effects of resource contention for tasks. However, the scheduling approach is not suitable if all tasks exhibit the same memory behavior, such as simulation tasks that execute the same application program.

For task scheduling, contention for communication resources is usually considered. For example, in [10], a model for communication contention is proposed that improves the accuracy of predicted execution times. The integration into scheduling methods is based on task duplication to avoid interprocessor communication and, thus, cannot directly be applied to contention of other hardware resources. Only few works consider contention for other resources. In [2], a contention aware scheduling algorithm for heterogeneous platforms is proposed, but in the context of achieving fault-tolerance by replicating tasks. In [13], the system resources required by tasks are modeled in order to constrain the number of tasks running concurrently. A reduction of the execution time was achieved for tasks that perform memory or file accesses. However, the approach requires that the system resources required by a task are specified manually with user annotations within the program code.

3   Multiprocessor Tasks and Heterogeneous Platforms

The efficient execution of multiprocessor tasks on heterogeneous platforms can be described as a scheduling problem. In the following, the scheduling of multiprocessor tasks and the modeling of the task runtimes is described.

3.1   Scheduling of Multiprocessor Tasks

The considered problem comprises n_T multiprocessor tasks $T_1, \ldots, T_{n_T}$. The term *multiprocessor task* describes a task that can be executed on an arbitrary number of processor cores. It is assumed that all tasks are independent from each other and that the number of utilized cores is fixed during the task execution. The execution of each multiprocessor task is non-preemptive, i.e. it can not be interrupted. For each task T_i, $i = 1, \ldots, n_T$, $t_{i,j}(p)$ denotes its parallel execution time on p cores of a compute node N_j, $j \in \{1, \ldots, n_N\}$. The modeling of the parallel execution time $t_{i,j}(p)$ is described in the following subsection.

The considered heterogeneous HPC platform consists of n_N compute nodes $N_1, \ldots, N_{n_N}$, each having a different computational speed. For each node N_j, $j \in \{1, \ldots, n_N\}$, its number of processor cores p_j and a performance factor f_j are given. The performance factor f_j describes the computational speed of the compute node N_j and is defined as the ratio between the sequential execution time of a task on a reference node N_r and the compute node N_j. Since the reference node is also used for the runtime modeling of the multiprocessor tasks, the compute node with the highest number of cores is used as reference node. It is assumed that each multiprocessor task can only be executed on a single node (e. g., OpenMP-based codes) and that each core can execute only one task at a time. Thus, each multiprocessor task might be executed on 1 to p_j cores of a node N_j, $j \in \{1, \ldots, n_N\}$. Depending on the number of utilized cores of a compute node, several tasks can be executed on a node at the same time.

The result of the scheduling is a schedule, which defines an assignment of the tasks T_i, $i = 1, \ldots, n_T$, to the compute nodes N_j, $j = 1, \ldots, n_N$. A schedule S includes for each task T_i, $i \in \{1, \ldots, n_T\}$, the information about the compute node and the number of cores to be utilized as well as the estimated start time s_i and finish time e_i. The total execution time $T_{max}(S)$ of a schedule S is defined as the difference between the earliest start time and latest finish time of all tasks. By assuming that the task execution starts at time 0, the total execution time corresponds to the latest finish time of all tasks, i. e. $T_{max}(S) = \max\limits_{i=1,\ldots,n_T} e_i$. The goal is to determine a schedule S such that $T_{max}(S)$ is as small as possible.

3.2   Runtime Modeling of Multiprocessor Tasks

Scheduling methods usually base their decisions on predictions of the execution times of the single task. A high accuracy and reliability of these predictions is required for achieving schedules with a lower total execution time. These predictions can, for example, be calculated regarding to a specific cost model or determined by benchmark measurements. Existing cost models for parallel programming, such as PRAM [9], BSP [11], or LogP [4], are not suitable for the considered scheduling of multiprocessor tasks. The PRAM model, for example, assumes a single shared memory with uniform access by each processor and, thus, heterogeneous platforms with distributed memory are not covered. Furthermore, all of the models calculate the cost of a parallel program based on its program structure and, thus, can not be used if this structure is unknown. In [1], a cost model is presented that uses the amount of work of each task in combination with the relative speed of each compute node. Since this model is designed for the execution of sequential tasks on multiprocessor architectures supported by accelerators, it is not suitable for the scheduling problem described above.

Since the program structures of the considered multiprocessor tasks are unknown, we use the following general runtime formula to model the execution time $t_{i,j}$ of each task T_i, $i \in \{1, \ldots, n_T\}$, on a compute node N_j, $j \in \{1, \ldots, n_N\}$ depending on the employed number of processor cores p:

$$t_{i,j}(p) = f_j \cdot (a_i/p + b_i + c_i \cdot \log p) \tag{1}$$

The parameter f_j denotes the performance factor of node N_j to account for the different computational speeds. The remaining part of Eq. (1) models the execution time of task T_i on the reference node. This part consists of a parallel computation time a_i that decreases linearly with the number of cores p, a constant sequential computation time b_i, and a parallelization overhead c_i that increases logarithmically with the number of cores p (e. g., for synchronization or communication). These components were chosen such that the runtime behavior of common parallel algorithms is covered. The parameters a_i, b_i, and c_i of a task T_i are determined through a least squares fit of the execution times measured on the reference node with different numbers of cores. In practice, these measurements have to be performed only for tasks with differing execution times.

4   A Resource Contention Aware Cost Model

Shared access to hardware resources can lead to increased execution times of tasks executed concurrently. In the following, a new resource contention aware cost model for predicting the execution time of such tasks is developed.

4.1   Measuring the Effects of Resource Contention

Since resource contention results from shared access to hardware resources, the specific effects on the execution time may depend on the type and number of tasks executed as well as on the hardware utilized. To investigate these effects, we consider three types of tasks. The specific data sizes of the tasks where chosen, such that effects due to data caching are avoided.

I/O bound: The *hdWrite* tasks are used to investigate resource contention due to concurrent hard disk accesses. Each task consists of writing data of size 300 MB to a file on the local hard disk. The parallel implementation as a multiprocessor task is based on MPI where each MPI process writes an equally sized part of the entire file using the function `MPI_File_write`.

Memory bound: The *memWrite* tasks are used to investigate resource contention for the memory bandwidth due to concurrent main memory accesses. Each task consists of writing random integers of size 12 GB to the main memory. The parallel implementation as a multiprocessor task is based on MPI, where each MPI process writes an equally sized share of the entire data.

Compute bound: Numerical simulations based on a *Finite Element Method (FEM)* code [3] are used as compute-intensive tasks. During the numerical optimization of lightweight structures, a large number of structure simulations for varied sets of manufacturing parameters have to be performed [5]. Each simulation applies a preconditioned conjugate gradient method on very large but sparse matrices. The FEM code is parallelized with OpenMP, thus leading to multiprocessor tasks that can be executed in parallel on a single compute node.

Figure 1 shows the sequential execution times for the different types of tasks depending on the number concurrently executed tasks on the same compute node. Each measurement is performed 5 times using the compute node `ws1` with

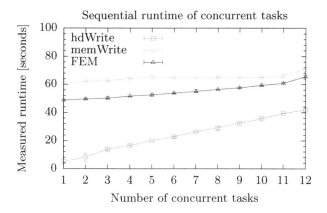

Fig. 1. Measured sequential runtime of different types of tasks on compute node `ws1`.

a total number of 12 cores (see Sect. 6.1). The results show that for each type of tasks, the execution times increase almost linearly with an increasing number of concurrently executed tasks. However, the slopes of the curves are different for each type of task. Further measurements have shown that the slope also differs for the same type of task between different compute nodes. These observations imply that the effects of resource contention depend on the type of the tasks, the number of concurrently executed tasks, and the compute node.

4.2 Runtime Modeling with Resource Contention

The effects of resource contention on the execution time of tasks is modeled separately for each type of task. For a fixed type of task, we introduce a *contention factor* c_j for each compute node N_j, $j \in \{1, \ldots, n_N\}$. This factor represents the linear slope of the sequential execution times that occurs for executing the tasks concurrently on the compute node N_j. The contention factors are determined by benchmark measurements as described in the previous subsection. Thus, the contention factor captures the entire effects of resource contention due to various hardware resources that may be utilized by a specific type of tasks.

To predict the impact of resource contention on the runtime of a task, the number of concurrently executed tasks on the same compute node has to be known. A task T_k, $k \in \{1, \ldots, n_T\}$ is executed concurrently to a task T_i, $i \in \{1, \ldots, n_T\}$, $i \neq k$, if the start time s_k of task T_k is smaller than the finish time e_i of task T_i and the finish time e_k of task T_k is larger than the start time s_i of task T_i. The period of time during which the two tasks T_k and T_i are executed concurrently lasts from their latest start time to their earliest finish time, i.e. $\min(e_k, e_i) - \max(s_k, s_i)$. During this time, the two tasks content for resources.

Let $K_{i,j}$ denote the set of tasks that are executed concurrently to a task T_i, $i \in \{1, \ldots, n_T\}$, on the compute node N_j, $j \in \{1, \ldots, n_N\}$. To include the effects of resource contention into the prediction of the execution time of the task T_i, its predicted runtime $t_{i,j}(p)$ (see Sect. 3.2) is increased by the additional time during which the task T_i is executed concurrently with the tasks $T_k \in K_{i,j}$. The specific time increase is calculated with the contention factor c_j for the type of tasks on compute node N_j. Thus, the contention aware execution time $\hat{t}_{i,j}(p)$ of task T_i executed on compute node N_j with p cores is modeled as follows:

$$\hat{t}_{i,j}(p) = t_{i,j}(p) + c_j \cdot \sum_{T_k \in K_{i,j}} (\min(e_k, e_i) - \max(s_k, s_i)) \tag{2}$$

4.3   Validation of the Runtime Modeling

In order to validate the accuracy of the proposed runtime modeling, several benchmark measurements have been performed for each of the three considered types of tasks, i.e. hdWrite, memWrite, and FEM. For each measurement a specific number of tasks (i.e., 10, 50, or 100) is executed on the compute node ws1. The number of cores p utilized by each multiprocessor task is chosen between 1 and 6 and each task is started as soon as the chosen number of cores was available. The total execution time of all tasks is measured and the difference to the prediction without resource contention according to Eq. (1) and with resource contention according to Eq. (2) is determined.

Table 1. Difference between measured and predicted execution times without and with resource contention depending on the type and number of tasks on compute node ws1.

Type of tasks		hdWrite			memWrite			FEM		
Number of tasks		10	50	100	10	50	100	10	50	100
Difference	Without contention	44.25	25.1	32.01	4.32	2.51	3.02	2.5	2.95	4.35
[%]	With contention	4.92	5.8	2.6	3.2	1.67	2.2	0.07	0.86	2.13

Table 1 shows the differences between measured and predicted execution times depending on the type and the number of tasks. For all types and numbers of tasks, the contention aware cost model leads to smaller differences in comparison to the cost model that neglects the effects resource contention. More exactly, the difference between measured and predicted execution times is always smaller than 6% with the contention aware cost model. The biggest improvement is achieved for the hdWrite tasks, where the difference without resource contention is up to about 45%. This corresponds to the previous results shown in Fig. 1, where a significant increase of the runtime was observed. However, even for the memWrite and FEM tasks, the contention aware cost model leads to better predictions of the execution times.

5   Resource Contention Aware Scheduling Methods

The contention aware cost model presented in the previous section has been integrated into two task scheduling methods. In the following, the two task scheduling methods and the necessary adaptions for the integration are described.

5.1   Task Parallel Execution

The task parallel scheduling scheme (TASKP) presented in [7] is a list scheduling algorithm that assigns each task to exactly one core (i. e., executed sequentially). All tasks are sorted in descending order based on their sequential runtimes. The algorithm iterates over the ordered tasks and selects one core to be utilized. The current task is then assigned to the core that provides the earliest finish.

5.2   Water-Level-Search Method

In [6], a heuristic method for scheduling parallel tasks onto heterogeneous compute resources called WATER-LEVEL-SEARCH (WLS) is proposed. Figure 2 shows the pseudocode of this method. The method uses a limit $\hat{m}$ for the predicted total execution time that must not be exceeded by the finish time of any task. An initial guess for this limit is based on the sequential runtimes of the tasks and the total compute capacity of all nodes (line 1). Afterwards, the WLS method performs a search for a better smaller limit that still allows to finish all tasks.

```
1  total execution time limit m̂ = ∑_{i=1}^{nT} t_{i,r}(1) / ∑_{j=1}^{nN} p_j f_j for reference node r
2  repeat
3  |    potential limits L = ∅
4  |    clear all assignments of tasks to nodes
5  |    for task T_i, i = 1, ..., nT, in descending order of t_{i,r}(1) do
6  |    |    for node N_j, j ∈ {1, ..., nN} and cores p = 1, ..., p_j do
7  |    |    |    select start time s_i such that p cores of node N_j are free
8  |    |    |    calculate finish time e_i = s_i + t_{i,j}(p)
9  |    |    |    add finish time e_i to the set of potential limits L
10 |    |    └    if e_i ≤ m̂ then assign T_i to p cores of N_j and quit the for-loop
11 |    |    if task T_i was not assigned then set m̂ to the smallest finish time
   |    └        calculated for task T_i and quit the for-loop if restart(i) returns true
12 until all task are assigned
13 repeat
14 |    total execution time limit m̂ = median of all potential limits L
15 |    clear all assignments of tasks to nodes
16 |    for task T_i, i = 1, ..., nT, in descending order of t_{i,r}(1) do
17 |    |    for node N_j, j ∈ {1, ..., nN} and cores p = 1, ..., p_j do
18 |    |    |    select start time s_i such that p cores of node N_j are free
19 |    |    |    calculate finish time e_i = s_i + t_{i,j}(p)
20 |    |    └    if e_i ≤ m̂ then assign T_i to p cores of N_j and quit the for-loop
21 |    if all task are assigned then remove all values greater than m̂ from L
22 |    else remove all values less than m̂ from L
23 until |L| ≤ 1
```

Fig. 2. Pseudocode of the WATER-LEVEL-SEARCH method.

The search for a better limit consists of two phases (lines 2–12 and lines 13–23). In each phase, the current limit $\hat{m}$ is used to determine an assignment of tasks to nodes and cores (lines 5–11 and lines 16–20). The assignment is determined by iterating over the tasks in descending order based on their sequential runtimes and for each tasks T_i, $i \in \{1, \ldots, n_T\}$, all compute nodes N_j, $j = 1, \ldots, n_N$, and their numbers of cores p_j are tested. This test consists of selecting a possible start time s_i and calculating the corresponding finish time e_i with the runtime formula $t_{i,j}(p)$ (lines 7–8 and lines 18–19). If the finish time e_i is valid for the current limit $\hat{m}$, then the task is assigned to the selected node and cores and then the next task is tested. Otherwise, the limit $\hat{m}$ is adapted and the assignment of tasks is restarted for all tasks. In the first phase, the limit is only increased and a set of potential limits L is created. In the second phase, a binary search among the potential limits in L is performed by repeatedly using the median of L as the current limit $\hat{m}$ (line 14) and adapting L accordingly (lines 21–22). The last value of L is the smallest limit $\hat{m}$ that was found and the corresponding assignment of tasks to nodes and cores is the determined schedule.

Determining an assignment in each phase depends linearly on the number of tasks n_T, the number of nodes n_N, and the highest number of cores of a node p_r. Restarting the assignment in the first phase is limited to at most $\log n_T$ times with a the *restart* function (line 11). The size of L depends linear on the number of tasks n_T, such that the binary search in the second phase requires $\mathcal{O}(\log n_T)$ steps. Thus, the overall complexity of the method is $\mathcal{O}(\log n_T \cdot n_T \cdot n_N \cdot p_r)$.

5.3   Integration of the Contention Aware Cost Model

Both methods use the runtime formula of $t_{i,j}(p)$ in Eq. (1) to predict the execution time of a task T_i, $i \in \{1, \ldots, n_T\}$, executed on compute node N_j, $j \in \{1, \ldots, n_N\}$ with p cores. To integrate the contention aware cost model described in Sect. 4, each occurrence of this usage is replaced by the new formula of $\hat{t}_{i,j}(p)$ in Eq. (2). Additionally, both methods use a list scheduling approach where tasks are assigned gradually to the compute resources. Thus, the number of tasks that are executed concurrently to a specific task that was already scheduled can increase during the scheduling. Since the contention aware cost model depends on this number, the start and finish time of an already scheduled task is recalculated whenever another task is assigned to the same compute node with an overlapping period of time.

For the WLS method, changing the finish times of tasks afterwards may lead to problems. For example, if the finish time of a task increases due to resource contention, then it might exceed the limit $\hat{m}$ that was used when the assignment of this task was determined. However, such a behavior conflicts with the assumption that a valid limit $\hat{m}$ allows to finish the execution of all tasks. To avoid such situations, the prediction of the finish time of a specific task uses always the maximum number of tasks that might be executed concurrently based on the number of currently available cores of the compute node.

6 Experimental Results

The proposed resource contention aware cost model has been integrated into the scheduling methods described in Sect. 5. The following experimental results compare the methods without and with the resource contention aware cost model.

6.1 Experimental Setup

The compute nodes of the heterogeneous compute cluster used for the measurements are listed in Table 2. The scheduling methods described in Sect. 5 have been implemented in Python. A Python script running on a separate node performs the execution of the tasks on the compute nodes via SSH connections. Each measurement is performed 5 times and the average values are shown.

Table 2. List of nodes of the utilized heterogeneous compute cluster.

Nodes	Processors	#Nodes × #processors × #cores	Total RAM	GHz
sb1	Intel Xeon E5-2650	$1 \times 2 \times 8$	60 GB	2.00
ws1,...,ws5	Intel Xeon X5650	$5 \times 2 \times 6$	32 GB	2.66
cs1,cs2	Intel Xeon E5345	$2 \times 2 \times 4$	16 GB	2.33

6.2 Performance Results with Benchmark and Simulation Tasks

The task parallel scheduling (TASKP) and the WATER-LEVEL-SEARCH method (WLS) without resource contention and with resource contention (i. e., TASKP-RC and WLS-RC) have been used to schedule the execution of different types of tasks. Figure 3 (top) shows the measured total runtimes for executing the hdWrite tasks (left) and the memWrite tasks (right) according to the determined schedules depending on the number of tasks. Up to 24 tasks of the corresponding type are executed on the compute nodes ws1 and ws2 with a total number of 24 cores. Using the contention aware scheduling methods leads to a significant reduction of the total runtimes with the hdWrite tasks. The biggest differences up to about 60% of the total runtime are achieved for the task parallel scheduling method (i. e., TASKP and TASKP-RC). With the contention aware cost model, both scheduling methods (i. e., TASKP-RC and WLS-RC) lead to about the same results. This behavior can mainly be attributed to the hardware resources utilized by the hdWrite tasks. The hard disk accesses are usually limited by the corresponding hard disk devices, thus leading to high contention for concurrent accesses and low benefits from parallelization. In comparison, the benefits of the contention aware cost model for the memWrite tasks are smaller. This behavior corresponds to the results shown in Fig. 1, where the effect of resource contention was also smaller for the memWrite tasks. However, there are still improvements of the total runtime for both contention aware scheduling methods.

Figure 3 (bottom left) shows measured total runtimes for executing the FEM simulation tasks according to the determined schedules depending on the number of tasks using all compute nodes of Table 2. The results confirm the improvements achieved with the contention aware cost model. Especially, if the number of tasks approaches the number of utilized cores (i. e., 92), both scheduling methods (i. e., TASKP-RC and WLS-RC) lead to a significant reduction of the total runtimes. In general, the results with the resource contention aware cost model show a more steady and less abrupt increase when the number of tasks is increased. Figure 3 (bottom right) shows the parallel speedups for executing 100 FEM simulation tasks according to the determined schedules depending on the number of utilized cores. Up to about 52 cores, there are only small differences between all scheduling methods. However, when all compute nodes are used, the resource contention aware cost model prevents a decrease of the speedup.

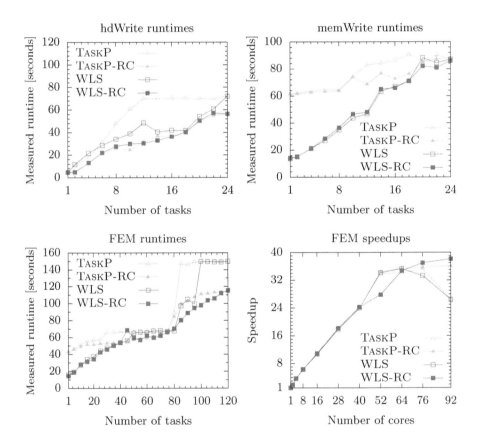

Fig. 3. Top: Measured total runtimes of hdWrite tasks (left) and memWrite tasks (right) depending on the number of tasks using all compute nodes ws1 and ws2. Bottom: Measured total runtimes of FEM simulation tasks depending on the number of tasks using all compute nodes of Table 2 (left) and parallel speedups for the execution of 100 FEM simulation tasks depending on the number of cores (right).

7   Conclusions

In this article, we investigated the effects of resource contention for the execution of multiprocessor tasks on heterogeneous platforms. The development of a contention aware cost model based on a task- and hardware-depending contention factor was described. The proposed cost model was used for the prediction of executions times of multiprocessor tasks and the integration into two existing scheduling methods was described. Measurements with benchmark tasks with hard disk and main memory accesses demonstrated that for both scheduling methods, a reduction of the total task runtimes could be achieved. Further results with FEM simulation tasks confirmed the performance improvements, especially due to a better utilization of hardware with high contention effects.

Acknowledgments. This work was performed within the Federal Cluster of Excellence EXC 1075 "MERGE Technologies for Multifunctional Lightweight Structures" and supported by the German Research Foundation (DFG).

References

1. Augonnet, C., Thibault, S., Namyst, R., Wacrenier, P.A.: StarPU: a unified platform for task scheduling on heterogeneous multicore architectures. Concurr. Comput. Pract. Exp. **23**(2), 187–198 (2011)
2. Benoit, A., Hakem, M., Robert, Y.: Contention awareness and fault-tolerant scheduling for precedence constrained tasks in heterogeneous systems. Parallel Comput. **35**(2), 83–108 (2009)
3. Beuchler, S., Meyer, A., Pester, M.: SPC-PM3AdH v1.0 - Programmer's manual. Preprint SFB/393 01–08, TU-Chemnitz (2001)
4. Culler, D., Karp, R., Patterson, D., Sahay, A., Schauser, K., Santos, E., Subramonian, R., von Eicken, T.: LogP: towards a realistic model of parallel computation. In: Proceedings of the 4th ACM SIGPLAN Symposium on Principles and Practice of Parallel Programming (PPOPP 1993), pp. 1–12. ACM (1993)
5. Dietze, R., Hofmann, M., Rünger, G.: Exploiting heterogeneous compute resources for optimizing lightweight structures. In: Proceedings of the 2nd International Workshop on Sustainable Ultrascale Computing Systems (NESUS 2015), pp. 127–134 (2015)
6. Dietze, R., Hofmann, M., Rünger, G.: Water-level scheduling for parallel tasks in compute-intensive application components. J. Supercomput. **72**, 4047–4068 (2016)
7. Dümmler, J., Kunis, R., Rünger, G.: A comparison of scheduling algorithms for multiprocessor tasks with precedence constraints. In: Proceedings of the High Performance Computing & Simulation Conference (HPCS 2007), pp. 663–669. ECMS (2007)
8. Feliu, J., Petit, S., Sahuquillo, J., Duato, J.: Cache-hierarchy contention-aware scheduling in CMPS. IEEE Trans. Parallel Distrib. Syst. **25**(3), 581–590 (2014)
9. Fortune, S., Wyllie, J.: Parallelism in random access machines. In: Proceedings of the 10th Annual ACM Symposium on Theory of Computing, pp. 114–118. ACM (1978)
10. Sinnen, O., To, A., Kaur, M.: Contention-aware scheduling with task duplication. J. Parallel Distrib. Comput. **71**(1), 77–86 (2011)

11. Skillicorn, D.B., Hill, J., McColl, W.: Questions and answers about BSP. Sci. Program. **6**(3), 249–274 (1997)
12. Subramanian, L., Seshadri, V., Kim, Y., Jaiyen, B., Mutlu, O.: MISE: providing performance predictability and improving fairness in shared main memory systems. In: Proceedings of the 19th International Symposium on High Performance Computer Architecture (HPCA 2013), pp. 639–650. IEEE (2013)
13. Tillenius, M., Larsson, E., Badia, R.M., Martorell, X.: Resource-aware task scheduling. ACM Trans. Embed. Comput. Syst. **14**(1), 5:1–5:25 (2015)
14. Zhuravlev, S., Saez, J.C., Blagodurov, S., Fedorova, A., Prieto, M.: Survey of scheduling techniques for addressing shared resources in multicore processors. ACM Comput. Surv. **45**(1), 4:1–4:28 (2012)

Hybrid CPU-GPU Simulation of Hierarchical Adaptive Random Boolean Networks

Kirill Kuvshinov[1]([✉]), Klavdiya Bochenina[1], Piotr J. Górski[2],
and Janusz A. Hołyst[1,2]

[1] ITMO University, Kronverkskiy av. 49, 197101 Saint Petersburg, Russia
kvkuvshinov@yandex.ru
[2] Faculty of Physics, Warsaw University of Technology,
Koszykowa 75, 00-662 Warsaw, Poland

Abstract. Random boolean networks (RBNs) as models of gene regulatory networks are widely studied by the means of computer simulation to explore interconnections between their topology, regimes of functioning and patterns of information processing. Direct simulation of random boolean networks is known to be computationally hard because of the exponential growth of attractor lengths with an increase of a network size. In this paper, we propose hybrid CPU-GPU algorithm for parallel simulation of hierarchical adaptive RBNs. The rules of evolution of this type of RBN makes it possible to parallelize calculations both for different subnetworks and for different nodes while updating their states. In the experimental part of the study, we explore the efficiency of OpenMP and CPU-GPU algorithms for different sizes of networks and configurations of hierarchy. The results show that a hybrid algorithm performs better for a smaller number of subnetworks while OpenMP version may be preferable for a limited number of nodes in each subnetwork.

1 Introduction

1.1 Motivation and Background

Nowadays data science provides tools that allow to observe stylized facts related to complex dynamics of various systems. However, in order to find out which of these features are important (in terms of a certain measure or behavior), one needs to create models. Models incorporate chosen system properties and as a result they are able to mimic and give better understanding of observed phenomena.

An example are Random Boolean networks (RBNs) used as models of gene regulatory networks [1–6]. An RBN is described by a triple (N, K_{in}, p) where N is a number of nodes, K_{in} is as number of directed connections going to each node and the parameter p will be described later. Each node i is in a time-dependent Boolean state $\sigma_i(t) \in \{0, 1\}$ and its state dynamics is governed by its Boolean function f_i. A Boolean function depends on states of all K_{in} nodes having a connection to the node i:

D. B. Heras and L. Bougé (Eds.): Euro-Par 2017 Workshops, LNCS 10659, pp. 403–414, 2018.
https://doi.org/10.1007/978-3-319-75178-8_33

$$\sigma_i(t+1) = f_i\left(\sigma_{i_1}(t), ..., \sigma_{i_{K_{in}}}(t)\right) \tag{1}$$

The Boolean function f_i of a given node is chosen randomly from a set of $2^{K_{in}}$ possible functions. As a result a space of possible networks is huge and such a simple approach may be used to model dynamics of complex structures [4]. Although Boolean functions are randomly chosen they do not have to be equally probable. Their distribution can be controlled for example [4,7] by the rule that the result of a Boolean function is 1 is equal to the parameter p

$$\forall i, P(f_i = 1) = p \tag{2}$$

If $p = 0.5$, then all functions are equally distributed. In the RBN dynamics it is assumed the nodes' states are updated simultaneously. The network state $\boldsymbol{\Sigma}(t) = \{\sigma_1, ..., \sigma_N\} \in \{0,1\}^N$ is deterministic, thus after a number of transient steps (T_0) an attractor of length T will be reached: $\boldsymbol{\Sigma}(T + t) = \boldsymbol{\Sigma}(t)$, where $t \geq T_0$. Depending on values of parameters (K_{in}, p) the RBN is said to be in the ordered, critical or chaotic regime. The relation between these parameters leading towards critical networks in the thermodynamic limit $(N \to \infty)$ is [6]

$$K_C(p) = \left(2p(1-p)\right)^{-1} \tag{3}$$

Networks with $Kin < K_C (Kin > K_C)$ are in the ordered (chaotic) regime.

The classical RBN concept has been modified to describe a more realistic dynamics of evolutionary systems. Evolutionary behavior can be introduced using adaptive RBNs (ARBNs) [8]. ARBNs tend to deactivate active nodes and activate inactive. This "steering" is done by adding and deleting links thus the dynamics is coevolutionary. Quick changes of nodes' states influence the network structure and network structure influences nodes' states. It has been shown [8] that ARBNs tend to achieve critical value of mean inconnectivity when the network size grows to infinity.

The structure of many real systems is hierarchical. Ideally the hierarchy would emerge by itself in a system. If this is not happening, one can build a hierarchical structure using one of the two approaches [9]:

1. A top-down approach. First, a whole network is created and then it is divided into subnetworks.
2. A bottom-up approach. First, the smallest unit (e.g. a node or a group of nodes) is created, and then similar units and links between them are added, which leads towards creating a unit of higher level. This step can be repeated which allows to create many levels of hierarchy. This approach will be used here.

Previously we have used a top-down approach [10] and created networks with two levels of hierarchy. Here, we introduce a new network type, which uses a bottom-up approach and creates a hierarchical system with unlimited number of hierarchy levels. In each step a new hierarchy level is created. Let H_i denote the ARBN structure of level i. In the step $(i + 1)$ the chosen number of similar structures are created. All subnetworks H_i form a new network H_{i+1}. Then the parameter p of each node is changed. In ARBNs the value of $p = 0.5$ has been used. If the probability p is modified, the Boolean functions become less random. However the number of active and inactive nodes are kept in the steady state, close to critical value. The change of p leads to the increase of mean connectivity (3). In this way we encourage nodes to create new links in a new level of hierarchy. Afterwards, the network evolves until the steady state according to the activity-dependent rewiring rule [8] is reached. The system evolution has one restriction: only the links between nodes from different structures H_i are allowed to be created or removed.

1.2   Related Work

The literature is replete with different modifications of the basic RBN model. Numerous studies (e.g. [8,10–13]) have been conducted to investigate ARBNs with a topology and/or Boolean functions which are subject to change according to the predefined rules. These rules are designed depending on the objectives of the network evolution. Bornholdt and Sneppen [11] use random modifications of connectivity matrix to model single species evolution. Activity-dependent rewiring rule (e.g. [8,12]) and model based on local information transfer [13] are used to move a system towards a critical state. An example of an ARBN representing collective behavior of economic agents can be found in [14]. Another strand of the literature considers particular network topologies especially those with non-trivial community structure. Authors of [15,16] investigate the effects of a modular topology on the properties of RBNs. Hierarchical ARBN as a system of several adaptive RBNs connected with permanent interlinks is proposed in [10]. Degree assortativity of RBNs is analyzed in connection with the stability [17] and the robustness of the signal-integration logic [18].

The majority of studies of RBNs (including those mentioned above) are focused on discovering the properties of networks rather than computational aspects of simulation. However, the efficiency of computational process is of crucial importance in this case due to the exponential growth of attractor lengths with an increase of network size, which hampers simulation of evolving RBNs larger than several hundreds of nodes. Regarding ARBNs, two main directions of speeding up the calculations can be distinguished: improving algorithms of attractor search and improving algorithms of network evolution. In addition, efficiency of different data types and data structures can be considered while implementing software for RBN simulation [19].

The problem of attractors search is usually tackled in two representations: to find a single attractor for a given initial state or to find all attractors of a given network. Along with sequential algorithms (e.g. [8,20] for single attractor search, [21–23] for multiple attractors search), parallel algorithms for both statements of the problem are presented in the literature. To perform multiple attractors search on a manycore architecture, authors of [24] propose to partition a Boolean network into several blocks consisting of the strongly connected components, which further can be processed in parallel. For single attractor search (which is used in ARBNs), GPGPU algorithm was proposed in [25] to update the states of vertices of RBN concurrently.

Design of efficient algorithms to simulate ARBNs is a challenging problem due to the data dependencies between consecutive epochs. For a non-modular ARBN, partially this problem can be solved by combining different ways to speed up calculations, namely, limiting the number of states updates, rewiring larger number of nodes per epoch and updating states of nodes in parallel. As it is shown in [25], this approach can increase the performance of simulation by several times. Unlike [25], the algorithms presented in this paper focus on Hierarchical ARBNs (HARBNs). HARBNs are formed by the bottom-up approach with simultaneously evolving independent submodules. To the best of our knowledge, up to now there have been no attempts to benefit from such a hierarchical organization of RBNs. In this paper, we propose several algorithms for parallel HARBN simulation, and compare their efficiency for different sizes of networks and configurations of hierarchy.

2   The Algorithms

2.1   Sequential Algorithm

The bottom-up approach of building a hierarchical structure comprises a consecutive merging of the subnetworks, starting from small disconnected units up through higher hierarchy levels to the resulting connected hierarchical RBN. According to the model, before the merger on each level can occur, the subnetworks have to reach the steady state in their independent evolution. During the evolution nodes lose and gain connections depending on their activity on the subnetworks' attractors.

Determining this activity is, essentially, the most computationally expensive part of the simulation. To find an attractor, one has to perform a number of state updates according to (1) to detect the repetition of the states: $\sigma_j(\lambda) = \sigma_j(\lambda + \mu) \, \forall j \in [1, N_{H_i}]$, where N_{H_i} is the number of nodes per subnetwork on a hierarchy level i. This repetition means that the network has reached its attractor, and λ and μ denote the lengths of a transient period and attractor respectively. At this point some nodes are rewired according to the ADRR, and the next epoch of evolution begins. The number of epochs required for the network to converge to the steady state grows with the size of the networks, along with the lengths of attractors and transients. Therefore, it is important for the efficient implementation to reduce the time that the attractor search takes.

The naive approach to find a network's attractor is to compare the current state of the network with all the previous ones. It implies $O((\lambda + \mu)^2)$ time and $O(\lambda + \mu)$ memory bounds. The complexity of the naive approach can be lowered by using hash-tables to store the previous states and perform a lookup operation to determine whether the current state has already been visited. In order to decrease both the complexity and memory requirements, one can use sequential heuristics of attractor search which are briefly described below.

Liu-Bassler's algorithm of attractor search was proposed in the paper introducing ARBNs [8]. The key idea of this approach is to set a number of checkpoints $T = (T_1, T_2, T_3, \ldots, T_k)$, and compare the states at each iteration to the states of the nodes at the latest checkpoint. Since the states of the attractor repeat infinitely, we can find attractors of maximum length $\mu_{\max} = T_k - T_{k-1}$ as long as the length of the transient period does not exceed $\lambda_{\max} = \sum_{i=1}^{k-2} T_i$. This way, although we may perform more state updates than in the naive algorithm, we make one comparison of states per iteration instead of $O(\lambda + \mu)$. The drawback of this approach is high dependency of its performance and $\mu_{\max}$ on the chosen values of the checkpoints: if the distance between the consecutive checkpoints is too large, it takes more time to be find short attractors than necessary. On the other hand, lowering the distance influences $\mu_{\max}$, which is especially undesirable when studying large networks.

Knuth's algorithm of attractor search [26], also known as "the tortoise and the hare algorithm". The algorithm uses two different instances of a Boolean network: for the first instance a single state update is performed per iteration, and two state updates are performed for the second instance. Using the observation that $\Sigma(\tau) = \Sigma(2 \cdot \tau)$ if and only if τ is a multiple of attractor length μ, an attractor will be found when states of the first and the second instances will be equal.

Summarizing, the sequential algorithm of HARBN simulation finds steady states of modules one after another, and during the evolution of each module states of nodes are also updated step by step. Sections 2.2 and 2.3 describe two parallel implementations of this algorithm: the one which processes distinct modules in different CPU threads, and the other which extends previous approach with simultaneous updates of nodes on GPU. We provide implementations for the Liu-Bassler's algorithm of attractor search, but both of them may also use Knuth's algorithm or any other heuristic for this purpose.

The notations used in the algorithms are explained in Table 1. If an index of a node is not given, a set of parameters for all the nodes in a module is meant (e.g. *StateSum*[m] is a set of variables keeping sums of states of distinct nodes of module m on the attractor).

2.2   OpenMP

As different modules of bottom-up HARBN evolve independently from each other until their steady state is reached, one can exploit the absence of data dependencies between subnetworks, and calculate them in parallel (Algorithm 1). Note that calculations of distinct epochs in different modules are independent, and there is no need to synchronize modules after the completion of each epoch.

While searching for an attractor, k checkpoints are examined at maximum (c denotes the index of the current checkpoint, and CS denotes the state of a module at c-th checkpoint). If the current state of the network is equal to the checkpoint state, the attractor is found. If the attractor is not found for the current interval, we set a new checkpoint. If the attractor was not found

Table 1. Description of parameters

Parameter	Description
N_M	The number of modules (subnetworks)
K_M	The number of nodes in each module
m	An index of a module, $m \in 0 \ldots N_M - 1$
i, j	Indices of nodes, $i, j \in 0 \ldots K_M - 1$
$AL[m][i]$	The adjacency list of i-th node of module m
$BF[m][i]$	The update function of i-th node of module m
$States[m][i]$	The initial state of i-th node of module m
$StateChanges[m][i]$	The number of state changes of i-th node of module m on the attractor
$StateSum[m][i]$	The sum of states of i-th node of module m on the attractor

after k checkpoints, we assume that the period of attractor is equal to $T_k - T_{k-1}$. The update of a node state is performed in a loop using the function *UpdateState* which takes as inputs the current state of a module, an index of a node, adjacency list and boolean functions of a module. *StateSum* and *StateChanges* are calculated to be used in activity-dependent rewiring rule.

2.3 Hybrid Approach

This section presents CPU-GPU algorithm for simulation of HARBN which incorporates both parallel calculation of different subnetworks and parallel update of nodes' states inside each subnetwork (Algorithm 2).

As in the OpenMP algorithm, evolution of distinct modules is performed independently. The difference with Algorithm 1 is in the implementation of the procedure of attractor search. While the main stages of Liu-Bassler's algorithm (e.g. examination of checkpoints) remain the same, states of nodes are updated simultaneously on GPU.

Liu-Bassler's algorithm of attractor search implies a synchronization after each state update of a subnetwork. GPU architecture offers two main ways to synchronize the threads of execution: block-level and kernel-level synchronization. The latter imposes a high performance penalty for kernel launches, which cancels out the speedup of the parallel implementation for small networks, where computational load per state update is low [25]. Block-level synchronization can be utilized in cases when the size of the simulated network does not exceed the maximum number of threads per block on the target platform.

As the epoch of evolution begins, the states of the nodes for each subnetwork are copied into the GPU device memory; the updated adjacency lists AL and boolean functions BF of the subnetworks are bound to a read-only texture memory to facilitate caching. Then, one block of K_M CUDA threads is launched

Data: $AL[m][i]$, $BF[m][i]$, $States[m][i]$ for $m \in 0 \ldots N_M - 1$, $i, j \in 0 \ldots K_M - 1$, $T = T_1, T_2, ..., T_k$, a number of epochs E
parallel for $m=0$ **to** $N_M - 1$:
 for $e = 1$ **to** E:
  $T_0 = 0$, $c = 0$, $CS = States[m]$, $found = false$;
  while $c < k$ **and** $!found$:
   fill $StateChanges[m]$, $StateSum[m]$ with zeros;
   for $t = T_c + 1$ **to** T_{c+1}:
    for $i = 0$ **to** $K_M - 1$:
     $prevS = S[i]$;
     $S[i] = \texttt{UpdateState}(S,i,AL[m],BF[m])$;
     $StateSum[m][i] \mathrel{+}= S[i]$;
     if $S[i] \neq prevS$:
      $StateChanges[m][i] \mathrel{+}= 1$;
    if $S = CS$:
     $\mu = t - T_c$;
     $found = true$; **break**;
   $c = c + 1$, $CS = S$;
  if $!found$:
   $\mu = T_k - T_{k-1}$
  Apply ADDR using μ, $StateSum[m]$, $StateChanges[m]$ ($AL[m]$ is updated);
  Assign new $BF[m]$, $States[m]$;

Algorithm 1. OpenMP algorithm for HARBN simulation (Liu-Bassler's method of attractor search), for a fixed hierarchy level

per each subnetwork to find the attractor. The state updates are performed in shared memory and the states are compared with the checkpoint state using either a block reduction or $\_\_\texttt{syncthreads\_all()}$ function depending on whether the latter is supported by the target platform (it is denoted as "**if all**" keyword in the algorithm description).

Some of the optimizations we applied are not shown in the Algorithm 2 for the sake of clarity. In particular, we store the previous and the current state of a node as one 32-bit integer in shared memory. In the $UpdateState$ function we read the previous state from the first word and write the new state to the second word of this integer at even iterations, and vice-versa at the odd ones. By doing this we can avoid the barrier before the actual state update and prevent the bank conflicts caused by misaligned access.

3 Experimental Study

3.1 Experimental Setup

The execution time of the algorithms described above highly depends on the lengths of attractors they aim to explore: the longer the attractor is, the more state updates are required to traverse through it and gather the statistics on

Data: $AL[m][i]$, $BF[m][i]$, $States[m][i]$ for $m \in 0 \ldots N_M - 1$, $i, j \in 0 \ldots K_M - 1$,
$T = T_1, T_2, \ldots, T_k$, a number of epochs E
parallel for $m=0$ **to** $N_M - 1$:
> **for** $e = 1$ **to** E:
>> copy $States[m]$ to device memory;
>> fill textures $AL_m = AL[m]$, $BF_m = BF[m]$;
>> **GPU parallel for** $i = 0$ **to** $K_M - 1$:
>>> **Thread local:** $T_0 = 0$, $c = 0$, $prevS_{m,i}$, $S_{m,i}$, $CS_{m,i}$,
>>> $StateChanges_{m,i} = 0$, $StateSum_{m,i} = 0$, μ, $found$;
>>> **Shared:** $SharedState_m[i]$;
>>> **Textures:** AL_m, BF_m;
>>> $found = false$;
>>> **while** $c < k$:
>>>> $StateChanges_{m,i} = 0$, $StateSum_{m,i} = 0$;
>>>> **for** $t = T_c + 1$ **to** T_{c+1}:
>>>>> $prevS_{m,i} = S_{m,i}$;
>>>>> $SharedState_m[i] = S_{m,i}$;
>>>>> **barrier**;
>>>>> $S_{m,i} = \mathtt{UpdateState}(SharedState_m, i, AL_m, BF_m)$;
>>>>> $StateSum_{m,i} \mathrel{+}= S_{m,i}$;
>>>>> **if** $S \neq prevS_i$:
>>>>>> $StateChanges_{m,i} \mathrel{+}= 1$;
>>>>>
>>>>> **barrier**;
>>>>> **if all** $S_{m,i} = CS_{m,i}$:
>>>>>> $\mu = t - T_c$;
>>>>>> $found = true$; **break**;
>>>>
>>>> $c = c + 1$, $CS = S$;
>>>
>>> **if** $!found$:
>>>> $\mu = T_k - T_{k-1}$;
>>>
>>> $StateChanges[m][i] = StateChanges_{m,i}$;
>>> $StateSum[m][i] = StateSum_{m,i}$;
>>
>> Apply ADDR using μ, $StateSum[m]$, $StateChanges[m]$ ($AL[m]$ is
>> updated);
>> Assign new $BF[m]$, $States[m]$;

Algorithm 2. Hybrid CPU-GPU algorithm for HARBN simulation (Liu-Bassler's method of attractor search), for a fixed hierarchy level

nodes' activity. In addition to that, after each epoch the network structure gets altered, and after a predefined number of epochs some networks are merged together according to the HARBN model. The diversity of the resulting network structures makes it impossible to predict the lengths of attractors, and, consequently, to effectively compare the execution times of the algorithms based on different realizations of the HARBN evolution process.

In order to obtain the quantitative performance characteristics, we measured the speedup per one state update. This measure, unlike total simulation time, does not depend on the attractor lengths, but takes into account the size and the structure of the simulated networks.

The experiments were conducted on the machines with Intel Core i7-3930K CPU (supports up to 12 parallel threads) and NVidia GeForce GT 640 GPU. In order to factor in the influence of the network structure, we run 100 epochs of evolution for different hierarchies. Then the execution time of each epoch was divided by the attractor length to estimate the time required for the state update. Only one hierarchy level was considered in each experiment.

3.2   Performance Results

In order to measure the speedup obtained by parallelizing the sequential algorithm with OpenMP and hybrid algorithm, we performed the simulations for networks with $N_M \in \{2, 4, 8, 16, 32, 64\}$ independent submodules and total number of nodes $N \in \{128, 512, 1024\}$.

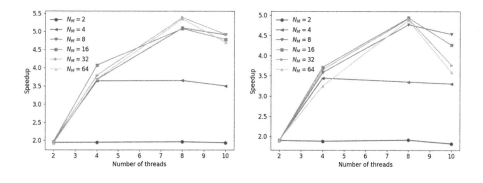

(a) Hierarchical system with 512 nodes   (b) Hierarchical system with 128 nodes

Fig. 1. The speedup of the OpenMP-based parallel algorithm

Figure 1 shows the speedup for different number of threads. For the number of modules less than a number of threads used (it can be clearly seen for $N_M = 2$ and $N_M = 4$) addition of supplementary threads has no positive effect on the performance. For the other cases ($N_M = 8; 16; 32; 64$), the best speedup (near 5) is achieved for 8 threads.

According to above results, using more than 8 threads to simulate hierarchical systems smaller than at least 512 nodes leads to a suboptimal performance. This is due to the little amount of computations that each thread performs, compared to the overhead for synchronization. It can be clearly seen in Fig. 1b, where the performance degradation is larger for hierarchical systems divided into more modules. Apart from that, the speedup is generally higher for networks with more independent submodules due to the large degree of parallelism.

Figure 2 demonstrates the results of comparison of hybrid and OpenMP algorithms for the networks with 512 (Fig. 2a) and 1024 (Fig. 2b) nodes with varying number of modules. In this figures we show the speedup for hybrid algorithm

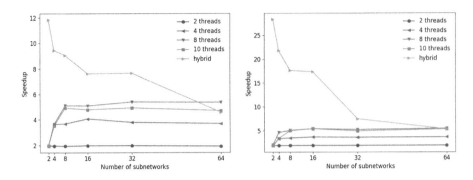

(a) Hierarchical system with 512 nodes   (b) Hierarchical system with 1024 nodes

Fig. 2. Performance comparison of hybrid and OpenMP algorithms

and for different number of threads for OpenMP algorithm (namely 2, 4, 8 and 10). These algorithms demonstrate opposite patterns of parallel performance with the growth of a number of subnetworks. The speedup for hybrid algorithm is the highest for 2 subnetworks (it outperforms OpenMP from 6 to 14 times in this case), and then monotonically decrease till it becomes lower than for OpenMP version. This is explained by the fact that the larger the number of nodes in each module the better effect is from updating their states in parallel: the proposed hybrid algorithm increased the average number of state updates per second from 37.07 (in the sequential version) to 1049.80 for a network consisting of 1024 nodes and 2 subnetworks. However, for a small number of nodes in each subnetwork (e.g. for $K_M = 4$ and $N_M = 64$ in Fig. 2a), the speedup from GPGPU calculations is insufficient. Finally, Fig. 2 shows that the speedup for OpenMP version saturates above a certain number of subnetworks (this number is related to the number of threads available).

4   Conclusion

Parallel simulation of adaptive random boolean networks is usually hampered by the linkages between consecutive epochs of their evolution (as the initial topology of RBN for a given epoch depends on a previous epoch). For the general case of synchronous evolving RBNs, one can exploit the fact that states of nodes are updated simultaneously during attractor search, thus providing the opportunity to use GPGPU capabilities.

In this study, we consider a particular type of ARBN with hierarchical modular structure which is created using a bottom-up approach. The number of hierarchy levels is built up step by step, and inside each fixed level the number of independent subnetworks (modules) are considered. Due to the absence of data dependencies between modules, it becomes possible to combine a parallel updating of nodes states with a parallel evolution of distinct modules.

The experimental part of the study demonstrates the comparison of OpenMP and hybrid CPU-GPU algorithms for varying sizes and hierarchies of networks. The results show that: (i) the more number of nodes in a module the better is the performance of the hybrid algorithm (up to 28x speedup for 1024 nodes), (ii) OpenMP algorithm may perform better when modules contain small number of nodes (because there is almost no effect of utilizing GPU in this case).

Acknowledgements. This research is financially supported by The Russian Science Foundation, Agreement 17-71-30029 with co-financing of Bank Saint Petersburg.

References

1. Kauffman, S.A.: Metabolic stability and epigenesis in randomly constructed genetic nets. J. Theor. Biol. **22**(3), 437–467 (1969)
2. Kauffman, S.A.: The ensemble approach to understand genetic regulatory networks. Physica A **340**(4), 733–740 (2004)
3. Gershenson, C.: Introduction to random Boolean networks. In: Workshop and Tutorial Proceedings, Ninth International Conference on the Simulation and Synthesis of Living Systems (ALife IX), pp. 160–173 (2004)
4. Drossel, B.: Random Boolean networks. Rev. Nonlinear Dyn. Complex. **1**, 69–110 (2008)
5. Cheng, D., Qi, H., Li, Z.: Random Boolean networks. In: Cheng, D., Qi, H., Li, Z. (eds.) Analysis and Control of Boolean Networks: A Semi-tensor Product Approach. Communications and Control Engineering, pp. 431–450. Springer, London (2011). https://doi.org/10.1007/978-0-85729-097-7_19
6. Aldana, M., Coppersmith, S., Kadanoff, L.P.: Boolean dynamics with random couplings. In: Kaplan, E., Marsden, J.E., Sreenivasan, K.R. (eds.) Perspectives and Problems in Nolinear Science, pp. 23–89. Springer, New York (2003). https://doi.org/10.1007/978-0-387-21789-5_2
7. Derrida, B., Pomeau, Y.: Random networks of automata: a simple annealed approximation. Europhys. Lett. (EPL) **1**(2), 45–49 (1986)
8. Liu, M., Bassler, K.E.: Emergent criticality from coevolution in random Boolean networks. Phys. Rev. E **74**(4), 041910 (2006)
9. Lane, D.: Hierarchy, complexity, society. In: Pumain, D. (ed.) Hierarchy in Natural and Social Sciences. Methodos Series, vol. 3, pp. 81–119. Springer, Dordrecht (2006). https://doi.org/10.1007/1-4020-4127-6_5
10. Górski, P.J., Czaplicka, A., Hołyst, J.A.: Coevolution of information processing and topology in hierarchical adaptive random boolean networks. Eur. Phys. J. B **89**(2), 1–9 (2016)
11. Bornholdt, S., Sneppen, K.: Neutral mutations and punctuated equilibrium in evolving genetic networks. Phys. Rev. Lett. **81**(1), 236 (1998)
12. Rohlf, T., Bornholdt, S.: Self-organized criticality and adaptation in discrete dynamical networks. In: Gross, T., Sayama, H. (eds.) Adaptive Networks. Understanding Complex Systems, pp. 73–106. Springer, Heidelberg (2009). https://doi.org/10.1007/978-3-642-01284-6_5
13. Haruna, T., Tanaka, S.: On the relationship between local rewiring rules and stationary out-degree distributions in adaptive random Boolean network models. In: ALIFE 14: The Fourteenth Conference on the Synthesis and Simulation of Living Systems, vol. 14, pp. 420–426. Citeseer (2014)

14. Paczuski, M., Bassler, K.E., Corral, Á.: Self-organized networks of competing Boolean agents. Phys. Rev. Lett. **84**(14), 3185 (2000)
15. Bastolla, U., Parisi, G.: The modular structure of Kauffman networks. Phys. D: Nonlinear Phenom. **115**(3–4), 219–233 (1998)
16. Poblanno-Balp, R., Gershenson, C.: Modular random Boolean networks. Artif. Life **17**(4), 331–351 (2011)
17. Pomerance, A., Ott, E., Girvan, M., Losert, W.: The effect of network topology on the stability of discrete state models of genetic control. Proc. Nat. Acad. Sci. **106**(20), 8209–8214 (2009)
18. Pechenick, D.A., Payne, J.L., Moore, J.H.: The influence of assortativity on the robustness of signal-integration logic in gene regulatory networks. J. Theor. Biol. **296**, 21–32 (2012)
19. Hawick, K.A., James, H.A., Scogings, C.J.: Simulating large random Boolean networks (2007)
20. Bhattacharjya, A., Liang, S.: Power-law distributions in some random Boolean networks. Phys. Rev. Lett. **77**(8), 1644 (1996)
21. Garg, A., Xenarios, I., Mendoza, L., DeMicheli, G.: An efficient method for dynamic analysis of gene regulatory networks and *in silico* gene perturbation experiments. In: Speed, T., Huang, H. (eds.) RECOMB 2007. LNCS, vol. 4453, pp. 62–76. Springer, Heidelberg (2007). https://doi.org/10.1007/978-3-540-71681-5_5
22. Zhao, Y., Kim, J., Filippone, M.: Aggregation algorithm towards large-scale Boolean network analysis. IEEE Trans. Autom. Control **58**(8), 1976–1985 (2013)
23. Zheng, D., Yang, G., Li, X., Wang, Z., Liu, F., He, L.: An efficient algorithm for computing attractors of synchronous and asynchronous Boolean networks. PLoS one **8**(4), e60593 (2013)
24. Guo, W., Yang, G., Wei, W., He, L., Sun, M.: A parallel attractor finding algorithm based on Boolean satisfiability for genetic regulatory networks. PLoS one **9**(4), e94258 (2014)
25. Kuvshinov, K., Bochenina, K., Górski, P.J., Hołyst, J.A.: Parallel simulation of adaptive random Boolean networks. Procedia Comput. Sci. **101**, 35–44 (2016)
26. Knuth, D.E.: The Art of Computer Programming: Seminumerical Methods, vol. 2. Addison-wesley, Boston (1981)

Benchmarking Heterogeneous Cloud Functions

Maciej Malawski$^{(\boxtimes)}$ ⬤, Kamil Figiela ⬤, Adam Gajek, and Adam Zima

Department of Computer Science, AGH University of Science and Technology,
Krakow, Poland
{malawski,kfigiela}@agh.edu.pl

Abstract. Cloud Functions, often called Function-as-a-Service (FaaS),
pioneered by AWS Lambda, are an increasingly popular method of running distributed applications. As in other cloud offerings, cloud functions are heterogeneous, due to different underlying hardware, runtime
systems, as well as resource management and billing models. In this
paper, we focus on performance evaluation of cloud functions, taking
into account heterogeneity aspects. We developed a cloud function benchmarking framework, consisting of one suite based on Serverless Framework, and one based on HyperFlow. We deployed the CPU-intensive
benchmarks: Mersenne Twister and Linpack, and evaluated all the major
cloud function providers: AWS Lambda, Azure Functions, Google Cloud
Functions and IBM OpenWhisk. We make our results available online
and continuously updated. We report on the initial results of the performance evaluation and we discuss the discovered insights on the resource
allocation policies.

Keywords: Cloud computing · FaaS · Cloud functions
Performance evaluation

1 Introduction

Cloud Functions, pioneered by AWS Lambda, are becoming an increasingly popular method of running distributed applications. They form a new paradigm,
often called Function-as-a-Service (FaaS) or serverless computing. Cloud functions allow the developers to deploy their code in the form of a function to the
cloud provider, and the infrastructure is responsible for the execution, resource
provisioning and automatic scaling of the runtime environment. Resource usage
is usually metered with millisecond accuracy and the billing is per every 100 ms
of CPU time used. Cloud functions are typically executed in a Node.js environment, but they also allow running custom binary code, which gives an opportunity for using them not only for Web or event-driven applications, but also for
some compute-intensive tasks, as presented in our earlier work [5].

As in other cloud offerings, cloud functions are heterogeneous in nature, due
to various underlying hardware, different underlying runtime systems, as well as
resource management and billing models. For example, most providers use Linux

D. B. Heras and L. Bougé (Eds.): Euro-Par 2017 Workshops, LNCS 10659, pp. 415–426, 2018.
https://doi.org/10.1007/978-3-319-75178-8_34

as a hosting OS, but Azure functions run on Windows. This heterogeneity is in principle hidden from the developer by using the common Node.js environment, which is platform-independent, but again various providers have different versions of Node (as of May 2017: for AWS Lambda – Node 6.10, for Google Cloud Functions – Node 6.9.1, for IBM Bluemix – Node 6.9.1, for Azure – 6.5.0.). Moreover, even though there is a common "function" abstraction for all the providers, there is no single standard API.

In this paper, we focus on performance evaluation of cloud functions and we show how we faced various heterogeneity challenges. We have developed a framework for performance evaluation of cloud functions and applied it to all the major cloud function providers: AWS Lambda, Azure Functions, Google Cloud Functions (GCF) and IBM OpenWhisk. Moreover, we used our existing scientific workflow engine HyperFlow [1] which has been recently extended to support cloud functions [5] to run parallel workflow benchmarks. We report on the initial results of the performance evaluation and we discuss the discovered insights on the resource allocation policies.

The paper is organized as follows. Section 2 discusses the related work on cloud benchmarking. In Sect. 3, we outline our framework, while in Sect. 4, we give the details of the experiment setup. Section 5 presents and discusses the results, while Sect. 6 gives a summary and outlines the future work.

2   Related Work

Cloud performance evaluation, including heterogeneous infrastructures has been subject of previous research. An excellent example is in [2], where multiple clouds are compared from the perspective of many-task computing applications. Several hypotheses regarding performance of public clouds are discussed in a comprehensive study presented in [3]. More recent studies focus e.g. on burstable [4] instances, which are cheaper than regular instances but have varying performance and reliability characteristics. Performance of alternative cloud solutions such as Platform-as-a-Service (PaaS) has also been analyzed. E.g. [6,8] focused on Google App Engine from the perspective of CPU-intensive scientific applications.

A detailed performance and cost comparison of traditional clouds with microservices and the AWS Lambda serverless architecture is presented in [10], using an enterprise application. Similarly, in [11] the authors discuss the advantages of using cloud services and AWS Lambda for systems that require higher resilience. An interesting discussion of serverless paradigm is given in [7], where the case studies are blogging and media management application. An example of price and performance of cloud functions is provided also in [9], describing Snafu, a new implementation of FaaS model, which can be deployed in a Docker cluster on AWS. Its performance and cost is compared with AWS Lambda using a recursive Fibonacci cloud function benchmark.

Up to our knowledge, heterogeneous cloud functions have not been comprehensively studied yet, which motivates this research.

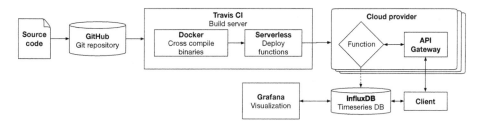

Fig. 1. Architecure of the cloud functions benchmarking framework based on Serverless Framework

3   Benchmarking Framework for Cloud Functions

For benchmarking cloud function providers, we used two frameworks. The first one is our new suite, designed specifically for this research, based on Serverless Framework. The second one uses our HyperFlow workflow engine [1,5].

3.1   Suite Based on Serverless Framework

The objective of this benchmarking suite is to execute and gather performance results of heterogeneous cloud function benchmarks over a long period of time. The suite has to run as a permanent service and execute selected benchmarks periodically. The results are then stored and available for examination. Our goal was to automate functions deployment as much as possible to improve results reproducibility. The architecture of the suite is shown in Fig. 1.

In order to deploy our benchmark suite we have used the Serverless Framework[1]. It provides a uniform way of setting up cloud functions deployment and supports, at the time of writing, AWS Lambda, IBM OpenWhisk and Azure Functions natively and Google Cloud Functions through an official plugin. In order to streamline our data taking process, we automated code deployment even further by setting up project on Travis continuous integration (CI), so that the code is automatically deployed on each cloud whenever we push new code to the Git repository. This also simplified security credentials management, since we do not need to distribute deployment credentials for each provider.

To address the heterogeneity of runtime environments underlying cloud functions, we have created dedicated wrappers for native binary that was executed by the function. We have used Docker to build binaries compatible with target environments. For Linux based environments, we use amazonlinux image to build a static binary that is compatible with AWS Lambda, Google Cloud Functions and IBM OpenWhisk. Azure Functions run in a Windows-based environment, thus it requires a separate binary. We used Dockcross[2] project that provides a suite of Docker images with cross-compilers, which includes a Windows target.

---

[1] https://serverless.com.
[2] https://github.com/dockcross/dockcross.

The Serverless Framework is able to deploy functions with all the necessary companion services (e.g. HTTP endpoint). However, we still had to adapt our code slightly for each provider, since the required API is different. For instance, AWS Lambda requires a callback when a function result is ready, while IBM OpenWhisk requires to return a Promise for asynchronous functions. The cloud platforms also differ in how $PATH and current working directory are handled.

The benchmarks results are sent to the InfluxDB time series database. We have also setup Grafana for convenient access to benchmark results. We implemented our suite in Elixir and Node.js. The source code is available on GitHub[3].

3.2   Suite Based on HyperFlow

For running parallel benchmarking experiments we adapted HyperFlow [1] workflow engine. HyperFlow was earlier integrated with GCF [5], and for this work it was extended to support AWS Lambda. HyperFlow is a lightweight workflow engine based on Node.js and it can orchestrate complex large-scale scientific workflows, including directed acyclic graphs (DAG).

For the purpose of running the benchmarks, we used a set of pre-generated DAGs of the fork-join pattern: the first task is a fork task which does not perform any job, it is followed by N identical parallel children of benchmark tasks running the actual computation, which in turn are followed by a single join task which plays the role of a final synchronization barrier. Such graphs are typical for scientific workflows, which often include such parallel stages (bag of tasks), and moreover are convenient for execution of multiple benchmark runs in parallel.

In the case of HyperFlow, the cloud function running on the provider side is a JavaScript wrapper (HyperFlow executor), which runs the actual benchmark, measures the time and sends the results to the cloud storage, such as S3 or Cloud Storage, depending on the cloud provider.

4   Experiment Setup

We configured our frameworks with two types of CPU-intensive benchmarks, one focused on integer and the other on floating-point performance.

4.1   Configuration of the Serverless Benchmarking Suite

In this experiment we used a random number generator, as an example of an integer-based CPU-intensive benchmark. Such generators are key in many scientific appliations, such as Monte Carlo methods, which are good potential candidates for running as cloud functions.

Specifically, the cloud function is a JavaScript wrapper around the binary benchmark, which is a program written in C. We used a popular Mersenne Twister (MT19937) random number generator algorithm. The benchmark runs

---

[3] https://github.com/kfigiela/cloud-functions.

approximately 16.7 milion iterations of the algorithm using a fixed seed number during each run and provides reproducible load.

We measure the execution time t_b of the binary benchmark from within the JavaScript wrapper that is running on serverless infrastructure, and the total request processing time t_r on the client side. We decided to deploy our client outside the clouds that were subject to examination. The client was deployed on a bare-metal ARM machine hosted in Scaleway cloud in Paris datacenter. The benchmark was executed for each provider every 5 min. We took multiple measurements for different memory sizes available: for AWS Lambda – 128, 256, 512, 1024, 1536 MB, for Google Cloud Functions – 128, 256, 512, 1024, 2048 MB, for IBM OpenWhisk – 128, 256, 512 MB. Azure Functions do not provide a choice on function size and the memory is allocated dynamically. The measurements: binary execution time t_b and request processing time t_r were sent to InfluxDB by the client. Since the API Gateway used in conjunction with AWS Lambda restricts request processing time to 30 s, we were not able to measure t_r for 128 MB Lambdas. Although the requests timeout on the API Gateway, the function completes execution. In this case, the function reports t_b time directly to InfluxDB.

On AWS Lambda functions were deployed in eu-west-1 region, on GCF functions were deployed in us-central1 region, on IBM OpenWhisk functions were deployed in US South region and on Azure function was deployed in US West region. Such setup results from the fact that not all of the providers offer cloud functions in all their regions yet.

We started collecting data on April 18, 2017, and the data used in this paper include the values collected till May 11, 2017.

4.2   Configuration of HyperFlow Suite

As a benchmark we used the HPL Linpack[4], which is probably the most popular CPU-intensive benchmark focusing on the floating point performance. It solves a dense linear system of equations in double precision and returns the results in GFlops. To deploy the Linpack on multiple cloud functions, we used the binary distribution from Intel MKL[5], version mklb_p_2017.3, which has binaries for Linux and Windows.

As benchmark workflows we generated a set of fork-join DAGs, with parallelism $N = [10, 20, ..., 100]$, thus it allowed us to run up to 100 Linpack tasks in parallel. Please note that in this setup all the Linpack benchmarks run independently, since cloud functions cannot communicate with each other, so this configuration differs from the typical Linpack runs in HPC centers which use MPI. Our goal is to measure the performance of individual cloud functions and the potential overheads interference between parallel executions.

The Linpack was configured to run using the problem size (number of equations) of $s \in \{1000, 1500, 2000, 3000, 4000, 5000, 6000, 8000, 10000, 12000, 15000\}$.

---

[4] http://www.netlib.org/benchmark/hpl/.
[5] https://software.intel.com/en-us/articles/intel-mkl-benchmarks-suite.

Not all of these sizes are possible to run on functions with smaller memory, e.g.
$4000 \times 4000 \times 8\,\text{Bytes} = 128\,\text{MB}$, so the benchmark stops when it cannot allocate
enough memory, reporting the best performance p_f achieved (in GFlops).

We run the Linpack workflows for each N on all the possible memory sizes
available on GCF (128, 256, 512, 1024, 2048 MB) and on AWS Lambda on sizes
from 128 to 1536 with increments of 64 MB.

On AWS Lambda functions were deployed in eu-west-1 region, on GCF functions were deployed in us-central1 region.

5   Performance Evaluation Results

Our benchmarks from the serverless suite run permanently and the original unfil-
tered data as well as current values are available publicly on our website[6]. They
include also selected summary statistics and basic histograms. The data can be
exported in CSV format, and we included the data in the GitHub repository.

Selected results are presented in the following Subsects. 5.1 and 5.2, while
the results of the Linpack runs using HyperFlow are given in Sect. 5.3.

5.1   Integer Performance Evaluation

The results of the integer benchmarks using Mersenne Twister random generator
are presented in Fig. 2. They are shown as histograms, grouped by providers and
function size. They give us interesting observations about the resource allocation
policies of cloud providers.

Firstly, the performance of AWS Lambda is fairly consistent, and agrees with
the documentation which states that the CPU allocation is proportional to the
function size (memory). On the other hand, Google cloud functions execution
time have multimodal distributions with higher dispersion. For example, for the
256 MB function, the execution time is most often around 27 s, but there is
another peak around 20 s, coinciding with the faster 512 MB function. Similarly,
the distribution for the slowest 128 MB function has multiple peaks, overlapping
with faster functions and reaching even the performance of the fastest 2048 MB
function. This suggests that GCF does not enforce strictly the performance limits, and opportunistically invokes smaller functions using the faster resources.

Regarding IBM Bluemix, the performance does not depend on the function
size, and the distribution is quite narrow, as in the case of AWS. On the other
hand, the performance of Azure has much wider distribution, and the average
execution times are relatively slower. This can be attributed to different hardware, but also to the underlying operating system (Windows) and virtualization.

5.2   Overheads Evaluation

By measuring the binary execution time t_b inside the functions as well as
the request processing time t_r (as seen from the client), we can also obtain

---

[6] http://cloud-functions.icsr.agh.edu.pl.

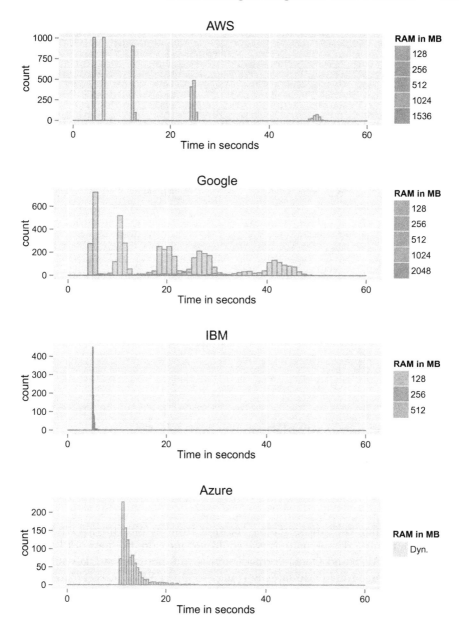

Fig. 2. Histograms of integer-based MT random number generator benchmark execution time vs. cloud function size. In the case of Azure memory is allocated dynamically. (Color figure online)

a rough estimate on total overhead $t_o = t_r - t_b$. The overhead includes: network latency, platform routing and scheduling overheads. Endpoints exposed by cloud providers are secured with HTTPS protocol. We warmed up the connection

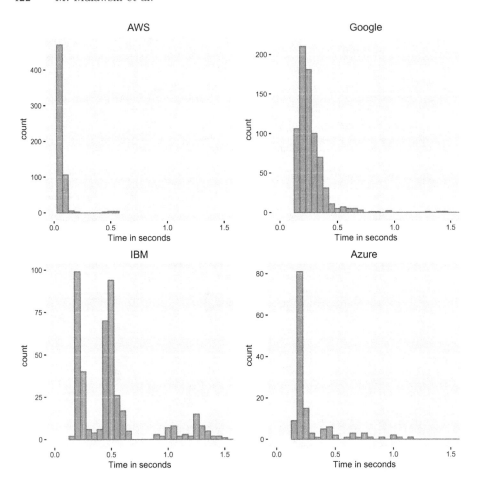

Fig. 3. Distribution of t_o overheads for cloud function providers.

before performing each measurement, so that we were able to exclude the TLS handshake from t_r. Unfortunately, we could not measure the network latency to the clouds as AWS and Google provide access to functions via CDN infrastructure. The average round trip latency (ping) to OpenWhisk was 117 ms and 155 ms to Azure (Fig. 3).

Histograms of t_o are presented in Fig. 2. One may observe that overhead is stable with a few outliers. However, for Bluemix one may see that there are two peaks in the distribution.

Furthermore, we measured t_r for requests targeting an invalid endpoint. This gives a hint on network latency under the assumption that invalid requests are terminated in an efficient way. The average results were consistent with typical network latency: for AWS Lambda – 43 ms, for Google Cloud Functions – 150 ms, for IBM Bluemix – 130 ms. However, for Azure the latency measured that way was 439 ms which is significantly larger than the network ping time.

5.3   Floating-Point Performance Evaluation

Results of the Linpack runs are shown in Fig. 4, as a scatter-plots where density of circles represents the number of data points. AWS data consists of over 12,000 points, and GCF of over 2,600 points. We show also histograms of subsets of these data.

In the case of AWS, we observe that the maximum performance grows linearly with the function size. There is, however, a significant portion of tasks that achieved lower performance. With the growing memory, we can see that the execution times form two clusters, one growing linearly over 30 GFlops, and one saturating around 20 GFlops.

In the case of GCF, we observe that the performance of tasks is clustered differently. The performance of one group of tasks grows linearly with memory. On the other hand, there is a large group of tasks, which achieve the top performance

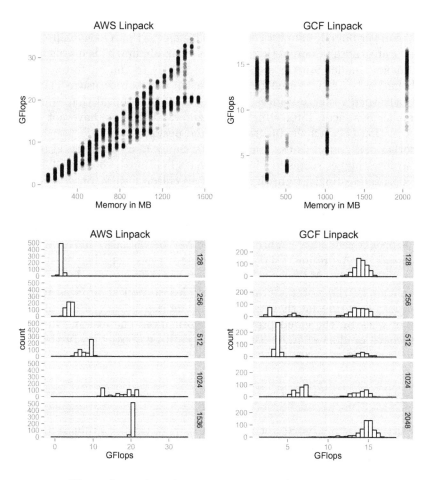

Fig. 4. Linpack performance versus cloud function size.

of 15 GFlops regardless of the function size. Interestingly, we observed that the smallest functions of 128 MB always achieved the best performance of about 14 GFlops.

To illustrate the multimodal nature of performance distribution curves of GCF, we show the results as histograms in Fig. 4 for selected memory siezes. As in the case of integer-based performance tests, the AWS Lambda show much more consistent results, while for GCF the performance points are clustered.

5.4 Discussion of Results

The most interesting observation is regarding the scheduling policies of cloud providers, as observed in both MT and Linpack experiments. Both GCF and AWS claim that the CPU share for cloud functions is proportional to the memory allocated. In the case of AWS we observe a fairly linear performance growth with the memory size, both for the lower bound and the upper bound of the plot in Fig. 4. In the case of GCF, we observe that the lower bound grows linearly, while the upper bound is almost constant. This means that Google infrastructure often allocates more resources than the required minimum. This means that their policy allows smaller functions (in terms of RAM) to run on faster resources. This behavior is likely caused by optimization of resource usage via reuse of already spawned faster instances, which is more economical that spinning up new smaller instances. Interestingly, for Azure and IBM we have not observed any correlation between the function size and performance.

Another observation is the relative performance of cloud function providers. AWS achieves higher scores in Linpack (over 30 GFlops) whereas GCF tops at 17 GFlops. Interestingly, from the Linpack execution logs we observed that the CPU frequency at AWS is 3.2 GHz, which suggests Xeon E5-2670 (Ivy Bridge) family of processors, while at GCF it is 2.1 GHz which means Intel Xeon E5 v4 (Broadwell). Such difference in hardware definitely influences the performance. These Linpack results are confirmed by the MT benchmark. Since we have not run Linpack on Azure and IBM yet, we cannot report on their floating point performance, but the MT results also suggest the differences in hardware.

Although we did not perform such detailed statistical tests as in [3], our observations confirm that there is not significant dependency of the time of day or day of week on the cloud providers performance. The existing fluctuations tend to have random characteristics, but it will be subject to further studies once we collect more data.

6 Summary and Future Work

In this paper, we presented our approach to performance evaluation of cloud functions. We described our performance evaluation framework, consisting of two suites, one using the Serverless Framework, and the one based on Hyper-Flow. We gave the technical details on how we address the heterogeneity of the environment, and we described our automated data taking pipeline. We made our experimental primary data available publicly to the community and we set up the data taking as a continuous process.

The presented results of evaluation using Mersenne Twister and Linpack benchmarks show the heterogeneity of cloud function providers, and the relation between the cloud function size and performance. We also revealed the interesting observations on how Amazon and Google differently interpret the resource allocation policies. These observations can be summarized that AWS Lambda functions execution performance is proportional to the memory allocated, but sometimes sightly slower, while for Google Cloud Functions the performance is proportional to the memory allocated, but often much faster.

Since this paper presents the early results of this endeavor, there is much room for future work. It includes the integration of HyperFlow with our serverless benchmarking suite, measurement of influence of parallelism, delays and warm-up times on the performance, possible analysis of trends as we continue to gather more data, as well as cost-efficiency analysis and implications for resource management.

Acknowledgements. This work was supported by the National Science Centre, Poland, grant 2016/21/B/ST6/01497.

References

1. Balis, B.: HyperFlow: a model of computation, programming approach and enactment engine for complex distributed workflows. Future Gener. Comput. Syst. **55**, 147–162 (2016)
2. Iosup, A., Ostermann, S., Yigitbasi, N., Prodan, R., Fahringer, T., Epema, D.: Performance analysis of cloud computing services for many-tasks scientific computing. IEEE Trans. Parallel Distrib. Syst. **22**(6), 931–945 (2011)
3. Leitner, P., Cito, J.: Patterns in the chaos - a study of performance variation and predictability in public IaaS clouds. ACM Trans. Internet Techn. **16**(3), 15:1–15:23 (2016). https://doi.org/10.1145/2885497
4. Leitner, P., Scheuner, J.: Bursting with possibilities - an empirical study of credit-based bursting cloud instance types. In: 8th IEEE/ACM International Conference on Utility and Cloud Computing, UCC 2015, Limassol, Cyprus, 7–10 December 2015, pp. 227–236 (2015). http://doi.ieeecomputersociety.org/10.1109/UCC.2015.39
5. Malawski, M.: Towards serverless execution of scientific workflows - HyperFlow case study. In: WORKS 2016 Workshop, Workflows in Support of Large-Scale Science, in Conjunction with SC 2016 Conference. CEUR-WS.org, Salt Lake City, November 2016
6. Malawski, M., Kuzniar, M., Wojcik, P., Bubak, M.: How to use Google app engine for free computing. IEEE Internet Comput. **17**(1), 50–59 (2013)
7. McGrath, M.G., Short, J., Ennis, S., Judson, B., Brenner, P.R.: Cloud event programming paradigms: applications and analysis. In: 9th IEEE International Conference on Cloud Computing, CLOUD 2016, San Francisco, CA, USA, 27 June – 2 July 2016, pp. 400–406. IEEE Computer Society (2016)
8. Prodan, R., Sperk, M., Ostermann, S.: Evaluating high-performance computing on Google app engine. IEEE Softw. **29**(2), 52–58 (2012)

9. Spillner, J.: Snafu: Function-as-a-Service (FaaS) runtime design and implementation. CoRR abs/1703.07562 (2017). http://arxiv.org/abs/1703.07562

10. Villamizar, M., Garces, O., Ochoa, L., Castro, H., Salamanca, L., Verano, M., Casallas, R., Gil, S., Valencia, C., Zambrano, A., Lang, M.: Infrastructure cost comparison of running web applications in the cloud using AWS lambda and monolithic and microservice architectures. In: 2016 16th IEEE/ACM International Symposium on Cluster, Cloud and Grid Computing (CCGrid), pp. 179–182, May 2016

11. Wagner, B., Sood, A.: Economics of resilient cloud services. In: 1st IEEE International Workshop on Cyber Resilience Economics, August 2016. http://arxiv.org/abs/1607.08508

Impact of Compiler Phase Ordering When Targeting GPUs

Ricardo Nobre[1,2](✉) , Luís Reis[1,2] , and João M. P. Cardoso[1,2]

[1] Faculty of Engineering of the University of Porto, Porto, Portugal
{ricardo.nobre,luis.cubal}@fe.up.pt, jmpc@acm.org
[2] INESC TEC, Porto, Portugal

Abstract. Research in compiler pass phase ordering (i.e., selection of compiler analysis/transformation passes and their order of execution) has been mostly performed in the context of CPUs and, in a small number of cases, FPGAs. In this paper we present experiments regarding compiler pass phase ordering specialization of OpenCL kernels targeting NVIDIA GPUs using Clang/LLVM 3.9 and the libclc OpenCL library. More specifically, we analyze the impact of using specialized compiler phase orders on the performance of 15 PolyBench/GPU OpenCL benchmarks. In addition, we analyze the final NVIDIA PTX assembly code generated by the different compilation flows in order to identify the main reasons for the cases with significant performance improvements. Using specialized compiler phase orders, we were able to achieve performance improvements over the CUDA version and OpenCL compiled with the NVIDIA driver. Compared to CUDA, we were able to achieve geometric mean improvements of 1.54× (up to 5.48×). Compared to the OpenCL driver version, we were able to achieve geometric mean improvements of 1.65× (up to 5.70×).

Keywords: GPU · Phase ordering · Optimization

1 Introduction

High Performance Computing (HPC) can offer Petaflops of performance by relying on increasingly more heterogeneous systems, such as the combination of Central Processing Units (CPUs) with accelerators in the form of Graphics Processing Units (GPUs) programmed with languages such as OpenCL [1] or CUDA [2]. Heterogeneous systems are widespread as a way to achieve energy efficiency and/or performance levels that are not achievable by a single device/architecture (e.g., matrix multiplication is much faster on GPUs than on CPUs for the same power/energy budget [3]). These accelerators offer a large number of specialized cores that the CPUs can use to offload computation that exhibits data-parallelism and often other types of parallelism as well (e.g., task-level parallelism). This adds an extra layer of complexity if one wants to target these systems efficiently, which in the case of HPC systems such as supercomputers is of

© Springer International Publishing AG, part of Springer Nature 2018
D. B. Heras and L. Bougé (Eds.): Euro-Par 2017 Workshops, LNCS 10659, pp. 427–438, 2018.
https://doi.org/10.1007/978-3-319-75178-8_35

utmost importance. An inefficient use of the hardware is amplified by the magnitude of such systems (hundreds/thousands of CPU cores and accelerators), with increasing utilization/power bill and/or cooling challenges as a consequence. In order to efficiently utilize the hardware resources, programmers need advanced compilers and they also need high levels of expertise. The programmer(s) and the compiler(s) have to be able to target different computing devices (CPU, GPU, and/or FPGA) and/or architectures (e.g., system with ARM or x86 CPUs) in a manner that achieves suitable results for certain metrics, such as execution time and energy efficiency.

Compiler users tend to rely on the standard compiler optimization levels, typically represented by flags such as GCC's -O2 or -O3. These flags represent fixed sequences of analysis and transformation compiler passes, also referred to as compiler phase orders. Programs compiled with these flags tend to outperform the unoptimized equivalent. However, there are often other assembly/binary representations of the source application in the solution space with higher performance than the ones achieved through the use of the standard optimization levels [4–8]. However, we can often achieve further performance, energy or power improvements by using specialized optimizing compiler sequences. Domains such as embedded systems or HPC tend to prioritize metrics such as energy efficiency that typically receive less attention from the compiler developers, so these domains benefit further from these specialized sequences [9].

Ideally, the standard compiler optimization levels would already correspond to the use of the best compiler phase selection/order for a given metric. However, there appears to be no single best phase order that applies to all programs. This is caused by the complex interactions between compiler passes. Some compiler passes negatively or positively interact with other compiler passes, resulting in the creation/destruction of optimization opportunities when executing the latter [11]. As such, a customized approach that produces different phase selections/orders for different functions/programs can lead to better performance.

Heterogeneous systems typically include a number of sub-devices with substantial differences. For this reason, different optimization strategies are needed for each computing component. With phase ordering, we can achieve closer-to-optimal optimization for these sub-devices, by specifying custom compiler sequences for each of them. This approach is orthogonal to other optimization strategies. For instance, it does not interfere with user and hardware optimizations. The use of compiler phase order specialization can reduce engineering costs. In a number of cases the same source code can be used when targeting architecturally different computing devices and/or different metrics through the use of different compiler phase orders. This reduces or mitigates the need to develop and maintain multiple versions of the same function/application.

The contributions of this paper are the following:

1. Compare performance between OpenCL and CUDA kernels implementing the same freely available and representative benchmarks (PolyBench/GPU) using recent NVIDIA drivers and CUDA toolchain, on an NVIDIA GPU with an up-to-date architecture (NVIDIA Pascal).

2. Assess the performance improvement that can be achieved using compiler pass phase ordering specialization with LLVM 3.9, in comparison with both use of that same LLVM compiler version without the use of phase ordering specialization and in comparison with the default OpenCL and CUDA kernel compilation strategies to NVIDIA GPUs.
3. Explain why the versions produced by phase selection/ordering specialization outperform the remaining ones, by analyzing the generated NVIDIA PTX assembly. We compare the specialized versions with CUDA's NVCC and OpenCL LLVM outputs.

Additionally, to the best of our knowledge this is the first work to present results of compiler pass phase ordering specialization targeting GPUs and considering OpenCL kernels.

The rest of this paper is organized as follows. Section 2 describes the methodology for the experiments presented in this paper. Section 3 presents the experimental results. Final remarks about the presented work and ongoing work are presented in Sect. 4.

2 Experimental Setup

We extended our compiler phase ordering Design Space Exploration (DSE) system [8] to support exploring compiler sequences targeting NVIDIA GPUs using Clang/LLVM and the libclc OpenCL library.

We used a workstation with an Intel Xeon E5-1650 v4 CPU, running at 3.6 GHz (4.0 GHz Turbo) and 64 GB of Quad-channel ECC DDR4 at 2133 MHz. For the experiments we relied on Ubuntu 16.04 64-bit with the NVIDIA CUDA 8.0 toolchain (released in Sept. 28, 2016) and the NVIDIA 378.13 Linux Display Driver (released in Feb. 14, 2017).

The GPU used for the experiments is a variant of the NVIDIA GP104 GPU in the form of an EVGA NVIDIA GeForce GTX 1070 graphics card (08G-P4-6276-KR) with a 1607 MHz/1797 MHz base/boost graphics clock and 8 GB of 256 bit GDDR5 memory with a transfer rate of 8008 MHz (256.3 GB/s memory bandwidth). The graphics card is connected to a PCI-Express 3.0 16x interface.

The GPU is set to persistence mode with the command `nvidia-smi -i <target gpu> -pm ENABLE`. This forces the kernel mode driver to keep the GPU initialized at all instances, avoiding the overhead caused by triggering GPU initialization at application start. The preferred performance mode is set to *Prefer Maximum Performance* under the *PowerMizer settings* tab in the *NVIDIA X Server Settings*, in order to reduce the occurrence of extreme GPU and memory frequency variation during execution of the GPU kernels.

In order to reduce DSE overhead, and given the fact that we found experimentally that multiple executions of the same compiled kernel on the GTX1070 GPU had a small standard deviation in relation to registered wall time, each generated code is only tested a single time during DSE. Only in a final phase on the DSE process are the top solutions executed 30 times and averaged in order to select a single compiler phase order. All execution time metrics reported (baseline CUDA/OpenCL and OpenCL optimized with phase ordering) in this paper correspond to the average over 30 executions.

2.1 Kernels and Objective Metric

In this paper we use the Polybench/GPU benchmark suite [10] kernels to assess the potential for improvement with phase ordering when targeting NVIDIA GPUs. We selected this particular benchmark as it is freely available and thus contributes to making the results presented in this paper reproducible.

We modified the benchmarks to ensure that the CUDA and OpenCL versions use the same floating-point precision. For instance, the OpenCL implementation of the original MVT kernel uses double floating point precision, while the CUDA implementation uses single precision. We performed the minimum of changes to ensure a fair comparison.

Polybench/GPU is a collection of codes implemented for GPUs using CUDA, OpenCL, and HMPP. This benchmark suite includes kernels from 15 benchmarks from different domains which represent computations that would be performed on GPUs in the context of HPC, including convolution kernels (2DCONV, 3DCONV), linear algebra (2MM, 3MM, ATAX, BICG, GEMM, GESUMMV, GRAMSCH, MVT, SYR2K, SYRK), datamining (CORR, COVAR), and stencil computations (FDTD-2D).

For our experiments we use both the CUDA and the OpenCL implementations available for each PolyBench/GPU benchmark. We rely on the default dataset shape so that reproducibility of our results (e.g., performance improvement using the specialized phase orders presented in this paper) is more straightforward.

2.2 Compilation and Execution Flow with Specialized Phase Ordering

We use Clang compiler's OpenCL frontend with the libclc library to generate an LLVM IR representation of a given input OpenCL kernel. The libclc library is an open source library with support for AMDGCN and NVPTX targets that implements functions as specified in OpenCL 1.1.

Then, we use the LLVM Optimizer tool (opt) to optimize the IR using a specific optimization strategy represented by a compiler phase order, and we link this optimized IR with the libclc OpenCL functions for our target using llvm-link. Finally, using Clang, we generate the NVIDIA PTX representation of the kernel from the LLVM bytecode resulting from the previous step, using the nvptx64-nvidia-nvcl target. PTX is NVIDIA's intermediate representation for GPU computations, and is used by NVIDIA's OpenCL and CUDA implementations. Although PTX is itself an IR and not a direct match to the code that is executed on the GPU, it is the closest we can get without direct access to the internals of NVIDIA's drivers.

Normally, programs that use OpenCL load the kernels and pass it to the clCreateProgramWithSource, which compiles them (*online compilation*). For specialized phase ordering, we instead compile the source code to PTX using Clang/LLVM and pass the PTX to the `clCreateProgramWithBinary` (*offline compilation*).

A compiler phase order represents not only the compiler passes to execute in the compiler pipeline, which can be in order of the hundreds, but also their order of execution. The fact that compiler passes are interdependent and interfere with each other's execution in ways that are difficult to predict can make it extremely hard to manually generate suitable compiler sequences. For the experiments presented in this paper, the OpenCL kernels from each of the PolyBench/GPU benchmarks were compiled/tested with a set of 10,000 randomly generated compiler phase orders (the same set was used with all OpenCL codes) composed of 256 LLVM pass instances (can include repeated calls to the same pass). Passes were selected from a list with all LLVM 3.9 passes except the ones that resulted in compilation and/or execution problems when used individually to compile the PolyBench/GPU OpenCL kernels.

2.3 Validation of the Code Generated After Phase Ordering

Each PolyBench/GPU benchmark has verification embedded in its code that consists in executing the OpenCL GPU kernel(s) followed by a functionally equivalent sequential C version on the CPU, and comparing the two. This alone poses a challenge, as CPU executing using the same parameters as the ones used for GPU execution takes a long time for a considerable number of the PolyBench/GPU benchmarks. This would have an unreasonable impact on the phase ordering exploration time.

To reduce the time for each DSE iteration, we separate the validation from the measurement phases. We validate the programs by executing on the CPU and GPU (as in the original PolyBench/GPU) with inputs that can be processed quickly. However, we also execute the same GPU code using the original inputs (without CPU validation) in order to measure the execution time.

We further reduce exploration time by checking whether an identical PTX file was previously generated. If so, we reuse the results (i.e., correctness and performance) from that previous execution.

At the end of phase ordering exploration, all compiler pass sequences that were iteratively tested during DSE are ordered by their resulting objective metrics. For the experiments presented in this paper, sequence/metric pairs are ordered from the one resulting in the fastest execution time to the one resulting in least performance. Then, as a final validation process, the optimized version that resulted in highest performance is executed with the original inputs on both the non-optimized CPU version and the optimized GPU version, and also with 30 randomly generated inputs that result in the same number of operations. We choose the fastest optimized version that passes validation.

This is performed to eliminate possible situations where a compiled PTX kernel gives correct results using a small input set but gives wrong results with the original input set.

The PolyBench/GPU kernels are mostly composed of floating-point operations and the result of floating-point operations can be affected by reordering operations and rounding. Because of this we allow for up to 1% difference between the outputs of CPU and GPU executions when testing if a given compiler phase order results in code that generates valid output.

3   Results

For each of the benchmarks, we measured the execution times for the CUDA version, the original OpenCL (from source), an offline compiled OpenCL without optimization, an offline compiled OpenCL with standard LLVM optimization levels (i.e., the best of -O1, -O2, -O3 and -Os for each benchmark, which we will refer to as -OX) and an offline compiled OpenCL with our custom compiler optimization phase orders resulting from DSE.

3.1   Performance Evaluation

We compared the results for the various versions of the benchmarks (offline OpenCL versions, OpenCL from source and CUDA) to determine how they perform. Using custom phase orders found by iterative compilation produced code that consistently outperforms the other OpenCL variants, and nearly always outperforms the CUDA version.

Figure 1 depicts the performance improvements with phase ordering over the OpenCL compiled online and CUDA baselines and the other OpenCL baselines (compiled with Clang/LLVM). With phase ordering specialization we were able to achieve a geometric mean performance improvement of 1.54× over the CUDA version and a performance improvement of 1.65× over the execution of the OpenCL kernels compiled from source. Additionally, code compiled with specialized phase ordering can be up to 5.48× and up to 5.70× faster than the respective CUDA implementation and the OpenCL compiled from source.

For the tested benchmarks, there were mostly no significant performance difference between the offline compilation model using Clang/LLVM without custom phase ordering and the OpenCL versions from source. There were exceptions, such as GESUMMV and SYR2K, that were 1.18× and 1.15× slower when using Clang/LLVM (with no optimization) to compile the kernels offline.

Using the LLVM standard optimization level flags did not result in noticeable improvements in terms of the performance of the generated code for most benchmarks. We believe this is because the PTX code is further aggressively optimized by the NVIDIA driver before generating the final assembly code for the target NVIDIA GPU [12], so effectively we are using LLVM only as a pre-optimizer.

For 2DCONV, FDTD-2D and SYR2K all of the standard optimization level flags (including -O0) resulted in the same code being generated. For benchmarks 2MM, 3DCONV, 3MM, ATAX, BICG, GEMM, GESUMMV, GRAMSCHM, MVT and SYRK, the optimization level flags lead to code that is different from the code without optimizations. CORR and COVAR are the only benchmarks for which different optimization level

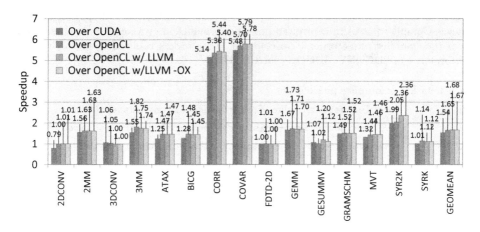

Fig. 1. Performance improvements from phase ordering with LLVM over CUDA implementations and OpenCL using the default online compilation pipeline for the NVIDIA GTX1070 GPU and over OpenCL to PTX compilation using Clang/LLVM without (OpenCL w/LLVM) and with standard optimization levels (OpenCL w/LLVM -OX).

flags produce different code. However, even in these benchmarks, the performance impact was minimal (within 1%).

For the GESUMMV and GRAMSCHM, there were significant performance improvements associated with the use of standard optimization levels. In the case of GESUMMV, the use the standard optimization levels resulted in 1.07× performance improvement over the non-optimized version. For GRAMSCHM, the non-optimized version was 1.04× faster than the versions produced by the optimization level flags.

The difference between the OpenCL baselines is that one represents the de facto OpenCL compilation flow (with compile from source) and the others represent the compilation using LLVM (with compile from binary) using the standard optimization level that results in the generation of code with highest performance on a kernel-by-kernel basis, and compilation using LLVM but with no optimization. Finally, on these benchmarks, performance with CUDA tends to be better than with OpenCL, if no specialized phase ordering is considered. The geometric mean (considering all 15 PolyBench/GPU benchmarks) of the performance improvement with CUDA (over OpenCL from source) is 1.07×. The 2DCONV, 3MM, ATAX, BICG and SYRK benchmarks are at least 1.1× faster in CUDA than with OpenCL. All other benchmarks with exception for 3DCONV and GESUMMV are still faster in CUDA than in OpenCL, although by a smaller margin.

Table 1 depicts LLVM 3.9 compiler phase orders found to have better performance than the OpenCL baseline that relies on Clang/LLVM and the libclc OpenCL library.

Table 1. Compiler phase orders that resulted in compiled kernels with highest performance. Compiler passes that resulted in no performance improvement were eliminated from the compiler phase orders. No compiler phase orders resulted in improving the performance of 2DCONV, 3DCONV or FDTD-2D.

Benchmark	Compiler phase order
2MM	`-cfl-anders-aa -dse -loop-reduce -licm -instcombine`
3MM	`-loop-reduce -gvn-hoist -reg2mem -cfl-anders-aa -sroa -licm`
ATAX	`-bb-vectorize -loop-reduce -licm -cfl-anders-aa`
BICG	`-gvn -loop-reduce -cfl-anders-aa -licm`
CORR	`-cfl-anders-aa -loop-reduce -gvn -loop-extract-single` `-loop-unswitch -loop-unswitch -ipsccp -reg2mem -licm` `-nvptx-lower-alloca`
COVAR	`-cfl-anders-aa -loop-unswitch -sink -loop-unswitch` `-loop-reduce -jump-threading -reg2mem -licm` `-nvptx-lower-alloca`
GEMM	`-cfl-anders-aa -print-memdeps -loop-reduce -licm`
GESUMMV	`-instcombine -reg2mem -instcombine -mem2reg -cfl-anders-aa` `-loop-reduce -nvptx-lower-alloca -gvn-hoist -licm`
GRAMSCHM	`-sink -reg2mem -licm -cfl-anders-aa -sroa`
MVT	`-gvn -loop-reduce -cfl-anders-aa -licm`
SYR2K	`-loop-reduce -loop-unroll -instcombine -loop-reduce -licm` `-cfl-anders-aa`
SYRK	`-licm -cfl-anders-aa -reg2mem -licm -sroa`

3.2   Analysis of the Results

We explain for each PolyBench/GPU benchmark what are the reasons behind the performance improvement achieved with phase ordering, comparing with the performance achieved with the OpenCL and CUDA baselines compiled with the NVIDIA driver. More specifically, we compare the PTX output resulting from OpenCL offline compilation with specialized phase ordering with PTX generated from OpenCL offline compilation without phase ordering and with PTX generated from the CUDA versions.

For 2DCONV, CUDA is 1.26× faster than the OpenCL version optimized with phase ordering. The compiler pass phase ordering DSE process was not able to find an LLVM sequence capable to optimize this benchmark. The main improvement of CUDA over OpenCL seems to be the generation of more efficient code for loads from global memory. Figure 2 shows the difference between the two approaches. Whereas load operations typically result in a single CUDA operation, the equivalent for OpenCL typically results in 5 PTX instructions. We believe this difference is the primary reason for CUDA's advantage over OpenCL.

For 2MM, the OpenCL version optimized with phase ordering is 1.63× and 1.56× faster than the OpenCL and CUDA baselines, respectively. The main

```
ld.global.f32      %f2, [%rd6+4]
```

(a) PTX load code generated from CUDA.

```
add.s32            %r17, %r14, %r1;
cvt.s64.s32        %rd16, %r17;
shl.b64            %rd17, %rd16, 2;
add.s64            %rd18, %rd1, %rd17;
ld.global.f32      %f2, [%rd18];
```

(b) PTX load code generated from OpenCL (-O3).

Fig. 2. PTX code for equivalent load operations, for CUDA and OpenCL with offline compilation (2DCONV benchmark)

reason for this speedup is the removal of store operations within the kernel loop. Both the OpenCL and the CUDA baseline versions of this kernel repeatedly overwrite the same element and this has a negative impact on performance.

The phase ordered version instead uses an accumulator register and performs the store only after all the loop computations are complete, which substantially reduces the number of costly memory accesses. It is unclear why the baseline OpenCL and CUDA versions do not perform this optimization. One possibility is that they are unable to determine that there are no aliasing issues. In the context of this benchmark, this assumption is correct in OpenCL 2.0, as any aliasing would result in a data race, which is undefined behavior [1]. We do not know if the optimization was applied because LLVM correctly discovered this fact, or if there is a bug that happened to result in correct code by accident. Even if the optimization turns out to be the result of a bug, we believe this speedup represents an opportunity for approaches based on *Loop Versioning* transformations. Although this benchmark uses two kernels, both are equivalent (the only difference being kernel and variable names), and thus the same analysis applies to both. There are two differences between the baseline CUDA and OpenCL compiled versions that can explain the different execution times. The first being the aforementioned issue with load instructions (see Fig. 2), the second being a different loop unroll factor as the phase ordered version based on OpenCL uses efficient load instructions, but also uses a loop unroll factor of 2 (while the CUDA version uses an unrolling factor of 8).

For 3DCONV, we were unable to achieve a speedup on this benchmark using any of the tested compiler phase orders, when compared with LLVM w/ or w/o the optimization level flags. We believe this happens because most of the time spent on the benchmark is due to global memory loads that are not removed or improved by any LLVM pass. Any optimization will only modify the rest of the code, which takes a negligible amount of time compared to the memory operations. There is a speedup from the use of the LLVM PTX backend compared with the OpenCL from source compilation path (1.05×) and the compilation from CUDA (1.06×).

On the 3MM benchmark, we were able to achieve speedups of $1.55\times$ and $1.82\times$ over the baseline CUDA and OpenCL version compiled from source, respectively. The main reason for the performance improvement is the removal of the memory store operation from the computation loop.

The OpenCL version of ATAX optimized with phase ordering achieves a speedup of $1.47\times$ and $1.25\times$ over the baseline OpenCL and CUDA versions, respectively. Once again, the phase ordered version is able to move memory stores out of the innermost loops of the kernels, which explains the speedups. The difference between the CUDA and the baseline OpenCL versions can be explained by a different loop unroll factor (2 for OpenCL, 8 for CUDA). The CUDA version uses the previously described simpler code pattern for memory loads compared to these baseline OpenCL versions, but the phase ordering version also uses an efficient memory load pattern.

On the BICG benchmark, we were able to achieve a speedup of $1.48\times$ over OpenCL, and $1.28\times$ over CUDA. The main differences between the versions are the memory stores in the kernel loop, the unroll factor and the inefficient memory access patterns in the baseline offline OpenCL versions.

The CORR benchmark is one of the benchmarks that benefits the most from phase ordering ($5.36\times$ and $5.14\times$ over baseline OpenCL from source and CUDA versions, respectively). Phase ordering is capable of moving global memory stores out of loops, which neither the CUDA version nor the baseline OpenCL versions do. In general, for this benchmark, the CUDA version tends to produce more compact load instructions and use higher loop unroll factors than the OpenCL versions.

COVAR and CORR use the same mean_kernel and reduce_kernel functions. However, this represents only a fragment of the total execution code, so the compiler sequences for the two benchmarks are different. Regardless, the same conclusions from CORR apply to COVAR: phase ordering removes global stores from the loop. COVAR improved by $5.7\times$ and $5.48\times$ with phase ordering specialization, compared with the OpenCL compiled from source and the CUDA version.

The functions of the FDTD-2D benchmark are very straightforward, with little potential for optimization. As such, phase ordering had no impact.

The performance differences for the GEMM benchmark ($1.73\times$ and $1.67\times$ over the OpenCL from source and the CUDA baselines) can be explained by the removal of the memory store operation from the kernel loop and the different pattern of memory load instructions.

There was only a small performance improvement for the GESUMMV benchmark ($1.07\times$ over CUDA and $1.02\times$ over the baseline OpenCL from source). The phase ordering sequence is able to extract the memory stores out of the main computation loop, but uses a smaller loop unroll factor (2) than the baseline OpenCL and CUDA versions (4 and 16, respectively).

We were able to obtain speedups of $1.49\times$ and $1.52\times$ over the baseline CUDA and OpenCL versions on the GRAMSCHM, respectively. Phase ordering is able to move the memory storage operations out of the loop. Aside from that, it uses the same load from memory instruction pattern and unroll factor as the baseline OpenCL versions.

The MVT benchmark benefits from phase ordering by a factor of $1.32\times$ and $1.44\times$ over the baseline CUDA and OpenCL versions. The main reason for this improvement is the extraction of the store operation from the computation loop.

The SYR2K benchmarks benefits from phase ordering by a factor of $1.99\times$ and $2.05\times$ over the baseline CUDA and OpenCL versions, respectively. In general, the same memory load pattern, loop unroll factor and loop invariant memory storage code motion conclusions apply to this benchmark. Phase ordering also seems to outline the segment of the code containing the kernel loop, but this does not seem to be the reason for the performance difference.

For the SYRK benchmark, phase ordering improves performance by $1.14\times$ over the OpenCL baseline compile from source. We could not achieve significant speedups over the CUDA version. Once again, the main reason for this improvement is the extraction of the store from the loop.

4   Conclusion

This paper showed that compiler pass phase ordering specialization allows achieving considerable performance improvements when compiling OpenCL kernels to NVIDIA GPUs. Using Clang/LLVM 3.9 and libclc we were able to improve the performance of code compiled from PolyBench/GPU OpenCL kernels to up to $5.70\times$ and $1.65\times$ on average over the default NVIDIA OpenCL compilation flow. The performance of OpenCL compiled with specialized compiler pass phase orders also tends to surpass the performance of CUDA implementations of the same kernels compiled with NVCC (from NVIDIA CUDA 8.0 toolchain). The use of phase ordering on top of the OpenCL versions of the kernels resulted in a maximum speedup of $5.48\times$ and a geometric mean speedup of $1.54\times$ when compared with the performance of the equivalent CUDA kernels compiled with NVCC.

We gave insights explaining why the OpenCL kernels compiled with LLVM specialized compiler pass phase orders tend to have considerably higher performance than both the kernels compiled with the traditional OpenCL compilation from source and the CUDA equivalent kernels. One of the optimizations with most impact in performance of the compiled OpenCL kernels over the performance resulting from OpenCL online compilation from source and the CUDA versions consists of moving memory writes out of inner loops of GPU kernels by using of an accumulator register. This avoids the overhead caused by repeated expensive global memory writes. The optimization can be performed even in cases where its correctness can not be proven at compilation time. This can be achieved with *Loop Versioning*, which consists of adding runtime checks that will result in the selection of what loop version (i.e., optimized or non-optimized) to execute at runtime.

We are currently evaluating the potential of compiler phase ordering for GPU energy consumption reduction, and how it correlates with performance as we previously did in the context of C code targeting x86 and ARM based systems [9]. Given the fact that GPUs are used in domains with energy (and power) concerns (e.g., HPC, embedded), there may be scenarios where it is acceptable to sacrifice performance for less total energy use.

We extended our DSE system to be able to target AMD GPUs, and we are currently exploring software optimization leveraged by compiler phase ordering specialization on these devices.

Acknowledgments. This work was partially supported by the TEC4Growth project, "NORTE-01-0145-FEDER-000020", financed by the North Portugal Regional Operational Programme (NORTE 2020), under the PORTUGAL 2020 Partnership Agreement, and through the European Regional Development Fund (ERDF). Reis acknowledges the support by FCT through PD/BD/105804/2014.

References

1. Khronos OpenCL Working Group. The OpenCL C Specification, Version 2.0 (2015)
2. Nickolls, J., et al.: Scalable parallel programming with CUDA. Queue **6**(2), 40–53 (2008)
3. Betkaoui, B., Thomas, D.B., Luk, W.: Comparing performance and energy efficiency of FPGAs and GPUs for high productivity computing. In: 2010 International Conference on Field-Programmable Technology, Beijing, pp. 94–101 (2010)
4. Kulkarni, S., Cavazos, J.: Mitigating the compiler optimization phase-ordering problem using machine learning. In: Proceedings of ACM International Conference on Object Oriented Programming Systems Languages and Applications, OOPSLA 2012, pp. 147–162. ACM, New York (2012)
5. Purini, S., Jain, L.: Finding good optimization sequences covering program space. ACM Trans. Archit. Code Optim. (TACO) **9**(4), 56:1–56:23 (2013)
6. Martins, L.G.A., et al.: Clustering-based selection for the exploration of compiler optimization sequences. ACM Trans. Archit. Code Optim. (TACO) **13**(1), 8:1–8:28 (2016)
7. Nobre, R., Martins, L.G.A., Cardoso, J.M.P.: Use of previously acquired positioning of optimizations for phase ordering exploration. In: Proceedings of the 18th International Workshop on Software and Compilers for Embedded Systems (SCOPES 2015), pp. 58–67. ACM, New York (2015)
8. Nobre, R., Martins, L.G.A., Cardoso, J.M.P.: A graph-based iterative compiler pass selection and phase ordering approach. In: Proceedings of 17th ACM Conference on Languages, Compilers, Tools, and Theory for Embedded Systems, LCTES 2016, pp. 21–30. ACM, New York (2016)
9. Nobre, R., Reis, L., Cardoso, J.M.P.: Compiler phase ordering as an orthogonal approach for reducing energy consumption. In: Proceedings of the 19th Workshop on Compilers for Parallel Computing, CPC 2016 (2016)
10. Grauer-Gray, S., et al.: Auto-tuning a high-level language targeted to GPU codes. In: Proceedings of Innovative Parallel Computing (InPar 2012) (2012)
11. Purini, S., Jain, L.: Finding good optimization sequences covering program space. ACM Trans. Archit. Code Optim. **9**(4), 23 (2013). Article 56
12. Parallel Thread Execution ISA Version 5.0. CUDA toolkit documentation. http://docs.nvidia.com/cuda/parallel-thread-execution/index.html

Evaluating Scientific Workflow Execution on an Asymmetric Multicore Processor

Ilia Pietri[1]([✉]), Sicong Zhuang[2,3], Marc Casas[2,3], Miquel Moretó[2,3][iD],
and Rizos Sakellariou[4][iD]

[1] Department of Informatics and Telecommunications, University of Athens,
Athens, Greece
ipietri@di.uoa.gr
[2] Barcelona Supercomputing Center (BSC), Barcelona, Spain
[3] Universitat Politecnica de Catalunya (UPC), Barcelona, Spain
[4] School of Computer Science, University of Manchester, Manchester, UK

Abstract. Asymmetric multicore architectures that integrate different types of cores are emerging as a potential solution for good performance and power efficiency. Although scheduling can be improved by utilizing an appropriate set of cores for the execution of the different jobs, determining frequency configurations is also crucial to achieve both good performance and energy efficiency. This challenge may be more profound with scientific workflow applications that consist of jobs with data dependency constraints. The paper focuses on deploying and evaluating the Montage scientific workflow on an asymmetric multicore platform with the aim to explore CPU frequency configurations with different trade-offs between execution time and energy efficiency. The proposed approach provides good estimates of workflow execution time and energy consumption for different frequency configurations with an average error of less than 8.63% for time and less than 9.69% for energy compared to actual values.

1 Introduction

Complex computational problems in many scientific fields, such as astronomy and physics, may consist of multiple computational steps (jobs) with data dependencies between them. For example, the output data of a program can be used as input from other programs. Scientific workflows [4] are commonly used to describe the computational jobs (tasks) and dependencies between them, separating the application development and execution. In this way, scientists can orchestrate the application components and provide a high level representation of the application independently of the particulars of the execution environment [5]. High performance computing (HPC) systems, including clusters, grids and clouds, have been widely used for the execution of workflow applications in order to improve application performance, by allocating a large number of resources to execute independent tasks (i.e., tasks without data dependencies

© Springer International Publishing AG, part of Springer Nature 2018
D. B. Heras and L. Bougé (Eds.): Euro-Par 2017 Workshops, LNCS 10659, pp. 439–451, 2018.
https://doi.org/10.1007/978-3-319-75178-8_36

between them) in parallel. However, optimizing the execution schedule of scientific workflows can be challenging, as the execution of a task can only start after the execution of its predecessors and data transfer have finished. This may result in idle slots between the execution of workflow tasks and wastage of resources.

When resources are heterogeneous, scheduling a workflow becomes particularly challenging, as many different combinations of the heterogeneous resources may be chosen. For example, the ARM big.LITTLE architecture is composed of fast and slow cores, which can additionally operate at different CPU frequencies. Although power consumption decreases for resources running at a lower computational speed (i.e. operating CPU frequency), overall energy consumption may increase. This is because computational speed may affect task execution time differently, depending on a task's characteristics. For example, the execution time of I/O bound tasks is not greatly affected from the reduction in CPU frequency, while the execution of CPU bound tasks may be greatly affected. As a result, gaps in the schedule due to idle time between the execution of the workflow's tasks may increase when resources operate at a lower computational speed. This may lead to significant idle energy, the energy spent while resources remain idle. Minimizing idle time, while balancing execution time and energy consumption, requires adjusted configurations combining fast and slow cores running at appropriate frequencies.

This paper carries out a set of real experiments to investigate the performance of a widely used scientific workflow application, Montage [9], using different CPU frequencies and different types of cores of an asymmetric multicore processor architecture. Energy consumption and task runtime models for the platform and for each type of core are proposed and validated using real measurements. Using these models, estimations of overall workflow execution time and energy consumption are obtained and compared with real measurements. To the best of our knowledge, this is the first paper evaluating the performance of a scientific workflow application on an ARM big.LITTLE platform.

In the rest of the paper, Sect. 2 gives background information on the architecture, the application model and the problem. Section 3 describes the models used to estimate execution time and energy required for the workflow execution under different frequency configurations. Section 4 evaluates the models on a real system. Section 5 concludes the paper.

2   Background

Architecture: The ARM big.LITTLE architecture is a system-on-chip technology for heterogeneous processing that uses two types of processors with different power and performance characteristics; ARM Cortex-A15 processors (Big out-of-order processors) for high performance processing and ARM Cortex-A7 processors (Little in-order processors) for power efficient processing. In the architecture used in this paper, each processor type contains four cores. The processors are coherently connected so that they can transfer information to each other. Also, the system provides frequency scaling capabilities, which allow to set CPU frequency individually for each core.

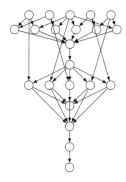

Fig. 1. Structure of a Montage workflow with 22 tasks.

Application Model: The paper assumes that a scientific workflow is modelled as a Directed Acyclic Graph (DAG) with the nodes being the tasks and the edges the data dependencies between them. The Pegasus Project [5] provides tools to generate abstract workflows: these are described in a form that includes information about the arguments required to run each task, their input and output files and data dependencies between them. These high-level abstract workflow descriptions are provided in DAX (directed acyclic graph in XML) files, which make use of a specific XML syntax for expressing the tasks, their arguments, files and dependencies between them. This information can be used to deploy and execute workflow applications on HPC systems in a way that data dependency constraints are respected. The scientific workflow application used in the paper is Montage, which is a real astronomy application that generates image mosaics of the sky [9]. A Montage workflow consists of collections of tasks (job classes) with different characteristics, such as task execution time and CPU utilization. Montage can be characterized as an I/O intensive application where most of the tasks have low CPU utilization and short runtime (in the order of seconds) as they mainly spend their execution time on I/O operations to read and write files. The tasks can be grouped into nine levels, each level corresponding to a different class of tasks. Figure 1 shows an example of a small Montage workflow with 22 tasks. In larger versions of Montage, the number of tasks of the first, second and fifth levels (counting from top to bottom) would increase further.

Problem Description: The problem of task scheduling onto heterogeneous HPC systems has been extensively studied [2,10–12,14,15], with several works focusing on multicore processors [1,3,8,10,16]. Some of the algorithms focus on optimizing application performance and execution time [10,12], while other works also consider energy and power optimization [1,8]. As heterogeneous multicore processing platforms integrating different types of processing cores are now used as a promising solution towards achieving different performance and power goals, there has been research on policies which aim to determine which types of cores are more appropriate for the scheduling of the applications or their parts [3,10,13]. For example, power-efficient cores may be used for the execution of memory-bound or non-critical jobs while fast cores may be more suitable for CPU-bound or critical jobs [3,13].

This scheduling problem becomes more complex, as one has to select an appropriate CPU frequency for each core. Clearly, there is a trade-off between energy and performance for different configurations. For example, using fast cores may result in small execution time but increased energy consumption. By lowering the CPU frequency of the cores, lower energy but longer execution time may be achieved. Solutions with even lower energy but significantly increased execution time may also be achieved using slow but power-efficient cores. If we consider all different configurations it is expected that some of them will result in sub-optimal solutions; these are solutions which are dominated by other solutions lying on a Pareto-front of the energy-performance trade-off space. Hence, the aim of the paper is to suggest approaches to explore the space of the CPU frequency combinations for the heterogeneous types of cores in order to find solutions with good performance and energy efficiency close to the pareto front. In contrast to heuristics-based related work [6], this paper proposes energy and execution time models to obtain estimations for a wide range of configurations, which are based on metrics monitored through real measurements from a small set of configurations. For example, runtime and power characteristics may be available from historical data and can be sufficient to provide estimations for frequencies between the extreme cases.

3   Modelling Execution Time and Energy Consumption

The idea in the paper is that given a predefined assignment policy for the mapping of the tasks to the cores, the execution of the workflow under different configurations can be modelled using task execution time and energy consumption estimations. The assignment policy and data dependency constraints between tasks specify the execution order of the tasks on the cores. Hence, task runtime estimations for each configuration can be used to specify the time slot required for the execution of each task. Also, power models can be used to estimate under different configurations the energy consumed when cores are idle or busy executing tasks. Based on such estimations, overall execution time and energy required to run the workflow is estimated.

3.1   Estimation of Execution Time

While frequency scaling may impact job performance, the increase in execution time is not proportional to the decrease in frequency as non-CPU activity, such as memory access, is not sensitive to frequency changes. Hence, different jobs may exhibit different performance slowdown depending on their CPU-boundedness. Assuming that we know the execution time of each task when the core it is assigned to operates at the maximum CPU frequency, task runtime estimations for different frequencies can be computed by:

$$taskRuntime_{t,f} = (\beta_t \cdot (\frac{f_{max}}{f} - 1) + 1) \cdot taskRuntime_{t,f_{max}}, \qquad (1)$$

where β_t, the CPU boundedness of task t, shows the performance sensitivity to frequency reduction [7]. The parameter β_t can be computed for each task based on measurements at the maximum and minimum operating frequency. In that way, task runtime estimations can be provided for different CPU frequencies (and for each type of core) by measuring task performance at the two extreme cases of operating the core, its maximum and minimum frequency. Then, the start time and finish time of each task in the schedule for a given assignment can be estimated recursively (Eqs. 2 and 3) based on the task runtime estimations. The start time of a task t is estimated as:

$$startTime_{t,f_t} = \begin{cases} \max_{\forall p \in pred_t} (finishTime_{p,f_p} + comCost_{p \to t}), & \text{if } pred_t \neq \emptyset \\ 0, & otherwise \end{cases}$$
(2)

where $pred_t$ includes the predecessors of the task at both the DAG and the core assigned. When the task has no predecessors at the DAG or the core, the start time of the task is zero. The communication cost from task p to task t, $comCost_{p \to t}$, is assumed to be zero, as tasks granularities are significantly larger than data transfer costs and there is a good interconnect. The finish time of a task t is estimated as:

$$finishTime_{t,f_t} = startTime_{t,f_t} + taskRuntime_{t,f_t}.$$
(3)

Overall workflow execution time for a given schedule is the finish time of the execution of the latest task:

$$makespan = \max_{\forall t \in w}(finishTime_{t,f_t}).$$
(4)

3.2   Estimation of Energy Consumption

The energy consumed during the execution of the workflow may vary between different execution schedules depending on the operating frequency of each core. The energy model used in this paper estimates the energy required under different frequency configurations taking into account the dynamic energy required for the execution of the tasks and the static energy of the system. Energy is the product of power and time. As frequency scaling does not affect non-CPU activity, power consumption at CPU (A7/A15 cluster) is modelled for the different frequency configurations, while power in the other system components, such as memory and GPU, is considered to be fixed, as it does not vary significantly between different frequency configurations. Note that CPU power consumption can be measured at the level of cluster and not individually per core. Power consumption at the A7/A15 cluster when running the task at a single core is modelled using a linear power model:

$$P_{f_t,t} = P_{base,t} + P_{dif,t} \cdot (\frac{f_t}{f_{min}} - 1),$$
(5)

where $P_{base,t}$ and $P_{dif,t}$ are parameters linearly fitted for each task t based on power measurements for the extreme cases of operating the cluster at minimum and maximum frequency supported. All the cores of the cluster operate at the same frequency level f_t. Power consumption while the cluster is not utilized (idle power) is also modelled for the different frequency configurations using a similar model:

$$P_{idle_{f_t}} = P_{base_{idle}} + P_{dif_{idle}} \cdot (\frac{f_t}{f_{min}} - 1), \qquad (6)$$

where $P_{base_{idle}}$ and $P_{dif_{idle}}$ are parameters fitted based on the power measurements at the minimum and maximum frequency supported for each core type (cluster).

Based on the power models above, the dynamic power required to run each task t on a core can be estimated by:

$$P_{dyn_{t,f_t}} = P_{f_t,t} - P_{idle_{f_t}}. \qquad (7)$$

Then, overall energy can be computed as:

$$E = \sum_{t \in w} (taskRuntime_{t,f} \cdot P_{dyn_{t,f}}) + P_{fixed} \cdot makespan, \qquad (8)$$

where P_{fixed} includes the idle power of the system (A7 and A15 cluster, memory and GPU) when the minimum frequency is set to the cores and the memory power required for the execution of the workflow.

The models described above are validated next and used to estimate overall workflow execution time and energy consumption.

4 Results

4.1 Methodology and Experimental Setup

Experiments are conducted on an ODROID-XU3 board that contains an eight-core Samsung Exynos 5422 processor of ARM big.LITTLE architecture with 2 Gbyte LPDDR3 RAM. The processor chip consists of a Cortex-A15 1.6 GHz quad core CPU and a Cortex-A7 1.4 GHz quad core CPU with a shared 2 MB and 512 KB L2 cache, respectively. Both CPUs, the Cortex-A15 cluster of four fast (or Big) cores and the Cortex-A7 cluster of four slow (or Little) cores, can be used in order to run simultaneously independent tasks of an application. Each core can be set to operate on a different number of CPU frequencies using the cpufreq driver. In the experiments, we varied the CPU frequency in the range of 0.8–1.6 GHz with a frequency step of 0.2 GHz for the fast cores and 0.8–1.3 GHz with a frequency step of 0.1 GHz for the slow cores, resulting in a total of five and six operating CPU frequency configurations, respectively.

For performance counter events we used perf, a performance monitoring tool for Linux, to collect various information about workflow execution, such as time duration and CPU utilization, and profile the application. Also, in order to estimate the energy consumed by the application at each configuration, power measurements are monitored using an energy daemon that reads power measurements at A7 cluster, A15 cluster, memory and GPU separately provided by INA-231 power sensors on the Hardkernel ODROID system every 0.27 sec. To do so, the sensors are enabled in advance. Regardless of the number of cores utilized, CPU power consumption is measured at the cluster level and per-core power monitoring is not supported. Overall energy consumption incurred during workflow execution (we refer to this as actual energy) is computed as the product of the average power consumption and workflow execution time, each one measured as above.

Two versions of the Montage workflow are used. The first version consists of 22 tasks and corresponds to the DAG shown in Fig. 1; this will be denoted by M_{22}. A second version of Montage with 65 tasks has more tasks at levels 1, 2, and 5 (counting from top to bottom), namely 15, 29, 15; we denote this version by M_{65}. In order to run a workflow on the platform, a script was written to manage the execution of the tasks using a statically predefined mapping policy. The tasks of each level are assigned statically to the CPU cores in a round-robin fashion, so that independent tasks can be executed in parallel; the mapping also specifies at what frequency each core runs. When a core is empty (no task has been assigned to it), the CPU frequency of the core is set to its minimum operating CPU frequency (0.8 GHz). Otherwise, the CPU frequency is set based on the predefined assignment policy. In each experiment, unless otherwise stated, four cores (two Big and two Little cores) from a total of eight available ones (four Big and four Little cores) are used to run the workflow. The script checks every t seconds if the execution of any running tasks finishes in order to start the execution of ready tasks (the successors of the tasks on the cores assuming that dependency constraints are met), adjusting the CPU frequency of the cores accordingly. The value of t is set close to the minimum task execution time so that performance overhead (in terms of both execution time and energy) but also the delay on triggering ready tasks is minimized. To do so, t is set equal to 0.2 and 0.5 secs for the small (22 tasks) and large (65 tasks) workflow, respectively. Also, the script runs at an idle core (a core that is not used for the execution of the workflow tasks) at minimum frequency so that the overhead is minimized.

Finally, we note that, unless otherwise stated, each experiment is repeated ten times and the average value of each metric is used to express the final results.

4.2 Validation of Task Runtime and Power Models

In this section, the power and task runtime models from Sect. 3 are validated. Task runtime estimations for homogeneous cores (cores of a single type operating at the same frequency) are computed using Eq. 1. To do so, each Montage workflow is executed using four homogeneous cores, alternatively four Big or four Little cores, for each available CPU frequency (five for Big and six for Little, as mentioned in Sect. 4.1) in order to collect information about the CPU utilization and runtime of the tasks. Parameter β_t is modelled as the average

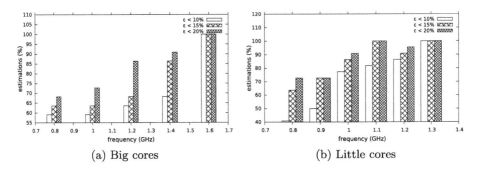

Fig. 2. Accuracy of task runtime estimation for each of the 22 tasks of M_{22}.

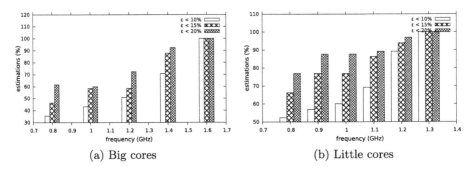

Fig. 3. Accuracy of task runtime estimation for each of the 65 tasks of M_{65}.

CPU utilization for each task at maximum frequency. Also, from the ten different runs for each experiment, the average runtime of each task is computed using the five smallest values so that any outliers (runs with poor performance) are not taken into account. Task runtime estimations are compared with the actual task runtimes at the different frequencies used. Figures 2 and 3 show the percentage of estimations with an error, ϵ, of less than 10, 15 and 20% for Big and Little cores for the small (M_{22}) and large (M_{65}) workflow, respectively. Large % errors are mostly related to small duration tasks, with a small impact on the overall workflow.

Experiments are also conducted to measure the power consumption of the A7/A15 cluster for different frequency configurations when running each workflow sequentially on a single core, as power consumption cannot be measured independently for each core. The parameters P_{base} and P_{dif} of the power model in Eq. 5 are fitted based on the power measurements at minimum and maximum frequency. Figures 4 and 5 show the percentage of power estimations with an error of less than 10, 15 and 20% at Big/Little cores (A7/A15 cluster) for the small and large workflow, respectively.

Finally, experiments are performed to profile idle power consumption and fit the parameters of the model in Eq. 6. For each experiment the CPU frequency of the Big/Little cores is set to the desired level and the `sleep` function is used for

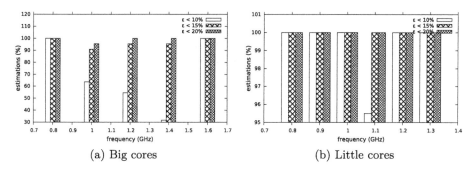

Fig. 4. Accuracy of power estimation for the M_{22} workflow.

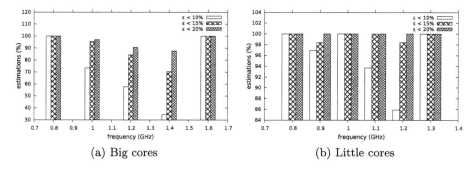

Fig. 5. Accuracy of power estimation for the M_{65} workflow.

10 sec to compute the average idle power consumption at the selected frequency. To do so, the energy daemon is triggered before and after the `sleep(10)` function to monitor the power measurements at the A7/A15 clusters (Big/Little cores). The parameters of the model, $P_{base_{idle}}$ and $P_{dif_{idle}}$, are fitted based on the power measurements at the minimum and maximum frequency for each core type. The results are compared with the actual measurements and the estimation error in idle power is less than 10% for all the frequency configurations used.

4.3 Workflow Energy and Execution Time Estimation

In this set of experiments we use as input parameters task runtime and power estimations when executing the workflow on homogeneous resources, Big or Little cores, in order to estimate overall workflow execution time and energy consumption when executing the workflow onto heterogeneous resources (combining two Big and two Little cores with different frequencies), based on the models in Sect. 4.2. These estimations are then compared with actual measurements. Delays that often happen in real environments, such as system overhead and job submission delays, are also incorporated. As mentioned in Sect. 4.1, the main script checks every t sec if the execution of any running tasks finishes in order to start the execution of ready tasks. This may cause delays in the assignment

Table 1. Overall execution time and energy estimations for the M_{22} workflow.

Configuration	Actual execution time (s)	Estimated execution time (s)	% error in execution time	Actual energy (J)	Estimated energy	% error in energy
L1.3B1.6	28.8	27.48	4.57	37.95	35.47	6.54
L1.3B1.4	29.5	28.56	3.19	35.11	33.01	6.00
L1.3B1.2	31.1	30.18	2.95	34.37	31.89	7.21
L1.3B1.0	33.6	33.97	1.11	32.33	30.88	4.48
L1.3B0.8	39.5	39.66	0.40	33.8	29.99	11.27
L1.2B1.6	29.2	26.63	8.81	38.44	34.27	10.84
L1.2B1.4	30	28.35	5.50	35.16	33.28	5.35
L1.2B1.2	31.9	30.50	4.38	33.98	31.46	7.40
L1.2B1.0	34.2	33.96	0.70	32.54	30.78	5.41
L1.2B0.8	39.7	38.46	3.13	32.16	29.11	9.49
L1.1B1.6	30.1	26.36	12.43	37.93	33.64	11.32
L1.1B1.4	31	28.76	7.23	35.22	32.79	6.89
L1.1B1.2	32.3	30.69	4.99	33.5	31.24	6.77
L1.1B1.0	34.7	34.95	0.72	31.48	30.77	2.25
L1.1B0.8	40.3	39.74	1.38	31.88	29.45	7.62
L1.0B1.6	31.1	27.38	11.96	37.86	33.96	10.29
L1.0B1.4	31.8	28.40	10.68	34.69	31.92	7.98
L1.0B1.2	32.9	31.23	5.07	33.53	31.29	6.69
L1.0B1.0	34.8	34.26	1.56	31.32	29.86	4.67
L1.0B0.8	39.9	39.74	0.40	31.09	29.01	6.68
L0.9B1.6	32.7	27.73	15.19	39.36	33.42	15.09
L0.9B1.4	33.3	28.54	14.29	35.35	31.49	10.92
L0.9B1.2	34.3	31.85	7.14	33.64	31.23	7.19
L0.9B1.0	36	35.79	0.60	31.63	30.54	3.44
L0.9B0.8	39.8	39.87	0.18	30.59	28.67	6.28
L0.8B1.6	34.1	30.07	11.81	38.73	34.46	11.04
L0.8B1.4	34.9	30.48	12.66	35.47	32.26	9.05
L0.8B1.2	36.1	31.98	11.42	33.83	30.81	8.91
L0.8B1.0	36.8	35.64	3.16	31.29	29.50	5.73
L0.8B0.8	40.7	40.93	0.57	30.43	28.75	5.51

of ready tasks. In order to account for such submission delays and the overhead imposed by the script, a random delay between $[0,t]$ is considered at the runtime estimated for each task. Also, an additional delay of about 1 sec is observed for the large workflow between the execution of subsequent tasks which appears to be due to the time required for the script to check the data dependency constraints between the tasks at the end of each time interval. Thus, a delay of

Table 2. Overall execution time and energy estimations for the M_{65} workflow.

Configuration	Actual execution time (s)	Estimated execution time (s)	% error in execution time	Actual energy (J)	Estimated energy	% error in energy
L1.3B1.6	116	100.13	13.68	128.55	112.11	12.79
L1.3B1.4	118.9	100.61	15.38	121.22	100.13	17.40
L1.3B1.2	122.5	104.71	14.52	114.08	95.62	16.19
L1.3B1.0	127.9	108.00	15.56	108.38	91.36	15.71
L1.3B0.8	135.2	113.07	16.37	103.36	89.04	13.86
L1.2B1.6	121.3	101.96	15.95	130.02	110.56	14.96
L1.2B1.4	124	103.14	16.83	118.62	99.50	16.12
L1.2B1.2	128.9	106.34	17.50	116.95	94.87	18.88
L1.2B1.0	132.2	110.93	16.09	107.65	91.14	15.34
L1.2B0.8	137.7	116.00	15.76	103.81	88.75	14.51
L1.1B1.6	108.1	103.77	4.01	110.12	108.56	1.42
L1.1B1.4	110.3	106.34	3.59	102.84	99.12	3.62
L1.1B1.2	113.4	107.45	5.25	96.91	93.47	3.55
L1.1B1.0	118.6	112.14	5.45	98.3	89.50	8.95
L1.1B0.8	123.9	118.31	4.51	93.94	88.22	6.09
L1.0B1.6	111.8	105.36	5.76	115.37	108.49	5.96
L1.0B1.4	115.2	107.34	6.82	107.53	98.31	8.58
L1.0B1.2	117.5	109.74	6.60	104.46	93.33	10.65
L1.0B1.0	121.8	114.33	6.13	98.94	88.90	10.15
L1.0B0.8	129.1	118.80	7.98	94.1	86.98	7.57
L0.9B1.6	116.3	111.81	3.86	116.45	109.73	5.77
L0.9B1.4	119.9	114.48	4.52	109.47	100.44	8.25
L0.9B1.2	123	118.19	3.91	103.04	95.93	6.90
L0.9B1.0	125.6	121.78	3.04	100.14	91.25	8.88
L0.9B0.8	133.6	125.85	5.80	95.14	88.90	6.56
L0.8B1.6	122.1	115.25	5.61	120.05	110.71	7.78
L0.8B1.4	118.26	117.93	0.28	98.35	100.43	2.12
L0.8B1.2	128.4	120.53	6.13	105.06	95.37	9.22
L0.8B1.0	132.6	124.63	6.01	99.18	91.53	7.72
L0.8B0.8	138.7	130.50	5.91	94.55	89.66	5.17

19 sec is added to the estimated workflow execution time for the large workflow. Finally, an extra amount of 0.036 W and 0.05 W for memory power, $P_{mem_{dyn}}$ in Eq. 8, is considered for each configuration, for the small and large workflow respectively, as average memory power did not vary significantly between the different configuration runs.

Tables 1 and 2 compare actual measurements with estimated values for each of the two workflows, M_{22} and M_{65}, for configurations of two Little (L) and two Big (B) cores at different frequencies (indicated by the number following L or B in the first column of the tables). In 38 of the 60 cases, the error for both execution time and energy consumption is less than 10%, with larger errors mostly related to extreme frequency choices. Across all 60 cases the average error is less than 8.63% for time and less than 9.69% for energy. This validates the main hypothesis: power and performance measurements at the minimum and maximum available CPU frequencies of the cores are sufficient to model energy and execution time with a reasonable precision for a wide range of configurations. Our models can be used for the appropriate selection of cores for heterogeneous platforms and the evaluation of different scheduling policies.

5   Conclusion

This work considered the problem of modelling and evaluating execution time and power/energy consumption of asymmetric multicore systems, using as a case study the execution of the Montage scientific workflow on an asymmetric multi-core processor of ARM big.LITTLE architecture. The approach described provides energy and execution time estimations for a wide range of CPU frequency configurations based on metrics monitored at a smaller set. Our approach allows users to select core and frequency configurations that achieve different trade-offs between execution time and energy consumption. Future work could investigate more elaborate modelling of system overheads to improve the accuracy of the estimations and can use such models to assess different scheduling policies.

Acknowledgment. This work was supported through a collaboration grant from HiPEAC (www.hipeac.net), the RoMoL ERC Advanced Grant (GA 321253), by the Spanish Ministry of Science and Innovation (contract TIN2015-65316-P), and by Generalitat de Catalunya (contracts 2014-SGR-1051 and 2014-SGR-1272).

References

1. Ahmad, I., Ranka, S., Khan, S.U.: Using game theory for scheduling tasks on multi-core processors for simultaneous optimization of performance and energy. In: Proceedings of the IPDPS, pp. 1–6. IEEE (2008)
2. Canon, L.C., Jeannot, E., Sakellariou, R., Zheng, W.: Comparative evaluation of the robustness of DAG scheduling heuristics. In: Gorlatch, S., Fragopoulou, P., Priol, T. (eds.) Grid Computing: Achievements and Prospects, pp. 73–84. Springer, Boston (2008). https://doi.org/10.1007/978-0-387-09457-1_7
3. Chronaki, K., Rico, A., Casas, M., Moreto, M., Badia, R., Ayguade, E., Labarta, J., Valero, M.: Task scheduling techniques for asymmetric multi-core systems. IEEE Trans. Parallel Distrib. Syst. **28**(7), 2074–2087 (2017)
4. Deelman, E., Gannon, D., Shields, M., Taylor, I.: Workflows and e-Science: an overview of workflow system features and capabilities. Future Gener. Comput. Syst. **25**(5), 528–540 (2009)

5. Deelman, E., Singh, G., Su, M.H., Blythe, J., Gil, Y., Kesselman, C., Mehta, G., Vahi, K., Berriman, G.B., Good, J.: Pegasus: a framework for mapping complex scientific workflows onto distributed systems. Sci. Program. **13**(3), 219–237 (2005)
6. Durillo, J.J., Nae, V., Prodan, R.: Multi-objective energy-efficient workflow scheduling using list-based heuristics. Future Gener. Comput. Syst. **36**, 221–236 (2014)
7. Etinski, M., Corbalan, J., Labarta, J., Valero, M.: Understanding the future of energy-performance trade-off via DVFS in HPC environments. J. Parallel Distrib. Comput. **72**(4), 579–590 (2012)
8. Ge, R., Feng, X., Cameron, K.W.: Modeling and evaluating energy-performance efficiency of parallel processing on multicore based power aware systems. In: Proceedings of the IPDPS, pp. 1–8. IEEE (2009)
9. Katz, D.S., Jacob, J.C., Deelman, E., Kesselman, C., Singh, G., Su, M.H., Berriman, G., Good, J., Laity, A., Prince, T.A.: A comparison of two methods for building astronomical image mosaics on a grid. In: Proceedings of the IEEE International Conference on Parallel Processing Workshops, pp. 85–94. IEEE (2005)
10. Kumar, R., Tullsen, D.M., Ranganathan, P., Jouppi, N.P., Farkas, K.I.: Single-ISA heterogeneous multi-core architectures for multithreaded workload performance. ACM SIGARCH Comput. Archit. News **32**(2), 64–75 (2004)
11. Li, K., Tang, X., Veeravalli, B., Li, K.: Scheduling precedence constrained stochastic tasks on heterogeneous cluster systems. IEEE TC **64**(1), 191–204 (2015)
12. Topcuoglu, H., Hariri, S., Wu, M.Y.: Performance-effective and low-complexity task scheduling for heterogeneous computing. IEEE TPDS **13**(3), 260–274 (2002)
13. Van Craeynest, K., Jaleel, A., Eeckhout, L., Narvaez, P., Emer, J.: Scheduling heterogeneous multi-cores through performance impact estimation (PIE). ACM SIGARCH Comput. Archit. News **40**(3), 213–224 (2012)
14. Von Laszewski, G., Wang, L., Younge, A.J., He, X.: Power-aware scheduling of virtual machines in DVFS-enabled clusters. In: Proceedings of the IEEE International Conference on Cluster Computing and Workshops, pp. 1–10. IEEE (2009)
15. Young, B.D., Pasricha, S., Maciejewski, A.A., Siegel, H.J., Smith, J.T.: Heterogeneous makespan and energy-constrained DAG scheduling. In: Proceedings of the Workshop on Energy Efficient High Performance Parallel and Distributed Computing, pp. 3–12. ACM (2013)
16. Zheng, W., Bao, W., Xu, C., Zhang, D.: Evaluation of the DAG ready tasks maximization algorithms in multi-core computing platforms. In: Proceedings of the CBD, pp. 110–115 (2016)

Operational Concepts of GPU Systems in HPC Centers: TCO and Productivity

Fabian P. Schneider[1] ⓘ, Sandra Wienke[1,2(✉)] ⓘ, and Matthias S. Müller[1,2] ⓘ

[1] IT Center, RWTH Aachen University, 52074 Aachen, Germany
fabian.schneider@rwth-aachen.de, {wienke,mueller}@itc.rwth-aachen.de
[2] JARA – High-Performance Computing, 52074 Aachen, Germany

Abstract. Nowadays, numerous supercomputers comprise GPUs due to promising high performance and memory bandwidth at low power consumption. With GPUs attached to a host system, applications could improve their runtime by utilizing both devices. However, this comes at a cost of increased development effort and system power consumption. In this paper, we compare the total cost of ownership (TCO) and productivity of different operational concepts of GPU systems in HPC centers covering various (heterogeneous) program execution models and CPU-GPU setups. Our investigations include runtime, power consumption, development effort and hardware purchase costs and are exemplified with two application case studies.

Keywords: TCO · Productivity · Multi-GPU · Operation
Procurement

1 Introduction

Over the last decade, the popularity of GPU-based supercomputers has increased due to their promising performance per watt ratio. Thus, nowadays, HPC centers often include GPU-based systems into their considerations for new hardware acquisitions. However, in tendering and procurement processes, HPC centers face the challenge to make an informed decision across available operational concepts of compute nodes with attached GPUs (here called *GPU nodes*). Operational concepts can vary in system configuration, i.e., number of CPU sockets and GPUs within a compute node, and the kind of GPU resource allocation.

The different operational concepts for GPU nodes are also apparent in the Top500 [21]: Titan (#3 system) deploys per GPU node one NVIDIA Kepler GPU attached to an AMD Opteron CPU that consists of two NUMA nodes [16]. Tsubame 2.5 (#40 system) employs three NVIDIA Kepler GPUs per (up to) two-socket Intel Westmere CPU in their GPU nodes. At RWTH Aachen University, the IT Center provides GPU nodes with either two NVIDIA Kepler or two Pascal GPUs attached to two-socket Intel CPUs. On all these HPC clusters, batch jobs are (currently) scheduled exclusively per GPU node [15,20]. However, from our experiences, users often run applications that are only capable of using a single

© Springer International Publishing AG, part of Springer Nature 2018
D. B. Heras and L. Bougé (Eds.): Euro-Par 2017 Workshops, LNCS 10659, pp. 452–464, 2018.
https://doi.org/10.1007/978-3-319-75178-8_37

GPU per node or do not efficiently run on more than one GPU per node. Other users only exploit the node's GPUs and leave the CPUs idling. One main reason for that is that they cannot or do not want to invest additional effort to leverage all GPUs and CPU cores within one node. Thus, from an HPC center perspective, operational concepts that consider single-GPU and multi-GPU nodes must be compared with respect to their total costs and obtained productivity. In the multi-GPU node configuration, the capabilities of GPU management in the job scheduler or virtualization possibilities can further play an important role.

In this paper, we compare different operational setups of GPU nodes with various program execution models in the context of our university HPC center. For instance, a GPU node comprising one GPU and one CPU socket executes either GPU-only or GPU-CPU hybrid programs; a GPU node with two GPUs and two CPU sockets may additionally run two independent program instances. We run a full productivity study including the system's total cost of ownership (TCO) with hardware costs, energy costs, and development costs for the parallelization of the applications and for further tuning to enable runs on multiple GPUs within a node. In detail, we investigate the productivity of a Conjugate Gradient (CG) solver and of a bio-medical real-world application on Intel Sandy Bridge and Broadwell servers combined with NVIDIA Kepler or Pascal GPUs.

The rest of the paper is structured as follow: Sect. 2 covers related work. In Sect. 3, we give an overview on the TCO model, derived productivity measure and corresponding assumptions and quantifications. In Sect. 4, we introduce the configurations representing our operational concepts of the GPU nodes. The parallelization of the CG solver and bio-medical application is described in Sect. 5. We present our results answering typical questions for GPU node operation in Sect. 6. Finally, we conclude with a recommendation for procurement in Sect. 7.

2   Related Work

While performance and power consumption of GPUs have been widely investigated in research, operational concepts of GPUs with respect to total costs and productivity have not been studied so far (to the best of our knowledge). Several works cover GPU resource management on the level of the operating system or job scheduler. For example, in [12], a CUDA wrapper library has been manually implemented to override CUDA device management calls enabling more than one user per GPU node with the given resource management constraints of the batch scheduler. Another solution for resource management is based on virtualization of GPUs that has been examined in numerous works. GViM [9] is based on Xen virtual machines. For decoupling GPUs and CPUs in resource allocation, the SLURM batch scheduler was extended with a new GPU device type in [11]. Basis for this remote GPU virtualization is rCUDA [17] that is also used in a runtime evaluation of different scenarios sharing single GPUs or accessing them remotely in another compute node [19]. While we focus on simple resource management strategies, more complex ones could be added later to our model.

TCO and productivity have been mainly studied in the context of the DARPA HPCS program [5] where most works have been published in a special issue journal [6] and cover (mathematical) models of productivity. These works only scarcely present quantifications of TCO parameters and do not apply their models to operational concepts of GPU nodes. In our previous works [24,25], we showed applicability of our TCO and productivity models to real-world HPC setups and compared costs per program run of real-world applications for (a single) GPU setup, CPU setup and Xeon Phi setup including development efforts [24].

The CG method [10] has been widely studied. A first multi-GPU implementation is given in [3], which still involved a workaround for double-precision calculations. Later multi-GPU implementations focus, e. g., on preconditioning [1], on automatic selection of the fastest of several kernels for the matrix-vector multiplication [4], or on improving the performance by reordering the matrix blocks [22]. A performance study of several kernels including CG with hybrid MPI-CUDA and MPI-OpenMP/CUDA computations is given in [14]. In [13], a heterogeneous implementation of a finite element method involving a CG algorithm on CPUs and GPU is analyzed aiming at a workload distribution that gives optimal performance and energy efficiency. However, the authors only use a single GPU and measure power using internal hardware counters instead of an external power meter. The CG algorithm newly developed in this work supports heterogeneous computations involving several CPU sockets and up to two GPUs. This implementation is highly tuned for our test systems and the structure of the used matrix, especially with respect to data transfers. Additionally, a reimplementation allowed us to track the development effort over time.

An algorithm for the bio-medical application and a shared-memory parallelization using OpenMP was developed in [2]. It was further tuned and ported with OpenCL and OpenACC to NVIDIA Fermi GPUs [26] and with OpenMP to the Intel Xeon Phi [18] in our previous works. In [24], the application's OpenMP and OpenACC implementations were compared with respect to TCO. However, the analyzed OpenACC implementation only utilized a single GPU and, thus, did not cover different operational GPU concepts. For our purposes, we developed a CUDA implementation while tracking development efforts. We tuned the code for the (newer) hardware supporting multi-GPU and heterogeneous computations using both the CPU as well as GPU architectures.

3   TCO and Productivity

For the comparison of different operational concepts of GPU nodes, we follow an integral approach from an HPC center perspective that is based on total ownership costs and productivity. These models are straightforward and fulfill all real-world procurement needs.

3.1   Model

Total costs of ownership represent the costs to acquire, operate and maintain HPC systems. Here, we follow the TCO model that we have created in [24,25].

Basically, we distinguish between one-time costs C_{ot} and costs per anno C_{pa} that depend on the number of compute nodes n and the system lifetime τ (e.g., 5 years) as shown in (1). One-time costs comprise costs for hardware acquisition, building, infrastructure, operating system (OS) and environment installation, and development effort needed to parallelize an application for the targeted HPC system and configuration. Annual costs cover maintenance costs for hardware, OS, environment and the application, as well as, energy costs and compiler/ software costs. To pay for these costs, HPC centers and institutes usually rely on federal, state and university funding that provide a fixed investment I so that an upper bound for total costs is given (see (2)). Using (2) and doing the math, we can compute the number of nodes n that can be purchased for a given fixed investment I and given system lifetime τ.

$$\text{TCO}(n, \tau) = C_{ot}(n) + C_{pa}(n) \cdot \tau \tag{1}$$

$$\text{TCO}(n, \tau) \leq I \tag{2}$$

To make an informed decision in a procurement, we do not only have to consider TCO but further need to account for the *benefit* that is gained by employing the HPC system. This can be done using a productivity metric that is economically the ratio of unit of outputs to unit of inputs. We use the productivity metric that we defined in [25], i.e., we take as value of an HPC system the number of application runs $r(n, \tau)$ that can be executed over the system's lifetime. Overall, productivity Ψ can then be expressed as:

$$\Psi(n, \tau) = \frac{value}{cost} = \frac{r(n, \tau)}{\text{TCO}(n, \tau)} \quad \text{with} \quad r(n, \tau) = \frac{\alpha \cdot \tau}{t(n)} \tag{3}$$

where $t(n)$ represents the application's runtime and α the system availability that accounts for downtimes or maintenance periods. While, formally, the runs of all applications executed on the HPC system should be summed up, we take a simplified approach here: We assume that only a single application is running for the whole system lifetime. Furthermore, we ignore any benefits gained through distributed large-scale runs, since we focus on the differences of operational concepts of GPU nodes. In this context, we investigate applications that run on a single node, but can be executed simultaneously similar to a parameter study.

3.2 Quantifications

For the application of the introduced TCO and productivity model to a real-world HPC setup, we make the following assumptions and quantifications based on our experiences from cluster procurement and operation at the IT Center of RWTH Aachen University which are also described in detail in [24].

Regarding the one-time costs, we take hardware list prices from our HPC vendors in 2013 and 2017. Building costs get amortized over 25 years and are, thus, referenced as annual costs here. Development costs are based on the effort spent for parallelizing and tuning the applications under investigation of a single experienced GPU developer so that effects on effort of varying programming skills are reduced. The corresponding salary of a full-time equivalent is derived from the funding guidelines of the German Science Foundation [8] and the European Commission's CORDIS [7]. Since our system administrations are experienced in running GPU clusters and have established an environment that can be easily rolled out to all nodes, we do not account for any additional environment costs. However, an implementation of flexible resource management into our LSF job scheduler is assumed to cost one administrator two person-days.

For the annual costs, we assume administrative costs of 83 € per compute node. We express the annual building costs with respect to the maximum power consumption of the given node configuration since the electrical supply is the limiting factor for housing machinery in the building. For the energy costs, we take 0.15 €/kWh with an estimated PUE of 1.5 in 2013. Furthermore, we divide both applications into a *serial* and *parallel part*. The former is not measured explicitly but assumed to have a fixed runtime with a power consumption corresponding to one fully-loaded core and the rest of the system idling. The parallel part corresponds to the actual work of the algorithm which is parallelized accross the devices. The runtime and power consumption are measured explicitly. As our systems have each two separate power supplies, the power consumption of both was measured on separate channels and summed up to obtain the final values. If the hardware setup contains less than two GPUs or CPU sockets, their idle power consumption is subtracted from the measured values.

Finally, we assume a fixed investment of 250 000 € from which we compute the number of nodes n. We set the system lifetime τ to 5 years and the system usage rate to 80 %.

4   GPU-CPU Configurations

For the comparison of TCO and productivity across different operational concepts of GPU nodes, we take two systems from the RWTH's compute cluster as basis from which we derive various GPU-CPU configurations, i.e., the combinations of different amounts of CPU sockets and GPU devices together with a suitable program execution model:

Kepler: 2 Intel Xeon E5-2680 CPUs @ 2.7 GHz (Sandy Bridge) with 2×8 cores, 2 NVIDIA K20Xm Kepler GPUs

Pascal: 2 Intel Xeon E5-2650 v4 CPUs @ 2.2 GHz (Broadwell) with 2×12 cores, 2 NVIDIA P100 Pascal GPUs.

As notation for the different GPU-CPU configurations, we use tuples of the form $(n_g, n_c) \in \{0, 1, 2\}^2$ with n_g denoting the number of involved GPUs and n_c the number of involved CPU sockets. This kind of tuple indicates that an executed program completely uses the given resources. The tuple $(\frac{1,1}{1,1})$ specifies the configuration with two parallel executions of the same application on 1 GPU and 1 CPU each. This configuration represents a job scheduler running two jobs in

Table 1. List of considered configurations

Config.	Description	Config.	Description
(0,2)	2 CPU sockets	$(2,^0/_1)$	2 GPUs, 1 idling CPU socket
$(^0/_2,2)$	2 CPU sockets, 2 idling GPUs	$(2,^0/_2)$	2 GPUs, 2 idling CPU sockets
$(1,^0/_1)$	1 GPU, 1 idling CPU socket	(2,2)	2 GPUs + 2 CPU sockets
(1,1)	1 GPU + 1 CPU socket	$(\frac{1,1}{1,1})$	$2 \cdot (1$ GPU + 1 CPU socket)
(1,2)	1 GPU + 2 CPU sockets		

parallel on a single node, each given one CPU socket and one GPU. The notation n'/n indicates that n GPUs or CPU sockets are available but only n' are used for program execution, i.e., $n - n'$ are idling. The purpose of these configurations is solely for comparison if GPUs are not used at all. All investigated configurations are summarized in Table 1. In the following, the term *device* is used as wildcard for either one GPU or all CPU sockets involved in program execution.

5   Applications

The CG and bio-medical application parallelized with OpenMP and CUDA are used to evaluate the different configurations. While we highly tuned these applications for the Kepler system, we have not yet focused on the Pascal architecture which is left for future work. However, we optimized the ratios for splitting the computations across the different devices. As common ground of both applications, we use a parallel first touch on the host to ensure data locality in the main memory of our cc-NUMA systems and pinned memory to increase the throughput of memory transfers between host and GPU memory. We apply asynchronous memory transfers and computations (where applicable) by using streams and events. Additionally, we hide latency of enqueuing kernels and memory copies on the GPUs by using separate host threads for the enqueuing operations.

5.1   Conjugate Gradient (CG)

First, we implement a double-precision CG algorithm for solving a linear equation system $A \cdot x = b$ [10]. We use the sparse symmetric positive definite Serena[1] matrix with $n \approx 1.4 \times 10^6$ rows, $nnz \approx 64.1 \times 10^6$ non-zeros, and a maximum of 249 non-zeros per row. To achieve the best data locality and performance on both device types, the matrix is stored in the compressed row storage format on the host with a memory footprint of roughly 775 MB, and in the ELLPACK-R format [23] on the GPUs (yielding 4.19 GB). The vectors have a size of ~90 MB.

On the host side, we use a task-driven approach for the matrix-vector multiplication with each task computing chunks of equal size. On the GPUs, we store the multiplication vector in texture memory to reduce the latency of the

---

[1] http://www.cise.ufl.edu/research/sparse/matrices/Janna/Serena.html.

unstructured accesses to this vector. Additionally, we use a Jacobi preconditioner to reduce the number of iterations in the algorithm until convergence. All operations of the algorithm are split row-wise across the available devices into disjoint chunks. Each chunk c contains the row indices R_c such that $\bigcup R_c = \{1, \ldots, n\}$. We exploit the matrix structure having most non-zeros close to the diagonal by minimizing vector data transfers for the matrix vector multiplication: At the beginning of the algorithm, the minimum and maximum column indices $t_c^{\min}, t_c^{\max}$ of non-zeros for each chunk c of the matrix are computed. Formally,

$$t_c^\lambda = \lambda(\{j \in \{1, \ldots, n\} \mid A_{i,j} \neq 0, i \in R_c\}) \text{ for } \lambda \in \{\min, \max\}$$
$$T_c = \{t_c^{\min}, t_c^{\min} + 1, \ldots, t_c^{\max} - 1, t_c^{\max}\} \setminus R_c$$

where T_c defines the set of indices of the vector that needs to be transferred to the device responsible for chunk c.

As our Kepler system does not support direct memory transfers between GPUs, we increase memory throughput by minimizing the transferred vector data between GPU and CPU so that additional main memory overheads are avoided. Thus, for hybrid multi-GPU computations, the first chunk refers to the first GPU, the middle one to the CPU, and the last chunk to the second GPU. Our Pascal system supports NVlink between GPUs and, thus, allows fast inter-GPU memory transfers. Therefore, in future, we will reorder the distribution for that architecture to take advantage of NVlink.

The analytical determination of the chunk sizes is challenging, as they are highly affected by the structure of the matrix and we hide some of the latency for copying the vector by doing it asynchronously to other computations. Thus, to obtain optimal work chunk distribution across devices, we benchmarked different values by running the algorithm with a small number of iterations.

The serial part of this algorithm includes reading the matrix file, conversion of matrix formats, allocation and initialization of vectors, and correctness checking of results. The time for these operations is assumed to have a fixed value of 20 s.

5.2 Neuromagnetic Inverse Problem (NINA)

The second application solves a real-world problem from the field of bio-medicine, namely the neuromagnetic inverse problem (NINA). The algorithm was originally implemented in MATLAB with the three most time-consuming parts computed in C, i. e., an objective function, and its first- and second-order derivatives. For simplicity, we assume a constant runtime of 46 s for the (serial) MATLAB part and imitate the original algorithmic optimization process implemented in MATLAB by executing all kernels one after the other for 1000 times. These three parts involve matrix vector operations and reductions with a mostly dense matrix of dimension $128 \times 512\,000$. This special matrix form hinders the effective usage of BLAS libraries, so that we had to manually optimize the algorithm.

Our best-effort performance was obtained with one block per row for the dense matrix vector multiplication. Additionally, we avoid delays by immediately starting the reduction kernels (per row) out of the multiplication kernels with dynamic parallelism. To coordinate the GPU computations without interfering with the other CPU computations, we use a dedicated CPU thread.

All operations are split row-wise across the different devices. As the matrix is stored in a dense fashion, the computation of every row takes the same time per device type, resulting in an equal number of rows for each GPU. As for CG, we used benchmarking to determine the number of rows computed by the CPU.

6 Productivity Results

We interpret our results with respect to typical questions for the operation of GPU nodes. Results of our runtime and power measurements are shown in Fig. 1 and for the productivity and programming effort in Fig. 2. While runtimes generally improved when going from Kepler to the Pascal system (without further tuning), heterogeneous computations involving more than one device do not perform well on Pascal. We assume that neglecting available memory bandwidth given by NVlink is one reason for that. Remember that presented results refer to 250 000 € of investment. Here, a potential budget increase does not cause any changes (saturation). If we decrease the budget, the results only change slightly.

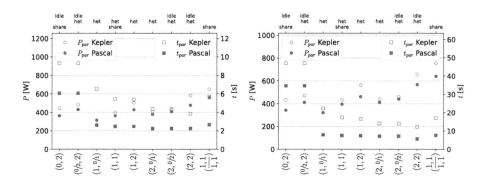

Fig. 1. Parallel runtime and power consumption: CG (left), NINA (right)

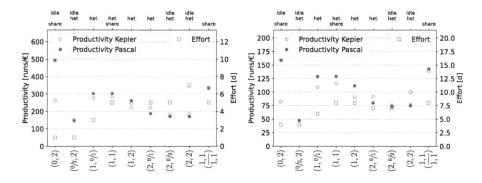

Fig. 2. Programming effort and productivity: CG (left), NINA (right)

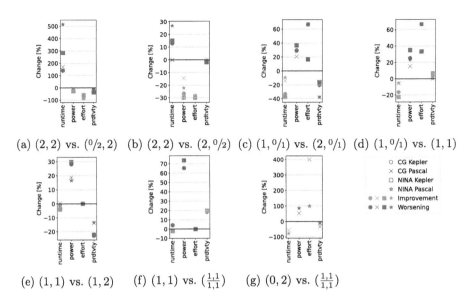

(a) $(2,2)$ vs. $(^0/2,2)$ (b) $(2,2)$ vs. $(2,^0/2)$ (c) $(1,^0/1)$ vs. $(2,^0/1)$ (d) $(1,^0/1)$ vs. $(1,1)$

(e) $(1,1)$ vs. $(1,2)$ (f) $(1,1)$ vs. $\left(\frac{1,1}{1,1}\right)$ (g) $(0,2)$ vs. $\left(\frac{1,1}{1,1}\right)$

Fig. 3. Detailed comparison of configurations

6.1   Cost of Idling Hardware

An interesting question for HPC centers procuring or operating GPU nodes is the cost or penalty if not all available devices are fully used by developers. For this investigation, we take as reference the hardware setup containing 2 GPUs and 2 CPU sockets – which is the default one at RWTH's compute cluster – and the execution concept using all of them, i. e., the configuration (2,2).

First, we compare the default configuration to $(^0/2,2)$ (cf. Fig. 3a). The idling GPUs decrease the performance significantly (up to 500 % with NINA on the Pascal system) but only reduce the power consumption by 10 % to 30 %. Hence, overall productivity is decreased with 2 idling GPUs by ~15 % with CG and ~40 % with NINA. With the same execution model exploiting only CPUs, but without any available GPUs in that node (configuration (0,2)), the productivity obviously increases again compared to $(^0/2,2)$ by about $\frac{3}{4}$ on Kepler and even ~230 % on Pascal (which is mainly due to omitting the GPU purchase costs).

On the other hand, if both GPUs are used and the CPU sockets are idling (configuration $(2,^0/2)$) (cf. Fig. 3b), the productivity is hardly affected (changes are below 3 %). This is because the runtime increases by at most one fourth, which is compensated by a lower power consumption by about the same factor.

6.2   Multiple (Heterogeneous) Devices

Next, we examine whether extra effort invested into enabling heterogeneous computing with more than one device pays off by additional productivity.

The sheer benefit of exploiting 2 GPUs per node can be investigated by comparison to the corresponding single-GPU setup – both with idling CPUs, i. e.,

$(1,^0/_1)$ vs. $(2,^0/_1)$ (cf. Fig. 3c). Surprisingly, we observe a productivity decrease with 2 GPUs by ~20 % on the Kepler system, and even 40 % on Pascal. Detailed examination shows that the (low) improvement in runtime (~35 % on Kepler and ~10 % on Pascal) cannot compensate for the increase in power consumption (around one fourth), programming effort, and purchase costs. While we assume to get better runtime on Pascal when leveraging NVlink, we will not be able to increase the runtime sufficiently to improve productivity due to the high serial runtime: e.g., if the assumption holds that 2 GPUs could halve the parallel runtime, the productivity decrease is still ~15 % on Kepler and ~35 % on Pascal.

As seen in the previous subsection, the productivity does not change much when adding 2 fully-utilized CPU sockets to 2 GPUs. A similar effect is evident when adding one fully-utilized CPU socket to one GPU, i.e., $(1,^0/_1)$ vs. $(1,1)$ (cf. Fig. 3d): The productivity slightly increases on Kepler (by ~5 %) and remains about the same on Pascal. To evaluate the worth of buying a two-socket (single-GPU) node vs. a one-socket (single-GPU) node, we compare the previous configuration $(1,1)$ to $(1,2)$ where both sockets are utilized (cf. Fig. 3e). Here, we see a productivity decrease by 13 % to 23 %, which is mainly due to the small runtime improvement (1 % to 4 %) compared to the higher power consumption (around 30 % on Kepler and 20 % on Pascal) and higher purchase cost.

6.3   Sharing GPU Nodes

The previous results lead us to the question whether we can increase productivity by sharing a single node containing 2 GPUs and 2 CPU sockets across multiple (simultaneous) program executions using disjoint devices (potentially) by multiple users. One solution for sharing nodes could be implemented based on the job scheduler's resource management capabilities for GPUs. We imitate this solution by running 2 programs in parallel on one node, each using one CPU socket and one GPU, i.e., configuration $(\frac{1,1}{1,1})$, and additionally assume further one-time costs for the administrative adoption of the batch scheduler.

On Kepler, this configuration delivers the highest productivity, as the runtime is about the same as for configuration $(1,1)$, – which is the configuration with the second highest productivity – but with two simultaneous program executions (cf. Fig. 3f). In return, the power consumption increases by only ~70 %, so the productivity increases by ~20 %. On Pascal, the configuration $(0,2)$ achieves the highest productivity, i.e., buying and utilizing GPUs at all seem not beneficial under the reservation that the codes have not been tuned for Pascal GPUs yet. However, the productivity of the sharing approach $(\frac{1,1}{1,1})$ is only 10 % lower with NINA, whereas about $^1/_3$ with CG (cf. Fig. 3g). The reason is the small runtime improvement (~80 % with NINA, ~60 % with CG) compared to the much higher power consumption (85 % or 55 %, respectively) and purchase costs. With further tuning for Pascal, we can probably reach a higher productivity with the shared approach. Note that effort needed for the adoption of the job scheduler is assumed to be low. More complex virtualization approaches will yield much higher one-time costs. Nevertheless, on Kepler, the sharing approach would still pay off if the administrative effort theoretically increased up to 130 person-days.

7   Conclusion

Concluding our productivity results, we give recommendations for hardware procurement choices and GPU system operations for HPC clusters. For this, we assume that at least one GPU per node should be available and that all cluster nodes have the same hardware setup. We base our suggestions on the case studies investigated, i. e., a CG solver and the real-world NINA application.

Since productivity decreases when using heterogeneous hardware setups, we recommend to buy only minimal nodes, containing only one GPU and one CPU socket. Furthermore, productivity is hardly affected by utilizing the CPU instead of letting it idle. Hence, it could be up to the programmer, to decide if he utilizes the CPU or not. Another approach can be taken by purchasing nodes with two GPUs and two CPU sockets and allow two programs from different users to exploit distinct devices on the node (e.g., by job scheduler resource management). In this way, even higher productivity results can be achieved as long as the additional administrative one-time effort to implement this is not prevailing.

In future, we will evaluate the productivity after tuning the applications for the Pascal architecture. Early results show a performance improvement of $\sim 19\%$ for CG utilizing NVlink in configuration $(2, 0)$. Additionally, we will analyze more applications, e. g., with lower serial fractions to achieve higher total speedups. Furthermore, we plan to lift the analysis to applications running across multiple nodes, i. e., with MPI+OpenMP+CUDA.

References

1. Ament, M., Knittel, G., Weiskopf, D., Strasser, W.: A parallel preconditioned conjugate gradient solver for the poisson problem on a multi-GPU platform. In: 2010 18th Euromicro Conference on Parallel, Distributed and Network-Based Processing, pp. 583–592 (2010)
2. Bücker, H., Beucker, R., Rupp, A.: Parallel minimum p-norm solution of the neuromagnetic inverse problem for realistic signals using exact Hessian-vector products. SIAM J. Sci. Comput. **30**(6), 2905–2921 (2008)
3. Cevahir, A., Nukada, A., Matsuoka, S.: Fast conjugate gradients with multiple GPUs. In: Allen, G., Nabrzyski, J., Seidel, E., van Albada, G.D., Dongarra, J., Sloot, P.M.A. (eds.) ICCS 2009 Part I. LNCS, vol. 5544, pp. 893–903. Springer, Heidelberg (2009). https://doi.org/10.1007/978-3-642-01970-8_90
4. Cevahir, A., Nukada, A., Matsuoka, S.: High performance conjugate gradient solver on multi-GPU clusters using hypergraph partitioning. Comput. Sci.- Res. Dev. **25**(1–2), 83–91 (2010)
5. Dongarra, J., Graybill, R., Harrod, W., Lucas, R., Lusk, E., Luszczek, P., Mcmahon, J., Snavely, A., Vetter, J., Yelick, K., Alam, S., Campbell, R., Carrington, L., Chen, T.Y., Khalili, O., Meredith, J., Tikir, M.: DARPA's HPCS program: history, models, tools, languages. In: Zelkowitz, M.V. (ed.) Advances in COMPUTERS High Performance Computing, vol. 72, pp. 1–100. Elsevier, Amsterdam (2008)
6. Dongarra, J.J., De Supinski, B.R. (eds.): International Journal of High Performance Computing Applications, vol. 18, no. 4. Sage Publications (2004)

7. European Commission - Community Research and Development Information Service (CORDIS): Guide to Financial Issues Relating to FP7 Indirect Actions (2014)
8. German Science Foundation (DFG): DFG Personnel Rates for 2017
9. Gupta, V., Gavrilovska, A., Schwan, K., Kharche, H., Tolia, N., Talwar, V., Ranganathan, P.: GViM: GPU-accelerated virtual machines. In: Proceedings of the 3rd ACM Workshop on System-Level Virtualization for High Performance Computing, pp. 17–24. ACM (2009). 1519141
10. Hestenes, M.R., Stiefel, E.: Methods of conjugate gradients for solving linear systems. Natl. Bur. Stand. **49**, 409–436 (1952)
11. Iserte, S., Castello, A., Mayo, R., Quintana-Orti, E.S., Silla, F., Duato, J., Reano, C., Prades, J.: SLURM support for remote GPU virtualization: implementation and performance study. In: 2014 IEEE 26th International Symposium on Computer Architecture and High Performance Computing, pp. 318–325 (2014)
12. Kindratenko, V.V., Enos, J.J., Shi, G., Showerman, M.T., Arnold, G.W., Stone, J.E., Phillips, J., Hwu, W.: GPU clusters for high-performance computing. In: 2009 IEEE International Conference on Cluster Computing and Workshops, pp. 1–8 (2009)
13. Lang, J., Rünger, G.: An execution time and energy model for an energy-aware execution of a conjugate gradient method with CPU/GPU collaboration. J. Parallel Distrib. Comput. **74**(9), 2884–2897 (2014)
14. Lu, F., Song, J., Yin, F., Zhu, X.: Performance evaluation of hybrid programming patterns for large CPU/GPU heterogeneous clusters. Comput. Phys. Commun. **183**(6), 1172–1181 (2012)
15. Oak Ridge National Laboratory: Job Resource Accounting. https://www.olcf.ornl.gov/support/system-user-guides/titan-user-guide/. Accessed 4 2017
16. Oak Ridge National Laboratory: XK7 (Titan) Node Description. https://www.olcf.ornl.gov/support/system-user-guides/accelerated-computing-guide. Accessed 4 2017
17. Pena, A.J., Reano, C., Silla, F., Mayo, R., Quintana-Orti, E.S., Duato, J.: A complete and efficient CUDA-sharing solution for HPC clusters. Parallel Comput. **40**(10), 574–588 (2014)
18. Schmidl, D., Cramer, T., Wienke, S., Terboven, C., Müller, M.S.: Assessing the performance of OpenMP programs on the Intel Xeon Phi. In: Wolf, F., Mohr, B., an Mey, D. (eds.) Euro-Par 2013. LNCS, vol. 8097, pp. 547–558. Springer, Heidelberg (2013). https://doi.org/10.1007/978-3-642-40047-6_56
19. Silla, F., Prades, J., Iserte, S., Reano, C.: Remote GPU virtualization: is it useful? In: 2016 2nd IEEE International Workshop on High-Performance Interconnection Networks in the Exascale and Big-Data Era (HiPINEB), pp. 41–48 (2016)
20. The Global Scientific Information and Computing Center (GSIC): TSUBAME 2.5 User's Guide: User Environment. http://tsubame.gsic.titech.ac.jp/docs/guides/tsubame2/html_en/resources.html. Accessed 4 2017
21. Top500-The List. https://www.top500.org/lists/2016/11/, November 2016
22. Verschoor, M., Jalba, A.C.: Analysis and performance estimation of the Conjugate Gradient method on multiple GPUs. Parallel Comput. **38**(10–11), 552–575 (2012)
23. Vázquez, F., Ortega, G., Fernández, J.J., Garzón, E.M.: Improving the performance of the sparse matrix vector product with GPUs. In: 10th IEEE International Conference on Computer and Information Technology, pp. 1146–1151 (2010)
24. Wienke, S., an Mey, D., Müller, M.S.: Accelerators for technical computing: is it worth the pain? A TCO perspective. In: Kunkel, J.M., Ludwig, T., Meuer, H.W. (eds.) ISC 2013. LNCS, vol. 7905, pp. 330–342. Springer, Heidelberg (2013). https://doi.org/10.1007/978-3-642-38750-0_25

25. Wienke, S., Iliev, H., an Mey, D., Müller, M.S.: Modeling the productivity of HPC systems on a computing center scale. In: Kunkel, J.M., Ludwig, T. (eds.) ISC High Performance 2015. LNCS, vol. 9137, pp. 358–375. Springer, Cham (2015). https://doi.org/10.1007/978-3-319-20119-1_26
26. Wienke, S., Springer, P., Terboven, C., an Mey, D.: OpenACC—first experiences with real-world applications. In: Kaklamanis, C., Papatheodorou, T., Spirakis, P.G. (eds.) Euro-Par 2012. LNCS, vol. 7484, pp. 859–870. Springer, Heidelberg (2012). https://doi.org/10.1007/978-3-642-32820-6_85

Large Scale Graph Processing in a Distributed Environment

Nitesh Upadhyay$^{(\boxtimes)}$, Parita Patel, Unnikrishnan Cheramangalath(iD),
and Y. N. Srikant

Indian Institute of Science, Bangalore, India
niteshu@iisc.ac.in

Abstract. Large graphs are widely used in real world graph analytics. Memory available in a single machine is usually inadequate to process these graphs. A good solution is to use a distributed environment. Typical programming styles used in existing distributed environment frameworks are different from imperative programming and difficult for programmers to adapt. Moreover, some graph algorithms having a high degree of parallelism ideally run on an accelerator cluster. Error prone and lower level programming methods (memory and thread management) available for such systems repel programmers from using such architectures. Existing frameworks do not deal with the accelerator clusters.

We propose a framework which addresses the previously stated deficiencies. Our framework automatically generates implementations of graph algorithms for distributed environments from the intuitive shared memory based code written in a high-level Domain Specific Language (DSL), *Falcon*. The framework analyses the intermediate representation, applies a set of optimizations and then generates Giraph code for a CPU cluster and MPI+OpenCL code for a GPU cluster. Experimental evaluations show efficiency and scalability of our framework.

Keywords: Distributed architecture · Accelerator · Cross-platform
Graph processing · DSL · Falcon

1 Introduction

Large scale graphs are generated and analyzed in various domains such as social networks, road networks, systems biology, and web graphs. Graph processing on a single machine becomes inefficient when the graph size exceeds the machine memory (due to high disk access latency). Graph processing is also inefficient because of irregular behaviour of graph algorithms. On the other hand, parallelism exhibited by graph algorithms improves performance [15]. To exploit the parallelism, modern distributed architectures such as multi-core CPU clusters and GPU clusters, are used.

In recent times, many frameworks for graph analytics in distributed environment such as Giraph [1], GraphLab [13], and PowerGraph [7], which target only

© Springer International Publishing AG, part of Springer Nature 2018
D. B. Heras and L. Bougé (Eds.): Euro-Par 2017 Workshops, LNCS 10659, pp. 465–477, 2018.
https://doi.org/10.1007/978-3-319-75178-8_38

multi-core CPU cluster, have been proposed. All these frameworks have their own specific unconventional programming style which is difficult for a programmer to comprehend and adopt.

To exploit the high degree of parallelism in graph algorithms, high performance compute resources such as GPUs are the most suitable targets. Moreover, large scale graph processing requires a distributed environment such as GPU clusters. Lower level APIs such as CUDA and OpenCL with Message Passing Interface (MPI) for communication among nodes facilitate programming in such environments. It is inconvenient for an amateur programmer to develop algorithms in such a language. A few challenges are summed up below.

- Thread management: Deciding the total number of threads and thread block size, and synchronizing threads.
- Memory management: Allocating and deallocating memory for a graph object and all its vertex and edge properties on GPU, copying a graph object to GPU from CPU and copying back the results.
- Debugging: Manual thread management and memory management make a program error prone and difficult to debug.
- Message passing: Deciding which data to communicate and to which nodes, preparing the data, and sending and receiving the data in appropriate buffers.
- Global variables: Absence of shared memory forces each node to keep a separate copy of each global variable and synchronize it whenever any node modifies its copy.

This paper presents a scalable framework which addresses the above discussed challenges of large scale graph processing in a distributed environment, i.e., CPU cluster and GPU cluster. The framework uses the front-end of Falcon DSL [18]. The framework traverses the Abstract Syntax Tree (AST) generated by Falcon [18], applies a set of optimizations and then generates Giraph [1] code for a CPU cluster and MPI+OpenCL code for a GPU cluster. Since our framework uses the constructs of Falcon [18], the programmer enjoys conventional, imperative, and shared memory programming style.

Our key contributions are as follows.

- We provide a multi-target code generator for any vertex-centric algorithm written in Falcon [18] that caters to CPU and GPU clusters.
- The framework analyses the DSL code and decides the graph object *properties* to be communicated, sends the messages, and synchronizes received message data with local data. Thus, it hides the complexity of message passing from the programmer.
- The framework applies a set of optimizations in order to minimize memory occupancy and communication latency.
- Experimental evaluations on CPU and GPU clusters shows scalability and efficiency of our framework.

2   Related Work

Green-Marl [9] and its extensions [10,16] target multi-core CPU, NVIDIA GPU and CPU cluster (Pregel [14]). Galois [12] provides C++ APIs to implement graph algorithms on a multi-core CPU. LonestarGPU [4] is a CUDA framework for graph algorithms and targets NVIDIA GPU. All of these DSLs and frameworks are either limited to a single node or do not target GPU cluster.

TOTEM [6] is a graph processing engine which targets hybrid architectures on a single node. It partitions the graph on multiple GPUs and CPU of a single node. Medusa [19] is a framework which generates graph algorithms implementations for multiple GPUs of a single node. Both, Totem and Medusa limit the graph size to the memory of the single node. Parallel Boost Graph Library [8] provides implementations of graph algorithms in a distributed environment. But it does not target GPU clusters.

There are many frameworks for graph processing in distributed environments, such as Pregel [14], Giraph [1], GraphLab [13], PowerGraph [7], GoFFish [17] etc. Pregel [14] and Giraph [1] adopt the Bulk Synchronous Parallel (BSP) model [5] and are scalable. Unlike Pregel [14], GraphLab [13] provides asynchronous and adaptive computation. It is suitable for graph algorithms where different parts of graph converge with dissimilar rates. PowerGraph [7] is an extended version of GraphLab [13]. It is desirable for natural graphs whose degree distribution follows a power law. GoFFish [17] is a sub-graph centric programming abstraction for distributed clusters. All these frameworks adopt unconventional programming models and target only CPU clusters. We generated code in Giraph because it offers high scalability. However, several other frameworks can also be targeted.

3   Background

3.1   Giraph

Giraph [1] is a scalable, efficient and fault-tolerant open-source implementation of Google's Pregel [14]. The collection of JAVA APIs available in Giraph [1] is useful to a programmer to implement graph algorithms on a Hadoop cluster. Giraph [1] has the following features.

– Bulk Synchronous Parallel model (BSP) [5] model: Giraph framework is built on the BSP model.
– Vertex-centric: Giraph algorithms are implemented in the form of *computation over vertices*. Algorithmic logic is written in a *single local compute function* (`BasicCompute.compute()`) which runs on every vertex in parallel. This function gets executed iteratively, and the program terminates when no communication happens and all vertices become inactive.

However, it poses the following challenges from a programming perspective.

- Programming in Giraph requires exclusive handling of *global variables* and *graph object properties*. A user must register them through an `Aggregator` in the global compute function (`MasterCompute.compute()`). Afterwards, these global variables and properties can be accessed and modified from both local and global functions.
- Since Giraph allows only a *single* `BasicCompute.compute()`, managing *multi-functions* is a difficult task. A global variable has to be maintained in the `MasterCompute.compute()` function. Depending on the value of this variable apt function is chosen in the *local compute function*.
- Programmer must explicitly implement *message type* through `Message` class and *vertex properties* through `Vertex` class.

```
1   class RBMC extends BasicCompute{        13   void shake3(Vertex v,Message m){...
2     void compute(Vertex v,Message m){     14   aggregate(RBMM.count,1);
3       int fun_call = getAggregatedValue    15   ...}
4       (RBMM.current_fun);                  16   }
5       switch(fun_call){                    17   class RBMM extends MasterCompute{
6         case 0: shake1(); break;           18     String count = "count";
7         case 1: shake2(); break;           19     String current_fun = "current_fun";
8         case 2: shake3(); break;           20     public void initialize(){
9       }                                    21       register(count);
10    }                                      22       register(current_fun);
11    void shake1(Vertex v,Message m){...}   23     }
12    void shake2(Vertex v,Message m){...}   24   }
```

Fig. 1. Giraph random bipartite matching code

Figure 1 shows the partial implementation of random bipartite matching in Giraph. This algorithm is a three-step handshake algorithm. In the first step, the left vertex sends a message to the right vertex. In second step, the right vertex accepts the message from any one of the left vertices randomly, and sends an acknowledgement. One of the edges is matched in the third step. Global variable `count`, which can be modified by any vertex, is registered in the `RBMMasterCompute` class. Also, *multi-functions* call is handled through `phase` aggregator. Its value gets modified in `MasterCompute.compute()` method which is not shown here. We have also omitted the implementations of `Vertex` and `Message` class, and other methods for brevity.

3.2   Falcon

Falcon [18], a graph DSL, extends C programming language and helps programmers to implement graph analysis algorithms intuitively. The front-end of the Falcon [18] compiler generates an AST. The back-end traverses the AST and generates OpenMP annotated C code for multi-core CPU and CUDA code for

NVIDIA GPU. Besides C data types, Falcon [18] has additional data types pertinent to graph algorithms such as *graph, vertex, edge, set* and *collection*. The user required to define parallelism explicitly through the parallel construct `foreach`.

4 Back-End of Our Framework

Our framework adopts the BSP model [5] where the computation of a graph algorithm occurs in a series of supersteps. Each superstep consists of the three following steps.

- Computation: Each node runs a *computation function* parallelly and independently.
- Communication: At the end of the computation, nodes communicate with each other.
- Synchronization: Each node synchronizes its local data with the received data.

Our framework uses the front-end of the Falcon compiler [18]. Front-end of Falcon parses the DSL code and generates an AST which is input to the back-end of our framework. Back-end compilation occurs in two phases. In the first phase, the AST is traversed to get some essential information such as the vertex or edge property to be communicated and the program location for the communication. In the second phase, optimizations are applied and efficient code is generated in Giraph for CPU cluster and MPI+OpenCL for heterogeneous cluster. The DSL programmer can enable or disable optimizations through command line switches.

Graph Storage and Partitioning for a Heterogeneous Cluster. Generated code stores the graph in Compressed Sparse Row (CSR) format. CSR format offers less storage overhead and favors memory coalescing compared to edge list and adjacency list representations. It keeps two arrays: `edges` and `indices`. `edges` array stores the destination vertices and weights of outgoing edges of each vertex. All the outgoing edges of each vertex are stored contiguously. `indices` array stores the index of the first outgoing edge (stored in `edges` array) of each vertex.

By default, our framework partitions the graph vertex-wise using the METIS tool [11]. A programmer can also use his/her own partitioning strategies. Each vertex belongs to a specific cluster node depending on its partition-id. Figure 2 shows graph partitioning on three nodes and graph storage at Node2 in CSR format. The input graph, which is shared among all nodes of a cluster, is read in parallel.

Multiple copies of a vertex property are stored in order to keep the vertex's property consistent across partitions. One *master copy* is stored at the node where the vertex belongs. Other copies (*duplicate copies*) reside at the nodes where the vertex is destination vertex of any inter-partition edge. As Fig. 2 suggests, the *master copies* of vertices v2 and v4 reside on Node2. Node2 also stores copies of vertices v3 and v5 whose *master copies* are stored at Node0 and Node1 respectively.

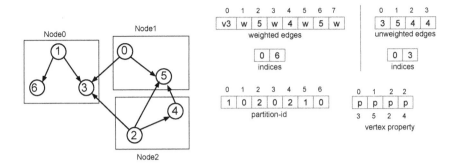

Fig. 2. Graph and its storage on Node2

4.1   Compilation for a GPU Cluster (MPI+OpenCL Code)

A heterogeneous cluster is composed of multiple nodes where each node can be any device such as CPU or accelerator, such as GPU, DSP, or FPGA. Usually, graph algorithms run on general purpose computing devices, i.e., CPU and GPU.

Typically, OpenMP is used to target the multi-core CPU nodes. CUDA is used to target the NVIDIA GPU nodes. But OpenCL is used to target both multi-core CPU and GPU devices of any vendor since it is an open, royalty-free, platform-agnostic and vendor-agnostic standard for programming on heterogeneous computation resources. Hence, we decided to generate code in OpenCL coupled with MPI which is a programming standard for a distributed architecture. Translations of some of the constructs are discussed below.

Parallel Regions: A Falcon programmer explicitly defines parallelism through the parallel construct `foreach`. Code enclosed in a `foreach` loop is translated to a kernel. The kernel will run in parallel on all local vertices. Since the execution of kernel comes under the *computation* step of the BSP model, it runs in parallel on all the nodes. Figure 3 shows the translation of `foreach` loop. t is a points iterator which iterates on all the vertices of the graph. Each vertex corresponds

```
1   //Falcon code
2   foreach(t In gr.points)
3     t.cc = Y;


1   //Giraph code
2   BasicCompute::compute(vertex){
3     if(getSuperStep==0)
4       vertex.getValue().cc = Y;
5   }
```

```
1   //OpenCL code
2   //kernel definition
3   _kernel void fun1(....){
4     int t_id = get_global_id(0);
5     cc[t_id+vertex_offset] = Y;
6   }
7   //kernel call
8   size = gr.no_of_part_vertices;
9   clEnqueueNDRangeKernel(..,&size,..);
```

Fig. 3. Falcon code and its equivalent generated Giraph and OpenCL code

to a thread, and all threads execute the loop body in parallel. The code enclosed in the `foreach` loop is translated to a kernel `fun1`. The kernel is called with the size of total number of vertices (lines 8–9).

Global Property and Variable: In a shared memory architecture, the scope of global variables and properties associated with a graph runs throughout the program. But in a distributed architecture, there is no memory which is accessible from all the nodes of the cluster. Hence, memory is allocated on all the nodes for all the global variables and properties. Whenever such a variable gets updated on any node, its value is broadcast to all the other nodes. If the operation applied on a global variable is `MIN`, `MAX`, `ADD` or `MUL`, then it can be applied in any order since these operations are associative and commutative. But, when `Assignment` operator is applied on a global variable, it gets written non-deterministically in any order.

Communication and Synchronization: In order to carry out communication in a distributed environment, a programmer needs to figure out data, program location, and source and destination nodes for the communication. Our framework automatically generates code to handle these issues from Falcon code. In the first phase of compilation, the AST is traversed to find out the required information for communication.

If any property is modified in a kernel, then that property needs to be communicated to the neighbours, and communication happens after the call to the kernel that modifies the property. Communication occurs between two nodes only if there is any inter-partition edge between them.

After the communication, received data is synchronized with local data based on the kind of operation applied on the property in the kernel code. This synchronization code is also generated by our framework.

4.2 Compilation for a CPU Cluster (Giraph Code)

Parallel Region: The code enclosed in a `foreach` loop is translated to the `BasicCompute.compute()` function of Giraph (as shown in Fig. 3). This function executes conceptually in parallel on all the vertices of graph.

Global Variables and Properties: Giraph offers `Aggregators` to handle global variables. Its value can be modified from either `BasicCompute.compute()` or `MasterCompute.compute()` function. `MasterCompute.compute()` function gets executed in the beginning of every superstep. Graph properties or global variables in Falcon are mapped to the `Aggregators` of Giraph. The first phase of compilation determines the type of `Aggregator` based on the type of the operation applied on global variable or graph object property. Table 1 depicts the operations and their equivalent `Aggregators`.

Table 1. Operations and their corresponding Aggregators

Expression	Type of Aggregator
MAX(gr.prop,k,change)	MaxAggregator
MIN(gr.prop,k,change)	MinAggregator
ADD(gr.prop,k)	SumAggregator
MUL(gr.prop,k)	ProductAggregator
gr.prop = k	OverwriteAggregator

Multi-functions: When multiple functions are called through parallel constructs in Falcon, they all are mapped to the same `BasicCompute.compute()` function. Our framework assigns numbers to all functions according to their calling order. Our framework also uses a `current_fun` variable (of type enum) to keep track of which function is being executed. Since `current_fun` is a global variable, it is modified through the `SumAggregator`. The `MasterCompute` `.compute()` function modifies the `current_fun` variable appropriately in the beginning of every superstep. Subsequently, `BasicCompute.compute()` function selects the function based on the value of `current_fun` variable.

Communication and Synchronization: Communication and synchronization are managed as stated in the GPU cluster compilation (Sect. 4.1).

5   Optimizations

5.1   Execute Only Active Vertices

Programmers often tend to write simple and unoptimized parallel code for traversal based graph algorithms that underperform and waste resources. However, better manual or optimized Falcon code can also be written.

   In traversal-based graph algorithms, all the vertices do not remain active in each iteration. In the generated code, active vertices can be tracked and kernel can be executed only on those vertices. In order to achieve this, the compiler associates a boolean property `is_Active` with each vertex that stores the status of the vertex. Initially, all the vertices have their `is_Active` flags set to false except for the starting point. Whenever a vertex's property gets updated, the status of that vertex is modified to active. When the execution of an active vertex is finished, its status is changed to inactive (false). The execution time of each iteration gets reduced because the number of active vertices is less than the total number of vertices. As a result, total execution time of the algorithm gets reduced significantly.

5.2   Discarding the Weight if Not Required

When a weighted graph is given as input to an algorithm that does not use the weight of an edge, storing the weight of edges does not serve any purpose.

Falcon uses the function `getWeight()` to access the weight of an edge. While traversing the AST, our compiler notes whether this function is called anywhere or not. Subsequently, this information is propagated to the code generator. The code generator generates code with the graph storage format accordingly and also alters the `READ` function appropriately. $|V| + 2 * |E|$ units of memory are required to store the graph G(V,E) in weighted CSR format while unweighted CSR format requires only $|V| + |E|$ units of memory. Our compiler optimization saves $|E|$ units of memory when the algorithm does not use weight of an edge. Thus larger graph can be accommodated on the given limited amount of memory. Furthermore, unweighted CSR format stores neighbors contiguously, unlike weighted CSR, where neighbors are stored alternatively. Thereby, it provides better cache locality and improves execution time.

5.3   Communicate Selective Data

Vertex's property has multiple copies as discussed in Sect. 4. One *master copy* is stored at the node where the vertex belongs. Other copies reside at the nodes where the vertex is the destination vertex of any inter-partition edge (referred here as *duplicate copy*). Whenever any *duplicate copy* is updated, that must be communicated to the *master copy* in order to preserve consistency. Some algorithms such as Pagerank update the *duplicate copy* in every iteration. However, other algorithms such as Single Source Shortest Path (SSSP) or Breadth First Search (BFS) do not update each *duplicate copy* in each iteration. Communicating all *duplicate copies* in each iteration is costly. Our optimization algorithm determines the updated duplicate copies and sends out only these. The compiler creates an extra copy of the property which stores previous value and compares it with the current value of the property to find out whether it is updated or not.

If an algorithm requires update of almost every *duplicate copy* in each iteration, then this optimization will not add any value and ends up performing slower than the unoptimized one (as illustrated in Table 4). Hence, this optimization has been made optional (through a command line switch).

6   Experimental Evaluations

Our framework generates Giraph code from Falcon code for a CPU cluster. It generates MPI+OpenCL for a heterogeneous cluster (OpenCL version 1.1). Table 2 shows the number of lines of code handwritten for Falcon, Giraph and MPI+OpenCL. Experiments on a GPU cluster have been carried out for five algorithms: BFS, SSSP, WCC, PR and RBM (Table 2). We used supercomputer Cray XC40 for experiments of the GPU cluster, where each node is having a NVIDIA Tesla K40 clocked at 706 MHz, with 2880 cores and 12 GB global memory. GPU cluster code is compiled with NVCC version 7.5. Experiments on CPU cluster are done for five algorithms: BFS, SSSP, PR, RBM and K-Core (Table 2). Our framework can generate code for any vertex-centric algorithm. An algorithm involving message-pulling can be indirectly supported in Giraph by storing all the in-neighbours of vertices. Graph mutation for GPU clusters is not supported in our framework. CPU cluster used for experiments consists of AMD CPUs, running Hadoop version 2.6.0. Each AMD CPU is an Opteron 6376 clocked at 1.40 GHz, with 8 cores and 32 GB RAM. K-Core algorithm mutates the graph structure and our framework for hybrid cluster does not support mutation of the graph. WCC algorithm is not implemented for CPU cluster because it involves message pulling, and Giraph does not directly support it.

Table 2. Graph algorithms and their lines of code [2]

Graph algorithm	Falcon	Giraph	MPI+OpenCL
Breadth First Search (BFS)	21	81	499
Single Source Shortest Path (SSSP)	21	81	310
Weakly Connected Components (WCC)	49	-	300
Pagerank (PR)	25	60	263
Random Bipartite Matching (RBM)	45	147	360
K-Core	32	82	-

Table 3. Graph inputs used in experiments

Graph	Type	No of nodes (in millions)	No of edges (in millions)
RD-1	Random	64	256
RD-2	Random	128	512
RM-1	Scale free (R-MAT)	60	300
RM-2	Scale free (R-MAT)	80	400
BP-1	Bipartite	64	256
BP-2	Bipartite	128	512
BP-3	Bipartite	256	1024

Table 3 shows the input graphs used for experiments. Random and R-MAT graphs have been generated using the GTgraph tool [3]. We synthesized bipartite graphs using the random function.

Figure 4 shows experimental evaluations on a GPU cluster with two, four and eight nodes. Time measured here for all the benchmarks includes only the computation and communication times after distributing the graph to the nodes. Speedup is shown with respect to two nodes. Figure 5 shows experimental evaluations on a CPU cluster with four, six, eight and ten nodes. Speedup is shown with respect to four nodes. Figures 4 and 5 show scalability of our framework. The scalability is not linear because with the increase in number of nodes of

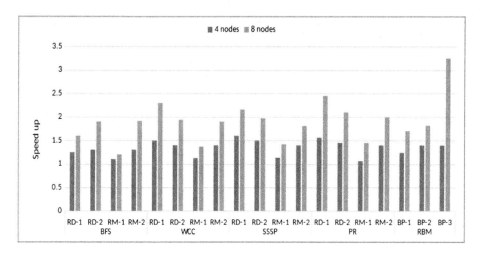

Fig. 4. Speedup over 2 nodes (MPI+OpenCL)

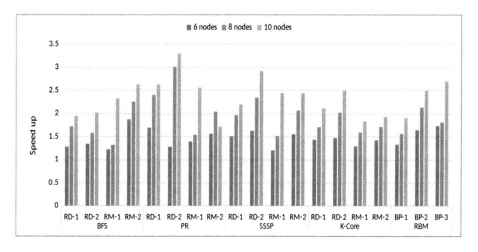

Fig. 5. Speedup over 4 nodes (Giraph)

cluster, the computation time decreases but the communication time increases. Also, we have compared compiler generated code with manual implementations of the above mentioned algorithms for both CPU and heterogeneous cluster and found that they perform similarly.

Table 4 shows the execution time for two implementations of the SSSP and the PR algorithms, one with *communicate-selective-data* optimization and the other without it.

Table 4. Execution time (in seconds) for generated optimized and unoptimized SSSP and PR algorithms on 2, 4 and 8 nodes of a GPU cluster

Graph	Optimized SSSP			Unoptimized SSSP			Optimized PR			Unoptimized PR		
	2	4	8	2	4	8	2	4	8	2	4	8
RD-1	14	11	8	90	57	41	144	105	78	142	95	62
RD-2	29	23	16	164	110	83	296	219	157	292	203	130
RM-1	11	11	9	49	44	35	110	182	109	103	108	78
RM-2	22	17	12	87	64	49	208	176	139	194	158	102

7   Conclusion

We proposed a framework for large scale graph processing on a distributed environment. It reuses the front-end of Falcon and generates Giraph implementations for a CPU cluster and MPI+OpenCL code for a heterogeneous cluster. Empirical results show scalability and efficiency of our framework.

References

1. Apache giraph project. http://giraph.apache.org
2. Distributed-falcon. https://github.com/niteshupadhyay/distributed-framework/
3. Bader, D.A., Madduri, K.: GTgraph: a synthetic graph generator suite. Atlanta, GA, February 2006
4. Burtscher, M., Nasre, R., Pingali, K.: A quantitative study of irregular programs on GPUs. In: Workload Characterization (IISWC), pp. 141–151. IEEE (2012)
5. Gerbessiotis, A.V., Valiant, L.G.: Direct bulk-synchronous parallel algorithms. In: Nurmi, O., Ukkonen, E. (eds.) SWAT 1992. LNCS, vol. 621, pp. 1–18. Springer, Heidelberg (1992). https://doi.org/10.1007/3-540-55706-7_1
6. Gharaibeh, A., Reza, T., Santos-Neto, E., Costa, L.B., Sallinen, S., Ripeanu, M.: Efficient large-scale graph processing on hybrid CPU and GPU systems. arXiv preprint arXiv:1312.3018 (2013)
7. Gonzalez, J.E., Low, Y., Gu, H., Bickson, D., Guestrin, C.: PowerGraph: distributed graph-parallel computation on natural graphs. In: OSDI, vol. 12, p. 2 (2012)
8. Gregor, D., Lumsdaine, A.: The parallel BGL: a generic library for distributed graph computations. In: POOSC (2005)
9. Hong, S., Chafi, H., Sedlar, E., Olukotun, K.: Green-Marl: a DSL for easy and efficient graph analysis. In: ACM SIGARCH Computer Architecture News, vol. 40, pp. 349–362. ACM (2012)
10. Hong, S., Salihoglu, S., Widom, J., Olukotun, K.: Simplifying scalable graph processing with a domain-specific language. In: CGO. ACM (2014)
11. Karypis, G., Kumar, V.: A fast and high quality multilevel scheme for partitioning irregular graphs. SIAM J. Sci. Comput. **20**(1), 359–392 (1998)
12. Kulkarni, M., Pingali, K., Walter, B., Ramanarayanan, G., Bala, K., Chew, L.P.: Optimistic parallelism requires abstractions. ACM SIGPLAN Not. **42**(6), 211–222 (2007)

13. Low, Y., Bickson, D., Gonzalez, J., Guestrin, C., Kyrola, A., Hellerstein, J.M.: Distributed GraphLab: a framework for machine learning and data mining in the cloud. Proc. VLDB Endow. **5**(8), 716–727 (2012)

14. Malewicz, G., Austern, M.H., Bik, A.J., Dehnert, J.C., Horn, I., Leiser, N., Czajkowski, G.: Pregel: a system for large-scale graph processing. In: Proceedings of the 2010 ACM SIGMOD ICMD, pp. 135–146. ACM (2010)

15. Pingali, K., Nguyen, D., Kulkarni, M., Burtscher, M., Hassaan, M.A., Kaleem, R., Lee, T.H., Lenharth, A., Manevich, R., Méndez-Lojo, M., et al.: The tao of parallelism in algorithms. ACM Sigplan Not. **46**(6), 12–25 (2011)

16. Shashidhar, G., Nasre, R.: `LightHouse`: an automatic code generator for graph algorithms on GPUs. In: Ding, C., Criswell, J., Wu, P. (eds.) LCPC 2016. LNCS, vol. 10136, pp. 235–249. Springer, Cham (2017). https://doi.org/10.1007/978-3-319-52709-3_18

17. Simmhan, Y., Kumbhare, A., Wickramaarachchi, C., Nagarkar, S., Ravi, S., Raghavendra, C., Prasanna, V.: *GoFFish*: a sub-graph centric framework for large-scale graph analytics. In: Silva, F., Dutra, I., Santos Costa, V. (eds.) Euro-Par 2014. LNCS, vol. 8632, pp. 451–462. Springer, Cham (2014). https://doi.org/10.1007/978-3-319-09873-9_38

18. Unnikrishnan, C., Nasre, R., Srikant, Y.: Falcon: a graph manipulation language for heterogeneous systems. ACM TACO **12**(4), 54:1–54:27 (2016)

19. Zhong, J., He, B.: Medusa: simplified graph processing on GPUs. TPDS **25**(6), 1543–1552 (2014)

LSDVE – Workshop on Large Scale Distributed Virtual Environments

Workshop on Large Scale Distributed Virtual Environments (LSDVE)

Workshop Description

The Fifth Workshop on Large Scale Distributed Virtual Environments (LSDVE 2017) has been held in Santiago De Compostela, Spain. For the fifth time, this workshop has been organized in conjunction with the Euro-Par annual series of international conferences. The main aim of the fifth edition of the workshop has been to provide a venue for researchers to present and discuss important aspects of large scale networked collaborative applications and of the platforms supporting them.

This year, the main theme of the workshop has been that of distributed networked application, with particular focus on the several novel applications recently emerged in this area: social networks, distributed payment systems, connected devices collaboration systems, and many other ones. These applications may greatly benefit from the support of different kinds of platforms, both cloud and peer to peer. An interesting technology recently adopted to handle cryptocurrencies (such as bitcoin) is the block-chain technology, that has now taken the more general role to handle several distributed applications. Furthermore, the analysis and validation of the huge amount of content generated by these applications asks for big data analysis and processing techniques. This workshop aims to provide a venue for researchers to present and discuss important aspects of large scale networked collaborative applications and of the platforms supporting them. The definition of these applications requires to afford several challenges, like the design of user interfaces, coordination protocols, and proper middle-ware and architectures. The workshop's aim is to investigate open challenges for such applications, related to both the applications design and to the definition of proper supports. Some important challenges are, for instance, adaptation of the classical block-chain technology to support collaborative applications, protocols design, distributed consensus algorithms, privacy and security issues.

LSDVE 2017 has been opened by the invited talk "Using Social Media Analysis to Discover Mobility Patterns in Public Events", given by Paolo Trunfio, University of Calabria, Cosenza, Italy. The first session of the workshop has presented papers regarding new technologies, like blockchains, while the second session social media applications and system issues.

We wish to thank all who helped to make this fifth edition of the workshop a success: Paolo Trunfio who accepted our invitation to give a talk, authors submitting papers, colleagues who refereed the submitted papers and attended the sessions, finally the Euro-Par 2017 organizers whose invaluable support greatly helped in the organisation of this fifth edition of the workshop.

Steering Committee

Laura Ricci	Department of Computer Science, Pisa, Italy
Alexandru Iosup	TU Delft, Delft, Netherlands
Radu Prodan	Inst. of Computer Science, Innsbruck, Austria

Program Chairs

Laura Ricci	Department of Computer Science, Pisa, Italy
Alexandru Iosup	TU Delft, Delft, Netherlands
Radu Prodan	Inst. of Computer Science, Innsbruck, Austria

Program Committee

Michele Amoretti	University of Parma, Italy
Emanuele Carlini	ISTI CNR, Pisa, Italy
Giuseppe Di Battista	University of Roma 3, Italy
Kalman Graffi	University of Dusseldorf, Germany
Barbara Guidi	University of Pisa, Italy
Alexandru Iosup	TU Delft, Holland
Jose A. F. de Macedo	Federal University of Ceará, Brasil
Andrea Marino	University of Pisa, Italy
Fabrizio Marozzo	University of Calabria, Italy
Pietro Michiardi	EURECOM, France
Alberto Montresor	University of Trento, Italy
Dana Petcu	West University of Timisoara, Romania
Radu Prodan	Inst. of Computer Science, Innsbruck, Austria
Laura Ricci	University of Pisa, Pisa, Italy

Appraising SPARK on Large-Scale Social Media Analysis

Loris Belcastro, Fabrizio Marozzo$^{(\boxtimes)}$, Domenico Talia, and Paolo Trunfio

DIMES, University of Calabria, Rende, Italy
{lbelcastro,fmarozzo,talia,trunfio}@dimes.unical.it

Abstract. Software systems for social media analysis provide algorithms and tools for extracting useful knowledge from user-generated social media data. ParSoDA (Parallel Social Data Analytics) is a Java library for developing parallel data analysis applications based on the extraction of useful knowledge from social media data. This library aims at reducing the programming skills necessary to implement scalable social data analysis applications. This work describes how the ParSoDA library has been extended to execute applications on Apache Spark. Using a cluster of 12 workers, the Spark version of the library reduces the execution time of two case study applications exploiting social media data up to 42%, compared to the Hadoop version of the library.

Keywords: Social data analysis · Scalability · Spark
Cloud computing · Parallel library · Big Data

1 Introduction

Every day, huge volumes of data are generated by users of social networks like Facebook, Twitter, Instagram and Flickr. Social media analysis aims at extracting useful knowledge from this big amount of data [3]. Social media analysis tools and algorithms have been used for the analysis of collective sentiments [15], for understanding the behavior of groups of people [5,6] or the dynamics of public opinion [2]. The use of parallel and distributed data analysis techniques and frameworks (e.g. MapReduce [10]) is essential to cope with the size and complexity of social media data. However, it is hard for many users to use such frameworks, mainly due to the programming skills necessary to implement the desired data analysis methods on top of them [18].

ParSoDA (Parallel Social Data Analytics) is a Java library for building parallel social media analysis applications, designed for simplifying the programming task necessary to implement these class of applications on parallel computing systems. To reach this goal, ParSoDA includes functions that are widely used for processing and analyzing data gathered from social media for finding different types of information (e.g., user mobility, user sentiments, topics trends). ParSoDA defines a general framework for a social data analysis application that includes a number of steps (data acquisition, filtering, mapping, partitioning,

© Springer International Publishing AG, part of Springer Nature 2018
D. B. Heras and L. Bougé (Eds.): Euro-Par 2017 Workshops, LNCS 10659, pp. 483–495, 2018.
https://doi.org/10.1007/978-3-319-75178-8_39

reduction, analysis, and visualization), and provides a predefined (but extensible) set of functions for each step. Thus, an application developed with ParSoDA is expressed by a concise code that specifies the functions invoked at each step. The library includes algorithms that are widely used on social media data for extracting different types of information. In a previous work [4], we presented the main features of ParSoDA and described how it can be used to execute parallel social data analysis on a Cloud system exploiting Apache Hadoop [19]. In this work we describe how the ParSoDA library has been extended to execute applications on Apache Spark [22]. Spark is one of the most popular framework for Big Data processing. Differently from Hadoop, in which intermediate data are always stored in distributed file systems, Spark stores data in main memory and processes it repeatedly so as to obtain better performance for some classes of applications (e.g., iterative machine learning algorithms and queries on data [20]).

We experimentally evaluated the scalability of the Spark version of ParSoDA proposed in this paper, compared to the previous Hadoop version of the library that has been presented in [4]. The experimental evaluation is based on two case study applications on social media data published in Flickr and Twitter. The first application aims at discovering sequential patterns from user movements, so as to find the common routes followed by users. The second application discovers the frequent sets of places visited by users. The ParSoDA library performance has been evaluated carrying out the data analysis applications both on a Hadoop and a Spark cluster deployed on the Microsoft Azure cloud platform. On a cluster using 12 workers, the Spark version of ParSoDA reduced the execution time up to 42% compared to the Hadoop version of the library.

The remainder of the paper is organized as follows. Section 2 discusses related work. Section 3 describes the ParSoDA library and the proposed integration with Spark. Section 4 presents the experimental evaluation of two case studies. Finally, Sect. 5 concludes the paper.

2   Related Work

Many professionals and researches are working on the design and implementation of tools and algorithms for extracting useful information from data gathered from social networks. In most cases the amount of data to be analyzed is so big that high performance computers, such as many and multi-core systems, Clouds, and multi-clusters, paired with parallel and distributed algorithms, are used by data analysts to reduce response time to a reasonable value [3].

Several research activities consider not only data analysis, but also providing solutions for building social data applications, with the aim of helping scientists to develop the different steps that compose social data mining applications without the need to implement common operations from scratch.

SOCLE [1] is a framework for expressing and optimizing data preparation in social applications. It is composed by a general-purpose three-layers architecture, an algebra, and a language to define operations for data preparation in social applications. As an example, SOCLE provides operators to remove all unnecessary information from data (data pruning), to add information by using external sources (data enrichment), to transform data values (data normalization). The authors examined the use of SOCLE for manipulating social data in two families of social applications, recommendation and analytics, but no studies have been performed to assess its scalability, and no details about framework requirements have been provided.

Cuesta et al. [9] proposed a framework for easing Twitter data extraction and analysis. In the proposed architecture the tweets, mined by the application through the Twitter APIs, are cleaned and then stored in a MongoDB database [7]. In addition to basic database operations (i.e. selection, projection, insertion, updating and deletion), the framework can be extended creating more complex aggregation MapReduce tasks in Python. By default, the framework provides researchers modules for executing sentiment analysis and generating reports.

SODATO (SOcial Data Analytics Tool) [12] is an on-line tool for helping researches on social data. It utilizes the APIs provided by social networks (i.e., currently, it supports only Facebook and Twitter) for collecting data; then, it provides a combination of web as well as console applications that run in batches for preprocessing and aggregating data for analysis. At the end of the analytics process, the results can be displayed using the integrated visualization module. SODATO provides methods for several kinds of analysis, such as sentiments analysis, keyword analysis, content performance analysis, social influencer analysis, etc.

You et al. [21] presented a framework, running on Clouds, for developing social data analysis applications for smarter cities, especially designed to support smart mobility. In particular, the framework is composed by five components (i.e., data collector, data preprocessor, data analyzer, data presenter, and data storage) that cover the whole data analysis lifecycle. The framework supports data collection from social networks (e.g., Twitter, Foursquare), by exploiting their public APIs, and from other Internet sources (e.g. website, blog, files). A component devoted to data preprocessing provides functions for data cleansing, filtering and normalization. Afterwards, the data analyzer component provides needed analysis methods (e.g. K-means, DBScan, and Self-organizing Map) to make some data analysis.

The main differences between ParSoDA and the systems described above (but the one by You et al. [21]), is that our system was specifically designed to build Cloud-based data analytics applications. To this end, it provides scalability mechanisms based on two of the most popular parallel processing frameworks (Hadoop and Spark), which are fundamental to provide satisfactory services as the amount of data to be managed grows.

3   The ParSoDA Library

ParSoDA (Parallel Social Data Analytics) is a Java library that includes algorithms that are widely used to process and analyze data gathered from social networks for extracting different kinds of information (e.g., user mobility, user sentiments, topic trends).

ParSoDA defines a general structure for a social data analysis application that is formed by the following steps:

- *Data acquisition:* during this step, it is possible to run multiple crawlers in parallel; the collected social media items are stored on a distributed file system (HDFS [17]).
- *Data filtering:* this step filters the social media items according to a set of filtering functions.
- *Data mapping:* this step transforms the information contained in each social media item by applying a set of map functions.
- *Data partitioning:* during this step, data is partitioned into shards by a primary key and then sorted by a secondary key.
- *Data reduction:* this step aggregates all the data contained in a shard according to the provided reduce function.
- *Data analysis:* this step analyzes data using a given data analysis function to extract the knowledge of interest.
- *Data visualization:* at this final step, a visualization function is applied on the data analysis results to present them in the desired format.

For each of these steps ParSoDA provides a predefined set of functions. Users are free to extend this set with their own functions. For example, for the data acquisition step, ParSoDA provides crawling functions for gathering data from some of the most popular social networks (Twitter and Flickr), while for the data filtering step, ParSoDA provides functions for filtering geotagged items based on their position, time of publication, and contained keywords.

Figure 1 presents the reference architectures describing how user applications based on the ParSoDA library are executed on the Hadoop and Spark frameworks, which allows implementing parallel and distributed applications with high level of scalability for several data mining tasks [8,22]. As shown in the figure, user applications can make use of ParSoDA and other libraries. Applications can be executed on a Hadoop or a Spark cluster, using YARN as resource manager and HDFS as distributed file system.

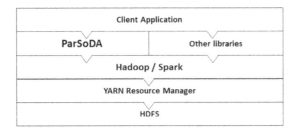

Fig. 1. Reference architecture

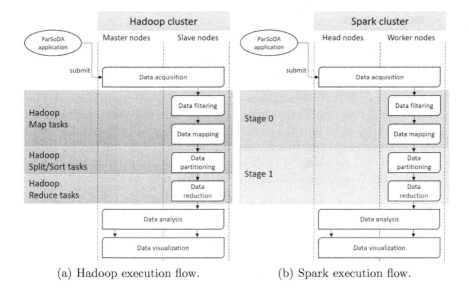

(a) Hadoop execution flow.   (b) Spark execution flow.

Fig. 2. Hadoop and Spark execution flows.

Figure 2 provides details on how applications are executed on a Hadoop or a Spark cluster. The cluster is formed by one or more master nodes, and multiple slave nodes. Once a user application is submitted to the cluster, its steps are executed according to their order (i.e., data acquisition, data filtering, etc.).

On a Hadoop cluster (see Fig. 2(a)), some steps are inherently MapReduce-based, namely: data filtering, data mapping, data partitioning and data reduction. This means that all the functions used to perform these steps are executed within a MapReduce job that runs on a set of slave nodes. Specifically: the data filtering and data mapping steps are wrapped within Hadoop Map tasks; the data partitioning step corresponds to Hadoop Split and Sort tasks; the data reduction step is executed as a Hadoop Reduce task. The remaining steps (data acquisition, data analysis, and data visualization) are not necessarily MapReduce-based. This means that the functions associated to these steps could be executed in parallel on multiple slave nodes, or alternatively they could be executed locally by the master node(s). The latter case does not imply that execution is sequential, because a master node could make use of some other parallel runtime (e.g., MPI).

On a Spark cluster (see Fig. 2(b)), the main steps are executed within two Spark stages that run on a set of worker nodes. A stage is a set of independent tasks executing functions that do not need to perform data shuffling (e.g., transformation and action functions). Specifically: data filtering and mapping are executed within the first stage (*Stage 0*), while data partitioning and reduction are executed within the second stage (*Stage 1*). Concerning the remaining steps (data acquisition, data analysis, and data visualization), the same considerations made for Hadoop apply to Spark.

4   Case Studies

We ran experiments to evaluate the scalability of the Spark version of ParSoDA proposed in this paper, in comparison with the previous Hadoop version of the library that has been presented in [4]. The experimental evaluation is based on two case studies based on the analysis of social media data published in Flickr and Twitter. The first application aims at discovering sequential patterns from user movements, so as to find the common routes followed by users. The second one aims at discovering the frequent sets of places visited by users. The analysis was carried out by analyzing 325 GB of social media data published in Flickr and Twitter from November 2014 to July 2016 that refer to the center of Rome.

4.1   Application Code

Listing 1.1 shows the code of the application for executing the sequential pattern mining. First, an instance of the *SocialDataApp* class must be created (*line 1*). Then a file containing the boundaries of the regions of interest (*RomeRoIs.kml*) is distributed to the processing nodes (*lines 2–3*). Afterwards, the different steps of the application are configured as described here:

1. *Data collection.* The names of two crawling classes (*FlickrCrawler* and *TwitterCrawler*) are defined in the *cFunctions* array (*line 4*). The parameters used to configure the instances of the two crawling classes are defined in the *cParames* array (*line 5*). The two arrays are then passed to the *setCrawlers* method (*line 6*).
2. *Data filtering.* Two filtering classes are specified: *IsGeotagged* and *IsInPlace* (*line 7*). The former filters data by keeping only geotagged items. The latter filters out data that are not in the center of Rome, which is defined by its geographical coordinates. The parameters of the two filtering functions are specified in the *fParams* array (*line 8*). The names of the filtering classes and associated parameters are then passed to the *setFilters* method (*line 9*).
3. *Data mapping.* The map class *FindPoI* (*line 10*), which does not require parameters to be instantiated (*line 11*), is specified. The mapping function defined in *FindPoI* assigns to each social media item the name of the place it refers to. To do this, it refers to the boundaries specified in the file defined at *line 2*. The name of the map class is then passed to the *setMapFunctions* method (*line 12*).
4. *Data partitioning.* The id of the user who posted a social media item is used as the *groupKey* (*line 13*), while the date and time when the social media item was posted is used as the *sortKey* (*line 14*). The two keys are then passed to the *setPartitioningKeys* method (*line 15*).
5. *Data reduction.* A reduce class, named *ReduceByTrajectories* (*line 16*), is specified to aggregate all the social media items posted by a single user, into a list of individual trajectories across places. The parameters of the reduce class are specified in the *rParams* string (*line 17*). In particular, it receives only a parameter t, which is the maximum time gap in hours that can be

taken for consecutive places in the same trajectory. The name of the reduce class and its parameters are then passed to the *setReduceFunction* method (*line 18*).

6. *Data analysis.* A data analysis class, named *PrefixSpan*, is specified (*line 19*). The class implements PrefixSpan [16], a scalable frequent sequence mining algorithm, built for Spark and included in the Spark Machine Learning library (MLlib), which takes as input a collection of sequences and mines frequent sequences. The parameters of data analysis class are specified in the *aParams* string (*line 20*). The name of the data analysis class and its parameters are then passed to the *setAnalysisFunction* method (*line 21*). In the Hadoop version of the application presented in [4], as data analysis class we used *MGFSM* [14], a scalable frequent sequence mining algorithm built for MapReduce.

7. *Data visualization.* The *SortResults* class is specified to perform the data visualization function (*line 22*). A configuration string *vParams*, containing the parameters of the data visualization class, is specified at *line 23*. The class receives two parameters: the key used to sort results (the sequence support) and the sort direction (descending order). The name of the data visualization class and its parameters are then passed to the *setVisualizationFunction* method (*line 24*).

Finally, the execution of the application is obtained by invoking the *execute* method (*line 25*).

```
 1 SocialDataApp app = new SocialDataApp("SPM - City of Rome");
 2 String[] cFiles = {"RomeRoIs.kml"};
 3 app.setDistributedCacheFiles(cacheFiles);
 4 String[] cFunctions = {"FlickrCrawler","TwitterCrawler"};
 5 String[] cParams = {"-lat 12.492 -lng 41.890 -radius 10 -startDate
       2016-07-31 -endDate 2014-11-01","-lat 12.492 -lng 41.890 -radius
       10 -startDate 2016-07-31 -endDate 2014-11-01"};
 6 app.setCrawlers(cFunctions,cParams);
 7 String[] fFunctions = {"IsGeotagged","IsInPlace"};
 8 String[] fParams = {"true","-lat 12.492 -lng 41.890 -radius 10"};
 9 app.setFilters(fFunctions, fParams);
10 String[] mFunctions = {"FindPoI"};
11 String[] mParams = null;
12 app.setMapFunctions(mFunctions, mParams);
13 String groupKey = "USER.USERID";
14 String sortKey = "DATETIME";
15 app.setPartitioningKeys(groupKey,sortKey);
16 String rFunction = "ReduceByTrajectories";
17 String rParams = "-t 5";
18 app.setReduceFunction(rFunction,rParams);
19 String aFunction = "PrefixSpan";
20 String aParams = "-maxPatternLength 5 -minSupport 0.01";
21 app.setAnalysisFunction(aFunction,aParams);
```

```
22 String vFunction = "SortBy";
23 String vParams = "-k support -d DESC";
24 app.setVisualizationFunction(vFunction,vParams);
25 app.execute();
```

Listing 1.1. An example of sequential pattern mining (SPM) application on Flickr and Twitter data from the City of Rome, written using the ParSoDA library.

The code for executing the frequent itemset analysis differs from that described above only for the used data analysis algorithm (*lines* 19–21). In particular, for extracting frequent sets of places from social media data, a parallel implementation of FP-Growth [11] called PFP [13], has been used both in the Spark- and in the Hadoop-version of the application.

4.2   Applications Results

A set of 24 popular places in the center of Rome have been considered to run the sequential pattern mining task and the frequent itemset discovery task, both implemented as ParSoDA applications. In the following, we discuss some of the most interesting results that have been obtained. Table 1 shows the top 5 places visited in Rome, with the corresponding support in the data. The Colosseum is the most visited place, followed by the St. Peter's Basilica.

Table 1. Top 5 places visited in Rome

Place	Support
Colosseum	21.7%
St Peter's Basilica	13.9%
Trastevere	8.7%
Pantheon	6.5%
Trevi Fountain	5.3%

Table 2. Top 5 frequent sets of places visited in Rome

Set of places	Support
Pantheon, St. Peter's Basilica, Colosseum	5.3%
Trevi Fountain, St. Peter's Basilica, Colosseum	4.5%
Roman Forum, St. Peter's Basilica, Colosseum	4.4%
Vatican Museums, St. Peter's Basilica, Colosseum	4.4%
Trevi Fountain, Pantheon, Colosseum	4.0%

Table 2 shows the most frequent itemsets of length 3 that have been discovered by the PFP algorithm. Set {*Pantheon, St. Peter's Basilica, Colosseum*} is the most frequent set of places visited by social users in Rome, with a support of 5.3%. Combining the information contained in Tables 1 and 2, an interesting result is that *Trastevere*, a popular district of Rome, is the third most visited place, but it is not present in any frequent itemset. This could happen because Trastevere is visited by people during the evening, for having a dinner in one of its many restaurants or pubs, but it is not part of common tourist routes during the daylight.

The sequential pattern analysis has been carried out for discovering the most frequent routes in Rome. In this experiment, it has been set a maximum time duration (gap) to move from a place to another of 5 h. This means that if the time distance between two contiguous places in sequence is greater than 5 h, they will belong to different sequences.

Figure 3(a) shows the top five visited places in Rome that have been found by the PFP algorithm. Figures 3(b), (c) and (d) show respectively the top five interesting patterns of length 3, 4, and 5, which have been found by the PrefixSpan algorithm. More detailed information about the most frequent patterns and the corresponding supports are reported in Table 3. Considering the sequential patterns of length 2, the sequence {*Colosseum → St. Peter's Basilica*} is the most frequent route among places in Rome, followed by 9.07% of users. The sequence {*Colosseum → Roman Forum → St. Peter's Basilica*} is the most frequent route of length 3, which is followed by 4.4% of users. Finally, the sequence {*Colosseum → Trevi Fountain → Pantheon → St. Peter's Basilica*} is the most frequent route of length 4 with a quite low support of 0.64%.

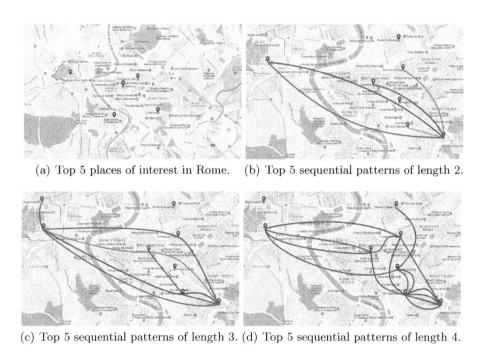

(a) Top 5 places of interest in Rome.   (b) Top 5 sequential patterns of length 2.

(c) Top 5 sequential patterns of length 3. (d) Top 5 sequential patterns of length 4.

Fig. 3. Sequential pattern mining application.

4.3   Scalability Evaluation

As mentioned before, we experimentally evaluated the scalability of the Spark version of ParSoDA proposed in this paper, compared to the previous Hadoop

Table 3. Top 5 sequential patterns of length 2, 3 and 4 across places in Rome

Sequential pattern	Support
Colosseum → St. Peter's Basilica	9.07%
St. Peter's Basilica → Colosseum	7.72%
Colosseum → Roman Forum	5.28%
Colosseum → Pantheon	4.44%
Colosseum → Trevi Fountain	4.19%
Colosseum → Roman Forum → St. Peter's Basilica	4.4%
Vatican Museums → St. Peter's Basilica → Colosseum	3.9%
Colosseum → Trevi Fountain → St. Peter's Basilica	3.7%
Colosseum → Roman Forum → Pantheon	3.6%
Colosseum → Pantheon → St. Peter's Basilica	3.6%
Colosseum → Trevi Fountain → Pantheon → St. Peter's Basilica	0.64%
Colosseum → Roman Forum → Trevi Fountain → San St. Peter's Basilica	0.61%
Colosseum → Roman Forum → Piazza Venezia → Piazza di Spagna	0.58%
Colosseum → Roman Forum → Piazza Venezia → St. Peter's Basilica	0.58%
Colosseum → Roman Forum → Pantheon → St. Peter's Basilica	0.58%

version of the library. The scalability was evaluated running the data analysis applications on the Microsoft Azure cloud. Specifically, we used one cluster equipped with 2 head nodes (each one having four 2.2 GHz CPU cores and 14 GB of memory), and 12 worker nodes (each one equipped with four 2.2 GHz CPU cores and 14 GB of memory). Here we present the results obtained with the sequential pattern mining application. The performance obtained with the frequent itemset applications are almost identical.

As shown in Fig. 4(a), the turnaround time of the Hadoop-based application decreases from about 54 min using two workers, to 10 min using 12 workers. The turnaround time of the Spark-based application decreases from about 32 min using two workers, to 9 min using 12 workers. Thus, using the same computing resources, the Spark version of ParSoDA results to be 8% (12 workers) to 42% (2 workers) faster than the Hadoop version. In terms of speedup (see Fig. 4(b)), Hadoop obtains a speedup ranging from 1.98 using 4 workers, to 5.37 using 12 workers. On the other hand, the Spark version achieves a lower relative speedup than Hadoop, as it passes from 1.74 using 2 workers, to 3.53 using 12 workers. This is due to the fact that the Spark version spends most of the time to load data in memory and to distribute it across the worker nodes. Thus, for such application, increasing the number of nodes beyond a certain number seems not have significant benefits. However, the advantage of Spark over Hadoop is significant in terms of absolute times reduction, as shown by the results presented in Fig. 4(a).

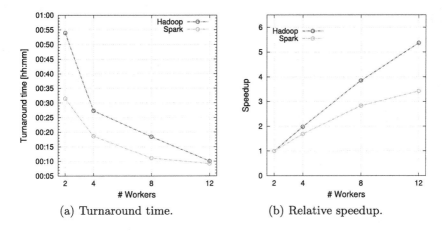

(a) Turnaround time.   (b) Relative speedup.

Fig. 4. Turnaround time and relative speedup of the sequential pattern mining application using Hadoop and Spark.

5   Conclusions

Social media analysis is an important research area aimed at extracting useful information from the big amount of data gathered from social networks. To cope with the size and complexity of social media data, the use of parallel and distributed data analysis techniques is fundamental. ParSoDA is a Java library that can be used for building parallel social data analysis applications. ParSoDA defines a general structure for a social data analysis application that includes a number of steps (data acquisition, filtering, mapping, partitioning, reduction, analysis, and visualization), and provides a predefined (but extensible) set of functions for each step. In a previous work [4], we described how ParSoDA can be used to run parallel social data analysis on the cloud using Hadoop.

In the present work we presented an extension of ParSoDA to execute applications on Spark. We experimentally evaluated the scalability of the Spark version of ParSoDA compared to the previous Hadoop version of the library. The experimental evaluation is based on two case study applications on social media data published in Flickr and Twitter. The ParSoDA library performance has been evaluated carrying out the data analysis applications both on a Hadoop and a Spark cluster deployed on the Microsoft Azure cloud platform. The results obtained on a cluster with 12 workers, showed that the Spark version of ParSoDA was able to reduce the execution time up to 42% compared to the Hadoop version of the library.

References

1. Amer-Yahia, S., Ibrahim, N., Kengne, C.K., Ulliana, F., Rousset, M.C.: Socle: towards a framework for data preparation in social applications. Ingénierie des Systèmes d'Information **19**(3), 49–72 (2014)
2. Anstead, N., O'Loughlin, B.: Social media analysis and public opinion: the 2010 UK general election. J. Comput.-Mediated Commun. **20**(2), 204–220 (2015)
3. Belcastro, L., Marozzo, F., Talia, D., Trunfio, P.: Big data analysis on clouds. In: Zomaya, A.Y., Sakr, S. (eds.) Handbook of Big Data Technologies, pp. 101–142. Springer, Cham (2017). https://doi.org/10.1007/978-3-319-49340-4_4. ISBN 978-3-319-49339-8
4. Belcastro, L., Marozzo, F., Talia, D., Trunfio, P.: A parallel library for social media analytics. In: The 2017 International Conference on High Performance Computing and Simulation (HPCS 2017), Genoa, Italy, 17–21 July 2017
5. Cesario, E., Congedo, C., Marozzo, F., Riotta, G., Spada, A., Talia, D., Trunfio, P., Turri, C.: Following soccer fans from geotagged tweets at FIFA world Cup 2014. In: Proceedings of the 2nd IEEE Conference on Spatial Data Mining and Geographical Knowledge Services, Fuzhou, China, pp. 33–38, July 2015. ISBN 978-1- 4799-7748-2
6. Cesario, E., Iannazzo, A.R., Marozzo, F., Morello, F., Riotta, G., Spada, A., Talia, D., Trunfio, P.: Analyzing social media data to discover mobility patterns at expo 2015: methodology and results. In: The 2016 International Conference on High Performance Computing and Simulation (HPCS 2016), Innsbruck, Austria, 18–22 July 2016
7. Chodorow, K.: MongoDB: The Definitive Guide. O'Reilly Media, Inc., Sebastopol (2013)
8. Chu, C., Kim, S.K., Lin, Y.A., Yu, Y., Bradski, G., Ng, A.Y., Olukotun, K.: Map-reduce for machine learning on multicore. Adv. Neural Inf. Process. Syst. **19**, 281 (2007)
9. Cuesta, Á., Barrero, D.F., R-Moreno, M.D.: A framework for massive Twitter data extraction and analysis. Malays. J. Comput. Sci. **27**, 1 (2014)
10. Dean, J., Ghemawat, S.: Mapreduce: simplified data processing on large clusters. In: Proceedings of the 6th Conference on Symposium on Operating Systems Design and Implementation, OSDI 2004, Berkeley, USA, p. 10 (2004)
11. Han, J., Pei, J., Yin, Y., Mao, R.: Mining frequent patterns without candidate generation: a frequent-pattern tree approach. Data Mining Knowl. Discov. **8**(1), 53–87 (2004)
12. Hussain, A., Vatrapu, R.: Social data analytics tool (SODATO). In: Tremblay, M.C., VanderMeer, D., Rothenberger, M., Gupta, A., Yoon, V. (eds.) DESRIST 2014. LNCS, vol. 8463, pp. 368–372. Springer, Cham (2014). https://doi.org/10.1007/978-3-319-06701-8_27
13. Li, H., Wang, Y., Zhang, D., Zhang, M., Chang, E.Y.: PFP: Parallel FP-growth for query recommendation. In: Proceedings of the 2008 ACM Conference on Recommender Systems, New York, NY, USA, pp. 107–114 (2008)
14. Miliaraki, I., Berberich, K., Gemulla, R., Zoupanos, S.: Mind the gap: large-scale frequent sequence mining. In: Proceedings of the 2013 ACM SIGMOD International Conference on Management of Data, pp. 797–808 (2013)
15. Pang, B., Lee, L.: Opinion mining and sentiment analysis. Found. Trends Inf. Retr. **2**(12), 1–135 (2008)
16. Pei, J., Han, J., Mortazavi-Asl, B., Wang, J., Pinto, H., Chen, Q., Dayal, U., Hsu, M.C.: Mining sequential patterns by pattern-growth: the prefixspan approach. IEEE Trans. Knowl. Data Eng. **16**(11), 1424–1440 (2004)

17. Shvachko, K., Kuang, H., Radia, S., Chansler, R.: The hadoop distributed file system. In: 2010 IEEE 26th Symposium on Mass Storage Systems and Technologies (MSST), pp. 1–10. IEEE (2010)
18. Talia, D., Trunfio, P., Marozzo, F.: Data Analysis in the Cloud. Elsevier, Amsterdam, October 2015
19. White, T.: Hadoop: The Definitive Guide, 1st edn. O'Reilly Media Inc., Sebastopol (2009)
20. Xin, R.S., Rosen, J., Zaharia, M., Franklin, M.J., Shenker, S., Stoica, I.: Shark: SQL and rich analytics at scale. In: Proceedings of the 2013 ACM SIGMOD Conference on Management of Data, pp. 13–24. ACM (2013)
21. You, L., Motta, G., Sacco, D., Ma, T.: Social data analysis framework in cloud and mobility analyzer for smarter cities. In: IEEE International Conference on Service Operations and Logistics, and Informatics, pp. 96–101, October 2014
22. Zaharia, M., Xin, R.S., Wendell, P., Das, T., Armbrust, M., Dave, A., Meng, X., Rosen, J., Venkataraman, S., Franklin, M.J., et al.: Apache spark: a unified engine for big data processing. Commun. ACM **59**(11), 56–65 (2016)

A Spatial Analysis of Multiplayer Online Battle Arena Mobility Traces

Emanuele Carlini[1]([✉])(iD) and Alessandro Lulli[2](iD)

[1] Istituto di Scienza e Tecnologia dell'Informazione (ISTI),
Consiglio Nazionale delle Ricerche (CNR), Pisa, Italy
emanuele.carlini@isti.cnr.it
[2] Department of Informatics, Bioengineering,
Robotics and System Engineering (DIBRIS),
University of Genova, Genoa, Italy
alessandro.lulli@dibris.unige.it

Abstract. A careful analysis and a deep understanding of real mobility traces is of paramount importance when it comes to design mobility models that aim to accurately reproduce avatar movements in virtual environment. In this paper we focus on the analysis of a specific kind of virtual environment, namely the Multiplayer Online Battle Arena (MOBA), which is a extremely popular online game genre. We performed a spatial analysis of about one hundred games of a popular MOBA, roughly corresponding to 4000 min of movements. The analysis revealed interesting patterns in terms of AoI observation, and the utilization of the map by the avatars. These results are effective building blocks toward the creation of realistic mobility models targeting MOBA environments.

1 Introduction

On-line gaming is one of the biggest entertainment industries and has seen a rise in popularity in the last decade, thanks to the widespread of fast home connections to the Internet all over the world. Such rise has naturally attracted research communities, as on-line games arguably represents the most widespread instance of what can be considered a virtual environment. Among the various genres, Multiplayer Online Battle Arena (MOBA) is one of the most popular in the current landscape of online gaming, targeting both casual and professional e-sport players. Games like Defense of the Ancients (DOTA) 2 [2] and Heroes of Newerth (HoN) [4] created huge communities of players that challenge themselves in countless player-vs-player matches. The business figures around MOBA are impressive and approaching those of classical sports: the most important MOBA related e-sport event, the DOTA 2's International, in 2016 had a prize pool of around $18M being the most prized e-sport event ever [3].

In this paper we present the methodology and the analysis of several spatial features in the movements of *avatar*, the virtual representation of the player in the game, in MOBA games. The analysis is based on around 98 replays of

© Springer International Publishing AG, part of Springer Nature 2018
D. B. Heras and L. Bougé (Eds.): Euro-Par 2017 Workshops, LNCS 10659, pp. 496–506, 2018.
https://doi.org/10.1007/978-3-319-75178-8_40

matches from HoN, which roughly correspond to 4 000 min of movements in the MOBA virtual environment. In particular, we analysed the following features: (i) how avatars are distributed in the map? (ii) how are populated the Area of Interest (AoIs) of the various avatars? (iii) how many avatars remains alone for a sufficient period of time?

The main intent of such analysis is to provide building blocks for the design of mobility models that capture the essence of movements in MOBA. In fact, one of the most active field of research in virtual environments has regarded the transition of virtual environments from client-server to distributed applications. Such approaches, broadly referred to as Distributed Virtual Environments (DVEs) [20]. The goal of this approach is to improve the scalability and the cost-effectiveness, by orchestrating the support of the virtual environments exploiting computational and network resources of the users of the DVE. In this context, an accurate representation of the movements of avatars is essential to properly design, validate and compare different DVE architectures. Specifically the analysis of AOIs and the position of the avatars provides indication on how many avatars share interests on the same parts of the virtual environment. This is of particular importance especially for those solutions in which the position of the avatars affects the performance of the DVE. For example, in Voronoi-based approaches, the management of the DVE is assigned to the machines where users are playing according to a tessellation of the virtual environment, which depends on the position of the avatars [12,21]. Upon avatars movements the assignment change accordingly, triggering a reconstruction in the distribution of the DVE.

To foster comparisons and further studies on common grounds, we made the traces publicly available [7].

2   Related Work

The analysis and mining of mobility traces with the aim of deriving common patterns and models is an important and large area of research, which considers both human and virtual mobility. In the context of DVEs, many works has focused on the analysis of one of the most popular and widespread online activity, which is online gaming. A common goal often found in such analysis is the modeling of avatars mobility. This can have two main directions (i) defining tools and mechanisms to easily replicate such mobility, (ii) testing and validation of various DVE frameworks and middlewares. The games subject of analysis of mobility traces have been many and of different kinds.

For example, in [15] Liang et al. propose a statistical analysis of Second Life [6] traces as well as a discussion on the implication about the design of a DVE framework. The analysis is performed characterizing both the mobility (avatar speed, pause time etc.) and contact patterns (AOI sizes, etc.), which represent good features when designing a mobility model. BlueBanana [14] is a mobility model for Second Life, in which players gather around a set of hotspots, which usually correspond to towns, or, in general, to points of interest of the virtual world. In [16,17] authors provide an analysis of avatar mobility for World of

Warcraft [1]. The analysis is focused on a particular area of the DVE where avatars battle for the control of several objectives. The paper presents a modeling of the avatars' behaviors in terms of hotspots, grouping and waypoints. Further, in [23] authors propose an enhancement of the random way point mobility model to better fit the behavior of players in the first person shooting game Quake 2 [5]. Among the features, they added various conditions for an avatar to be stationary, an hotspot popularity and non-straight movement paths.

In the context of MOBA, several works on trace analysis and mining has been recently carried out, due to the massive popularity gained by this online game genre. Few works focus on the modelling of movements in the context of designing AI agents playing DOTA 2 simulating human choices and behaviour, such as in [19]. This work targets a specific MOBA (i.e. DOTA 2) and therefore considers many features that are specific to it. Many works focus on understanding which movement (and sometimes actions) patterns characterizes high skilled players in the context of a MOBA game. Cavadenti et al. [10] built a reference model considering the actions and movements of expert players, and then analyses MOBA traces looking for features that differentiate them from non expert players. Drachen et al. [11] analysed MOBA traces to extract the spatial features of teams as whole, such as the distance between members of the same team and members of different teams, in order to highlight the difference between expert and non-expert players. In a similar way, Rioult et al. [22] analysed several topological and spatial movement features of MOBA traces, trying to find a correlation between the features and the winning or losing. Those works analyzes the traces in order to recognize if the movement patterns have some features that can explain winning or losing in a MOBA games. Even if we share some mechanisms and underlying core principle with some of these works, our direction is different: indeed our analysis is toward those features that characterize the movement essence of MOBA's avatar, with the goal of creating a mobility model that embed such essence.

3   Multiplayer Online Battle Arenas

Multiplayer Online Battle Arena (MOBA) is a genre of online games in which players control a single character in one of two factions. The objective is to destroy the opposing faction structures, usually following predetermined paths.

A MOBA map is generally a squared area, in which avatars move mostly along predetermined paths that go thorough faction structures, which, in turn, represent landmarks. Figure 1 shows the map of two popular MOBA games *Heroes of Newerth* and *League of Legends*. Generally, in a MOBA game, avatars start weak and acquire power and abilities over time, by completing various objectives. This kind of advancements affects the strategy of the players with as a consequence on the relationships among players and their movements. There exists several variables that affect avatar mobilities: (i) the phase of the game, (ii) the typology of the avatar, (iii) the level of skills acquired by the avatar.

The behaviour of the avatar changes during each phase, according to the relationship they have with the other avatars and landmarks.

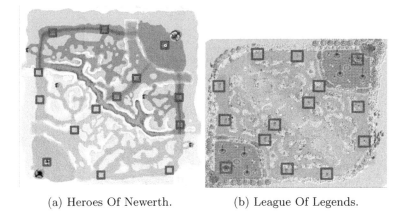

(a) Heroes Of Newerth.   (b) League Of Legends.

Fig. 1. Examples of MOBA games map, landmarks are represented as squares

For what concern the typology of the avatar, these games are played in a modality called 5-vs-5 matches. In this scenario ten players form two teams of five players each. Each player selects an avatar represented by a hero to combat before the real match starts. Each hero has different characteristics. Due to this, each hero is expected to have different play styles and tactics in matches. For example, there are hero called *tanker* who have short-ranged attack ability and excel at surviving combats. Another type of heroes are called *supports* who are weak when alone but can help allies and slow down opponents movements.

Finally, each game is independent from another and avatar starts each game from scratch. The skills of each hero must be improved during the game and the level of them affect the play style and how the avatar moves. For instance, an hero able to increase rapidly its power is probably interested in moving towards the enemy to destroy them. On the other hand, an avatar slow into increase his skills is likely to run away during a fight.

4   The Dataset

In this paper we propose an aggregate analysis of 98 traces from a popular MOBA. The dataset containing all traces, including the data about the AoI statistics and the movement of the player is publicly available [7]. The archive is organized a set of directories, with each directory corresponding to a single trace. Each directory contains three files, whose format and description is presented in Table 1.

The movements happen over a squared map of 15500 × 15550 points. The AoI of avatars is set at 800 points, as it is the most common range for interaction with objects and other players. The position of the avatars is sampled 20 times per second (once every 0.05) seconds.

Table 1. Trace format description

File name	Content description
Avatars	Position of avatars at every time frame in csv format
	time: the time frame considered
	id: the id of the avatar
	x: the x-axis coordinate at the frame
	y: the y-axis coordinate at the frame
aoiStatAVG	Aggregated statistics for avatars AOI in csv format
	time: the time frame considered
	pop_mean, pop_std: aoi population average and st. deviation
	cr_mean, cr_std: avatar contact rate average and st. deviation
	cd_mean, cd_std: avatar contact duration average and st. deviation
	lone: number of lone avatars
Tessellation	Avatars presence over the map as a grid of 100×100 tiles. Matrix of numeric values

4.1   AoI Measures

In the dataset we provide an analysis of movement traces in terms of the relationships of avatars among each other by exploiting the concepts of AOIs and avatar contact. To extract these measures we exploited TRACE [8], a tool for the visualization and analysis of mobility traces for virtual environments.

Several of the measures considered can be found in researches related to ad-hoc networks, especially in terms of *contacts* among entities [13]. In such context, contacts are important as they represent the moment when two entities can communicate and exchange data. Rather differently, from a DVE perspective, contacts among avatars are important, because two contacting avatars share the same spatial interest, and their knowledge can be useful to each other. Therefore, the rate and the duration of contacts can impact both on the design and the behaviour of a DVE architecture. For example, in scenarios in which avatars work as points of centralization for their AOI [9], the analysis of contacts and AOIs are crucial measures. We gather four metrics about AOI and AOI contacts: population size, loneliness, contacts rate and contacts duration.

We define P_a as the set of avatars in a's AOI (excluding a) during an interval period T. AP is defined as the average AOI population for all the avatar in the virtual environment.

$$AP = \frac{1}{N} \sum_{n=1}^{N} |P_n| \tag{1}$$

When $|P_a| = 0$ an avatar is said to be alone, with L being the set of alone avatars. We register an AOI contact when an avatar enters in the AOI of another avatar. We represents with C_a the amount of AOI contacts experienced by an avatar a during an interval period T. The average contact rate CRA is the average number of new AOI contacts experienced by all avatars in the DVE during T, and it is defined as following:

$$CRA = \frac{1}{N} \sum_{n=1}^{N} \frac{C_n}{T} \tag{2}$$

Similarly, the average AOI contact duration CDA is the average of all the terminated contacts of all avatars during T. A terminated contact is registered by TRACE when an avatar exits from the AOI of another one. It is defined as following:

$$CDA = \frac{1}{N} \sum_{n=1}^{N} \frac{\sum_{z \in Z_n} z \times \Delta t}{|Z_n|} \tag{3}$$

where Z_n is the set of all terminated contacts of avatar n.

We record the values for the above metrics during the generation of the traces. Such statistics, are stored in the same archive with the mobility trace itself for later use and comparison.

5   Trace Analysis

In this section we describe how we perfomed the analysis of the traces for the MOBA game "Heroes of Newerth". We start describing the methodology to extract the mobility traces from real game replay and converting them in analyzable traces in Sect. 5.1. In the remain of the section we describe the analysis we performed on such traces: (i) several details about the traces in Sect. 5.2, (ii) an analysis about the AoI of the avatars in Sect. 5.3, and (iii) an analysis on the hotspots identified using the traces in Sect. 5.4.

5.1   Methodology

In this paper we presents the analysis of 98 traces from the MOBA "Heroes of Newerth" (HoN). The traces have been scraped from replays downloaded from the official servers of the game on April 2012, when the popularity of HoN was at its maximum. We used a Python script to transform the replays into movement traces.

Next, in order to analyse the trace we make use of TRACE[1]. TRACE is a Java software library for the generation of avatar movement traces aimed to an easy integration and portability among different systems and approaches.

We extended TRACE with an additional mobility model called *HoN-Mimic* able to mimic the movements loaded by the replays of HoN. We choose this approach for the following advantages:

---

[1] https://github.com/hpclab/trace.

– we can compare *HoN-Mimic* with all the mobility models built-in in TRACE;
– we can automatically extract several metrics provided by TRACE;
– using TRACE permits us to convert the replays of HoN in a format similar to other mobility models for an easier integration in third-party softwares.

In the following we describe the type of data and the information we extracted from the traces.

5.2   Trace Length

In the dataset analysed, the length of the traces varied from 22701 to 91285 frames, correspondent respectively to matches with a duration of 19 to 76 min. The average observed duration is of 48124 frames, which corresponds around to 40 min. The total duration of observed traces is around 4000 min. By analysing the probability distribution histogram of the duration, the best fit is a Nakagami distribution [18] with a shape parameter of 0.62 Fig. 2 shows the histograms and the fitting distribution.

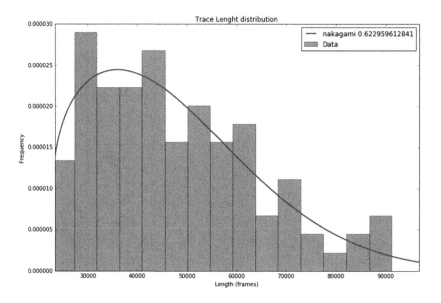

Fig. 2. Distribution of length of the traces

5.3   AoI Analysis

We have performed an analysis of the proximity of avatars in terms of their average AoI population AP, as it is described in Sect. 4.1. The objective of this analysis is to identify how the AoI population changes in the different phases of the game.

To conduct the analysis we have measured the average AP of each trace in every frame. More formally, the value for the global AP_T at the frame n is defined as:

$$AP_T(n) = \frac{1}{N} \sum_{i=0}^{K} AP_i(n) \tag{4}$$

where $AP_i(n)$ is the average AoI population for the trace i at frame n, and K is the total number of traces.

In order to compute a meaningful result of the AP metric it is required that all the traces have the same length. This is due to the fact that if the traces do not have the same length we are not able to compare different traces because the phases of each trace could be not aligned. Therefore, we normalize the traces performing a linear interpolation, such that:

$$y_i = \frac{y_{i-1} + y_{i+1}}{x_{i+1} - x_{i-1}} \tag{5}$$

The results of the analysis are presented in Fig. 3. From the images, we can distinguish the phases that characterize a typical MOBA game, as mentioned in Sect. 3, and how the avatars of different faction relate to each other. Apart from the initial phase, in which all the avatars are clustered together at the start of the game, we can observe the following phases:

- *beginning* (from the 3000th up to the 30000th frame): in this phase each player tries to acquire skills and power as fast as possible, usually traveling alone or together with few components of its faction. Generally in this phase the contact with players of the opposite faction is avoided and battle among avatars are fast. This phase is then characterized by low AoI population (average below 1) and around half of avatar travelling alone.
- *skirmish* (from the 30000th frame up to the 85000th frame): this is the longest phase of the game, in which avatars coordinates in small groups to defeat opponent's structures at the hotspots or battle against other group of avatars. In this phase we can observe a steady increase of the average population with a consequent decrease of lone avatars.
- *final battle* (from the 85000th frame to the end): in the last phase, the majority of the avatars of both the teams aggregate in large groups to achieve the final objective. This phases sees a drastic diminishing of lone avatars and a rapid growth of the AoI population.

5.4   Hotspot Analysis

We performed an analysis of the movement of avatars in order to verify if the landmarks in the game, as described in Sect. 3, actually represent actual hotspots in terms of mobility. Our analysis focus on understanding the position, importance and size of hotspots. To this end, we divided the map into a grid of

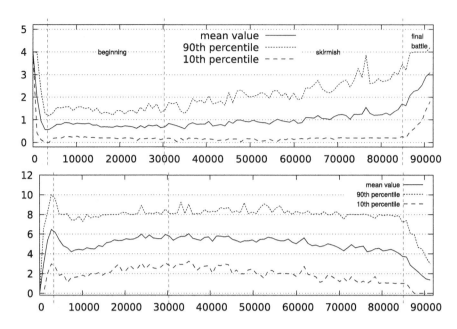

Fig. 3. Average AoI population and avatar loneliness over time

100×100 tiles, all of the same dimensions. For each trace, we counted the presence of avatars for each tile, and then averaged the count for each tile considering all traces.

Figure 4 presents an heat map depicting for each tile the amount of avatars traveling in that specific portion of the map during the game. It is possible to identify mainly 6 hotspots relative to the following position in game: (i) the two team bases, respectively at the top right and bottom left corner, (ii) the three points where the avatars of opposing teams meet since the beginning (the center of the map, the top left corner and the bottom right corner), (iii) and one more hotspot where "Kongor" is positioned. Kongor is an avatar controlled by the artificial intelligence of the game, it is the toughest unit in the map and killing him gives the team a significant advantage. This is the motivation because this area is usually patrolled by the teams.

It is interesting to note also that the majority of the trajectories of the avatars mainly follow predetermined paths between the hotspots. This observation is important in terms of the design of a mobility model, as it allows to use direct paths from one hotspot to another. It worth to notice that this is the same assumption also made from other mobility models for other games, such as Blue Banana [14] for Second Life.

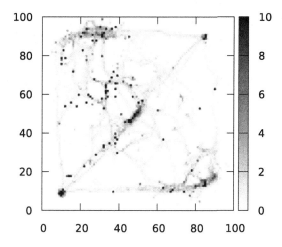

Fig. 4. Hotspot analysis. The heat map represents the average avatar population presence in each tile

6   Conclusion

This paper presented a spatial analysis of movement traces taken from matches of HoN, a MOBA online game. We make use of several metrics in order to detect the characteristics of these games. In particular we identified different phases during a match and how the avatars behave in the different situations. Our analysis span a large number of real traces of the HoN game. We collected such traces and we make them freely available. Our extensive analysis can be a starting point to define novel mobility models able to mimic the behavior of the avatars in the MOBA games. In addition, even if the main motivation of this work is oriented toward the definition of a mobility model, the presented analysis can serve other purposes, such as the creation of AI agents that actually play MOBA games [19], and the inference of the level of ability of MOBA players by the analysis of their movements [10].

References

1. Blizzard Entertainment, World of Warcraft Website. https://worldofwarcraft.com. Accessed 09 Apr 2017
2. Dota 2 - Defense of the Ancient. http://blog.dota2.com/. Accessed 26 May 2017
3. Dota 2 Breaks its Own Record for Biggest Prize Pool in e-sports. https://www.theverge.com/2016/7/26/12266152/dota-2-the-international-6-prize-pool-record. Accessed 07 May 2017
4. Heroes of Newerth. http://www.heroesofnewerth.com/. Accessed 26 May 2017
5. Quake 2. http://store.steampowered.com/app/2320/QUAKE_II/. Accessed 26 May 2017
6. Second Life Official Website. http://secondlife.com/. Accessed 09 Apr 2017

7. Carlini, E., Lulli, A.: Data used for submission entitled "A spatial analysis of Multiplayer Online Battle Arena mobility traces", May 2017. https://doi.org/10.5281/zenodo.583600

8. Carlini, E., Lulli, A., Ricci, L.: TRACE: generating traces from mobility models for distributed virtual environments. In: Desprez, F., et al. (eds.) Euro-Par 2016. LNCS, vol. 10104, pp. 272–283. Springer, Cham (2017). https://doi.org/10.1007/978-3-319-58943-5_22

9. Carlini, E., Ricci, L., Coppola, M.: Reducing server load in MMOG via P2P gossip. In: Proceedings of the 11th Annual Workshop on Network and Systems Support for Games, p. 11. IEEE Press (2012)

10. Cavadenti, O., Codocedo, V., Boulicaut, J.F., Kaytoue, M.: What did i do wrong in my MOBA game? Mining patterns discriminating deviant behaviours. In: 2016 IEEE International Conference on Data Science and Advanced Analytics (DSAA), pp. 662–671. IEEE (2016)

11. Drachen, A., Yancey, M., Maguire, J., Chu, D., Wang, I.Y., Mahlmann, T., Schubert, M., Klabajan, D.: Skill-based differences in spatio-temporal team behaviour in defence of the ancients 2 (DotA 2). In: 2014 IEEE Games Media Entertainment (GEM), pp. 1–8. IEEE (2014)

12. Hu, S.Y., Chen, H.F., Chen, T.H.: VON: a scalable peer-to-peer network for virtual environments. IEEE Netw. **20**(4), 22–31 (2006)

13. Khelil, A., Marron, P.J., Rothermel, K.: Contact-based mobility metrics for delay-tolerant ad hoc networking. In: 13th IEEE International Symposium on Modeling, Analysis, and Simulation of Computer and Telecommunication Systems, pp. 435–444. IEEE (2005)

14. Legtchenko, S., Monnet, S., Thomas, G.: Blue banana: resilience to avatar mobility in distributed MMOGs. In: 2010 IEEE/IFIP International Conference on Dependable Systems and Networks (DSN), pp. 171–180. IEEE (2010)

15. Liang, H., De Silva, R.N., Ooi, W.T., Motani, M.: Avatar mobility in user-created networked virtual worlds: measurements, analysis, and implications. Multimedia Tools Appl. **45**(1–3), 163–190 (2009)

16. Miller, J.L., Crowcroft, J.: Avatar movement in world of warcraft battlegrounds. In: Proceedings of the 8th Annual Workshop on Network and Systems Support for Games, p. 1. IEEE Press (2009)

17. Miller, J.L., Crowcroft, J.: Group movement in world of warcraft battlegrounds. Int. J. Adv. Media Commun. **4**(4), 387–404 (2010)

18. Nakagami, M.: The m-distribution-a general formula of intensity distribution of rapid fading. In: Statistical Method of Radio Propagation (1960)

19. do Nascimento Silva, V., Chaimowicz, L.: On the development of intelligent agents for MOBA games. In: 2015 14th Brazilian Symposium on Computer Games and Digital Entertainment (SBGames), pp. 142–151. IEEE (2015)

20. Ricci, L., Carlini, E.: Distributed virtual environments: from client server to cloud and P2P architectures. In: 2012 International Conference on High Performance Computing and Simulation (HPCS), pp. 8–17. IEEE (2012)

21. Ricci, L., Carlini, E., Genovali, L., Coppola, M.: AOI-cast by compass routing in Delaunay based DVE overlays. In: 2011 International Conference on High Performance Computing and Simulation (HPCS), pp. 135–142. IEEE (2011)

22. Rioult, F., Métivier, J.P., Helleu, B., Scelles, N., Durand, C.: Mining tracks of competitive video games. AASRI Procedia **8**, 82–87 (2014)

23. Tan, S.A., Lau, W., Loh, A.: Networked game mobility model for first-person-shooter games. In: Proceedings of 4th ACM SIGCOMM Workshop on Network and System Support for Games, pp. 1–9. ACM (2005)

Long Transaction Chains and the Bitcoin Heartbeat

Giuseppe Di Battista$^{(\boxtimes)}$ ⓘ, Valentino Di Donato ⓘ, and Maurizio Pizzonia ⓘ

Department of Engineering, Roma Tre University, Rome, Italy
{gdb,didonato,pizzonia}@ing.uniroma3.it

Abstract. Over the past few years a persistent growth of the number of daily Bitcoin transactions has been observed. This trend however, is known to be influenced by a number of phenomena that generate long transaction chains that are not related to real purchases (e.g. *wallets shuffling* and *coin mixing*). For a transaction chain we call *transaction chain frequency* the number of transactions of the chain divided by the time interval of the chain. In this paper, we first analyze to which extent Bitcoin transactions are involved in high frequency transaction chains, in the short and in the long term. Based on this analysis, we then argue that a large fraction of transactions do not refer to explicit human activity, namely to transactions between users that trade goods or services. Finally, we show that most of the transactions are involved into chains whose frequency is roughly stable over time and that we call *Bitcoin Heartbeat*.

Keywords: Bitcoin · Cryptocurrency · Transaction graph

1 Introduction

Bitcoin is the most popular decentralized digital currency and it is the largest of its kind in terms of total market value. As of May 2017, the total number of bitcoins in circulation correspond to over 28B US dollars. As opposed to traditional currencies, Bitcoin does not rely on a trusted entity like a bank or governmental authority. Instead, it is based on an open social model of trust and on incentivized collaboration. After an initial period when it was only known to a small group of enthusiasts and libertarians, Bitcoin has recently gained considerable popularity. According to the "State of Bitcoin" [2], nowadays more than 100,000 merchants accept payments in Bitcoin. Developers started to add it in their applications as a standard form of payment and financial institutions have recently launched initiatives to explore its potential.

The average number of daily Bitcoin transactions, as of May 2017, is somewhere around 280,000. This number is known to be heavily influenced by a number of phenomena. Wallets shuffling and coin mixing are just two examples of activities that generate transactions that are not directly related to real purchases of goods or services. Another example comes from the activity of some

D. B. Heras and L. Bougé (Eds.): Euro-Par 2017 Workshops, LNCS 10659, pp. 507–516, 2018.
https://doi.org/10.1007/978-3-319-75178-8_41

exchanges (i.e., organizations that allow users to trade Bitcoin for fiat currency and vice versa) that use long transaction chains to issue payments to customers that decide to withdraw Bitcoins. This kind of organizations aggregate several deposits into a single large transaction and repeatedly issue payments spending the large change of the previous transaction at each step. Although these long transaction chains are triggered by human activity (i.e., by users that decide to trade Bitcoins), they are still generated by a automatic mechanisms that inflate the raw number of daily Bitcoin transactions associated to the explicit exchange of goods or services between users.

On top of this it is also believed that organizations with interests in Bitcoin generate transactions with the mere objective of attracting investors and inflating the exchange rate. Being generated by computer programs, these "artificial" transactions often introduce in the blockchain regular patterns. Visual systems [5,9] and previous analytical papers [10,14] have pinpointed various suspicious structures ranging from binary tree-like distributions, fork-merge patterns, long and "peeling" chains [10].

In this paper we focus on long transaction chains and consider the frequency at which these chains evolve over time. In brief, we label each transaction with its *LLC*, namely with the *length of the longest chain* the transaction lays on, and we analyze the statistical distribution of the *LLC*s using both short and long intervals of time. We therefore introduce the concept of *Bitcoin Heartbeat*, namely an average measure of the pace at which long chains in Bitcoin have grown over the history.

The paper is structured as follows. Section 2 gives a short description of the Bitcoin transaction graph. Section 3, after providing the reader with some context on long transaction chains, shows the results of our experiments on the distribution of long chains. Section 4 focuses on a specific set of transactions and analyzes how the chains they lay on change through time. Section 5 introduces the concept of Bitcoin Heartbeat. Section 6 concludes the paper.

2   The Bitcoin Transaction Graph

In this section we give a simplified description of Bitcoin transactions and we define the Bitcoin transaction graph. For a broader introduction to Bitcoin see e.g. the original paper [11] and recent surveys [4,16].

A *transaction* (in what follows *tx*) t has a set of inputs $i_t^1, \ldots, i_t^h$ and a set of outputs $o_t^1, \ldots, o_t^k$, each associated with a cryptographic identifier, called *address*, and a bitcoin amount. A tx transfer bitcoins from its inputs to its outputs. Outputs of txs are denoted *txos*. At a certain time T, each txo of a tx t can be unspent (*utxo*) or spent (*stxo*). The only way to spend a utxo o_t of t is to use it as the input $i_{t'}$ of a tx t' (with $t \neq t'$). In this way, bitcoins flowing from one tx to the other create the so called "chain of ownership".

As the authors of [13] we define a directed graph, called *Transaction graph* (*tx-graph*), as follows. Nodes are txs. Nodes t and t' are connected by a directed edge (t, t') if one output o_t of t is used as an input $i_{t'}$ of t'. More precisely, the tx-graph is acyclic, because transactions are never issued twice and it is a multigraph, since several outputs of t can correspond to several inputs of t'. For the sake of simplicity, we will refer to the tx-graph without the attributes "directed", "acyclic" and "multi". An example of a tx-graph can be found in Fig. 1. The above defined graph differs from the *user-graphs* defined for example in [6,7,12] where nodes represent users and edges represent transactions involving pairs of users. The user-graph is obtained by contracting the tx-graph thanks to a heuristic described in [13]. The rule establishes that all the addresses associated to all the inputs of a multi-input tx belong to the same user and can be therefore clustered together. An example of a user-graph can be found in Fig. 2. For the rest of this paper we will always refer to the raw tx-graph.

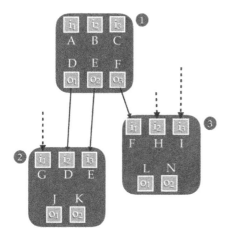

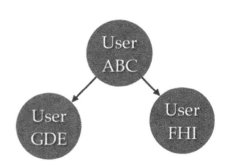

Fig. 1. An example of tx-graph with 3 txs (1, 2 and 3). Tx 1 has 3 inputs (i_1, i_2 and i_3) associated to the addresses A, B and C and 3 outputs (o_1, o_2 and o_3) associated to D, E and F. These outputs are spent in txs 2 and 3. Some inputs of txs 2 and 3 come from outputs of txs that are not part of the drawing (dashed arrows).

Fig. 2. The corresponding user-graph obtained by heuristic described in [13]. Addresses associated to all the inputs of the 3 txs are grouped into single nodes. For the purpose of this paper we do not consider these types of graphs.

The Blockchain is divided into "pages" called *blocks*. Each block contains, roughly, the txs issued in a time interval of ten minutes. The block sequence number is its *height*. For a tx t we denote $b(t)$ the block of t. As of May 2017, the Blockchain consists of about 460,000 blocks and contains about 220 M txs, that is the number of nodes of the tx-graph.

Given a set S of txs, the subgraph of the tx-graph *induced* by S is the graph whose nodes coincide with S and whose edges are the edges of the tx-graph between vertices of S. For a given pair of blocks (b', b'') such that $b' < b''$ we define $G(b', b'')$, as the tx-graph induced by the txs t_i s.t. $b' \leq b(t_i) \leq b''$.

3   Long Transaction Chains

Understanding whether a chain of txs has been generated automatically or it reflects a chain of human purchases is a challenging task. In fact, the "chain of ownership" naturally introduces long chains in the tx-graph. What is often not natural is the velocity at which these chains are generated. With this in mind, Blockchain.info [1] has developed a heuristic to rule out high velocity chains that are probably not in a one-to-one correspondence with chains of real purchases of goods and services[1]. The heuristic works as follows. Each 24 h a counter resets and keeps track of the lengths of the new chains looking at how many times tx outputs are spent on the same day. Data are summarized in Fig. 3. This simple heuristic provides a first estimate of the extent of the phenomena we are looking at: only about 40% of the total number of daily txs do not belong to chains longer than 10.

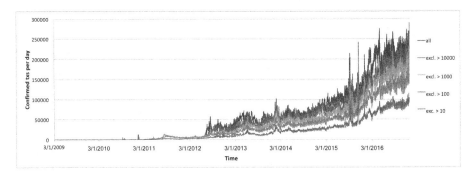

Fig. 3. Number of confirmed txs per day. Red series includes all the txs; green (grey, yellow, blue) series excludes txs belonging to chains longer than 10000 (1000, 100, 10). (Color figure online)

3.1   What Happens in a Day

To understand the nature of long tx chains in Bitcoin, we designed Algorithm 1. Such algorithm receives as input the tx-graph $G(b', b'')$, for a pair of blocks (b', b''), and labels each node v of $G(b', b'')$ with a quantity LLC that represents the length of the longest chain of $G(b', b'')$, vertex v belongs to. In the algorithm with the word "source" ("sink") we refer to nodes with in-degree (out-degree) equal to zero. LLC labeling is computed by leveraging a topological ordering algorithm described in [15].

We performed a first experiment computing graph $G_1 = G(417113, 417256)$ which correspond approximately to 24 h of activity. We then ran Algorithm 1 to

---

[1] From Blockchain.info: *"There are many legitimate reasons to create long transaction chains; however, they may also be caused by coin mixing or possible attempts to manipulate transaction volume."*

Algorithm 1. Label nodes with their LLC

1: **procedure** LABELNODES(*txGraph*)
2:     Label each source node of *txGraph* with attribute *backward* initialized to 0
3:     Label each sink node of *txGraph* with attribute *forward* initialized to 0
4:     *sortedNodes* ← topologicalSort(*txGraph*)   ▷ based on a description from [15]
5:     **for** *n* in *sortedNodes* **do**
6:         **if** predecessors(*n*).length ≠ 0 **then**
7:             *bPredecessors* ← List of backward attributes of all predecessors of *n*
8:             *txGraph*.getNode(*n*).backward ← max(*bPredecessors*) + 1
9:     **for** *n* in reverse(*sortedNodes*) **do**
10:         **if** successors(*n*).length ≠ 0 **then**
11:             *fSuccessors* ← List of forward attributes of all successors of *n*
12:             *txGraph*.getNode(*n*).forward ← max(*fSuccessors*) + 1
13:     **for** *n* in *txGraph*.nodes() **do**
14:         *n*.LLC ← sum(*n*.forward + *n*.backward)

---

label each node with its LLC. G_1 has 219,084 nodes and 264,084 edges. About 10% of the nodes (20,975) have $LLC = 0$ and about 7% of the nodes (15,775) have $LLC = 1$. Figure 4 shows the probability density function of LLC using logarithmic scales on both axes. We left out of the chart nodes with $LLC = 0$ or 1 in order to be able to draw on logarithmic axes. We also computed a power trendline for values of LLC lower than 100 (see the dashed red line on the chart and the equation in the top-right corner). We found out that the left part of the distribution seems to be following a power-law (we recall that straight lines on doubly logarithmic axes are equivalent to exponentially decreasing curves on linear axes). We ran the same experiment on 30 different, randomly selected days obtaining very similar charts and interpolations. Additionally, Fig. 5 shows the cumulative distribution function of LLC. We can observe that about 60% of the daily txs have $LLC \leq 200$ and that about 90% of them have $LLC \leq 700$.

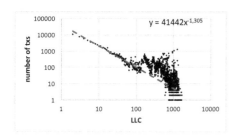

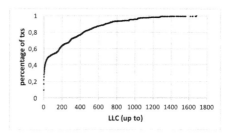

Fig. 4. Probability density function of LLC on 144 blocks using log scales. (Color figure online)

Fig. 5. Cumulative distribution function of LLC on 144 blocks.

3.2   Extending the Analysis to a Wider Range of Blocks

To better understand the LLC distribution, we computed graph $G_2 = G(413000, 419143)$ referred to 6144 consecutive blocks (this number corresponds to the maximum blocks we managed to load in the memory of a single machine) and we ran Algorithm 1. Graph G_2 has 9,344,879 nodes and 18,375,705 edges. Txs for which $LLC = 0$ are 0.49% of the total whereas txs for which $LLC = 1$ are 0.27% of the total. Figure 6 shows the probability density function of LLC. Values on the y-axis have been normalized by multiplying them by 144/6144 where 144 is the average number of blocks per day and 6144 is the number of considered blocks. We have therefore obtained the average number of transactions per day (y-axis) with a certain value of LLC (x-axis). We can observe that also in this case, values of LLC lower than about 100 seem to be following a power-law and that even though values are much higher, the interpolated trendline for values lower than 100 has essentially the same shape and slope as before. The CDF instead (reported in Fig. 7), has a very different shape. This can be explained as follows: even if the number of nodes, that is the average number of txs per day, is roughly the same as the previous experiment, the set of edges increased quite a lot, since its number grows non linearly with the number of involved blocks. We have that 10% of the samples have $LLC \leq 20,000$, whereas 50% have $LLC \leq 50,000$.

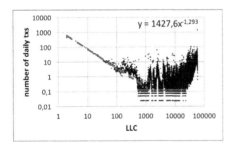
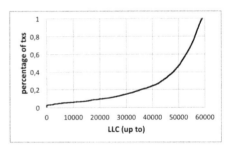

Fig. 6. Probability density function of frequency of LLC on 6144 blocks.

Fig. 7. Cumulative distribution function of LLC on 6144 blocks.

3.3   Trying to Separate Human and Non-human Activity

As reported in [8], power-law distributions have been termed "the signature of human activity". As it is clear from Figs. 4 and 6, the probability density functions of LLC for our experiments do not exhibit the classical power-law shape in their entirety. In particular our distributions lack very long steady tails. In fact, for values higher than about 100, LLC does not seem to follow any regular trendline. Looking at Figs. 4 and 6 we suspect that the power-law portions of the distributions represent human activity whereas the rest represent algorithmically generated txs. Zooming into the figures, we observed that for values higher than about 100, a series of consecutive peaks appear. Such peaks might be interpreted as a sequence of automatic phenomena, each of which introduces at its own frequency new "artificial" transactions in the blockchain. Examples of these peaks can be observed in Fig. 8 where we zoomed into Fig. 6 and we considered the number of daily txs for which $1000 \leq LLC \leq 10000$.

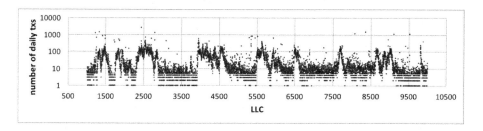

Fig. 8. Zoom of Fig. 6 showing number of daily txs with $1000 \leq LLC \leq 10000$. X-axis uses a linear scale and y-axis uses a logarithmic scale.

4   A Deeper Analysis of a Specific Set of Transactions

In this section we describe the outcome of an experiment aimed at understanding how LLC values change over time for a specific set of txs. We decided to deepen the analysis on a recent block and arbitrarily selected block $B = 416000$. The number of txs in B is 1205. We computed graphs $G_k = G(B - k + 1, B + k)$ with $k = 3, 6, 12, \ldots, 1536, 3072$. Such graphs refer to sequences of blocks "centered" around B, including a number of blocks that grows exponentially. We therefore obtained graphs $G(415998, 416003)$, $G(415995, 416006), \ldots, G(414465, 417536), G(412929, 419072)$ where the first graph refers to 6 blocks (corresponding to about one hour of activity) and the last graph refers to 6144 blocks (corresponding to about 42 days of activity). For each G_k we computed with Algorithm 1, the LLC value for each tx in B. Then we normalized such values, i.e., we computed $(LLC \times 144)/b$, where b is the number of blocks of G_k obtaining the txs per day (TPD) belonging to the longest chain traversing each tx. Figure 9 shows the evolution of TPD for every tx in B. In order to be able to represent null values on logarithmic axes we changed them to be 0.01.

Interestingly, TPD for almost all txs, in the long run, converges to a value included in [300, 1300] as indicated by the red bar in the top-right corner of the figure. This suggests that, after some time, most txs in B will be connected to chains that evolve at the pace of h TPDs, with $h \in [300, 1300]$. Note that, for each graph G_k (see Fig. 9) there is a certain number of txs that "get in the game", i.e., txs whose TPD for the graph G_k is 0 and for the subsequent graph is $\neq 0$. We say that such txs "wake up". We drew in red those txs "waking up"

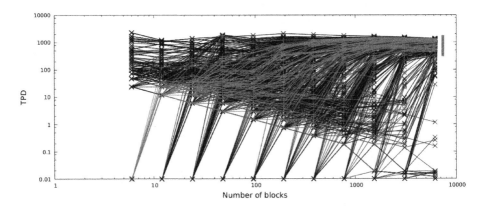

Fig. 9. Evolution of the transactions per day for a specific set of txs. Each point in the plot refers to a specific transaction t of B. Its x-value is the number of blocks of a graph G_k. Its y-value is the TPD for t in G_k. Each tx is represented by a set of points, each showing its TPD in a graph G_k. Such points are linked by a curve. The red curves refer to txs that "wake up" in G_6 (in one hour). (Color figure online)

in graph G_6. We decided to pay specific attention to those txs because, in a sense, they start belonging to some chains exactly at the same time. Txs with this characteristic will be the object of our last experiment.

5   The Bitcoin Heartbeat

In this section we describe our last experiment aimed at investigating how the interval h, introduced in Sect. 4 changed in the Bitcoin history. We considered as a starting date Jan. 2011 because looking at the numbers [3] in this month the number of daily Bitcoin transaction started to be steadily above 1000. Following the same procedure of Sect. 4, we built 22 families of graphs such that each of them refers to 6144 consecutive blocks. The 22 families of graphs correspond to intervals of blocks centered in a random block of the first day of the months Feb., May, Aug. and Nov. of years 2011–2015 and partially 2016 (only Feb. and May). The considered intervals span in total about 141,000 blocks. We then built, for each family, a charts similar to the one of Fig. 9. In particular for each family we only considered txs "waking up" when graph G_6 of the family is taken into account. Finally, we computed one h-interval for each family of graphs as in the previous section, restricting the attention to those txs.

Since the h-interval is the set of frequency values where txs tend to converge over time, we call its average value the *Bitcoin Heartbeat*. Figure 10 shows the evolution of the Bitcoin heartbeat. Note that, in the figure, frequencies are normalized to txs per hour rather than to TPDs as in Fig. 9. Each point represents the frequency at which on average, LLC values of "waking up" txs grow in an hour. In May 2016 we were standing around 52. This means that at the given pace, on average, tx chains get longer by about 1248 (i.e., 52×24) TPDs.

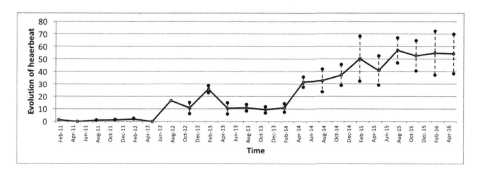

Fig. 10. Evolution of the Bitcoin heartbeat. x-axis is labeled with time. y-axis with the frequency at which on average, *LLC* values of "waking-up" txs grow in one hour. The standard deviation, for each average value is represented using vertical dashed lines.

6   Conclusions

In this paper we have analyzed long chains in the Bitcoin transaction graph performing several experiments each spanning a considerable amount of time and involving a large number of blocks.

The experiments put in evidence what follows. (i) The distribution of the lengths of the longest chains passing through transactions exhibit a shape that is hard to believe to be produced by explicit human activities. In fact, it consists of a low frequency portion that resembles a power-law distribution and an high frequency portion that contains several peaks. (ii) If we consider a sufficiently large amount of time the transactions surprisingly tend to be traversed by long chains with frequencies distributed in a somehow small interval. We call the average of such interval *Bitcoin Heartbeat*. (iii) The Bitcoin Heartbeat has a rather stable value that has slowly grown in the recent Bitcoin history.

Although our observations highlight some interesting properties of the tx-graph we believe that further reasoning is needed about the found results. We believe that a better understanding of the dynamics taking place in Bitcoin has two positive side effects. On one hand it stimulates new research in the field and on the other hand it leads to a more conscious digital economy.

References

1. Blockchain.info. https://blockchain.info/
2. Coindesk. http://www.coindesk.com/state-of-bitcoin-blockchain-2016/
3. Evolution of the number of bitcoin transactions. https://blockchain.info/it/charts/n-transactions?timespan=all
4. Bonneau, J., Miller, A., Clark, J., Narayanan, A., Kroll, J.A., Felten, E.W.: SoK: research perspectives and challenges for bitcoin and cryptocurrencies. In: 2015 IEEE Symposium on Security and Privacy, pp. 104–121, May 2015
5. Di Battista, G., Di Donato, V., Patrignani, M., Pizzonia, M., Roselli, V., Tamassia, R.: Bitconeview: visualization of flows in the bitcoin transaction graph. In: 2015 IEEE Symposium on Visualization for Cyber Security (VizSec), pp. 1–8 (2015)

6. Di Francesco Maesa, D., Marino, A., Ricci, L.: Uncovering the Bitcoin Blockchain: an analysis of the full users graph. In: 2016 IEEE International Conference on Data Science and Advanced Analytics (DSAA), pp. 537–546, October 2016
7. Di Francesco Maesa, D., Marino, A., Ricci, L.: Data-driven analysis of bitcoin properties: exploiting the users graph. Int. J. Data Sci. Anal. (2017). https://doi.org/10.1007/s41060-017-0074-x
8. Fabrikant, A., Koutsoupias, E., Papadimitriou, C.H.: Heuristically optimized trade-offs: a new paradigm for power laws in the internet. In: Widmayer, P., Eidenbenz, S., Triguero, F., Morales, R., Conejo, R., Hennessy, M. (eds.) ICALP 2002. LNCS, vol. 2380, pp. 110–122. Springer, Heidelberg (2002). https://doi.org/10.1007/3-540-45465-9_11
9. McGinn, D., Birch, D., Akroyd, D., Molina-Solana, M., Guo, Y., Knottenbelt, W.: Visualizing dynamic bitcoin transaction patterns. Big Data http://hdl.handle.net/10044/1/32752
10. Meiklejohn, S., Pomarole, M., Jordan, G., Levchenko, K., McCoy, D., Voelker, G.M., Savage, S.: A fistful of bitcoins: characterizing payments among men with no names. In: Proceedings of the ACM Internet Measurement Conference, IMC, pp. 127–140 (2013)
11. Nakamoto, S.: Bitcoin: a peer-to-peer electronic cash system (2008). http://www.bitcoin.org/bitcoin.pdf
12. Ober, M., Katzenbeisser, S., Hamacher, K.: Structure and anonymity of the bitcoin transaction graph. Future Internet **5**(2), 237–250 (2013). http://www.mdpi.com/1999-5903/5/2/237
13. Reid, F., Harrigan, M.: An analysis of anonymity in the bitcoin system. In: 2011 IEEE Third International Conference on Privacy, Security, Risk and Trust and 2011 IEEE Third International Conference on Social Computing, pp. 1318–1326, October 2011
14. Ron, D., Shamir, A.: Quantitative analysis of the full bitcoin transaction graph. In: Sadeghi, A.-R. (ed.) FC 2013. LNCS, vol. 7859, pp. 6–24. Springer, Heidelberg (2013). https://doi.org/10.1007/978-3-642-39884-1_2
15. Skiena, S.S.: The Algorithm Design Manual, 2nd edn. Springer Publishing Company, Incorporated, London (2008). https://doi.org/10.1007/978-1-84800-070-4
16. Yli-Huumo, J., Ko, D., Choi, S., Park, S., Smolander, K.: Where is current research on blockchain technology?—a systematic review. PLoS One **11**(10), 1–27 (2016)

Dynamic Community Analysis in Decentralized Online Social Networks

Barbara Guidi[(✉)], Andrea Michienzi, and Giulio Rossetti

Department of Computer Science, University of Pisa,
Largo B. Pontecorvo, 56127 Pisa, Italy
{guidi,rossetti}@di.unipi.it, a.michienzi@studenti.unipi.it

Abstract. Community structure is one of the most studied features of Online Social Networks (OSNs). Community detection guarantees several advantages for both centralized and decentralized social networks. Decentralized Online Social Networks (DOSNs) have been proposed to provide more control over private data. One of the main challenge in DOSNs concerns the availability of social data and communities can be exploited to guarantee a more efficient solution about the data availability problem. The detection of communities and the management of their evolution represents a hard process, especially in highly dynamic social networks, such as DOSNs, where the online/offline status of user changes very frequently. In this paper, we focus our attention on a preliminary analysis of dynamic community detection in DOSNs by studying a real Facebook dataset to evaluate how frequent the communities change over time and which events are more frequent. The results prove that the social graph has a high instability and distributed solutions to manage the dynamism are needed.

Keywords: Decentralized Online Social Networks · P2P
Dynamic community · Data availability

1 Introduction

Static features, such as clustering coefficient or centrality of Online Social Networks (OSNs) have been largely studied. In particular, the community structure is one of the most studied feature of OSNs and it has attracted wide attention. The general notion of community refers to the fact that nodes tend to form clusters which are more densely interconnected through social relationships, relatively to the rest of the network. Communities reflect the behaviour of users and a high percentage of shared contents are generated by communities (or groups) of social users. During the last ten years, the increase of the amount of social data produced by social users, has put users inside several privacy issues. Centralized solutions for OSNs have been considered the main weak point in the problem of guarantee a certain level of privacy. To overcome this issue, decentralized solutions, known as Decentralized Online Social Networks (DOSNs), have been proposed. The decentralization includes several benefits, in particular in terms

© Springer International Publishing AG, part of Springer Nature 2018
D. B. Heras and L. Bougé (Eds.): Euro-Par 2017 Workshops, LNCS 10659, pp. 517–528, 2018.
https://doi.org/10.1007/978-3-319-75178-8_42

of privacy preserving, but it introduces new challenges that have to be faced. In particular, the problem of data availability is one of the most important ones. Current proposals manage the problem of data availability through a user-centric point of view, and no approaches take into account groups (or communities) of users.

Several studies are proposed to manage the community detection in dynamic environments, such as Mobile Social Networks or Opportunistic Networks. However these studies manage scenarios in which mobile devices make contact with each other and they consider a community as a group of connected nodes.

By considering the importance of a community-centric point of view and the high level of dynamism in DOSNs, this work proposed a preliminary study of dynamic communities by using a real Facebook dataset. In detail, we define a set of community change events that are important to manage the data availability problem and we study the dynamic communities in ego networks to evaluate how frequent the communities change over time and which events are more frequent. All our studies show the need of a distributed approach to manage the problem of the high instability of the social graph over time when we consider the online presence of users.

The important contribution of this work is that, even we consider a specific scenario, our contribution could be applied to other distributed systems, by taking into account the specific constraints.

This paper is organized as follow. In Sect. 2 we describe the related work. In Sect. 3 we introduce the dynamic community analysis in DOSNs. A preliminary analysis is showed in Sect. 4. Finally, conclusions and future work are presented in Sect. 5.

2   Related Work

In this section we describe the two fields involved in our work. First of all, we introduce current DOSN proposals by describing their characteristics. Afterwards, we describe the state of art in the dynamic community detection field.

2.1   DOSN's Approaches

DOSNs [7] have been proposed in order to overcome the privacy issues of the centralized OSNs. The decentralization of most of the current proposals is implemented by a P2P network. Diaspora[1], with about 669,000 users, is one of the most successful DOSN proposal currently active and deployed in a decentralized way. PeerSoN [2] is one of the most well-known DOSN after Diaspora. It is implemented as a two-tier system in which the first tier is used for the lookup service, instead the second tier is used for the communication between peers and the exchange of users' profile. SafeBook [6] uses a social overlay named *Matryoshkas*, which is composed by concentric rings of peers built around each

---

[1] https://joindiaspora.com/.

peer. The social overlay guarantees a trusted data storage and an obscure communication through indirection. LifeSocial [10] proposes a solution to the privacy issue by using public-private key pairs to encrypt profile data which are store in a DHT. DiDuSoNet [12] is built on a Dunbar-based social overlay and it is focused on the data availability issue by introducing the concept of Point of Storage (PoS). The number of replicas each profile has is minimized by considering only two replicas. A similar approach is Cachet [17] which replicates profiles on the DHT. Cachet does not minimize the number of replicas and it does not manage the problem of consistency raised to keep all replicas up-to-date.

2.2 Dynamic Community Detection

Dynamic Community Discovery is a relatively novel task in complex network analysis [1,3], its goal being identify and track trough time clusters of highly connected nodes in a dynamic network. In a preliminary survey [14] two high level categories of online Dynamic Community Discovery algorithms are identified depending on how the community evolution is handled: (i) *Temporal Smoothness* approaches run the community discovery process from scratch on each graph evolution step (e.g. network snapshot); (ii) *Dynamic Updates* approaches incrementally update the communities as time goes by looking both at their previous states and at novel network perturbations. In static community discovery a formal and shared definition of community is still missing: such ill-posedness applies even to the dynamic extension of the problem, thus leading to several detection and quality criteria. Since there are countless ways to define what a dynamic community should look like most of the literature on the subject focus not on reaching consensus on community topology but on the description of approaches able to track elementary communities evolution patterns. Following such rationale, several works converged on the definition and adoption of a stable set of events that can be used to describe dynamic community life-cycles [4,18,19]: Birth, Death, Growth, Contraction, Merge, Split.

3 Towards the Dynamic Community Analysis in DOSNs

Several approaches propose to manage the problem of community detection in social networks take into account the evolution of the social graph in term of friendship relationship (or co-authorships [21,22]), or in term of interactions between users (or call graphs [11]).

Focusing on a single user, its friendship relationships do not change so frequently. Instead, interactions of each nature (calls, emails, posts, tweets, etc.) suffer of a different level of dynamism. However, the study of the interactions graph represents a different evaluation of the social graph, because the interaction graph is an abstraction of the social graph that should be represented as a weighted and usually directed graph [13]. In a distributed system which wants to provide social services, such as a DOSN, an interest evaluation concerns the study of dynamic community by considering the temporal behaviour of users.

As showed in our previous work [20], the static view of an ego network and as a consequence its communities are completely different when we consider the time-varying ego network.

In the follow, we describe more in detail our DOSN's architecture by explaining how our architecture is organized. Moreover, we explain the problem of data availability, which is the main goal treated by our DOSN [12]. Finally, we give our definition of the events occurred during the normal activity of a DOSN which involve the dynamic communities.

3.1 DOSN: Our Scenario

A current trend of DOSNs is the usage of a social overlay which represents in some way the friendship relationships between users. The network topology resulting is generally known as a Friend to Friend network (F2F) in which users only make direct connections with people they know. Usually in OSNs, the social graph of each user is referred by using a well-known social network model known as *Ego Network*. The *Ego Network* [15] of a user represents a structure built around the ego which contains his direct friends, known as *alters* and may also include information about the direct connections between the alters. Formally, each vertex $u \in V$ can be seen as an *ego* and $EN(u) = (V_u, E_u)$ is the ego network of u where $V_u = \{u\} \cup \{v \in V | (u, v) \in E\}$, $E_u = \{(a, b) \in E | \{a, b\} \subseteq V_u\}$ and E is the set of edges present in the original graph. $N(u) = V_u - \{u\}$ is the set of adjacent nodes of u.

A F2F network can be formally represented by using an *Ego Network* to model the social graph and we assume a one-to-one mapping between the users of the OSN and the nodes of the DOSN [12].

3.2 Data Availability Problem

Data availability is a real hard problem for every distributed environment. Replication is the most used technique to manage this challenge.

In our scenario, the problem has a big constraint inserted to maintain a high level of privacy inside the system. The constraint concerns how data should be stored: replica nodes are chosen by exploiting friendship relations.

To manage the problem of data availability, proper techniques must be introduced in order to ensure that data of the ego users will be available on a subset of their alters.

In our previous works [9,12], we have exploited a friendship-based replication schema. A friendship-based replication schema chooses replica nodes by taking into account the friendship relationships between users. Indeed, consider an ego node e, only its friend nodes can be chosen to be its replica nodes.

This replication schema is applied also in other DOSN proposals, such as My3 [16]. However, the data availability could be guided from both friendship relationships and a content-based point of view. For sake of clarity, a content based point of view concerns the problem to find group of users which are interest to a same content to minimize the number of replicas. Groups of users can be defined with a *community* and this approach can be named as a *community-based replication technique*. The presence of densely connected groups of nodes can be exploited to increase the level of data availability and to minimize the replicas. A possible approach could be exploit the community structure to store at least one replica of the whole profile or of interest content for the users belonging to the community. As discussed in Sect. 3, ego networks in DOSNs suffer of a high level of dynamism and for this reason, we are interested in studying how communities evolve during the online activity of the system due to the online/offline of users to understand which community change events could happen and the frequency of them.

3.3 Dynamic Community Analysis in DOSNs

A real interest in studying the dynamic community in distributed environment is to understand how the network changes and in particular, after defining what we intend as community, how the community evolves during the time. In this paper a community is identified with nodes that are densely linked to each other, directly or through other nodes. We represent an ego network e as a set of n snapshots $(EG_1^e, EG_2^e, ..., EG_n^e)$. Each snapshot of an ego network e at time i, identified as EG_i^e, contains a set of communities $C = (C_i^1, C_i^2, ..., C_i^m)$ We are interest to evaluate the evolution of communities in term of the community change events explained in detail in [22]. For sake of readiness, communities events are merge, split, death, and birth. To evaluate the similarity between communities, we use a revised version of the similarity metric proposed in [22]. Consider an ego network e and two snapshot EG_i^e and EG_j^e, the revised similarity metric is introduced by the Eq. (1),

$$sim(C_{i-1}^p, C_i^q) = \frac{|V_{i-1}^p \cap V_i^q|}{max(|V_{i-1}^p|, |V_i^q|)} \tag{1}$$

where C_i^q is the community q included in EG_i^e and C_{i-1}^p is the community p included in EG_{i-1}^e. Instead, V_{i-1}^p is the set of nodes contained in C_{i-1}^p and V_i^q is the set of nodes contained in C_i^q.

Thanks to this similarity metric, each community in a time instant i is compared with each community of the time instant $i - 1$.

Moreover, we need to redefine all the possible community change events (merge, split, death, birth) to be applied in a DOSN. We propose our definition of the four events:

- *Birth:* we say that a community C_i^p is born at time i if, given the set of communities $C_{i-1}^* = \{C_{i-1}^1, C_{i-1}^2, \cdots, C_{i-1}^k\}$ at time $i - 1$, $\forall C_{i-1}^j \in C_{i-1}^*$, we have that $sim(C_i^p, C_{i-1}^j) = 0$. This means that all the communities discovered at the previous time instant $(i - 1)$ do not share any node with C_i^p.
- *Death:* we say that a community C_{i-1}^p is dead at time i if, given the set of communities $C_i^* = \{C_i^1, C_i^2, ..., C_i^k\}$ at time i, $\forall C_i^j \in C_i^*$, we have that

$sim(C_{i-1}^p, C_i^j) = 0$. This means that all the communities discovered at time i do not share any node with C_{i-1}^p.

- *Merge:* we say that a set of communities $C_{i-1}^* = \{C_{i-1}^1, C_{i-1}^2, \ldots, C_{i-1}^k\}$ merge into a community C_i^p if, for each community $C_{i-1}^j \in C_{i-1}^*$, we have that $sim(C_{i-1}^j, C_i^p) \geqslant k$, where k is the similarity threshold defined in [22]. This means that k% of mutual friends between C_i^p and each community in C_{i-1}^* are included in C_i^p.
- *Split:* we say that a community C_{i-1}^p splits into a set of communities $C_i^* = \{C_i^1, C_i^2, \ldots, C_i^n\}$ if, for each community $C_i^j \in C_i^*$, we have that $sim(C_i^j, C_{i-1}^p) \geqslant k$ where k is the similarity threshold as described in [22]. This means that a community C_i^p is divided in a set of community identified by C_{i-1}^*.

3.4   How Community Change Events Affect the Data Availability

In this study we refer to the events proposed in [22] and we do not consider the event *survive*, usually referred as *growth* and *shrink*, because it is less relevant in term of data availability, due to the fact that this event gives little information about the evolution of the communities in the network.

Considering the problem of data availability in DOSNs and our proposed community-based replication technique explained in Sect. 3.2, the events *birth*, *death*, *split* and *merge* can affect the level of availability and the number of replicas. *Birth* events are critical and they are one of the main issue that has to be faced. Indeed, a newly formed community may have little to no information about the most fresh contents created by the ego and nodes inside such communities must find a way to retrieve it. *Death* events are reported mainly to give us more information about node churn in such dynamic context, but are no concern in a replication technique because offline nodes do not need any content. *Merge* and *split* events are important because, in the former case, nodes that belong to different communities converge in the same community, so they should merge the available information and probably a few replicas of data can be dropped. In the latter case, splitted communities suggest that communities may become more distant over time, so the content may need to be redistributed and replicated over the newly formed communities.

4   A Case Study: Facebook

To evaluate the dynamics in OSNs, we study Facebook through our dataset retrieved by a Facebook application, called SocialCircles![2].

As described in [8], SocialCircles! was able to retrieve the following sets of information from registered users:

Friendship. We obtained friends of registered users and the friendship relations existing between them.

---

[2] https://www.facebook.com/SocialCircles-244719909045196/.

Online presence. We monitored the chat status of users in Facebook. The presence status is identified with 0 if user is offline, 1 if user is in active state and 2 if user is idle.

We were able to obtain two different datasets, the first one introduced in [8] and a second one composed by 240 users monitored for 32 consecutive days. In detail, we sampled all the registered users and their friends every 5 min, for 32 days (from 9 March to 10 April 2015). Using this methodology we were able to access the temporal status of about 240 registered users and of their friends (for a total of 78.129 users).

A discrete time model is used to represent the online/offline status of the users during the simulation. In particular, each day of the monitored period consists of a finite number of time slots (i.e., 288 time slots each of 5 min), for a total number of 9251 time slots in the whole monitored period.

Figure 1 shows the number of online users for each time slot. The figure shows that there is a clear periodic pattern, probably reflecting the day/night cycle. By analyzing the amount of users online for each time slot, we can see that we have at most around 18000 online users, roughly 23% of the total amount, and at least 3000, 3.8% of the total amount of users.

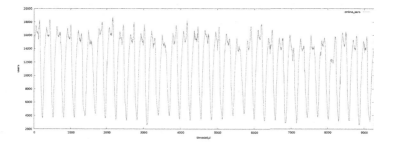

Fig. 1. Online users count during the observed period

4.1   Dynamic Community Evaluation

For the community discovery algorithm, we choose DEMON [5] among the many that are present in literature. The main reason is that we define a community as a group of clustered nodes that is the community structure found by the label propagation implemented in DEMON. Moreover, DEMON is computationally not expensive. Indeed, it is theoretically linear in time. For the community similarity computation, we are interested only in computing the similarity value for each community at time i, with all the communities at time $i - 1$. This saves a lot of computation of similarity between communities that do not belong to adjacent time slots. We computed the community events as described in Sect. 3 considering two different sets of communities:

– All: in this case we considered all the communities of all ego networks during the observed period of time of 32 days;
– Selected: consider only the communities in the time slots where the related ego was offline (inter-arrival session slots).

With this differentiation we aim to capture a generic, global view of the dynamism of the network in the first case, and a more specific, critical view in the second case. It is very important to understand how the network evolves in time, also when it is not strictly needed for the data availability problem because we need to handle churn.

As a preliminary analysis, we computed some statistical measures on the number and size of the dynamic communities to compare them with the static communities. Table 1 reports the measures for all communities, while Table 2 reports the same measures for the static communities. By analyzing the dynamic results, we can say that the network is, as expected, very shattered and not even close to the static view. When considering the number of communities, the high value of standard deviation with respect to the average, suggests that in some particular time slots some ego networks have no community at all. In the static case we have a lower maximum value and an higher average with respect to the dynamic case, which suggests that it is very unlikely to have a dynamic ego network that is similar to the static one. Also the size statistics confirms this fact: static communities tend to be larger than the dynamic ones. We can explain the difference in the two results by recalling the fact that we have at most less than a forth of the users online, as reported in Fig. 1.

Table 1. Statistical measures on number and size of all dynamic communities

	Min	Max	Mean	Std. deviation
Number	0	104	2.2814344395195665	3.75809047211548
Size	4	452	17.643563738762122	22.10944505125662

Table 2. Statistical measures on number and size of static communities

	Min	Max	Mean	Std. deviation
Number	1	26	9.49583333333333	4.401405173746986
Size	4	1894	99.38788942518802	141.28948531026552

To better understand how the events are arranged during the observed time (Tables 3 and 4), we decided to make some plots. Figure 2 shows the arrangements of the events when considering all communities of all time slots while Fig. 3 shows the events for the selected communities. Both the figures show that there is a temporal pattern in the results, suggesting that the behaviour follows

Table 3. Statistical measures on community events of all dynamic communities

Event	Min	Max	Mean	Std. deviation
Split	0	173	61.90498324505457	38.221971154669156
Merge	0	170	61.961301480920845	38.21300775550354
Death	0	117	39.51551183655814	15.25082726706613
Birth	0	98.0	39.51940330775052	16.40523076472613

Table 4. Statistical measures on community events of selected dynamic communities

Event	Min	Max	Average	Std. deviation
Split	0	122	44.72067884553051	26.444005572482837
Merge	0	124	44.78207761323137	26.432679749759142
Death	0	80	26.160415090260557	12.350502534938407
Birth	0	58	26.152307858609966	12.836074158727344

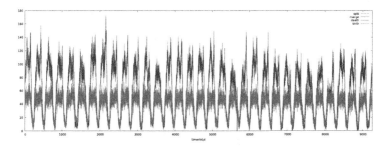

Fig. 2. Community events for each time slot of all dynamic communities

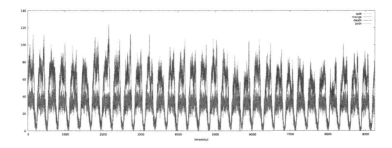

Fig. 3. Community events for each time slot of selected dynamic communities

a daily cycle, confirming the results in Fig. 1. Moreover, on the peaks, the number of merge/split events are roughly double the number of death/birth events, while in the nadirs the number of merge/split events are slightly less than the number of death/birth events. By taking a closer look at the arrangements of the events, we may also observe that peaks and nadirs of merge and split events are slightly moved on the right with respect to the ones of birth and death events, which means that, before observing a variation on the number of split and merge events, we should see a variation in the number of birth and death events. It is also worth noticing that, as expected, at each drop of the events corresponds a peak in deaths, which probably means that we are approaching the night time slots. Dually, at each increase of events, we usually see a peak of birth events, which should correspond to the time slots where people wake up. Another important result is that the two graphs look similar which is sign that the network behaves in the same way both when the ego is online or offline. This is of interest in the sense that all the analysis can be done regardless that an ego is online or not.

Finally, since the events follow a daily cycle, we are interested to see how this events are related to the presence of users on the network. From a comparison between Figs. 2 and 3 with Fig. 1 we can see that the more users are online, the more events are observed in the network. This means that, in a community-based replication technique, choosing the replicas when there are less users on the network is somewhat easier because the network is more stable in terms of communities, while, on the other hand, when there are a lot of users online, we need to handle more community events, especially split and merge events.

5 Conclusion and Future Works

In this paper we propose a preliminary analysis of dynamic community due to the online/offline status of users in DOSNs. In detail, we focus our attention of the data availability problem that is one of the most important problems in DOSNs and we propose a set of community change events which are important in our scenario. We analyze both how and the frequency of these events by exploiting a real Facebook dataset gathered by our Facebook application (SocialCircles). Results show that DOSNs are affected by a high dynamism and a community-based replication schema needs to be supported by a distributed algorithm able to manage the dynamism of communities. By analyzing the dynamic results, we show that the network is very shattered and not even close to the static view. Moreover, the community change events introduced in this paper have a temporal pattern that is similar to the temporal user behaviour and, in a community-based replication technique, when there are less users the network is more stable in terms of communities, while, when there are a lot of users online, we need to handle more community events. We plan a deep analysis of the instability of the social graph due to the online/offline status of users. In particular, we plan to develop a distributed algorithm to detect the dynamic community, which can be used to address the problem of data availability.

References

1. Aynaud, T., Fleury, E., Guillaume, J.L., Wang, Q.: Communities in evolving networks: definitions, detection, and analysis techniques. In: Mukherjee, A., Choudhury, M., Peruani, F., Ganguly, N., Mitra, B. (eds.) Dynamics On and Of Complex Networks, vol. 2, pp. 159–200. Springer, New York (2013). https://doi.org/10.1007/978-1-4614-6729-8_9

2. Buchegger, S., Schioberg, D., Vu, L., Datta, A.: Implementing a P2P social network - early experiences and insights from PeerSoN. In: Second ACM Workshop on Social Network Systems (Co-located with EuroSys 2009) (2009)

3. Cazabet, R., Amblard, F.: Dynamic community detection. In: Alhajj, R., Rokne, J. (eds.) Encyclopedia of Social Network Analysis and Mining, pp. 404–414. Springer, New York (2014). https://doi.org/10.1007/978-1-4614-6170-8

4. Cazabet, R., Amblard, F., Hanachi, C.: Detection of overlapping communities in dynamical social networks. In: 2010 IEEE Second International Conference on Social Computing (SocialCom), pp. 309–314. IEEE (2010)

5. Coscia, M., Rossetti, G., Giannotti, F., Pedreschi, D.: DEMON: a local-first discovery method for overlapping communities. In: Proceedings of the 18th ACM SIGKDD, KDD 2012 (2012)

6. Cutillo, L.A., Molva, R., Strufe, T.: Safebook: a privacy-preserving online social network leveraging on real-life trust. Commun. Mag. **47**(12), 94–101 (2009)

7. Datta, A., Buchegger, S., Vu, L.H., Strufe, T., Rzadca, K.: Decentralized online social networks. In: Furht, B. (ed.) Handbook of Social Network Technologies and Applications, pp. 349–378. Springer, Boston (2010). https://doi.org/10.1007/978-1-4419-7142-5_17

8. De Salve, A., Dondio, M., Guidi, B., Ricci, L.: The impact of user's availability on on-line ego networks: a Facebook analysis. Comput. Commun. **73**, 211–218 (2016)

9. De Salve, A., Guidi, B., Mori, P., Ricci, L.: Distributed coverage of ego networks in F2F online social networks. In: 2016 International IEEE Conferences on Ubiquitous Intelligence and Computing, Advanced and Trusted Computing, Scalable Computing and Communications, Cloud and Big Data Computing, Internet of People, and Smart World Congress (UIC/ATC/ScalCom/CBDCom/IoP/SmartWorld), pp. 423–431 (2016)

10. Graffi, K., Gross, C., Mukherjee, P., Kovacevic, A., Steinmetz, R.: LifeSocial. KOM: a P2P-based platform for secure online social networks. In: Peer-to-Peer Computing, pp. 1–2. IEEE (2010)

11. Greene, D., Doyle, D., Cunningham, P.: Tracking the evolution of communities in dynamic social networks. In: Proceedings of the 2010 International Conference on Advances in Social Networks Analysis and Mining, ASONAM 2010, pp. 176–183 (2010)

12. Guidi, B., Amft, T., De Salve, A., Graffi, K., Ricci, L.: DiDuSoNet: a P2P architecture for distributed dunbar-based social networks. Peer-to-Peer Netw. Appl. **9**(6), 1–18 (2015)

13. Guidi, B., Conti, M., Ricci, L.: P2P architectures for distributed online social networks. In: 2013 International Conference on High Performance Computing and Simulation (HPCS), pp. 678–681. IEEE (2013)

14. Hartmann, T., Kappes, A., Wagner, D.: Clustering evolving networks. In: Kliemann, L., Sanders, P. (eds.) Algorithm Engineering. LNCS, vol. 9220, pp. 280–329. Springer, Cham (2016). https://doi.org/10.1007/978-3-319-49487-6_9

15. Marsden, P.: Egocentric and sociocentric measures of network centrality. Soc. Netw. **24**(4), 407–422 (2002)
16. Narendula, R., Papaioannou, T.G., Aberer, K.: My3: a highly-available P2P-based online social network. In: 2011 IEEE International Conference on Peer-to-Peer Computing (P2P), pp. 166–167. IEEE (2011)
17. Nilizadeh, S., Jahid, S., Mittal, P., Borisov, N., Kapadia, A.: Cachet: a decentralized architecture for privacy preserving social networking with caching. In: Proceedings of the 8th International Conference on Emerging Networking Experiments and Technologies, CoNEXT 2012, pp. 337–348. ACM (2012)
18. Palla, G., Barabási, A.L., Vicsek, T.: Quantifying social group evolution. Nature **446**(7136), 664–667 (2007)
19. Rossetti, G., Pappalardo, L., Pedreschi, D., Giannotti, F.: Tiles: an online algorithm for community discovery in dynamic social networks. Mach. Learn. **106**(8), 1213–1241 (2017)
20. Salve, A.D., Guidi, B., Ricci, L.: Evaluation of structural and temporal properties of ego networks for data availability in DOSNs. Mob. Netw. Appl. 1–12 (2017)
21. Takaffoli, M., Rabbany, R., Zaïane, O.R.: Community evolution prediction in dynamic social networks. In: 2014 IEEE/ACM International Conference on Advances in Social Networks Analysis and Mining (ASONAM), pp. 9–16 (2014)
22. Takaffoli, M., Sangi, F., Fagnan, J., Zäıane, O.R.: Community evolution mining in dynamic social networks. Procedia-Soc. Behav. Sci. **22**, 49–58 (2011)

Multi-objective Service Oriented Network Provisioning in Ultra-Scale Systems

Dragi Kimovski$^{(\boxtimes)}$, Sashko Ristov, Roland Mathá, and Radu Prodan

Distributed and Parallel Systems, Institute of Informatics,
University of Innsbruck, Innsbruck, Austria
dragi@dps.uibk.ac.at

Abstract. The paradigm of ultra-scale computing has been recently pushed forward by the current trends in distributed computing. This novel architecture concept is focused towards a federation of multiple geographically distributed heterogeneous systems under a single system image, thus allowing efficient deployment and management of very complex architectures applications. To enable sustainable ultra-scale computing, there are multiple major challenges, which have to be tackled, such as, improved data distribution, increased systems scalability, enhanced fault tolerance, elastic resource management, low latency communication and etc. Regrettably, the current research initiatives in the area of ultra-scale computing are in a very early stage of research and are predominantly concentrated on the management of the computational and storage resources, thus leaving the networking aspects unexplored. In this paper we introduce a promising new paradigm for cluster-based Multi-objective service-oriented network provisioning for ultra-scale computing environments by unifying the management of the local communication resources and the external inter-domain network services under a single point of view. We explore the potentials for representing the local network resources within a single distributed or parallel system and combine them together with the external communication services.

Keywords: Inter-domain network provisioning
Multi-objective optimization · Machine learning

1 Introduction

In order to successfully handle the growth of data volume and maintain computational performance on large scales, it is essential for the emerging hardware and software systems to be re-evaluated to handle the foreseen challenges introduced by the large scale distributed environments. The emerging field of ultra-scale computing aims at tackling these rather ambitious challenges by paving the road for the development of highly distributed architectures, spawning over multiple administrative domains [1]. The paradigm of ultra-scale computing has been recently pushed forward by the current trends in distributed computing,

© Springer International Publishing AG, part of Springer Nature 2018
D. B. Heras and L. Bougé (Eds.): Euro-Par 2017 Workshops, LNCS 10659, pp. 529–540, 2018.
https://doi.org/10.1007/978-3-319-75178-8_43

and to some extend in high-performance computing (HPC), focused towards a federation of multiple geographically distributed heterogeneous systems under a single system image, thus allowing efficient deployment and management of very complex architectures [2].

Unfortunately, supporting the evolution of the ultra-scale systems requires immense research activities focused towards development of domain-specific tools and architectures for enabling robust computing solutions through multi-domain cooperative approaches. To enable sustainable ultra-scale computing, there are multiple major challenges, which have to be tackled, such as, improved data distribution and data locality, increased systems scalability, enhanced fault tolerance and availability, elastic resource management, low latency inter-domain communication and etc.

Regrettably, all promising research initiatives in the area of distributed ultra-scale computing are in a very early stage of research and are predominantly concentrated on the inter-domain management of the computational and storage resources, thus leaving the networking aspects unexplored. As a result, multiple challenges in terms of description, allocation, operation and management of network services and resources, especially in heterogeneous distributed and parallel environments, have been neglected and remained unexplored till today.

In this paper we introduce a promising new paradigm for Multi-objective service-oriented network provisioning for ultra-scale computing environments by unifying the management of the local communication resources and the external inter-domain network services under a single point of view. We explore the potentials for representing the local network resources within a single distributed or parallel system and combine them together with the external communication services. The composition of the local resources and external services will result in the creation of an inter-domain communication environment called *communication super-service*. The introduction of such a paradigm will enable transparent deployment of highly adaptive service-based virtual networks, spawning across various domains and system architectures.

In order to enable efficient and low latency provisioning of network super-services we utilize algorithms and techniques from the field of multi-criteria optimization and clustering. More concretely, we have exploited current clustering techniques to initially divide the available network services and resources based on the user's preferences. Afterwards, multi-objective optimization and non-domination sorting algorithms, together with novel decision making strategy, are used to provide a set of "optimal" trade-off combination of network services and network resources. In what follows a detailed description and comprehensive evaluation of the proposed communication super-service provisioning is provided.

2   Related Work

Recently, promising new research initiatives have been started in the European research community, focused towards solving the issues that prevent efficient management of the network resources in an inter-domain environment. One of these initiatives is the SSICLOPS project, which aims at developing novel techniques for management of software-defined networks within federated Cloud infrastructures [3]. Furthermore, the BEACON research project [4] targets a virtualization layer on top of heterogeneous underlying physical networks, computing and storage infrastructures, providing automated federation of applications across different Clouds and data centers. Significant research progress has also been reported in the literature. The authors in [6] introduced a novel approach for designing Cloud systems, developed around the notion of robust virtual network infrastructure capable of specifying complex interconnection topologies. A promising architectural solution for Cloud service provisioning was proposed in [7] relying on service-based IP network virtualization. Within this research initiative, various management schemes have been designed and implemented, such as novel resource description and abstraction mechanisms, complex virtual network request methods, and a resource broker mechanism called "Marketplace". The work in [8] proposes an OpenFlow service based network virtualization framework for supporting Cloud infrastructures and presents promising new network abstraction methods for virtualization of the physical infrastructure. Furthermore, the innovative virtual network provisioning approach in [9] comprises an elasticity-aware abstraction model and virtual network service provisioning method that allows for elastic network scaling in relation to the communication load in the data center or Cloud infrastructure. Lastly, the authors in [10] proposed an adaptive virtual resource provisioning method capable of adapting in response to the demand for virtual network service requests, extended to support fault-tolerance embedding and provisioning algorithm.

In spite of these important advances, the management and utilization of the network resources are still in an early stage of research. Currently, even within a single Cloud environment or multi-cluster infrastructure, the guarantees on the Quality-of-Service (QoS) on the communication infrastructure are limited. For example, in the current Cloud architectures, only minimal bandwidth is assured per Virtual Machine (VM), without considering the communication latency [11]. Moreover, the current research advances have been only focused towards overcoming the barriers that limit the efficient utilization of the interconnection resources in Cloud environment, which neglect the requirements of the high-performance community for low latency communication between heterogeneous distributed and parallel systems.

3 Background

3.1 Multi-objective Optimization

In this work we utilize multiple concepts from the area of multi-objective optimization to enable efficient network services provisioning in ultra-scale systems. In general, optimization is a process of identifying one or multiple solutions, which correspond to the extreme values of two or more objective functions within given constraints set. In the cases in which the optimization task utilizes only a single objective function it results in a single optimal solution. Moreover, the optimization can also consider multiple conflicting objectives simultaneously. In those circumstances, the process will usually result in a set of optimal trade-off solutions, so-called Pareto solutions. The task of finding the optimal set of Pareto solutions is known in the literature as a multi-objective optimization [12].

The multi-objective optimization problem usually involves two or more objective functions which have to be either minimized or maximized. The problem of optimization can be formulated as: $min/max(f_1(Y), f_2(Y), \ldots, f_n(Y))$, where $n \geq 2$ is the number of objectives functions f that we want to minimize or maximize, while $Y = (y_1, y_2, \ldots, y_k)$ is a region enclosing the set of feasible decision vectors.

Even though the above formulation of the multi-objective optimization is without any constraints, this is hardly the case when real-life optimization problems are being considered. The real-life problems are typically constrained by some bounds, which divide the search space into two regions, namely feasible and infeasible region.

3.2 Clustering

In the Big Data era the vital tool for dealing with large data-sets is the concept of classification or grouping of data objects into a set of categories or clusters. The classification of the objects is conducted based on the similarity or dissimilarity of multiple features that describe them. Those differences are usually generalized as proximity in accordance to certain standards or rules. Essentially, the classification methods can be divided into two categories, namely supervised and unsupervised [5]. In supervised classification, the features' mapping from a set of input data vectors is classified to a finite set of discrete labeled classes and it is modeled in terms of some mathematical function. On the other hand, in unsupervised classification, called clustering, no labeled data-sets are available. The aim of the clustering is to separate a finite unlabeled data-sets into a finite and discrete set of clusters. For the purposes of our work, we utilize distance and similarity based clustering algorithms, such as k-means, which allow for low-latency coarse-grained clustering [16].

4   System Architecture

To tackle the issues that limit the possibilities for transparent inter-domain communication we present a use-case scenario for the proposed multi-objective provisioning environment. Furthermore, based on the use-case scenario the top-level view architecture of the proposed system is provided.

The use-case of the proposed environment can be identified in the field of distributed ultra-scale computing. More concretely, the future large-scale systems have been foreseen as a heterogeneous fusion of the tightly coupled HPC systems and loosely coupled Cloud infrastructures, interconnected by external network infrastructures provided on the network-as-a-service basis. The heterogeneity of such platforms can pose many challenges for efficient and low latency communication between processes located in different domains and systems. For example, let us assume that we have distributed application located at two distant geographical locations, where both computing systems are of different architecture. The current state-of-the-art technology will only allow for a high-level protocol, such as TCP, to be used over the shared Internet network in order to provide a communication channel between the application components. This may induce high latency and low communication bandwidth. Contrary, the proposed architecture aims at utilizing the high bandwidth communication systems, based on the network-as-a-service paradigm, and combine them with the local network resources to achieve better communication performance.

In relation to the use-cases, we envision the proposed system, depicted in Fig. 1, as a full environment capable of providing a universal backbone for super-service network provisioning. Essentially, the environment allows for the network service providers, together with local system administrators, to register the offered services, including the functional parameters, to a specific database. After the proper description of the available services, they are clustered in multiple classes based on the functional parameters, such as latency and bandwidth. The given set of services is then provided to the multi-objective service composition module, which explores for an optimized combination of services and resources that meet the performance requirements. Subsequently, this mapping, or more concretely combination of services is provisioned to the application that required it.

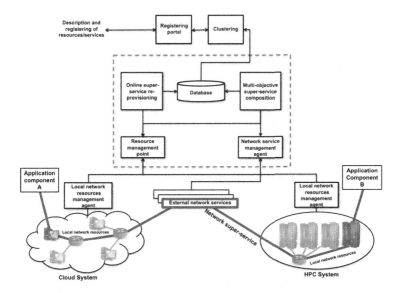

Fig. 1. Top level view of the multi-objective super-service provisioning architecture

Furthermore, based on the previous usage data, a separate re-provisioning module continuously gazes for degraded communication performance. Based on the provided data, this module utilizes the same multi-objective core algorithm to re-provision the given super-service if some faults are imminent or there are many QoS violations.

4.1 Multi-objective Super-Service Provisioning

The system design of the proposed super-service provisioning environment is modular in nature, encapsulating variety of different components which interact by exchanging structured information on the available network services and resources. Each component in the system provides specific functions, which are essential for the normal functioning of the provided network resources. The core of the proposed environment is based upon multi-objective optimization module, capable of composing various network resources and service into a compound network super-service.

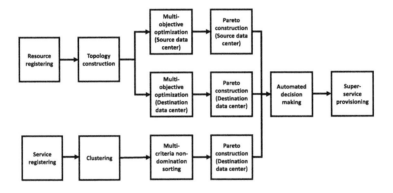

Fig. 2. Multi-objective super-service provisioning model

The process of network service and resource composition, depicted on Fig. 2, is divided into two distinctive stages: resource provisioning (see Sect. 4.2) and service provisioning (see Sect. 4.3). The two stages are conducted in parallel and separate Pareto fronts are constructed for the network services and source/destination network resources. The automated decision making considers the independent Pareto fronts, together with the user's a-priory preferences, to complete the process of super-service provisioning.

4.2 Network Resource Provisioning

During this process the registered network resources are fetched from the database and a set of starting "candidate" routes is constructed, both for the source and destination data-centers or clusters. This information is then used as an input for two separate multi-objective optimization processes based on the NSGA-II algorithm [15]. The NSGA-II is an evolutionary optimization algorithm, therefore it requires proper representation of the routes that will be optimized as individuals in the algorithm's population. For our purposes we represent the routes as a directed vectors containing all channels, switches and router through which the data will be send within the source or destination system.

Each of these processes is focused on finding a set of optimal "trade-off" routes in relation to the communication bandwidth and latency within the local source and destination systems respectively. The optimization processes result in two separate Pareto fronts, which are later used during the decision making (see Sect. 4.4). Every solution in the Pareto represents a possible internal route through which a virtual channel can be established within the source and destination large scale computational centers.

4.3   Network Service Clustering and Provisioning

In parallel to the previous described stage, the registered network services are clustered each time a new service has been added to the database by utilizing k-means clustering technique [16]. This technique has been selected primary because it requires low computational resources for small number of clusters. In our case, we create three different clusters of services in relation with the following objectives: communication latency and network bandwidth. This allows us to initially prioritize the services in relation to the given objectives, thus reducing the execution time of the computational costly non-domination sorting algorithms.

In relation to the clustering objectives, we divide the registered network service in the following categories:

- **High-bandwidth/low-latency:** this cluster encompasses the services which provide the best communication latency and bandwidth rates. Usually these network services induce higher financial costs.
- **Medium-to-low-bandwidth/low-latency:** this cluster provides low latency, similar to the previous one, however with reduced bandwidth. The network services belonging to this cluster are usually more cost effective, compared to the first cluster.
- **Low-bandwidth/low-latency:** the last cluster encompasses the network services that are not capable of providing sufficiently high bandwidth or low latency. The services belonging to this cluster are discarded and not used during the following process of non-domination sorting.

Afterwards, the feasible clusters are sorted based on non-domination multiple-criteria sorting algorithm, resulting in a separate Pareto fronts for each of the clusters. In the case of the non-domination sorting we consider three objectives: communication latency, network bandwidth and financial costs. To be more concrete, the utilization of the clustering techniques allows for the services to be classified in a coarse-grained manner, while the non-domination sorting enables fine-grained selection of the most optimal network services.

The process of service clustering and sorting is only conducted when new service has been added or the functional parameters of some service have been changed. The constructed Pareto front during this process is later utilized for the automated decision making (see Sect. 4.4).

4.4   Automated Decision Making

The basic prerequisite of the multi-objective super-service provisioning is the implementation of Automated Decision Making (ADM). Due to the basic requirements for low provisioning latency it is essential to enable efficient decision making techniques. To this end, we have implemented a simple and computationally efficient a-priori ADM procedure, which takes into consideration the user's preferences. During the process of automated decision making, the Pareto fronts from the source and destination routes and networks services are considered independently. Consequently, from the three Pareto fronts separate solutions are selected and are then joined together to provide the final solution on how to provision the super-service. The proposed ADM process assumes that all solutions in the Pareto front belong to the same cluster. Based on this assumption, we find the centroid of the Pareto front. Afterwards, we map the centroid to the objectives' axis. This allow us to divide the objective space and the Pareto solutions into distinctive regions. More concretely if a solution is located within the parallels of the centroid it is considered that it belongs in the "balanced" region. The solutions which are within the centroid's parallel in one objective dimension, but not in the other are consider to belong to the "objective's priority" region. For illustration, Fig. 3 shows the division of the solutions in two-dimensional space in relation to the centroid of the Pareto front.

In order to perform the final decision, the ADM relies on the user's preferences, i.e. which objective function should be given priority. In the case of our implementations, this could be communication latency, network bandwidth or service cost. If the user gives a strong priority towards a single objective,

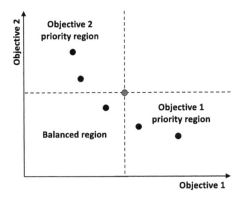

Fig. 3. Automated decision making

then only the solutions in the given "objective's priority" region are considered. Afterwards, within this region we measure the distance of every solution to the centroid. Based on the distance, in the preferred objective dimension, we sort and weight the solutions and select the one closest to the objective weight preferred by the user.

5   Experimental Evaluation

The experimental evaluation of the proposed concept of super-service provisioning was conducted based on a monitoring data-sets provided by RIPE NCC [17] and CEDEXIS [18]. The data-sets include comprehensive information on the response time, communication bandwidth and communication latency of multiple Cloud service providers from around the world. With respect to the implementation of the super-service provisioning algorithm, we have utilized the jMetal framework [13] for the purposes of multi-objective optimization and the Waikato environment for knowledge analysis [14] for the clustering.

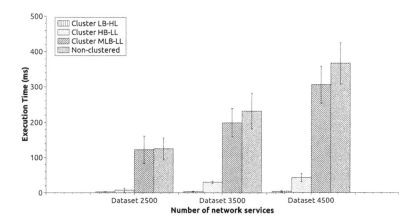

Fig. 4. Scalability of the clustered non-domination service sorting

As previously described, the process of super-service selection is conducted in two independent stages, therefore requiring distinctive set of evaluation experiments. The service non-domination sorting and Pareto construction has been evaluated on the basis of the degree of scalability for various cluster-sizes, while the behavior of the source and destination route multi-objective provisioning algorithm has been examined from multiple aspects, including solutions quality, scalability and computational performance.

To begin with, we evaluated the scalability and computational performance of the non-domination service sorting and selection algorithm by considering three distinctive data-sets with varying sizes from 2500 to 4500 network services. The data-sets were clustered in three categories: high-bandwidth/low-latency with relative size of 12%, medium-to-low-bandwidth/low-latency with relative size of 85% and low-bandwidth/high-latency with relative size of 3%. The clustering time for all data-sets was below 2 ms and was included in the total service sorting time. Figure 4 shows the correlation between the average sorting time for the full sets of non-clustered and clustered network services. It is evident that the clustering reduces the execution time of the multi-objective non-domination sorting, compared to the non-clustered datasets, from 20% to more than 1100% in the cases when small clusters have been created.

The process of source and destination network resource provisioning has higher computational complexity, compared to the service non-domination sorting, therefore requiring more comprehensive experimental evaluation. Figure 5 shows the correlation between the execution time of the multi-objective optimization algorithm and the length of the network route, for two different population sizes and evaluation limits. It can be easily observed that the optimization algorithm scales very good for different route lengths, with latencies ranging from 70 to 100 ms for routes with 30 hops. Furthermore, Fig. 6 provides detailed information on the quality of the provided routes for different optimization parameters. The Hypervolume indicator was used to represent the quality of the Pareto set of solutions provided by the multi-objective algorithm. The presented results show that the quality of the Pareto routes decreases by up to 10% with the increase of the number of hops, which can be considered as satisfactory.

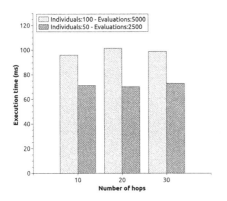
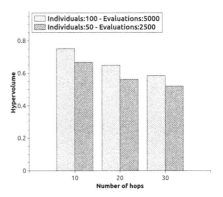

Fig. 5. Scalability of the resource provisioning multi-objective algorithm

Fig. 6. Solutions quality of the resource provisioning multi-objective algorithm

In order to prevent the decrease of the quality of the Pareto front, in the cases when the number of hops in the route is higher, the number of individuals or evaluations for the multi-objective algorithm can be increased. Unfortunately, this can increase the execution time exponentially, which is not adequate for low-latency processes. Figure 7 shows the relation between the number of individuals/evaluations and the execution time for a fixed route of 30 hops. Furthermore, Fig. 8 provides comparison between the number of individuals/evaluations and

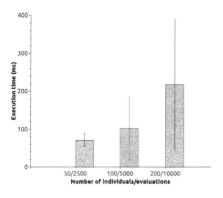

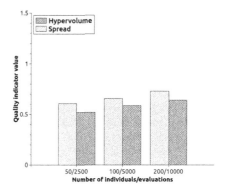

Fig. 7. Correlation between the execution time and the number of individuals/evaluations for fixed route size

Fig. 8. Correlation between the solutions quality and the number of individuals/evaluations for fixed route size

the quality of solutions. The quality of the solutions in this case was evaluated based on two indicators: hypervolume and spread. Overall, it can be determined, that in the cases when higher quality routes are required, higher number of individuals can be used with a penalty on the execution time.

6   Conclusion

This paper introduces a promising new paradigm of super-service provisioning for ultra-scale computing environments by unifying the management of the local communication resources and the external inter-domain network services under a single point of view. The research work has resulted in a development of an efficient technique for network services clustering and non-domination sorting, multi-objective network resource provisioning and a-priory automated decision making.

The presented paradigm has been evaluated based on a real-life monitoring data-sets. As our research deals with the utilization of clustering algorithms for reducing the complexity of multi-objective optimization problems, we present an experimental results that demonstrate the ability of our approach to provide an adequate super-service provisioning in inter-domain systems. The initial results confirm the scalability of the implemented algorithms and highlight the benefits arising from utilizing clustering for multi-objective non-domination sorting and optimization.

Acknowledgments. This work is being accomplished as a part of project *ENTICE: "dEcentralised repositories for traNsparent and efficienT vIrtual maChine opErations"*, funded by the European Union's Horizon 2020 research and innovation programme under grant agreement No. 644179.

References

1. Mihajlovic, M., Bongo, L., Ciegis, R., Frasheri, N., Kimovski, D., Kropf, P., Margenov, S., Neytcheva, M., Rauber, T., Runger, G., Trobec, R., Wuyts, R., Wyrzykowski, R., Gong, J.: Applications for ultra-scale computing. Supercomput. Front. Innov. **2**(1), 19–48 (2015)
2. Celesti, A., Tusa, F., Villari, M., Puliafito, A.: How to enhance cloud architectures to enable cross-federation. In: IEEE CLOUD (2010)
3. Vincenzo, M., Rizzo, L., Lettieri, G.: Flexible virtual machine networking using netmap passthrough. In: IEEE Symposium on Local and Metropolitan Area Networks (2016)
4. Moreno-Vozmediano, R., et al.: BEACON: a cloud network federation framework. In: Celesti, A., Leitner, P. (eds.) ESOCC 2015. CCIS, vol. 567, pp. 325–337. Springer, Cham (2016). https://doi.org/10.1007/978-3-319-33313-7_25
5. Xu, R., Wunsch, D.: Survey of clustering algorithms. IEEE Trans. Neural Netw. **16**(3), 645–678 (2005)
6. Araujo, W., Granville, L.Z., Schneider, F., Dudkowski, D., Brunner, M.: Rethinking cloud platforms: network-aware flexible resource allocation in IaaS clouds. In: IFIP/IEEE Symposium on Integrated Network Management (2013)
7. Bo, P., Hammad, A., Nejabati, R., Azodolmolky, S., Simeonidou, D., Reijs, V.: A network virtualization framework for IP infrastructure provisioning. In: IEEE Conference on Cloud Computing Technology and Science (2011)
8. Jon, M., Jacob, E., Sanchez, D., Demchenko, Y.: An OpenFlow based network virtualization framework for the cloud. In: IEEE Conference on Cloud Computing Technology and Science (2011)
9. Meng, S., Xu, K., Li, F., Yang, K., Zhu, L., Guan, L.: Elastic and efficient virtual network provisioning for cloud-based multi-tier applications. In: Conference in Parallel Processing - ICPP (2015)
10. Ines, H., Louati, W., Zeghlache, D., Papadimitriou, P., Mathy, L.: Adaptive virtual network provisioning. In: ACM SIGCOMM Workshop on Virtualized Infrastructure Systems and Architectures (2010)
11. Jeffrey, M., Popa, L.: What we talk about when we talk about cloud network performance. ACM SIGCOMM Comput. Commun. Rev. **42**(5), 44–48 (2012)
12. Branke, J., et al. (eds.): Multiobjective Optimization: Interactive and Evolutionary Approaches, vol. 5252. Springer, Heidelberg (2008). https://doi.org/10.1007/978-3-540-88908-3
13. Durillo, J.J., Nebro, A.J.: jMetal: a Java framework for multi-objective optimization. Adv. Eng. Softw. **42**(10), 760–771 (2011)
14. Garner, S.R.: Weka: the waikato environment for knowledge analysis. In: New Zealand Computer Science Research Students Conference (1995)
15. Deb, K., Pratap, A., Agarwal, S., Meyarivan, T.A.M.T.: A fast and elitist multi-objective genetic algorithm: NSGA-II. IEEE Trans. Evol. Comput. **6**(2), 182–197 (2002)
16. Kanungo, T., Mount, D.M., Netanyahu, N.S., Piatko, C.D., Silverman, R., Wu, A.Y.: An efficient k-means clustering algorithm: analysis and implementation. IEEE Trans. Pattern Anal. Mach. Intell. **24**(7), 881–892 (2002)
17. RIPE Network Coordination Centre. https://atlas.ripe.net/
18. CEDEXIS. https://www.cedexis.com/

Resilience – Workshop on Resiliency in High Performance Computing with Clouds, Grids, and Clusters

Resilience 2017: Tenth Workshop on Resiliency in High Performance Computing in Clouds, Grids, and Clusters

Workshop Description

Clouds, Grids, and Clusters are three different computational paradigms with the potential to support High Performance Computing (HPC) and enterprise IT infrastructure. Currently, they consist of hardware, management, and usage models particular to different computational regimes (e.g., high performance cluster systems designed to support tightly coupled scientific simulation codes typically utilize high-speed interconnects and commercial cloud systems designed to support software as a service (SAS) typically do not). However, in order to support HPC, all must at least utilize large numbers of resources and hence effective HPC in any of these paradigms must address the same issue of resiliency at a very large-scale.

Recent trends in HPC systems have clearly indicated that future increases in performance, in excess of those resulting from improvements in single-processor performance, will be achieved through corresponding increases in system scale, i.e., using a significantly larger component count. As the raw computational performance of the world's fastest HPC systems increases from today's current multi-petascale to next-generation exascale capability and beyond, their number of computational, networking, and storage components will grow from the ten-to-one-hundred thousand compute nodes of today's systems to several hundreds of thousands of compute nodes in the foreseeable future. This substantial growth in system scale, and the resulting component count, poses a challenge for HPC system and application software with respect to reliability, availability and serviceability (RAS).

Resilience is a critical challenge as HPC systems continue to increase component counts, individual component reliability decreases, and software complexity increases. Application correctness and execution efficiency, in spite of frequent faults, errors, and failures, is essential to ensure the success of the extreme-scale HPC systems, cluster computing environments, Grid computing infrastructures, and Cloud computing services.

Resilience for HPC systems encompasses a wide spectrum of fundamental and applied research and development, including theoretical foundations, fault detection and prediction, monitoring and control, end-to-end data integrity, enabling infrastructure, and resilient solvers and algorithm-based fault tolerance. This workshop brings together experts in the community to further research and development in HPC resilience and to facilitate exchanges across the computational paradigms of extreme-scale HPC, cluster computing, Grid computing, and Cloud computing.

The goal of this workshop is to bring together experts in the area of fault tolerance and resilience for HPC to present the latest achievements and to discuss the challenges ahead. The Resilience 2017 workshop program included presentations of four high-quality peer-reviewed papers as well as an opportunity for discussions among the participants from research, academia, and industry.

Workshop Chairs

Stephen L. Scott   Tennessee Tech University and Oak Ridge National
                                Laboratory, USA
Chokchai (Box) Leangsuksun   Louisiana Tech University, USA

Workshop Program Chairs

Patrick G. Bridges   University of New Mexico, USA
Christian Engelmann   Oak Ridge National Laboratory, USA

Program Committee (PC)

Ferrol Aderholdt   Oak Ridge National Laboratory, USA
Dorian Arnold   University of New Mexico, USA
Rizwan Ashraf   Oak Ridge National Laboratory, USA
Wesley Bland   Intel Corporation, USA
Hans-Joachim Bungartz   Technical University of Munich, Germany
Franck Cappello   Argonne National Laboratory and University
                                of Illinois at Urbana-Champaign, USA
Marc Casas   Barcelona Supercomputer Center, Spain
Zizhong Chen   University of California at Riverside, USA
Robert Clay   Sandia National Laboratories, USA
Miguel Correia   Universidade de Lisboa, Portugal
Nathan DeBardeleben   Los Alamos National Laboratory, USA
James Elliott   Sandia National Laboratories, USA
Kurt Ferreira   Sandia National Laboratories, USA
Michael Heroux   Sandia National Laboratories, USA
Saurabh Hukerikar   Oak Ridge National Laboratory, USA
Dieter Kranzlmueller   Ludwig-Maximilians University of Munich, Germany
Sriram Krishnamoorthy   Pacific Northwest National Laboratory, USA
Ignacio Laguna   Lawrence Livermore National Laboratory, USA
Scott Levy   University of New Mexico, USA
Kathryn Mohror   Lawrence Livermore National Laboratory, USA
Christine Morin   INRIA Rennes, France
Dirk Pflueger   University of Stuttgart, Germany
Nageswara Rao   Oak Ridge National Laboratory, USA
Alexander Reinefeld   Zuse Institute Berlin, Germany

Understanding and Improving the Trust in Results of Numerical Simulations and Scientific Data Analytics

Franck Cappello$^{(\boxtimes)}$, Rinku Gupta, Sheng Di, Emil Constantinescu,
Thomas Peterka, and Stefan M. Wild

Mathematics and Computer Science Division, Argonne National Laboratory,
9700 South Cass Avenue, Argonne, IL 60439, USA
{cappello,rgupta,sdi1,emconsta,tpeterka,wild}@mcs.anl.gov

Abstract. With ever-increasing execution scale of parallel scientific simulations, potential unnoticed corruptions to scientific data during simulation make users more suspicious about the correctness of floating-point calculations than ever before. In this paper, we analyze the issue of the trust in results of numerical simulations and scientific data analytics. We first classify the corruptions into two categories, nonsystematic corruption and systematic corruption, and also discuss their origins. Then, we provide a formal definition of the trust in simulation and analytical results across multiple areas. We also discuss what kind of result accuracy would be expected from user's perspective and how to build trust by existing techniques. We finally identify the current gap and discuss two potential research directions based on existing techniques. We believe that this paper will be interesting to the researchers who are working on the detection of potential unnoticed corruptions of scientific simulation and data analytics, in that not only does it provide a clear definition and classification of corruption as well as an in-depth survey on corruption sources, but we also discuss potential research directions/topics based on existing detection techniques.

Keywords: Trust · Numerical simulation · Data analytics

1   Introduction

Today and future scientific simulations or data analytics are facing a huge risk with potential unnoticed corruptions because of ever-increasing execution scale and more and more complicated system architecture. Multiple examples of hardware bugs in floating-point units and software bugs in application stack make users more suspicious about the correctness of floating-point calculations. In 2004 the AMD Opteron had an instruction bug that could result in succeeding instructions being skipped or an incorrect address size or data size being used [4]. Other bugs were reported in the Opteron processor in 2012 and 2014 [3].

© Springer International Publishing AG, part of Springer Nature 2018
D. B. Heras and L. Bougé (Eds.): Euro-Par 2017 Workshops, LNCS 10659, pp. 545–556, 2018.
https://doi.org/10.1007/978-3-319-75178-8_44

In this paper, we investigate several key aspects of the trust that a user can give to the results of numerical simulations and scientific data analytics. The notion of trust is related to the integrity of numerical simulations and data analytics applications and not on whether the application actually completes.

To simplify the presentation without loss of generality, we consider that trust in results can be lost (or the results' integrity impaired) because of any form of corruption happening during the execution of the numerical simulation or the data analytics application. In general, the sources of such corruption are threefold: errors, bugs, and attacks. Current applications are already using techniques to deal with different types of corruption, but these techniques are not all-encompassing. The current level of trust that a user has in the results is at least partially founded on ignorance of this issue or the hope that no undetected corruptions will occur during the execution.

So far, there have been a lot of research studying the trust/reliability issue, such as detection of silent data corruptions (SDC) in numerical simulations (to be detailed in Sect. 6). However, there are no specific surveys to categorize, formalize the research from the perspective of technical background and summarize the corresponding solutions comprehensively. The work in this paper aims to fill this gap.

In this paper, we look at (1) exploring the sources of trust loss; (2) reviewing the definitions of trust in several areas; (3) providing numerous cases of result alteration, some of them leading to catastrophic failures; (4) examining the current notion of trust in numerical simulation and scientific data analytics; (5) providing a gap analysis; and (6) suggesting two important research directions and their respective research topics. We also, specifically, suggest recommendations for developing a more scientifically grounded notion of trust in aforementioned applications. We first formulate the problem and show that it goes beyond previous questions regarding the quality of results such as Verification and Validation (V&V), uncertainty quantification, and data assimilation. We then explore the complexity of this difficult problem, and we sketch complementary general approaches to address it.

The product of simulation or of data analytic executions is the final element of a potentially long chain of transformations, where each stage has the potential to introduce harmful corruptions. These corruptions may produce simulation results that deviate from the user-expected accuracy without notifying the user of this deviation. There are many potential sources of corruption before and during the execution; consequently, in this paper we do not focus on the protection of the end result after the execution (latter is covered in the paper [10], through the notion of provenance and trustable communications and storage).

2   Corruption Classification and Origins

In this section, we focus on corruptions that stay unnoticed. The corruptions for which significant research efforts are needed in the context of trust are those that corrupt the results in a harmful way but are not detected by hardware, software, or the users. We consider two main classes of corruptions: nonsystematic and systematic.

Nonsystematic corruptions are those affecting an execution in a unique way; that is, the probability of repetition of the exact same corruption in another execution is very low. A harmful corruption is manifested as an alteration of one of more data elements. Origins of such corruptions may be radiations (cosmic ray, alpha particles from package decay), bugs in some paths of nondeterministic executions, attacks targeting executions individually, and other potential sources.

Systematic corruptions (including conception/model errors and epistemic uncertainties) affect multiple executions of the same code, with the same input parameters, in the same way. The harmful corruption also is manifested as an alteration of one of more data elements. Executions do not need to be identical to produce the same corruptions because of possible uncertainty of the input/execution data or so. Origins of these corruptions are twofold: (1) bugs or defects (hardware or software) that are exercised the same way by executions (different executions will execute a same code region or the same instruction that will cause the same corruption) and (2) attacks that will consistently affect executions the same way.

A question that usually arises is that is **the trust in numerical results a real problem?** We argue that trust is a serious and insufficiently recognized problem. For a list of software bugs that impacted users in domains such as space exploration and telecommunications, see [1].

Two serious issues could be raised because of such unnoticed corruptions.

1. A large number of executions may have been corrupted before the discovery; bad decisions may have been taken [2]; and it might be difficult after-the-fact to check whether executions have actually been corrupted or not, without heavy checking (e.g., re-executing the simulations entirely)
2. Even if silent corruptions do not lead to accidents, they may lead to significant productivity losses.

3   Definition of Trust in Multiple Areas (Computer Science, Sociology, Economy)

All types of corruptions mentioned in this paper are considered as part of the general dependability problem as formulated in the paper [12]: "the ability to deliver service that can justifiably be trusted". Table 1 shows the relation between dependability, survivability, and trustworthiness, as mentioned in the paper [12]: the three concepts essentially cover equivalent goals and threats.

A survey of definitions related to dependability and trustworthiness is presented in the paper [13]. In that survey, trust depends on many elements: safety, correctness, reliability, availability, confidentiality/privacy, performance, certification, and security.

Multiple definitions of trust [6] are relative to other contexts: social sciences, psychology, philosophy, and economics. The definitions that may help address

Table 1. Relation between dependability, survivability, and trustworthiness

Concept	Dependability	Survivability	Trustworthiness
Goal	(1) ability to deliver service that can justifiably be trusted; (2) ability of a system to avoid failures that are more frequent or more severe than is acceptable to the user(s)	capability of a system to fulfill its mission in a timely manner	assurance that a system will perform as expected
Threats present	(1) development faults (e.g., software flaws, hardware errata, malicious logic); (2) physical faults (e.g., production defects, physical deterioration); (3) interaction faults (e.g., physical interference, input mistakes, attacks, including viruses, worms, and intrusions)	(1) attacks (e.g., intrusions, probes, denials of service); (2) failures (internally generated events due to, e.g., software design errors, hardware degradation, human errors, corrupted data); (3) accidents (externally generated events such as natural disasters)	(1) hostile attacks (from hackers and insiders); (2) environmental disruptions (accidental disruptions, either manmade or natural); (3) human and operator errors (e.g., software flaws, mistakes by human operators)
Reference	this paper	"Survivable network systems" (Ellison el al. 1999)	"Trust in cyberspace" (Schneider 1999)

the trust problem in our context are the following: "One party (trustor) is willing to rely on the actions of another party (trustee)" and "The trustor is uncertain about the outcome of the other's actions; they can only develop and evaluate expectations".

Although there exist several metrics for trust [7] and approaches to building trust, there is no consensus on or norm for which metrics should be used in which case. In numerical simulation and scientific data analytics, there is a lack of trust metrics that could be used to quantitatively compute and express the trustworthiness of the execution results.

4   Building Trust in Application Results

The trust in the results of numerical simulation and data analytics execution is related to two main notions: correctness of computation and integrity of the execution stack. However, neither of them could be proven formally for nontrivial execution scenarios. To address this issue, users have to develop a process to build trust in their execution results.

The simple pattern of building trust generally involves the following process. The users first start with the smallest-scale, simplest problem that can be reasonably modeled, and compare the output with expectations. The simulation is then repeatedly scaled up in complexity and size (both simulation size and system size), while repeating the comparisons of output with expectations. Any odd or unexpected behavior is scrutinized and assumed to be an error until demonstrated otherwise.

4.1   Expected Result Accuracy

Expected result accuracy is application dependent. Some applications are sensitive to the details of calculation; for example, they can even act as tests of the randomness of the pseudo-random number generator used. Other applications model systems following a trajectory to an attractor state and small perturbations to that trajectory have no impact on the final outcome. During the execution, accuracy is affected by round-off errors; such errors accumulate, and the expected accuracy at the end of the execution is much lower than the machine precision. Typical expected accuracies at the end of the execution are 10^{-6} for the HACC cosmology code executions and 10^{-8} for Nek5000 computational fluid dynamics executions.

At its most fundamental, expected result accuracy can be defined as follows: If the corruption of the data does not result in any measurable changes to any physically meaningful statistics of the simulation between a run that contained the corruption and a run that does not, then the user's expectation of accuracy has been satisfied. This definition suggests that research should focus on detecting corruptions that make the end results diverge from the expected user accuracy, as did by the adaptive impact-driven SDC detector [18].

4.2   How Existing Techniques Help Building Trust

Verification and validation form the basis for building trust in codes and the models underlying them. We follow the convention of [16], whereby validation determines the faithfulness of the mathematical/computational models to the real world and verification determines the faithfulness of the code to the mathematical/numerical models. While solution verification techniques quantify the accuracy at which algorithms solve the model, code verification techniques certify that a code is a truthful implementation of the algorithms themselves. Following best practices (e.g., unit and regression testing) and standards for software design is a common, although incomplete, attempt toward verification.

Another common software development technique for building trust is to incorporate physical, mathematical, and numerical knowledge alongside a computation in order to flag potential errors. Examples in the course of a computation can include ensuring that mass or other quantities are conserved, that two linear basis vectors remain orthogonal, and that an accumulated remainder term lies below a round-off bound.

Uncertainty quantification is an umbrella term for several activities involved in improving the trust in the simulations and data in the hope of accounting for all sources of uncertainty involved in the simulation of real-world/physical quantities. Several techniques are used to improve the trust in the numerical model, data, and simulation productivity under random effects. For example, gridded or complete data sets are constructed from sparse data by solving inverse problems. Simulations are corrected (or guided) by using data through a process referred to as data assimilation. Complex mathematical models and models that are used to represent real processes that are not well understood typically use parameterizations. Parameterizations are surrogate models that depend on a set of parameters that do not necessarily have a physical meaning. These parameters are usually calibrated by solving a parameter estimation problem. Although UQ techniques are often segregated along domain science and scientific community lines, they support a common mathematical formulation and are often used in tandem or in a manner that is not always transparent.

5   Gap Analysis

Many techniques are already applied from the hardware to the application in order to detect corruptions. These techniques do not cover all potential sources of corruptions, however, and large gaps put execution results at risk.

Harmful nonsystematic corruptions (undetected corruptions that corrupt execution results in a non-noticeable way) can be detected by classic approaches such as replication or algorithm-based fault tolerance (ABFT). Replication is too expensive in our domain to be applied on all executions, however, and ABFT covers only the data protected by the ABFT scheme: other application data are not protected. Ensemble computations also offer a way to deal with nonsystematic corruptions, since statistical analysis of the ensemble results may detect or absorb the corruptions.

Harmful systematic corruptions are not detected by replication because replication detects errors by comparing identical (or comparable) executions. Since the systematic corruptions will affect replicated executions the same way, the comparison of executions will not detect any corruption. Ensemble computations will suffer the same limitation and will not be able to detect or absorb such corruptions.

One approach to detect systematic corruptions, called n-version programming [11], was proposed three decades ago. In this approach, which has some similarity with the notion of alternates in recovery blocks [21], the results of the executions of multiple different versions responding to the same specification are compared in order to detect potential corruptions. The higher the diversity of the versions (from hardware to application), the higher is the chance of detecting corruptions. This approach does not seem applicable in our domain, however, because of the cost of developing multiple versions of all levels of the stacks, from the hardware to the application. Moreover, it has been demonstrated experimentally that different versions may suffer the same bugs (and lead to the same corruptions) [19].

Formal validation and verification often presuppose the availability of a correct reference solution that can be used to assess model accuracy and code correctness. Although codes can be designed to capture these subsystems as special cases, the potential for increased trust is rarely deemed to outweigh the resulting efficiency loss; and this gap widens at scale. As highlighted in the paper [16], problem classes for which formal V&V methods exist (e.g., quantifying the numerical error in the solution of linear elliptic PDEs) seldom overlap with the complex simulations performed for DOE.

Uncertainty quantification considers that the hardware and the software stack produce correct results. Uncertainty quantification is almost entirely focused on addressing randomness introduced through the mathematical model. In general, all algorithms assume that the hardware/software stack produces asymptotically correct, if not exact, results. In the presence of numerical errors or spurious software, outcomes can lead to biases in UQ that render the analysis useless or can have a significant detrimental effect on trust.

6   Analysis of Research Directions and Solution

Since the trust problem spans all layers of the stack, from the hardware to the application, and is related to many aspects of numerical simulation and data analytics (modeling, initial conditions, numerical accuracy, parametric settings, etc.), we believe that holistic approaches, considering all potential sources of corruptions, have a better chance of succeeding. Figure 1 presents complementary research directions.

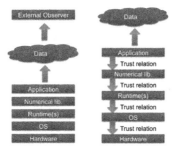

Fig. 1. Complementary research directions to address the trust problem

The first direction performs on-line verification by using an external algorithmic observer that does not trust the execution stack. During the execution, the transformations applied by the hardware and software stack to the data are verified against trusted models run by the observer. This direction is close to n-version programming but uses verification algorithms much simpler than the execution stack (the external algorithmic observer method assumes that the observer is simpler to code than the full execution stack, hence can be more easily

Table 2. Advantages and drawbacks of two research directions

	External observer	Trust relations
Detection approach	Simulation and observer are checking each other	Checking object results
Detection assumptions	External observer is correct (should be verified, validated)	All verifications and reputation calc. are correct
Detection latency	Short (depends on sampling rate, typically 1 appl. iteration)	Long (actual detection could be long: months)
Timeliness of notification after detection	Short (one iteration to next)	Short (immediate upper layer)
Time to build trust	Low (trust depends on verisimilitude of results not on components)	High (h/w and s/w components need to acquire trust level)
Targeted level of trust	User-expected accuracy	Machine precision (modulo round-off errors)
Dev. time and cost	Low (requires only to develop the observer)	High (affects all layers of the stack)
Tolerance	High (corruptions of the appl. data lower than user-expected accuracy are tolerated)	Low (any corruption at object level is suspicious since the consequence on appl. data is unknown)

verified). The second direction establishes trust relations between levels of the execution stack. Establishing these trust relations may involve thorough verification of each level, reputation mechanisms, and layer-level on-line verification. Table 2 shows the advantages and drawbacks of the two directions.

6.1 External Algorithmic Observer

The external observer approach is similar to the simplex architecture technique for critical systems [22]. It is also similar in principle to a direction developed for cyber security at the UIUC/Information Trust Institute where the predictable/expected behavior of a system is defined and used for detecting anomalies [9]. The main idea is that the external observer checks that the observed execution respects constraints set by the developer of the application/user.

In our context, the external algorithmic observer executes a model of the data transformation performed by the application. There are several related techniques proposed recently. Di et al. [17] proposed a silent data corruption detection method with error-feedback control and even-sampling for HPC applications. It is designed particularly for iterative scientific simulations with multiple time steps/snapshots generated. The detection performs the data prediction mainly along the time series dimension for each data point in each snapshot. Based on that work, they further proposed an improved solution [18] by taking into account only significant corruptions regarding their impact on the final execution results. They also proposed an adaptive solution allowing each process/rank to select the best-fit prediction method based on its dynamic local dataset, significantly improving the detection ability and lowering the memory cost meanwhile. In absolute terms, Experiments with about 20 benchmarks indicate that it can detect 80–99.99% of influential SDCs with the false positive rate reduced to 0–1% in most cases. In addition, Berrocal et al. [15] explored partial replication to improve lightweight silent data corruption detection for HPC Applications.

Alternatively, the detection model could be derived from observed properties of the data transformation [17], learned using some machine leaning algorithms, or could implement a simpler version of the model used in the application [14, 24]. The critical point is that the application and the external model should be diverse enough that they would not be affected by systematic corruptions in the same way. In principle this approach allows a very large spectrum of model complexities (compute and memory complexities) that could go up to the complexity of the application plus the stack running the application. Since we cannot afford such complexity in our domain, however, the research should focus on models of a much lower complexity.

Low-complexity models implement trade-offs between complexity, accuracy, and other properties. For example, the model proposed by Benson et al. [14] relaxes numerical stability assuming that (1) the model can be restarted at each step from the verified results of application at the previous step and (2) corruptions happening in one step are detected in the same step. In Di et al.'s work [17], the model computes only local predictions for the next simulation step, from the application results at the current step (one step prediction), leveraging the spatiotemporal continuity present in many applications simulating physics phenomena. This model does not compute solutions of the equations governing the simulation; rather, it verifies that the simulation respects a particular physics property between steps.

Because the model is purposely simpler than the simulation, the data produced by the model diverges slightly from the one of the application. Therefore, the detection cannot be based on perfect comparison. A tolerance margin should be considered that controls the detection accuracy that conditions the number of false positives (detection of a corruptions that did not happen) and false negatives (nondetection of corruptions that actually happened). Other metrics include overhead in execution time and overhead in memory occupation (the model needs memory space for its execution). The tolerance margin should avoid false detection due to the natural divergence between the model and the application. It also should be lower than the user-expected accuracy in order to ensure that corruptions exceeding the user-expected accuracy will be detected.

An important advantage of this approach is that by being much simpler than the simulation stack, the software implementing the model is also easier to verify and to protect. For example, the multiversion programming approach is not applicable to the simulation stack but it is applicable to the software implementing the model. Several implementations of the same model or several different models could be executed and compared. Because the software implementing the model has a low compute complexity, in principle, it could be executed on a more secure environment, such as a secure processor. This allows increasing the trust in the model itself.

6.2 Trust Relations

The direction based on trust relations is more mature in the sense that a large body of research has been devoted to this topic in computer science. The DOE report on Cybersecurity for Scientific Computing Integrity [10] provides considerable coverage of the issues and approaches related to this direction. This section complements the report by providing additional analysis and references.

To simplify the presentation, we call an "object" any piece (or layer) of software of hardware that needs to be trusted. The trust relation direction supposes at least (1) a way to certify that each used object is actually the object it is supposed to be, (2) a method to evaluate a level of trust for each object involved in the execution, (3) a metric of the level of trust, and (4) a way to protect the trust level acquired by an object.

Considering points (1) and (4), the Trust Computing Group [5] has produced the Trusted Platform Module (TPM) specification [8], which is an ISO/IEC international standard. This specification details embedded crypto capability that supports user, application, and machine authentication. More than 500 million PCs have shipped with TPM. One application of TPM is the verification of the integrity of the platform to ensure no unauthorized changes have occurred in the BIOS, disk master boot record, boot sector, operating system, and application software. We believe that points (1) and (4) can leverage this well-established technology to reduce the risk of attack-induced corruptions. However, TPM does not protect against sophisticated attacks, and some TPM circuits showed vulnerability [23,26].

Regarding point (2), the evaluation of the trust level of an object could rely on extensive verification and validation of that object by a combination of formal verification when applicable and empirical methods (checking against known results, checking results against actual measurements). In principle the external observer approach can be applied for each object. However, modeling the data transformation of some functions in order to perform effective and efficient detection may require a model complexity close to that of the function.

Regarding point (3), the trust metrics could have multiple dimensions (such as time since first trusted, time since last verification, number of independent verifications, or number of validations). The trust metrics would help compute a trust level for the whole execution (a function of the trust of each object involved in the execution). Thus, a user could explore different combinations of objects for a given overall trust level. Conversely, the user could explore different combinations of objects and their impact on the overall trust score. Researchers in security and networking domains [20,25] have already investigated this problem: they represent objects in a graph where edges are trust relations and the trust evaluation is modeled as a path problem on a directed graph.

All these precautions will not avoid corruptions from a highly trusted object, however, because verification and validation cannot test exhaustively the behavior of all objects. This fact motivates research in the context of trust relations beyond reputation or research, in order to develop new reputation techniques.

7 Conclusion

In this paper, we analyze the research issue of the trust in numerical simulation results and scientific data analytics and identify possible research directions based on existing state-of-the-art solutions. A classic assumption that users make when running numerical simulations and data analytics is that floating-point computations are correct. Unfortunately, multiple examples of hardware bugs in floating-point units and software bugs in application stack make users more suspicious about the correctness of floating-point calculations. A significant issue for hardware bugs is that the time until the detection and the time between the detection of the issue and the repair could be very long. At the application level, fixing bugs that lead to corruptions in a version of a software does not mean that the number of corruptions would be lower accordingly. Parameterization defects leading to wrong results could be considered as a form of user-level corruptions. There are two possible research directions/solutions about the detection of corruptions: (1) performing on-line verification by using an external algorithmic observer that does not trust the execution stack; (2) establishing trust relations between levels of the execution stack.

Acknowledgments.. This material was based upon work supported by the U.S. Department of Energy,Office of Science, Advanced Scientific Computing Research Program, under Contract DE-AC02-06CH11357.

References

1. http://en.wikipedia.org/wiki/List_of_software_bugs . Accessed 08 May 2017
2. Disasters in bad numerical computing. http://www.iro.umontreal.ca/~mignotte/IFT2425/Disasters.html. Accessed 08 May 2017
3. Opteron bugs. https://access.redhat.com/solutions/918043. Accessed 08 May 2017
4. Opteron REP bug. http://www.theinquirer.net/inquirer/news/1042490/amd-opteron-bug-cause-incorrect-results. Accessed 08 May 2017
5. Trust Computing Group. http://www.trustedcomputinggroup.org/. Accessed 08 May 2017
6. Trust in Social Sciences. http://en.wikipedia.org/wiki/Trust_(social_sciences). Accessed 08 May 2017
7. Trust Metrics. http://en.wikipedia.org/wiki/Trust_metric. Accessed 08 May 2017
8. Trusted Platform Module (TPM) Specification. http://www.trustedcomputinggroup.org/resources/tpm_main_specification. Accessed 08 May 2017
9. TWC: Small: behavior-based zero-day intrusion detection for real-time cyber-physical systems. https://www.collectiveip.com/grants/NSF:1423334. Accessed 08 May 2017

10. ASCR Cybersecurity for Scientific Computing Integrity, February 2015. http://www.osti.gov/scitech/servlets/purl/1223021
11. Avizienis, A.: The N-version approach to fault-tolerant software. IEEE Trans. Softw. Eng. **11**(12), 1491–1501 (1985)
12. Avižienis, A., Laprie, J.-C., Randell, B.: Dependability and its threats: a taxonomy. In: Jacquart, R. (ed.) Building the Information Society. IIFIP, vol. 156, pp. 91–120. Springer, Boston (2004). https://doi.org/10.1007/978-1-4020-8157-6_13
13. Becker, S., Hasselbring, W., Paul, A., Boskovic, M., Koziolek, H., Ploski, J., Dhama, A., Lipskoch, H., Rohr, M., Winteler, D., Giesecke, S., Meyer, R., Swaminathan, M., Happe, J., Muhle, M., Warns, T.: Trustworthy software systems: a discussion of basic concepts and terminology. SIGSOFT Softw. Eng. Notes **31**(6), 1–18 (2006)
14. Benson, A.R., Schmit, S., Schreiber, R.: Silent error detection in numerical time-stepping schemes. Int. J. High Perform. Comput. Appl. **29**(4), 403–421 (2015)
15. Berrocal, E., Bautista-Gomez, L., Di, S., Lan, Z., Cappello, F.: Exploring partial replication to improve lightweight silent data corruption detection for HPC applications. In: Dutot, P.-F., Trystram, D. (eds.) Euro-Par 2016. LNCS, vol. 9833, pp. 419–430. Springer, Cham (2016). https://doi.org/10.1007/978-3-319-43659-3_31
16. National Research Council: Assessing the Reliability of Complex Models: Mathematical and Statistical Foundations of Verification, Validation, and Uncertainty Quantification. The National Academies Press, Washington, D.C. (2012). https://www.nap.edu/catalog/13395/assessing-the-reliability-of-complex-models-mathematical-and-statistical-foundations
17. Di, S., Berrocal, E., Cappello, F.: An efficient silent data corruption detection method with error-feedback control and even sampling for HPC applications. In: 2015 15th IEEE/ACM International Symposium on Cluster, Cloud and Grid Computing, pp. 271–280, May 2015
18. Di, S., Cappello, F.: Adaptive impact-driven detection of silent data corruption for HPC applications. IEEE Trans. Parallel Distrib. Syst. **27**(10), 2809–2823 (2016). https://doi.org/10.1109/TPDS.2016.2517639
19. Knight, J.C., Leveson, N.G.: An experimental evaluation of the assumption of independence in multiversion programming. IEEE Trans. Softw. Eng. **12**(1), 96–109 (1986)
20. Levien, R., Aiken, A.: Attack-resistant trust metrics for public key certification. In: Proceedings of the 7th Conference on USENIX Security Symposium, SSYM 1998, vol. 7, pp. 18–18. USENIX Association, Berkeley (1998)
21. Randell, B., Xu, J.: The evolution of the recovery block concept. In: Software Fault Tolerance, pp. 1–22. Wiley (1994)
22. Sha, L.: Using simplicity to control complexity. IEEE Softw. **18**(4), 20–28 (2001)
23. Sparks, E.R.: A security assessment of trusted platform modules. Technical report TR2007-597, Dartmouth College, Computer Science, Hanover, NH, June 2007
24. Subasi, O., Di, S., Bautista-Gomez, L., Balaprakash, P., Unsal, O., Labarta, J., Cristal, A., Cappello, F.: Spatial support vector regression to detect silent errors in the exascale era. In: 2016 16th IEEE/ACM International Symposium on Cluster, Cloud and Grid Computing (CCGrid), pp. 413–424 May 2016
25. Theodorakopoulos, G., Baras, J.S.: On trust models and trust evaluation metrics for ad hoc networks. IEEE J. Sel. A. Commun. **24**(2), 318–328 (2006)
26. Türpe, S., Poller, A., Steffan, J., Stotz, J.-P., Trukenmüller, J.: Attacking the BitLocker boot process. In: Chen, L., Mitchell, C.J., Martin, A. (eds.) Trust 2009. LNCS, vol. 5471, pp. 183–196. Springer, Heidelberg (2009). https://doi.org/10.1007/978-3-642-00587-9_12

Pattern-Based Modeling of High-Performance Computing Resilience

Saurabh Hukerikar$^{(\boxtimes)}$ and Christian Engelmann

Computer Science and Mathematics Division, Oak Ridge National Laboratory,
Oak Ridge, TN, USA
{hukerikarsr,engelmann}@ornl.gov

Abstract. With the growing scale and complexity of high-performance computing (HPC) systems, resilience solutions that ensure continuity of service despite frequent errors and component failures must be methodically designed to balance the reliability requirements with the overheads to performance and power. Design patterns enable a structured approach to the development of resilience solutions, providing hardware and software designers with the building block elements for the rapid development of novel solutions and for adapting existing technologies for emerging, extreme-scale HPC environments. In this paper, we develop analytical models that enable designers to evaluate the reliability and performance characteristics of the design patterns. These models are particularly useful in building a unified framework that analyzes and compares various resilience solutions built using a combination of patterns.

Keywords: High-performance computing · Resilience · Patterns
Performance · Reliability · Modeling

1   Introduction

Many of the choices that drive hardware and software component designs in emerging extreme-scale high-performance computing (HPC) systems are made to deliver maximum application performance, but are also subject to the constraints of cost, power and reliability. While HPC system architectures have evolved significantly over the past decade, these constraints are expected to force

This work was sponsored by the U.S. Department of Energy's Office of Advanced Scientific Computing Research. This manuscript has been authored by UT-Battelle, LLC under Contract No. DE-AC05-00OR22725 with the U.S. Department of Energy. The United States Government retains and the publisher, by accepting the article for publication, acknowledges that the United States Government retains a non-exclusive, paid-up, irrevocable, world-wide license to publish or reproduce the published form of this manuscript, or allow others to do so, for United States Government purposes. The Department of Energy will provide public access to these results of federally sponsored research in accordance with the DOE Public Access Plan (http://energy.gov/downloads/doe-public-access-plan).

© Springer International Publishing AG, part of Springer Nature 2018
D. B. Heras and L. Bougé (Eds.): Euro-Par 2017 Workshops, LNCS 10659, pp. 557–568, 2018.
https://doi.org/10.1007/978-3-319-75178-8_45

further dramatic changes to the system stack to achieve exascale performance. Recent system architectures have emphasized increasing on-chip and node-level parallelism in addition to complex memory architectures consisting of deeper hierarchies and diverse technologies [12]. The software infrastructure, including the system software, middleware and tools, has continued to evolve to keep up with these changes to the system architectures to drive application performance on these extreme-scale computers.

The reliability and availability of the recent generation of HPC systems have been degrading in comparison to their predecessors [6]. This trend is projected to cause future extreme-scale systems to experience unprecedented rates of faults, which will make it difficult to accomplish productive work. The increasingly complex, multicomponent hardware and software environment only makes the challenge of detection of faults in a timely manner, containment of error propagation and mitigation of the impact of error and failure events more difficult. Resilience solutions must protect the correctness of HPC applications in the presence of faults, errors and failures arising from a multitude of sources, including the system environment, the interactions between platform hardware and system software components and applications, and variability in behavior of hardware components, while seeking to limit the performance and power overhead they impose on the system.

To navigate the complexities of this emerging landscape of HPC design, we proposed a structured approach to designing HPC resilience solutions based on the concept of design patterns [9]. In general, a design pattern is a general reusable solution to a commonly occurring problem within a given context in any design discipline. A pattern provides a description or template for how to solve a problem that may be adapted to specific context. Resilience patterns describe solutions to confront faults and their consequences. The patterns describe techniques for detection, containment and mitigation of faults, errors and failure events. They can be instantiated at any layer of the system stack. The resilience design patterns serve as building block elements for designing complete solutions, and are useful for the exploration of design alternatives for a target HPC system environment and application workload. Section 2 describes the concept of patterns and summarizes the different types of resilience patterns that are organized in a catalog.

The development of resilience solutions through composition of various design patterns lends structure to the design and implementation process by compelling designers to consider the key issues of protection coverage, fault model, handling capability, etc. However, objectively selecting pattern solutions that have been examined and utilized successfully in a specific context with the intention of adapting them to a new architecture or software environment of a future system requires criteria based on a quantitative foundation. Mathematical models of hardware or software components, or even entire HPC systems, which are solved either analytically or through discrete event simulation, are useful to HPC designers for predicting resilient behavior of the system in the presence of various fault, error and failure events, without having to build the component or system. This paper develops models for analytical evaluation of reliability and performance measures of the various resilience design patterns in our pattern catalog. These models are presented in Sect. 3. The models are designed to capture the interaction between the resilient behavior and the performance overhead incurred by instantiating a specific pattern. Section 4 discusses approaches to calculate reliability and performance of a solution built by combining several patterns.

2 Background: Resilience Design Patterns

2.1 Concept

Design patterns identify the key aspects of a solution to common problem, and presents the solution in the form of an abstract description, which provides designers with guidelines on how to address the problem. Patterns capture the best-known techniques to solve a problem. We developed resilience design patterns [9] to support a systematic approach to designing and implementing new resilience solutions and adapting existing solutions to future extreme-scale architectures and software environments.

The patterns describe the design decisions and trade-offs that must be considered when applying a pattern solution to a specific context. The descriptions encourage designers to reason about the impact of applying a solution on a system's performance scalability and power consumption overhead as well as consider implementation issues. Based on the patterns, we developed a framework that enables designers to comprehensively evaluate the scope of protection domain and the handling efficiency of resilience solutions.

The basic template of a resilience design pattern is defined in an event-driven paradigm, in which each resilience design pattern consists of a *behavior* and a set of *activation* and *response interfaces*. The patterns present solutions to specific problems in detecting, recovering from, or masking a fault, error or failure event. The pattern descriptions are abstract and they may be implemented by HPC applications' algorithms, numerical libraries, system software, or even in the hardware architectures. We have organized the resilience design pattern as a catalog that contains detailed descriptions of the patterns. The catalog is available as a specification document [8], in which each resilience pattern is presented using a structured format to enable designers to quickly discover whether the pattern solution is suitable to the problem being solved.

2.2 Classification

We developed a pattern classification scheme that organizes the resilience patterns in a layered hierarchy, in which each level addresses a specific aspect of the problem. The classification enables designers to separately reason about the patterns that define the scope of the protection domain and those that define the semantics of the detection, containment and mitigation. The hierarchical

organization of the patterns permits system architects to work on the overall
organization of the solutions by analyzing the integration of various resilience
patterns across the system stack while designers of individual hardware and
software components can focus on implementation of the patterns.

Resilience in the context of HPC systems and its applications has two key
dimensions: (1) forward progress of the system; (2) data consistency in the system. Based on these factors, we organize the resilience design patterns into two
major categories, **state** patterns and **behavioral** patterns. The behavioral patterns identify detection, containment, or mitigation actions that enable a system
to cope with the presence of a fault, error, or failure event. These patterns are
organized hierarchically and they include **strategy**, **architectural** and **structural** patterns.

The strategy patterns define high-level polices of a resilience solution. Their
descriptions are deliberately abstract to enable hardware and software architects
to reason about the overall organization of the techniques used and their implications on the full system design. These patterns describe the overall structure of
the solution and the key attributes of the solution and their capabilities independent of the layer of system stack and hardware/software architectural features.
The architectural patterns convey specific methods necessary for the construction of a resilience solution. They explicitly convey the type of fault, error or
failure event that they handle and provide detail about the key components and
connectors that make up the solution. The structural patterns provide concrete
descriptions of the solution rather than high-level strategies. They comprise of
instructions that may be implemented in hardware/software components. While
the strategy and architectural patterns serve to provide designers with a clear
overall framework of a solution and the type of events that it can handle, the
structural patterns express the details so they can contribute to the development
of complete working solutions.

2.3   Designing Resilience Solutions Using Patterns

Each pattern in the resilience design pattern catalog presents a solution to a
specific problem in detecting, containing or mitigating a fault, error or failure
event. In order to construct complete resilience solutions designers must identify
patterns that provide each of these capabilities and apply them to a well-defined
protection domain. Therefore, a complete solution consists of at least one state
pattern (defining scope of the protection domain), and one or more behavioral
patterns (supporting a combination of detection, containment and mitigation
solutions).

For hardware and software designers to make practical use these patterns in
the development of resilient versions of their designs, we have developed a design
framework that a set of guidelines are necessary to combine the patterns and
refine their implementations. The framework is based on design spaces that are
arranged in a hierarchy. By working through the design spaces, designers can
convert initial outline of the resilience solution into a concrete implementation

by considering the layer of abstraction for the pattern implementation, scalability of the solution, portability to other architectures, dependencies on any hardware/software features, flexibility to adapt the solution to accelerated fault rates, capability to handle other types of fault and error events, the performance and performance overheads.

3   Reliability and Performance Models for Resilience Design Patterns

The models are intended to be useful for predicting the reliability and performance characteristics of solutions built using design patterns in a notional extreme-scale system that may use different plausible architectures and configurations that consist of different node counts, and may use different software environments. Therefore, we present the analytic models for the various architecture patterns in our catalog because these patterns explicitly specify the type of event that they handle and convey details about the handling capabilities and the components that make up the solution in a manner independent of the layer of system stack and hardware/software architectural features. For the checkpoint and rollback pattern, we present models for the derivative structural patterns due to their widespread use in HPC environments. The models for the patterns provide a quantitative analysis of the costs and benefits of instantiating specific resilience design patterns. The models may be applied to an individual hardware or software component, which is a sub-system, or to a full system that consists of a collection of nodes capable of running a parallel application.

Although the future extreme-scale systems may not look at all like the systems of today, we assume that the notional system consists of multiple processing nodes, and that the parallel application partitions the work among tasks that run on these nodes that cooperate via message passing to synchronize. Therefore, we use the following notation in the descriptions of the models: N: number of tasks/processes in the parallel application; M: total number of messages exchanged between the tasks/processes of the application; P: the number of processors in the system; T_{system}: the operation time of the system, or the execution time of an application.

In general, we assume that the event (whether fault, error or failure) arrivals follow a Poisson process, the probability of an event is F(t). The reliability of the system is:

$$R(t) = 1 - F(t) \tag{1}$$

which indicates the probability that the system operates correctly for time t.

If the scope of the system captured by the state pattern has an exponential event distribution, the reliability of the system takes the form:

$$R(t) = 1 - e^{-t/\eta} \tag{2}$$

where η is the mean time to interrupt of the system, which may be calculated as the inverse of the failure rate of the system.

3.1 Fault Diagnosis Pattern Model

The fault diagnosis pattern identifies the presence of the fault and tries to determine its root cause. Until a fault has not activated into an error it does not affect the correct operation of the system, and therefore the pattern makes an assessment about the presence of a defect based on observed behavior of one or more system parameters. To incorporate this pattern in an HPC environment requires inclusion of a monitoring component. The pattern uses either effect-cause or cause-effect analysis on the observed parameters of a monitored system to infer the presence of a fault. The performance overhead of this pattern may be expressed as:

$$T_{system} = T_0 + \sum_{k=1}^{n} t_{inference}/\beta \tag{3}$$

where n is the number of observed parameters of the monitored system and β is the frequency of polling the monitored system. Since the pattern only identifies faults, but does not remedy them, there is no tangible improvement in reliability of the system when this pattern is instantiated.

3.2 Reconfiguration Pattern Model

The reconfiguration pattern entails modification of the interconnection between components in a system, such that isolates the component affected by a fault, error or failure event, preventing it from affecting the correct operation of the overall system. The pattern may cause the system to assume one of several valid configurations that are functionally equivalent to the original system configuration, but results in system operation at a degraded performance level.

To simplify the derivation of the reliability and performance models, we assume that the system consists of n identical components. The performance of the system for the loss of a single component may be expressed as:

$$T_{system} = T_{FF} + (1 - T_{FF}).\frac{n-1}{n} + T_R \tag{4}$$

where T_{FF} represents the operational time before the occurrence of the event, and T_R is the system downtime on account of the delay for reconfiguring the n − 1 components.

The reliability of the system may be expressed as:

$$R(n,t) = 1 - \prod_{i=1}^{n}(1 - R_i(t)) \tag{5}$$

This equation assumes that the fault events are independent and are exponentially distributed.

3.3 Rollback Recovery Pattern Model

The checkpoint-recovery architectural pattern is based on the creation of snapshots of the system state and maintenance of these checkpoints on a persistent storage system during the error- or failure-free operation of the system. Upon detection of an error or a failure, the checkpoints/logged events are used to recreate last known error- or failure-free state of the system, after which the system operation is restarted. The rollback recovery pattern is a derivative of the checkpoint-recovery provides rollback recovery, i.e., based on a temporal view of the system's progress, the system state recreated during the recovery process is a previous correct version of the state of the system.

The pattern requires interruption of the system during error or failure-free operation to record the checkpoint, which incurs an overhead. Therefore, the operational lifetime of the system can be partitioned into distinct phases, which include the regular execution phase (o), the interval for creating checkpoints (δ), and the interval for recovery upon occurrence of an event (γ) to account for the operational state lost on account of the event.

The performance of the system in absence of any error or failure events may be expressed as:

$$T_{system} = o + \delta/r \tag{6}$$

where r is the rate of checkpointing.

The performance of the system in the presence of failure events, assuming an exponential event rate of $e^{-t/\eta}$ (η is the mean time to interrupt of the system) may be modeled as:

$$T_{system} = (T_{FF} + \gamma)/\eta \tag{7}$$

where $T_{FF} = o + \delta/r$.

The reliability of a system using the rollback recovery pattern may be modeled as:

$$R(t) = 1 - e^{-(T_{FF} + \gamma)/\eta} \tag{8}$$

for systems in which an event occurs before the interval $T_{FF} + \gamma$, and η is the mean time to interrupt.

3.4 Roll-Forward Recovery Pattern Model

The roll-forward pattern is a structural pattern, which is also a derivative of the checkpoint recovery pattern. It uses either checkpointing or log-based protocols to record system progress during error- or failure-free operation. The recovery entails the use of checkpointed state and/or logging information to recreate a stable version of the system identical to the one right before the error or failure occurred. The roll-forward pattern may also use online recovery protocols that use inference methods to recreate state.

The roll-forward pattern also requires the system to record system and/or message state during fault-free operation. The system performance may be calculated using:

$$T_{system} = o + \delta/r \tag{9}$$

where r is the rate of checkpointing or message logging.

The performance of the system in the presence of failure events may be captured using:

$$T_{system} = (T_{FF} + \gamma)/\eta \tag{10}$$

where $T_{FF} = o + \delta/r$.

When the roll-forward pattern instantiation uses message logging, the term δ in these equations is calculated as the logging interval: $\delta = M.t_{logging}$.

The reliability of the system that uses the rollforward pattern capability may be modeled as:

$$
\begin{aligned}
R(t) &= 1 - e^{-(T_{FF}+M.t_{logging})/\eta}[\text{for message logging implementations}] \\
&= 1 - e^{-(T_{FF}+\gamma)/\eta}[\text{for checkpointing implementations}]
\end{aligned} \tag{11}
$$

assuming an exponential event arrival and η is the mean time to interrupt of the system.

3.5   Redundancy Pattern Model

The redundancy pattern is based on a strategy of compensation since it entails creation of a group of N replicas of a system. The replicated versions of the system are used in various configurations to compensate for errors or failures in one of the system replicas, including fail-over, active comparison for error detection, or majority voting for detection and correction by excluding the replica whose outputs fall outside the majority. The use of the redundancy pattern incurs overhead to the system operation independent of whether an error or failure event occurs.

For parallel application, the overhead depends on the scope of replication, which may include aspects such as the amount of computation performed by the tasks, the communication between them, etc. The overhead also depends on factors such as the degree of redundancy, placement of the replicas on the system resources. Therefore, to develop a precise mathematical model that represents each of these factors is complex. To simplify the analysis, we partition the operation time of the system into the ratio of the time spent on the redundant operation $\mathcal{A}$ and the time. This partitioning can be logically defined by the scope of the state patterns; $(1 - \mathcal{A})$ is the fraction outside the scope of the state pattern, for which no redundancy is applied. Since the term t is taken as the base execution time of the application, the time $\mathcal{A}.t$ is the time of system operation for which redundancy is applied, while $(1 - \mathcal{A}).t$ is the remaining time. The term d refers to the degree of redundancy, i.e., the number of copies of the pattern behavior that are replicated.

$$T_{system} = T_S.((1 - \mathcal{A}) + \beta.\mathcal{A})) + T_{MV} \tag{12}$$

where β is 1 when the state pattern is replicated in a space redundant manner and is equal to d when applied in a time redundant manner. The term T_S is serial operation time of the system and the term T_{MV} represents the time spent by the majority voting logic to detect output mismatches.

Assuming the mean time to interrupt of the system that uses the redundancy pattern is λ, then the reliability of the system may expressed as:

$$R(t) = 1 - \prod_{i=1}^{d} t/\lambda = 1 - (t/\lambda)^d \tag{13}$$

3.6   Design Diversity Pattern Model

When a design bug exists in a system design or configuration, an error or failure during system operation is often unavoidable. Therefore, the detection and mitigation of the impact of such errors or failures is critical. The n-version design pattern applies distinct implementations of the same design specification created by different individuals or teams. The N versions of the system are operated simultaneously with a majority voting logic is used to compare the results produced by each design version. Due the low likelihood that different individuals or teams make identical errors in their respective implementations, the pattern enables compensating for errors or failures caused by a bug in any one implementation version.

Assuming that there are n versions of the system scope encapsulated by the state pattern, $1 \geq i \leq n$, then the probability that only version i executes its function correctly while the remaining versions produce an incorrect outcome:

$$P(A) = \sum_{k=1}^{n+1} P(A_k) \tag{14}$$

where the $P(A_k)$ is the probability that only the version A_k out of the n versions produces the correct outcome, while the remaining versions produce an incorrect outcome.

The probability density function (PDF) describing the probability of failure occurring during the system operation may be expressed as:

$$P(t) = ((1 - P(V)) \sum_{k=1}^{n+1} P(A_k) + P(V)) \tag{15}$$

where the $P(V)$ represents the probability that the majority voting procedure cannot select the correct result from at least two correct versions. Therefore, the reliability of the system using the n-version design at time t may be calculated in terms of this probability:

$$R(t) = 1 - ((1 - P(V)) \sum_{k=1}^{n+1} P(A_k) + P(V)).F(t) \tag{16}$$

where $F(t) = e^{-t/\eta}$ is the failure rate assuming exponential event arrival rate.

4   Model-Based Evaluation of Resilience

The design of complete resilience solutions often requires the composition of multiple resilience design patterns. In a complex HPC environment with numerous hardware and software pattern instantiations in the various components, the resilience to different fault events is managed by this well-defined system of patterns. To developed a combined evaluation of the reliability and performance characteristics of a real system that consists of several pattern solutions implemented across the system stack requires composition of the pattern models.

For the simplified case of a system configuration that consists of N independent components or tasks such that, if any one of the system components or tasks fails, the entire system fails, the overall reliability of the system may be modeled as:

$$R_{system} = R_1 \times R_2 \times R_3 \times \ldots R_N \tag{17}$$

where the reliability R_i of a component is a function of the resilience pattern that it instantiates. For such a configuration, the performance overhead of applying patterns to the N components in the system is additive.

For more intricate analytic evaluation of the performance and reliability, more complex models must be developed. There are several paradigms that are useful for this purpose, including fault trees, block diagrams, reliability & task graphs, Markov & semi-Markov chains, stochastic Petrinets, etc. Analytical models that use Markov models are useful to model the intricate dependencies between the pattern solutions in a complex multicomponent HPC environment. Markov chains are state-space-based methods that consist of states representing various conditions associated with the system, and the transition between states, which represent the changes in system state or configuration due to the occurrence of a simple or compound event such as the malfunction or failure of one or more components in the system. The assessment of system resilience using Markov models for a multicomponent HPC environment that experiences different modes of faults, as well as a model for the combined evaluation of performance and reliability is the subject of ongoing research.

5   Related Work

Much research has been done on modeling techniques and tools that are useful for reliability and performance analysis of various computing systems and applications. These approaches may broadly be categorized into [11]: (i) *structural modeling*, which highlights the relationships between the system components using representations such as block diagrams, reliability graphs and fault trees. These models assume stochastic independence between system components; (ii) *state-space models*, which model the dependencies among system components and use representations such as Markov chains. These models are significantly more complex due to the need for as many as 2^n states in the Markov representation for n system components; and, (iii) *hierarchical models*, which balance the speed of analysis with the accuracy of the model by combining abstract structural models with the detailed Markov models [7]. There have also been several advances in performability analysis, which aim to model the interaction between failure recovery behavior and performance in a composite manner [1,13].

Due to the dominance of checkpoint and rollback approaches in high-performance computing systems, several approaches have been proposed for calculating the reliability and performance measures of systems that use this solution. Analytic models have been developed for determining the optimum intervals for checkpoints [14]. For applying such analysis to large-scale cluster-based HPC systems, the model has been adapted to meet the goal of minimizing the overall application run time [2]. For understanding the viability of rollback recovery on extreme-scale systems, models for prediction of its performance have been proposed. This model was developed to evaluate the rollback recovery solution for petascale HPC systems [5]. An optimal checkpoint and rollback model has been devised that incorporates a reliability function obtained from the analysis of historical failure data from the system event log files [10]. There have also been efforts to develop models that analyze the combination of checkpoint restart with redundancy techniques for MPI applications [4], and for multilevel checkpointing solutions [3].

6   Conclusion

For future extreme-scale HPC systems, designers will be required to work within tight constraints of cost, power and reliability to achieve greater performance. The use of design patterns enables the exploration of alternative solutions for a specific context and provides a framework to combine individual patterns into complete solutions. The performance and reliability models for resilience design patterns presented in this paper allow us to develop measures to analyze the solutions built using the patterns. While these models for the architecture patterns are not detailed enough and refining them will lead to considerable added complexity, they predict the implications of selecting specific combination of patterns for the reliability and performance of a system in a given context. The models developed in this paper are designed to be useful for simulation frameworks to examine the effectiveness of a resilience solution for specific fault models and fault rates, as well as to measure the performance and reliability characteristics of the pattern-based solution for different system architectures, software environments and application workloads.

Acknowledgements. This material is based upon work supported by the U.S. Department of Energy, Office of Science, Office of Advanced Scientific Computing Research, program manager Lucy Nowell, under contract number DE-AC05-00OR22725.

References

1. Beaudry, M.D.: Performance-related reliability measures for computing systems. IEEE Trans. Comput. **C–27**(6), 540–547 (1978)
2. Daly, J.: A higher order estimate of the optimum checkpoint interval for restart dumps. Future Gener. Comput. Syst. **22**(3), 303–312 (2006)
3. Di, S., Bautista-Gomez, L., Cappello, F.: Optimization of a multilevel checkpoint model with uncertain execution scales. In: Proceedings of the International Conference for High Performance Computing, Networking, Storage and Analysis, SC 2014, pp. 907–918 (2014)
4. Elliott, J., Kharbas, K., Fiala, D., Mueller, F., Ferreira, K., Engelmann, C.: Combining partial redundancy and checkpointing for HPC. In: 2012 IEEE 32nd International Conference on Distributed Computing Systems, pp. 615–626, June 2012
5. Elnozahy, E.N., Plank, J.S.: Checkpointing for peta-scale systems: a look into the future of practical rollback-recovery. IEEE Trans. Dependable Secure Comput. **1**(2), 97–108 (2004)
6. Geist, A.: How to kill a supercomputer: dirty power, cosmic rays, and bad solder. IEEE Spectr. (2016)
7. Geist, R., Trivedi, K.S.: Reliability estimation of fault-tolerant systems: tools and techniques. Computer **23**(7), 52–61 (1990)
8. Hukerikar, S., Engelmann, C.: Resilience design patterns: a structured approach to resilience at extreme scale (version 1.1). Technical report ORNL/TM-2016/767, Oak Ridge National Laboratory, Oak Ridge, TN, USA, December 2016
9. Hukerikar, S., Engelmann, C.: Resilience design patterns: a structured approach to resilience at extreme scale. Supercomput. Front. Innov. **4**(3), 1–38 (2017)
10. Liu, Y., Nassar, R., Leangsuksun, C., Naksinehaboon, N., Paun, M., Scott, S.: A reliability-aware approach for an optimal checkpoint/restart model in HPC environments. In: 2007 IEEE International Conference on Cluster Computing, pp. 452–457, September 2007
11. Pham, H.: Reliability Modeling, Analysis and Optimization. World Scientific Publishing, Singapore (2006)
12. Shalf, J., Dosanjh, S., Morrison, J.: Exascale computing technology challenges. In: Palma, J.M.L.M., Daydé, M., Marques, O., Lopes, J.C. (eds.) VECPAR 2010. LNCS, vol. 6449, pp. 1–25. Springer, Heidelberg (2011). https://doi.org/10.1007/978-3-642-19328-6_1
13. Trivedi, K.S., Malhotra, M.: Reliability and performability techniques and tools: a survey. In: Walke, B., Spaniol, O. (eds.) Messung, Modellierung und Bewertung von Rechen- und Kommunikationssystemen. INFORMAT, pp. 27–48. Springer, Heidelberg (1993). https://doi.org/10.1007/978-3-642-78495-8_3
14. Young, J.W.: A first order approximation to the optimum checkpoint interval. Commun. ACM **17**(9), 530–531 (1974)

On the Resilience of Conjugate Gradient and Multigrid Methods to Node Failures

Carlos Pachajoa and Wilfried N. Gansterer$^{(\boxtimes)}$

University of Vienna, Faculty of Computer Science, Vienna, Austria
{carlos.pachajoa,wilfried.gansterer}@univie.ac.at

Abstract. In this paper, we examine the inherent resilience of multigrid (MG) and conjugate gradient (CG) methods in the search for algorithm-based approaches to deal with node failures in large parallel HPC systems. In previous work, silent data corruption has been modeled as the perturbation of values in the work arrays of a MG solver. It was concluded that MG recovers fast from errors of this type. We explore how fast MG and CG methods recover from the loss of a contiguous section of their working memory, modeling a node failure. Since MG and CG methods differ in their convergence rates, we propose a methodology to compare their resilience: Time is represented as a fraction of the iterations required to reach a certain target precision, and failures are introduced when the residual norm reaches a certain threshold. We use the two solvers on a linear system that represents a model elliptic partial differential equation, and we experimentally evaluate the overhead caused by the introduced faults. Additionally, we observe the behavior of the conjugate gradient solver under node failures for additional test problems. Approximating the lost values of the solution using interpolation reduces the overhead for MG, but the effect on the CG solver is minimal. We conclude that the methods also have the inherent ability to recover from node failures. However, we illustrate that the relative overhead caused by node failures is significant.

Keywords: Node failure · Conjugate gradient · Multigrid · Resilience

1 Introduction

With HPC systems growing in scale, the probability of a failure occurring in a computer component during an application's lifetime is expected to increase. Therefore, an algorithm's ability to deal with lost or corrupted data gains importance, particularly in the case of future exascale systems [14, Sect. 1.1].

In this work, we examine the inherent resilience of the multiplicative geometric multigrid method [15] and the conjugate gradient method [12] applied to the solution of linear systems defined by a sparse, positive-definite matrix. The CG method is widely used in the solution of such systems, while geometric MG is an optimal solver for matrices arising from certain physical problems.

© Springer International Publishing AG, part of Springer Nature 2018
D. B. Heras and L. Bougé (Eds.): Euro-Par 2017 Workshops, LNCS 10659, pp. 569–580, 2018.
https://doi.org/10.1007/978-3-319-75178-8_46

We do not consider checkpointing solutions to the node-failure problem in this paper. We focus on better understanding the inherent resilience of the algorithms instead. External checkpointing is expensive and incurs on overhead even if no fault occurs.

We are interested in the effects of the starting vector of the solver, the size of the lost region and its location in the domain, and of the way the iterand is reconstructed after a node failure. Where applicable, we also investigate the effect of different preconditioners. We use our own implementations of geometric MG and CG. We also use PETSc [5,6] for experiments with the preconditioned CG method.

1.1 Previous Work

In [11], Mishra and Banerjee explore the application of Algorithm-Based Fault Tolerance [10] (ABFT) to the detection of faults introduced in the interpolation and restriction operations of MG. Their model problem is the two-dimensional Poisson equation. They introduce separate checksums for the relaxation, restriction and interpolation steps, created by adding up the elements of the solution and residual arrays, which can be used to check for faults incurred during any of the steps.

In [8], Casas et al. explore the impact of silent data corruption in an algebraic MG solver. The errors are introduced in the machine instructions, weighting the probability of an error according to the number of cycles it uses. By replicating pointers to the storage arrays, they show that MG has some inherent fault tolerance, reducing the count of segmentation faults with overheads smaller than the undisturbed runtime of the application.

Agullo et al. present interpolation strategies to accelerate the recovery of Krylov solvers in [1,2]. In their work, they consider node failures as well. They reconstruct the solution approximation of a lost node with a process which they call linear interpolation that depends on the structure of the matrix. In this paper, we perform linear interpolation to reconstruct the lost elements in the iterand without using information from the iteration matrix. Such a strategy is expected to have significantly lower communication and computation costs.

In [3], Ainsworth and Glusa present a two-grid model that takes silent data corruption into account. They conclude that the two-grid method is not resilient and propose a way to solve the problem by protecting the interpolation operation. In [4], Altenbernd and Göddeke propose a way to detect and correct soft failures for the *full approximation scheme* variant of MG by exploiting invariants in the maps between levels.

In this paper, we extend earlier work by investigating the influence of (i) the position of the node failure, (ii) the initial guess and (iii) different recovery strategies.

2   Model Setup

Our results are based on simulating parallel execution of the algorithms based on the model setup summarized in the following.

Sets of contiguous grid points are assigned to different nodes of a parallel machine. In order to apply the matrix-vector products used by the iterative solvers, some communication is necessary between the nodes, and the required information to be sent and received depends on the sparsity pattern of the matrix.

To ease the application of geometric MG, we use a grid of equally spaced points. The number of grid points is $2^k + 1$, for a given $k \in \mathbb{N}$, such that the number of segments of the domain is 2^k and can be successively divided by two to form coarser grids. Now, we consider the grids of two consecutive levels. We call the one in the higher level the *fine grid*, and the one in the coarser level the *coarse grid*. With this setup, the distance between grid points in the fine grid is $h = \frac{1}{2^k}$, The coarse grid is composed of 2^{k-1} segments and $2^{k-1} + 1$ grid points. We let each node work on an index set of 2^l grid points for a given $l \in \mathbb{N}, l < k$ for the fine grid, except for the node in charge of the leftmost index set, which works with $2^l + 1$ grid points. This grid-point distribution is used also for all arrays in the CG method when solving the discretized Poisson equation.

Parallel MG methods also require a strategy to distribute grid points of coarser grids to the workers. The number of grid points decreases rapidly when moving to coarser grids. If each worker is responsible for the same subdomain in all grid levels, the communication to computation ratio becomes very high. Better approaches to deal with this problem are proposed in [15, Sect. 6.3.2]. The agglomeration strategy [15, Fig. 6.8] merges subdomains such that the workers are responsible for a comparable number of nodes, representing a larger subdomain.

We also apply the CG method to matrices from the SuitSparse Matrix Collection [9]. More details are provided in Sect. 4.1. Here, the size of the index set of a node is set to $2^{-m} \times$ size of the domain for some $m \in \mathbb{N}$, and the data of the node is aligned such that the leftmost element of the array lies in the position $i \times 2^{-m} \times$ size of the domain, $i \in \{0, 1, ..., 2^m - 1\}$.

Our experiments are not run in a parallel machine. A node failure is represented by disturbing entries of the iterand as described in the following section.

Modeling the Failure of a Node

Our experiments introduce perturbations in a contiguous section of the fine-grid solution array of the solver. This perturbation models a node failure and the consequent loss of the information it holds. We assume that the system is notified about the lost node and a spare node takes over the work for its index set. In each experiment, we observe the residual after the data of a node is lost. Node failures are introduced only once in each experiment, at different cycles of the MG algorithm or at iterations that reach a given threshold in the relative residual norm for CG.

We also assume that the right-hand-side vector is backed up only once, when the solver starts, and it can be restored cheaply. We further assume that the sparse system matrix can also be stored and restored in the case of a failure. In the case of the discretized Poisson equation, it is represented as a linear operator, completely described with very few parameters and can be replicated in every node, according to a matrix stencil.

3   Algorithms Investigated

On the one hand, we consider multiplicative geometric multigrid. This variant of multigrid is not optimal for work in parallel (particularly if different workers take care of different grid levels [15, Sect. 6].) However, we use it as a first approximation to the subject. We use a damped Jacobi smoother with a damping parameter $\omega = \frac{2}{3}$, and V-cycles (see [15, p. 46]) as the recursion strategy. The solution is smoothed twice both before restriction and further twice after interpolation. The coarsest grid consists of three grid points and is solved exactly.

On the other hand, we consider the CG method without preconditioning for the discretized Poisson problem, and with Jacobi and Gauss-Seidel preconditioners for some test problems from the SuitSparse Matrix Collection [9]. When applied to the Poisson problem, two common preconditioners, Jacobi and incomplete LU factorization, do not produce interesting results. The former does not improve the convergence, since the system matrix is not diagonally dominant, while the latter conditions the problem perfectly, because the LU decomposition of the problem matrix has the same sparsity pattern as the original matrix. Solving the system without preconditioning still provides information the performance of the algorithm, albeit for a less favorable eigenvalue distribution.

3.1   Recovery Strategies

With a perturbation to its current approximation, MG will still converge to the solution provided that the spectral radius of the system matrix is less than one, the right hand side is restored and additional MG cycles are conducted. The solver can converge from lost information in nodes if the initial guess in the region is set to valid real numbers (see [7, p. 17]). This is equivalent to starting the method from a different initial approximation.

The CG method also requires that its search directions are A-orthogonal to each other, as it was shown in [13]. This can be achieved by restarting the residual and search direction vectors after a node failure. This solution is, however, not optimal: The CG method is not stateless and, in order to reproduce its trajectory to the solution, we require the iterand and search direction corresponding to a time before the perturbation, the latter of which acts as the state of the solver. In the event of a node failure, a part of the search direction is lost as well. For better results, the search direction should be reconstructed along with the iterand. A solver that overcomes this limitation and is more resilient to node failures is currently being investigated.

In this paper, we consider two strategies to reconstruct the iterand after a node failure: (a) The grid points corresponding to the lost node are set to zero and (b) The grid points corresponding to the lost node are linearly interpolated from the values neighboring the domain which are available on the neighbors of the failed node.

Notice that these two recovery strategies require very little additional communication between nodes: Filling the arrays in the replacement node with zeros requires no additional communication, and to perform a linear interpolation we require only the corresponding values in the boundaries of the neighbors.

We are not concerned with recovery strategies for the coarser levels of MG. In the event of a node failure, we restart from a new approximation of the solution in the fine grid and the information of the coarser grids is recomputed in the solution process.

The linear interpolation approach does not translate directly to higher dimensions. In that case, a different approach, such as solving the Poisson equation for the smaller system with Dirichlet boundary conditions, could be applied to reconstruct the iterand.

4 Experimental Setup

4.1 Test Problems

Discretized Poisson Equation. Our first model problem is the one-dimensional Poisson equation with Dirichlet boundary conditions:

$$x : [0,1] \to \mathbb{R}, \quad \Delta x = f, \quad x(0) = x(1) = 0. \tag{1}$$

The equation is discretized using a uniform grid and finite differences, producing the three-point stencil $\frac{1}{h^2} \begin{bmatrix} 1 & -2 & 1 \end{bmatrix}$, where h is the distance between two neighboring grid points.

We fix the problem size to $2^{16} + 1$ grid points and the right-hand side is taken to be a vector of ones. We examine cases where the elements of the starting vector are set to zero or drawn from a uniform probability distribution in the interval $[-0.5, 0.5]$.

The problem is then divided into workers that will take a set of grid points of size 2^6, 2^{10} and 2^{14}. Node failures are introduced at the edge of the domain or at its center. We terminate the iteration once the relative residual norm $\|r\|/\|b\|$ is below 10^{-5}, where b is the right-hand side vector resulting from the discretization of f. In each experiment, a single node is lost at a given time step.

We simulate node failures at fixed V-cycles in MG and store the values of the relative residual norm before perturbing the solution. In CG, we introduce failures when the residual reaches the values stored in the MG run. The location of the failed nodes and the number of lost grid points are the same for each case. This way, we can compare the two methods.

More General Sparse Matrices. For CG, we also experiment with positive-definite, full-rank matrices obtained from the SuitSparse Matrix Collection [9]. Properties of the matrices that we use for these experiments are summarized in Table 1.

With the more complex sparsity patterns of these matrices, the effects of preconditioners, such as Gauss-Seidel and Jacobi, is more interesting.

All entries of the right-hand side vector are set to one. We consider that the solver has converged when the relative residual norm $\|r\|/\|b\|$ goes below 10^{-15}. Again, starting vectors are set to zero or drawn from a uniform probability distribution in the interval $[-0.5, 0.5]$.

Table 1. Positive definite matrices from [9] used in the CG experiments.

Name	bcsstk28	mhd4800b
Application	Solid mechanics	Magnetohydrodynamics
Rows × columns	4410 × 4410	4800 × 4800
Non-zeros	219024	27520

4.2   Overhead Metric

We do not model the communication between the nodes or the runtime of the application. Instead, our metric is based on the number of iterations (or MG V-cycles) necessary to reach a given relative residual norm. Aspects such as bandwidth and latency can have an impact on the runtime of the application, but the number of cycles necessary to reach the desired precision is proportional to the runtime and, given the same parameters and initial conditions, it is deterministic.

We measure the impact of a node failure with the relative overhead in the number of iterations or V-cycles necessary to reach convergence. We define the following metric: *relative overhead due to a node failure* $= \frac{i_f + i_r - i_0}{i_0}$, according to the definitions shown in Fig. 1.

Thus, the relative overhead reflects how many additional iterations are required to reach the target relative residual norm in comparison to a solver that did not suffer a node failure. A relative overhead of less than one means that the solver converges after a node failure to the correct solution in less iterations than what restarting the method would require.

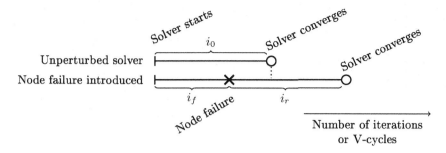

Fig. 1. Measurements used to define overhead metrics for CG and MG. The variable i_0 represents the number of iterations/V-cycles that an unperturbed solver requires to converge, i_f is the number of iterations/V-cycles before a node failure occurs, and i_r is the number of iterations/V-cycles to reach convergence after a node failure.

5   Experimental Results

Poisson Problem. Node failures cause a spike in the relative residual norm right after they occur. As depicted in Fig. 2, such a failure is not significant if it occurs soon enough during the solution process, when the error is not dominated by the loss of the information of the failing node but by the initial approximation.

A summary of the results is shown in Fig. 3. We see that the relative overhead of MG decreases linearly with the logarithm of the relative residual norm when the node failure was introduced.

The slope of the curves for MG is almost constant in all the cases. This is related to the reduction in the residual norm at a constant convergence rate depicted in Fig. 2. This rate of convergence is constant and depends on the eigenvalues of the matrix and the operators used in the method. Introducing an error in the MG solver sets the relative residual close to a "ceiling" value that depends on the size of the lost region, and from there, the relative residual norm continues its reduction at the same rate as before.

The relative residual norm at the start of the experiments is smaller in scenarios with a zero initial approximation, so the corresponding plots do not display failures introduced at larger residuals. The matrix of the problem increases the norm of vectors with high-frequency components. Therefore, we can expect this difference, because a starting vector composed of random values as we build it contains power in the high frequencies.

The overhead of MG is very high in experiments with a zero initial guess and where lost data is filled with zeros. This can be explained, again, with the spectrum of the matrix: Entering a region of zeros in the iterand will add high-frequency components that increase the residual norm by a large amount, above the residual for the initial guess of zeros. The time required to converge at a constant convergence rate is then longer than for the unperturbed problem.

For MG, the influence of the location of the failure is important only if the subdomain is reconstructed by filling with zeros. If linear interpolation is used, there is little variation in the curves between the left and the right columns of

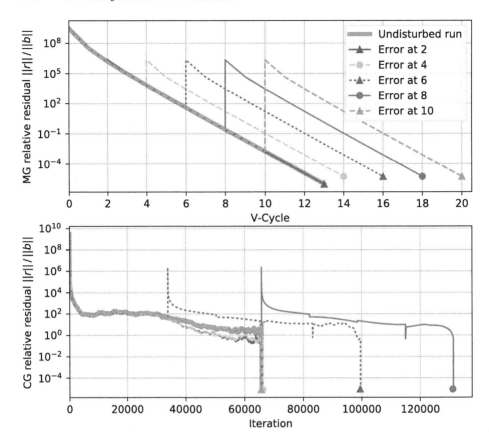

Fig. 2. A single case of the comparison between MG (above) and CG (below) for a problem size of $N = 2^{16} + 1$. The entries of the initial approximation to the solution are random, following a uniform distribution in $[-0.5, 0.5]$. A region of size 2^{14} is lost at the edge of the domain when the responsible node fails. The recovery strategy is to initialize the values in the affected region with zeros and resume the solver. The introduction of faults appear as spikes in the corresponding curve.

the plot. We have analytical results that show that, if the information of the lost nodes is reconstructed using linear interpolation and if the right-hand side is constant, the location of the lost subdomain does not affect the overhead for the Poisson problem. We cannot show details due to lack of space.

In general, the larger the region where the data is lost, the greater the overhead. There is an exception for MG if we set the values to zero for an index set in the middle of the domain. Then, the overhead for a large error in the center is slightly smaller.

The CG curves in Fig. 3 show very little variation for different sizes of the lost subdomain. In the experiments where the initial approximation is zero the behavior is similar for variations in all other parameters: The overhead is close to two (meaning that it takes about three times the number of iterations of the

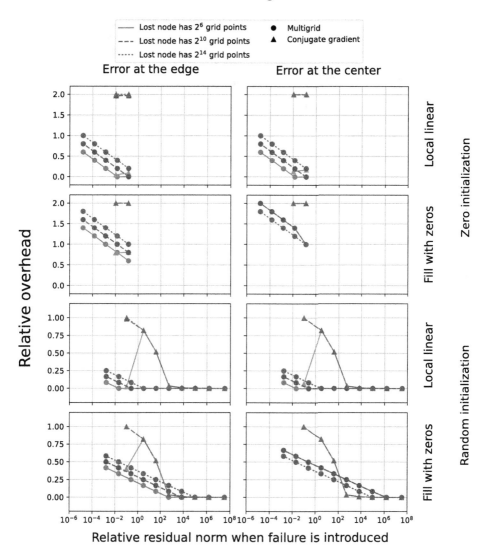

Fig. 3. Overhead of introducing node failures in the Poisson problem. Both CG and MG are represented. *Fill with zeros* and *Local linear* refer to the reconstruction of the lost values by setting them to zero and performing linear interpolation, respectively. Some of the curves overlap.

unperturbed solver to converge), and the solver remains in a narrow interval of relative residual norms before converging suddenly.

Other Test Problems. To test the influence of the preconditioner on the CG method, we run experiments using the Krylov solver facilities of PETSc. Summaries of the results are presented in Fig. 4, showing only results for the cases with a random initial guess.

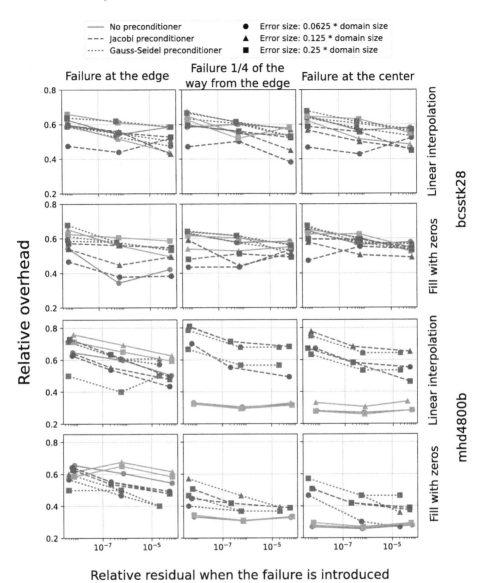

Fig. 4. Overhead of the methods for the matrices bcsstk28 and mhd4800b in comparison to their reference run, in which no node failures are introduced. All depicted experiments are started with a random initial guess, with values drawn from a uniform distribution in $[-0.5, 0.5]$. *Fill with zeros* and *Linear interpolation* refer to the reconstruction of the lost values by filling the values for the index set with zeros and performing linear interpolation, respectively.

Our first observation is that, for the two matrices, the overhead remains under one in all experiments. We see for matrix mhd4800b that, as the node failure moves to the center of the domain, performing linear interpolation actually increases the overhead of the solver. Also, when the node failure happens close to the center, the smallest overhead results from using no preconditioner.

Results for experiments with a zero vector as initial approximation are not shown due to lack of space, but they yield the same conclusions.

6   Conclusions

We have investigated some recovery strategies to be employed if a node in a parallel computer fails, represented by the loss of a contiguous set of indices in the approximation to the solution. We explored scenarios using conjugate gradient and geometric multigrid methods.

The results for the Poisson problem give an idea of the behavior of the solvers after recovering from node failures. For scenarios where a zero vector is the initial approximation to the solution, the closeness of the iterand to the solution has a great impact on the overhead caused by a node failure for the MG method, but it barely has an impact for CG. On the other hand, CG seems to be more sensitive to variations in the size of the index set of the lost node.

The relative overhead tends to be smaller if the initial guess is randomized. In this situation, the relative overhead caused by a node failure for the CG solver is not affected considerably by the size of the lost region, but increases if the failure occurs in later stages of the process and is, in general, greater than the relative overhead of MG.

Our experiments with more general test problems resulted in smaller relative overheads (below one). They also show that using no preconditioning produces a smaller relative overhead if the node failure happens closer to the center of the domain for one of our test matrices.

For some experiments on the Poisson problem, the relative overhead of MG is greater than the one of CG. We aim to explore more efficient recovery strategies for node failures for both methods.

Acknowledgement. This work has been supported by the Vienna Science and Technology Fund (WWTF) through project ICT15-113.

References

1. Agullo, E., Giraud, L., Guermouche, A., Roman, J., Zounon, M.: Towards resilient parallel linear Krylov solvers: recover-restart strategies. Research Report RR-8324, INRIA, July 2013
2. Agullo, E., Giraud, L., Guermouche, A., Roman, J., Zounon, M.: Numerical recovery strategies for parallel resilient Krylov linear solvers. Numer. Lin. Algebra Appl. **23**(5), 888–905 (2016)
3. Ainsworth, M., Glusa, C.: Is the multigrid method fault tolerant? The two-grid case. SIAM J. Sci. Comput. **39**(2), C116–C143 (2017)

4. Altenbernd, M., Göddeke, D.: Soft fault detection and correction for multigrid. Int. J. High Perform. Comput. Appl. (2017). https://doi.org/10.1177/1094342016684006

5. Balay, S., Abhyankar, S., Adams, M.F., Brown, J., Brune, P., Buschelman, K., Dalcin, L., Eijkhout, V., Gropp, W.D., Kaushik, D., Knepley, M.G., McInnes, L.C., Rupp, K., Smith, B.F., Zampini, S., Zhang, H., Zhang, H.: PETSc users manual. Technical report ANL-95/11 - Revision 3.7, Argonne National Laboratory (2016)

6. Balay, S., Gropp, W.D., McInnes, L.C., Smith, B.F.: Efficient management of parallelism in object oriented numerical software libraries. In: Arge, E., Bruaset, A.M., Langtangen, H.P. (eds.) Modern Software Tools in Scientific Computing, pp. 163–202. Birkhäuser Press, Boston (1997). https://doi.org/10.1007/978-1-4612-1986-6_8

7. Briggs, W., Henson, V., McCormick, S.: A Multigrid Tutorial, 2nd edn. SIAM, Philadelphia (2000)

8. Casas, M., de Supinski, B.R., Bronevetsky, G., Schulz, M.: Fault resilience of the algebraic multi-grid solver. In: Proceedings of the 26th ACM International Conference on Supercomputing, ICS 2012, pp. 91–100. ACM (2012)

9. Davis, T.A., Hu, Y.: The University of Florida sparse matrix collection. ACM Trans. Math. Softw. **38**(1), 1:1–1:25 (2011)

10. Huang, K.H., Abraham, J.A.: Algorithm-based fault tolerance for matrix operations. IEEE Trans. Comput. **33**(6), 518–528 (1984)

11. Mishra, A., Banerjee, P.: An algorithm-based error detection scheme for the multigrid method. IEEE Trans. Comput. **52**(9), 1089–1099 (2003)

12. Saad, Y.: Iterative Methods for Sparse Linear Systems, 2nd edn. SIAM, Philadelphia (2003)

13. Sao, P., Vuduc, R.: Self-stabilizing iterative solvers. In: Proceedings of the Workshop on Latest Advances in Scalable Algorithms for Large-Scale Systems, ScalA 2013, pp. 4:1–4:8. ACM (2013)

14. Snir, M., Wisniewski, R.W., Abraham, J.A., Adve, S.V., Bagchi, S., Balaji, P., Belak, J., Bose, P., Cappello, F., Carlson, B., Chien, A.A., Coteus, P., DeBardeleben, N.A., Diniz, P.C., Engelmann, C., Erez, M., Fazzari, S., Geist, A., Gupta, R., Johnson, F., Krishnamoorthy, S., Leyffer, S., Liberty, D., Mitra, S., Munson, T., Schreiber, R., Stearley, J., Hensbergen, E.V.: Addressing failures in exascale computing. Int. J. High Perform. Comput. Appl. **28**(2), 129–173 (2014)

15. Trottenberg, U., Oosterlee, C.W., Schüller, A.: Multigrid. Academic Press, Cambridge (2001)

It's Not the Heat, It's the Humidity: Scheduling Resilience Activity at Scale

Patrick M. Widener[✉], Kurt B. Ferreira, and Scott Levy

Sandia National Laboratories, Center for Computing Research,
Albuquerque, NM, USA
{pwidene,kbferre,sllevy}@sandia.gov

Abstract. Maintaining the performance of high-performance computing (HPC) applications with the expected increase in failures is a major challenge for next-generation extreme-scale systems. With increasing scale, resilience activities (e.g. checkpointing) are expected to become more diverse, less tightly synchronized, and more computationally intensive. Few existing studies, however, have examined how decisions about scheduling resilience activities impact application performance. In this work, we examine the relationship between the duration and frequency of resilience activities and application performance. Our study reveals several key findings: (i) the aggregate amount of time consumed by resilience activities is not an effective metric for predicting application performance; (ii) the duration of the interruptions due to resilience activities has the greatest influence on application performance; shorter, but more frequent, interruptions are correlated with better application performance; and (iii) the differential impact of resilience activities across applications is related to the applications' inter-collective frequencies; the performance of applications that perform infrequent collective operations scales better in the presence of resilience activities than the performance of applications that perform more frequent collective operations. This initial study demonstrates the importance of considering *how* resilience activities are scheduled. We provide critical analysis and direct guidance on how the resilience challenges of future systems can be met while minimizing the impact on application performance.

Keywords: Resilience · Scheduling · Performance · Collectives

1 Introduction

Fault tolerance is a key challenge to building exascale systems. Next-generation systems are projected to have dramatically higher node counts than today's

---

Sandia National Laboratories is a multimission laboratory managed and operated by National Technology and Engineering Solutions of Sandia, LLC., a wholly owned subsidiary of Honeywell International, Inc., for the U.S. Department of Energy's National Nuclear Security Administration under contract DE-NA0003525.

D. B. Heras and L. Bougé (Eds.): Euro-Par 2017 Workshops, LNCS 10659, pp. 581–592, 2018.
https://doi.org/10.1007/978-3-319-75178-8_47

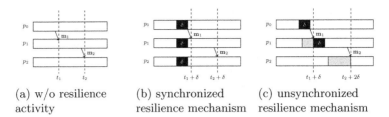

(a) w/o resilience   (b) synchronized   (c) unsynchronized
activity   resilience mechanism   resilience mechanism

Fig. 1. Example of how delays introduced by unsynchronized resilience mechanisms may propagate along application communication dependencies. The processes p_1, p_2, and p_3 exchange two messages m_1 and m_2 in each of the three scenarios. The black regions marked with a white δ denote the execution of coordinated (subfigure (b)) and uncoordinated (subfigure (c)) resilience activities. The grey regions denote periods in which the execution of a process is stalled due to an unsatisfied communication dependency.

largest systems. The complexity and component count of individual nodes are also projected to grow. These two trends mean that future systems will experience more frequent failures than current systems. Moreover, power optimizations (e.g., decreases in supply voltages) may further increase failure rates. Advances in component technology and system design mean that these systems may fail in new and different ways. In addition to fail-stop faults (e.g., node failure), Byzantine faults [18] due to silent data corruption may also be prevalent [3].

Currently, coordinated checkpoint/restart (cCR) [5] is the most commonly-used method for addressing failures on large-scale HPC systems. However, because the overhead of cCR grows as systems increase in size there is concern that cCR will no longer be a viable option for exascale systems [6]. First, the overhead of coordinating among application processes to determine when to take a checkpoint is expected to be prohibitive. Second, cCR (and checkpoint/restart in general) is only capable of handling fail-stop faults; by itself, it is not able recover from silent errors that may cause the application to produce incorrect results. Finally, as failures become more frequent, resilient operation may require a non-trivial amount of on-node computation to ensure that the application can continue to make meaningful progress. The combination of these factors means that resilience methods on future systems will be more diverse, less tightly synchronized, and more computationally intensive.

Significant effort has been devoted to developing alternatives to cCR that are able to effectively address failures on next-generation systems [6,8,19]. However, few of these existing studies have examined how decisions about scheduling resilience activities may impact application performance. The mechanism by which independently-scheduled resilience activities affect application performance is analogous to the impact of operating system noise on HPC applications, *see e.g.*, [7]. Drawing on this analogy, Fig. 1 illustrates how applications may be affected by the degree to which resilience activities are synchronized across processes. Figure 1a represents the execution of a simple application running without resilience on three processes: p_0, p_1, and p_2. Time progresses from left to right. These processes exchange two messages, m_1 and m_2, at times t_1 and t_2, respectively. For the purposes of this discussion, we assume that these messages represent tight dependencies: the receiving process will immediately stall if the expected message is delayed. Figure 1b shows how the application's execution is affected when the delays introduced by resilience are perfectly synchronized. Because each process is delayed by the same amount at the same time, the inter-process timings are preserved. In contrast, Fig. 1c demonstrates the potential impact of allowing resilience mechanisms to execute in the absence of inter-process synchronization. For example, if the execution of the application on p_0 is delayed by the execution of a fault tolerance mechanism, then it may delay the transmission of message m_1. As a consequence, process p_1 stalls waiting for the arrival of this message. Moreover, this delay may ultimately propagate to process p_2 because of its dependency on communication from process p_1.

In this paper, we investigate how decisions about scheduling resilience activities affect application performance. Specifically, our initial study yields several key findings:

– The aggregate amount of time spent on resilience activities is not an effective metric for predicting application performance at scale (Sect. 3.1).
– The duration of interruptions due to resilience activities has the greatest influence on application performance; shorter, but more frequent, interruptions are correlated with better application performance (Sect. 3.1).
– The differential impact of resilience activities across applications is related to the applications' inter-collective frequencies; the performance of applications that perform infrequent collective operations scales better in the presence of resilience activities than the performance of applications that perform more frequent collective operations (Sect. 3.2).

This study of the importance of considering *how* resilience activities are scheduled has wide-ranging implications for fault-tolerant computing in general. It also provides critical analysis and direct guidance on how the resilience challenges of future systems can be met while ensuring that overheads remain tolerable.

2   Experimental Approach

2.1   Modeling Local Checkpoint/Restart

In general, the communication structure of Message Passing Interface (MPI) programs cannot be determined offline because message matches cannot be established statically [2]. This makes modeling application performance analytically challenging even if all parameters of the application (e.g., the complete communication structure and all relative inter-process timings) are known. We therefore use a validated discrete-event simulation framework to evaluate the impact of local checkpointing activities on the performance of real applications.

Our simulation-based approach models checkpointing activities as CPU detours: periods of time during which the CPU is taken from the application and used to compute and commit checkpoint data. This approach allows a level of fidelity and control not always possible in implementation-based approaches. It also allows us to examine simulated systems much larger than those generally available.

Our simulation framework is based on LogGOPSim [13] and the tool chain developed by Levy et al. [20]. LogGOPSim uses the LogGOPS model, an extension of the well-known LogP model [4], to account for the temporal cost of communication events. An application's communication events are generated from traces of the application's execution. These traces contain the sequence of MPI operations invoked by each application process. LogGOPSim uses these traces to reproduce all communication dependencies, including indirect dependencies between processes which do not communicate directly.

LogGOPSim can also extrapolate traces from small application runs; a trace collected by running the application with p processes can be extrapolated to simulate performance of the application running with $k \cdot p$ processes. The extrapolation produces exact communication patterns for MPI collective operations and approximates point-to-point communications [13]. The validation of LogGOPSim and its trace extrapolation features have been documented previously [13]. Similarly, its ability to accurately predict local checkpointing overheads has also been documented [8,20].

2.2   Simulating Different Resilience Schedules

To simulate the impact of depriving the application of CPU cycles in order to perform local resilience operations (like checkpoints), LogGOPSim accepts a *resilience activity trace*: an ordered list of events, expressed as the start time and duration of each event. We use three different aggregate resilience activity percentages (1%, 5%, and 10%), each representing an aggregate amount of computation time taken away from the application over the course of the entire run. These aggregate amounts are then scheduled along a spectrum from high frequency, low duration detours to low frequency, high duration detours. The sum total of noise in each schedule equals the given aggregate percentage.

We make two simplifying assumptions in our investigation. First, we assume no failures. While including failures would not change our overall message and results, we disregard them in order to better understand the measured overheads. Second, we assume no additional interference events occur in the run of the application (e.g. slowdowns due to true operating system noise).

In the remainder of the paper, we present results from simulation experiments based on the behavior of a set of four workloads. These workloads were chosen to be representative of scientific applications that are currently in use and computational kernels thought to be important for future extreme-scale computational science. They include:

– LAMMPS: A scientific application developed by Sandia National Laboratories to perform molecular dynamics simulations. For our experiments, we used the *Lennard-Jones*(LJ) and *2D crack* potentials [24].

- HPCCG: A conjugate gradient solver from the Mantevo suite of mini-applications [12].
- LULESH: An application that represents the behavior of a typical hydrocode [17].

LAMMPS is an important U.S. Department of Energy (DOE) application which runs for long periods of time on production machines and exhibits a range of different communication structures. HPCCG represents an important computational pattern in key HPC applications. LULESH is a proxy for important exascale applications developed by the DOE's Exascale Co-Design Center for Materials in Extreme Environments (ExMatEx).

3   Results and Discussion

Our experiments explored the effect of different strategies for scheduling resilience activities on the runtime of our chosen workloads. To make our results applicable across a wide range of resilience strategies and application requirements, we used three general classes of resilience-related activity. These classes are characterized by the percentage of total application runtime taken up by resilience activity; we studied cases where 1%, 5%, and 10% of application time was used.

For each case, we explored different representations of the actual resilience activity. While the total time taken for resilience might sum up to, say, 5% of application runtime, the *frequency* and *duration* of those activities can vary depending on overall resilience strategy, hardware capabilities, contention for storage, and other factors. We have explored the tradeoffs between frequency and duration in uncoordinated checkpointing systems in previous work [8,25]. We focused in these experiments, however, on modeling this tradeoff more abstractly.

We generated a *detour list* for a set of discrete frequency/duration combinations in each of the 1%, 5%, and 10% cases. A detour list consists of a set of pairs (*timestamp, duration*) indicating when each detour begins and how long it lasts, representing the particular frequency/duration tradeoff for a particular scenario. We then conducted simulations using execution traces of our chosen workloads and each detour list, simulating the execution of the workload in the presence of the indicated resilience activity pattern and (implicitly) amount. For each case, we simulated the effects of the following combinations of detour frequency and duration: 100 KHz/110 ns, 10 KHz/1.1 μs, 1 KHz/11 μs, 100 Hz/110 μs, and 10 Hz/1.1 ms. While not all of these combinations of detours and resilience activity amounts may represent conditions that occur in practice, our goal in this work is to explore the nature of the tradeoffs in this space rather than examine the effects of particular ones on applications or systems in detail.

We present results for all of our chosen workloads with 32Ki simulated processes, and due to technical constraints, for 3 workloads with 64Ki simulated processes[1].

---

[1] We use the binary prefixes defined by the International Electrotechnical Commission (IEC). For example, 1Ki processes denotes $2^{10} = 1024$ processes.

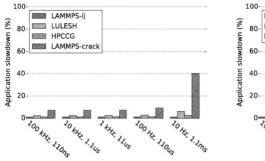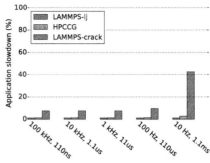

(a) 1% resilience activity, 32Ki processes.   (b) 1% resilience activity, 64Ki processes.

Fig. 2. 1% resilience activity with varying frequency/duration compositions.

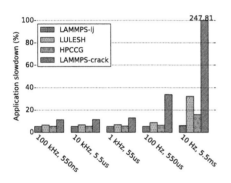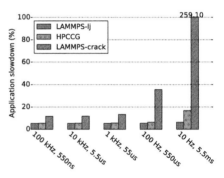

(a) 5% resilience activity, 32Ki processes.   (b) 5% resilience activity, 64Ki processes.

Fig. 3. 5% resilience activity with varying frequency/duration compositions. The bars for LAMMPS-crack at 10 Hz/5.5 ms in each plot have been truncated; the magnitude is displayed as an annotation in the plot.

3.1   Discussion

The results of our experiments are presented in Figs. 2, 3 and 4. These figures plot the total application time-to-solution slowdown for each scenario. The most general result of note from these figures is that each application behaves differently under each resilience activity schedule, with LAMMPS-crack showing the greatest impacts and LAMMPS-lj showing the least. Also of significance is that the composition of a resilience activity (the frequency and duration) has a greater effect on application runtime than does the aggregate amount of that resilience activity. This is easily visible in all of the cases (Figs. 2, 3 and 4), where increasing the duration of detours eventually results in significant slowdowns for all our tested workloads, even as the total time taken in detours remains the same. Similar results were observed at the two different simulated process counts we

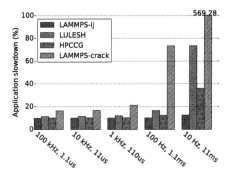 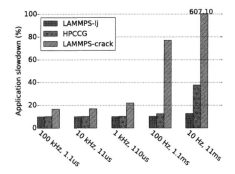

(a) 10% resilience activity, 32Ki processes.   (b) 10% resilience activity, 64Ki processes.

Fig. 4. 10% resilience activity with varying frequency/duration compositions. The bars for LAMMPS-crack at 10 Hz/11 ms in each plot have been truncated; the magnitude is displayed as an annotation in the plot.

studied, implying that the effect of increasing duration appears to be generally insensitive to application size.

Our results also raise the possibility that there may not be a strictly linear relationship between application slowdown and the proportion of runtime spent servicing each detour event. In other words, a factor of 5 increase in duration between two cases, does not imply a factor 5 overall slowdown in application performance. In fact, in most cases it is strictly less. Lastly, it is important to note that for each of the aggregate noise cases (1%, 5% and 10%), there exists a fine-grained schedule that significantly reduces overall impact and therefore can possibly be exploited by future applications.

3.2 Application Inter-collective Times

In this section, we examine the reasons behind the differential performance impact across applications described in the previous section. Specifically, we examine the relationship between application performance and the application's inter-collective period.

Figure 5 shows the discrete cumulative distribution functions (CDF) of the inter-collective periods for the MPI collective operations performed by each of our workloads. In this figure, a point at (x, y) indicates that, for a given application, at least $(x * 100)\%$ of the inter-collective times are smaller than y seconds. For example, Fig. 5d shows that for LULESH 100% of the inter-collective times for `MPI_Allreduce()` are less than 150 ms.

Our first observation is that `MPI_Allreduce()` is the most common collective operation for all four workloads. In fact, for LULESH and HPCCG, MPI_-

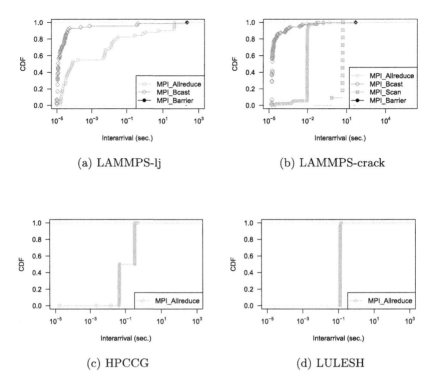

Fig. 5. Discrete cumulative distribution function (CDF) of the MPI collective inter-arrival time for each application. NOTE: the CDF for MPI_Barrier() is represented by a single point for both LAMMPS-crack and LAMMPS-lj because only two such operations occur during their execution.

Allreduce() is the only collective operation.[2] The next observation is that the frequency of MPI_Allreduce() varies significantly between applications:

- in HPCCG, the inter-collective times for MPI_Allreduce() are bimodal: approximately half are between 40 and 50 ms, and approximately half are between 300 and 500 ms;
- in LAMMPS-crack, 80% of the MPI_Allreduce() inter-collective times are between 9 and 10 ms, but there are also a small number inter-collective periods that exceed 150 ms;
- in LAMMPS-lj, half of the MPI_Allreduce() inter-collective times are between 10 and 100 ms, but more than 10% are in excess of 5 s; and
- in LULESH, all of the MPI_Allreduce() inter-collective times are approximately 100 ms.

---

[2] Although MPI_Allreduce() is the only collective operation that we observed in our experiments, the occurrence of MPI collective operations may depend on the inputs provided to the application.

We also observe from these CDFs that for the total aggregate noise cases, applications which perform more frequent collective operations are slowed down more by resilience activities that are longer in duration but occur less frequently. The exact interplay between inter-collective periods and resilience activity durations is beyond the scope of this paper, but is fertile ground for future investigation.

4   Related Work

In this paper, we study how the schedule of a general resilience mechanism can influence HPC application performance. To the best of our knowledge, no published works explicitly examine the influence of schedules. In this section we attempt to provide an overview of more loosely-related work.

Our study has origins in published research that characterizes application behavior in the presence of OS noise [7]. Collectively, this research shows that the pattern of OS noise events determines the impact on application performance and the benefits of coordination. Moreover, it shows that the duration of an OS noise event can significantly slowdown application performance.

Closely related, Ferreira et al. [8] studied the effects of communication on uncoordinated checkpointing at scale. This previous work makes a number of contributions that relate directly to the present paper. First, the authors show, contrary to previous work in the area, that a completely uncoordinated local checkpointing protocol can lead to significant application slowdown at scale. These local checkpoints can lead to process delays that can propagate through messaging relations (typically MPI collectives) to other processes causing a cascading series of delays. To ameliorate these slowdowns, the authors demonstrate how a hierarchical (or clustered) checkpointing approach [11] typically used to reduce message log volumes also can be effective at reducing impacts from local checkpoints. While our work has antecedents in this previous work, we investigate the role of fine-grained scheduling in reducing overheads for local resilience approaches.

Checkpoint/restart protocols in HPC systems have been extensively studied. There are many descriptions of the foundations of both coordinated and uncoordinated CR protocols available in the literature [16,21]. Beyond uCR and cCR, many other checkpoint/restart protocols have been proposed. Alvisi et al. examined the performance impact of coarse-grained communication patterns on the performance of three communication-induced checkpoint/restart (ciCR) algorithms [1]. ciCR uses the application's communication patterns to avoid checkpoints that cannot be used to recover a consistent global state. Hierarchical checkpointing attempts to group application processes into clusters that communicate frequently with each other [11,22]. cCR is used within a cluster and uCR plus message logging is used between clusters. Because the number of processes in a cluster is smaller than the total application, contention for filesystem resources is reduced. Also, because most of the communication is within a cluster, the volume of message log data is also reduced.

Significant research has been conducted on how to reduce checkpoint commit time. The approaches that have arisen out of this research include: compression [14], exploiting faster storage media [23], excluding unchanged memory contents from checkpoints [9,10], and de-duplication [15].

In this paper, we extend the results of these studies of checkpointing and general resilience mechanisms to examine how best to schedule these activities to reduce application performance. Specifically, we show that, as a whole, lowering the duration of each resilience event is more important to performance than decreasing the frequency.

5   Conclusion

Near-future HPC application developers will need to understand the performance implications of their design choices. This is especially true for applications implementing fault-tolerance strategies, as predicted scalability ceilings force exploration of alternate approaches. The work we describe in this paper contributes in several ways. We have presented a simulation-based approach for examining the tradeoffs between resilience activity duration and frequency, without regard to a particular resilience strategy. Our results reinforce earlier performance characterizations of uncoordinated checkpointing which suggested that detour duration has greater impact than detour frequency. This paper confirms this result for a range of frequency/duration compositions of a particular detour profile.

We intend to pursue several directions of future work based on this research. One is characterization of the relationship between the overall amount of resilience activity and the duration of detours for particular applications. *Can an application's communication pattern suggest, a priori, how resilience activities should be scheduled to minimize the impact on application performance?* We also plan to extend our study to additional workloads and a wider range of application sizes.

References

1. Alvisi, L., Elnozahy, E., Rao, S., Husain, S., de Mel, A.: An analysis of communication induced checkpointing. In: Twenty-Ninth Annual International Symposium on Fault-Tolerant Computing, 1999. Digest of Papers, pp. 242–249 (1999)
2. Bronevetsky, G.: Communication-sensitive static dataflow for parallel message passing applications. In: Proceedings of the 7th annual IEEE/ACM International Symposium on Code Generation and Optimization, pp. 1–12. IEEE Computer Society (2009)
3. Cappello, F., Geist, A., Gropp, W., Kale, S., Kramer, B., Snir, M.: Toward exascale resilience: 2014 update. Supercomput. Front. Innov. **1**(1) (2014). http://superfri. org/superfri/article/view/14
4. Culler, D., Karp, R., Patterson, D., Sahay, A., Schauser, K.E., Santos, E., Subramonian, R., von Eicken, T.: LogP: towards a realistic model of parallel computation. In: Proceedings of the Fourth ACM SIGPLAN Symposium on Principles and Practice of Parallel Programming, PPOPP 1993, pp. 1–12. ACM, New York (1993). https://doi.org/10.1145/155332.155333

5. Elnozahy, E.N., Alvisi, L., Wang, Y.M., Johnson, D.B.: A survey of rollback-recovery protocols in message-passing systems. ACM Comput. Surv. **34**(3), 375–408 (2002)

6. Ferreira, K., Riesen, R., Stearley, J., Laros III, J.H., Oldfield, R., Pedretti, K., Bridges, P., Arnold, D., Brightwell, R.: Evaluating the viability of process replication reliability for exascale systems. In: Proceedings of the ACM/IEEE International Conference on High Performance Computing, Networking, Storage, and Analysis, (SC 2011), November 2011

7. Ferreira, K.B., Bridges, P., Brightwell, R.: Characterizing application sensitivity to OS interference using kernel-level noise injection. In: Proceedings of the 2008 ACM/IEEE conference on Supercomputing, p. 19. IEEE Press (2008)

8. Ferreira, K.B., Levy, S., Widener, P., Arnold, D., Hoefler, T.: Understanding the effects of communication and coordination on checkpointing at scale. In: Proceedings of the International Conference for High Performance Computing, Networking, Storage and Analysis (SC 2014), pp. 883–894. IEEE Press (2014)

9. Ferreira, K.B., Riesen, R., Brighwell, R., Bridges, P., Arnold, D.: libhashckpt: hash-based incremental checkpointing using GPU's. In: Cotronis, Y., Danalis, A., Nikolopoulos, D.S., Dongarra, J. (eds.) EuroMPI 2011. LNCS, vol. 6960, pp. 272–281. Springer, Heidelberg (2011). https://doi.org/10.1007/978-3-642-24449-0_31

10. Gioiosa, R., Sancho, J.C., Jiang, S., Petrini, F., Davis, K.: Transparent, incremental checkpointing at kernel level: a foundation for fault tolerance for parallel computers. In: Proceedings of the 2005 ACM/IEEE Conference on Supercomputing, p. 9. IEEE Computer Society (2005)

11. Guermouche, A., Ropars, T., Brunet, E., Snir, M., Cappello, F.: Uncoordinated checkpointing without domino effect for send-deterministic MPI applications. In: International Parallel Distributed Processing Symposium (IPDPS), pp. 989–1000, May 2011

12. Heroux, M.A., Doerfler, D.W., Crozier, P.S., Willenbring, J.M., Edwards, H.C., Williams, A., Rajan, M., Keiter, E.R., Thornquist, H.K., Numrich, R.W.: Improving performance via mini-applications. Technical report, Sandia National Laboratories (2009)

13. Hoefler, T., Schneider, T., Lumsdaine, A.: LogGOPSim - simulating large-scale applications in the LogGOPS model. In: Proceedings of the 19th ACM International Symposium on High Performance Distributed Computing, pp. 597–604. ACM, June 2010

14. Ibtesham, D., Arnold, D., Bridges, P.G., Ferreira, K.B., Brightwell, R.: On the viability of compression for reducing the overheads of checkpoint/restart-based fault tolerance. In: 2012 41st International Conference on Parallel Processing (ICPP), pp. 148–157. IEEE (2012)

15. Islam, T.Z., Mohror, K., Bagchi, S., Moody, A., De Supinski, B.R., Eigenmann, R.: McrEngine: a scalable checkpointing system using data-aware aggregation and compression. In: 2012 International Conference for High Performance Computing, Networking, Storage and Analysis (SC), pp. 1–11. IEEE (2012)

16. Johnson, D.B., Zwaenepoel, W.: Recovery in distributed systems using asynchronous message logging and checkpointing. In: Proceedings of the Seventh Annual ACM Symposium on Principles of Distributed Computing, pp. 171–181 (1988)

17. Karlin, I., Bhatele, A., Chamberlain, B.L., Cohen, J., Devito, Z., Gokhale, M., Haque, R., Hornung, R., Keasler, J., Laney, D., Luke, E., Lloyd, S., McGraw, J., Neely, R., Richards, D., Schulz, M., Still, C.H., Wang, F., Wong, D.: LULESH programming model and performance ports overview. Technical report, LLNL-TR-608824, Lawrence Livermore National Laboratory, December 2012
18. Lamport, L., Shostak, R., Pease, M.: The Byzantine generals problem. ACM Trans. Program. Lang. Syst. (TOPLAS) 4(3), 382–401 (1982)
19. Levy, S., Ferreira, K.B., Bridges, P.G.: Improving application resilience to memory errors with lightweight compression. In: SC16: International Conference for High Performance Computing, Networking, Storage and Analysis, pp. 323–334. IEEE (2016)
20. Levy, S., Topp, B., Ferreira, K.B., Arnold, D., Hoefler, T., Widener, P.: Using simulation to evaluate the performance of resilience strategies at scale. In: 2013 SC Companion: High Performance Computing, Networking, Storage and Analysis (SCC). IEEE (2013)
21. Maloney, A., Goscinski, A.: A survey and review of the current state of rollback-recovery for cluster systems. Concurr. Comput. Pract. Exp. 21(12), 1632–1666 (2009)
22. Monnet, S., Morin, C., Badrinath, R.: A hierarchical checkpointing protocol for parallel applications in cluster federations. In: Proceedings of 18th International Parallel and Distributed Processing Symposium, p. 211. IEEE (2004)
23. Moody, A., Bronevetsky, G., Mohror, K., de Supinski, B.R.: Design, modeling, and evaluation of a scalable multi-level checkpointing system. In: Proceedings of the 2010 ACM/IEEE International Conference for High Performance Computing, Networking, Storage and Analysis (SC10), SC 2010, pp. 1–11. IEEE Computer Society, Washington, DC (2010). https://doi.org/10.1109/SC.2010.18
24. Plimpton, S.: Fast parallel algorithms for short-range molecular-dynamics. J. Comput. Phys. 117(1), 1–19 (1995)
25. Widener, P.M., Ferreira, K.B., Levy, S.: Horseshoes and hand grenades: the case for approximate coordination in local checkpointing protocols. In: Desprez, F. (ed.) Euro-Par 2016. LNCS, vol. 10104, pp. 623–634. Springer, Cham (2017). https://doi.org/10.1007/978-3-319-58943-5_50

ROME – Workshop on Runtime and Operating Systems for the Many-core Era

Fifth Workshop on Runtime and Operating Systems for the Many-core Era (ROME 2017)

Workshop Description

Since the beginning of the multicore era, parallel processing has become prevalent across the board. However, in order to continue a performance increase according to Moore's Law, a next step needs to be taken: away from common multicores towards innovative many-core architectures. Such systems, equipped with a significant higher number of cores per chip than multicores, pose challenges in both hardware and software design. On the hardware side, complex on-chip networks, scratchpads, hybrid memory cubes, non-volatile memory and stacked memory, as well as deep cache-hierarchies and novel cache-coherence strategies will enrich the current research areas in the future.

However, the ROME workshop (Runtime and Operating Systems for the Many-core Era) focuses on the software side because without complying system software, runtime and operating system support, all these new hardware facilities cannot be exploited. Hence, the new challenges in hardware/software co-design are to step beyond traditional approaches and to venture new programming models and operating system designs in order to exploit the theoretically available performance of future hardware as effectively and power-aware as possible.

For the fifth time already, the ROME workshop was held in conjunction with the Euro-Par annual series of international conferences. Appropriately for this milestone, this year's ROME workshop at the Euro-Par 2017 in Santiago de Compostela featured a lot of seminal and technical discussions and highly interesting presentations. The organizers were particularly very happy that Balazs Gerofi from the System Software Research Team of the RIKEN Advanced Institute for Computational Science volunteered to deliver the invited keynote talk about *Diverse Workloads need Specialized System Software: An approach of Multi-kernels and Application Containers*. In addition, a second invited talk, delivered by Michael Voss from Intel, enriched the regular workshop program composed of six selected paper presentations.

Upon the call for papers, the program committee received five contributions. Each submitted paper was assigned to at least four PC members for review and some particularly disputed papers were subject to even more reviews. The assignment of papers to reviewers was done according to the overall research interests and expertise of each PC member. The reviewers were encouraged to give a detailed review in order to justify their vote. The final acceptance/rejection decision was discussed and appointed by the workshop organizers and was based on the weighted scores assigned by the reviewers. Eventually, four high-quality papers could be accepted for presentation in two sessions at the workshop. In addition, two further paper presentations were moved from the canceled PISCES workshop (Processors, Interconnects, Storage and Caches for Exascale Systems) to a third session led by the ROME workshop chairs.

Program Chairs

Stefan Lankes   RWTH Aachen University
Carsten Clauss   ParTec Cluster Competence Center GmbH

Program Committee

Jens Breitbart   TU München
Carsten Clauss   ParTec Cluster Competence Center GmbH
Florian Kluge   Universität Augsburg
Stefan Lankes   RWTH Aachen University
Timothy G. Mattson   Intel Labs
Jörg Nolte   BTU Cottbus
Lena Oden   Argonne National Laboratory
Antonio J. Peña   Barcelona Supercomputing Center
Swann Perarnau   Argonne National Laboratory
Andreas Polze   Hasso-Plattner-Institute
Pablo Reble   RWTH Aachen University
Bettina Schnor   University of Potsdam
Oliver Sinnen   University of Auckland
Christian Terboven   RWTH Aachen University
Josef Weidendorfer   TU München
Carsten Weinhold   TU Dresden

Additional Reviewers

Steffen Christgau   University of Potsdam
Randolf Rotta   BTU Cottbus

Program Chairs of PISCES Workshop

Julio E. Sahuquillo   Universidad Politécnica de Valencia, Spain
Manuel E. Acacio   University of Murcia, Spain

Reviewers of PISCES Papers

Manuel E. Acacio
Francisco Alfaro
Pierfrancesco Flogia
Salvador Petit
Juan Piernas
Antonio Portero

Data Partitioning Strategies for Stencil Computations on NUMA Systems

Frank Feinbube, Max Plauth$^{(\boxtimes)}$, Marius Knaust, and Andreas Polze

Operating Systems and Middleware Group,
Hasso Plattner Institute for Software Systems Engineering,
University of Potsdam, Potsdam, Germany
{frank.feinbube,max.plauth,marius.knaust,
andreas.polze}@hpi.uni-potsdam.de

Abstract. Many scientific problems rely on the efficient execution of stencil computations, which are usually memory-bound. In this paper, stencils on two-dimensional data are executed on NUMA architectures. Each node of a NUMA system processes a distinct partition of the input data independent from other nodes. However, processors may need access to the memory of other nodes at the edges of the partitions. This paper demonstrates two techniques based on machine learning for identifying partitioning strategies that reduce the occurrence of remote memory access. One approach is generally applicable and is based on an *uninformed search*. The second approach caps the search space by employing *geometric decomposition*. The partitioning strategies obtained with these techniques are analyzed theoretically. Finally, an evaluation on a real NUMA machine is conducted, which demonstrates that the expected reduction of the remote memory accesses can be achieved.

Keywords: NUMA · Stencil computation · Data partitioning

1 Introduction

Stencils on two-dimensional data are a major field of research. [2,6,16,19] Several scientific problems are solved with the help of stencils, ranging from image processing to fluid simulations. For instance, stencils are used to solve partial differential equations (PDEs) numerically [15] and linear equations with the *Jacobi method* [8]. Stencil computations iteratively update each cell of an input data matrix, using only a neighborhood of cells at a time to obtain the values. In real-world applications, this often leads to high computational intensities, which is why stencils are usually executed in a parallel fashion. Causing a high load on the memory channel, stencil computations are usually memory-bound.

Comprised of multiple processors and dedicated memory units, modern non-uniform memory access (NUMA) architectures facilitate massively data-parallel computations. With this set-up, processors can access their local memory fast and independently from other processors. Remote physical memory can still

© Springer International Publishing AG, part of Springer Nature 2018
D. B. Heras and L. Bougé (Eds.): Euro-Par 2017 Workshops, LNCS 10659, pp. 597–609, 2018.
https://doi.org/10.1007/978-3-319-75178-8_48

be accessed via inter-chip interconnects. However, *remote* memory access bears higher latencies and reduced bandwidth.

When executed on NUMA architectures, stencil computations require that the input data grid is *partitioned* such that each processor can perform a distinct portion of the computation in parallel to one another. When a processor updates cells at the border of its data partition, neighboring cells might not be located in the node's local memory. Hence, expensive access to remote data partitions is inevitable. The number of remote memory accesses is greatly influenced by the specific *shape* of the partitions, which raises the question which partitionings are most suitable for stencil computations on NUMA systems.

This work aims at finding partitionings that reduce the occurrence of remote memory access on modern NUMA systems. For this purpose, a technique based on evolutionary algorithms is devised to search for optimized partitionings. Building on this approach, a second technique is developed that solves the partitioning problem geometrically. Based on findings from experiments with the two techniques, the partitionings are elucidated further from a theoretical perspective. Finally, a practical evaluation on a real NUMA hardware shows that the number of remote memory accesses can indeed be decreased with the presented approaches.

The remainder of the paper is organized as follows: Sect. 2 presents related work. Section 3 describes two approaches how machine learning can be applied to acquire suitable data partitionings. Section 4 provides a theoretical analysis of the communication cost and compares the state of the art partitioning to the proposed partitioning for 5-point stencils. Section 5 assesses the performance on a four-node NUMA system. Finally, Sect. 6 summarizes this paper and highlights key results.

2   Related Work

Here, we provide a brief overview of preceding work dealing with performance optimization techniques for stencil computations and NUMA systems. At an abstract level, *vectorization* [6] and *blocking* [19] are the two general approaches for optimizing stencil computations. Nguyen et al. combined both spatial and temporal blocking to optimize stencil computations [11]. Dursun et al. concluded that the advantage of blocking is highly dependent on finding the right block size [4]. Strzodka et al. introduced an approach called CORALS, which combines temporal blocking with vectorization [18]. Shaheen and Strzodka analyzed the effect of CORALS on NUMA systems [16]. However, the approach turns out not to be scalable on NUMA architectures.

Datta conducted research on stencil code optimizations and provided basic recommendations for NUMA systems [2]. Plauth et al. evaluated methods for introducing NUMA-awareness to the SIFT algorithm, which also employs stencil computations [13]. In a subsequent project, these findings resulted in a framework that assists C++ developers in maintaining NUMA-awareness, however the focus has shifted away from stencil computations [5].

Partition Shapes. An alternative way to approach performance optimization is to focus on the communication cost by optimizing the shape of the input data partitions.

In 1986, Reed et al. [14] studied the characteristics of rectangular, triangular, and hexagonal spatial partitionings. The authors defined computation as a function of a partition's area and communication as a function of the partition's perimeter. They found that for 5-point stencils, hexagonal partitions yield the highest ratio of computation to communication. The authors evaluate the partitionings and show that good performance can only be achieved when considering the combination of stencil, partitioning, and system architecture. In 1991, Abraham and Hudak [1] extended this research by introducing algorithms to automatically partition the input data based on rectangular and hexagonal shapes.

In 2010, Orozco et al. [12] studied a number of different tilings for stencil computations. They provided a proof that a diamond shaped partition has the optimal ratio of computation to communication and describe how input data can be partitioned accordingly for a system with 64 processors. Their performance evaluation demonstrated the efficiency and performance of the diamond tiling in comparison to the other partitioning approaches.

In 2014, DeFlumere [3] showed that – by the example of matrix multiplication algorithms – the optimal partitioning for large processor numbers is not optimal for smaller processor numbers or systems with heterogenous processors and systems with differing communication topologies.

Inspired by these findings, we studied the optimal partitionings for systems with a small number of computational nodes – such as processors or NUMA nodes. We show that while the optimal partitioning approach for large processor counts is known to be diamonds, a small number of processors or NUMA nodes require a different tiling.

3   Evolutionary Approaches

We discuss two approaches for applying machine learning to find suitable data partitioning strategies for stencil computations on NUMA systems. The first approach can be considered an *uninformed search*, which is applicable to a wide range of algorithms. The second approach takes the special characteristics of the 5-point stencil into account to produce a more efficient albeit less general solution by implementing a *geometric decomposition*.

Given *input matrices* of arbitrary type and a *latency matrix* indicating a NUMA topology, the evolutionary algorithms try to produce an optimal index range mapping matrix indices to NUMA nodes. Both approaches aim at minimizing the total occurrence of remote memory access in scenarios where the stencil computation is distributed across multiple NUMA nodes.

3.1   Uninformed Search

The *uninformed search* is suitable for various algorithms as it is provided with a function describing the *access pattern*. It is implemented as an evolutionary algorithm that works by iteratively selecting the best individual and then creating multiple mutations of it yielding the individuals of the next generation. An individual represents a system instance, which holds a collection of nodes and a partitioning. The individuals are rated by a cost function that iterates over each cell and, depending on the partitioning, lets the according node apply the access pattern (for instance, a stencil function), and counts remote accesses. The accumulated cost of remote accesses during an individual's simulation step represents its fitness value. The cost for performing the access on the corresponding remote node is based on the *latency matrix* of the NUMA topology. In the mutation step, new individuals are created based on the parent allocation by randomly exchanging cells with different processor assignments. Parallelization is achieved using the *parallel mode* of `libstd++`, which is a parallel implementation of most of the algorithms found in the C++ Standard Library.

Optimization Strategies. In order to speed up the evolutionary algorithm, some problem-specific optimizations are applied. Thereby, the resolution of the input data can be increased, which allows for the timely computation of partitionings with more nodes. In this implementation, an elitist selection is implemented by employing a Bernoulli distribution to decide whether the parent individuals should become part of the new generation or not.

With some states, performing single mutations always reduces the fitness value, while performing multiple mutations at once may result in a better partitioning. To overcome local minima, it is often necessary to mutate cells that are located close to each other. This is achieved by using a normal distribution around the first change to determine areas for the subsequent changes. In order to scale, the standard deviation of the distribution is inferred from the input data size and the number of nodes.

The algorithm sometimes moves away from the best partitioning instead of refining it, even when elitist selection is applied. While this is intended behavior to escape local minima, it might lead to a longer runtime, especially in the late phase when only refinements are required. A strategy to address this problem is to reset the population with mutations of the best known solution up to that point in time. These resets are performed based on the number of generations that have passed since the best known solution was replaced with a better one. Furthermore, the frequency of these resets is decreased when they do not lead to a successful outcome.

Results. As illustrated in Fig. 1, the results yielded by this approach corroborate the findings pointed out by Reed et al. [14], i.e. that diagonal partition borders are preferable since neighboring cells along diagonal borders share a common remote cell that both are accessing.

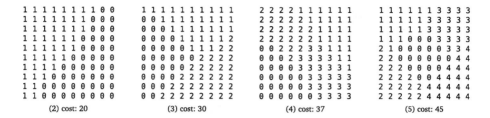

```
1 1 1 1 1 1 1 1 0 0      1 1 1 1 1 1 1 1 1 1      2 2 2 2 1 1 1 1 1 1      1 1 1 1 1 1 3 3 3 3
1 1 1 1 1 1 1 0 0 0      0 0 1 1 1 1 1 1 1 1      2 2 2 2 2 1 1 1 1 1      1 1 1 1 1 3 3 3 3 3
1 1 1 1 1 1 1 0 0 0      0 0 0 1 1 1 1 1 1 1      2 2 2 2 2 2 1 1 1 1      1 1 1 1 1 3 3 3 3 3
1 1 1 1 1 1 0 0 0 0      0 0 0 0 1 1 1 1 1 2      2 2 2 2 2 1 1 1 1 1      1 1 1 0 0 0 3 3 3 3
1 1 1 1 1 0 0 0 0 0      0 0 0 0 0 1 1 1 2 2      0 0 2 2 2 3 3 1 1 1      2 1 0 0 0 0 0 3 3 4
1 1 1 1 0 0 0 0 0 0      0 0 0 0 0 0 2 2 2 2      0 0 0 2 3 3 3 3 1 1      2 2 0 0 0 0 0 0 4 4
1 1 1 0 0 0 0 0 0 0      0 0 0 0 0 2 2 2 2 2      0 0 0 0 3 3 3 3 3 1      2 2 2 0 0 0 0 4 4 4
1 1 0 0 0 0 0 0 0 0      0 0 0 0 2 2 2 2 2 2      0 0 0 0 0 3 3 3 3 3      2 2 2 0 0 4 4 4 4 4
1 1 0 0 0 0 0 0 0 0      0 0 0 2 2 2 2 2 2 2      0 0 0 0 0 3 3 3 3 3      2 2 2 2 4 4 4 4 4 4
1 1 0 0 0 0 0 0 0 0      0 0 2 2 2 2 2 2 2 2      0 0 0 0 0 0 3 3 3 3      2 2 2 2 4 4 4 4 4 4
    (2) cost: 20              (3) cost: 30              (4) cost: 37              (5) cost: 45
```

Fig. 1. Partitionings yielded using *uninformed search* for a 5-point stencil on two to five nodes with fully-connected topology and square-shaped input data.

Unfortunately, the evolutionary technique reaches its limits soon with higher input data resolutions, which are necessary to find configurations with more nodes. Due to the search space explosion, partitionings with many nodes can hardly be represented without rasterization artifacts on smaller resolutions. Nevertheless, the experiments led to some interesting insights, which the *geometric decomposition* approach is taking advantage of.

3.2 Geometric Decomposition

To overcome the limitation imposed by the search space, the *geometric decomposition* works with geometric shapes instead of a raster of discrete cells. The idea is depicted in Fig. 2. In order to partition a given outline shape into polygons, a configurable number of straight lines are randomly placed to subdivide the space. The resulting fragments (referred to as *atomic polygons*) are then combined to as many shapes as there are NUMA nodes in the system. For this purpose, all combinations are evaluated to determine the best candidate. More optimized partitionings can be found by performing these steps multiple times with different random lines. To further refine the partitionings obtained using this technique, the geometric approach employs a local search.

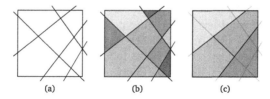

(a)   (b)   (c)

Fig. 2. Geometric approach: Random lines are generated (a) to fragment the space into *atomic polygons* (b), which are merged to match the node count (c).

To find the best partitioning given the initial randomly generated lines, a cost function is developed that expresses remote access to other nodes in a continuous, two-dimensional space. A consequence of this approach is that the areas of the partition shapes are not necessarily the same size. Therefore, not only the remote communication cost have to be minimized but also the variation between the area sizes. To improve the efficiency of our approach, we refine the best results by applying random changes to the angle and distance of the lines following the principle of simulated annealing [9].

To map the resulting shapes to an actual NUMA system, the shapes are converted to a discrete partitioning through rasterization.

Cost Function. The cost of remote communication in the geometric approach are caused by the *edges* shared by adjacent polygons with different labels. Mapped to cell grids, polygon edges can be seen as rasterized line segments spanning Δx cells horizontally and Δy cells vertically. Without loss of generality, assume that $\Delta x > 0$, $\Delta y > 0$, and $\Delta x \geq \Delta y$. Seen from the node having the lower right partition, there are $\Delta x + \Delta y$ remote accesses to the node having the upper left partition – in general, $|\Delta x| + |\Delta y|$. However, some of the remote accesses are performed *twice* and can hence be fetched from the cache. This always amounts to $\min(|\Delta x|, |\Delta y|)$ cached remote cost. Thus, the cost for remote access is:

$$|\Delta x| + |\Delta y| - \min(|\Delta x|, |\Delta y|) = \max(|\Delta x|, |\Delta y|) \tag{1}$$

When considering polygon edges as rasterized line segments of infinite resolution, the cost of a polygon edge $e = (p_1, p_2)$ becomes:

$$\text{cost}(e) = \text{cost}((p_1, p_2)) = \max(|p_{1,x} - p_{2,x}|, |p_{1,y} - p_{2,y}|) \tag{2}$$

Abraham and Hudak come to similar conclusions [1]. For a single atomic polygon $A = (e_1, e_2, \ldots)$, the communication cost caused by remote accesses from *inside* the polygon is:

$$\text{cost}(A) = \sum_{e \in A} \text{cost}(e) \tag{3}$$

In principle, the remote communication cost of the *entire* geometric partitioning would be the sum of the cost of all atomic polygons. However, some edges could have been subject to merging polygons in order to match the number of available nodes. Figure 3a indicates merged edges using the same color for adjacent polygons. The cost of these merged edges $m_1, m_2, \ldots$ have to be subtracted from the total remote communication cost – once for each of both adjacent atomic polygons. Additionally, the border edges of the outline shape do not contribute any cost, as accesses are neither performed from inside the outline shape to the outside nor the other way around. For this reason, the cost of the outline shape's border edges is subtracted as well.

With atomic polygons $\underline{A} = (A_1, A_2, \ldots)$, merged edges $M = (m_1, m_2, \ldots)$, and outline edges $O = (o_1, o_2, \ldots)$, the total cost are then:

$$\text{cost}(\underline{A}, M, O) = \sum_{A \in \underline{A}} \text{cost}(A) - 2 * \sum_{m \in M} \text{cost}(m) - \sum_{o \in O} \text{cost}(o) \tag{4}$$

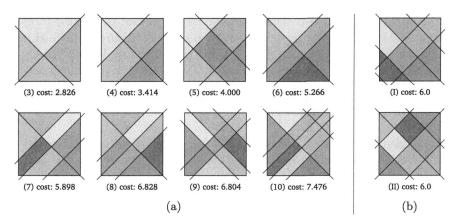

Fig. 3. The best partitionings found by the geometric approach for three to ten nodes (a). Two partitionings for eight nodes with diamond shapes (b).

Since the geometric approach does *not* guarantee that all partition shapes have the same area, the presented implementation uses a *score* function to simultaneously minimize the cost function as well as the variation between the partition shapes' areas. Assuming the areas of the smallest and biggest shape are $\mathrm{area_{min}}(\underline{A}, M)$ and $\mathrm{area_{max}}(\underline{A}, M)$, respectively, the total score is defined as:

$$\mathrm{score}(\underline{A}, M, O) = \mathrm{cost}(\underline{A}, M, O) * \frac{\mathrm{area_{max}}(\underline{A}, M)}{\mathrm{area_{min}}(\underline{A}, M)} \qquad (5)$$

Results. Figure 3a shows the best partitionings found for three to ten nodes on square-shaped data when *only diagonal lines* were used. Diagonal lines were used since they have lowest remote communication cost – while the restriction improves the efficiency of the geometric approach.

Notably, the results for three to five nodes almost match the results obtained with the uninformed search. In the experiments, two patterns recurred frequently: a two-part stripe pattern and a diamond pattern.

Two-Part Diagonal Stripe Pattern. An interesting finding is that all partitionings with an even number of nodes seem to follow a similar pattern. The partition shapes form diagonal stripes, each cut in half by a single diagonal line that ranges from one corner to the opposite one.

Diamond Pattern. For configurations with eight nodes, two better results exist. When allowing the algorithm to generate more random lines, the patterns in Fig. 3b emerge. It is interesting to observe that in these cases, triangular shapes in the corners and diamond-like structures in the middle seem to be preferable.

Hierarchical Application. The geometric technique can be applied to hierarchical NUMA topologies. In such cases, each partition is further divided into sub-partitions, using the same approach. Using this technique, large NUMA systems with hierarchical topologies (such as the SGI UV300H [17]) can be handled.

4   Theoretical Analysis

In this section, we provide a theoretical analysis of the partitionings observed in Sect. 3. Optimal communication cost is obtained when maximizing the area of the partitions in relation to the perimeter. When rectangular partition shapes are assumed, squares are the optimal rectangular partitioning for 5-point stencils [14]. However, partitioning a given outline with just squares is only possible for n NUMA nodes with $n = k^2$ for some $k \in \mathbb{N}^+$.

For our four-node test system, a square-based partitioning is trivial: Each shape is circumvented by four edges of length $\frac{a}{2}$, where a is the side length of the two-dimensional input matrix. Each edge amounts to the cost of a ($\frac{a}{2}$ once for both of the adjacent squares). The total cost are $\text{cost} = 4\left(2 * \frac{a}{2}\right) = 4a$.

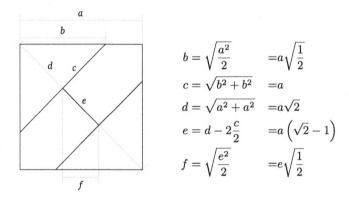

$$b = \sqrt{\frac{a^2}{2}} \qquad = a\sqrt{\frac{1}{2}}$$

$$c = \sqrt{b^2 + b^2} \qquad = a$$

$$d = \sqrt{a^2 + a^2} \qquad = a\sqrt{2}$$

$$e = d - 2\frac{c}{2} \qquad = a\left(\sqrt{2} - 1\right)$$

$$f = \sqrt{\frac{e^2}{2}} \qquad = e\sqrt{\frac{1}{2}}$$

Fig. 4. Pattern yielded by the geometric approach, labeled with length ratios.

Next, we consider the non-rectangular four-node pattern with the lowest cost yielded by the geometric approach (see Fig. 4). As shown in Eq. 6, the communication cost amount to $3.414a$, which is less than the cost of the *rectangular partitioning* ($4a$). Notice that this calculation expects caching to be present. As only diagonal lines occur in the pattern, both projections would have the same length.

$$\text{cost} = 2 * b + 2 * (b + f) = \left(\sqrt{2} + 2\right)a = 3.414a \qquad (6)$$

5   Evaluation

Here, we evaluate the approaches presented in Sect. 3 using a fully connected four-node NUMA system (see Table 1) with a 5-point cross-type stencil being applied to square-shaped data. This evaluation is based on the partitionings discussed in Sect. 4. Based on the theoretical analysis, we expect that the remote access cost of the partitioning pattern roughly amount to about 85% (based on the ratio $\frac{3.414a}{4.0a}$) of the cost of the rectangular reference partitioning.

Table 1. Detailed specifications of the reference system.

	HPE ProLiant DL580 G9 Server
CPU	4 × Intel Xeon E7-8890 v3 (Haswell), 18C/36T, 2.5 GHz
Memory	16 × 8 GB DDR4-1600 reg. ECC DIMM
Topology	4 Sockets, Fully interconnected, RMA Penalty: ca. 1.4 [7]

To verify this hypothesis, the number of remote accesses is counted while performing the stencil computation. In order to reduce noise in the measurement, the simulation of the stencil operation only performs the memory accesses without executing the actual computation.

5.1   Method of Measurement

While the stencil operation is not required to be computed for evaluation purposes, it is important to make sure that memory accesses are still performed. In particular, the compiler must not optimize any memory access away. To have full control over the implementation inline assembler is used.

To evaluate the effect of the refined partitioning, it necessary to count how many remote memory accesses are performed by the nodes. For this purpose, off-core hardware performance counters are used. To filter off-core response events, certain fields in the *model-specific registers* (MSR) have to be configured. With this mechanism at hand, it is possible to tailor a special filter suited to measuring memory accesses on remote nodes regarding data and not instructions. Linux perf is used to access the off-core performance counters.

In order to measure only the impact of the introduced partitioning pattern, it is necessary to eliminate all other factors on the number of remote memory accesses. For this reason, prefetchers are disabled in the evaluation, even though they would have an effect in practice. Furthermore, automatic NUMA balancing is disabled to make sure the Linux kernel does not interfere with the memory placement. Lastly, functions have been implemented that verify that thread bindings and memory allocations are performed as expected.

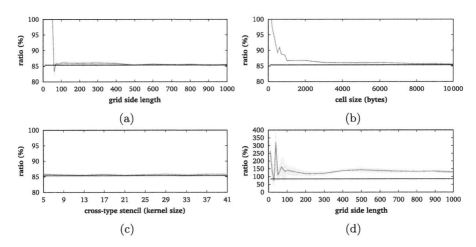

Fig. 5. For larger input grid sizes (a) and larger cell sizes (b), the theoretically computed improvement of the remote communication cost is achieved. Increasing the kernel size has no effect (c). However, when data is written locally, the cache coherence protocol introduces additional remote accesses (d).

5.2   Results

In our measurements, a 5-point cross-type stencil is applied to a two-dimensional input matrix. The geometric partitioning and the rectangular partitioning from Sect. 4 are both tested and the impact of input data grid size, cell size and kernel size are investigated.

Dimension of the Input Data Grid. The cell size was fixed at 10 kB, and the side length ranged from 10 to 1000 cells. The anticipated value of 85% is reached starting at resolutions of 100×100 (see Fig. 5a). This value cannot be obtained with smaller side lengths, presumably because the resolution is not high enough and introduces aliasing artifacts.

Variable Cell Size. The grid dimension is fixed to 1000×1000, and the cell size is varied from 10 to 10000 bytes. At around 3 kB, the expected improvement regarding the number of remote memory accesses is almost reached (see Fig. 5b). Additional investigations are necessary to identify why the improvements do not affect smaller cell sizes.

Kernel Size of the Cross-Type Stencil. A grid of 1000×1000 cells of size 5 kB is used and the stencil size ranges from 5 to 41 to evaluate the impact of the stencil size. The result shows that the kernel size does not influence the obtained improvement concerning the number of remote memory accesses (see Fig. 5c).

Additional Observations. When actual computations are performed, data is written locally in addition to reading remote data. This results in increased node-interconnect utilization, likely to be caused by cache coherency traffic among nodes (see Fig. 5d). To represent real world scenarios more accurately, the theoretical model needs to be extended to incorporate the remote accesses introduced by the cache coherency protocol.

Furthermore, the findings of this evaluation lead to the question which actual systems could benefit from the newly found partitioning patterns. Even with a well-suited system, the positive effects of the partitionings highly depend on the exact configuration, as Reed et al. [14] noticed as well. Partitioning patterns need to be tailored to the exact number of NUMA nodes and the caching behavior. Otherwise, applying the partitioning patterns can be counterproductive. While the *geometric decomposition* approach is more efficient, the flexibility of the *uninformed search* approach allows the consideration of further system characteristics, such as cache line sizes, in its fitness function.

6   Conclusions

With NUMA architectures, accesses to the memory of remote nodes bear higher latencies than local accesses. Multiple solutions were developed with the objective of finding data partitionings that reduce the demand of remote memory accesses during the execution of stencil operations.

First, an uninformed search technique based on evolutionary algorithms was developed. This approach was conceived to make as little assumptions about the data, memory access patterns, and the system configuration as possible. Even though the evolutionary technique is limited to small data grid resolutions due to the large search space, multiple recurring partitioning patterns could be observed. Building on these findings, a second, geometric approach was devised. This technique is based on the temporary assumption that the input data grid is a resolutionless, two-dimensional space. In this space, partitionings are searched for by fragmenting the space into simple, polygonal shapes. A new cost function was introduced in order to translate the concept of remote memory demands to this continuous representation. The implementations of each approach are available online[1]. They are discussed in detail in [10].

A novel partitioning pattern for a four-node NUMA system is identified, analysed and evaluated – showing the projected communication cost reduction to 85%. Furthermore the impact of various scaling factors was evaluated. To provide consistent performance improvements in real world scenarios, the influence of the cache coherency protocol has to be further investigated.

Acknowledgement and Disclaimer. This paper has received funding from the European Union's Horizon 2020 research and innovation programme 2014–2018 under grant agreement No. 644866. This paper reflects only the authors' views and the European Commission is not responsible for any use that may be made of the information it contains.

---

[1] https://gitlab.com/hpi-osm/stencil-partitioning.

References

1. Abraham, S.G., Hudak, D.E.: Compile-time partitioning of iterative parallel loops to reduce cache coherency traffic. IEEE Trans. Parallel Distrib. Syst. **2**(3), 318–328 (1991)
2. Datta, K.: Auto-tuning Stencil Codes for Cache-Based Multicore Platforms. Ph.D. thesis, University of California, Berkeley (2009)
3. DeFlumere, A.: Optimal partitioning for parallel matrix computation on a small number of abstract heterogeneous processors. Ph.D. thesis, University College Dublin (2014)
4. Dursun, H., Nomura, K.I., Wang, W., Kunaseth, M., Peng, L., Seymour, R., Kalia, R.K., Nakano, A., Vashishta, P.: In-core optimization of high-order stencil computations. In: PDPTA, pp. 533–538 (2009)
5. Hagen, W., Plauth, M., Eberhardt, F., Polze, A.: PGASUS: a framework for C++ application development on NUMA architectures. In: 2016 Fourth International Symposium on Computing and Networking (CANDAR), pp. 368–374. IEEE, Hiroshima, November 2016
6. Henretty, T., Veras, R., Franchetti, F., Pouchet, L.N., Ramanujam, J., Sadayappan, P.: A stencil compiler for short-vector SIMD architectures. In: Proceedings of the 27th International ACM Conference on International Conference on Supercomputing, pp. 13–24. ACM (2013)
7. Hewlett-Packard Development Company: Red Hat Linux NUMA Support for HP ProLiant Servers. Technical report. (2013). Accessed 1 Feb 2017
8. Jacobi, C.G.J.: Über ein leichtes Verfahren die in der Theorie der Säcularstörungen vorkommenden Gleichungen numerisch aufzulösen. Journal für die reine und angewandte Mathematik **30**, 51–94 (1846)
9. Kirkpatrick, S., Vecchi, M.P., et al.: Optimization by simulated annealing. Science **220**(4598), 671–680 (1983)
10. Knaust, M.: Partitioning 2D Data for Stencil Computations on NUMA Systems. Master's thesis, Hasso Plattner Institute, University of Potsdam (2016)
11. Nguyen, A., Satish, N., Chhugani, J., Kim, C., Dubey, P.: 3.5-D blocking optimization for stencil computations on modern CPUs and GPUs. In: Proceedings of the 2010 ACM/IEEE International Conference for High Performance Computing, Networking, Storage and Analysis, pp. 1–13. IEEE Computer Society (2010)
12. Orozco, D., Garcia, E., Gao, G.: Locality optimization of stencil applications using data dependency graphs. In: Cooper, K., Mellor-Crummey, J., Sarkar, V. (eds.) LCPC 2010. LNCS, vol. 6548, pp. 77–91. Springer, Heidelberg (2011). https://doi.org/10.1007/978-3-642-19595-2_6
13. Plauth, M., Hagen, W., Feinbube, F., Eberhardt, F., Feinbube, L., Polze, A.: Parallel implementation strategies for hierarchical non-uniform memory access systems by example of the scale-invariant feature transform algorithm. In: IEEE International Parallel and Distributed Processing Symposium Workshops, pp. 1351–1359. IEEE, Chicago, May 2016
14. Reed, D.A., Adams, L.M., Patrick, M.L.: Stencils and problem partitionings: their influence on the performance of multiple processor systems. IEEE Trans. Comput. **100**(7), 845–858 (1987)
15. Roth, G., Mellor-crummey, J., Kennedy, K., Brickner, R.G.: Compiling stencils in high performance Fortran. In: Supercomputing 1997: Proceedings of the 1997 ACM/IEEE conference on Supercomputing, pp. 1–20. ACM Press (1997)

16. Shaheen, M., Strzodka, R.: NUMA aware iterative stencil computations on many-core systems. In: 2012 IEEE 26th International Parallel and Distributed Processing Symposium (IPDPS), pp. 461–473. IEEE (2012)
17. Silicon Graphics International Corp: SGI UV 300H for SAP HANA (2015)
18. Strzodka, R., Shaheen, M., Pajak, D., Seidel, H.P.: Cache oblivious parallelograms in iterative stencil computations. In: Proceedings of the 24th ACM International Conference on Supercomputing, pp. 49–59. ACM (2010)
19. Wellein, G., Hager, G., Zeiser, T., Wittmann, M., Fehske, H.: Efficient temporal blocking for stencil computations by multicore-aware wavefront parallelization. In: 33rd Annual IEEE International Computer Software and Applications Conference, COMPSAC 2009, vol. 1, pp. 579-586. IEEE (2009)

Delivering Fairness on Asymmetric Multicore Systems via Contention-Aware Scheduling

Adrian Garcia-Garcia⬤, Juan Carlos Saez(✉)⬤, and Manuel Prieto-Matias⬤

Facultad de Informática, Complutense University of Madrid, Madrid, Spain
{adriagar,jcsaezal,mpmatias}@ucm.es

Abstract. Asymmetric single-ISA multicore processors (AMPs), which integrate high-performance big cores and low-power small cores, were shown to deliver better energy efficiency than symmetric multicores for diverse workloads. Previous work has highlighted that this potential of AMP systems can be realizable with help from the OS scheduler. Notably, delivering fairness on AMPs still constitutes an important challenge, as it requires the scheduler to accurately track the progress of each thread as it runs on the various core types throughout the execution. In turn, this progress depends on the speedup that an application derives on a big core relative to a small one. While existing fairness-aware schedulers take application relative speedup into consideration when tracking progress, they do not cater to the performance degradation that may occur naturally due to contention on shared resources among cores, such as the last-level cache or the memory bus. In this paper, we propose CAMPS, a contention-aware fair scheduler for AMPs. Our experimental evaluation, which employs real asymmetric hardware and scheduler implementations in the Linux kernel, demonstrates that CAMPS improves fairness by 10.6% on average with respect to a state-of-the-art fairness-aware scheme, while delivering higher throughput.

Keywords: Asymmetric multicore · OS scheduling · Fairness
Linux kernel

1 Introduction

Previous research has shown that asymmetric single-ISA (instruction set architecture) multicore processors (AMPs), which integrate a mix of complex high-performance big cores and power-efficient small cores on the same chip, can deliver higher performance per watt than their symmetric counterparts for diverse workloads [8,15]. To bring the potential of AMPs to unmodified applications, the operating system has to face a number of challenges [9], some of which must be properly addressed by the OS scheduler [10].

Most asymmetry-aware schedulers have been designed to optimize the system throughput for multi-application workloads [3,7,8,12]. To this end, the scheduler must devote big cores to running applications that use these cores efficiently,

© Springer International Publishing AG, part of Springer Nature 2018
D. B. Heras and L. Bougé (Eds.): Euro-Par 2017 Workshops, LNCS 10659, pp. 610–622, 2018.
https://doi.org/10.1007/978-3-319-75178-8_49

since they derive performance improvements (speedup) relative to running on small cores [8]. Further throughput gains can be obtained by using big cores to accelerate different scalability bottlenecks present in parallel programs [6, 12].

Unfortunately, asymmetry-aware schedulers that strive to optimize throughput alone are known to be inherently unfair [14]. Unfairness gives rise to a number of undesirable effects on multicore systems [5, 18]. For example, equal-priority applications may not experience the same performance degradation (slowdown) when running together relative to the performance observed when each application runs alone on the AMP. Moreover, when attempting to optimize throughput, the completion time of an application on an AMP may largely depend on its co-runners [14]. These issues make priority-based scheduling policies ineffective, reduce performance predictability, and can lead to wrong billings in commercial cloud-like computing services, where users are charged for CPU hours.

These QoS-related issues can be addressed on AMPs via fairness-aware scheduling algorithms [3, 9, 14, 16]. Most of these algorithms rely on tracking the progress that individual threads make when running on the various core types throughout the execution, and attempt to deliver fairness by swapping threads between different cores based on the observed progress. In tracking progress, existing schedulers [14, 16] factor in the slowdown that a thread experiences when it is mapped to a small core, which can differ greatly across applications and vary over time as a program goes through different execution phases [3, 12]. Notably, these schedulers do not consider the performance degradation that comes from contention on the shared resources among cores, which may also lead to unfairness [5, 20]. In current AMP hardware [2, 4], clusters of cores of the same type typically share a last-level cache and other memory-related resources. Applications running on the various cores may contend for shared resources, which could degrade their performance in an uneven and unpredictable way [5, 18–20].

To address this shortcoming, we propose CAMPS, an OS-level contention-aware scheduler for AMPs that seeks to optimize fairness while maintaining acceptable throughput. CAMPS is equipped with a novel mechanism to approximate a thread's current slowdown, which leverages past performance history gathered at runtime in low contention scenarios. Unlike other schedulers, CAMPS does not need special hardware extensions [16] or platform-specific prediction models [7, 12, 14] to function. Instead, it relies on performance counters available in commercial hardware, which makes the scheduler highly portable across architectures. To assess the effectiveness of our proposal, we implemented it in the Linux kernel and evaluated it on a real AMP platform that features an ARM big.LITTLE processor [2]. Our analysis reveals that CAMPS improves fairness by 10.6% on average compared to a state-of-the-art fairness-aware scheduling scheme [14], and at the same time improves throughput by up to 17%.

The rest of the paper is organized as follows. Section 2 motivates our proposal and discusses related work. Section 3 outlines the design of the CAMPS scheduler. Section 4 showcases our experimental results and Sect. 5 concludes.

2   Background and Related Work

In this section we first introduce the notion of fairness used in our work, and discuss the challenges associated with determining the slowdown at runtime. We then present a brief experimental study that showcases the main observation we exploit to determine the slowdown on-line on AMPs, and discuss related work.

2.1   Fairness on AMPs and Determining the Slowdown

Previous research on fairness for CMPs [5,18] and AMPs [6,14,16] define a scheme as fair if equal-priority applications in a multi-program workload suffer the same slowdown due to sharing the system. To cope with this notion of fairness, we turned to the lower-is-better *unfairness* metric [5]:

$$Unfairness = \frac{MAX(Slowdown_1, ..., Slowdown_n)}{MIN(Slowdown_1, ..., Slowdown_n)} \tag{1}$$

where n is the number of applications in the workload and $Slowdown_i = CT_{sched,i}/CT_{alone,i}$. In turn, $CT_{sched,i}$ denotes the completion time of application i under a given scheduler, and $CT_{alone,i}$ is the completion time of application i when running alone on the AMP (with all the big cores available).

The slowdown of an individual thread (or that of a single-threaded application) observed during a certain execution phase can be defined in terms of the number of instructions per second (IPS) as follows:

$$Slowdown = IPS_{alone}/IPS_{sched} \tag{2}$$

where IPS_{alone} represents the number of instructions per second observed for the specific phase when the thread runs alone on the system, and IPS_{sched} denotes the IPS achieved by the thread when it runs the same execution phase, but in the context of a multi-program workload under a given scheduling algorithm.

In this work, we assume that the IPS_{alone} on an AMP is maximized when the thread runs on a high-performance big core in isolation. That is the case across all the applications explored in our experiments. We should also highlight that in the context of multi-threaded programs, the IPS can be a somewhat misleading performance metric, since a thread can exhibit a high IPC when busy waiting (spinning) for other threads to arrive at a synchronization point (e.g. barrier). To make the OS scheduler aware of these situations, where threads do no useful work, our scheduling scheme leverages spin notifications from the user-level runtime system by following a similar approach to that proposed in [13].

Delivering fairness entails ensuring that the slowdown accumulated by the various application threads throughout the execution remains as even as possible [5,14,16,18], while maintaining acceptable throughput. To this end, the scheduler must be equipped with a mechanism to determine a thread's slowdown at runtime. However, measuring the slowdown directly by using Eq. 2 is difficult in practice; while a thread's IPS_{sched} can be easily obtained via performance counters, accurately determining IPS_{alone} online is a challenging task, even on symmetric CMPs [20]. For that reason, existing scheduling algorithms for symmetric CMPs typically rely on estimation models to approximate IPS_{alone} [18], or employ different heuristics to determine the degree of performance degradation indirectly via contention-related metrics [20]. Unfortunately, these scheduling algorithms are not suitable for AMPs, as they assume that the key performance metrics used to drive scheduling decisions (e.g., IPC or LLC miss rate) do not vary across cores when the application runs alone on the system. On current AMP hardware [2,4,15], this assumption is not valid, as cores may exhibit different microarchitectural features and cache sizes [7,14].

Recently proposed fairness-aware schedulers for AMPs [14,16], implicitly rely on the assumption that the performance degradation experienced by a thread on an AMP (relative to its solo execution) is negligible when it runs on a big core, even if it runs simultaneously with other threads. Thus, a thread's slowdown is estimated to be 1 when it runs on a big core; and the thread's big-to-small performance ratio – also referred to as the *speedup factor* (SF) [12] – is used to approximate the slowdown when the thread runs on a small core. In turn, the SF can be determined online by various means, such as direct measurement (IPC sampling) [3,8], prediction models based on hardware counters [7,12,14] or by leveraging special hardware extensions [16].

2.2 Performance Impact of Shared Resource Contention on AMPs

Assuming that a thread's slowdown is negligible when it runs on a big core (as done in [14,16]) is unrealistic in scenarios where threads heavily contend for shared resources with each other. To illustrate this fact, we analyzed the slowdown experienced by different single-threaded applications under varying degree of contention. Our analysis reveals that contention-related degradation can be substantial, and should be accounted for to avoid unfairness.

For our experiment, we used two AMP configurations based on the ARM Juno development board [2] – equipped with a mix of Cortex A57 and Cortex A53 cores, and the Intel QuickIA prototype [4], a dual-socket system featuring an Intel Atom N330 processor and a Xeon E5450 processor. The ARM-based configuration – presented in more detail in Sect. 4, features two big cores and four little cores. The Intel-based configuration integrates two big and two small cores. On both asymmetric platforms, the set of cores of the same type (big or small), which make up a cluster, share a last-level cache (L2) and a bus interface (FSB on Intel, AMBA on ARM) with the remaining cores in the cluster. Both platforms integrate a single DRAM controller shared among all cores.

Our experiment consists in measuring the slowdown experienced by diverse programs when mapped to a big core and run simultaneously with a different number of instances of an aggressor application. As the aggressor, we used the bandwidth benchmark [19], which causes substantial contention on the LLCs, shared buses and DRAM controller. On our platforms, we observed that this benchmark is capable of causing even a higher degree of contention than the one generated by highly memory-intensive SPEC CPU benchmarks, such as lbm.

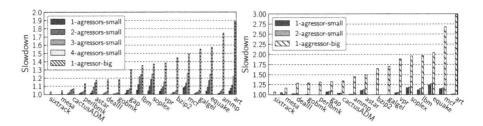

Fig. 1. Slowdown experienced by various benchmarks when running together with several instances of `bandwidth` on the Juno board (left) and the Intel QuickIA (right).

Figure 1 shows the slowdown (relative to the solo execution) that different applications experience when running simultaneously with several instances of the `bandwidth` application. Note that we measured the slowdown for all benchmarks in the SPEC CPU2000 and CPU2006 suites, but due to space constraints we only display the results for a few representative benchmarks that cover the full spectrum of slowdown values observed on both AMP platforms.For each benchmark, which is always assigned to a big core in our experiments, we explored different scenarios. In the first one, denoted as "1-aggressor-big" in Fig. 1, the benchmark runs simultaneously with one instance of `bandwidth`, which is also mapped to a big core; the small cores remain idle in this case. In the remaining scenarios, labeled as "N-aggressors-small", N instances of `bandwidth` are mapped to small cores; thus, in leaving one big core unused, we remove contention on the LLC and the bus interface associated with the big core cluster, but not on the DRAM controller (shared among all cores).

As is evident, the performance penalty that a thread may suffer on a big core due to interference with memory-intensive threads mapped to big cores is much greater (up to 1.89x on the ARM platform, and 2.98x on the Intel platform) than the degradation that comes from placing multiple aggressors on small cores (up to 1.26x, reached with the highest number of simultaneous small-core aggressors possible). This stems from two main factors. First, the contention on the LLC and on the shared bus (big-core cluster) is removed completely in the "N-aggressors-small" scenarios. Second, we observed that the pressure a single aggressor puts on the shared memory resources is higher when it runs on a big core than on a small one. We hypothesized that this has to do with the fact that in-order small cores cannot handle multiple outstanding cache misses, leading to a smaller bus and memory bandwidth utilization, and as a result to a smaller degree of contention. This observation suggests that monitoring the IPS of a thread when it runs on a big core in a contention-free scenario on a big cluster (e.g. with the other big cores idle) could be a good estimate for IPS_{alone}. Our scheduling proposal leverages this observation to approximate the slowdown.

We also observe that some programs, such as `sixtrack` or `mesa`, experience very low slowdown when executed together with memory-intensive aggressors. As pointed out in [18,20], CPU-intensive applications with a very small working set and good cache locality, or those that do not use the memory hierarchy substantially, do not experience significant performance penalty due to contention. As in [18], our scheduling proposal uses the bus transfer rate (BTR) to identify scenarios where threads are unlikely to suffer from contention when running on a big core. In our platforms, the BTR is measured as follows: $(bus\_read\_accesses * LLC\_cache\_line\_size * processor\_freq) / total\_cycle\_count$.

2.3   Related Work

The first approach to fairness-aware scheduling on AMPs was an asymmetry-aware Round-Robin (RR) scheduler that simply fair-shares big cores among applications by triggering periodic thread migrations [3]. Fair-sharing big cores has proven to provide better performance and more repeatable completion times across runs on AMPs than default schedulers in general-purpose OSes [9,11], which are largely asymmetry agnostic. For this reason, RR has been widely used as a baseline for comparison [3,12]. Note, however, that RR and other schemes that also rely on fair sharing big cores, such as A-DWRR [9] do not take into account the fact that applications derive different speedup factors when using big cores on the platform, and that these speedups may vary over time. This leads to degrading fairness and throughput [14].

Currently, the state-of-the-art OS-level fairness-aware scheduling scheme is ACFS [14]. To optimize fairness, ACFS leverages per-thread speedup factor (SF) values to continuously track the relative progress that each thread in the workload makes on the AMP, and enforces fairness by evening out the slowdown observed across applications. A thread's SF is determined online by feeding a platform-specific estimation model with the values of different performance metrics gathered via hardware counters. In [14] the authors experimentally demonstrated that ACFS clearly outperforms previous fairness-aware scheduling schemes, such as RR [3], Equal-Progress [16], and A-DWRR [9], for a wide range of workloads running on real asymmetric hardware. The main limitation of ACFS [14] (also present in previous schemes [16] based on thread progress tracking mechanisms), is the fact that the scheduler does not take shared-resource contention effects into consideration. As our experiments reveal, failing to cater to the degradation that comes from contention leads the scheduler to exhibit unfair behavior when multiple memory-intensive programs are included in the workload. CAMPS effectively improves fairness in this scenario.

3   The CAMPS Scheduler

CAMPS consists of two components: the *performance monitor* and the *core scheduler*. The performance monitor continuously gathers the value of various runtime metrics for each thread in the workload using performance counters, and feeds the core scheduler with critical information it needs, such as estimates of threads' slowdowns. The *core scheduler* assigns threads to big and small cores so as to preserve load balance in the system, and swaps threads between cores when necessary to ensure that applications achieve similar progress on the AMP.

In the remainder of this section we first describe the mechanism used by CAMPS to predict a thread's slowdown at runtime. Then we outline the progress tracking mechanism and discuss how fairness is enforced via thread swaps.

3.1 Determining the Slowdown at Runtime

The *performance monitor* approximates a thread's current slowdown by using Eq. 2; the actual IPS is measured with performance counters, and IPS_{alone} is estimated by using a *history table* maintained for each thread at runtime. This table stores IPS values observed in past execution phases when the thread was mapped to a big core in a low-contention scenario. As shown in Sect. 2, when a thread runs on a big core, the performance degradation that comes from interference with small-core threads is typically very low. Based on this observation, big-core low-contention IPS values are used to approximate the IPS_{alone}.

To detect low-contention scenarios on a big core, the scheduler leverages the heuristics based on the bus transfer rate (BTR) metric proposed in [17,18]. Essentially, a thread whose BTR is smaller than a given *low_btr* threshold are not likely to suffer noticeably from contention. In a similar vein, when the aggregate BTR across threads running a given core cluster falls below a given *high_btr* threshold we can assume that degradation due to contention will be very low [18]. These thresholds can be quickly determined via synthetic benchmarks [17,18]. If low-contention scenarios do not occur naturally as a result of the thread-to-core assignments performed by CAMPS, the core scheduler will enter a special mode (described later), which introduces low-contention scenarios artificially.

Indexing a thread's history table, which is necessary to approximate the slowdown and to record new IPS samples, requires the performance monitor to figure out whether information on the current program phase already exists in the table or not. To this end, we leverage a variant of the phase-detection mechanism used in a previous work [1]. In that work, the scheduler continuously monitors the percentage of instructions of different types (int/FP, load, store, branches, etc.) retired during the last sampling period, which make up a *instruction type vector* (ITV). Specifically, if the Manhattan distance of the ITVs for two performance samples (collected at different intervals) is smaller than a threshold, then both samples are assumed to belong to the same phase. Unfortunately, this scheme cannot be implemented in the real AMP platform we used, as the Performance Monitoring Unit is not equipped with the necessary performance events. To overcome this issue, we adapted this approach by monitoring two alternative *control metrics* along with the thread's BTR and its IPS: the number of L1 cache accesses per 1K instructions, and the percentage of branches retired over the total instruction count. As the instruction composition, the value of these two control metrics for a specific phase remain the same under different levels of shared resource contention, and more importantly, they do not vary significantly across core types. In addition, we observed that the value of these metrics changes dramatically when an application enters a new execution phase exhibiting a different degree of memory intensity and branch-prediction related behavior, which have a great impact on cross-core performance on AMPs [7,14]. These facts make the selected *control metrics* very suitable to index the table.

The history table is updated at the end of a monitoring interval in which the thread ran on a big core cluster in a low-contention scenario. If there is not any information of the current phase, a new IPS entry is created; otherwise the existing is updated with a running average of the low-contention IPS values recorded for that phase. When the thread runs on a small core, or a big core under potential contention, CAMPS accesses the history table to estimate the slowdown. If the IPS for the current phase is found in the table (i.e. *phase hit*), the slowdown is estimated with the ratio of the IPS value retrieved from the table, and the current IPS value measured in the last sampling interval. Otherwise (i.e. *phase miss*), the slowdown is approximated with the ratio of the average IPS samples stored in the history table, and the current IPS value.

3.2   Progress Tracking and Enforcing Fairness

CAMPS's core scheduler maintains a progress counter for each thread referred to as `amp_progress`, which enables the scheduler to track progress and enforce fairness. This counter tracks how much progress the thread has made thus far relative to the progress that would have resulted from running it on a big core the whole time in isolation. When a thread runs for a clock *tick* on a given core type, the scheduler increments `amp_progress` by $\Delta_{\text{amp\_progress}}$, defined as follows:

$$\Delta_{\text{amp\_progress}} = (100 \cdot W_{\text{def}}) / (CS \cdot W_t) \qquad (3)$$

where W_t is the thread's weight, derived directly from the application priority (set by the user); W_{def} is the weight of applications with the default priority; and CS is the thread's current slowdown as estimated by the *performance monitor*.

The definition of $\Delta_{\text{amp\_progress}}$ is very similar to the formula that the ACFS scheduler [14] uses to update progress counters. The main difference lies in how the CS factor is defined. ACFS assumes that a thread's current slowdown is always 1 (no performance degradation) when it runs on a big core, and uses the thread speedup factor (predicted via a platform-specific model) to approximate the slowdown when the thread runs on a small core. In doing so, ACFS does not take shared resource contention into consideration when updating progress. This aspect is factored in by CAMPS, as the slowdown is determined by comparing the thread's actual performance with an estimate of IPS_{alone}.

Threads mapped to big cores by the scheduler typically make faster progress than threads running on small ones, which causes unfairness. Note that the CS factor (slowdown) is usually bigger when the thread runs on a small core; thus, progress counters of small-core threads are incremented at a slower pace than that of big-core threads. CAMPS strives to enforce fairness by evening out the progress counter across threads. To make this possible, it may need to perform thread swaps (migrations) between different core types every so often. Like ACFS, CAMPS swaps a thread running on a big core with another thread running on a small core when the difference of their progress counters exceeds a given threshold. Specific instructions are provided in [14] for selecting the most appropriate value of this threshold for a given platform.

We found that relying on progress counters alone (as ACFS does) is ineffective in the event that a contention-sensitive application and an aggressor are mapped to the big-core cluster simultaneously. As shown in Sect. 2, this may slow down contention-sensitive applications substantially. To overcome this issue, CAMPS uses the BTR-based heuristics [18] to detect high contention scenarios, and favors those threads swaps that contribute to reducing contention on the big core cluster (e.g. a big-core aggressor thread is migrated to a small core). The main goal of this is to reduce the slowdown experienced by threads mapped to the big-core cluster simultaneously, and in turn, to improve fairness and throughput.

Finally, it is worth noting that when the number of memory-intensive threads in the workload is high, low contention scenarios may not occur that often. In these cases, CAMPS transitions into a non-work-conserving (NWC) mode in which low contention scenarios are created artificially. To control transitions into this special mode, the scheduler operates as follows. Every time that a thread completes k consecutive monitoring intervals (being k a configurable parameter), CAMPS calculates the thread's phase-hit rate and the number of IPS samples that were inserted into the history table over that time period. If the phase-hit rate is not high enough (falls below 80% in our experimental platform) and not a single IPS sample was inserted in the table during that period, the scheduler enters the NWC mode. When in this mode, if the thread was not running on a big core already, it will be swapped with a big-core thread to preserve load balance; in doing so, CAMPS tries to select a memory-intensive thread as the swap partner, so as to reduce contention on the big core cluster. If a low-contention scenario is still not present on the big-core cluster, the scheduler will disable as many big cores as necessary (for a very short period of time) to mimic such a scenario. Making this possible comes down to disabling only a few big cores: those where potentially aggressor (high-BTR) threads are running at this point. The scheduler transitions back into the normal operating mode when (1) a number of IPS samples have been gathered, or (2) when the thread blocks/exits.

4   Experimental Evaluation

We compare the effectiveness of CAMPS with that of two previously proposed fairness-aware schedulers for AMPs: ACFS [14] and an asymmetry-aware Round-Robin (RR) scheme [3]. We opted to use RR instead of the default OS scheduler, which is known to deliver highly variable completion times for compute-intensive workloads [11]. For the sake of completeness, we also experimented with a scheduler that attempts to optimize throughput by preferentially running on big cores those applications that derive a higher big-to-small speedup [7,12]. We will refer to this scheduler as *HSP* (High SPeedup). All the schemes considered in our study were implemented as a separate scheduling class in the Linux kernel v3.10. Except for RR, all the schedulers rely on performance monitoring counters (PMCs) to function. Our implementation of HSP and ACFS determine threads' speedup factors on-line by monitoring different PMC events, and by feeding an estimation model with the obtained event counts, as described in [11].

Table 1. Multi-application workloads

Name	Applications	Name	Applications
W1	GemsFDTD, equake, soplex, milc, povray, bzip2	W13	GemsFDTD, bwaves, gamess, hmmer, crafty, astar
W2	galgel, hmmer, soplex, lbm, fma3d, bzip2	W14	bzip2, bwaves, hmmer, lucas, gobmk, gzip
W3	galgel, equake, gamess, lbm, bzip2, astar	W15	soplex, art, vortex, lbm, fma3d, gobmk
W4	twolf, bwaves, equake, soplex, astar, gobmk	W16	galgel, equake, hmmer, lbm, fma3d, h264ref
W5	GemsFDTD, bwaves, equake, povray, fma3d, astar	W17	bwaves, equake, gamess, povray, astar, libquantum
W6	bwaves, equake, gamess, lbm, fma3d, bzip2	W18	GemsFDTD, galgel, gamess, hmmer, astar, libquantum
W7	GemsFDTD, applu, perlbmk, sixtrack, astar, gzip	W19	swim, mcf, perlbench, h264ref, gobmk, gzip
W8	bwaves, perlbmk, povray, fma3d, astar, gzip	W20	galgel, equake, hmmer, povray, mgrid, gobmk
W9	galgel, perlbmk, sixtrack, mgrid, astar, libquantum	W21	galgel, equake, hmmer, bzip2, perlbench, h264ref
W10	GemsFDTD, vortex, perlbmk, fma3d, astar, gzip	W22	galgel, equake, gamess, hmmer, sixtrack, povray
W11	bzip2, equake, hmmer, vortex, crafty, astar	W23	gamess, art, bzip2, gobmk, sixtrack, vortex
W12	gamess, hmmer, soplex, art, astar, gzip	W24	galgel, gamess, hmmer, povray, perlbench, gobmk

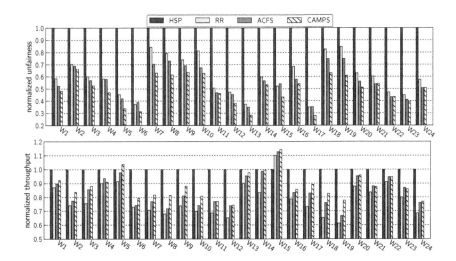

Fig. 2. Unfairness and throughput for workloads in Table 1

To assess the effectiveness of the various algorithms, we employed multi-application workloads consisting of compute-intensive benchmarks from different benchmarks suites (SPEC CPU, PARSEC, etc.) running on two real AMP platforms with different number of cores. Due to space constraints however, we could only include the discussion for the results of workloads consisting of single-threaded programs, and running on the ARM Juno board [2]. In using this kind of workloads, we ensure a fair comparison against HSP, RR and ACFS, as these schemes were evaluated before using similar workloads [3,7,14]. The ARM Juno board used for our experiments features a big.LITTLE processor that consists of two Cortex A57 "big" cores (running at 1.10 GHz) and four Cortex A53 "small" cores (running at 850 MHz). Each core has a private L1 cache and shares a last-level (L2) cache with the other cores of the same type. Specifically, big cores share a 2 MB/16-way L2 cache, and small ones feature a 1 MB/16-way cache.

For the evaluation on the Juno board, we randomly built 24 program mixes that combine a different number of *light-sharing* programs – whose performance does not suffer noticeably under contention, and *memory-intensive* programs, which are subject to high contention-related performance degradation or put significant pressure on shared resources. Table 1 displays the workloads sorted in descending order by the number of memory-intensive programs they include. Figure 2 reports the unfairness and throughput values for each workload and scheduler, normalized with respect to the results of the HSP scheduler. To assess throughput we employed the *Aggregate Speedup* (ASP) metric as in [11,14].

The results illustrate that optimizing one metric may lead to substantial degradation of the other metric. This is consistent with what was observed in previous work [11,14], which underscores that fairness and throughput are largely conflicting optimization goals on AMPs. As is evident, the HSP scheduler, which strives to optimize throughput achieves the best ASP values for the most workloads, at the expense of the worst unfairness numbers (the higher, the worse) across the board. Conversely, the remaining schedulers (fairness aware), achieve substantial reductions in unfairness vs. HSP (up to 72% – CAMPS under W17), at the cost of potentially high throughput degradation (up to 38% – RR, W19).

ACFS, RR and CAMPS exhibit a clear trend across the board. Specifically, for most workloads ACFS delivers better throughput and higher reductions in unfairness than RR. This is the expected behavior since ACFS takes applications' big-to-small speedups into consideration when distributing big-core cycles among applications, whereas RR does not. Despite the higher throughput, the fact that ACFS does not take contention effects into consideration, leads it similar unfairness figures to those of RR in some cases (e.g. W4-W6, W15 or W17). By contrast, our proposal (CAMPS) is able to reduce unfairness even further: by up to 11% with respect to ACFS (W17) and by up to 28% relative to RR (W19). At the same time, CAMPS is capable to reap higher throughput gains. Notably, under those workloads with a low degree of contention (W20-W24) – due to the small number of memory-intensive applications, CAMPS and ACFS perform very similarly. This demonstrates that our proposal is also suitable for low-contention scenarios, as it delivers similar unfairness and throughput figures to ACFS, which provides the best results under these circumstances [14]. All in all, CAMPS achieves an average 10.6% reduction in unfairness with respect to ACFS while improving throughput by up to 17% (4% average increase).

Finally, we also observed that HSP is especially affected by contention effects under workloads W5 and W13-W15, where the two applications with the highest speedup constitute a pair consisting of an aggressor and a contention-sensitive program. In these cases, HSP maps these conflicting applications simultaneously to the two available big cores very often. Despite the fact that the applications derive benefits from running on a big core alone, they also contend for shared resources, which gives rise to throughput degradation. Fairness-aware schedulers mitigate this issue by swapping threads between core types every so often, which reduces the amount of time that the conflicting applications are mapped together on the same cluster; this contributes to improving throughput. Specifically, the results reveal that all fairness-aware schedulers reap high normalized throughput figures under these workloads (W5, W13-W15). More importantly, our proposal, is able to outperform HSP for some of these conflicting workloads (W5 and W15). This is possible thanks to the fact that CAMPS swaps threads based on their observed progress and by catering to the degree of contention.

5   Conclusions

In this paper, we have proposed CAMPS, an OS-level fairness-aware scheduler for asymmetric single-ISA multicores. Unlike other fairness-conscious asymmetry-aware schemes [3,14,16], our approach effectively caters to the performance degradation that comes from contention on shared resources among cores. CAMPS accurately tracks the progress that the various threads in the workload make when running on the different core types throughout the execution, and enforces fairness by evening out the progress across threads. To this end, CAMPS approximates the current slowdown of an application thread by comparing its actual performance, with the performance observed in the past for the thread when it ran on a big core in low contention scenarios. Notably, our proposal does not require special hardware extensions [16] or platform-specific speedup-prediction models [7,14] to function. Instead, CAMPS relies on performance counters available in commercial AMP platforms, which makes it portable across CPU architectures. We implemented CAMPS in the Linux kernel and assessed its effectiveness on a real AMP system that features an ARM big.LITTLE processor. An extensive comparison was performed with existing asymmetry-aware schedulers [3,7,14,16]. Our experiments reveal that CAMPS outperforms the state-of-the-art fairness-aware scheme – ACFS [14] – in both fairness and throughput.

Acknowledgements. This work has been supported by the EU (FEDER) and the Spanish MINECO under grant TIN 2015-65277-R.

References

1. Annamalai, A., et al.: An opportunistic prediction-based thread scheduling to maximize throughput/watt in AMPS. In: Proceedings of PACT 2013, pp. 63–72 (2013)
2. ARM: Juno ARM development platform. http://infocenter.arm.com/help/topic/com.arm.doc.subset.boards.juno/index.html (2014)
3. Becchi, M., Crowley, P.: Dynamic thread assignment on heterogeneous multiprocessor architectures. In: Proceedings of CF 2006, pp. 29–40 (2006)
4. Chitlur, N., et al.: QuickIA: exploring heterogeneous architectures on real prototypes. In: Proceedings of HPCA 2012, pp. 1–8 (2012)
5. Ebrahimi, E., et al.: Fairness via source throttling: a configurable and high-performance fairness substrate for multi-core memory systems. In: Proceedings of ASPLOS 2010, pp. 335–346 (2010)
6. Joao, J.A., et al.: Utility-based acceleration of multithreaded applications on asymmetric CMPs. In: Proceedings of ISCA, vol. 13, pp. 154–165 (2013)

7. Koufaty, D., et al.: Bias scheduling in heterogeneous multi-core architectures. In: Proceedings of EuroSys 2010, pp. 125–138 (2010)

8. Kumar, R., et al.: Single-ISA heterogeneous multi-core architectures for multi-threaded workload performance. In: Proceedings of ISCA 2004, pp. 64–75 (2004)

9. Li, T., et al.: Operating system support for overlapping-ISA heterogeneous multi-core architectures. In: Proceedings of HPCA 2010, pp. 1–12 (2010)

10. Mittal, S.: A survey of techniques for architecting and managing asymmetric multicore processors. ACM Comput. Surv. **48**(3), 45:1–45:38 (2016)

11. Saez, J.C., et al.: On the interplay between throughput, fairness and energy efficiency on asymmetric multicore processors. Comput. J. (to appear)

12. Saez, J.C., et al.: A comprehensive scheduler for asymmetric multicore systems. In: Proceedings of EuroSys 2010, pp. 139–152 (2010)

13. Saez, J.C., et al.: Operating system support for mitigating software scalability bottlenecks on AMPs. In: Proceedings of the CF 2010, pp. 31–40 (2010)

14. Saez, J.C., et al.: Towards completely fair scheduling on asymmetric single-ISA multicore processors. J. Parallel Distrib. Comput. **102**, 115–131 (2017)

15. Samsung: benefits of the big.LITTLE architecture. http://www.samsung.com/semiconductor/minisite/Exynos/data/benefits.pdf. Accessed 10 Jan 2015

16. Van Craeynest, K., et al.: Fairness-aware scheduling on single-ISA heterogeneous multi-cores. In: Proceedings of PACT 2013, pp. 177–187 (2013)

17. Xu, D., et al.: On mitigating memory bandwidth contention through bandwidth-aware scheduling. In: Proceedings of PACT 2010, pp. 237–248 (2010)

18. Xu, D., et al.: Providing fairness on shared-memory multiprocessors via process scheduling. In: Proceedings of SIGMETRICS 2012, pp. 295–306 (2012)

19. Yun, H., et al.: PALLOC: DRAM bank-aware memory allocator for performance isolation on multicore platforms. In: Proceedings of RTAS 2014, pp. 155–166. IEEE (2014)

20. Zhuravlev, S., et al.: Survey of scheduling techniques for addressing shared resources in multicore processors. ACM Comput. Surv. **45**(1), 4:1–4:28 (2012)

Powernightmares: The Challenge of Efficiently Using Sleep States on Multi-core Systems

Thomas Ilsche[1]([envelope]), Marcus Hähnel[2], Robert Schöne[1], Mario Bielert[1],
and Daniel Hackenberg[1]

[1] Center for Information Services and High Performance Computing (ZIH),
Technische Universität Dresden, 01062 Dresden, Germany
{thomas.ilsche,robert.schoene,mario.bielert,
daniel.hackenberg}@tu-dresden.de
[2] Operating Systems Group, Technische Universität Dresden,
01062 Dresden, Germany
marcus.haehnel@tu-dresden.de

Abstract. Sleep states are an important and well-understood feature of modern server and desktop CPUs that enable significant power savings during idle and partial load scenarios. Making proper decisions about how to use this feature remains a major challenge for operating systems since it requires a trade-off between potential energy-savings and performance penalties for long and short phases of inactivity, respectively. In this paper we analyze the default behavior of the Linux kernel in this regard and identify weaknesses of certain default assumptions. We derive pathological patterns that trigger these weaknesses and lead to 'Powernightmares' during which power-saving sleep states are used insufficiently. Our analysis of a workstation and a large supercomputer reveals that these scenarios are relevant on real-life systems in default configuration. We present a methodology to analyze these effects in detail despite their inherent nature of being hardly observable. Finally, we present a concept to mitigate these problems and reclaim lost power saving opportunities.

Keywords: Linux · Sleep state · Energy efficiency
Power consumption

1 Introduction

As energy is one of the major cost factors in data-center operations, CPU developers are constantly pushing towards more aggressive techniques to scale power consumption with system load. One aspect to achieve this so called *power proportionality* is the reduction of power consumption during idle phases. These phases represent a major fraction of the run-time of desktop systems and are also noteworthy in the server domain. How deep a CPU sleeps determines how much power it consumes, but also how long it takes to wake up from its slumber.

© Springer International Publishing AG, part of Springer Nature 2018
D. B. Heras and L. Bougé (Eds.): Euro-Par 2017 Workshops, LNCS 10659, pp. 623–635, 2018.
https://doi.org/10.1007/978-3-319-75178-8_50

For example, depending on the depth of the sleep a typical Haswell server may consume 73 W in idle and wake up within 25 μs or consume 126 W and wake up within 2 μs [3]. The challenge for an operating system (OS) is to ensure that as much time as possible is spent sleeping as deeply as possible, while satisfying the latency requirements of the system. The job of the idle governor is to strike this balance. When investigating unexpected high power usage of one of our test systems, we found that sometimes the default governor in Linux does not let the system sleep as deeply as desirable for prolonged idle phases—it caused a *Powernightmare*. The same effect was found in our petascale production HPC system. We traced the cause of this inefficiency, and developed a mitigation that wakes the system from its nightmare and lets it sleep well again.

The remainder of this work is structured as follows: We explain the details of sleep states of modern CPUs and their use by the OS in Sect. 2, followed by a description of the problem and when it occurs in the wild in Sect. 3. We discuss possible solutions and describe and evaluate our mitigation approach in Sect. 4 before we conclude and give an outlook on future work in Sect. 5.

2   Background and Related Work

The ACPI standard [1] describes different power saving mechanisms. This includes P-states, which are implemented via voltage and frequency scaling (DVFS), T-states, which are implemented via clock modulation, and C-states that are typically implemented via clock gating [15, Sect. 5.2.1.1] and power gating [15, Sect. 5.3.2]. The four different C-states *C0* to *C3* are distinguished by ACPI. Higher C-state numbers refer to deeper sleep states with lower power consumption and longer wake-up latencies.

2.1   Hardware Perspective on C-States

Contemporary Intel server CPUs implement C-states per core and per package, referred to as *CC*-states and *PC*-states, respectively. Only the former can be directly influenced by the OS, while the latter are enabled by hardware under specific circumstances. The CC-state is the lowest of the selected C-states among all hardware threads on the core. Similarly, the PC-state is determined by the lowest CC-state of all cores incorporated on the package [6,7, Sect. 4.2.5].

Modern Intel server CPUs implement at least four CC-states: *CC0*, *CC1*, *CC3*, and *CC6* [6,7, Sect. 4.2.4]. The processor core is active and executes instructions in CC0. In CC1 the processor core is still active and caches are not flushed. The additional *C1E* does not differ from CC1 for the core itself, but allows the package to enter *PC1E*, if all cores are in C1E or higher. In CC3, core clocks are stopped, and caches are flushed. In CC6, the core applies power gating, storing its internal state to a dedicated SRAM. The architectural state is restored when the core returns to a lower CC-state. Another feature, called *delayed deep C-states (DDCst)* is described in [7, Sect. 4.2.4.5]. Here lower CC-states are used for a short period of time before switching to higher C-states.

To the best of our knowledge, a documentation of the mechanisms of newer Intel server processors is currently not available. However, since they are handled like their predecessors and their desktop counterparts, one can assume that the general mechanisms are the same.

There are six different PC-states [7, Sect. 4.2.5]: PC0, PC1, PC1E, PC2, PC3, and PC6. Similarly to CC0, PC0 refers to the normal operation of the package. While in PC1, "No additional power reduction actions are taken" [6, Sect. 4.2.5], core voltage and frequencies are reduced in PC1E. In PC3 and PC6 the last level cache becomes inaccessible, voltages are lowered, and the power consumption of uncore components is reduced [7, Sect. 4.2.5].

Higher C-states provide a significant power saving potential, at the cost of higher exit latencies [13]. Intel describes hardware mechanisms that counter inefficient usages of C-states [14]. These mechanisms, called *promotion* and *demotion*, use hardware loops to track C-state residency history and automatically re-evaluate OS decisions. For promotion, the hardware automatically increases the C-state, for demotion it lowers the C-state. Intel desktop processors and previous server processors include a feature called *C1E auto-promotion* [6,7, Sect. 4.2.4]. There is no promotion to higher PC-states than PC1E. The processor core can perform demotion by choosing: (1) CC3 instead of the requested CC6, and (2) CC1 instead of CC6/CC3. To correct wrong decisions demotions can be reverted by a mechanism called *undemotion*. Whether promotion, demotion, and undemotion are enabled is encoded in the PKG_CST_CONFIG_CONTROL register. On Intel processors, C-states can be requested by the OS in the form of a hint argument to the mwait instruction.

2.2 Idle Power Conservation Techniques in Linux

An important feature of modern Linux systems is the so called *dyntick-idle* mode, also called *nohz* mode or *tickless*. This feature reduces the number of scheduling-clock interrupts for idle cores as opposed to having regular scheduling ticks, e.g., every 4 ms. In dyntick-idle mode, a core can remain in idle indefinitely. This is the default behavior on modern systems [9].

Whenever a core has no task to be scheduled, an idle state is selected. The cpuidle *governor* implements the selection policy while the cpuidle *driver* implements the architecture-specific mechanism to request an idle state from the CPU [10]. In our evaluation, we focus on high performance systems with Intel processors, using the intel_idle driver. Idle states correspond to C-states. Linux currently provides two governors to select idle states.

The ladder governor evaluates on each call whether the previous C-state was predicted correctly and increases or decreases the depth stepwise. Pallipadi et al. [10, Sect. 4.1] describe that while "this works fine with periodic tick-based kernels, this step-wise model will not work very well with tickless kernels".

The menu governor, which is the default on tickless Linux systems, combines several factors as a heuristic. It uses an *energy break even point* based on the target_residency provided by the architecture specific cpuidle driver. The challenge is to predict the upcoming idle duration.

The prediction algorithm starts with the known *next timer event,* and applies a correction factor based on an exponential moving average on how accurate this prediction was in the past. Idle times predicted to be longer than 50 ms are always considered to be perfect, on grounds that longer sleeping times provide no additional power improvement. Additionally, the *repeatable-interval-detector* records the duration of 8 previous intervals and uses their average. Up to two high values are ignored if the variance across all eight values would be too high. If the variance is still too high among the six lowest previous times, this predictor is ignored, otherwise the minimum of the next timer event and the repeatable-interval-detector is used.

Further, the `menu` governor tries to *limit the performance impact* by choosing C-states with shorter exit latencies on busy systems. Based on the load average and number of IO wait tasks, a `performance_multiplier` limits the ratio of predicted idle time and exit latency. A device or user can request a maximum DMA latency for QOS purposes (`PM_QOS_CPU_DMA_LATENCY`). The latency requirement is the minimum of both values. Finally, the `menu` governor selects the highest enabled C-state with a `target_residency` of no more than the predicted idle time and an `exit_latency` that does not exceed the latency requirement.

The heuristic relies on many values that have been determined experimentally. Since its last big change[1] in 2009, the `menu` governor has operated like that. In principle, the `ladder` governor has not changed since 2007. In our work, we focus on tickless systems running the `menu` governor, since it is essential from an energy-efficiency perspective to avoid unnecessary scheduling-clock interrupts.

Considering the impact on performance and power consumption, the `cpuidle` governor was a research target before. Roba and Baruch [11] propose two possible improvements for the C-state selection heuristic claiming a constant improvement of 10% for their combination. One approach is based on machine learning, the other tries to improve the responsiveness of the already existing repeatable-interval-detector in the `menu` governor. Kanev et al. [8] conducted a state-of-the-art study for typical datacenter applications. They argue that "the maximum improvement for both power and latency with a single policy is unlikely" and thus the `menu` governor is a compromise in-between. Given the strict latency requirements in the datacenter domain, Kanev et al resort to DVFS for power savings. However, both works focus more on improving latency instead of energy.

3   Analysis of Inconsistent Power Saving in Idle

In this section, we identify inefficient power saving decisions in Linux and demonstrate how to trigger the effect. We also show real world occurrences on an individual machine and across a production HPC system.

---

[1] cpuidle: fix the menu governor to boost IO performance: https://git.kernel.org/pub/scm/linux/kernel/git/torvalds/linux.git/commit/?id=69d25870f20c4b2563304f2b79c5300dd60a067e.

Table 1. Properties of systems under test

	Testsystem *Diana*	HPC system *Taurus*
CPU	2 × Xeon E5-2690 v3	2 × Xeon E5-2680 v3
Measurement	Per socket at 500 kSa/s [4]	Per socket at 100 Sa/s
	System (AC) at 20 Sa/s	Node (DC) at 1000 Sa/s [2]
Kernel Version	4.11.0-rc8 (8b5d11e)	2.6.32 (Bull SCS4 / RHEL 6.8)
Total system power consumption in different states		
All cores C6	73.9 W (total system)	87.0 W (total node)
Core 0 C1E, others C6	106.3 W (total system)	n/a*
All cores C1E	126.1 W (total system)	130.8 W (total node)

*The old kernel does not support disabling C-states for individual cores.

3.1   Observation

During energy efficiency research on a system with sophisticated power measurement instrumentation [4], we have observed an unexpected behavior: Even
though the system is specifically configured for low idle power consumption, i.e.
few interrupts, the power consumption during idle phases was erratic. While the
baseline idle power is 73 W, sometimes after inconspicuous activities, the total
power consumption remained over 100 W for several seconds. This happened
during times without any explicit activity on the system and was observed by
the external power measurement. The behavior persisted across a wide range of
recent and historic kernel versions. We also observed this effect on a production
HPC system. The underlying issue eluded investigation for a while, in particular
because any active measurement directly impacted the effect under investigation.

3.2   Experimental Platform

For reproduction and analysis of the effect we used two systems: a workstation
for energy measurements (*Diana*) and a node of a petascale production HPC
system (*Taurus*). Both are equipped with dual socket Intel Haswell-EP CPUs
and sophisticated energy measurement instrumentation (see Table 1). All energy
measurements are calibrated and verified to high accuracy [2,4,5]. On *Diana* we
use the high resolution socket power measurements when observing small time
scales. Full system (AC) measurement allows us to perform analysis at larger
time scales. We fixate the core frequency with the userspace P-state governor
and disable HyperThreading to reduce the variance of the measurements. Most
of our observations relate to PC1E or higher, in which power consumption is not
affected by core frequency.

3.3   Tools to Isolate the Effect

To isolate the effect, we combined existing and newly implemented kernel trace-
points, measurement of C-state residencies via the `x86_adapt` kernel module [12],

and high resolution power measurements. The `power/cpu_idle` (for older kernels `power/power_start`) tracepoint provides the selected C-state for each idle governor decission. The `sched/sched_switch` tracepoint correlates tasks with the CPU they are scheduled on. We added a `power/menu_idle` tracepoint to record the internal decision parameters of the heuristic within the `menu` governor.

Since we want to observe an idle system, we designed the measurement to avoid activities as much as possible. Tracepoint events are recorded by the kernel in a ring buffer. The measurement threads idle in `poll()` until the buffer is nearly full. The only regular interruption is from reading the C-state residency counters of the CPU via `x86_adapt` every 5333 ms. Even the activity of the measurement process itself is recorded through the scheduling events. Power measurements are recorded externally and merged into a common trace file after the experiment.

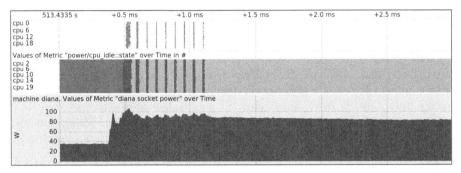

(a) Repeatedly sleeping for short intervals causing an idle time misprediction. Top: scheduled tasks per CPU, middle: core C-state requested by the `menu` governor (active [blue], C1E [green], C6 [red]), bottom: power consumption. Note that only socket power measurements are available at this time granularity.

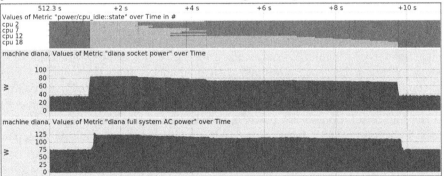

(b) Full duration of the Powernightmare: requested idle states, power consumption of both sockets and full system.

Fig. 1. A synthetically triggered Powernightmare on *Diana*. (Color figure online)

3.4   Cause, Trigger, and Contributing Factors

The cause of the unusual high idle power consumption is a severe underestimation of the upcoming idle time by the **menu** governor. Its heuristic has to resort to historic knowledge, as not all events can be known in advance.

```
#include <unistd.h>
int main() {
  #pragma omp parallel
  while (1) {
    for (int i = 0; i < 8; i++) {
      #pragma omp barrier
      usleep(10);
    }
    sleep(10);
  }
}
```

Listing 1. Code to reproduce underestimation of the **menu** governor

Bursts of activity with short idle times after which the CPU idles for a long time can confuse the heuristic. Based on the observation of recent idle times, the heuristic concludes that a short idle time will follow, regardless of the next known timer event being far in the future. Moreover, due to discarding long intervals in cases of high variance, the algorithm will often not correct its prediction after the first long idle time. As up to two outliers are ignored by the heuristic, it can take up to three consecutive wake-up events to recover from a misprediction. If a CPU goes into a shallow sleep state but stays there for a long time, it wastes power because it could be sleeping much deeper. We call this a *Powernightmare*.

We use the code from Listing 1 to reliably trigger a Powernightmare. This code repeatedly sleeps for a very short time tricking the **menu** governor into predicting an upcoming short idle phase, hence requesting a low C-state. An execution of this code is shown in Fig. 1a. Our test system *Diana* is optimized for little background activity, tasks are scheduled infrequently. Therefore it takes up to 10 s before all involved cores are able to end their Powernightmare—especially because it takes up to three wake-up events to correct the misprediction (see Fig. 1b). During the shown Powernightmare, the idle consumption increases from 73 W to 125 W–109 W, depending on the number of cores in CC1. As long as at least one core is in CC1 state, the respective socket cannot enter the PC6 state, wasting most of the energy saving potential. The hardware C-state residency counters are consistent with the selected C-states by the **menu** governor.

We have seen Powernightmares being triggered in normal operation. On the production HPC system *Taurus* it occurs regularly when no jobs are running on a node. Figure 2a shows a scheduling pattern that happens every 25 s. This regular activity is related to the parallel Lustre filesystem and the interaction of its pinger thread (**ll_ping**), the OFA Infiniband network driver (**kiblnd_sd**), and PortalRPC daemon tasks for each CPU (**ptlrpcd**). As shown in Fig. 2b, several cores remain in C1 for up to one second[2]. Due to regular background activity, the Powernightmare rarely lasts more than one second on this system.

There are various other causes for Powernightmares on our test systems. Most of the time, the cause is communication between user and/or kernel tasks scheduled on different cores, such as **systemd-journald** and I/O related kernel

---

[2] The **power/power_start** tracepoint event does not distinguish between C1 and C1E.

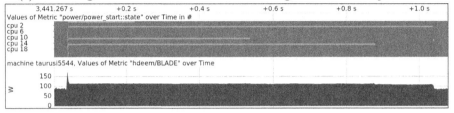

(a) Scheduling of Lustre related kernel tasks causing an idle time misprediction.

(b) After the Lustre ping (short power spike) several cores remain in C1 (green) instead of C6 (red) for ≈1 s causing increased node power consumption.

Fig. 2. A Powernightmare in normal idle on a *Taurus* HPC node. (Color figure online)

tasks. Another example are updates from a GNU `screen` status bar that affect a shell process and the kernel task handling the respective tty, all waiting for one another for very short time periods. Further causes invole reading model specific registers, which is done by a kernel worker scheduled on the specific core.

We also observed Powernightmares on an Intel Xeon Phi 7210 machine. However, the impact there is reduced, due to recurrent events on all cores every 100 ms, which allows the governor to correct a misprediction within 300 ms.

4   Optimization and Results

We identify several approaches to address the problem of wasted energy due to Powernightmares. Further we describe our selected solution and evaluate it.

4.1   Approaching the Problem

Changing task behavior to avoid triggering a Powernightmare. In many cases it would be possible to tune the applications or kernel tasks such that they no longer trigger an idle time misprediction. For instance, pinning tasks that communicate with each other on the same core could prevent short sleep times while one task is waiting for the other. The pattern exhibited by Lustre involving several kernel tasks per core appears to have significant potential for general improvement. However modifying a wide variety of legacy code is intractable as a solution. Even for newly written software, the complex interactions between different components make it hardly feasible to address the problem this way.

Improving the idle time prediction. A C-state governor must function with incomplete information. It is conceivable to improve the prediction in some cases, e.g., using improved heuristics or software hints. However, there will never be perfect information about upcoming events in general. Applications or outside influences such as network packets cannot be generally predicted.

Biasing the prediction error. It would be possible to tune the heuristic towards over-predicting idle times instead of under-predicting them. The resulting energy savings come at the cost of increased latency. This trade-off could be tunable according to user preferences. One aspect that can certainly be improved is to not generally discard long idle times as outliers in the analysis of recent history.

C-state selection by hardware. For Intel processors, the C-state requested by the `mwait` command is only a hint to the hardware, which may chose to override this decision. However, current Intel processors offer no feature to automatically promote the cores into CC3 or higher. A possibility would be to always request the highest C-state and then relying on auto-demotion or delayed deep C-states for low latency as well as auto-undemotion for low power. Then the OS would no longer be able to enforce latency requirements.

Mitigating the impact. As any modification of the heuristic cannot improve every possible situation, we focus on mitigating the impact of a misprediction. A simple workaround is a program that runs a thread pinned to each core which sleeps for 10 ms in an endless loop. Using a kernel with regular scheduling clock ticks has a similar effect. This avoids staying in an inefficient sleep state for a long time but comes at the cost of a permanent background noise. And while it may save power in some situations, it does increase idle power measurably compared to perfect deep sleeping. Inspired by this workaround, we describe a solution in the `menu` governor without the disadvantages.

4.2   Fallback Timer

To mitigate the effect while avoiding permanent background noise, a core has to wake up from a shallow sleep state only. To achieve this in the `menu` governor, we set a special *fallback timer* if there is a very large factor between the next known timer event and the predicted idle time. This fallback timer is set so that if the prediction heuristic was right, the core wakes up before the timer triggers. We then cancel the additional timer to avoid generating noise. If the heuristic was wrong, the programmed wake-up allows to go into a higher C-state and continue sleeping with lower power consumption. To achieve this, we instruct the kernel to ignore the recent residency history for the upcoming idle state selection. We choose to use the *hrtimer* API of the Linux kernel for our implementation. Regular timers have too low resolution and will miss their deadline by a significant margin on tickless kernels, which would render our solution ineffective.

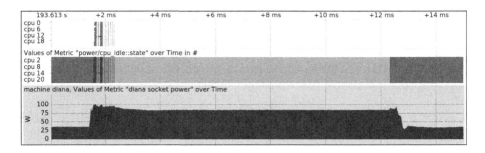

Fig. 3. The fallback timer corrects a wrong C-state selection after 10 ms of shallow sleep. Timeline diagram from top to bottom: scheduling activity, core C-states (active [blue], C1E [green], C6 [red]), power measurements. Note that only socket power measurements are available at this time granularity. (Color figure online)

4.3   Verification

To determine the effectiveness of our solution, we compare an unmodified kernel against a patched kernel with enabled fallback timer. We compare normal idle with no user activity and the worst-case trigger workload as described in Listing 1. Powernightmares that occur in normal operation often exhibit a strong variance and depend on many environmental factors. For the sake of statistical significance and reproducibility, we focus the quantitative verification on the simple synthetic workload, that is >99.99% idle, and normal idle configuration.

Figure 3 shows the timeline of a mispredicted idle time. While all cores enter C1E after the trigger executes, the fallback timer is activated and all cores can enter a higher C-state. The duration of 10 ms for the fallback timer is an initial estimate and can be further experimentally refined or dynamically adapted based on target residencies. Figure 4 shows the statistical density distribution of power consumption samples during 20 min. If the trigger workload is active every 10 s, the average system power consumption with the unmodified kernel is 119 W. The modified kernel with active fallback timer reduces the average power to 74.3 W. During normal idle, in which only few Powernightmares occur, the system consumes 75.5 W with the unmodified kernel and 73.9 W with the fallback timer. The difference is hardly statistically significant, but the amount of outliers is reduced and the standard deviation decreases from 8.1 W to 3.5 W by using the fallback timer. With tickless disabled, which also implies the `ladder` governor, the unmodified kernel is not affected by Powernightmares. The regular timer interrupts increase idle power to 78.5 W. The trigger workload does not increase that further. Our results show that the fallback timer prevents Powernightmares, without causing additional power-overhead in normal idle configurations.

We have not observed any other occurrences of Powernightmares when using the fallback timer. Due to the production nature of the system, we could not apply the patch to *Taurus*. A fair comparison would also require to back-port the patch to the old kernel version normally used on the system.

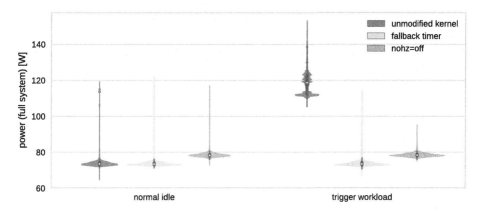

Fig. 4. Combined violin-/box-plot of the *Diana* power consumption during idle and trigger workload using an unmodified Linux kernel, our patched kernel with fallback timer, and an unmodified kernel with disabled tickless (`nohz=off`).

On our system, it takes on average 1735 cycles (0.67 μs) to program a fallback timer. Since the core has no scheduled task a that point, this cost does not impact performance but represents a small energy overhead. When waking up before a set fallback timer triggers, canceling it takes 390 cycles (0.15 μs). This time is added to the wake-up transition latency, which is up to 2.1 μs on our system for C1 and 15 μs for C3 [3], not considering the remaining time spent in the Linux kernel after the wake-up. Considering that this only applies whenever the governor has to deal with conflicting information and the overhead is an order of magnitude lower than existing latencies, we conclude that the negative impact is insignificant for all practical purposes.

5   Summary and Outlook

In this study, we described and analyzed a pattern of inefficient use of sleep states that leads to a significant waste of energy on idle systems. We developed a methodology and open-source tools[3] to carefully observe these anomalies without altering them. Our investigation reveals that a misprediction of the default Linux idle governor can cause the system to enter an inappropriate C-state. In particular, systems with little background activity can stay in this shallow sleep state for ten seconds or more, wasting significant energy-saving potential. We designed a solution to mitigate the negative effects by setting a fallback timer if the idle governor is unsure about the duration of a sleep phase. This allows the system to enter a deep sleep instead of remaining in a shallow sleep state for a long time. We demonstrated that our implementation[4] effectively reduces the average power consumption without notable negative side-effects.

---

[3] https://github.com/tud-zih-energy/lo2s/tree/powernightmares.

[4] https://github.com/tud-zih-energy/linux/tree/menu_idle_fallback_timer.

While this study focuses on HPC systems, the effects discussed are not necessarily limited to a specific architecture. The same imperfect idle governor runs on millions of mobile devices that all rely on effective sleep-state use to conserve battery life. Since core numbers continue to increase in most devices, so does the likelihood that at least one will sleep badly and thus prevent shared resources from saving power. The impact of our work increases with the gap of power consumption between different sleep states. Further efforts to save energy, which rely on increasing the time spent continuously in idle, would be very susceptible to Powernightmares. Our work therefore contributes to the energy-proportionality for a variety of modern and future systems.

Acknowledgement. This work is supported in part by the German Research Foundation (DFG) within the CRC 912 - HAEC and by the European Union's Horizon 2020 program in the READEX project (grant agreement number 671657). The authors thank Thomas Kissinger for the report and initial discussion that led to this investigation.

References

1. Advanced Configuration and Power Interface (ACPI) Specification, Revision 6.1, January 2016. uefi.org. Accessed 30 Jan 2017
2. Hackenberg, D., Ilsche, T., Schuchart, J., Schöne, R., Nagel, W.E., Simon, M., Georgiou, Y.: HDEEM: high definition energy efficiency monitoring. In: International Workshop on Energy Efficient Supercomputing (E2SC) (2014). https://doi.org/10.1109/E2SC.2014.13
3. Hackenberg, D., Schöne, R., Ilsche, T., Molka, D., Schuchart, J., Geyer, R.: An energy efficiency feature survey of the Intel Haswell processor. In: IEEE International Parallel and Distributed Processing Symposium Workshop (IPDPSW) (2015). https://doi.org/10.1109/IPDPSW.2015.70
4. Ilsche, T., Hackenberg, D., Graul, S., Schuchart, J., Schöne, R.: Power measurements for compute nodes: improving sampling rates, granularity and accuracy. In: International Green and Sustainable Computing Conference (IGSC) (2015). https://doi.org/10.1109/IGCC.2015.7393710
5. Ilsche, T., Schöne, R., Schuchart, J., Hackenberg, D., Simon, M., Georgiou, Y., Nagel, W.E.: Power measurement techniques for energy-efficient computing: reconciling scalability, resolution, and accuracy. In: Second Workshop on Energy-Aware High Performance Computing (EnA-HPC) (2017, accepted for publication)
6. Intel Corporation: Desktop 4th Generation Intel Core Processor Family, Desktop Intel Pentium Processor Family, and Desktop Intel Celeron Processor Family, Datasheet, vol. 1 of 2, March 2014. intel.com. Accessed 12 Aug 2016
7. Intel Corporation: Intel Xeon Processor E5–1600/E5-2600/E5-4600 v2 Product Families, Datasheet, vol. One of Two, March 2014. intel.com. Accessed 12 Aug 2016
8. Kanev, S., Hazelwood, K., Wei, G.Y., Brooks, D.: Tradeoffs between power management and tail latency in warehouse-scale applications. In: IEEE International Symposium on Workload Characterization (IISWC) (2014). https://doi.org/10.1109/IISWC.2014.6983037
9. McKenney, P.E.: NO_HZ: Reducing Scheduling-Clock Ticks. kernel.org. Accessed 09 May 2017

10. Pallipadi, V., Li, S., Belay, A.: cpuidle: do nothing, efficiently. In: Proceedings of the Ottawa Linux Symposium (OLS) (2007). kernel.org. Accessed 12 Jan 2017

11. Roba, A., Baruch, Z.: An enhanced approach to dynamic power management for the Linux cpuidle subsystem. In: IEEE International Conference on Intelligent Computer Communication and Processing (ICCP) (2015). https://doi.org/10.1109/ICCP.2015.7312712

12. Schöne, R., Molka, D.: Integrating performance analysis and energy efficiency optimizations in a unified environment. Comput. Sci.-Res. Dev. **29**(3–4), 231–239 (2014). https://doi.org/10.1007/s00450-013-0243-7

13. Schöne, R., Molka, D., Werner, M.: Wake-up latencies for processor idle states on current x86 processors. Comput. Sci.-Res. Dev. **30**(2), 219–227 (2014)

14. Song, J.: System and method for processor utilization adjustment to improve deep c-state use, 1 January 2013. US Patent 8,347,119

15. Weste, N.H.E., Harris, D.M.: CMOS VLSI Design - A Circuits and Systems Perspective, 4th edn. Pearson, London (2011). https://doi.org/10.1177/002072098602300231

Help Your Busy Neighbors: Dynamic Multicasts over Static Topologies

Robert Kuban[✉][iD], Randolf Rotta[iD], and Jörg Nolte

Brandenburg University of Technology Cottbus-Senftenberg, Cottbus, Germany
{robert.kuban,randolf.rotta,joerg.nolte}@b-tu.de

Abstract. Acknowledged multicasts, e.g. for software-based TLB invalidation, are a performance critical aspect of runtime environments for many-core processors. Their latency and peak throughput highly depend on the topology used to propagate the events and to collect the acknowledgements. Based on the assumption of an inevitable interrupt latency, previous work focused on very simple flat topologies. However, the emergence of simultaneous multi-threading with locally shared caches enables interrupt-free multicasts. Therefore, this paper explores and re-evaluates the design space for dynamic multicast groups based on combining shared memory with active messages and helping mechanisms. We expect this new approach to considerably improve the scalability of acknowledged multicasts on many-core processors.

Keywords: Multicast · Shared memory · Many-core · TLB shootdown

1 Introduction

Multicasts send a message to a selected group of receivers. One of its most important uses in operating systems is the software-controlled invalidation of caches, most notably the invalidation of Translation Lookaside Buffer (TLB) entries after changes to shared address spaces [3–5,18,19,22]. Although a number of mechanisms have been proposed, often a variant of the TLB shootdown algorithm [4] is used. The most costly operation in such algorithms is the handling of inter-processor interrupts (IPIs) [3,5,18], which were necessary in order to enforce the multicast's completion.

Multi- and many-core architectures provide a large number of processor cores. For example, the Intel XeonPhi processors contain more than 60 cores with four hardware threads per core. This poses a scalability challenge [8]: The propagation and acknowledgment overhead per multicast and the number of concurrent multicasts grow with the number of threads. In addition, dynamic membership updates in multicast groups can become more frequent.

One worst case scenario is bulk synchronous parallel processing: All threads may reconfigure their part of the shared address space after a synchronizing barrier. Restricting the updates to a few single manager threads would miss

© Springer International Publishing AG, part of Springer Nature 2018
D. B. Heras and L. Bougé (Eds.): Euro-Par 2017 Workshops, LNCS 10659, pp. 636–647, 2018.
https://doi.org/10.1007/978-3-319-75178-8_51

parallelization benefits and complicate the applications. Likewise, introducing partitioned address spaces [8] would require careful use by the applications.

Many applications do not need all of the available hardware threads to fully utilize the numeric execution resources [7]. With simultaneous multi-threading (SMT) [21] the threads in a core share the local caches and, most importantly, the TLB. Hence, with minimal hardware support, an idle thread can invalidate its neighbor thread's TLB entries without interrupting the currently running application.

This paper proposes an interrupt-free TLB invalidation algorithm that exploits dedicated hardware threads for cross-thread invalidation on shared TLBs in order to avoid disturbing application threads. Interrupt-free multicasts raise the question, whether tree- or ring-based multicast topologies can outperform conventional flat approaches and provide better trade-offs between latency and throughput. Hence, the potential performance gains on the Intel XeonPhi Knights Corner many-core processor are evaluated. However, complex multicast topologies increase the costs of dynamic membership updates [1] and do not necessarily reflect the hardware's optimal topology. Consequently, this paper compiles a number of strategies that exploit shared memory to skip non-members dynamically on top of an optimized static topology.

The paper is structured as follows: Sect. 2 surveys related work on multicasts and TLB invalidation mechanisms. Section 3 outlines an interrupt-free invalidation algorithm which uses that the TLB is shared between multiple hardware threads. Section 4 explores the design space for dynamic multicast algorithms that operate on top of static topologies. Section 5 evaluates the potential performance gains and compares dynamic multicasts over static topologies against adapted topologies.

2   Preliminary and Related Work

The first subsection surveys related work on multicast algorithms and topologies. Then, their application to TLB invalidation on multi-core processors is reviewed.

2.1   Multicast Topologies

Multicast algorithms distribute messages to multiple receivers over unicast networks. In the *propagation* phase, the message is delivered to each receiver. This can be carried out in parallel by letting intermediate receiver or support nodes forward the message, which forms the logical *multicast topology*. A preemptive *notification*, e.g. via interrupt signals, ensures the timely forwarding and processing on all receivers. After *processing* the message at each receiver, an *acknowledgment* of the global completion is returned to the multicast's sender, for example, to ensure ordering. This can be achieved by aggregating the individual acknowledgments along the multicast topology.

The choice of the topology provides different performance trade-offs. The *throughput*, as number of concurrent multicasts per time unit, is limited by the node with the highest per-message processing overhead and the most congested network link. The overhead roughly increases with the number of direct successors, which favors the simple ring topology. The *latency*, as time between issuing the multicast and receiving the acknowledgment, depends on the time needed to propagate the messages and acknowledgments on the longest path. This favors flat tree topologies. Finally, the *reconfiguration overhead* describes the cost of inserting and removing receivers in the multicast group. Adapting the logical topology appropriately to the network's physical topology tends to come with high construction overhead, which favors simple topologies like rings [1].

A wide range of literature exists on the construction of optimal topologies. A recent review for many-core architectures can be found in [11]. Low-latency strategies have been found for many network topologies [10] and performance models such as the POSTAL model [2,6] and the LogP model [12]. Fractional trees [15] provide a trade-off between latency and throughput in sparsely connected networks. Similarly, diamond rings [13] balance both by unifying acknowledgment and propagation in a ring-like topology.

A model for optimizing the throughput is the k-item broadcast problem in which the number of rounds to multicast k messages should be minimized. Santos [17] provide a near optimal solution in the LogP model and the circulant graphs [20] in the simultaneous send–receive model. However, the 2Tree algorithms [16] are easier to implement while achieving near optimal throughput.

This paper does not aim to identify the best topology. Instead, the focus lies on re-evaluating how much the choice of topology matters on many-core processors with dynamic multicast groups. Additional optimizations are available on cache-coherent shared memory systems. Instead of the message-based aggregation of the acknowledgments, tree combining [23] by a hierarchy of counters in shared memory can be more efficient.

2.2   Multi-core TLB Invalidation

The translation lookaside buffer (TLB) is a small cache that speeds up the mapping from logical to physical addresses and access permissions. Each core contains one or more local TLBs. For various reasons, the TLBs in many-core architectures are not invalidated by the hardware's cache-coherence. Instead, the operating system has to send invalidation requests to all cores (or hardware threads) that currently use the affected address space. Especially when removing mappings, the sender has to wait for the global completion in order to ensure that all threads can no longer access the removed pages.

Thus, the TLB invalidation is a major application of acknowledged multicasts. Dynamic groups are maintained in order to not bother unrelated threads and reduce the system noise. Several algorithms have been proposed in the literature [3–5,18,19,22] and, often, a variant of [4] is used, which sequentially sends interrupts to all cores to be invalidated. Barrelfish is a notable exception by building efficient multicast topologies from a hardware description using a constraint solver [3]. However, in scenarios where membership can change rapidly rebuilding the entire topology would not be efficient. The following summarizes the algorithm used by Linux 4.11 on x86 architectures[1].

Each hardware thread owns a linked list as a task queue and an array of pre-allocated per-thread task structures. The tasks consist of a list handle for the task queue, a function pointer, a generic argument pointer for the function, and an acknowledgment flag. The interrupt handler processes each task from its queue and sets the flag. The multicast groups are maintained as bit mask in each address space. By iterating over the mask, the task for each receiver is initialized and enqueued. Then, an interrupt is sent to each receiver by either sending individual interrupts or using hardware multicast support if available. Finally, the mask is iterated again to wait on each acknowledgment flag.

In conclusion, concurrent multicasts are propagated in parallel with minimal overhead for the receiver. This results in good throughput and simplicity but comes with high overhead on the sender side and, hence, high latency.

As preliminary work we investigated the relevant parameters of a 60-core Intel XeonPhi 5110P (KNC) processor with 1.053 GHz clock using microbenchmarks. Hence, one processor cycle equates to roughly one nanosecond. The message transmission overhead is around 1200 cycles. Sending an interrupt between cores takes around 400 cycles and the next interrupt can be sent when the interrupt controller is ready again after approximately 1000 cycles. The interrupt latency from issuing the signal to reaching the interrupt handler was around 1000 cycles.

Typical HPC application on this processor use 60–120 application threads. Hence, sending the 60–120 messages sequentially would take 72k–144k cycles. Sending the interrupts sequentially would cost another 60k–120k cycles. By interleaving the interrupt and message transmissions, this could be reduced to 24k–48k cycles. In summary, a TLB invalidation across 120 threads would take at least 264k cycles (250 µs) without the acknowledgment when using a flat topology. This is 10x higher than other multicast topologies on the same processor, see for example [11,13].

3   Interrupt-Free TLB Invalidation

This section outlines an interrupt-free invalidation algorithms that avoids operation system noise on application threads. It exploits that multiple hardware threads share a TLB. Many applications do not need all of the available hardware threads to fully utilize the numeric execution resources [7]. Thus, one thread per core can be *dedicated* to the propagation and processing of TLB invalidation multicast messages and other operating system tasks.

The first challenge is to avoid interrupting the applications running at a core. Therefore, the dedicated thread must invalidate the TLB entries for the core's neighbor threads without sending interrupts. This can be achieved by exploiting that threads using exactly the same address space share their TLB entries and, thus, invalidation requests through the INVLPG instruction become effective for the neighbor threads. On x86 processors that support process context

---

[1] Function smp_call_function_many() in kernel/smp.c.

identifiers (PCIDs), the PCID of the target address space can be used for invalidation through the `INVPCID` instruction. Finally, reverse-engineering of the TLB structure can be exploited [9].

The x86 PCIDs are currently not used by Linux because the overhead of multicasts to unused address spaces would quickly offset the performance gain. However, the Alpha architecture has a similar feature called address space numbers (ASNs). There, Linux maintains a small per-core mapping from used address spaces to their local ASN. Invalidation multicasts are received only for the actively used address space(s). The others are invalidated upon reloading if a generation counter inside the address space indicates a skipped invalidation. The same approach can be used for interrupt-free TLB invalidation on x86 by tracking the PCIDs on the core level instead of individual hardware threads.

The invalidation requests need to be multicasted only to the non-sleeping cores. Each core's dedicated system thread checks if one of its application threads is affected. Cores waking up from deep sleep invalidate their TLBs anyway.

The second challenge is to avoid sending an interrupt to the dedicated thread. On processors with `MONITOR/MWAIT` support, the behavior of `MWAIT` ensures that the dedicated thread directly continues its execution whenever a message arrives in its queue. Without such support, the operating system can implement a similar behavior by polling. The dedicated thread goes to sleep when all application threads are idle, and is woken up by the first resuming application thread. Multicasts should skip cores that are in deep sleep, which is achieved by the mechanisms presented in the next section.

4   Dynamic Membership in a Static Broadcast Topology

Hierarchical multicast topologies may outperform the conventional simple flat algorithm used by Linux. However, complex topologies increase the cost of dynamic membership updates. On the other hand, using a static topology, similar to a broadcast, bothers non-member threads and leads to high latencies for small groups. Therefore, mechanisms are needed that emulate dynamic multicast groups on top of a static hardware-optimized broadcast topology.

The basic idea is to decouple the logical from the physical topology: The role of intermediate non-member nodes that should not receive a multicast can be taken over by other nodes via shared memory. The logical topology can contain additional support nodes that do not represent actual processor cores or hardware threads.

This enables three mechanisms: *Shared Memory Acknowledgment* and *Helping* avoid bothering non-member nodes by taking over their role. *Skipping* can speed up the helping by jumping over larger subgroups of non-member nodes.

The first subsection defines the necessary node types for such topologies. Then, the three mechanisms are discussed in more detail.

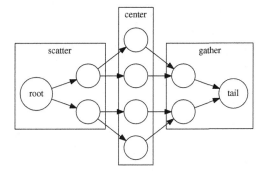

Fig. 1. An example topology labeled with node types.

4.1   Node Types for Hierarchical Topologies

In Fig. 1, the three nodes types are illustrated by an example topology: *Scatter* nodes have a single predecessor and multiple successors. Their role is to parallelize the multicast's propagation. *Gather* nodes have multiple predecessors and a single successor. Their role is to distribute the aggregation of the acknowledgements. *Center* nodes are in-between by having just a single predecessor and successor. The *root* of the topology is a node without predecessor. At the opposite end, the *tail* node has no successor and its role is to notify the multicast's source about the global completion.

Places represent the possible multicast receivers. For example, these can be processor cores or hardware threads. A *multicast group* is the set of places that shall process each multicast exactly once. The membership information needs to be readable from all places and can be implemented, for example, by an array of membership flags in shared memory. Each node of the topology is assigned to a place. *Member* nodes belong to places that are part of the multicast group. Some topologies require additional *support* nodes, which never will be a member of the multicast group to prevent repeated processing of the same message.

In tree topologies, for example, the tree leaves become center nodes. Each intermediate tree node consists of a scatter node and a supporting gather node. On member scatter nodes, the message can be first forwarded, then processed, and, after that, acknowledged to the associated gather node. In contrast, ring-alike topologies have no support nodes. Their gather nodes can be members and are responsible for message processing on their assigned place. Here, all member nodes have to forward the message only after processing, because the propagation of the message implicitly acknowledges that it has been processed.

4.2   Shared Memory Acknowledgment (SmAck)

Gather nodes aggregate the acknowledgment from their predecessors. In a pure message passing implementation, each predecessor would send an acknowledgment message, which is counted by the gather node. Such message transmissions over shared memory would cause more cache traffic than simply decrementing a shared counter. With SMACK, each predecessor decrements the gather node's atomic counter via shared memory. Only when it reaches zero, a single message is sent to the gather node.

4.3   Helping Non-member Nodes (Help)

Multicasts should not disrupt places that are currently not members of the multicast group. With a static topology however the respective non-member nodes are still needed for propagation and acknowledgment aggregation. Each node can check another node's membership via shared memory. The HELP mechanism forwards messages only to member nodes. For non-member successors, the sender node performs the successor's propagation or aggregation role.

In other words, each node traverses the topology recursively along its non-member nodes and propagates the multicast message only to members. In combination with SMACK, this strategy reduces the acknowledgment aggregation on *support* gather nodes to the classic tree combining [23].

4.4   Skipping Non-member Subgroups (Skip)

The HELP mechanism has a drawback: With many non-member nodes, a few nodes will have to scan most of the membership flags and carry out most or all message transfers. As highlighted in Fig. 2, pairs of gather and scatter nodes recursively form brackets around a smaller group of nodes. The SKIP mechanism uses this information to jump over entire hierarchical subgroups if such a subgroup contains no member. Checking a large set of membership flags at each node would be inefficient. Instead, tree combining [23] can be applied to track the membership state of each subgroup hierarchically.

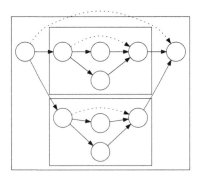

Fig. 2. An example skipping hierarchy. The dotted arrows indicate skip targets.

5   Evaluation

This section evaluates the performance of dynamic multicast groups on top of static topologies with focus on the latency. Our basic assumption is that cross-thread TLB invalidation has negligible overhead compared to the multicast itself. This allows to implement a better portable benchmark based on multicasts without actual TLB invalidation. As described in Sect. 2.2, interrupt-based multicasts work the same just with additional latency along the longest path.

The first subsection summarizes the benchmark setup and the second subsection presents the latency results. This evaluation has obvious room for improvement: Comparing the overhead of group membership updates, integrating latency-optimized trees [11], and investigating the throughput with 2Tree algorithms [16] is open for future work.

5.1   Setup

The benchmark environment is based on user-space threads on top of Linux. Each thread is pinned to an individual hardware thread using a affinity mask. The multicast is propagated through active messages via shared memory FIFO queues based on [14]. All experiments were performed on a 60-core Intel XeonPhi 5110P (KNC) processor with 1.053 GHz clock. For this platform, one thread per core is used and each polls actively for messages with a delay of 200 cycles when its queue is empty. If available, as in the more recent Intel XeonPhi Knights Landing architecture, MONITOR/MWAIT can be used to minimize the polling overhead.

The impact of the multicast group size is compared for $n = 2, 4, 8, 16, 32, 60$ members. For each size, 32 configurations are generated by selecting random members and the measurement is repeated 16 times for each configuration. The median over all measurements is used to reduce the impact of the operating system noise. The STATIC variant uses a single topology across the 60 cores for all group sizes. In contrast, the DYNAMIC variant uses smaller topologies that span just the members.

Different topologies are used to investigate the impact on the multicast mechanisms and the general benefit of deeper topologies compared to the classic flat TLB invalidation. The FLAT topology, see Fig. 3(a), mimics the conventional strategy as described in Sect. 2.2. The acknowledgments are counted in a single support node. The TREE topology, see Fig. 3(b), uses a 2-ary balanced tree. Finally, the DIAMOND topology, see Fig. 3(c), is based on diamond rings, in which the gather nodes are responsible for their own cores.

As baseline mechanism, SMACK uses just shared memory acknowledgment to decrease the amount of messages sent to gather nodes. The HELP mechanism combines helping and shared memory acknowledgment. Finally, the SKIP mechanism combines skipping, helping, and shared memory acknowledgment. Because there are no non-member nodes in the topologies of the DYNAMIC variant, SKIP does not provide any benefits there and HELP just implements tree combining for the gather phase.

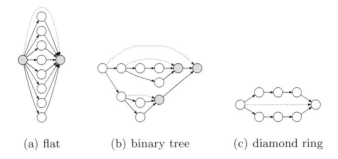

(a) flat   (b) binary tree   (c) diamond ring

Fig. 3. Topologies for 8 threads. Helper nodes are grey, dotted arrows indicate possible skipping paths.

5.2   Results

Figure 4 shows the results of the latency benchmark. The columns represent the three topologies (FLAT, TREE, DIAMOND) and the rows represent the three mechanisms (SMACK, HELP, SKIP). The circles represent the DYNAMIC topology variants that consist only of the group members, and the triangles denote the STATIC variant that includes all 60 cores. The x-axis is the size of the multicast groups and the y-axis shows the medium latency.

The latency of the SMACK mechanism on the DYNAMIC topologies increases linearly with the group size for the flat topology and logarithmically for the hierarchical typologies. With the STATIC variant, the latency is almost constant with a median around 77k cycles for FLAT, 39k for TREE, and 38k for DIAMOND. This can be expected because it involves all 60 cores independent of the group size. Thus, the overhead for a single message is around 1280 cycles based on the FLAT topology. The longest path in the TREE and DIAMOND topologies is 6 scatter nodes with 2 messages per node plus 6 gather nodes. This predicts a latency of 23k cycles. The remaining 16k cycles might be caused by additional overhead from navigating through the more complex topology.

The latency of the HELP mechanism on the DYNAMIC topologies is roughly equal to the pure SMACK mechanism, except on the TREE topology. The STATIC variants have a much higher latency than the DYNAMIC variants. On the STATIC TREE topology, the latency decreases from 38k to 31k cycles for growing group size. For all 60 members on the TREE topology, HELP is 8k cycles faster than pure SMACK. This difference can be attributed to the tree combining during the gather phase. Based on the large difference on the FLAT topology, it seems that the membership test of our implementation has a high overhead. This equally impacts the STATIC HELP on the other topologies. With growing group size, this overhead is hidden by the parallel propagation.

The STATIC SKIP mechanism performs similar to the DYNAMIC HELP on each topology but has slightly higher overhead. Compared to STATIC HELP on the TREE and DIAMOND topology, it has a much smaller latency for small groups. On the FLAT topology, SKIP never happens as long as there is at least one

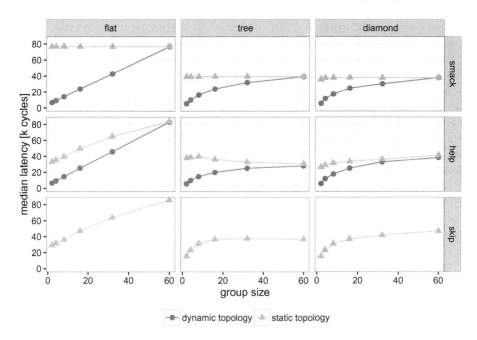

Fig. 4. Median latency for the different topologies and propagation mechanisms.

member. SKIP actually eliminates the overhead of the STATIC HELP mechanism on small groups. However, this advantage vanishes for larger group sizes. There, the additional overhead to check for possible skipping becomes visible.

In summary, HELP on the TREE topology performed best for the DYNAMIC variant and SKIP on the TREE topology performed best for the STATIC variant. The difference is negligible for large groups. For groups with just two members, the DYNAMIC variant (5.6k cycles) is 3x faster than the STATIC variant (15.5k cycles). However, the static variant has likely a larger overhead for topology updates when the group changes, which was not evaluated in this paper.

Comparing the FLAT versus TREE topology, the latency can be halved from 77k to 37k. Of course this difference increases with the number of cores or hardware threads. Interrupts during the propagation would increase the latency to 78k on the FLAT and up to 43k on the TREE topology. Hierarchical topologies benefit more from interrupt-free multicasts than the conventional flat approach.

6   Conclusions

The first part of the paper examined TLB shootdowns as a practical example for invalidation multicasts on many-core processors. We proposed an interrupt-free TLB invalidation algorithm that exploits simultaneous multiprocessing by dedicating superfluous hardware threads to the multicast processing. Similar algorithms are applicable to other kinds of locally shared caches, for example non-coherent instruction caches. Such interrupt-free multicasts reduce the operating system noise by not interrupting applications.

The second part evaluated the potential performance gains on the Intel XeonPhi Knights Corner many-core processor with focus on hierarchical multicast topologies and strategies that exploit shared memory to skip non-members dynamically on top of an optimized static topology. The results show that the latency can be significantly reduced for large groups (2x for 60 cores) and benefits more from interrupt-free propagation than the conventional flat approach. Therefore, TLB shootdowns should be redesigned for many-core processors. The impact on the peak throughput needs further investigation.

Acknowledgments. This work was supported by the German Research Foundation (DFG) under grant no. NO 625/7-2. We thank our students Martin Messer and Stefan Hertrampf for supporting the implementation and evaluation.

References

1. Baldi, M., Ofek, Y.: Ring versus tree embedding for real-time group multicast. In: Proceedings of Eighteenth Annual Joint Conference of the IEEE Computer and Communications Societies, INFOCOM 1999, vol. 3, pp. 1099–1106. IEEE (1999). https://doi.org/10.1109/INFCOM.1999.751665
2. Bar-Noy, A., Kipnis, S.: Designing broadcasting algorithms in the postal model for message-passing systems. Math. Syst. Theory **27**(5), 431–452 (1994). https://doi.org/10.1007/BF01184933
3. Baumann, A., Barham, P., Dagand, P.E., Harris, T., Isaacs, R., Peter, S., Roscoe, T., Schüpbach, A., Singhania, A.: The multikernel: a new OS architecture for scalable multicore systems. In: Proceedings of the ACM SIGOPS 22nd Symposium on Operating Systems Principles, SOSP 2009, pp. 29–44. ACM (2009)
4. Black, D.L., Rashid, R.F., Golub, D.B., Hill, C.R.: Translation lookaside buffer consistency: a software approach. In: Proceedings of ASPLOS-III, vol. 17, no. 2, pp. 113–122 (1989). https://doi.org/10.1145/68182.68193
5. Boyd-Wickizer, S., Chen, H., Chen, R., Mao, Y., Kaashoek, F., Morris, R., Pesterev, A., Stein, L., Wu, M., Dai, Y., Zhang, Y., Zhang, Z.: Corey: an operating system for many cores. In: Proceedings of the 8th USENIX Conference on Operating Systems Design and Implementation, OSDI 2008, pp. 43–57. USENIX Association, Berkeley (2008). https://www.usenix.org/conference/osdi-08/corey-operating-system-many-cores
6. Bruck, J., Coster, L.D., Dewulf, N., Ho, C.T., Lauwereins, R.: On the design and implementation of broadcast and global combine operations using the postal model. IEEE Trans. Parallel Distrib. Syst. **7**(3), 256–265 (1996). https://doi.org/10.1109/71.491579
7. Fang, J., Varbanescu, A.L., Sips, H.J., Zhang, L., Che, Y., Xu, C.: An empirical study of Intel Xeon Phi abs/1310.5842 (2013). http://arxiv.org/abs/1310.5842
8. Gerofi, B., Shimada, A., Hori, A., Ishikawa, Y.: Partially separated page tables for efficient operating system assisted hierarchical memory management on heterogeneous architectures. In: 2013 13th IEEE/ACM International Symposium on Cluster, Cloud and Grid Computing (CCGrid), pp. 360–368 (2013). https://doi.org/10.1109/CCGrid.2013.59
9. Gras, B., Razavi, K., Bosman, E., Bos, H., Giuffrida, C.: ASLR on the line: Practical cache attacks on the MMU. In: NDSS (2017). https://www.vusec.net/download/?t=papers/anc_ndss17.pdf

10. Hedetniemi, S.M., Hedetniemi, S.T., Liestman, A.L.: A survey of gossiping and broadcasting in communication networks. Networks **18**(4), 319–349 (1988). https://doi.org/10.1002/net.3230180406

11. Kaestle, S., Achermann, R., Haecki, R., Hoffmann, M., Ramos, S., Roscoe, T.: Machine-aware atomic broadcast trees for multicores. In: Proceedings of the 12th USENIX Conference on Operating Systems Design and Implementation, OSDI 2016, pp. 33–48 (2016). https://www.usenix.org/conference/osdi16/technical-sessions/presentation/kaestle

12. Karp, R.M., Sahay, A., Santos, E.E., Schauser, K.E.: Optimal broadcast and summation in the LogP model. In: Proceedings of the Fifth Annual ACM Symposium on Parallel Algorithms and Architectures, SPAA 1993, pp. 142–153. ACM, New York (1993). https://doi.org/10.1145/165231.165250

13. Nürnberger, S., Rotta, R., Drescher, G., Danner, D., Nolte, J.: Diamond rings: acknowledged event propagation in many-core processors. In: Hunold, S., et al. (eds.) Euro-Par 2015. LNCS, vol. 9523, pp. 722–733. Springer, Cham (2015). https://doi.org/10.1007/978-3-319-27308-2_58

14. Oyama, Y., Taura, K., Yonezawa, A.: Executing parallel programs with synchronization bottlenecks efficiently. In: Proceedings of International Workshop on Parallel and Distributed Computing for Symbolic and Irregular Applications (PDSIA 1999), pp. 182–204 (1999)

15. Sanders, P., Sibeyn, J.F.: A bandwidth latency tradeoff for broadcast and reduction. Inf. Process. Lett. **86**(1), 33–38 (2003). https://doi.org/10.1016/S0020-0190(02)00473-8

16. Sanders, P., Speck, J., Träff, J.L.: Two-tree algorithms for full bandwidth broadcast, reduction and scan. Parallel Comput. **35**(12), 581–594 (2009). https://doi.org/10.1016/j.parco.2009.09.001. Selected papers from the 14th European PVM/MPI Users Group Meeting

17. Santos, E.E.: Optimal and near-optimal algorithms fork-item broadcast. J. Parallel Distrib. Comput. **57**(2), 121–139 (1999). https://doi.org/10.1006/jpdc.1999.1529

18. Stets, R., Dwarkadas, S., Hardavellas, N., Hunt, G., Kontothanassis, L., Parthasarathy, S., Scott, M.: CASHMERE-2L: software coherent shared memory on a clustered remote-write network. ACM SIGOPS Oper. Syst. Rev. **31**(5), 170–183 (1997). https://doi.org/10.1145/269005.266675

19. Teller, P.J.: Translation-lookaside buffer consistency. Computer **23**(6), 26–36 (1990). https://doi.org/10.1109/2.55498

20. Träff, J.L., Ripke, A.: Optimal broadcast for fully connected processor-node networks. J. Parallel Distrib. Comput. **68**(7), 887–901 (2008). https://doi.org/10.1016/j.jpdc.2007.12.001

21. Tullsen, D.M., Eggers, S.J., Levy, H.M.: Simultaneous multithreading: maximizing on-chip parallelism. In: 25 Years of the International Symposia on Computer Architecture (Selected Papers), ISCA 1998, pp. 533–544. ACM, New York (1998). https://doi.org/10.1145/285930.286011

22. Villavieja, C., Karakostas, V., Vilanova, L., Etsion, Y., Ramirez, A., Mendelson, A., Navarro, N., Cristal, A., Unsal, O.S.: DiDi: mitigating the performance impact of TLB shootdowns using a shared TLB directory. In: 2011 International Conference on Parallel Architectures and Compilation Techniques, pp. 340–349 (2011). https://doi.org/10.1109/PACT.2011.65

23. Yew, P.C., Tzeng, N.F., Lawrie, D.H.: Distributing hot-spot addressing in large-scale multiprocessors. IEEE Trans. Comput. **C−36**(4), 388–395 (1987). https://doi.org/10.1109/TC.1987.1676921

UCHPC – Workshop on Unconventional High Performance Computing

UnConventional High Performance Computing 2017 (UCHPC17)

Workshop Description

Recent issues with the power consumption of conventional HPC hardware results in both new interest in accelerator hardware and in usage of mass-market hardware originally not designed for HPC. The most prominent examples are GPUs, but FPGAs, DSPs and embedded designs are also possible candidates to provide higher power efficiency, as they are used in energy-restricted environments, such as smartphones or tablets. The so-called "dark silicon" forecast, i.e. that not all transistors may be active at the same time, may lead to even more specialized hardware in future mass-market products. Exploiting this hardware for HPC can be a worthwhile challenge.

As the word "UnConventional" in the title suggests, the workshop focuses on usage of hardware or platforms for HPC, which are not (yet) conventially used today, and may not be designed for HPC in the first place. Reasons for its use can be raw computing power, good performance per watt, or low cost in general. To address this unconventional hardware, often, new programming approaches and paradigms are required to make best use of it. Another focus of the workshop is on innovative, (yet) unconventional new programming models, and algorithms (e.g. Big Data) exploiting unconventional HPC hardware or software. To this end, UCHPC tries to capture solutions for HPC which are unconventional today but could become conventional and significant tomorrow, and thus provide a glimpse into the future of HPC.

This year was the 10th time the UCHPC workshop took place, and it is the 8th time in a row it is co-located with Euro-Par (each year since 2010). Before that, it was held in conjunction with the *International Conference on Computational Science and Its Applications 2008* and with the *ACM International Conference on Computing Frontiers 2009*. However, UCHPC is a perfect addition to the scientific fields of Euro-Par, and this is confirmed by the continuous interest we see among Euro-Par attendees for this workshop.

While the general focus of the workshop is fixed, the topic actually is a moving target. GPUs were quite unconventional for HPC a few years ago, but today a notable portion of the machines in the Top500 list is making use of them. Due to raising costs for energy consumption, low-power processors and hardware specialized for specific tasks – including FPGAs – are a hot topic in HPC nowadays. The raising interest in FPGAs can be seen in that more than half of the papers accepted for UCHPC 2017 did research on embracing FPGAs for HPC. Furthermore, a lot of energy may be wasted in not using the right interface between hardware and software. It can help a lot to design both sides together to reach new performance peaks. To this end, we invited Miquel Moreto (from the Barcelona Supercomputing Center/UPC) to give a keynote on "Co-Designing HPC Architectures and the Runtime System". He also talked about the started project for an European HPC platform where FPGAs play a central role.

These post-workshop proceedings include the final versions of the papers presented at UCHPC and accepted for publication. They take the feedback from reviewers and workshop audience into account.

The workshop organizers/program chairs want to thank the authors of the papers for joining us in Santiago de Compostela, the program committee for doing the hard work of reviewing all submissions, the conference organizers for providing such a nice venue, and last but not least the large number of attendees again this year.

Steering Committee

Jens Breitbart	Bosch Driver Assistance, Germany
Anders Hast	Uppsala University, Sweden
Josef Weidendorfer	Technische Universität München, Germany
Jan-Philipp Weiss	COMSOL, Sweden

Program Chairs

Jens Breitbart	Bosch Driver Assistance, Germany
Josef Weidendorfer	Technische Universität München, Germany

Program Committee

Michael Bader	Technische Universität München, Germany
Denis Barthou	University of Bordeaux, France
Alex Bartzas	National Techn. University of Athens, Greece
Michaela Blott	Xilinx, Ireland
Jens Breitbart	Technische Universität München, Germany
Georgios Dimitrakopoulos	Democritus University of Thrace, Greece
Karl Fürlinger	Ludwig-Maximilians-Univ. München, Germany
Frank Hannig	University of Erlangen-Nuremberg, Germany
Anders Hast	Uppsala University, Sweden
Paul Keir	University of the West of Scotland, UK
Rainer Keller	Hochschule für Technik Stuttgart, Germany
Gaurav Khanna	University of Massachusetts Dartmouth, USA
Stefan Lankes	RWTH Aachen, Germany
Manfred Mücke	Materials Center Leoben, Austria
Yannis Papaefstathiou	Technical University of Crete, Greece

Bertil Schmidt	University of Mainz, Germany
Carsten Trinitis	Technische Universität München, Germany
Josef Weidendorfer	Technische Universität München, Germany
Jan-Philipp Weiss	COMSOL, Sweden
Peter Zinterhof jun.	University of Salzburg, Austria

Accelerating the 3-D FFT Using a Heterogeneous FPGA Architecture

Matthew Anderson[(✉)], Maciej Brodowicz, Martin Swany, and Thomas Sterling

School of Informatics and Computing, Center for Research in Extreme Scale Technologies, Indiana University, Bloomington, IN 47408, USA
andersmw@indiana.edu

Abstract. Future Exascale architectures will likely make extensive use of computing accelerators such as Field Programmable Gate Arrays (FPGAs) given that these accelerators are very power efficient. Oftentimes, these FPGAs are located at the network interface card (NIC) and switch level in order to accelerate network operations, incorporate contention avoiding routing schemes, and perform computations directly on the NIC and bypass the arithmetic logic unit (ALU) of the CPU. This work explores just such a heterogeneous FPGA architecture in the context of two kernels that are driving applications in leadership machines: the 3-D Fast Fourier Transform (3-D FFT) and Asynchronous Multi-Tasking (AMT). The machine explored here is a DataVortex system which consists of conventional processors but with programmable logic incorporated in the memory architecture. The programmable logic controls the network and is incorporated both in the network interface cards and the network switches and implements a contention avoiding network routing. Both the 3-D FFT and AMT kernels show compelling performance for deployment to FFT driven applications in both molecular dynamics and density functional theory.

Keywords: FFT · FPGA · Heterogeneous systems
Asynchronous multitasking · High radix networks
Contention avoiding routing

1 Introduction

Future Exascale architectures will likely make extensive use of computing accelerators such as Field Programmable Gate Arrays (FPGAs) given that these accelerators are very power efficient. Oftentimes, these FPGAs are located at the network interface card (NIC) such as in the NetFPGA project [16] which has generated a large body of research on ways this configuration can improve networks. Programmable logic at the NIC not only offloads computation from the CPU to the NIC, but also enables more complicated routing schemes and topologies that can reduce contention at the scales Exascale researchers attempt to address. This work explores just such a heterogeneous FPGA architecture in

© Springer International Publishing AG, part of Springer Nature 2018
D. B. Heras and L. Bougé (Eds.): Euro-Par 2017 Workshops, LNCS 10659, pp. 653–663, 2018.
https://doi.org/10.1007/978-3-319-75178-8_52

the context of two kernels that are driving applications in leadership machines: the 3-D Fast Fourier Transform (3-D FFT) and Asynchronous Multi-Tasking (AMT).

The 3-D FFT kernel is a well known high performance computing (HPC) benchmark and is a key kernel in a wide range of HPC applications including molecular dynamics and density functional theory. AMT kernels, on the other hand, come from those emerging runtime models which combine multithreading with some form of message-driven computation. These runtime models, sometimes referred to as "Asynchronous Multi-Tasking" or "AMT", feature the ability to express and perform fine grain thread parallelism in the context of distributed computation while also supporting the coarse grained parallelism of conventional parallel programming practice. Some examples of experimental AMT implementations include OCR [7], Legion [6], the Habanero family of languages [23,25,29,33], the Grappa framework for distributed shared memory [30], HPX [3,4], Qthreads [8], X10 [10], and Charm++ [1]. An emerging challenge for AMT implementations is that they generate a large number of small messages when operating in the modality of fine grain computation. While this may present a problem for a conventional system, a heterogeneous FPGA architecture is better equipped to handle this modality of operation.

The machine explored in this work is a DataVortex 200 series [2] which consists of conventional processors but with programmable logic incorporated in the memory architecture. The programmable logic controls the network and is incorporated both in the network interface cards and the network switches and implements a contention avoiding network routing. In June 2016 a DataVortex 200 series ranked 20th in the Green Graph 500 list [22] achieving 8.39 MTEPS per Watt.

For the 3-D FFT kernel, the expanded memory hierarchy in the network serves to significantly accelerate global memory rotations resulting in a significant speedup in FFT performance. For the AMT kernel, the incorporation of programmable logic directly controlling the network enables high memory bandwidth for small message sizes. These traits may prove crucial for applications in an Exascale setting.

This work is structured as follows. Related work is given in Sect. 2, followed by a detailed description of the prototype system and qualitative analysis of the potential of this type of architecture for Exascale in Sect. 3. Section 4 explores AMT runtime system requirements for dynamic applications and presents microbenchmark results empirically exploring small message behavior on the machine. Section 5 introduces the 3-D FFT kernel and explores the performance of this kernel in both a conventional and FPGA accelerated modality. The conclusions and directions for future work are given in Sect. 6.

2   Related Work

The incorporation of programmable logic into network interface cards has become extremely popular. The open source NetFPGA project [16] has been cited in hundreds of academic works and is an open source field programmable gate array (FPGA) PCI Express board with Gigabit or Ten Gigabit Ethernet networking ports. This project has enabled hundreds of groups to experiment with programmable logic at the network interface card level with SRAM for data rearrangement and buffering. There are also many vendors selling PCI Express boards with programmable logic for building systems like the prototype system explored in this work including Bittware [12] and Alpha Data [11]. The widespread adoption of this technology for networks itself suggests the importance of studying a prototype system for potential Exascale use. The use of FPGAs for low-latency contention avoiding networking designs has already been adopted by high frequency traders in the financial industry [26,28].

Concurrent with the massive interest in programmable logic in network cards is the large body of topology work aimed at improving communication bandwidth through the elimination of link contention. Some examples of adaptive routing schemes to avoid contention include those of Reed [32], Deniziak and Tomaszewski [19] and Zhao et al. [36]. Topologies matter for performance and this is especially well illustrated in the Dragonfly work [24]. A significant strength of the prototype system explored in this work is the contention-avoiding topology.

3 Experimental Setup

The prototype system for exploring the FFT and AMT kernels is the DataVortex 200 series system described here. The system consists of 8 nodes with one Intel Xeon E5-1630v3 operating at 3.7 GHz per node and 8 FPGA-based network interface cards. Each of these cards is an Altera Stratix 5 A7 FPGA and has 32 MB of SRAM. These network interface cards are connected to a switchboard consisting of four Altera Stratix 5 B6 FPGAs. The cards operate at a throughput of 550 million packets/sec and are connected across the PCIe 3.0 controller using eight lanes with an aggregate packet bandwidth of 35.2 GB/s in each direction for the entire 8 nodes. For network comparison studies, the prototype system also contains Mellanox Infiniband cards (Connect-X 3 VPI) to provide a redundant network against which to compare performance. The *stream* benchmark [9] on a single core of the prototype system indicates a sustained memory bandwidth of 14.5 GB/s.

All results in this work originate from the prototype system including both the AMT and FFT control cases which do not use programmable logic with SRAM and the DataVortex FPGA architecture cases which do. Due to the small size of the prototype system, there is no expected performance impact from the contention avoiding routing at the prototype system scale. The contention avoiding routing algorithm implemented is that of Reed [32]. In both the AMT and FFT kernels, the SRAM of the FPGAs is heavily utilized in order to accelerate strided memory accesses in conjunction with network operations. The small message behavior of the FPGA driven network is key for just the AMT kernel. Small messages are a key component of AMT runtime systems and have shown significant potential for improving the scalability and performance of scaling constrained applications [18,34].

4   Asynchronous Multi-tasking Kernel

Asynchonrous Multi-Tasking runtime systems frequently target medium to fine grain thread parallelism rather than the coarse-grained process parallelism employed in conventional parallel programming practices. This approach can significantly improve efficiency in algorithms with irregular and time-varying execution properties and show promise for Exascale usage. However, dynamic task and resource management execution for fine grain thread parallelism also results in a large number of small messages rather than the relatively small number of large messages that frequently appears when using conventional parallel programming practice. An example of this is illustrated in Fig. 1. Figure 1 shows a visualization of the sparsity pattern of network communication and size of messages for two different execution modalities of the Livermore Unstructured Lagrangian Explicit Shock Hydrodynamics (LULESH) mini-application. LULESH [5] is a proxy application representing a commonly used kernel in scientific computation intended to better measure and reflect realizable performance on high performance computing architectures than benchmarks such as High Performance Linpack (HPL) [20] while also serving as a performance measure for potential Exascale architectures and to optimize for power, energy, and performance [27]. The two different execution modalities explored are coarse grain parallelism as typified using conventional parallel programming practice and asynchronous multi-tasking for fine grain parallelism and the modalities were explored using the SST/macro simulator [21] where MPI was used for the

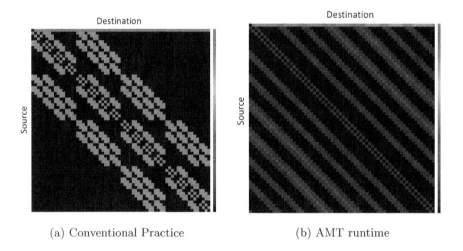

(a) Conventional Practice   (b) AMT runtime

Fig. 1. A visualization of the sparsity pattern of network communication and size of messages for the LULESH mini-application for both coarse grained conventional practice and a fine grained AMT approach. The color indicates the size of the messages with red being the largest and black being zero size. The conventional practice shows fewer but larger mesages while the AMT approach shows many more messages of much smaller size. (Color figure online)

conventional approach and HPX was used for the AMT approach. LULESH performance and network behavior were simulated on 64 nodes of a Cray XE6 for both modalities with significant overdecomposition in the AMT modality. The AMT approach generates significantly many more smaller messages than the conventional approach. Most networks, however, show their best efficiency with fewer, larger messages. In order to explore typical AMT behavior, the AMT kernel explored in this section is alltoall communication limited to 8 byte messages.

The prototype system programmable logic network shows behavior substantially different from conventional networks and favors large numbers of small messages such as what is seen in AMT runtime executions like that of Fig. 1. Alltoall communication bandwidth for 8 byte messages comparing infiniband and the programmable logic network of the prototype system is shown in Fig. 2. For many small messages the programmable logic network significantly increases communication bandwidth for typical AMT execution modalities. This characteristic may become an important feature for future Exascale architectures and is a natural consequence of the programmable logic network created for the prototype system here.

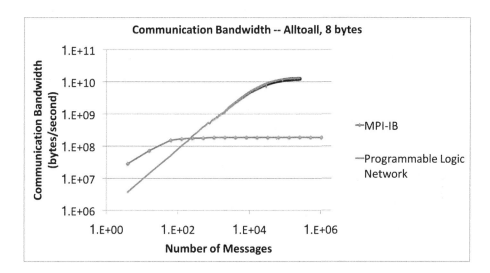

Fig. 2. Alltoall communication bandwidth for 8 byte messages comparing infiniband and the programmable logic network of the prototype system. For many small messages such as that in the AMT modality of Fig. 1, the programmable logic network has the benefit of not only employing contention avoiding routing but also increasing communication bandwidth for AMT execution modalities.

5   3-D Fast Fourier Transform

The 3-D Fast Fourier Transform (FFT) is a key scientific computing kernel used in many widely used software frameworks and toolkits. Some of these include widely used molecular dynamics toolkits such as NAMD [31] and Gromacs [14] and Density Functional Theory toolkits such as VASP [17]. In NAMD, the smooth Particle-Mesh Ewald method [35] is critically dependent on the distributed 3-D FFT implementation for both performance and scalability. The 3-D FFT is also an important kernel for computational fluid dynamics simulations. Any potential Exascale architecture will need to compute the 3-D FFT extremely efficiently as well as strong scale without generating a lot of network contention.

Among the many ways to implement a 3-D FFT, several global memory rotations are usually implemented so that a 1-D FFT is applied along 1-D lengths of data that are stored consecutively in memory for fast access. No strided memory accesses occur this way and such 3-D FFT implementations are very fast. However, such global memory rotations are expensive requiring both a large alltoall operation and some data reordering. The incorporation of SRAM in the programmable logic network enables the network to also perform such a memory rotation when taking each of the x, y, and z FFTs and thereby compute the FFTs using the fastest memory layout possible. These rotations are illustrated in Fig. 3. The 3-D data is decomposed across the distributed memory system in just one dimension giving each CPU access to the entire fast dimension domain memory each time an FFT is computed. The initial memory layout has fastest access in the z direction and so the z FFT is computed first. The first rotation then places fastest memory access in the x direction for computing the x FFT. The second rotation places the fastest memory access in the y direction for computing the y FFT. The last rotation returns the memory to the original layout. Rotations in memory and FFT computations are entirely overlapped due to the expanded memory hierarchy in the network.

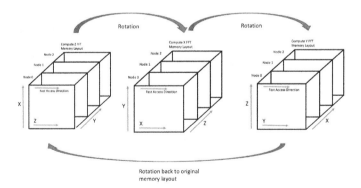

Fig. 3. The programmable logic network and associated SRAM are used to perform quick memory rotations and network communication for optimal memory layout of FFT computations. For a memory layout that begins with fastest access in the z direction, the z FFT is computed first. The first rotation then places fastest memory access in the x direction for computing the x FFT. The second rotation places the fastest memory access in the y direction for computing the y FFT. The last rotation returns the memory to the original layout.

For comparison purposes, the FFT kernel on the programmable logic network is compared against performance from the widely used MPI-FFTW library [13] and the FFT NAS Parallel Benchmark [15]. All of the comparison cases using MPI-FFTW or the NAS Parallel Benchmark were conducted on the prototype system but used the infiniband network. Figure 4 gives the time to solution for a fixed problem size, 1024^3 3-D FFT run from 1 to 8 nodes on the prototype system for complex double precision. In this figure, the lower the time to solution, the better the result. The programmable logic network version significantly outperforms the MPI-FFTW comparison in each case by around a factor of 4 or 5. The performance of the programmable logic network FFT is also better even on a single node, reflecting the usage of the fast programmable logic SRAM for data rearrangement and optimal FFT computation even while not in a distributed modality. Figure 5 gives the strong scaling speedup for the complex double 3-D FFT calculations. The programmable logic network FFT scales linearly with the number of nodes in both cases in addition to giving the significant performance advantage illustrated in Fig. 4.

The NAS Parallel Benchmark for FFT enables a comparison in terms of GFlops with the programmable logic network FFT. This comparison is shown in Fig. 6. In these results, several different problem sizes were explored consistent with NAS PB classes A–D while the programmable logic network FFT was performed at cubic sizes. In each case, the entire 8 node system was used. The performance improvement when using the programmable logic network versus

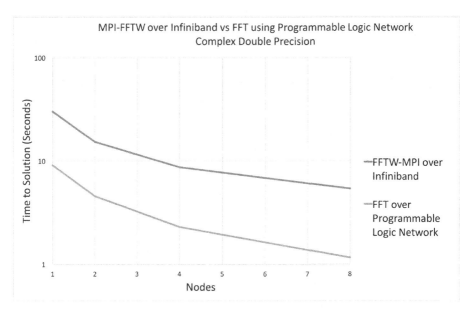

Fig. 4. Strong scaling result showing the time to solution between a 1024^3 complex double 3-D FFT using either MPI-FFTW over infiniband or the FFT with the programmable logic network. In this plot, the lower the line, the faster the time to solution and the better the result. All simulations used the prototype system. The scaling comparison for this data is found in Fig. 5.

the NAS PB over infiniband is between a factor of 3 and 4. The peak sustained performance for the programmable logic network version of the 3-D FFT was 163.1 GFlops over 8 nodes.

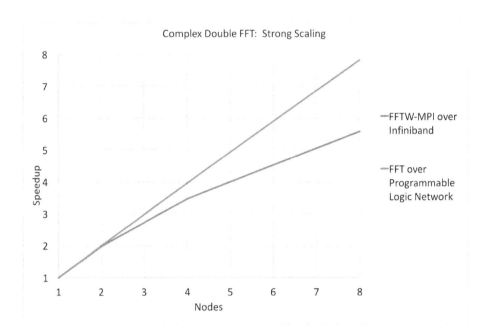

Fig. 5. Strong scaling result showing the speedup between a 1024^3 complex double 3-D FFT using either MPI-FFTW over infiniband or the FFT with the programmable logic network. In this plot, the higher the line, the better the scalability and the result. All simulations used the prototype system. The time to solution comparison for this data is found in Fig. 4.

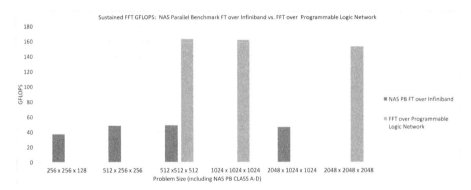

Fig. 6. A comparison of sustained GFlops for the FFT operation comparing the NAS Parallel FT Benchmark over Infiniband with the FFT over the programmable logic network. All results used the prototype system and use the the full system (8 nodes). Multiple 3-D problem sizes are explored. The NAS parallel FT benchmark peaks at 49 GFlops while the FFT over the programmable logic network peaks at 163 GFlops.

6   Conclusions

Because it is expected that FPGAs will likely play a significant role in reducing power consumption in emerging and future supercomputers, this work has explored a heterogeneous FPGA machine which incorporates programmable logic that both expands the memory architecture and controls the network. Two application motivated scientific computing kernels were explored on a small 8 node prototype system: an AMT kernel consisting of alltoall with 8 byte messages and the 3-D fast Fourier transform. While the AMT kernel tested the small message communication bandwidth capability of the system, the 3-D FFT kernel tested the global memory rotation capability of the system in order to accelerate performance over conventional practice.

High communication bandwidth for small messages was explored due to its importance for asynchronous multi-tasking runtime systems which target medium to fine grain thread parallelism and generate large numbers of small messages. This was demonstrated explicitly in this work using the SST/macro simulator. AMT runtime systems may become key components of the Exascale software stack both to improve efficiency and programmability. The FPGA machine was able to significantly outperform the equivalent infiniband 8 byte message alltoall. While a conventional application running on a conventional machine addresses this performance issue through message coalescence, AMT applications will often opt to avoid coalescence for greater overlap of computational phases. In this modality, the FPGA machine shows promise.

Fast rotations in conjunction with the programmable logic network enable a very fast algorithmic approach to 3-D FFT's so that the memory layout is arranged for optimal access at the same time the network exchanges necessary data between nodes. This results in performance improvements of as much as a factor of 5 over conventional practice in computing 3-D FFT's for the small prototype system in this work. Future work will directly explore the performance impact of this architecture on molecular dynamics toolkits like NAMD and density functional theory toolkits like VASP.

References

1. Charm++. http://charm.cs.illinois.edu/research/charm/
2. Datavortex. http://www.datavortex.com/
3. HPX. http://stellar.cct.lsu.edu/tag/hpx/
4. HPX-5. http://hpx.crest.iu.edu
5. Hydrodynamics Challenge Problem. Technical report LLNL-TR-490254, Lawrence Livermore National Laboratory
6. Legion programming system. http://legion.stanford.edu/
7. Open Community Runtime. https://01.org/open-community-runtime
8. Qthreads. http://www.cs.sandia.gov/qthreads/
9. Stream benchmark. https://www.cs.virginia.edu/stream/
10. X10. http://x10-lang.org/
11. Alpha data (2016). www.alpha-data.com

12. Bittware (2016). www.bittware.com
13. FFTW (2016). www.fftw.org
14. GROMACS (2016). www.gromacs.org
15. NAS parallel benchmarks (2016). https://www.nas.nasa.gov/publications/npb.html
16. NetFPGA project (2016). netfpga.org
17. VASP (2017). www.vasp.at
18. Anderson, M., Brodowicz, M., Kulkarni, A., Sterling, T.: Performance modeling of gyrokinetic toroidal simulations for a many-tasking runtime system. In: Jarvis, S.A., Wright, S.A., Hammond, S.D. (eds.) PMBS 2013. LNCS, vol. 8551, pp. 136–157. Springer, Cham (2014). https://doi.org/10.1007/978-3-319-10214-6_7
19. Deniziak, S., Tomaszewski, R.: Contention-avoiding custom topology generation for network-on-chip. In: Proceedings of the 2009 12th International Symposium on Design and Diagnostics of Electronic Circuits and Systems, DDECS 2009, pp. 234–237. IEEE Computer Society, Washington, DC, USA (2009). https://doi.org/10.1109/DDECS.2009.5012136
20. Dongarra, J.: Performance of various computers using standard linear equations software. Technical report CS-89-85, University of Tennesse Computer Science (2014). http://www.netlib.org/benchmark/performance.pdf
21. Hendry, G., Rodrigues, A.: SST: a simulator for exascale co-design. In: Proceedings of the ASCR/ASC Exascale Research Conference (2012)
22. Hoefler, T.: Seventh green graph 500 list (2016). http://green.graph500.org/
23. Imam, S., Sarkar, V.: Habanero-Java library: a Java 8 framework for multicore programming. In: 11th International Conference on the Principles and Practice of Programming on the Java Platform: Virtual Machines, Languages, and Tools (PPPJ 2014), September 2014
24. Kim, J., Dally, W.J., Scott, S., Abts, D.: Technology-driven, highly-scalable Dragonfly topology. In: Proceedings of the 35th International Symposium on Compute Architecture, ISCA 2008. IEEE (2008)
25. Kumar, V., Zheng, Y., Cave, V., Budimlic, Z., Sarkar, V.: HabaneroUPC++: a compiler-free PGAS library. In: 8th International Conference on Partitioned Global Address Space Programming Models (PGAS14), October 2014
26. Leber, C., Geib, B., Litz, H.: High frequency trading acceleration using FPGAs. In: 2011 21st International Conference on Field Programmable Logic and Applications, pp. 317–322, September 2011
27. Leon, E., Karlin, I., Grant, R.: Optimizing explicit hydrodynamics for power, energy, and performance. In: 2015 IEEE International Conference on Cluster Computing (CLUSTER), pp. 11–21, September 2015
28. Lockwood, J., Gupte, A., Mehta, N., Vissers, K.A.: A low-latency library in FPGA hardware for high-frequency trading. In: IEEE 20th Annual Symposium on High-Performance Interconnects, pp. 9–16, August 2012
29. Majeti, D., Sarkar, V.: Heterogeneous Habanero-C (H2C): a portable programming model for heterogeneous processors. In: Programming Models, Languages and Compilers for Manycore and Heterogeneous Architectures (PLC), May 2015
30. Nelson, J., Holt, B., Myers, B., Briggs, P., Ceze, L., Kahan, S., Oskin, M.: Grappa: a latency-tolerant runtime for large-scale irregular applications. In: International Workshop on Rack-Scale Computing (WRSC w/EuroSys), April 2014
31. Phillips, J.C., Braun, R., Wang, W., Gumbart, J., Tajkhorshid, E., Villa, E., Chipot, C., Skeel, R.D., Kale, L., Schulten, K.: Scalable molecular dynamics with NAMD. J. Comput. Chem. **26**, 1781–1802 (2005)

32. Reed, C.: Means and apparatus for a scaleable congestion free switching system with intelligent control III, US Patent 7835278, November 2010

33. Sarkar, V.: Habanero-Scala: Async-finish programming in Scala. In: The Third Scala Workshop (Scala Days 2012), April 2012

34. Treichler, S., Bauer, M., Aiken, A.: Realm: an event-based low-level runtime for distributed memory architectures. In: Proceedings of the 23rd International Conference on Parallel Architectures and Compilation, PACT 2014, pp. 263–276. ACM, New York, NY, USA (2014). https://doi.org/10.1145/2628071.2628084

35. Essmann, U., Perera, L., Berkowitz, M.L., Darden, T., Lee, H., Pedersen, L.G.: A smooth particle mesh Ewald method. J. Chem. Phys. **103**, 8577–8593 (1995)

36. Zhao, J., Zhou, Q., Cai, Y.: Fast congestion-aware timing-driven placement for island FPGA. In: Proceedings of the 2009 12th International Symposium on Design and Diagnostics of Electronic Circuits and Systems, DDECS 2009, pp. 24–27. IEEE Computer Society, Washington, DC, USA (2009). https://doi.org/10.1109/DDECS.2009.5012092

Evaluation of a Floating-Point Intensive Kernel on FPGA

A Case Study of Geodesic Distance Kernel

Zheming Jin[✉], Hal Finkel, Kazutomo Yoshii, and Franck Cappello

Argonne National Laboratory, Argonne, IL 60439, USA
{zjin,hfinkel,kazutomo,cappello}@anl.gov

Abstract. Heterogeneous platforms provide a promising solution for high-performance and energy-efficient computing applications. This paper presents our research on usage of heterogeneous platform for a floating-point intensive kernel. We first introduce the floating-point intensive kernel from the geographical information system. Then we analyze the FPGA designs generated by the Intel FPGA SDK for OpenCL, and evaluate the kernel performance and the floating-point error rate of the FPGA designs. Finally, we compare the performance and energy efficiency of the kernel implementations on the Arria 10 FPGA, Intel's Xeon Phi Knights Landing CPU, and NVIDIA's Kepler GPU. Our evaluation shows the energy efficiency of the single-precision kernel on the FPGA is 1.35X better than on the CPU and the GPU, while the energy efficiency of the double-precision kernel on the FPGA is 1.36X and 1.72X less than the CPU and GPU, respectively.

Keywords: HPC · FPGA · Floating-point operation · OpenCL

1 Introduction

Compared to central processing units (CPUs) and graphics processing units (GPUs), field programmable gate arrays (FPGAs) have major advantages in reconfigurability and performance achieved per watt. This development flow has been augmented with high-level synthesis (HLS) flow that can convert programs written in a high-level programming language to Hardware Description Language (HDL) [1]. Using high-level programming languages such as C, C++, and OpenCL for FPGA-based development could allow regular software developers, who have little FPGA knowledge, to take advantage of the FPGA-based application acceleration.

OpenCL is an open-source standard for data-parallel heterogeneous computing, which supports CPUs, GPUs, FPGAs, and other accelerators. OpenCL specifies functionality that vendors need to implement for their hardware features and programming interfaces. In addition, OpenCL makes it easier for a portable design across multiple hardware platforms and allows developers to optimize the functions for a specific architecture.

The Intel FPGA SDK for OpenCL supports their Cyclone-, Stratix-, and Arria-series FPGA platforms [2–4]. Xilinx offers a complete SDAccel development

© Springer International Publishing AG, part of Springer Nature 2018
D. B. Heras and L. Bougé (Eds.): Euro-Par 2017 Workshops, LNCS 10659, pp. 664–675, 2018.
https://doi.org/10.1007/978-3-319-75178-8_53

environment for OpenCL-based application acceleration on their Kintex-series and Virtex-7 FPGA products [5].

Recent publications [6–9] on optimizing OpenCL applications on FPGAs show that there are few detailed analyses of the mapping of various floating-point operations to FPGAs for a floating-point intensive kernel. The analysis and evaluation of mapping floating-point operations described in a high-level programming language to hardware are important because a user can optimize a design that enables the compiler to reduce FPGA resource usage and increase performance.

To this end, this paper presents our research on the evaluation of a floating-point intensive kernel compiled with the Intel FPGA SDK for OpenCL employing the Nallatech 385A FPGA board. The analyses of this kernel reveal how the compiler optimizes the single- and double-precision kernels and maps each floating-point arithmetic operation in the kernel to the corresponding hardware floating-point operator.

The kernel is representative of other floating-point intensive kernels. As far as the authors know, it has not been evaluated previously on the FPGA-based computing platform. In this paper, we first introduce the kernel identified in a geographical information system (GIS) and analyze the FPGA designs generated by the compiler. Then we measure the kernel execution time and the floating-point error rate of the FPGA implementations. Finally, we compare the performance and energy efficiency of the kernels on the Arria 10 FPGA, the Intel Xeon Phi Knights Landing CPU, and the NVIDIA's K80 GPU.

2   Background

As a brief overview of the OpenCL programming model, an OpenCL application consists of host and kernel programs. Its host program is written in standard C/C++ that runs on most modern microprocessors. The host allocates data arrays in the global memory that will be read by the kernel. When the data are ready for the kernel, the host launches the kernel that will be executed on the FPGA device(s). A kernel typically executes computation by reading data from global memory as specified by the host, processing it, and then writing the results back into global memory. When the results are ready, they can be read by the host for validation and post-processing.

Intel and Xilinx websites provide OpenCL literature on implementation, low-level optimization, and programming interfaces for their hardware features. In many cases, an optimized kernel with loop unrolling, vectorization, and compute-unit duplication can achieve better performance on FPGAs, but the resource usage of the resulting implementations limits the degree of task and data parallelism. In addition, the modules in the low-level kernel system architecture – including the memory access interface, local memory usage, work-group dispatch, and the interconnection network – affect kernel performance.

3 Related Work

Underwood showed that the use of FPGAs is promising for running applications with floating-point addition, multiplication and division [10]. Since then, FPGAs have been gradually decreasing the gap to GPUs and many-core CPUs for particular applications in terms of peak performance, power consumption, and sustained performance. [11].

In [12], the authors showed that the performance of the double-precision floating-point matrix multiplication on FPGAs has a 3.48X improvement over that of the processor, while the power per GFLOP of the FPGA is 7.64X lower than that of the processor. In addition, the FPGA slices of the 64-bit floating-point addition unit and multiplication unit is on average 2.5X and 3.1X more than those of the 32-bit floating-point units, respectively. Due to the FPGA size constraint, the authors only studied the floating-point add and multiply units.

In [13], the authors presented application characteristics to FPGA, CPU, and GPU platform mapping using three applications. For their future work, they suggested a direct comparison between CUDA and a high-level language for FPGAs.

In [6], the authors demonstrated that the OpenCL-based FPGA implementation of a fractal encoding kernel is 3X and 114X faster than a GPU and a multi-core CPU, respectively, while consuming 12% and 19% of the power, respectively. They compared the results on Altera Stratix IV 530 and Stratix V A7 FPGAs with a NVIDIA Fermi C2075, a 40 nm GPU; and an Intel Xeon W3690 host processor, a 32 nm CPU. Our FPGA results on the Arria 10 GX1150 are compared against the NVIDIA K80, a 28 nm GPU; and an Intel Xeon Phi Knights Landing 7210, a 14 nm CPU. This takes into account technological advances in the hardware platforms.

In [9], the authors implemented the Monte Carlo simulations option pricing with three HLS tools from Altera, Xilinx, and Maxeler, and compared the results among FPGA, CPU, and GPU accelerator platforms. Their results showed that the HLS tools are suited to accelerating parallel-friendly algorithms. The study, however, didn't analyze how floating-point operators in the kernel are implemented on each FPGA board.

The OpenCL kernels in the CHO benchmark [14] contain implementations of IEEE-standard double-precision floating-point operations using 64-bit integers, but none of the kernels have floating-point computations. For a subset of the OpenCL-based Rodinia benchmark suite, the authors achieved 3.4X greater energy efficiency using a Stratix V FPGA in comparison to a NVIDIA K20c GPU [8]. Due to the compiler and board support package issues for their Arria-10 FPGA board at the time, the results may not reflect the best performance for each kernel.

A key to efficient FPGA implementation for complicated floating-point operations is to use multiplier-based algorithms to leverage the large amount of hardened DSP resources integrated into the FPGA devices [15]. For example, Arria 10 FPGAs— Intel's first FPGAs that natively support single-precision floating-point computation using dedicated hardened circuitry—delivers 3.8X increased performance and 3.6X better energy efficiency than the Stratix V results for the SGEMM kernel [16].

When implementing real-word large floating-point functions on an FPGA, a general rule of thumb is that the clock speed of a design implementation would degrade as

```
void
geodesic_distance (TYPE * restrict lat1,
                    TYPE * restrict lon1,
                    TYPE * restrict lat2,
                    TYPE * restrict lon2,
                    TYPE * restrict out)
{   ---- BB0 ----
  i = get_global_id(0) ;  // return work-item ID
  rad_lon1 = lon1[i] * TO_RADIAN ;
  rad_lat1 = lat1[i] * TO_RADIAN ;
  rad_lon2 = lon2[i] * TO_RADIAN ;
  rad_lat2 = lat2[i] * TO_RADIAN ;

  tu1 = COMPRESSION_FACTOR * sin ( rad_lat1 ) /
                             cos ( rad_lat1 ) ;
  tu2 = COMPRESSION_FACTOR * sin ( rad_lat2 ) /
                             cos ( rad_lat2 ) ;

  cu1 = 1.0 / sqrt ( tu1 * tu1 + 1.0 ) ;
  su1 = cu1 * tu1 ;
  cu2 = 1.0 / sqrt ( tu2 * tu2 + 1.0 ) ;
  s = cu1 * cu2 ;
  baz = s * tu2 ;
  faz = baz * tu1 ;
  x = rad_lon2 - rad_lon1 ;
  ---- BB1 ----
  do  {
    sx = sin ( x ) ;
    cx = cos ( x ) ;
    tu1 = cu2 * sx ;
    tu2 = baz - su1 * cu2 * cx ;
    sy = sqrt ( tu1 * tu1 + tu2 * tu2 ) ;
    cy = s * cx + faz ;
    y = atan2 ( sy, cy ) ;
    sa = s * sx / sy ;
    c2a = - sa * sa + 1.0;
    cz = faz + faz ;
    if ( c2a > 0.0 ) cz = -cz / c2a + cy ;
    e = cz * cz * 2.0 - 1.0 ;
    c = ( ( -3.0 * c2a + 4.0 ) * FLATTENING + 4.0 ) * c2a *
      FLATTENING / 16.0 ;
    d = x ;
    x = ( ( e * cy * c + cz ) * sy * c + y ) * sa ;
    x = ( 1.0 - c ) * x * FLATTENING + rad_lon2 - rad_lon1 ;
  } while ( fabs ( d - x ) > EPS ) ;
  ---- BB2 ----
  x = sqrt ( ELLIPSOIDAL * c2a + 1.0 ) + 1.0 ;
  x = ( x - 2.0 ) / x ;
  c = 1.0 - x ;
  c = ( x * x / 4.0 + 1.0 ) / c ;
  d = ( 0.375 * x * x - 1.0 ) * x ;
  x = e * cy ;
  s = 1.0 - e - e ;
  s = ( ( ( ( sy * sy * 4.0 - 3.0 ) * s * cz * d / 6.0 - x ) *
      d / 4.0 + cz ) * sy * d + y ) * c * POLAR_RADIUS ;
  out[i] = s;
}
```

Fig. 1. Pseudocodes for the geodesic distance kernel.

FPGA resource utilization rises above 70–80%. This high-resource utilization often requires more effort spent on placement, routing, and timing optimization. Intel FPGA SDK for OpenCL version 16.0.2 Pro Prime, for example, fails to generate FPGA implementations for two kernels in the CHO benchmark due to routing congestion [17]. In addition, floating-point results generally do not strictly match across different heterogeneous computing platforms. For example, Leeser et al. give an example of the numerical accuracy difference in the sequential and parallel versions of a floating-point intensive program [18] when analyzing the behavior of an OpenCL floating-point benchmark on different heterogeneous architectures.

4 OpenCL Kernel Implementation

4.1 Kernel Description

The geodesic distance kernel calculates the distance between two geographic coordinates on the earth's surface. Earth's shape is modelled as an ellipsoid. The shortest distance between two points along the surface of an ellipsoid is along the geodesic. The methods for computing the geodesic distance are available in GIS, software libraries, standalone utilities, and online tools [19]. The OpenCL kernel is based on the open-source implementation [20] of the solution to the inverse geodesic problem [21].

Figure 1 presents the pseudocodes for the kernel. Each coordinate of a point is represented as latitude and longitude in degrees. The default type of the coordinate is double-precision floating-point type. The kernel is composed of three building blocks (BB0, BB1 and BB2) annotated in Fig. 1, and is floating-point intensive with more than 100 floating-point arithmetic operations.

4.2 Analyses of Kernel Implementations

The Intel FPGA SDK for OpenCL compiler generates three block modules in Verilog HDL corresponding to the three building blocks in the kernel. Table 1 shows the number of double-precision floating-point operator instances in the Verilog HDL codes generated by the compiler without any floating-point optimization options enabled. From the arithmetic expressions in the BB0, the compiler instantiates four divide operators (dp_div), two square root operators (dp_sqrt) and two combined sine and cosine operators (dp_sincos) in the HDL library of the Intel FPGA SDK for OpenCL. There are only 12 multiplications in the BB0, but the number of instantiated multipliers (dp_mul) is 13. The generated Verilog HDL code reveals that the compiler performs a global optimization to include the multiplication "su1 * cu2" from the BB1, as "su1", "cu2", and their product have no dependency with other variables in the BB1.

For the BB1, the compiler produces the expected number of operators for sincos, atan2, and sqrt operations. The compiler, however, instantiates 18 multipliers, less than the number of multiplications in the expressions. The compiler optimizes away the multiplications in "cz * 2.0" and "−3.0 * c2a". For the divide operations, the compiler instantiates two dividers and converts the "divide by 16.0" operation to an adjustment to the exponent of the result.

Table 1. Number of double-precision floating-point operators instantiated by the compiler without using floating-point optimization

Operator	BB0	BB1	BB2	Total
dp_mul	13	18	13	44
dp_div	4	2	3	9
dp_sincos	2	1	0	3
dp_atan2	0	1	0	1
dp_sqrt	2	1	1	4

Table 2. Number of double-precision floating-point operators instantiated by the compiler using option "–fpc"

Operator	BB0	BB1	BB2	Total
dp_div	4	2	3	9
dp_sincos	2	1	0	3
dp_atan2	0	1	0	1
dp_sqrt	2	1	1	4
int_mul	13	18	13	44

For the BB2, the compiler attempts to optimize away the "multiply by constant" operations and is able to factor out the common product "x * x" in the block. Therefore, the compiler instantiates 13 multiply operators. For the divide operations, the compiler does not optimize away the "x/6.0", as "x/6" is not precisely equivalent to "x * 1/6.0". Therefore, three dividers are instantiated.

Overall, the compiler instantiates 44 multiply, nine divide, three sincos, one atan2, and four square root operators. It does not instantiate other floating-point operators from the HDL IP library. Instead, they are directly implemented using combinational and sequential logics. While the compiler supports the optimization option of replacing a * b + c with a multiply-and-add (MAD) operator, a double-precision MAD operator is not available in the IP library.

The Intel FPGA OpenCL programming guide [22] describes how users can reduce the amount of floating-point hardware resources with the "–fpc" option of the compiler command. The option removes floating-point rounding options and conversions whenever possible.

Table 2 shows the number of double-precision floating-point operators of each type instantiated by the compiler when using the optimization option. The option removes intermediary roundings and conversions when possible and changes the rounding modes to round towards zero for multiply and add operations. Compared to the results in Table 1, the option directs the compiler to instantiate 44 54 × 54-bit integer multiply operators because mantissa multiplication requires a 54 × 54-bit hardware multiplier.

While another floating-point optimization option, "–fp_relaxed", can lead to more efficient hardware resource usage by relaxing the order of arithmetic floating-point operations, the FPGA resource usage report does not show resource reduction for the kernel.

For the single-precision floating-point kernel, Table 3 shows the number of operators of each type instantiated by the compiler without any floating-point optimization options enabled. The compiler instantiates multiply (sp_mul), add (sp_add), subtract (sp_sub), and compare (sp_cmp) operators from the IP library. The compiler optimizes the multiply and add operations with multadd (a * b + c) and dot2 (a * b + c * d) operators. Compared to the double-precision implementations, the compiler can generate high-performance hardened floating-point implementations by taking advantage

Table 3. Number of single-precision floating-point operators instantiated by the compiler.

Operator	BB0	BB1	BB2	Total
sp_mul	13	16	13	42
sp_add	1	4	6	11
sp_sub	1	4	4	9
sp_multadd	2	6	3	11
sp_div	4	2	3	9
sp_sincos	2	1	0	3
sp_dot2	0	1	0	1
sp_atan2	0	1	0	1
sp_sqrt	2	1	1	4
sp_cmp	0	2	0	2

of the native floating-point operators offered by Arria 10 FPGA devices [23]. The compiler, however, does not discover additional multiply and add operations using the "-cl-mad-enable" optimization flag. When the optimization option "–fpc" or "–fp-relaxed" is enabled for the single-precision floating-point kernel, the compiler may ignore the option and generate the same Verilog HDL codes.

5   Experimental Results

5.1   Experimental Setup

We chose the Intel Xeon Phi Knights Landing (KNL) 7210 processor with 64 cores and four threads per core as the target CPU, with high-bandwidth on-package memory in cache mode. The program is compiled using an Intel C compiler, version 2018 Beta, with the "-O3" option, OpenMP, and AVX-512 SIMD instruction enabled. Its system thermal design power is 215 W, and its idle CPU package power is approximately 60 W [24].

We chose the NVIDIA K80 with 2,496 cores as the target GPU. Its peak performance is 2.8 TFLOPS for double-precision, and 0.95 TFLOPS for single-precision. The GPU's power limit is 149 W with an idle power of 74.15 W with persistence mode enabled. The program is compiled with CUDA Toolkit 7.5.

We used the Intel's FPGA SDK for OpenCL version 16.0.2 Pro Prime to compile the OpenCL kernels into the hardware configuration files. The target FPGA board is a Nallatech 385A, a PCIe-based FPGA accelerator card that features an Arria 10 GX1150 FPGA device, PCIe x8 Generation 3 host interface, and two banks of 4 GB DDR3 memory. The theoretical peak floating-point performance of the Arria10 chip is 1.5 TFLOPS, and the theoretical peak memory bandwidth is approximately 34 GB/s. The FPGA board's idle power is 27.3 W.

The input test data are retrieved from Maxmind's world cities database [25] that includes city, region, country, latitude, and longitude. In our experiment, we extracted 2^{21} cities with unique locations around the world. We chose four cities (Mumbai,

Sydney, Federal District Mexico, and London) from which the kernel computed distances to each of the 2^{21} cities.

5.2   Resource Usage, Performance, and Power

Tables 4 and 5 show the FPGA resource usage of double- and single-precision implementations of the kernel respectively. Replication of the compute unit is represented as "cuX", where X indicates the replication times. The maximum frequency (Fmax) of the double-precision kernels is approximately 230 MHz. Since each compute unit requires 515 DSPs, and there are a total of 1,518 DSPs on the target device, only two duplicate kernels (cu2) can be implemented. The approximate 30% logic utilization for each kernel also constrains the number of duplicate kernels. Compared to the double-precision floating-point kernel, the single-precision version can accommodate nine duplicate compute units (cu9), as shown in Table 5. However, the Fmax decreases from 280 MHz to 212 MHz, as the number of compute units increase from one to nine.

The kernel execution time is a performance metric that measures the execution time of a kernel on an FPGA device. Figure 2 shows that the kernel execution time of a single double-precision compute unit is 198.9 ms and 196.9 ms for cu1 (without –fpc) and cu1(–fpc), respectively. For two compute units, the kernel execution time depends on the local work size. When the local work size ranges from 2^4 to 2^{20}, the kernel execution time reaches the minimum values of 100.5 ms and 103.5 ms, respectively.

For one single-precision compute unit (cu1), as shown in Fig. 3, the execution time of the kernel is 75 ms, 62% less than the execution time of the double-precision kernel. For multiple compute units, the kernel execution time also depends on the local work size. The kernel execution time reaches the minimum values of 21.1 ms for cu4 when the local work size is 2^{14}, and 13 ms for cu9 when the local work size is 2^8.

The FPGA power consumption results of the double- and single-precision floating-point kernel are shown in Figs. 4 and 5, respectively. When there is one compute unit, the power is 35.6 W and 34.7 W for the double-precision floating-point kernel and its resource-optimized version, respectively. The power of one single-precision floating-point kernel is only 30.7 W. The power increases to the

Table 4. Resource usage and maximum frequency of the double-precision kernel implementations.

	cu1	cu1 (fpc)	cu2	cu2 (fpc)
Logic utilization	36%	28%	61%	45%
Memory bits	14%	14%	22%	21%
RAM blocks	25%	25%	44%	38%
#DSPs	515	515	1030	1030
Fmax (MHz)	230	233	227	221

Table 5. Resource usage and maximum frequency of the single-precision kernel implementations.

	cu1	cu4	cu9
Logic utilization	15%	28%	49%
Memory bits	8%	12%	17%
RAM blocks	18%	35%	63%
#DSPs	160	640	1440
Fmax (MHz)	280	255	212

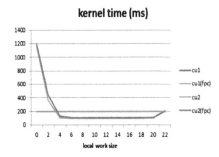

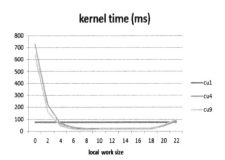

Fig. 2. Kernel execution time of the double-precision implementations. The local work size in the x axis indicates $2^{\text{local work size}}$.

Fig. 3. Kernel execution time of the single-precision implementations. The local work size in the x axis indicates $2^{\text{local work size}}$.

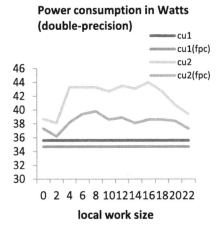

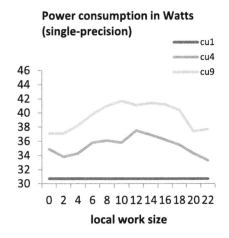

Fig. 4. Power consumption of the double-precision kernel implementations. The local work size in the x axis indicates $2^{\text{local work size}}$.

Fig. 5. Power consumption of the single-precision kernel implementations. The local work size in the x axis indicates $2^{\text{local work size}}$.

maximum 44 W for two double-precision compute units and a maximum of 41.7 W for nine single-precision compute units. While reducing the FPGA resource usage can effectively reduce the power, the results show that power consumption is also related to local work size for multiple compute units.

6   Comparison of CPU, GPU, and FPGA Results

In our experiment, the execution time of the kernel averages over 256 iterations. The CPU power is measured with an in-house energy trace utility, the GPU power is measured with the NVIDIA Management Library, and the FPGA power is measured with Nallatech's board support package. For the GPU implementations, we use standard math functions instead of floating-point intrinsic functions [26]. In addition, we do not employ any floating-point optimizations provided by the CPU and GPU compilers.

As shown in Table 6, the CPU consumes the highest power (190 W), the FPGA the lowest power (44 W). Due to the DSP and logic resource constraints on the FPGA device, its execution time is more than 5X slower than the CPU and GPU for the double-precision kernel, and less than 3.25X slower for the single-precision kernel. The execution time on the GPU and CPU differ by approximately 1 ms for each kernel.

We define *energy efficiency* as the number of normalized distance calculations in millions in a second per watt:

$$\text{Energy efficiency} = \frac{n}{\text{kernel time} \times \text{maximum power} \times 1.0E6} \quad (1)$$

where n is the normalized size of the input data (i.e., a pair of double-precision coordinates equivalent to two pairs of single-precision coordinates).

As shown in Fig. 6, the GPU has the best energy efficiency (6.51) for the double-precision kernel, while the FPGA has the best energy efficiency (15.36) for the single-precision kernel. The energy efficiency of the single-precision kernel is better than that of the double-precision kernel on each platform. The energy efficiency of the single-precision kernel on the FPGA is 1.35X better than the K80 and KNL7210, while the energy efficiency of the double-precision kernel on the FPGA is 1.36X and 1.72X less than the CPU and GPU, respectively.

Table 6. Performance and energy efficiency of CPU, GPU and FPGA for the double-precision (DP) and single-precision (SP) kernels.

	CPU_{DP}	CPU_{SP}	GPU_{DP}	GPU_{SP}	FPGA_{DP}	FPGA_{SP}
Execution time (ms)	18.3	4	17.7	5.4	100.5	13
Maximum power (W)	190	190	145.5	136.7	44	42

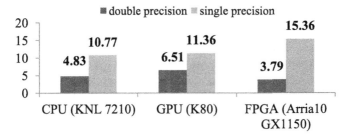

Fig. 6. Million distance calculations per watt for the single-precision and double-precision kernels on the three platforms.

7 Conclusion

We introduce the floating-point intensive geodesic distance kernel, analyze the FPGA designs generated by the compiler, and evaluate the kernel performance, resource usage, and error rate for the FPGA implementations. Two compute units can be realized for the double-precision version of the kernel on the Arria 10 GX1150, while nine can be used for the single-precision version. Single-precision floating-point computation is suitable for the current generation of FPGA devices, based on FPGA performance, resource usage, and energy efficiency of single- and double-precision floating-point kernel implementations.

In the case of the geodesic distance kernel, the energy efficiency of the single-precision kernel is 1.35X better than the GPU and CPU, while the energy efficiency of the double-precision kernel is 1.36X and 1.72X less.

The FPGA results are promising as the upcoming 14-nm Stratix 10 GX FPGA devices are power aware [27] and provide more DSPs, memory, and adaptive logic resources [28]. The GX 2800 device, for example, has 933,120 ALMs, 5,760 DSPs and 11,721 M20 memory blocks, which will allow more than double the compute units to be implemented for the kernel.

Acknowledgement. We thank the anonymous reviewers and the shepherd for their comments. This research used resources of the Argonne Leadership Computing Facility, which is a DOE Office of Science User Facility supported under Contract DE-AC02-06CH11357.

References

1. Koch, D., Hannig, F., Ziener, D. (eds.): FPGAs for Software Programmers. Springer, Cham (2016). https://doi.org/10.1007/978-3-319-26408-0
2. Intel FPGA SDK for OpenCL Cyclone V SoC Getting Started Guide. Intel (2017)
3. Intel FPGA SDK for OpenCL Stratix V Network Reference Platform Porting Guide. Intel (2017)
4. Intel FPGA SDK for OpenCL Arria 10 GX FPGA Development Kit Reference Platform Porting Guide. Intel (2017)
5. Wirbel, L.: Xilinx SDAccel Whitepaper. Xilinx (2014)
6. Chen, D., Singh, D.: Fractal video compression in OpenCL: an evaluation of CPUs, GPUs, and FPGAs as acceleration platforms. In: Proceedings of 18th Asia and South Pacific Design Automation Conference, pp. 297–304 (2013)
7. Fifield, J., et al.: Optimizing OpenCL applications on Xilinx FPGA. In: Proceedings of 4th International Workshop on OpenCL. ACM, New York (2016)
8. Zohouri, H.R., et al.: Evaluating and optimizing OpenCL kernels for high performance computing with FPGAs. In: International Conference for High Performance Computing, Networking, Storage and Analysis, Salt Lake City, UT, pp. 409–420 (2016)
9. Inggs, G., et al.: Is high level synthesis ready for business? A computational finance case study. In: 2014 International Conference on Field-Programmable Technology (FPT), Shanghai, pp. 12–19 (2014)

10. Underwood, K.: FPGAs vs. CPUs: trends in peak floating-point performance. In: Proceedings of 12th ACM International Symposium on Field-Programmable Gate Arrays, pp. 171–180. ACM Press (2004)
11. Véstias, M., Neto, H.: Trends of CPU GPU and FPGA for high-performance computing. In: 2014 24th International Conference on Field Programmable Logic and Applications, pp. 1–6 (2014)
12. Govindu, G., et al.: Area and power performance analysis of floating-point-based application on FPGAs. In: Proceedings of 7th Annual Workshop High-Performance Embedded Computing, USA (2003)
13. Che, S., et al.: Accelerating compute-intensive applications with GPUs and FPGAs. In: Symposium on Application Specific Processors, USA, pp. 101–107 (2008)
14. Ndu, G., et al.: CHO: towards a benchmark suite for OpenCL FPGA accelerators. In: 3rd IWOCL International Workshop on OpenCL, California, USA (2015)
15. Taking Advantage of Advances in FPGA Floating-Point IP Cores. Altera (2009)
16. Enabling High-Performance Floating-Point Designs. Intel (2016)
17. Jin, Z., et al.: Evaluation of CHO benchmarks on the Arria 10 FPGA using the Intel FPGA SDK for OpenCL. Argonne Leadership Computing Facility, Argonne National Laboratory, ANL/ALCF-17/4 (2017)
18. Leeser, M., et al.: OpenCL floating point software on heterogeneous architectures–portable or not. In: Workshop on Numerical Software Verification (NSV) (2012)
19. Wikipedia Webpage: https://en.wikipedia.org/wiki/Geographical_distance
20. GpsDrive Homepage: http://www.gpsdrive.de/
21. Geographiclib Homepage: https://geographiclib.sourceforge.io/2009-03/geodesic.html
22. Intel FPGA SDK for OpenCL Programming Guide. UG-OCL002. Intel (2016)
23. Arria 10 Native Floating-Point DSP IP Core User Guide. Intel (2016)
24. Jeffers, J., et al.: Intel Xeon Phi Processor High Performance Programming: Knights Landing Edition. Morgan Kaufmann Publishers, San Francisco (2016)
25. Maxmind Database Homepage: https://www.maxmind.com/en/free-world-cities-database
26. CUDA C Programming Guide. NVIDIA (2017)
27. Leveraging the Intel HyperFlex FPGA Architecture in Intel Stratix 10 Devices to Achieve Maximum Power Reduction. Intel (2016)
28. Stratix 10 GX/SX Device Overview. Intel (2016)

Shallow Water Waves on a Deep Technology Stack: Accelerating a Finite Volume Tsunami Model Using Reconfigurable Hardware in Invasive Computing

Alexander Pöppl[1]([envelope])(iD), Marvin Damschen[2], Florian Schmaus[3],
Andreas Fried[2], Manuel Mohr[2], Matthias Blankertz[2], Lars Bauer[2],
Jörg Henkel[2], Wolfgang Schröder-Preikschat[3], and Michael Bader[1]

[1] Department of Informatics, Technical University of Munich,
Boltzmannstraße 3, 85748 Garching bei München, Germany
{poeppl,bader}@in.tum.de
[2] Department of Informatics, Karlsruhe Institute of Technology,
Kaiserstraße 12, 76131 Karlsruhe, Germany
{damschen,fried,manuel.mohr,lars.bauer,henkel}@kit.edu,
matthias.blankertz@student.kit.edu
[3] Department of Computer Science 4, Friedrich-Alexander University
Erlangen-Nürnberg (FAU), Martensstr. 1, 91058 Erlangen, Germany
{schmaus,wosch}@cs.fau.de

Abstract. Reconfigurable architectures are commonly used in the embedded systems domain to speed up compute-intensive tasks. They combine a reconfigurable fabric with a general-purpose microprocessor to accelerate compute-intensive tasks on the fabric while the general-purpose CPU is used for the rest of the workload. Through the use of *invasive computing*, we aim to show the feasibility of this technology for HPC scenarios. We demonstrate this by accelerating a proxy application for the simulation of shallow water waves using the *i*-Core, a reconfigurable processor that is part of the invasive computing multiprocessor system-on-chip. Using a floating-point custom instruction, the entire computation of numerical fluxes occurring in the application's finite volume scheme is performed by hardware accelerators.

Keywords: Invasive computing · High Performance Computing
Tsunami simulation · Reconfigurable processor
Resource-aware computing

1 Introduction

General-purpose graphics processing units (GPGPUs) and accelerator cards such as the Intel Xeon Phi have brought heterogeneity to today's High Performance Computing (HPC). While these accelerators focus on general-purpose

© Springer International Publishing AG, part of Springer Nature 2018
D. B. Heras and L. Bougé (Eds.): Euro-Par 2017 Workshops, LNCS 10659, pp. 676–687, 2018.
https://doi.org/10.1007/978-3-319-75178-8_54

computations to provide benefits for a wide range of applications, the emerging application-specific accelerators like Google's Tensor Processing Unit [16] or Microsoft Catapult [20] offer an additional performance increase at a reduced power consumption. In contrast to HPC, application-specific accelerators are used commonly in the domain of embedded systems in the form of application-specific integrated circuits (ASICs), application-specific instruction-set processors (ASIPs) or reconfigurable architectures [27]. The latter combine the performance and power consumption benefits of application-specific accelerators with the applicability of general purpose architectures by employing a reconfigurable fabric (FPGA) that can be flexibly configured to host application-specific accelerators at runtime. Accelerator cards featuring a reconfigurable fabric ("fabric" hereafter) have been used in HPC before. However, such a *loose coupling* of CPU and fabric introduces high latencies between accelerators and computations on the CPU, thus impairing the performance benefits. In the embedded systems domain, *reconfigurable processors* are a well-researched architecture that couples a CPU and a fabric on the same chip. This gives accelerators direct access to the CPU-internal state, a so-called *tight coupling*. Therefore, reconfigurable processors provide acceleration with a low latency (of few CPU cycles) and provide a performance benefit even when accelerating computations of only a few hundred cycles.

Our contribution is an integrated demonstration of a reconfigurable HPC system consisting of custom hardware, operating system, compiler, and application. We employ *invasive computing* [26], which allows us to program our system in a *resource-aware* way: The applications can explore available resources at runtime and allocate them exclusively for the duration of an upcoming computation. We first introduce how invasive computing is supported throughout our technology stack. Then, we present our case study of computing shallow water waves on the heterogeneous InvasIC multi-processor system-on-chip (MPSoC). Finally, we detail how we accelerate the shallow water wave computations using *i*-Core, a processor with reconfigurable accelerators that is part of the invasive computing multiprocessor system-on-chip.

2   The Invasive Computing Stack

The governing thought of invasive computing is to grant applications, running on a massively-parallel computer, temporary exclusive access to resources like processor, communication channels and memory [9,26]. A set of granted resources is called a *claim*. Applications allocate claims by *invading* resources, and then *infect* them with a program to run. Finally, the application *retreats* from its claim, freeing the resources.

Realizing this programming model requires support from the hardware architecture, the operating system, the compiler and the application. Figure 1 shows a high-level overview of the invasive computing technology stack providing that support. Its components will be introduced in the following.

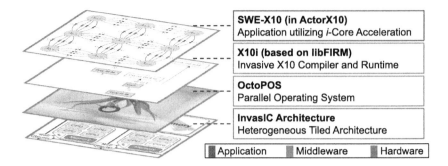

Fig. 1. High-level overview of the invasive computing technology stack. It targets challenges to support invasive computing at the architectural, runtime/compiler and programming level.

2.1 The InvasIC Hardware Architecture

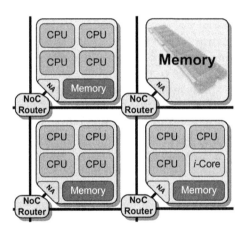

Fig. 2. Overview of the InvasIC hardware architecture used in our work

InvasIC [14] is a heterogeneous Multiprocessor System-on-Chip (MPSoC). It consists of tiles of different types that are interconnected using a network-on-chip (NoC). Within this work, we employ three types of tiles for the Shallow Water Equations (see Sect. 3). (i) RISC tiles contain several RISC cores that communicate over a shared bus, (ii) *i*-Core tiles contain RISC cores and an *i*-Core, a RISC core with reconfigurable hardware accelerators that are accessible through instruction-set extensions (see Sect. 4) and (iii) memory tiles that provide DDR memory. The hardware architecture used in this work is shown in Fig. 2. The RISC cores within these tiles are LEON3 CPU cores (available as part of the Gaisler GRLIB [11]) that implement the SPARC V8 ISA. Each core on a tile has dedicated L1 data and instruction caches. Additionally, the cores on a tile share an L2 cache and a tile local memory (TLM). The TLM is a freely accessible, low-latency and high-throughput scratchpad memory. All tiles are able to access larger amounts of memory (compared to the TLM) provided by memory tiles, and additionally the TLMs of other tiles. This tile-external memory is accessed through a network adapter (NA) providing access to the invasive Network on Chip (*i*NoC) and cached by the L2 cache. Further details on the architecture can be found in [14, 26].

While the i-Core offers a strict superset of the LEON3's functionality, and may hence be used just like a normal LEON3, special care has to be taken when features unique to the i-Core are used: (i) An application can store intermediate state that depends on the i-Core so that parts of the further execution need to be scheduled on the i-Core (ii) Using accelerators, i-Cores can process much more computations than the LEON3 cores in the same amount of time. Simply accessing global memory during these computations leads to memory being the performance bottleneck. We detail challenges (i) and (ii) in Sects. 4.1 and 4.2, respectively.

2.2 The Invasive Operating System – OctoPOS

OctoPOS [19] is a parallel operating system (POS) for the invasive programming paradigm. It was designed and tailored to run on systems with 1000+ cores and therefore implements a non-traditional threading scheme: Instead of long-running threads, parallelized control flows are represented as short snippets of code called i-lets. Similar to fibers [25], i-lets use cooperative scheduling and mostly run to completion. The exclusive access to resources combined with the mostly-run-to-completion property of i-lets relieves us from the requirement of temporal isolation through preemption. This in turn avoids frequent context switches. A run-to-completion i-let leaves no state on the stack upon termination, which allows OctoPOS to recycle the used stack for the next i-let. Hence, a single stack can be used by multiple i-lets. This approach makes them lightweight and inexpensive to create, schedule, and dispatch when compared to traditional threads.

The cooperative scheduling is based around a synchronization primitive called *signal* which is a *private semaphore* [13] implemented in a wait-free [15] manner. When an i-let performs a blocking operation, its execution context is saved. This is the only case that necessitates a binding of the i-let to its stack.

2.3 The Invasive Language

The invasive hardware platform offers a global address space, but caches are not coherent between tiles. The Asynchronous Partitioned Global Address Space (APGAS) model [23] and its implementation in X10 [24] are a good fit for this use-case. Threads within a single address space partition[1] may freely access each others' memory, while accesses between partitions require the programmer to invoke a special operation[2]. We associate each tile with an APGAS address space partition. Thus, APGAS ensures the separation of cache coherence regions.

To transmit data between partitions, the sender flushes its cache to global memory. The receiver then clones the data into its partition. This offers an API similar to shared memory access to the user program and is more efficient than message passing.

---

[1] An X10 *place*.
[2] `at`-expression for place-shifting.

We have developed a custom X10 compiler based on libFIRM [7] in order to implement X10 on top of the OctoPOS API, mapping X10's activities directly to i-lets [18]. Moreover, we have extended X10 to *Dynamic X10* [6] which supports the dynamic resource changes effected by `invade` and `retreat`.

3   Shallow Water Equations in X10

Shallow Water Equations in X10 (SWE-X10) is a proxy application for the computation of shallow water waves, a model that may be used to predict the propagation of a tsunami wave given the initial water displacement. Shallow water waves are governed by a system of hyperbolic partial differential equations. They are a set of conservation laws for water height (h), and horizontal (hu) and vertical (hv) momenta. Enriched with source terms ($S(x, y, t)$) for bathymetry and Coriolis Forces, they are used to capture not just the propagation of tsunami waves, but also the inundation of coastal regions [8,17].

$$\begin{bmatrix} h \\ hu \\ hv \end{bmatrix}_t + \begin{bmatrix} hu \\ hu^2 + \frac{1}{2}gh^2 \\ huv \end{bmatrix}_x + \begin{bmatrix} hv \\ huv \\ hv^2 + \frac{1}{2}gh^2 \end{bmatrix}_y = S(x, y, t) \tag{1}$$

Equation (1) displays the shallow water equations. For their numeric solution, we use a finite volume scheme on a Cartesian grid with piecewise constant unknown quantities and an explicit Eulerian time step [17]. We use

$$Q_{i,j}^{(n+1)} = Q_{i,j}^{(n)} - \frac{\Delta t}{\Delta x}\left(\mathcal{A}^+\Delta Q_{i-\frac{1}{2},j}^{(n)} + \mathcal{A}^-\Delta Q_{i+\frac{1}{2},j}^{(n)}\right) \tag{2}$$
$$- \frac{\Delta t}{\Delta y}\left(\mathcal{B}^+\Delta Q_{i,j-\frac{1}{2}}^{(n)} + \mathcal{B}^-\Delta Q_{i,j+\frac{1}{2}}^{(n)}\right)$$

to calculate the new values for the unknown quantities h, hu, hv and b in cell (i, j) at time step $n + 1$, $Q_{i,j}^{(n+1)}$ based on the values of the previous time step. To this end, we need to determine the fluxes of unknown values into and out of each cell for each of the cell's borders. In Eq. (2), this is reflected by $\mathcal{A}^\pm\Delta Q_{i\pm\frac{1}{2},j}^{(n)}$ and $\mathcal{B}^\pm\Delta Q_{i,j\pm\frac{1}{2}}^{(n)}$ for the vertical and horizontal fluxes, respectively. These fluxes can be computed by solving the Riemann problem at the cell boundary. SWE-X10 includes several approximate Riemann solvers. Here, we focus on the fWave solver [3] that we accelerate using the i-Core.

SWE-X10 is written in X10 using the ActorX10 framework [21,22]. Figure 3 depicts a high-level overview of the actor graph. Using actors, we are able to parallelize the application while avoiding data races and without having to distinguish between shared and distributed memory. Each actor is assigned a single patch of the overall grid, and data between patches is exchanged using channels. The actor uses a *patch calculator* to compute the updates for the grid points of a patch. By employing resource-aware programming (see Sect. 2.3), we show how specialization of the patch calculator enables support for hardware accelerators so that each instance fully exploits the available resources.

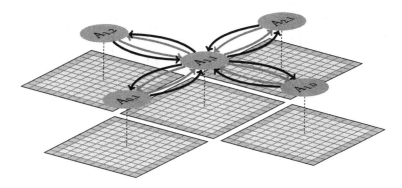

Fig. 3. Grid and actor graph. Five actors (orange) are shown, together with their respective patches (blue). Between each two neighboring actors there are four channels, one pair for simulation data and another for coordination data. (Color figure online)

4   Accelerating SWE-X10 Using *i*-Core

The *i*-Core is a runtime-reconfigurable processor, i.e., it combines a processor core (here: LEON3) with application-specific hardware accelerators. In contrast to application-specific processors (ASIPs), hardware accelerators are not fixed at design time. Instead, they can be reconfigured – even at runtime – to accelerate any given application by the use of a reconfigurable fabric (FPGA). Hardware accelerators are utilized by so-called *custom instructions* (CIs) that extend the ISA of the processor core. A CI invokes execution of a microprogram on the *CI Execution Controller*. Using the microprogram, the CI Execution Controller takes care of data transfers between accelerators and accelerator execution. Thus, a CI can utilize, potentially in parallel, one or more accelerators. The microprogram implementing a specific CI is obtained by scheduling the CI's data flow graph (representing the computations performed by the CI) onto accelerators that are available on the reconfigurable fabric in a specific configuration (see [5] for details). CIs can read inputs from the CPU register file and write results back to it (*tight coupling* of the reconfigurable fabric). A CI can access the whole memory hierarchy through the CPU's cache controller. Additionally, the reconfigurable fabric is directly connected to the TLM using two 128-bit-wide memory ports with a single cycle latency. Therefore, the TLM provides a much higher bandwidth for CIs than accessing the 32-bit-wide system bus. The protocol of invoking CIs from the CPU pipeline is similar to invoking multicycle instructions such as integer division from the standard ISA (Fig. 4).

As the invasive computing paradigm guarantees isolation of resources between applications, each application can adapt the *i*-Core and configure application-specific hardware accelerators that provide maximum benefits for the respective application (in terms of performance but also non-functional properties like worst-case execution time [12]). For accelerating compute-intensive floating-point-based applications like SWE-X10, we introduce a set of pipelined floating-point accelerators that implement generic floating-point operations as

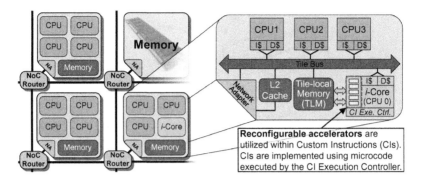

Fig. 4. Overview of the InvasIC architecture with a detailed view of the i-Core tile

Table 1. Pipelined floating-point accelerators available for i-Core. CIs can utilize multiple accelerators in parallel. Thus, configuring highly-utilized accelerators multiple times can benefit a CI's latency.

Accelerator	Operations	Min./Max. latency[1]	Initiation interval
FP_MAC	Add/subtract, multiply, multiply-accumulate	3/5	2
FP_DIV	Divide, reciprocal	6/6	2
FP_SQRT	Square root	5/5	2
FP_UTIL	Min/max, absolute and compare $(<,>)$	3/3	2

[1] Clock cycles on the reconfigurable fabric

listed in Table 1 (details on a previous version of FP_MAC can be found in [4]). To accelerate SWE-X10, we implemented the fWave solver as a CI (fwave) for i-Core. The fwave instruction performs all 54 floating-point operations of the fWave solver as a single CI using our floating-point accelerators. This results in a data-flow graph that consists of 97 nodes (operations) including memory accesses, address generation, communication between accelerators and accelerator execution. On our current i-Core prototype within the InvasIC architecture, we instantiate i-Core using five reconfigurable containers. We utilize these containers for SWE-X10 to configure the following accelerators: 2×FP_MAC, 1×FP_DIV, 1×FP_SQRT and 1×FP_UTIL. The reconfigurable fabric needs to be configured once at application startup, which takes ca. 5.5 ms at a reconfiguration bandwidth of 100 MB/s. This configuration enables us to schedule the 97 operations of fwave onto the accelerators in a microprogram consisting of 41 steps. Pipelining is very beneficial for fwave: when disabling it, the number of steps almost doubles (>71 steps). Each step of the microprogram takes 2 clock cycles (at maximum 100 MHz) on the reconfigurable fabric. In total, the 54 floating-point operations of the fWave solver are executed in 82 cycles using fwave and our pipelined floating-point accelerators on i-Core.

CIs like `fwave` are provided to the X10 programmer using wrapper methods that are inlined by the compiler. Thus, we can directly access the CIs from X10 with minimal overhead.

4.1   Adaptions to the OctoPOS Operating System

To maximize the utilization of the available resources on the InvasIC architecture, the OctoPOS scheduler has to be able to schedule i-lets over CPU cores that feature instruction set extensions. More specifically, the instruction set of the LEON3 is a strict subset of the instructions provided by the i-Core. As a consequence, i-lets that rely on the availability of i-Core CIs have to be scheduled on an i-Core that is configured accordingly, as the invocation of the CI would cause an *illegal instruction* trap otherwise. i-lets that only contain standard SPARC-V8 instructions can be executed on i-Cores as well.

We therefore allow i-lets to be assigned to a team which may have a different *scheduling domain* than non-team members. The scheduler ensures that team members are only executed on cores belonging to the team's scheduling domain. Unlike the original team concept [10], i-lets can be dynamically (re-)assigned to a team. This enables the dynamic pinning of i-lets to a set of cores. An application is thus able to create scheduling domains that only contain its invaded i-Cores. By pinning i-lets containing CIs to such a scheduling domain, it is ensured that those i-lets do not trap, while other i-lets are still scheduled on all available cores.

4.2   Adaptions in SWE-X10

SWE-X10 only required very minor code changes to make it compatible with the APIs exposed by the invasive X10 compiler, and therefore most of the work was spent optimizing the performance on i-Core. In SWE-X10, the computational hotspot is the calculation of fluxes between cell boundaries, $\mathcal{A}^{\pm}\Delta Q^{(n)}_{i\pm\frac{1}{2},j}$ and $\mathcal{B}^{\pm}\Delta Q^{(n)}_{i,j\pm\frac{1}{2}}$, in Eq. (2). As mentioned in Sect. 3, the code utilizes, amongst others, the fWave approximate Riemann solver to compute these net updates. The aforementioned CI of the i-Core may be used as a drop-in replacement for the X10 implementation of the fWave solver. However, this way the i-Core does not benefit from its high-bandwidth connection to the TLM, but accesses data from global memory.

Therefore, we created a specialized subclass with an implementation of the iteration optimized for the i-Core that buffers data in the TLM. The size of that memory is limited. Thus, it is impossible to retain the entire patch in the TLM. Instead, we load the data row-wise, using a triple buffering scheme with a *previous*, a *current* and a *next* row. The i-let graph for the scheme is shown in Fig. 5. A task depends on all tasks that are connected to it by an incoming edge. The iteration starts by synchronously loading the first two rows into the TLM ($L_{(0)}$ and $L_{(1)}$), followed by the computation of the horizontal fluxes for row 0 ($H_{(0)}$). Now, we perform the loop for rows 1 to N, N being the number of rows in a patch. In each iteration n, we asynchronously load the next row ($L_{(n+1)}$) into memory and perform the vertical flux computations on the previous and the current row $(V_{(n-1,n)})$. After the computation is completed, we may asynchronously start the write of the previous row back to the global memory $(S_{(n-1)})$ and perform the horizontal flux computation on the current row $(H_{(n)})$. After clearing the previous row $(C_{(n-1)})$ and, in case of $n = N - 1$, writing back the next row $(S_{(n+1)})$, the loop returns to the beginning.

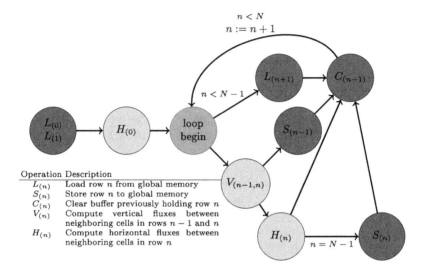

Fig. 5. i-let graph for the i-Core patch calculator. Nodes that are not (transitively) connected may be executed in parallel. Nodes performing I/O operations are depicted in blue, while nodes performing a computation are depicted in orange. Edges annotated with a condition are only taken if the condition is met. (Color figure online)

5   Results

First, we evaluate the performance benefits and resource utilization on the reconfigurable fabric of executing the fWave solver kernel using the i-Core CI compared to execution in software on the LEON3 CPU with different variants of floating-point support. Afterwards, we evaluate the performance of computing one simulation step of a whole patch (see Sect. 3) on the i-Core compared to the LEON3 CPU utilizing its high-performance floating-point unit (FPU-HP).

Table 2 shows execution time and resource utilization results for the fWave solver kernel. Compared to a standard LEON3 with FPU-HP (fastest floating-point support variant that also utilizes most resources), i-Core is 7.5 times faster and 3.8 times more efficient in the use of lookup tables (LUTs) on the Xilinx Virtex-7 (floating-point operations per second/LUTs).

Table 3 shows the execution time of one iteration of the patch calculators that perform 7140 to 7320 calls to the previously evaluated fWave solver (depending on the patch characteristics). The baseline is execution on the LEON3 with FPU-HP utilizing global memory. Buffering data in the TLM results in a speedup of

Table 2. Execution time and resource utilization results for the fWave solver kernel executed in software (without floating-point unit (FPU), with "lite" FPU and "high-performance" FPU from Gaisler) compared to `fwave` CI on i-Core. Results were obtained using GRLIB on a Xilinx VC707 board (Virtex-7 FPGA) at 75 MHz.

	LEON3 − no FPU		LEON3 + FPU-lite		LEON3 + FPU-HP		i-Core	
Execution	$[\mu s]$	Speedup	$[\mu s]$	Speedup	$[\mu s]$	Speedup	$[\mu s]$	Speedup
Time[1]	183.6	1	14.9	12.3	9.8	18.7	1.3	141
Resource	LUTs	DSPs	LUTs	DSPs	LUTs	DSPs	LUTs	DSPs
Utilization	9,103	4	12,756	4	23,949	20	37,658	24
Resource	$\frac{FLOPS}{LUTs}$	$\frac{FLOPS}{DSPs}$	$\frac{FLOPS}{LUTs}$	$\frac{FLOPS}{DSPs}$	$\frac{FLOPS}{LUTs}$	$\frac{FLOPS}{DSPs}$	$\frac{FLOPS}{LUTs}$	$\frac{FLOPS}{DSPs}$
Efficiency	27.8	73,529	248	906,040	203.8	275,510	780.3	1,730,769

[1] Average over 1024 measurements

1.75×. Execution on the i-Core utilizing global memory speeds up the computation by 2×. Both optimizations combined alleviate the memory bottleneck for the i-Core and we achieve a speedup of 4.82× in total.

Table 3. Patch calculator execution time on the LEON3 (with FPU-HP) compared to execution time on the i-Core, with data in global DDR RAM or buffering in the tile-local memory (TLM). Results were obtained using the InvasIC Hardware Prototype on a Synopsis CHIPit system consisting of four Xilinx XC5VLX330 (Virtex-5 FPGA) at 25 MHz.

	LEON3 − global		LEON3 − TLM		i-Core − global		i-Core − TLM	
Execution	[ms]	Speedup	[ms]	Speedup	[ms]	Speedup	[ms]	Speedup
Time[1]	2049	1	1169	1.75	1017	2.01	425	4.82

[1] Average over 200 measurements

6   Related Work

SWE-X10 is based on the C++-application SWE [2,8], a code based on the finite volume scheme described by LeVeque [17]. SWE features a modular approach, with one patch per MPI rank. It has been executed on Xeon CPUs [2], Tesla GPUs [8] and the Xeon Phi [2]. In contrast to SWE-X10, SWE uses a global communication approach, and does not have lazy activation.

ElasticX10 [1] also allows for a dynamic and asynchronous change in the amount of places. Compared to this, Dynamic X10 offers more stability: Places change in a predictable fashion, as the application itself drives the change in resources, i.e., it is *resource aware*, enabling it to maximize its performance.

Compared to other reconfigurable processors [27], i-Core has the unique feature that its CIs are not implemented as one monolithic accelerator, but using microcode to utilize multiple accelerators. This enables to implement the same functionality with more or less accelerators and enables to opt for a different tradeoff between CI latency and fabric area allocated at runtime.

In contrast to our work, FPGA accelerators such as Microsoft Catapult [20] are coupled loosely to the CPU, and only effectively speed up large computations. Application specific accelerators such as the Tensor Processing Unit [16] are not reconfigurable.

7   Conclusion

In this contribution, we have demonstrated the applicability of techniques from embedded computing, such as application-specific hardware reconfiguration and control over the entire technology stack, to HPC. Using the i-Core's tightly-coupled reconfigurable fabric, we were able to implement an fWave approximate Riemann solver in hardware. Thus, we accelerated the computation of fluxes between cell boundaries, the computational hotspot of SWE-X10, by a factor of 4.82 over the baseline solution using the LEON3's high-performance floating point unit, while utilizing resources on a reconfigurable fabric more efficiently (in terms of LUTs and DSPs). This contribution demonstrates the feasibility of accelerating HPC applications using a reconfigurable processor.

Acknowledgments. This work was supported by the German Research Foundation (DFG) as part of the Transregional Collaborative Research Centre "Invasive Computing" (SFB/TR 89).

References

1. Elastic   X10.   http://x10-lang.org/documentation/practical-x10-programming/ elastic-x10.html. Retrieved 9 May 2017
2. Bader, M., Breuer, A., Hölzl, W., Rettenberger, S.: Vectorization of an augmented Riemann solver for the shallow water equations. In: Proceedings of 2014 International Conference on High Performance Computing and Simulation (HPCS 2014), pp. 193–201. IEEE (2014)
3. Bale, D.S., LeVeque, R.J., Mitran, S., Rossmanith, J.A.: A wave propagation method for conservation laws and balance laws with spatially varying flux functions. SIAM J. Sci. Comput. **24**(3), 955–978 (2003)
4. Bauer, L., Grudnitsky, A., Damschen, M., et al.: Floating point acceleration for stream processing applications in dynamically reconfigurable processors. In: IEEE Symposium on Embedded Systems for Real-time Multimedia (ESTIMedia), October 2015
5. Bauer, L., Shafique, M., Henkel, J.: A computation- and communication-infrastructure for modular special instructions in a dynamically reconfigurable processor. In: International Conference on Field Programmable Logic and Applications, pp. 203–208. IEEE (2008)
6. Braun, M., Buchwald, S., Mohr, M., Zwinkau, A.: Dynamic X10: resource-aware programming for higher efficiency. Technical report 8, Karlsruhe Institute of Technology (2014). (X10 2014)
7. Braun, M., Buchwald, S., Zwinkau, A.: Firm—a graph-based intermediate representation. Technical report 35, Karlsruhe Institute of Technology (2011)

8. Breuer, A., Bader, M.: Teaching parallel programming models on a shallow-water code. In: Proceedings of 2012 11th International Symposium on Parallel and Distributed Computing, ISPDC 2012, pp. 301–308. IEEE Computer Society (2012)

9. Bungartz, H.J., Riesinger, C., Schreiber, M., et al.: Invasive computing in HPC with X10. In: Proceedings of 3rd ACM SIGPLAN X10 Workshop, X10 2013, pp. 12–19. ACM, New York (2013)

10. Cheriton, D.R., Malcolm, M.A., Melen, L.S., Sager, G.R.: Thoth, a portable real-time operating system. Commun. ACM **22**(2), 105–115 (1979)

11. Cobham Gaisler AB: GRLIB IP library user's manual. Technical report, Göteborg, Sweden, January 2016. Version 1.5.0: http://www.gaisler.com/products/grlib/grlib.pdf. Retrieved 2 May 2017

12. Damschen, M., Bauer, L., Henkel, J.: Extending the WCET problem to optimize for runtime-reconfigurable processors. ACM Trans. Archit. Code Optim. **13**(4), 45:1–45:24 (2016)

13. Dijkstra, E.W.: The structure of the "THE"-multiprogramming system. Commun. ACM **11**(5), 341–346 (1968)

14. Henkel, J., Herkersdorf, A., Bauer, L., et al.: Invasive manycore architectures. In: Proceedings of 17th Asia and South Pacific Design Automation Conference (ASP-DAC), pp. 193–200, January 2012

15. Herlihy, M.: Wait-free synchronization. ACM Trans. Prog. Lang. Syst. (TOPLAS) **13**(1), 124–149 (1991)

16. Jouppi, N.P., Young, C., Patil, N., et al.: In-datacenter performance analysis of a tensor processing unit. arXiv preprint arXiv:1704.04760 (2017)

17. LeVeque, R.J., George, D.L., Berger, M.J.: Tsunami modelling with adaptively refined finite volume methods. Acta Numerica **20**, 211–289 (2011)

18. Mohr, M., Buchwald, S., Zwinkau, A., et al.: Cutting out the middleman: OS-level support for X10 activities. In: Proceedings of 5th ACM SIGPLAN X10 Workshop, X10 2015, pp. 13–18. ACM, New York (2015)

19. Oechslein, B., Schedel, J., Kleinöder, J., et al.: OctoPOS: a parallel operating system for invasive computing. In: Proceedings of International Workshop on Systems for Future Multi-core Architectures (SFMA), pp. 9–14. EuroSys (2011)

20. Ovtcharov, K., Ruwase, O., Kim, J.Y., et al.: Accelerating deep convolutional neural networks using specialized hardware. Microsoft Research Whitepaper, vol. 2, no. 11 (2015)

21. Pöppl, A., Bader, M., Schwarzer, T., Glaß, M.: SWE-X10: simulating shallow water waves with lazy activation of patches using ActorX10. In: Proceedings of 2nd International Workshop on Extreme Scale Programming Models and Middleware (ESPM2), pp. 32–39. IEEE, November 2016

22. Roloff, S., Pöppl, A., Schwarzer, T., et al.: ActorX10: an actor library for X10. In: Proceedings of 6th ACM SIGPLAN X10 Workshop (X10). ACM (2016)

23. Saraswat, V., Almasi, G., Bikshandi, G., et al.: The asynchronous partitioned global address space model. Technical report, Toronto, Canada, June 2010

24. Saraswat, V., Bloom, B., Peshansky, I., et al.: X10 language specification, December 2015. Version 2.5: http://x10-lang.org. Retrieved 5 May 2017

25. Tanenbaum, A.S.: Modern Operating Systems, pp. 859–860. Prentice Hall, Upper Saddle River (2009)

26. Teich, J., Henkel, J., Herkersdorf, A., Schmitt-Landsiedel, D., Schröder-Preikschat, W., Snelting, G.: Invasive computing: an overview. In: Hübner, M., Becker, J. (eds.) Multiprocessor System-on-Chip, pp. 241–268. Springer, New York (2011). https://doi.org/10.1007/978-1-4419-6460-1_11

27. Tessier, R., Pocek, K., DeHon, A.: Reconfigurable computing architectures. Proc. IEEE **103**(3), 332–354 (2015)

Linking Application Description with Efficient SIMD Code Generation for Low-Precision Signed-Integer GEMM

Günther Schindler[1]([✉]), Manfred Mücke[2], and Holger Fröning[1]

[1] Institute of Computer Engineering, Ruprecht Karls University, Heidelberg, Mannheim, Germany
{guenther.schindler,holger.froening}@ziti.uni-heidelberg.de
[2] Materials Center Leoben Forschung GmbH, Leoben, Austria
manfred.muecke@mcl.at

Abstract. The need to implement demanding numerical algorithms within a constrained power budget has led to a renewed interest in low-precision number formats. Exploration of the degrees of freedom provided both by better support for low-precision number formats on computer architectures and by the respective application domain remains a most demanding task, though.

In this example, we upgrade the machine learning framework Theano and the Eigen linear algebra library to support matrix multiplication of formats between 32 and 1 bit by packing multiple values in a 32-bit vector. This approach keeps all the optimizations of Eigen to the overall matrix operation, while maximizing performance enabled through SIMD units on modern embedded CPUs. With respect to 32-bit formats, we achieve a speedup between 0.45 and 21.17 on an ARM Cortex-A15.

1 Introduction

Digital computers implement computer arithmetic over finite number sets. The past decades saw improved support for higher-precision number formats resulting in native support of double-precision (64-bit) floating-point on almost all computing platforms from supercomputers to desktops and mobile devices. Recently, though, there is a substantial interest in reduced-precision number formats to execute demanding algorithms within limited time, memory, or power budgets. The key driver for this development are complex algorithms executed on mobile platforms, for instance for speech recognition, computer vision, or augmented reality. An extreme example of this trend are binarized neural networks [3], in which the weights and activations are represented by either a plus one or a minus one, allowing storing each parameter in a single bit.

Driven by various trends, including big data, deep learning, and a steadily increasing resolution in image processing, the complexity of applications continues to grow. This applies to computational complexity, algorithmic complexity,

© Springer International Publishing AG, part of Springer Nature 2018
D. B. Heras and L. Bougé (Eds.): Euro-Par 2017 Workshops, LNCS 10659, pp. 688–699, 2018.
https://doi.org/10.1007/978-3-319-75178-8_55

and memory complexity. At the same time, algorithms continue to rely heavily on Basic Linear Algebra Subroutines (BLAS) like matrix-vector or matrix-matrix multiplication. As an example, a trained neural network uses matrix-vector and matrix-matrix operations for the inference, in which new information is detected. As the number of layers for neural networks is continuously growing, up to extreme examples including 100 or 1000 layers [8], the execution time and memory footprint for such a workload increases accordingly. Unfortunately, single-thread performance is stagnating since the end of Dennard scaling, and now performance scaling usually requires parallelization.

Short-vector units (also known as single-instruction multiple-data – or SIMD – units) exploit the low cost of data-level parallelism in current CMOS processes. SIMD units are ubiquitous in current architectures from server CPUs to microcontrollers. They typically support multiple number formats with throughput doubling at half of the bit width. While the performance of SIMD units looks good on paper, the challenge is to map numerical algorithms to matching number formats and to exploit the complex instruction sets.

Quantization is a form of lossy data compression, with the benefit of lower memory footprint and lower computational complexity. While originally studied in the context of computer arithmetic, it can also be seen in the context of approximate computing, which also looks at different techniques like logic design [13] and architecture [4], as well as software aspects including data type qualifiers [10] and loops [11].

This work is motivated by the wish to use complex (BLAS-based) algorithms for highly resource-constrained systems with limited computational performance. ARM architectures dominate many domains of embedded computing today. We see ARM-based CPUs as a viable option that should be explored initially, as they offer in comparison to specialized processors a relatively high productivity, versatility and rather unconstrained memory capabilities. By computing locally on the mobile device, one avoids traffic to cloud-based processing solutions, and especially the need for online connectivity. Under real-time constraints or security considerations this might be a strong argument. We assume that selected application domains are able to map relevant tasks onto lower-precision number format. We are concerned with the question how lower-precision number formats can be effectively used. That includes direct use at the application level as well as resulting low-level code making best use of available SIMD units.

Here, we report insights from our explorations and optimizations to enable ARM processors to efficiently perform computations on extremely quantized data. In particular, the main contributions of this work are as follows:

- A review of architectural support in embedded ARM processors for computations based on extreme forms of quantizations, in particular non-standard representations
- The design, optimization, and evaluation of building blocks for efficient quantized computations

– Based on our findings, a discussion of the implications with regard to the compute stack, or how to extend the compute stack to allow generalized forms of such computations.

The remainder of this work is structured as follows: Sect. 2 provides a background on matrix multiplication, ARM processors, and NEON vector instructions. Section 3 describes our solution in detail and explains optimizations. Next, Sect. 4 reports performance results. We discuss our observations in Sect. 5 before we conclude in Sect. 6.

2   Background

In this section, we shortly introduce the necessary background in combination with the most important related work.

2.1   Implementation and Optimization of GEMM

One of the key operations in linear algebra is General Matrix Multiply (GEMM). GEMM is implemented in BLAS. GEMM takes two two-dimensional arrays of size $M \times N$ and $N \times K$ as inputs and returns a two-dimensional array of size $M \times K$. The values of the output matrix are calculated as shown in Eq. 1, with A and B as input arrays and C as output array.

$$c_{i,j} = \sum_{n=1}^{N} a_{i,n} * b_{n,j} \tag{1}$$

Thus, GEMM consists of iterating over the input arrays and applying Multiply-Accumulate (MAC) operations. Despite the simplicity of the GEMM algorithm it requires multiple, hardware-dependent optimization techniques in order to achieve high performance on any given architecture. Modern compilers are capable of detecting cache ineffective source code or integrate some autovectorization, but this is usually not sufficient to reach state-of-the-art performance for GEMM. Thus, libraries like Eigen, Atlas, or OpenBLAS focus on highly optimized BLAS algorithms [6]. For instance, the Eigen library implements a hand-tuned GEMM that exploits a variety of optimizations for a set of SIMD-capable processors [7].

2.2   ARM Processors and Their SIMD Extensions

Single Instruction Multiple Data (SIMD) refers to a vectorization technique that enables the computation of multiple data elements with a single instruction. With the introduction of the ARMv7 architecture, ARM processors supports a SIMD extension named NEON [1,2] to accelerate media applications. NEON is able to process 128 bit wide vectors and supports 16×8-bit, 8×16-bit, 4×32-bit, and 2×64-bit integer and floating-point operations. With the upcoming introduction of the ARMv8-A architecture and its Scalable Vector Extension (SVE), ARM is extending the vector processing capabilities for vector lengths that scale from 128 to up to 2048 bit.

2.3   ARM NEON ISA Review

Table 1 summarizes the most important NEON instruction for the MAC operation, relevant to implement GEMM for different number formats.

Table 1. Instruction overview for the MAC operation

Operation	Instruction	Description
Multiplication	VMLA	Multiplies the elements of two vectors and accumulates the elements of a third vector - Supports 32/16/8 bit
	VMUL	Multiplies the elements of two vectors - Supports 32/16/8 bit
	VMULL	Multiplies the elements of two vectors and doubles the bit width - Supports 32/16/8 bit
	VAND + VEOR	Bitwise logic instruction - Supports 32/16/8 bit
Reduction	VPADDL	Adds adjacent pairs of elements of a vector - Supports 32/16/8 bit
	VPADAL	Adds adjacent pairs of elements of a vector and accumulates the result by elements of a second vector - Supports 32/16/8 bit
	VCNT	Counts the number of set bits of a vector - Supports 8 bit
Accumulation	VADD	Adds the elements of two vectors - Supports 32/16/8 bit

All instruction listed in Table 1 support the full NEON-SIMD width of 128 bit with the exception of *VMULL*. Due to bit-width doubling, this instruction can only process 64-bit vectors.

2.4   Relevant Libraries

Libraries supporting reduced-precision computations are relatively sparse. The MPFR C++ library [9] which is built upon the MPFR library [5] supports multiprecision floating-point number formats and is available as support module for the Eigen library. A library supporting reduced-precision GEMM is Google's Gemmlowp[1] which is integrated in the application framework Tensorflow and supports 8-bit representation. The library currently supports CPUs and is optimized for NEON and SSE vectorization. ARM's Compute Library[2] supports reduced-precision GEMM for 16-bit representation and is supported for NEON-capable processors.

---

[1] https://github.com/google/gemmlowp.
[2] https://github.com/ARM-software/ComputeLibrary.

3   Reduced-Precision Signed-Integer GEMM on ARM NEON

Specialized BLAS libraries are pervasively used to improve execution time of numerical algorithms. Impressive results up to achieving almost theoretical peak performance exist. However, specialized BLAS libraries generally support single- and double-precision floating-point only. They typically lack any support for lower-precision number format.

In this work, we show the optimization potential of a signed-integer GEMM on a NEON-capable ARM processor. We use 32-, 16-, 8-, 2-, 1-bit signed integer, and show how NEON SIMD instructions allow for fast data-parallel computation of GEMM. We extend the Eigen BLAS library, which has demonstrated competitive performance and is widely used, for low-precision integers. In particular, we show that support for reduced-precision number formats can be implemented by leaving most of the algorithm untouched and only adapting the highest and lowest level of the operator. Finally, we integrate this extension in the mathematical expression framework Theano [12] to maximize the usability of such custom forms of representations.

To benefit from the advantages of lower-precision number formats, it is necessary to implement operators that can handle these kinds of representation. For the GEMM example we can simply extend the equation by another summation loop as shown in Eq. 2, with W representing the full-precision bit width divided by the reduced-precision bit width.

$$c_{i,j} = \sum_{n=1}^{N} a_{i,n} * b_{n,j} = \sum_{n=1}^{N/W} \sum_{w=1}^{W} a_{i,n+w} * b_{n+w,j} \tag{2}$$

We can furthermore simplify this equation by packing W values from a and b to a^{packed} and b^{packed} and overwriting the MAC operation (Eq. 3).

$$c_{i,j} = \sum_{n=1}^{N/W} a_{i,n}^{packed} * b_{n,j}^{packed} \tag{3}$$

Within the MAC operation, W scalar products can be vectorized in SIMD fashion and summed up using reduction. As a result, we can extend the Eigen GEMM operator to support reduced precision by overwriting the MAC operation, packing W reduced-precision values into a single full-precision value, and dividing the matrix depth N by W.

In order to integrate the reduced-precision operator into Theano, we propose the following workflow: the value packing is performed within Theano and the packed matrices are propagated via references to Eigen's GEMM operator. Then, Eigen performs its high-level transformations and forwards the data in form of 128-bit vectors to the customized MAC operator. Finally, the MAC operator performs the actual computations by exploiting optimized code on SIMD units.

3.1   Implementation

We use the NEON SIMD-MAC operation to evaluate the scalar product of the input vectors a and b, followed by accumulating the result by input vector c. The

SIMD-MAC operation is illustrated in Fig. 1 on the example of $int8\_t$ input representation. As can be seen, the scalar product of two vectors is implemented by pairwise multiplying elements of input vectors a and b. The results of the multiplication are reduced into a $int32\_t$ intermediate representation and accumulated by elements of input vector c. Input and output vectors for the MAC operations are mapped to the full NEON-SIMD width of 128 bit, with precision depend type for a and b ($int32x4\_t$, $int16x8\_t$, $int8x16\_t$, $int4x32\_t$, $int2x64\_t$, and $int1x32\_t$) and full-precision type $int32x4\_t$ for input vector c and output vector.

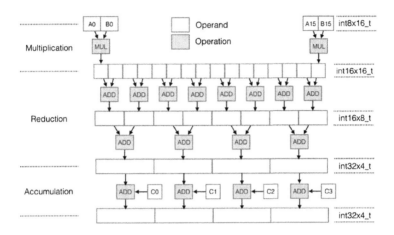

Fig. 1. Simplified illustration of the MAC operation for int8_t representation

A performance-sensitive pitfall of the MAC operation is bit-width doubling when performing the multiplication in order to avoid integer overflows. Bit-width doubling is performed for $int16\_t$, $int8\_t$, and $int4\_t$ input representation. $int2x64\_t$ and $int1x32\_t$ representations cannot cause overflows since the result's range is identical with the input range ($+1$, -1 and -1, 0, $+1$).

3.2 Supporting Different Bit Widths

The baseline implementation of the MAC operation assumes input vectors a and b of type $int32x4\_t$. For this case, NEON includes the Fused-Multiply-Accumulate (FMA) instruction, which is able to multiply and accumulate 4 operands (128-bit vector) in one instruction.

int16x8_t and int8x16_t MAC: NEON also includes FMA instructions for 16-bit and 8-bit representations. However, the FMA instructions are not applicable here because the reduction has to be performed after the multiplication and before the accumulation.

Thus, we use a multiplication instruction with bit-width doubling. Since instructions with bit-width doubling only can process 64-bit vectors, the multiplication of the highest and lowest 64 bit of input vectors a and b has to be performed sequentially. Then, both resulting vectors are sequentially reduced by adding adjacent pairs of elements (one reduction layer for $int16x8\_t$ MAC and two reduction layers for $int8x16\_t$ MAC). Finally, both resulting vectors are combined to a single vector and its values are summed up.

int4x32_t MAC: While 16-bit and 8-bit representation is supported inherently by NEON, it lacks support for 4-bit formats. In particular, the extraction of $int4\_t$ values from the input vectors causes a high instruction overhead. In order to perform the extraction, we mask out even and odd indexed $int4\_t$ values from the 128-bit input vectors a and b via bit-wise logic operations and split the values into two separate 128-bit vectors. Once the extraction is done, the obtained vectors can be simply multiplied without bit-width doubling. Then, a three-layer reduction is performed before the resulting vector elements are summed up.

int2x64_t MAC: The multiplication of the $int2x64\_t$ MAC is realized by evaluating the resulting positive and negative values separately via bit-wise logic operations (AND, XOR). Then, a 8-bit population count is performed to count the positive and negative values within a 8-bit vector. The resulting positive values are subtracted by the resulting negative values. Two reduction levels transform the $int8x16\_t$ representation into a $int32x4\_t$ intermediate representation and accumulate the vector by elements of input vector c.

int1x128_t MAC: For the $int1x128\_t$ MAC, we use the approach proposed by Courbariaux et al. [3]. The basic idea is to replace the actual multiplications of input vectors a and b with bit-wise XOR operations and perform the reduction via population count. Since NEON includes only a 8-bit population count, we use two further reduction levels to reduce the results into a $int32x4\_t$ intermediate representation. Afterwards the result is accumulated by input vector c.

3.3   Optimizing Reduction Overhead

Halving the bit representation causes an additional reduction layer within the MAC operation to obtain a 32-bit intermediate representation. In most cases, this 32-bit intermediate representation cannot be avoided without causing an overflow. However, $int1\_t$ and $int2\_t$ representation differ because the multiplication results are in between -1 and $+1$.

As shown in Sect. 3.2, the first reduction layer of $int1\_t$ and $int2\_t$ MAC is performed via 8-bit population count. Considering that the scalar product of a row vector and a column vector takes N (matrix depth) accumulations of a maximum value of 8, the maximum scalar value is $N * 8$ for the first reduction layer and $N * 16$ for the second reduction layer. Therefore, a reduced bit width $(Width)$ for the intermediate representation is sufficient if $N < \frac{2^{Width}}{Width}$ holds.

Using this observation, we can modify the GEMM implementation for $int1\_t$ and $int2\_t$ input representation to dynamically adapt among 32-bit, 16-bit, and 8-bit intermediate representation by only evaluating the matrix' depth. Consequently, compared to 32-bit intermediate representation, a 16-bit intermediate representation requires one reduction layer less, and an 8-bit intermediate representation requires two reduction layer less. Obviously, the resulting representation of this optimization differs from the expected output representation. Thus, the last MAC operation of the scalar product of a row vector and a column vector has to reduce the intermediate representation to a 32-bit output representation. As a result, the computational complexity of the reductions can be reduced from $O(n^2)$ to $O(n)$ which directly translates into a significant performance improvement for small $(N < 32)$ and mid-sized $(N < 4096)$ matrices.

4   Performance Results

In this section we report execution times and memory footprint of our reduced-precision signed-integer GEMM Eigen extension. We compare the results to Eigen's $int32\_t$ GEMM.

All results are obtained via averaging on a system with a 2.32 GHz ARM quad-core Cortex-A15 CPU and 2 GB DDR3L memory. The C++ source code with NEON intrinsics is compiled using GNU g++ (version 4.8.4) with the following command-line switches set: Optimization level: -Ofast, OpenMP parallelization: -fopenmp.

Table 2 summarizes the results of the signed-inter GEMM operator. The execution time refers to the required time to perform the pure matrix multiplication without memory allocation and value packing.

Table 2. Summary of the obtained results: execution time and speed-up over int32_t representation

Size	Metric	$int32\_t$	$int16\_t$	$int8\_t$	$int4\_t$	$int2\_t$	$int1\_t$
128 × 128	Time	0.18 ms	0.37 ms	0.16 ms	0.22 ms	0.12 ms	0.05 ms
	Speedup	1.00	0.48	1.06	0.81	1.43	3.61
256 × 256	Time	1.34 ms	2.94 ms	1.26 ms	1.66 ms	0.44 ms	0.08 ms
	Speedup	1.00	0.46	1.07	0.85	3.10	17.09
512 × 512	Time	11.54 ms	24.02 ms	10.03 ms	12.92 ms	3.27 ms	0.54 ms
	Speedup	1.00	0.48	1.15	0.89	3.52	21.17
1024 × 1024	Time	90.10 ms	192.08 ms	81.63 ms	104.03 ms	26.17 ms	4.73 ms
	Speedup	1.00	0.47	1.11	0.87	3.43	18.99
2048 × 2048	Time	0.70 s	1.52 s	0.61 s	0.83 s	0.20 s	0.04 s
	Speedup	1.00	0.46	1.10	0.85	3.45	19.81
4096 × 4096	Time	5.53 s	12.15 s	5.10 s	6.57 s	1.60 s	0.26 s
	Speedup	1.00	0.46	1.09	0.84	3.43	20.83
8192 × 8192	Time	44.72 s	97.36 s	40.88 s	52.53 s	12.74 s	3.11 s
	Speedup	1.00	0.45	1.10	0.85	3.50	14.34

The expected execution time of the core code sequence can be estimated using instruction latency data from the ARM Technical Reference Manual [1]. Table 3 summarizes the estimated and the actual speed-up of the GEMM operator for different input representations, compared to $int32\_t$ representation. As can be seen, the expected speed up is achieved in most cases with the exception of small matrices ($<256 \times 256$) combined with $int1\_t$ and $int2\_t$ representation. This is caused by Eigen optimizations which enforce padding of small matrices.

Table 3. Expected and actual speed up of the signed-integer GEMM derived from the required cycles of the MAC operation

Input rep.	Cycles	Estimated speed-up	Observed speed-up
$int32x4\_t$	6	1	1
$int16x8\_t$	30	0.40	0.45–0.48
$int8x16\_t$	36	0.67	1.06–1.15
$int4x32\_t$	69	0.70	0.81–0.89
$int2x64\_t$	39	2.46	1.43–3.52
$int1x128\_t$	15	12.80	3.61–21.17

Figure 2 shows the improvement of reduced representation over full representation in terms of memory footprint and execution time for signed integer GEMM. The line showing the theoretical improvement assumes that reducing the bit representation by a certain factor results in a performance improvement

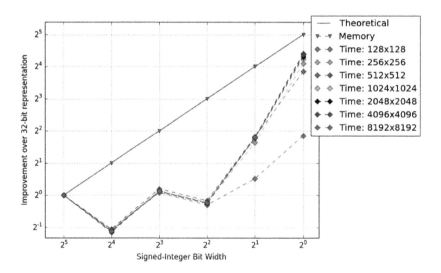

Fig. 2. Memory footprint and execution time of 32-bit and reduced-precision signed integer GEMM

of the same factor. Obviously, the memory footprint improvement meets the expected theoretical improvement since halving the bit representation results in half the memory usage.

There is a significant gap between theoretical improvement and the improvement of execution time. In particular, for $int16\_t$, $int8\_t$, and $int4\_t$, the GEMM only performs similar or even worse compared to $int32\_t$. Besides the additional reduction overhead, this is mainly due to instruction serialization caused by bit-width doubling when the multiplication is performed. As can be seen, bit representations without the need of bit-width doubling ($int2\_t$ and $int1\_t$) are clearly superior. The simplicity of computing the $int1\_t$ MAC combined with the reduction optimization (discussed in Sect. 3.3) shows its advantage by nearly reaching the theoretical improvement.

5 Discussion

The suggested GEMM implementation avoids integer overflows within the MAC operator and therefore produces the same results as the full-precision operator. The drawback of this design is that it results in a mismatch between input and output representation and, most importantly, requires bit-width doubling in most of the cases. As we have seen, bit-width doubling leads to a significant performance penalty.

In future work, we plan to show how quantization information can be propagated from the application framework to the operator and extend our custom-precision GEMM to also support custom quantization. The current implementation uses a 32-bit data type ($int32_t$) as a container to transparently transport short vectors of lower-precision data from the application framework (Theano) via Eigen to actual code, exploiting SIMD units on selected architectures (value packing). Value packing is required since lower-precision types are not known and therefore not interpretable by the application framework and Eigen. However, high-level transformations of matrix operators are optimized on a fixed size (e.g. SIMD width or cache size) and not a specific data type. As a consequence, this approach enables the use of these existing transformations on collections of values packed into 32-bit. Obviously the packed format reduces the granularity of matrix operations in the application framework and Eigen from single value to up to 32 values (in the case of 1-bit data types) and, thus, inhibits other operations on the matrices. Currently we rely on packing/unpacking the data whenever reduced-/full-precision operators are used. This approach benefits from a reduced execution time, but the advantage of a reduced memory footprint is partially lost when the data has to be unpacked.

Ultimately, the number format should therefore be interpretable by other matrix operators. This could be achieved by matrix operators supporting a generic (precision-agnostic) data type. The GNU MPFR library [5] implements multiple-precision floating-point (i.e. with user-defined mantissa and exponent) computations with correct rounding. Many interfaces to MPFR exist. The mpfr::real class[3] and bigfloat library implement full-featured interfaces (i.e. keeping all the format information) to C++ and Python respectively. The MPFR project webpage lists two linear algebra libraries compatible with some MPFR APIs:

- The ALGLIB.NET project implements multiple-precision linear algebra using MPFR[4]
- Eigen, a C++ template library for linear algebra, via Pavel Holoborodko's MPFR C++ wrapper [9]

In future work, we plan to use and explore effects on the performance of the Eigen MPFR wrapper.

6   Conclusion

We presented and discussed an approach of extending linear-algebra operators to support reduced-precision representations. Using the example of signed-integer GEMM, we showed that the highly optimized Eigen library can be extended by only modifying the MAC operation and packing several reduced-precision values into a 32-bit value. We reviewed the NEON ISA and showed its applicability to support reduced-precision arithmetic. Based on our findings, we optimized the MAC operation for NEON-capable processors and integrated our implementation into Eigen's GEMM operator and interfaced the operator to the application framework Theano.

Our results show that selected reduced-precision number formats can benefit from reduced GEMM execution time on NEON units. In particular, the performance of $int1\_t$ and $int2\_t$ GEMM is promising, and matches well with the rising interest on these data formats in the machine-learning community [3,14]. 16-, 8-, and 4-bit signed integer GEMM, however, show no performance advantage over 32-bit for this ARM architecture. Better support for reduction operations would be needed to achieve performance improvements for these number formats.

Last, we would like to encourage developers of BLAS libraries and application frameworks to design software with consideration for custom/reduced precision, as support for these representations is mostly not present today.

Acknowledgments. The main author is sponsored by the German Research Foundation (DFG). The financial support by the Austrian Federal Government, within the framework of the COMET Funding Programme is gratefully acknowledged. We also acknowledge the valuable discussions with various people, including Franz Pernkopf and Matthias Zöhrer (Graz University of Technology, Austria), and Michaela Blott (Xilinx).

---

[3] http://chschneider.eu/programming/mpfr_real/.
[4] www.alglib.net.

References

1. ARM: Cortex-A9 NEON Media - technical reference manual. Technical report (2008)
2. ARM: Introducing NEON - development article. Technical report (2009)
3. Courbariaux, M., Bengio, Y.: BinaryNet: training deep neural networks with weights and activations constrained to +1 or −1. CoRR (2016)
4. Esmaeilzadeh, H., Sampson, A., Ceze, L., Burger, D.: Architecture support for disciplined approximate programming. SIGPLAN Not. **47**(4), 301–312 (2012)
5. Fousse, L., Hanrot, G., Lefèvre, V., Pélissier, P., Zimmermann, P.: MPFR: a multiple-precision binary floating-point library with correct rounding. Research report RR-5753, INRIA (2005)
6. Goto, K., van de Geijn, R.A.: Anatomy of high-performance matrix multiplication. ACM Trans. Math. Softw. **34**(3), 12:1–12:25 (2008)
7. Guennebaud, G., Jacob, B., et al.: Eigen v3 (2010). http://eigen.tuxfamily.org
8. He, K., Zhang, X., Ren, S., Sun, J.: Deep residual learning for image recognition. CoRR arXiv:1512.03385 (2015)
9. Holoborodko, P.: MPFR C++ (2008–2012). http://www.holoborodko.com/pavel/mpfr/
10. Sampson, A., Dietl, W., Fortuna, E., Gnanapragasam, D., Ceze, L., Grossman, D.: EnerJ: approximate data types for safe and general low-power computation. In: Proceedings of 32nd ACM SIGPLAN Conference on Programming Language Design and Implementation, PLDI 2011. ACM, New York (2011)
11. Sidiroglou-Douskos, S., Misailovic, S., Hoffmann, H., Rinard, M.: Managing performance vs. accuracy trade-offs with loop perforation. In: Proceedings of 19th ACM SIGSOFT Symposium and the 13th European Conference on Foundations of Software Engineering, ESEC/FSE 2011. ACM, New York (2011)
12. Theano Development Team: Theano: A Python framework for fast computation of mathematical expressions, May 2016. arXiv e-prints arXiv:1605.02688
13. Venkataramani, S., Sabne, A., Kozhikkottu, V., Roy, K., Raghunathan, A.: Salsa: systematic logic synthesis of approximate circuits. In: Proceedings of 49th Annual Design Automation Conference, DAC 2012, pp. 796–801. ACM, New York (2012)
14. Zhu, C., Han, S., Mao, H., Dally, W.J.: Trained ternary quantization. CoRR (2016)

Complementary Papers

Complementary Papers

The Euro-Par workshops presented in this volume were selected out of submissions made in February. Two additional workshops were also selected at that time. They issued a call for submissions, and evaluated the submitted papers exactly the same as the other workshops. The final number of papers accepted by their respective program committees was found to be too low by the Euro-Par workshop organization committee to deserve their organization at the conference. However, even though those workshops were not formally organized, the papers were presented within other neighboring workshops, for the interest of the audience. We call those papers "complementary papers".

Here is the list of those complementary papers:

- *Efficient Implementation of Data Objects in the OSD+-based Fusion Parallel File System*. Juan Piernas and Pilar González-Férez. Presented at the ROME workshop.
- *A formula-driven scalable benchmark model for ABM, applied to FLAME GPU*. Eidah Alzahrani, Paul Richmond and Anthony J H Simons. Presented at the APPT workshop.
- *PhotoNoCs: Design Simulation Tool for Silicon Integrated Photonics Towards Exascale Systems*. Juan-José Crespo, Francisco Alfaro and José L. Sánchez. Presented at the UCHPC workshop.
- *On the Effects of Data-aware Allocation on Fully Distributed Storage Systems for Exascale*. Jose A. Pascual, Caroline Concatto, Joshua Lant and Javier Navaridas. Presented at the ROME workshop.

We would like to thank the organizers of the workshops which attracted and selected those complementary papers for their work. Their dedication fully contributed to the overall quality of the scientific program of the Euro-Par workshops. We would also like to thank the organizers of the hosting workshops who included those complementary papers into their program, providing them with the scientific visibility they deserve. Finally, we would like to express our commitment providing all participants, the authors as well as the attendants, with the best environment for their scientific advances.

A Formula-Driven Scalable Benchmark Model for ABM, Applied to FLAME GPU

Eidah Alzahrani[1,2]([✉]), Paul Richmond[1], and Anthony J. H. Simons[1]

[1] Department of Computer Science, The University of Sheffield, Sheffield, UK
E.alzahrani@sheffield.ac.uk
[2] Al Baha University, Al Bahah, Saudi Arabia

Abstract. Agent Based Modelling (ABM) systems have become a popular technique for describing complex and dynamic systems. ABM is the simulation of intelligent agents and how these agents communicate with each other within the model. The growing number of agent-based applications in the simulation and AI fields led to an increase in the number of studies that focused on evaluating modelling capabilities of these applications. Observing system performance and how applications behave during increases in population size is the main factor for benchmarking in most of these studies. System scalability is not the only issue that may affect the overall performance, but there are some issues that need to be dealt with to create a standard benchmark model that meets all ABM criteria. This paper presents a new benchmark model and benchmarks the performance characteristics of the FLAME GPU simulator as an example of a parallel framework for ABM. The aim of this model is to provide parameters to easily measure the following elements: system scalability, system homogeneity, and the ability to handle increases in the level of agent communications and model complexity. Results show that FLAME GPU demonstrates near linear scalability when increasing population size and when reducing homogeneity. The benchmark also shows a negative correlation between increasing the communication complexity between agents and execution time. The results create a baseline for improving the performance of FLAME GPU and allow the simulator to be contrasted with other multi-agent simulators.

Keywords: Agent based modelling · Benchmarking
Multi-agent systems

1 Introduction

Agent-based modelling (ABM) systems (also known as multi-agent systems) have become a popular technique to study complex systems in various domains, such as biology, social sciences and business complexity. ABM can be defined as a modelling paradigm used to simulate the actions and reactions of individual entities and to measure their effects on the whole system. Many phenomena,

© Springer International Publishing AG, part of Springer Nature 2018
D. B. Heras and L. Bougé (Eds.): Euro-Par 2017 Workshops, LNCS 10659, pp. 703–714, 2018.
https://doi.org/10.1007/978-3-319-75178-8_56

even complex ones, can be described as systems of autonomous agents following a number of rules to communicate with each other [14].

According to Macal and North [13,14], the structure of an agent-based model is based on three elements: (1) the number of agents, their attributes and behaviours; (2) the agents' relationships and the mechanisms with which they interact with others; and (3) each agent's environment, the actions and reactions of the agent with respect to its environment and other agents. By identifying and programming these elements, a model designer can easily create an ABM that simulates reality.

There are a number of popular agent-based modelling and simulation frameworks that are used to build models such as Swarm, NetLogo, Repast and MASON. The limitations of scalability and performance in these systems prevent modellers from simulating complex systems at very large scales. This is because some of these frameworks were designed to be run on a single CPU architecture and some of them cannot deal with a large number of agents within one model. For this reason, a number of platforms and simulators were implemented to deal with such systems. Repast HPC [28], D-Mason and FLAME GPU [23] are examples of these kinds of platforms that use parallel and distributed approaches to run simulations.

There have been several studies in the literature reporting computational performance in most ABM frameworks [2,7,11] for specific models. Varying the population size to measure system scalability is the most common benchmark. A benchmarking process is an excellent method to discover the characteristics of simulator performance, but unfortunately, so far there is no standard method to benchmark simulation tools. Thus there is a need to design a benchmark model that meets complexity and scalability standards. The OpenAB community[1] summarised a number of criteria that may affect the performance as follows:

– Arithmetic intensity: the computational complexity of an agent or population.
– Scale: varying population size.
– Model memory: the internal memory requirements of an agent or population.
– Inter-connectivity: the level of communication between agents.
– Homogeneity: divergence of behaviour within an agent or population.

This paper proposes a benchmark model that allows each of these criteria to be tested and we have implemented this model in FLAME GPU. The main contribution of this paper is creating a benchmark model that can be a standard to measure the execution efficiency of the existing ABM systems. This new model will be able to examine the following elements: system scalability, system homogeneity, and the ability to handle an increase in the level of agents' communications and agents' internal memories. The results will give insight into the performance characteristics of simulations and provide a baseline for which to measure simulator improvements.

---

[1] http://www.openab.org/.

2   Related Work

Numerous ABMs have been used to address a number of issues such as testing and analysing simulation tools and comparing ABM platforms, and they have been used as teaching tools for modelling real systems. This section reviews some of these models and their purposes.

Railsback et al. [17] proposed a simple model called StupidModel that can be easily implemented on any ABM platform. This model contains a number of versions to increase simulation complexity, starting from moving agents to a full predator-prey model. StupidModel was developed to be a teaching model for ABM platforms such as NetLogo and Swarm. It is also used as a benchmark model to compare modelling capabilities and performance between several ABM platform [11,12,18,27].

Predator-prey is the most commonly used model in the field of ABM and simulation. Developed by Alfred Lotka (1925) and Vito Volterra (1926), it is based on two differential equations to describe the dynamics of predator-prey behaviour. The basic rules of predator-prey in ABM can be summarised as follows: (1) two types of populations represent prey and predator agents; (2) the prey population will increase by moving to food resources and decrease by being eaten by the predators; (3) the predator population will increase by eating the prey and will decrease by starvation; and (4) both populations are moving randomly and following simple rules to communicate with the environment and with each other.

Several studies have reported comparisons of execution efficiencies between ABM platforms using predator-prey models [7,23]. Execution efficiencies have also been used as a benchmark to show the modelling ability of Repast Simphony [28] and by Borshchev and Filippov [3] to compare three approaches to simulation modelling: System Dynamics, Discrete Events and ABM.

The Sugarscape model is an artificial society model presented by Epstein and Axtell in their book *Growing Artificial Societies: Social Science from the Bottom Up* [6]. This model was replicated by several ABM platforms such as NetLogo[2], MASON [2] and Repast [24]. Agents in the basic Sugarscape model follow very simple rules. They move towards deserted areas with high levels of sugar resources. The Sugarscape Wealth Distribution model, as described by Epstein and Axtell, has more complexity in the relations between agents.

Boids is an artificial life model developed by Reynolds [20,21] that describes the behaviour of flocking of fish or birds. According to Reynolds (2001), flocking is an example of emergence, by which the interactions of simple local rules produce a complex global behaviour. There are three simple steering behaviours that an agent in the Boids model can follow: (1) alignment, which is steering towards the average heading of nearby neighbours; (2) separation, steering to avoid crowding nearest neighbours; and (3) cohesion, steering to move toward the average position of the immediate flockmates [19]. Flocking models

---

[2] http://ccl.northwestern.edu/netlogo/models/community/Sugarscape.

have been used widely to measure the modelling ability of some ABM platforms [8,15,18,23].

Rousset et al. [26] used their reference model [25] to benchmark 10 existing platforms that support parallel and distributed systems. The reference model they used is based on three main behaviours for each agent: (1) agent perception, (2) agent communication and (3) agent mobility. This benchmark model is used to evaluate the ability of each platform regarding their parallelism support. A large and growing body of literature has focused on the comparison between parallel and serial execution methods to run simulation [1,4,5,7,11,16]. All ABMs reviewed above were used as benchmarks for two purposes; to evaluate modelling capabilities of platforms and/or to make comparisons between simulators. Observing system performance and how applications behave during increases in population size is the main factor for benchmarking in most of these studies. System scalability is not the only issue that may affect the overall performance, but there are some issues that need to be dealt with to create a standard benchmark model that meets all ABM criteria.

3 The Benchmark Model

Our model is based on the concept of particle-based simulation which represents each molecule in the system as an individual entity. This entity has attributes, such as position, velocity and type of molecule. Entity movements and the reactions within the system will be computed using these attributes through methods to update system behaviour. The representation of the molecule (agent) will follow Brownian Dynamics methods, where each agent is represented as a point-like particle moving randomly in the environment.

This type of model is relevant to a wider class of ABMs. For example, both cellular models and social system models have similar behaviours, when considered from the view point of mobile agents with local interactions, birth and death and binding (combining). To make this model more complex and to meet all the criteria highlighted above, we propose a reaction-diffusion like model with different rules. Our model is able to convert formula syntax (such as $A + B = C$) that represents a chemical reaction to a number of mobile agents that can communicate with each other and captures important characteristics of ABM.

A simple reaction will occur when one A molecule combines with one B molecule to produce a C molecule, assuming that $A + B = C$ represents the relationship between the three molecules. The model that resulted from the given example above contains three agents A, B, and C as follows: agent A (master agent), agent B (slave agent) and agent C (combined agent). Each of these agent specifications is defined by a set of variables and functions that help to establish the simulation. At the beginning of the simulation, agents A and B are moving randomly, and both agents are communicating with each other looking for the closest complementary agent. Agent B will send its location and then agent A will choose the closest B and replied with the ID of closest B. Once the ID of B is confirmed both agents will die and produce the new agent C.

3.1   Implementation

This section consists of three parts: (1) an overview of FLAME GPU, (2) how the benchmark model is implemented using FLAME GPU and (3) model generation. The FLAME GPU framework [22] is a template for agent-based simulation on the Graphics Processing Unit (GPU). It consists of a number of X-agents (the agent representation of an X-machine [10]) specifications. Each instance of an x-agent has its own memory that holds a set of variables. All instances of x-agents have transition functions that can read and write to their memory a start state and an end state. Agents can communicate by sending and receiving messages and their functions can read and write these messages at any time between start and end states for each agent. Creating a model using FLAME GPU is very similar to the original FLAME[3] which required writing the model specification in XML format within an X-Machine Mark-up Language (XMML) document. However, the syntax that is used to write the model in FLAME GPU uses an extended version of the FLAME XML schema. The GPUXMML extension outlines the GPU specific model description elements such as the maximum size of an agent memory [22]. This allows a formal agent specification to be transformed to optimised C-based CUDA code through GPU-specific templates.

The FLAME GPU implementation of the above example consists of three agents A, B, and C. Each agent is defined by a set of variables, transition functions, start and end states, and communication messages as shown in Table 1. The representation of agents as a state machine is shown in Fig. 1. During a single iteration of the simulation, each type of agent will move from the starting state to the end state, completing each function in turn. The diagram is divided into three parts, each part showing the agent-transition functions and the communication dependency messages (green) for each agent.

At the beginning of the simulation, agents A and B are moving randomly using their move functions to update their locations during each cycle, as shown in Fig. 2 Part A. Agent B will use send_locationB to output a locationB message holding all B information (agent ID, location, etc.). Agent A after that will get all B's locations using a need_locationB function that inputs the locationB message. This function will calculate the distance between A and B and then compare it with the binding radius. If the distance is less than or equal to the binding radius, the internal memory of A will be updated (the state variable will be set equal to 2, the defined value of binding (2 is the defined value of the combined state.), and the closest ID and the closest point will be stored). The send_bindB function will output bindB messages holding the updated information for agent A (only messages that have the state variable equal to 2 as a function condition (*An agent function condition indicates that the agent function should only be applied to agents which meet the defined condition which are in the correct state specified by current State* [22])). In the next step, the receive_bindB function will input bindB messages to check for the closest A that is ready to combine. B's internal memory will be updated (the state variable

---

[3] http://flame.ac.uk/.

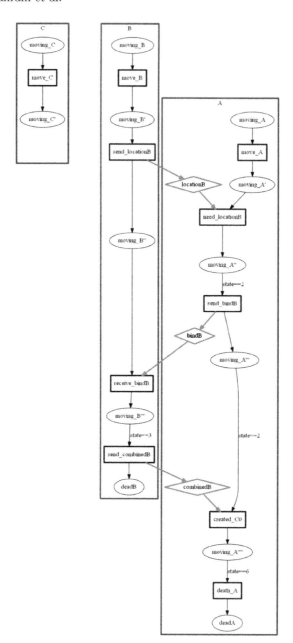

Fig. 1. State graph of the model that represents $A + B = C$. (Color figure online)

will be set to 3 (3 is the defined value of the dead state.), and the closest ID and closest point will be stored) after finding the closest A that is ready to combine. The **send_combinedB** function will output combinedB messages that meet the

Table 1. Agent specifications

Agent Type	Internal Memory	Function Name	Function Description

Master agent	Agent ID
	`Agent Position:`
	X,Y,Z
	`Closest_id`
	`Closest_point`
	state
		1.`move_A`
		2.`need_locationB`
		3. `send_bindB`
		4. `created_C`
		5. `death_A`
			1.To update A's location
			2.Choose closest B
			3.Send request to closest B
			4.Output agent C
			5.Remove agent A from simulation

Slave agent	Agent ID
	`Agent position:`
	X,Y,Z
	`Closest_id`
	`Closest_point`
	state
		1.`move_B`
		2.`send_locationB`
		3. `receive_bindB`
		4.`send_combinedB`
			1.To update B's location
			2.Send B location
			3.Verify and choose closest A that is ready to bind.
			4.Send notification to A to combine and then remove agent B from the simulation

Combined agent	Agent ID
	`Agent position:`
	X,Y,Z
	`Closest_id`
	`Closest_point`
	state
		`move_C`	To update C's location

condition (the state variable is equal to 2), and the B agent will be removed from the simulation. The next function will be `created_C`. This function will input combinedB messages (only messages that meet the condition that the state is equal to 3), output agent C, and update A's internal memory (the state variable will be updated to meet the next function condition). All A's that meet the condition of `death_A` will be removed at this stage. A visualisation of the model after a number of iterations is shown in Fig. 2 Part B.

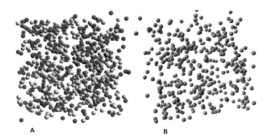

Fig. 2. Part A: Screenshot of the first iteration showing agents A (red) and B (yellow) moving randomly. Part B: Screenshot after 100 iterations showing agents C (blue) moving randomly and two of A (red) and two of B (yellow) still moving. (Color figure online)

To save time and effort, and to implement several chemical reactions at the same time automatically, a model generator is needed. This section presents a FLAME GPU model generator that can easily convert lines of formula syntax into movement models of agents. This generator after parsing the syntaxes will output three files that are required to run a FLAME GPU model: (1) a FLAME GPU XML model (XMLModelFile.xml) file that consists of model specifications, (2) a function.c file that holds the scripted agent functions, and (3) initial values of each agent for the simulation state data which is stored in a FLAME GPU XML file (0.xml).

4   Benchmarking Results

The model generator helped to vary the model in a different way and allowed modelling of different types of chemical reaction. FLAME GPU version 1.4.3 was used for the performance benchmarking on a NVIDIA GeForce GTX 970 GPU with 1665 CUDA cores and 4 GB of memory. This section shows four different benchmarks to measure FLAME GPU framework performance.

Divergence within a population: The purpose of this benchmark is to observe the system performance when doubling the number of equations. This benchmark starts with a simple model with three types of agent, ten agent functions and three type of message and ends with more than 40 agent types, 150 agent functions, and 45 message types. Adding more equation input lines (every line contains three different types of agent) increases the execution time linearly with a value of regression $\simeq 0.9945$, as shown in Fig. 3 (axis x1 against axis y1). processing time increases by $\simeq 0.5$ a second with the addition of a new equation. This benchmark was implemented using an agent population of 2000 for each type of agent with the same environment size, and each simulation was performed for 100 iterations.

Divergence within an agent: This benchmark gives us the average execution time for increasing slave agent types (more chemicals per line). This experiment will increase divergence within the master agent of this line. Adding a new chemical will extend the master agent functions, and that means more functions in each layer every cycle. In FLAME GPU function layers represent the control flow of simulation processes [9]. All agent functions are executed in a sequential order to complete one iteration and by adding more functions for the same agent that will increase execution time in every iteration. This can be observed in the results in Fig. 3 (axis x2 against axis y2). The processing time is increasing linearly by increasing chemicals per line given a value of the regression equal to 0.9956. This benchmark was implemented using an agent population of 2000 for each type of agent with the same environment size, and each simulation was run for 100 iterations.

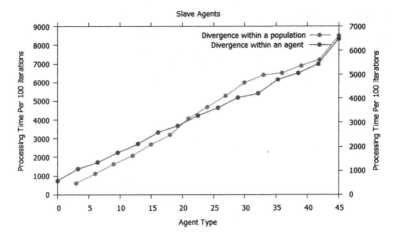

Fig. 3. Processing time of the same environment size against the type of agent that have been added at every step (appears with a red line). Processing time of the same environment size against the number of slave agents that has been added every time (appears with a blue line). (Color figure online)

Population sizes: The goal of this benchmark is to measure the ability of this model to scale to examine ABM systems scalability. The population size of each agent type starts with 4,096 agents and ends with 262,144 agents. This benchmark uses $A + B = C$ as an example to run this experiment for 100 iterations each time. The performance of implementing our model on FLAME GPU with respect to agent population size is shown in Fig. 4 with linear correlation coefficient equal to 0.9811.

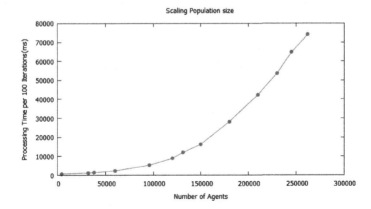

Fig. 4. Increasing population size led to increased processing time.

Level of communication and complexity: Two changes have been made to agent behaviour to slow down the simulation and add extra arithmetic intensity within agent functions: (1) decreased interaction radius and (2) decreased agent movement speed. Figure 5 (axis x1 against axis y1) shows the relationship between decreasing the interaction radius and increasing processing time to produce 50 agents C from the $A + B = C$ equation with same movement speed. This experiment allows agents to move for a longer time until reaching the needed radius, during this movement, several operations occur such as calculating agent position, sending and receiving messages between agents looking for the nearest agent to combine with. The next experiment is shown in Fig. 5 (axis x2 against axis y2), which shows the relationship between slowing down the agent speed the number of iterations required to produce 50 agents. This experiment has been implemented with a constant radius and same environment size. Slowing down the movement speed allows additional operations during the simulation and this help to measure the ability of the system to handle many computational operations for a long time and how to manage using the resources.

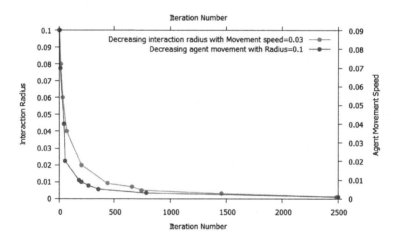

Fig. 5. Decreasing interaction radius led to increased time to produce 50 agents (appears with a red curve). Decreasing agent movement speed led to increased time to produce 50 agents (appears with a blue curve) (Color figure online)

5   Conclusion

This paper presents the implementation of a new benchmark model using FLAME GPU. The aim of this model is to measure the following elements: system scalability, system homogeneity, and the ability to handle increases in the level of agent communications and model complexity. Unfortunately, measuring the ability to handle increases in the internal memory requirements of an agent or population was not covered by this paper. However, it will be involved in our future work.

Four benchmark experiments have been carried out, demonstrating the ability of this benchmark model to examine each element. The first two experiments focused on increasing agent and population divergence, and this led to increased the execution time due to the additional agent functions, messages and communication information that is held by these messages. The third experiment showed that we could easily scale the population size of this model to measure the system scalability. The results showed that scaling the population size led to varying the execution time from 0.5 s per 100 iterations for 4069 agents till 72 s per 100 for 262144 agents. In the last experiment, computational complexity was added by decreasing the value of two variables that are used within agent functions to update agents behaviour. This experiment causes the model to reach a steady state at a slower rate, this allows assessment of the system capabilities.

Divergence is known to reduce performance in GPU simulations and our benchmark model confirms this. The obtained results will be used for assessing simulator improvements to achieve improved scaling with respect to divergence and better overall performance for increasing the population size. The performance results obtained indicate that our benchmark model is a suitable model to be used as an experimental tool to evaluate modelling capabilities of an ABM system if it is replicated in a suitable way.

References

1. Aaby, B.G., Perumalla, K.S., Seal, S.K.: Efficient simulation of agent-based models on multi-GPU and multi-core clusters. In: Proceedings of 3rd International ICST Conference on Simulation Tools and Techniques, p. 29. ICST (Institute for Computer Sciences, Social-Informatics and Telecommunications Engineering) (2010)
2. Bigbee, A., Cioffi-Revilla, C., Luke, S.: Replication of sugarscape using MASON. In: Terano, T., Kita, H., Deguchi, H., Kijima, K. (eds.) Agent-Based Approaches in Economic and Social Complex Systems IV, vol. 3, pp. 183–190. Springer, Tokyo (2007). https://doi.org/10.1007/978-4-431-71307-4_20
3. Borshchev, A., Filippov, A.: From system dynamics and discrete event to practical agent based modeling: reasons, techniques, tools. In: Proceedings of 22nd International Conference of the System Dynamics Society, vol. 22 (2004)
4. Deissenberg, C., Van Der Hoog, S., Dawid, H.: EURACE: a massively parallel agent-based model of the European economy. Appl. Math. Comput. **204**(2), 541–552 (2008)
5. Dematte, L.: Parallel particle-based reaction diffusion: a GPU implementation. In: 2010 9th International Workshop on Parallel and Distributed Methods in Verification and 2nd International Workshop on High Performance Computational Systems Biology, pp. 67–77. IEEE (2010)
6. Epstein, J.M., Axtell, R.: Growing Artificial Societies: Social Science from the Bottom Up. Brookings Institution Press, Washington, DC (1996)
7. Fachada, N., Lopes, V.V., Martins, R.C., Rosa, A.C.: Towards a standard model for research in agent-based modeling and simulation. PeerJ Comput. Sci. **1**, e36 (2015)
8. Goldsby, M.E., Pancerella, C.M.: Multithreaded agent-based simulation. In: Proceedings of 2013 Winter Simulation Conference: Simulation: Making Decisions in a Complex World, pp. 1581–1591. IEEE Press (2013)

9. Grimm, V., Railsback, S.F.: Individual-Based Modeling and Ecology. Princeton Series in Theoretical and Computational Biology. Princeton University Press, Princeton (2005)
10. Ipate, F., Holcombe, M.: A method for refining and testing generalised machine specifications. Int. J. Comput. Math. **68**(3-4), 197–219 (1998)
11. Lysenko, M., D'Souza, R.M., et al.: A framework for megascale agent based model simulations on graphics processing units. J. Artif. Soc. Soc. Simul. **11**(4), 10 (2008)
12. Lytinen, S.L., Railsback, S.F.: The evolution of agent-based simulation platforms: a review of NetLogo 5.0 and ReLogo. In: Proceedings of 4th International Symposium on Agent-Based Modeling and Simulation, p. 19 (2012)
13. Macal, C.M., North, M.J.: Agent-based modeling and simulation. In: Winter Simulation Conference, pp. 86–98 (2009)
14. Macal, C.M., North, M.J.: Tutorial on agent-based modelling and simulation. J. Simul. **4**(3), 151–162 (2010)
15. North, M.J., Tatara, E., Collier, N.T., Ozik, J., et al.: Visual agent-based model development with repast simphony. Technical report, Argonne National Laboratory (2007)
16. de Paiva Oliveira, A., Richmond, P.: Feasibility study of multi-agent simulation at the cellular level with FLAME GPU. In: FLAIRS Conference, pp. 398–403 (2016)
17. Railsback, S., Lytinen, S., Grimm, V.: StupidModel and extensions: a template and teaching tool for agent-based modeling platforms. Swarm Development Group (2005). http://condor.depaul.edu/~slytinen/abm
18. Railsback, S.F., Lytinen, S.L., Jackson, S.K.: Agent-based simulation platforms: review and development recommendations. Simulation **82**(9), 609–623 (2006)
19. Reynolds, C.W.: Boids: background and update (2001). www.red3d.com/cwr/boids
20. Reynolds, C.W.: Big fast crowds on PS3. In: Proceedings of 2006 ACM SIGGRAPH Symposium on Videogames, pp. 113–121. ACM (2006)
21. Reynolds, C.W.: Flocks, herds and schools: a distributed behavioral model. ACM SIGGRAPH Comput. Graph. **21**(4), 25–34 (1987)
22. Richmond, P.: Flame GPU technical report and user guide (CS-11-03). Technical report, Department of Computer Science, University of Sheffield (2011)
23. Richmond, P., Romano, D.: Template-Driven Agent-based Modeling and Simulation with CUDA. Applications of GPU Computing Series, GPU Computing Gems Emerald Edition, pp. 313–324 (2011)
24. Robertson, D.A.: Agent-based models to manage the complex. Manag. Org. Complex.: Philos. Theory Appl. **24**, 417–430 (2005)
25. Rousset, A., Herrmann, B., Lang, C., Philippe, L.: A survey on parallel and distributed multi-agent systems. In: Lopes, L., et al. (eds.) Euro-Par 2014. LNCS, vol. 8805, pp. 371–382. Springer, Cham (2014). https://doi.org/10.1007/978-3-319-14325-5_32
26. Rousset, A., Herrmann, B., Lang, C., Philippe, L.: A survey on parallel and distributed multi-agent systems for high performance computing simulations. Comput. Sci. Rev. **22**, 27–46 (2016)
27. Standish, R.K.: Going stupid with EcoLab. Simulation **84**(12), 611–618 (2008)
28. Tatara, E., North, M., Howe, T., Collier, N., Vos, J., et al.: An introduction to repast simphony modeling using a simple predator-prey example. In: Proceedings of Agent 2006 Conference on Social Agents: Results and Prospects (2006)

PhotoNoCs: Design Simulation Tool for Silicon Integrated Photonics Towards Exascale Systems

Juan-Jose Crespo$^{(\boxtimes)}$, Francisco J. Alfaro-Cortés, and José L. Sánchez

High-Performance Networks and Architectures (RAAP) Group,
University of Castilla-La Mancha, Albacete, Spain
{juanjose.gcrespo,fco.alfaro,jose.sgarcia}@uclm.es
http://www.i3a.uclm.es/raap/

Abstract. The need to greatly increase the number of compute nodes to design exascale systems raises numerous challenges that must be solved to obtain an efficient system in terms of cost, energy consumption and performance. Data movement is a critical barrier toward realizing exascale computing systems, and therefore the interconnection network is a key component of these systems. Among the different technologies that could contribute to an efficient interconnect, photonics is perhaps the most disruptive, due to its capabilities to generate, transmit, and receive high bandwidth signals with superior power efficiencies and inherent immunity to degradation. However, photonic interconnects lack from practical buffering, which make these networks circuit switched in its essence. Therefore, new network architectures are required, both to satisfy the requirements of data transfers between nodes and between the multiple computing resources of each multicore node. This paper presents *PhotoNoCs* as a tool which helps the computer architect to design and test new approaches of photonics interconnection systems at different levels: On-chip networks for multicore architectures and off-chip networks for the whole supercomputer.

Keywords: Photonics · SiP · On-chip · Exascale

1 Introduction

Progress in scientific fields including clime, aerospace, biotechnology, and energy, depends largely on the ability to perform costly and complex simulations. Supercomputers are the only viable option to support such computations, and intense research is focusing in increasing the computing capability of these systems. In fact, the main objective is the design of exascale systems, for which it becomes necessary greatly increase the number of compute nodes. This raises numerous challenges that must be solved to obtain an efficient system in terms of cost, energy consumption and performance. Some of these challenges are: scalable system software, resilience and correctness, programming systems, energy efficiency, or interconnect technology.

© Springer International Publishing AG, part of Springer Nature 2018
D. B. Heras and L. Bougé (Eds.): Euro-Par 2017 Workshops, LNCS 10659, pp. 715–724, 2018.
https://doi.org/10.1007/978-3-319-75178-8_57

A significant growth in parallelism implies the system performance is greatly determined by the communication generated when running the parallel applications, even more than the arithmetic operations. Note that data transfers exist at several levels: between compute and storage nodes, between compute nodes, and between the multiple computing resources of each multicore node. Therefore, data movement is a critical barrier toward realizing the exascale systems, and thus the interconnection network is a key component of exascale systems.

Moving to exascale systems seems that it will not be possible with a traditional incremental strategy, and significant qualitative changes will be necessary. In the case of the interconnect systems, different technologies to the traditional ones could contribute to achieve this objective. Photonics is perhaps the most disruptive technology, due to its capabilities to transmit, and receive high bandwidth signals with higher power efficiency and immunity to degradation.

Significant progress has been made over the past decade in optical device integration [13–15].

However, photonic devices are different in how they function, and exploiting all its advantages would require a significant change in how on- and off- chip interconnects are designed. Nevertheless, this paradigm has some challenges to be addressed, for example, optical signals cannot be buffered nor processed without being converted first to the electronic domain. This requires new proposals to solve these issues.

In this work, we present *PhotoNoCs* [4] as a tool to fullfil the need for a design tool at different levels, ranging from on-chip networks, to off-chip networks and switch design schemes based on silicon photonics. We also evaluate a particular switch design using *PhotoNoCs* to probe its new capabilities.

The structure of this paper is as follows: Sect. 2 gives an overview of the simulation tool *PhotoNoCs* and its main features. It also provides a background to understand the building blocks behind photonic technology that allows the integration of complex devices. Section 3 provides a review on recent microring-based switches, and it focuses on a particular design to be evaluated in Sect. 4 using *PhotoNoCs*. Finnally conclusions are presented in Sect. 5.

2   PhotoNoCs Simulator

The PhotoNoCs simulator is developed using *OMNeT++ v5.0*, an extensible, modular, component-based C++ simulation library and framework, primarily for building network simulators. This choice is motivated by the fundamental requirements behind the PhotoNoCs project: reusability of models, modular architecture and scalable performance with low memory footprint.

As depicted in Fig. 1, PhotoNoCs is composed of different blocks, being each of them focused on a single aspect of the system. The gray-colored blocks are provided by the *OMNeT++* framework.

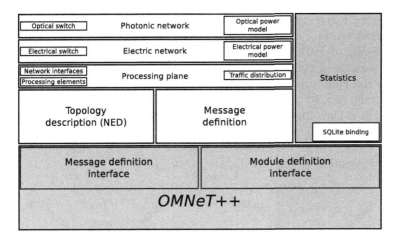

Fig. 1. Block diagram of the PhotoNoCs design.

2.1 Main Features

Each block shown in Fig. 1 provides new functionality to the simulation tool. For the sake of brevity, only those characteristics used for this work are described:

1. **Photonic network:** Several photonic devices are integrated into PhotoNoCs, the vast majority are based on the *Photonic Device Library* from the project *PhoenixSim* [2]. Using these devices, the programmer can study different switch designs based on these devices and simulate them. PhotoNoCs then reports several metrics as described in Sect. 2.3.
2. **Electric network:** Components and example modules are implemented such as buffers, arbiters, electrical crossbars, etc. All of these modules are ready to work together to simulate electrical networks (mainly NoCs).
3. **Processing plane:** Processors and network interfaces are also modelled. At the moment, processors are responsible for generating messages, such generation can be based on traces or synthetic traffic. Network interfaces are implemented to support electrical, and also optical networks, separately or both at the same time. In the later case, a selection policy must be configured to select through which network data is transferred (such policies are available in the tool).
4. **Topology description:** Because of its modular nature, each module, being optical switches, or any other module, can be connected using the skeletons provided in the simulation tool. Progammers can configure any topology using the Network Description (NED) language provided by *OMNeT++*.

2.2 The Building Block: Silicon Photonic Microring Based 2 × 2 Switch

This section explains the fundamentals of the basic building block used in this work, the silicon photonic microring based 2 × 2 switch. This component is accurately modelled in the simulation tool PhotoNoCs, and it is the baseline for complex devices.

The design of a silicon photonic microring-based 2×2 switch is shown in Fig. 2. It is made of two silicon microrings and two crossing silicon waveguides.

When the rings are ON resonance with a given input signal, the signal is coupled to the ring, to be coupled to the second waveguide. As shown in Fig. 2(b), the signal goes through the Out_2 port.

On the other hand, as shown in Fig. 2(a) if the rings are OFF resonance with the input signal, the signal passes through the switching element remaining on the same waveguide, it goes through the Out_1 port.

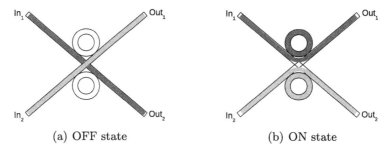

(a) OFF state   (b) ON state

Fig. 2. Silicon photonic microring based 2×2 switch: (a) microring based 2×2 switch in its OFF state; and (b) microring based 2×2 switch in its ON state.

It is worth mentioning that both input signals can be dropped into or allowed to pass both rings simultaneously, this builds a full 2×2 switching element.

2.3   Performance Metrics

This section describes a set of physical metrics that characterizes the performance of photonic network designs. The following metrics are calculated by the *PhotoNoCs* tool and reported for each type of loss depending on the device physical properties (Sect. 4).

- **Insertion Loss:** This is the power attenuation incurred by an optical signal along its path of propagation. Photonic transmission must be realized without signal regeneration because of the difficulties in creating silicon-based optical amplifiers. Therefore, *insertion loss* should be as low as possible.
  Then, it is clear that the complexity and size of a network is limited by the insertion loss since a photonic link can only exhibit a certain amount of loss before the signal becomes too weak to be received properly.
- **Optical Loss Budget:** This metric represents the difference of the maximum injectable laser power into the network and the minimum detectable power at the receivers. The maximum injectable laser power is limited by the threshold of undesirable nonlinear optical effects in silicon, which deteriorate

signal integrity when the signal power is too high.

Wavelength Division Multiplexing (WDM) [1] must be taking into account if used, although it enables data signals to be transmitted in parallel across different wavelength channels, the total optical power (sum across all present wavelength channels) must still remain below this nonlinear limit.

In Eq. 1 is used to calculate the Optical Loss Budget. Where P is the power threshold of the laser source, S is the photodetector sensitivity, IL_{max} is the worst-case optical path insertion loss, and n specifies the amount of wavelengths used.

$$P - S \geq IL_{max} + 10 \log_{10}(n) \tag{1}$$

- **Crosstalk:** Leakage of a small portion of power from signals to intersecting waveguides along its path of propagation. At a given waveguide intersection, signals coming from different waveguides will leak a small portion of power to the other waveguides. This also occurs at resonator-based switches due to imperfect coupling of the wavelength channels.

  If a device is modeled as having N ports from which an optical signal can ingress or egress, then the message can receive crosstalk from up to $N - 1$ foreign messages. If M is the set of signals present in the device and P_k is the power of signal k, then the crosstalk seen by signal s is given by Eq. 2.

$$C_s = \sum_{k \in M, k \neq s} \frac{P_k}{IL(p_{k.in}, p_{s.out})} \tag{2}$$

Function $IL(p_{k.in}, p_{s.out})$ calculates the insertion loss (a portion of the original signal power) between two ports of the device. $p_{k.in}$ denotes the input port of any signal other than s, and $p_{s.out}$ is the output port of signal s.

3 Microring-Based Switches

This section reviews developments in microring-based switches for silicon photonic interconnection networks in many-core computing systems.

Microring-based array filters and switches for multiple-input multiple-output (MIMO) optical interconnects have long attracted research interest. There have been several array structures design proposals in different materials including silicon [3,5–7,9–12].

In this work, to show the simulation tool capabilities, a switch design has been selected, as shown in Fig. 3. Due to lack of space, only *silicon-on-insulator (SOI)* designs are studied.

3.1 Optical Hitless Switch

The optical hitless switch shown in Fig. 3, proposed in [11] is a spatially non-blocking optical 4 × 4 switch to be used in integrated photonic networks.

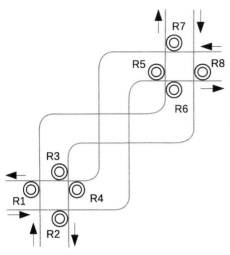

Fig. 3. Optical hitless switch [11].

Table 1. Physical paths microring configuration.

		Input			
		N	S	E	W
Output	N	-	None	R7	R5
	S	None	-	R4	R2
	E	R8	R6	-	None
	W	R3	R1	None	-

Table 2. Non overlapping combinations of I/O ports.

		Input				Rings used
		N	S	E	W	
Configuration	1	W	N	S	E	R3, R4
	2	W	E	N	S	R3, R6, R7, R2
	3	W	E	S	N	R3, R6, R4, R5
	4	S	N	W	E	None
	5	S	W	N	E	R1, R7
	6	S	E	W	N	R6, R5
	7	E	W	S	N	R8, R1, R4, R5
	8	E	W	N	S	R8, R1, R7, R2
	9	E	N	W	S	R8, R2

The routing is accomplished by having one dedicated waveguide for each input-output combination. Note that signals are never routed back through their direction of origin nor to the same direction as another signal.

The previous paragraph states that switching multiple signals through this switch should be performed in a way that for a given signal s to be sent through output port o, there must not be any other signal r to be sent through the same output port o.

Table 1 shows the microrings to be configured to allow any given combination of I/O ports. On the other hand, the possible 9 combinations of I/O ports which avoid overlaps on the waveguides used by each flow of data have been included in Table 2.

4   Evaluation

This section describes the study performed to evaluate the switch design shown in Sect. 3.1 as well as the capabilites of the simulation tool.

The switch is shown in Fig. 4. The modulator bank needed to inject multiple wavelengths λ_n into the waveguide is located at the south port of the switch. The parameters used to characterize the physical properties of the photonic devices and types of losses are summarised in Tables 3 and 4.

The switch design has been tested under three different situations that can arise depending on the output port trying to forward the data. The switch design shown in Fig. 4 has the modulator located at its south I/O port. This allows to test three different switching configurations:

Table 3. Physical properties of the photonic devices.

Property	Value
Laser power	10 dBm
Modulator ring diameter	3 μm
2 × 2 switch rings diameter	50 μm

Table 4. Characterization of the types of losses.

Type of loss	Value
Propagation	$1.5 * 10^{-4}$ dB/um
Pass by ring (OFF)	$5.0 * 10^{-3}$ dB
Drop into ring (ON)	0.5 dB
Crossing (at 90°)	0.15 dB
Bending	$5.0 * 10^{-3}$ dB

1. **StoN:** Data going from the South port to the North port, Fig. 4(a).
2. **StoW:** Data going from the South port to the West port, Fig. 4(b).
3. **StoE:** Data going from the South port to the East port, Fig. 4(c).

The previous switching configurations are sufficient to characterize this particular switch design. Because the optical hitless switch design is inherently symmetric, every possible situation is represented with the previous ones.

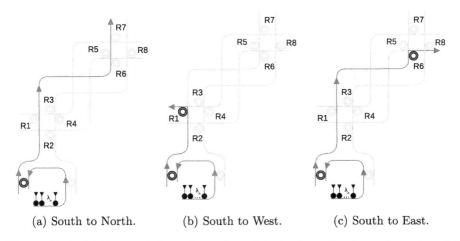

(a) South to North.   (b) South to West.   (c) South to East.

Fig. 4. Optical hitless switch configurations: (a) South to North configuration; (b) South to West configuration; and (c) South to East configuration.

Performance results in terms of signal loss and power are shown in Fig. 5. Similar results are drawn from each configuration in Fig. 5(a), (b) and (c). Pass by off resonance rings and propagation losses both develop an exponential increase as the number of wavelengths used rises. Other sources of signal loss such as crossings, bendings and drop into rings on resonance do not depend on the number of wavelengths used, this is due to the use of *broadband* microrings in the design.

The fact that passing through rings off resonance (*Pass By Ring* in the graphs) and the propagation loss rise with the number of wavelengths used is due to the modulator. Modulator microrings have a fixed wavelength resonance (*narrowband* microrings), which causes an increase of the number of microrings needed as the number of wavelengths increases (each microring modulates a single wavelength).

Moreover, because more microrings are needed as the number of wavelengths increases, it also has an impact on the modulator design, having to increase the physical length of the waveguides to go through these microrings.

On the other hand, Fig. 5(d) shows that communication is not feasible using more than 128 wavelengths, if we consider a photodectector sensitivity of 13.1 dBm as reported in [8].

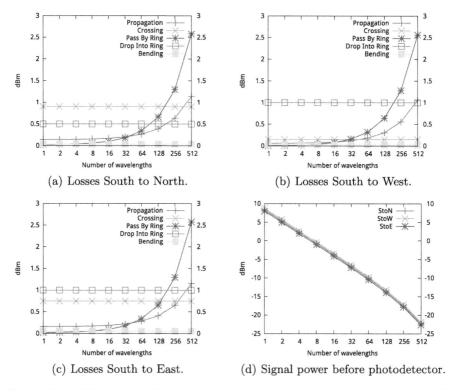

(a) Losses South to North.

(b) Losses South to West.

(c) Losses South to East.

(d) Signal power before photodetector.

Fig. 5. Optical hitless switch performance as number of optical signals increase: (a) losses going from South to North; (b) losses going from South to West; (c) losses going from South to East; and (d) signal power for each configuration before reaching the photodetector.

Finally, Fig. 6 shows for each switch configuration the different sources of signal loss. Signal loss due to crossings is most significant going from one side to the opposite of the switch (South to North, Fig. 4(a)), and also, going to the East (Fig. 4(c)).

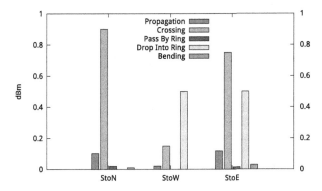

Fig. 6. Loss sources for each switch configuration.

We can conclude that modulator losses as shown in Fig. 5(a), (b) and (c) and also losses due to waveguide crossings and bendings, as shown in Fig. 6, are the main sources of signal loss for this switch design.

5   Conclusions

This work presents a detailed characterization of an optical switch design using the tool *PhotoNoCs*, an event-driven simulator developed in $C++$ using the framework *OMNeT++*.

First, an overview of the simulation tool and its components have been described, showing how PhotoNoCs allows to simulate traditional Networks-on-Chip. However, PhotoNoCs is not limited to NoCs but it also carries detailed simulation of emerging technologies such as optical communications, allowing the study and design of different networks and devices (such as switches) to be applied both, on-chip and off-chip networks.

Results show that PhotoNoCs is able to simulate sofisticated communication mechanisms with high accuracy due to fine-grained details implemented together with high level of parametrization and modular design. These features make PhotoNoCs an effective simulation tool for the manycore design space research towards the exascale era.

Acknowledgements. This work has been supported by the Spanish MECD and European Commission (FEDER funds) under the project TIN2015-66972-C5-2-R; and by the JCCM under the project PEII-2014-028-P. Juan-Jose Crespo is also funded by the Spanish MECD under national grant (FPU) FPU15/03627.

References

1. Beausoleil, R.G., Ahn, J., Binkert, N., Davis, A., Fattal, D., Fiorentino, M., Jouppi, N.P., McLaren, M., Santori, C., Schreiber, R.S., et al.: A nanophotonic interconnect for high-performance many-core computation. In: 16th IEEE Symposium on High Performance Interconnects, HOTI 2008, pp. 182–189. IEEE (2008)
2. Chan, J., Hendry, G., Biberman, A., Bergman, K., Carloni, L.P.: PhoenixSim: a simulator for physical-layer analysis of chip-scale photonic interconnection networks. In: Proceedings of the Conference on Design, Automation and Test in Europe, pp. 691–696. European Design and Automation Association (2010)
3. Chang, S.J., Ni, C.Y., Wang, Z., Chen, Y.J.: A compact and low power consumption optical switch based on microrings. IEEE Photonics Technol. Lett. **20**(12), 1021–1023 (2008)
4. Crespo, J.J., Alfaro Cortes, F.J., Sanchez Garcia, J.L.: PhotoNoCs: un simulador de redes ópticas para CMPs. Jornadas de Paralelismo, pp. 509–516 (2015). ISBN: 978-84-16017-52-2
5. Goebuchi, Y., Hisada, M., Kato, T., Kokubun, Y.: Optical cross-connect circuit using hitless wavelength selective switch. Opt. Express **16**(2), 535–548 (2008)
6. Goebuchi, Y., Kato, T., Kokubun, Y.: Multiwavelength and multiport hitless wavelength-selective switch using series-coupled microring resonators. IEEE Photonics Technol. Lett. **19**(9), 671–673 (2007)
7. Kaźmierczak, A., Drouard, E., Briere, M., Rojo-Romeo, P., Letartre, X., O'Connor, I., Gaffiot, F., Lisik, Z.: Optimization of an integrated optical crossbar in SOI technology for optical networks on chip. J. Telecommun. Inf. Technol. 109–114 (2007)
8. Koester, S.J., Schow, C.L., Schares, L., Dehlinger, G., Schaub, J.D., Doany, F.E., John, R.A.: Ge-on-SOI-detector/Si-CMOS-amplifier receivers for high-performance optical-communication applications. J. Lightwave Technol. **25**(1), 46–57 (2007)
9. Little, B., Chu, S., Pan, W., Kokubun, Y.: Microring resonator arrays for VLSI photonics. IEEE Photonics Technol. Lett. **12**(3), 323–325 (2000)
10. Shacham, A., Bergman, K., Carloni, L.P.: On the design of a photonic network-on-chip. In: Proceedings of the First International Symposium on Networks-on-Chip, pp. 53–64. IEEE Computer Society (2007)
11. Sherwood-Droz, N., Wang, H., Chen, L., Lee, B.G., Biberman, A., Bergman, K., Lipson, M.: Optical 4 × 4 hitless silicon router for optical Networks-on-Chip (NoC). Opt. Express **16**(20), 15915–15922 (2008)
12. Soref, R.A., Little, B.E.: Proposed N-wavelength M-fiber WDM crossconnect switch using active microring resonators. IEEE Photonics Technol. Lett. **10**(8), 1121–1123 (1998)
13. Vlasov, Y., Green, W.M., Xia, F.: High-throughput silicon nanophotonic wavelength-insensitive switch for on-chip optical networks. Nat. Photonics **2**(4), 242–246 (2008)
14. Watts, M.R., Trotter, D.C., Young, R.W., Lentine, A.L.: Ultralow power silicon microdisk modulators and switches. In: 2008 5th IEEE International Conference on Group IV Photonics, pp. 4–6. IEEE (2008)
15. Xu, Q., Manipatruni, S., Schmidt, B., Shakya, J., Lipson, M.: 12.5 Gbit/s carrier-injection-based silicon micro-ring silicon modulators. Optics Express **15**(2), 430–436 (2007)

On the Effects of Data-Aware Allocation on Fully Distributed Storage Systems for Exascale

Jose A. Pascual$^{(\boxtimes)}$, Caroline Concatto, Joshua Lant, and Javier Navaridas

Computer Science School, The University of Manchester, Manchester, UK
{jose.pascual,caroline.concatto,joshua.lant,
javier.navaridas}@manchester.ac.uk

Abstract. The convergence between computing- and data-centric work-loads and platforms is imposing new challenges on how to best use the resources of modern computing systems. In this paper we show the need of enhancing system schedulers to differentiate between compute- and data-oriented applications to minimise interferences between storage and application traffic. These interferences can be especially harmful in systems featuring fully distributed storage systems together with unified interconnects, such as our custom-made architecture ExaNeSt. We analyse several data-aware allocation strategies, and found that such strategies are essential to maintain performance in distributed storage systems.

Keywords: Near-data computing · Scheduling · Resource allocation

1 Introduction

Traditional supercomputers have been used to execute large computing-intensive parallel applications such as scientific codes. However, nowadays new types of data-oriented applications are becoming increasingly popular. In contrast with traditional HPC codes, they have to process massive amounts of scientific or business-oriented data and, hence, impose completely different needs to the computing systems.

Indeed, new hardware and software are being developed to suit these necessities, such as our novel, custom-made architecture, ExaNeSt [13]. We are working on the design and construction of a prototype capable of reaching Exascale computation using tens of millions of interconnected low-power-consumption ARM cores [1]. To support such kind of data-intensive applications we are leveraging a unified, low-latency interconnect and a fully distributed storage subsystem with data spread across the nodes. This greatly contrasts with traditional supercomputers and datacentres that rely on Storage Area Networks (SAN) to access the data with separate networks for I/O, system management and application traffic.

A fully distributed file system allows for near-data computation reducing the great overheads of moving data from centralized storage to the compute nodes. A

D. B. Heras and L. Bougé (Eds.): Euro-Par 2017 Workshops, LNCS 10659, pp. 725–736, 2018.
https://doi.org/10.1007/978-3-319-75178-8_58

single, consolidated interconnect offers enormous power-savings when compared with multi-network designs. While these design decisions do, indeed, allow us to cope with power and cost design constraints, they also exacerbate the challenges arising from workload convergence as storage traffic will be distributed all across the system which can interfere negatively with application traffic. We show that job scheduling, in particular the allocation phase where resources are assigned to applications, can have a huge impact on performance.

This is precisely our objective: understanding to what extent the mix of application and storage traffic interfere with each other and how this affects performance. Hence, we conducted an extensive evaluation of data-aware allocation strategies for data-intensive applications which take into consideration the location of both storage devices and data when deciding where application tasks will be allocated. For completeness, we compare these allocation strategies with a baseline HPC SAN-based system. Our evaluation relies on a novel, generic application model that generates synthetic workloads mimicking different types of application, i.e. I/O-, computation- or communication-intensive.

Results show that application performance can be severely degraded when mixing both types of traffic, unless careful allocation of resources is orchestrated, but also that proper resource allocation can outperform traditional storage approaches.

The rest of the paper is organized as follows. In Sect. 2 we discuss some previous works on data-aware allocation for large-scale computing system. Following in Sect. 3 we provide an overview of the architecture of ExaNeSt, specifically the storage and interconnection subsystems. We continue in Sect. 4 explaining the scheduling process and the simple allocation strategies considered in this paper. Then in Sect. 5 we present the experimental framework used to asses the impact of these strategies on the performance of the applications. These results are analysed and discussed in Sect. 6. We close the paper with Sect. 7 which highlights some concluding remarks and sets some future lines of research arising from the findings of this work.

2   Related Work

To the best of our knowledge this is the first time that a fully distributed storage subsystem based on high-performance solid state devices has been leveraged with a unified interconnect that handles both application and storage traffic in the context of high-performance computing system. Hence, there is no previous work tackling resource allocation when such a specific architecture is considered.

Some similar works are focused on allocating applications close to the data either in memory (Spark, see [20,21]) or in storage (Hadoop, see [4,8,10,24]). In all cases the authors present scheduling techniques to maintain data locality in either Hadoop-like or Spark-like clusters. Regarding traditional clusters, the insufficiency of traditional CPU-oriented batch schedulers was exposed and Stork, a scheduler that uses a job's description language to manage data location, was proposed [14]. Other works try to assign the application to the node where the data is mapped or at least, as close as possible [22]. Other approaches try to maintain the locality dynamically based on the status of the system and the network [11]. A detailed overview of data-aware scheduling can be found in [7].

There exist also plenty of previous work centred around the allocation and mapping of applications to reduce the overhead of inter-process communications, mainly within the realms of HPC systems and parallel applications (e.g. MPI-based). These disregard data locality as the proportion of storage traffic is negligible and, indeed, dealt with by a separate network, as explained above. Many authors [6,17,18] analyse the extent that inter-application interference has on their performance. In order to minimise this interference, many non-contiguous [12,19] and contiguous [18,19] allocation strategies have been proposed for a range of topologies. Similarly, other works [2,5,17] have tried to reduce intra-application contention using different techniques to map the tasks of the application onto the previously selected nodes. This paper motivates the need for merging these two approaches so to obtain the benefits of minimizing both inter-process and storage interferences.

3   The ExaNeSt Architecture

In this section we describe ExaNeSt's architecture. One of the main novelties of our design is the affordance of non-volatile storage devices [23] (NVM) within compute nodes so to reduce latency and energy by exploiting data-locality. Compute nodes will access the storage subsystem transparently using BeeGFS [3], a high performance parallel filesystem that is in charge of reading and writing data between the local NVMs and the external storage system.

In Fig. 1 we depict an overview of the model we use in this paper for the storage subsystem which is based on the typical datacentre storage architecture. In the right side we can see the computing elements (circles) and the NVM devices connected directly to them (squares). Compute nodes access remote NVMs through our custom-made interconnection network (IN, hereafter) which is also used for

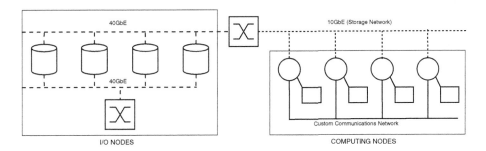

Fig. 1. Visual representation of the ExaNeSt storage architecture. The local NVMs are attached to the computing nodes sharing the main interconnect (solid). An Ethernet network is provided for persistent data storage (dashed).

interprocess-communication (solid lines). NVMs access the external storage back-end, in the left, using an independent storage network (dashed lines). For simplicity, in this work we have modelled the external storage network as a 10 GB Ethernet network which connects the compute nodes to the storage servers using a front-end 10 GB switch (this network is only to be used for I/O operations from/to the persistence storage when applications start/end the execution). As we try to model a realistic high performance system we also model a 40 GB back-end network which is in charge of data replication within the storage servers. The operation of this storage system is the typical in big datacenters [15]: when a computing node writes to disk, one of the servers will be chosen and data-replication to other servers (the number of replicas is configurable) will occur in the background without requiring user-intervention. In case of read operations the computing elements will access several storage servers (the number of replicas) and perform the operation in parallel, in order to improve the throughput. Note that although we have used this standard model for the storage subsystem, the architecture of the persistent storage is still an open question in ExaNeSt; and more efficient solutions are likely to be implemented in the final prototype.

For the purpose of this work, we define data to be **cached** if it is in main memory which allows very fast access to the data (we assume an average bandwidth of 10 GB/s) and **non-cached** if it is in an NVM. Also we define data as being **local** if it is located in the node where it is needed or **remote** if it is located in a nearby node where it can be retrieved from using the IN (performed transparently by BeeGFS). Finally data available only in central storage is denoted as **Central**. Therefore there are 5 possibilities when applications access data:

- **Local access, cached data:** This is the fastest access mode. As data are local and cached in main memory, the only limiting factors will be the latency (very low) and bandwidth (very high) of the memory.
- **Local access, non-cached data:** In this case the data are local but not in RAM. Therefore access to the NVM device is required. The limiting factors are the latency (low) and bandwidth (high) of the NVM.
- **Remote access, cached data:** In this case data is not available locally requiring access through the IN, so the limiting factor in this case will be the latency and bandwidth of the main IN, which is highly affected by external factors that could degrade its performance such as traffic interference.
- **Remote access, non-cached data:** This is the worst possible situation. The access to the IN is required because the data are not local but, in this case, both the remote NVM and the IN can become the limiting factor.
- **Central access:** We differentiate two different scenarios here. In ExaNeSt, BeeGFS access the external storage when applications start or finish execution, transferring data between persistent storage and the NVMs, so that applications always access data from the NVMs. The baseline configuration (SAN), represents an scenario where the applications do not use the NVMs so all accesses are done against the external storage; i.e., the SAN will be accessed whenever applications require to read or write data.

4   Scheduling and Resource Allocation Strategies

The scheduling process in a supercomputer involves, at least, three different stages. Applications are submitted to scheduling queues where, following some scheduling policy [9] such as FCFS, Backfilling or Shortest Job First (SJF), they are selected to be executed. After this stage, the allocator must find a set of suitable resources (physical nodes) usually fulfilling some constraints imposed by the application such as available memory, number of cores, type of architecture, etc. Finally the tasks (instances) of the application are mapped to those resources. In this Section we focus on the allocation stage in order to analyse the impact of data location on the performance of the applications.

Once an application has been selected to be run, the allocator will select a set of computing nodes to place the tasks of the application. In that moment, the application will request access to the required data and BeeGFS will load it from persistent storage into local storage. Ideally all the data will be local to each application, meaning that all accesses will be performed within local NVMs. However in a real system with many applications running concurrently and data-oriented applications demanding immense storage space, local-only accesses could be impossible to accomplish. Figure 2 represents the three possible types of storage assignment based on the interference they create in the interconnect:

- **Local:** All the local storage devices are available to load the data for the application. This is the ideal scenario where all the storage traffic remains local and, hence, there is no traffic interference.
- **Internal:** In this case only some of the local storage devices are available. This situation could happen if other applications have requested some of these storage devices previously. This will impose some intra-application interference, but will not generate inter-application interference if the applications are allocated consecutively.

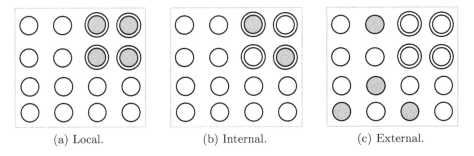

(a) Local.   (b) Internal.   (c) External.

Fig. 2. Examples of application allocation. Double-circled nodes represent the nodes assigned for compute whilst grey circles represent these for storage. Note that the 2D mesh is used for illustration purposes only.

– **External:** Some (or all) the storage devices are outside of the partition assigned to the application. Now, remote accesses to the data will generate intra- and inter-application interference.

As discussed, the assignment of the storage devices to applications depends on both internal and external factors. Internal factors are the storage space required by the application which could be larger than that available within the local NVMs and the way data is partitioned which could impose access to remote NVMs. External factors are caused by other applications using NVMs outside of their local nodes. This will lead to fragmentation making new applications to allocate storage in remote NVMs instead of in local ones (already busy). In the long run this may end up with no application being able to use local NVMs.

These factors motivate the need of resource allocation policies in order to minimize both fragmentation and interference among traffic of different applications. To this end, the scheduler (allocator) should be enhanced to incorporate knowledge about the data access patterns of the applications and about the physical topology of the network. In this work, we consider two very simple allocation strategies for typical HPC topologies: fat-tree and 3D torus. These strategies will use contiguous partitions, in which the communications of the applications remain internal within the assigned nodes. Strategies to look for contiguous partitions can be found in [16,18,19]. The second strategy is random, that mimics the behaviour of a datacenter not using any locality-aware allocation. At any rate, neither of these strategies considers the actual communication patterns or the data access patterns of the applications and so there is no attempt to reduce internal contention. Of course, we envision both reducing both external and internal contention through optimised allocation essential to take advantage of the colossal raw computing power of Exascale systems. Indeed, part of our current work is the design of strategies that take into account specific information of the applications in order to select the best set of nodes to allocate them, see e.g., [17]. This selection will consider several application metrics with the goal of reducing the interference between inter- and intra-application storage and communication traffic.

5   Experimental Set-Up

In this section we present the simulation environment used to evaluate the effects of the allocation policies. First we describe the experimental environment which is composed of the INRFlow simulator and our data-intensive application models. We conclude the section describing the set of experiments performed.

The evaluation has been carried out using INRFlow, our in-house developed simulator. INRFlow models the behaviour of parallel systems, including the topology (link arrangement), the applications and workload generation and the scheduling policies (selection, allocation and mapping) and measures several static (application-independent) and dynamic (with applications) properties.

Given the wide variety of applications that we need to consider (HPC from several scientific domains, big data analytics, etc.) and their different needs in terms of communication and storage, we have constructed a generic application model based on Markov chains which can be fine-tuned to model different application types by changing transition probabilities. Figure 3 shows the model we constructed based on an analysis of ExaNeSt's applications.

The model is composed of 6 states each of them representing the different types of operations that can go on during the execution of an application in the ExaNeSt platform. Note that storage traffic has been split into two different states in order to be able to model applications with varying IO needs (e.g. read- or write-intensive, or more balanced access to storage). In particular for this work we use read-write balanced I/O-intensive applications (75% storage *versus* 25% of computation and communications, 12.5% each), leaving other types of applications, in particular actual applications, as future work.

We evaluate two different types of scenarios. First we measure the runtime of a single application when multiple access modes are used. In particular, we measure the impact of accessing cached and non-cached data, of having a varying number of remote NVMs and of hitting in RAM with different frequency. In this scenario the applications run in isolation without any interference. The effect of interferences is evaluated in the second set of experiments in which we run several applications concurrently using two simple allocation strategies.

All the experiments have been carried out using two different INs. The first set uses a 4:3-fat-tree and a (4×4×4) torus both with 64 nodes each. The second uses a 8:3-fat-tree and a (8×8×8) torus with 512 nodes. In this case we use a larger network to execute four 128-node applications concurrently.

We consider three storage strategies: **CACHE** is the optimal case in which all the data is available in the local device, **SAN** where all I/O operations are done against the SAN and, finally, **STG-**k in which k NVMs have been allocated for the application and the required data are spread among them. If k is equal to the number of nodes it represents Local allocation, otherwise it represents Internal allocation (as discussed above). External allocation is not considered in this paper for the sake of brevity.

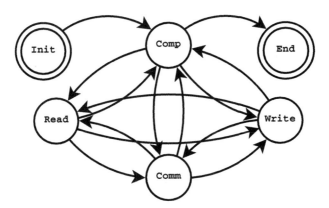

Fig. 3. Representation of the Markov chain used to generate synthetic applications. For the sake of clarity transition probabilities between states are omitted.

6   Analysis of the Results

In this section we analyse the results in terms of runtime (time required to process all the events in the trace). For the sake of brevity we only present results obtained with the fat-tree using consecutive placement, but all other results (tori and random allocation) are consistent with the ones discussed here.

6.1   Single Application Scenario

Let us start analysing the impact of accessing the NVM device where the required data is not mapped in main memory. In Fig. 4 we have represented the runtime with varying percentages of cached data access; 0 indicates that 0% of the operations are in memory, i.e., we have to always access the storage subsystem, to 100% in which all the data is accessed using main memory.

Results clearly show that when misses occur, that is, when the data must be loaded from disk, the performance is degraded. This effect is more evident in remote nodes due to the use of the unified network but it also occurs when the storage device is local. However in that case the effect is less evident due to the low latency and high bandwidth of the devices. From the results we can also notice the effects on the performance of remote accesses comparing the STG-64 and CACHE strategies. Although both strategies use 64 NVMs devices, the use of the interconnect to access 50% of the data has severely degraded the performance of the application increasing the runtime, in average, one order of magnitude.

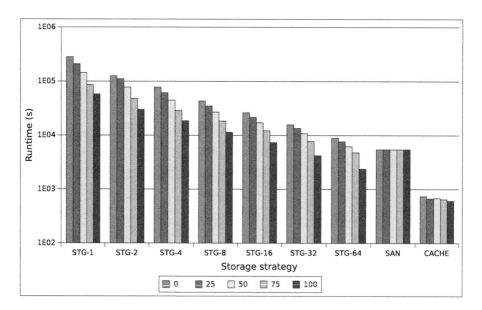

Fig. 4. Runtime of one applications running in a 64 nodes network for 50% of accesses to remote nodes and several ratios of accesses to main memory (0, 25, 50, 75 and 100%).

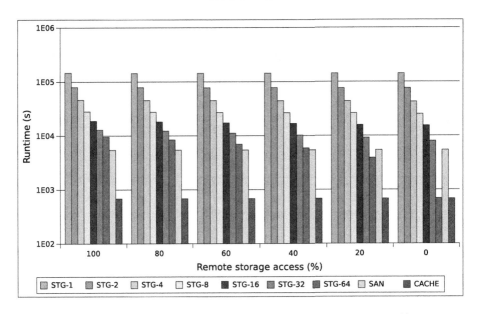

Fig. 5. Runtime of one applications running in a 64 nodes network for 50% of accesses to main memory and several ratios of accesses to remote nodes using 9 storage strategies (STG-{1, 2, 4, 8, 16, 32, 64}, SAN and CACHE).

Now let us analyse the impact of accessing remote storage devices. Figure 5 shows results for a configuration using 50% of accesses to main memory (cached data) and varying the amount of accesses to remote nodes from 0% to 100%. Results are very clear, showing that accessing remote storage devices does not comes without tremendous overheads. The worst case happens when just one NVM is used and all the tasks access it to retrieve the data, with the subsequent contention in the IN and the NVM. Increasing the number of storage devices makes the traffic spread through the IN, therefore reducing contention. In this scenario and in the one shown previously, the CACHE strategy is the best performer showing that locality for the data (both in memory and in the network) is required to take advantage of the distributed storage. Regarding the SAN access strategy, it was expected to perform well because it relies on a completely independent and high performance network and features immense bandwidth to the permanent storage. However, even in this case, STG-64 can outperform it when accessing mostly cached-data.

At any rate, having a single application running in a large parallel system is uncommon. For this reason, in the next section we will explore the effects of multiple applications accessing the storage subsystem concurrently.

6.2 Multi-application Scenario

Figure 6 shows the results for the multi-application scenario using contiguous allocation. Due to space constraints we omit the results for the random

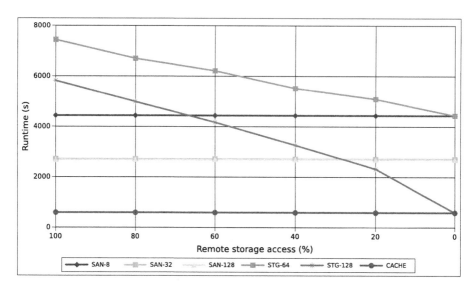

Fig. 6. Runtime of four applications running concurrently in a 512-node fat-tree using 75% of cached data and a varying percent of accesses to remote storage.

allocation, but the conclusions are akin to these presented here. As we can see, when several applications compete for the network, reducing the number of remote accesses, below 20–40% remarkably improves the performance of the applications. Regarding the number of I/O servers for the SAN strategy, we have evaluated several configurations (we only show here the use of 8, 32 and 128 I/O servers). Looking at the results it is clear that the SAN approaches perform well but at the cost of increasing the number of I/O servers. Notice that here we match the number of computing nodes with the size of the applications; this is possible for small networks as the one shown here, but clearly unaffordable for larger networks. In that case the SAN will become a bottleneck for applications.

If we focus on the STG strategies, we can see that if the number of accesses to remote NVMs is reduced below 25% the runtimes are shortened considerably, outperforming even the biggest SAN when the STG-128 strategy is used. The best performer is again the CACHE strategy that minimizes the use of the network for storage traffic. Notice that these results consider 75% of cached-data.

In summary, from all the results, we can conclude that when keeping all the data local is not possible, reducing the number of accesses to remote storage device is critical to maintain the performance. In any case, if good locality is achieved, the ExaNeSt storage subsystem can outperform classic storage systems based on SANs. We want to remark SAN-based systems require the number of I/O servers to scale with the number of compute nodes in order to keep up with the performance levels, which will be unaffordable for Exascale-capable computing systems. Alternatively, the performance of the I/O infrastructure will be degraded as systems grow. This evaluation remains as future work.

7 Conclusions and Future Work

In this work we have presented the storage architecture of ExaNeSt composed of fast NVM devices attached to the computing nodes. These devices provide to the applications low latency and high bandwidth for accessing the data. However, as this system will use a unified interconnect for all types of traffic, we wanted to measure to what extent the performance of the applications could be degraded and if the addition of specific data-aware allocation policies to the scheduling system could help alleviating this effect.

First we have seen how much accessing storage devices instead of *hot* data mapped into main memory affects the performance. Then, we looked at the effects of accessing remote storage devices. Finally, we assessed the effects of inter-application interferences. Our results show the potential benefits that exploiting locality when mapping data would bring when employing data-locality aware allocation functions in fully-distributed storage systems.

This has been just a preliminary study to assess whether specific storage allocation policies can benefit the execution of the applications in ExaNeSt and other systems using unified interconnects. In future works we will evaluate much larger networks executing a mix of applications such as communication- and computation-oriented applications. We also plan to develop specific allocators to optimise the assignment of resources that take into account both the storage and application traffic in order to improve application performance.

Acknowledgement. This work was funded by the European Union's Horizon 2020 research and innovation programme under grant agreement No 671553.

References

1. ARM. https://www.arm.com
2. Balzuweit, E., et al.: Local search to improve coordinate-based task mapping. Parallel Comput. **51**, 67–78 (2016)
3. BeeGFS. https://www.beegfs.com
4. Bezerra, A., et al.: Job scheduling for optimizing data locality in Hadoop clusters. In: 20th European MPI Users' Group Meeting, EuroMPI 2013, pp. 271–276. ACM, New York, NY, USA (2013)
5. Bhatele, A., et al.: Mapping applications with collectives over sub-communicators on torus networks. In: International Conference on High Performance Computing Networking, Storage and Analysis, SC 2012, Salt Lake City, UT, p. 97 (2012)
6. Bhatele, A., et al.: There goes the neighborhood: performance degradation due to nearby jobs. In: International Conference for High Performance Computing, Networking, Storage and Analysis, SC 2013, Denver, CO, USA, pp. 41:1–41:12 (2013)
7. Caíno-Lores, S., Carretero, J.: A survey on data-centric and data-aware techniques for large scale infrastructures. Int. J. Comput. Electr. Autom. Control Inf. Eng. **10**(3), 517–523 (2016). http://waset.org/Publications?p=111
8. Chen, T.Y., et al.: LaSA: A locality-aware scheduling algorithm for Hadoop-MapReduce resource assignment. In: 2013 International Conference on Collaboration Technologies and Systems (CTS), pp. 342–346, May 2013

9. Feitelson, D.G., Rudolph, L., Schwiegelshohn, U.: Parallel job scheduling – a status report. In: Feitelson, D.G., Rudolph, L., Schwiegelshohn, U. (eds.) JSSPP 2004. LNCS, vol. 3277, pp. 1–16. Springer, Heidelberg (2005). https://doi.org/10.1007/11407522_1

10. Hammoud, M., Sakr, M.F.: Locality-aware reduce task scheduling for MapReduce. In: International Conference on Cloud Computing Technology and Science, CLOUDCOM 2011, pp. 570–576, Washington, DC, USA (2011)

11. Jin, J., et al.: Bar: An efficient data locality driven task scheduling algorithm for cloud computing. In: CCGRID, pp. 295–304. IEEE Computer Society (2011). http://dblp.uni-trier.de/db/conf/ccgrid/ccgrid2011.html#JinLSDX11

12. Johnson, C.R., Bunde, D.P., Leung, V.J.: A tie-breaking strategy for processor allocation in meshes. In: 39th International Conference on Parallel Processing, ICPP Workshops, San Diego, California, USA, pp. 331–338 (2010)

13. Katevenis, M., et al.: The ExaNeST project: interconnects, storage, and packaging for exascale systems. In: Euromicro Conferene on Digital System Design (DSD) (2016)

14. Kosar, T., Balman, M.: A new paradigm: data-aware scheduling in grid computing. Future Gener. Comput. Syst. **25**(4), 406–413 (2009)

15. Mellanox. https://www.mellanox.com/related-docs/whitepapers/WP_Deploying_Ceph_over_High_Performance_Networks.pdf

16. Pascual, J.A., Miguel-Alonso, J., Lozano, J.A.: Strategies to map parallel applications onto meshes. In: de Leon F. de Carvalho, A.P., Rodríguez-González, S., De Paz Santana, J.F., Rodríguez, J.M.C. (eds.) Distributed Computing and Artificial Intelligence. Advances in Intelligent and Soft Computing, vol 79, pp. 197–204. Springer, Heidelberg (2010). https://doi.org/10.1007/978-3-642-14883-5_26

17. Pascual, J.A., Miguel-Alonso, J., Lozano, J.A.: Optimization-based mapping framework for parallel applications. J. Parallel Distrib. Comput. **71**(10), 1377–1387 (2011)

18. Pascual, J.A., Miguel-Alonso, J., Lozano, J.A.: Locality-aware policies to improve job scheduling on 3D tori. J. Supercomput. **71**(3), 966–994 (2015)

19. Pascual, J.A., Navaridas, J., Miguel-Alonso, J.: Effects of topology-aware allocation policies on scheduling performance. In: Frachtenberg, E., Schwiegelshohn, U. (eds.) JSSPP 2009. LNCS, vol. 5798, pp. 138–156. Springer, Heidelberg (2009). https://doi.org/10.1007/978-3-642-04633-9_8

20. Power, R., Li, J.: Piccolo: building fast, distributed programs with partitioned tables. In: Proceedings of the 9th USENIX Conference on Operating Systems Design and Implementation, OSDI 2010, pp. 293–306 (2010)

21. Santos-Neto, E., Cirne, W., Brasileiro, F., Lima, A.: Exploiting replication and data reuse to efficiently schedule data-intensive applications on grids. In: Feitelson, D.G., Rudolph, L., Schwiegelshohn, U. (eds.) JSSPP 2004. LNCS, vol. 3277, pp. 210–232. Springer, Heidelberg (2005). https://doi.org/10.1007/11407522_12

22. Topcuouglu, H., Hariri, S., Wu, M.: Performance-effective and low-complexity task scheduling for heterogeneous computing. IEEE Trans. Parallel Distrib. Syst. **13**(3), 260–274 (2002)

23. Xu, Q., et al.: Performance analysis of NVMe SSDs and their implication on real world databases. In: Proceedings of the 8th ACM International Systems and Storage Conference, SYSTOR 2015, pp. 6:1–6:11. ACM, New York, NY, USA (2015)

24. Zhang, X., et al.: An effective data locality aware task scheduling method for MapReduce framework in heterogeneous environments. In: International Conference on Cloud and Service Computing, CSC 2011, pp. 235–242. Washington, DC, USA (2011)

Efficient Implementation of Data Objects in the OSD+-Based Fusion Parallel File System

Juan Piernas$^{(\boxtimes)}$ and Pilar González-Férez

Departamento de Ingeniería y Tecnología de Computadores,
Universidad de Murcia, Murcia, Spain
{piernas,pilar}@ditec.um.es

Abstract. OSD+s are enhanced object-based storage devices (OSDs) able to deal with both data and metadata operations via data and directory objects, respectively. So far, we have focused on designing and implementing efficient directory objects in OSD+s. This paper, however, presents our work on also supporting data objects, and describes how the coexistence of both kinds of objects in OSD+s is profited to efficiently implement data objects and to speed up some common file operations. We compare our OSD+-based Fusion Parallel File System (FPFS) with Lustre and OrangeFS. Results show that FPFS provides a performance up to 37× better than Lustre, and up to 95× better than OrangeFS, for metadata workloads. FPFS also provides 34% more bandwidth than OrangeFS for data workloads, and competes with Lustre for data writes. Results also show serious scalability problems in Lustre and OrangeFS.

Keywords: FPFS · OSD+ · Data objects · Lustre · OrangeFS

1 Introduction

File systems for HPC environment have traditionally used a cluster of data servers for achieving high rates in read and write operations, for providing fault tolerance and scalability, etc. However, due to a growing number of files, and an increasing use of huge directories with millions or billions of entries accessed by thousands of processes at the same time [3,8,12], some of these file systems also utilize a cluster of specialized metadata servers [6,10,11] and have recently added support for distributed directories [7,10].

Unlike those file systems, that have separate data and metadata clusters, our in-house Fusion Parallel File System (FPFS) uses a single cluster of *object-based storage device+* (OSD+) [1] to implement those clusters. OSD+s are improved OSDs that handle not only data objects (as traditional OSDs do) but also directory objects. Directory objects are a new type of object able to store file names and attributes, and support metadata-related operations. By using OSD+s, an FPFS metadata cluster is as large as its data cluster, and metadata is effectively distributed among all OSD+s comprising the system. Previous results show that OSD+s have a small overhead, and provide a high throughput [1,2].

© Springer International Publishing AG, part of Springer Nature 2018
D. B. Heras and L. Bougé (Eds.): Euro-Par 2017 Workshops, LNCS 10659, pp. 737–747, 2018.
https://doi.org/10.1007/978-3-319-75178-8_59

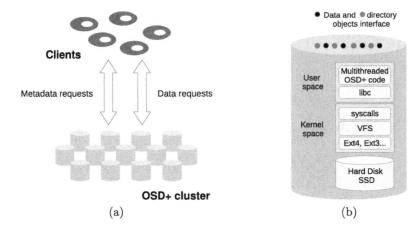

Fig. 1. (a) FPFS's overview. Each OSD+ supports both data and metadata operations. (b) Layers implementing an OSD+ device.

So far, we have focused on the development of the metadata part of FPFS. In this paper, however, we describe how we implement the support for data objects. We show that the utilization of a unified data and metadata server (i.e., an OSD+ device) provides FPFS with a *competitive advantage* with respect to other file systems that allows it to speed up some file operations.

We evaluate the performance and scalability of FPFS with data-object support through different benchmarks, and, for the first time, we compare those results with that obtained by OrangeFS [10] and Lustre [7], which only recently have added stable support for distributed directories (and, in the case of Lustre, for a metadata cluster too). Results show that, for metadata-intensive workloads, FPFS provides a throughput that is, at least, one order of magnitude better than that of OrangeFS and Lustre. For workloads with large files and large data transfers, FPFS can obtain a bandwidth up to 34% better than the bandwidth achieved by OrangeFS, and can compete with Lustre in data writes. Interestingly, results have also spotted some scalability problems of OrangeFS and Lustre that severely affect their performance in metadata workloads.

2   Overview of FPFS

FPFS [1] uses a single kind of server, called OSD+ device, that acts as both data and metadata server (see Fig. 1(a)). This approach consequently enlarges the metadata cluster's capacity that becomes as large as the data cluster's. Moreover, having a single cluster increases system's performance and scalability, since there will not be underutilized data or metadata servers.

Traditional OSDs deal with *data objects* that support operations like creating and removing objects, and reading/writing from/to a specific position in an object. We extend this interface to define *directory objects*, capable of managing directories. Therefore, OSD+ devices also support metadata-related operations like creating and removing directories and files, getting directory entries, etc.

Since there exist no commodity OSD-based disks (note that Seagate's Kinetic drives are not full-fledged OSD devices), we use mainstream computers for implementing OSD+s (see Fig. 1(b)). Internally, a local file system stores the objects; we profit this by *directly mapping* operations in FPFS to operations in the local file system, thus reducing the overhead introduced by FPFS.

A directory object is implemented as a regular directory in the local file system of its OSD+. Any directory-object operation is directly translated to a regular directory operation. The full pathname of the directory supporting a directory object is the same as that of its corresponding directory in FPFS. Therefore, the directory hierarchy of FPFS is imported within the OSD+s by partially replicating its global namespace.

For each regular file that a directory has, the directory object conceptually stores its attributes, and the number and location of the data objects that store the content of the file. The exceptions are size and modification time attributes of the file, which are stored at its data object(s). These "embedded i-nodes" are i-nodes of empty files in the local file system; the number and location of the data objects are also stored in those empty files as extended attributes.

When a metadata operation is carried out by a single OSD+ (`creat`, `unlink`, etc.), the backend file system itself ensures its atomicity and POSIX semantics. Only for operations like `rename` or `rmdir`, that usually involve two OSD+s, the participating OSD+s need to deal with concurrency and atomicity by themselves through a three-phase commit protocol [9], without client involvement.

FPFS distributes directory objects (and so the file-system namespace) across the cluster to make metadata operations scalable with the number of OSD+s, and to provide a high performance metadata service. For the distribution, FPFS uses the deterministic pseudo-random function CRUSH [11] that, given a hash of a directory's full pathname, returns the ID of the OSD+ containing the corresponding directory object. This allows clients to directly access any directory *without performing a path resolution*. Thanks to CRUSH, migrations and imbalances when adding and removing devices are minimized. FPFS manages renames and permission changes via lazy techniques [4].

FPFS also implements management for huge directories, or *hugedirs* for short, which are common for some HPC applications [8]. FPFS considers a directory is huge when it stores more than a given number of files. Once this threshold is exceeded, the directory is shared out among several nodes [2].

A hugedir is supported by a *routing OSD+* and a group of *storing OSD+s*. The former is in charge of providing clients with the hugedir's distribution information. The storing OSD+ store the directory's content. A routing object can also be a storing object. The storing objects work independently of each other, thereby improving the performance and scalability of the file system.

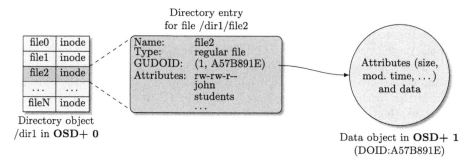

Fig. 2. A regular file in FPFS. The directory entry contains the i-node and also a reference to the data object.

3 Data Objects

Data objects are storage elements able to store information of any kind. They can also have associated attributes that users can set and get. Data objects support different operations, being the reading and writing of data the most important. Data objects receive an ID, which we call *data object ID* (DOID), when they are created. These DOIDs allow us to unequivocally identify an object inside a given device, although there can be duplicated DOIDs among different devices. Therefore, a data object is globally identifiable by means of its DOID and the ID of the device holding it. We call this pair (device ID, data object ID) a *globally unique data object ID* (GUDOID).

3.1 Data Objects of a Regular File

When a regular file is created in FPFS, three related elements are also created: a directory entry, an i-node and a data object. From a conceptual perspective, the i-node is embedded into the directory entry, so these two elements are stored together in the corresponding directory object, while the data object is stored separately. Figure 2 depicts this situation.

FPFS can use two different policies for selecting the OSD+ to store the data object of a file: *same OSD+* and *random OSD+*. The former, used by default, stores a data object in the OSD+ of the directory object storing its file's entry. This approach reduces the network traffic during file creations because no other OSD+s participate in the operation. The latter chooses a random OSD+ instead. This second approach can potentially achieve a better use of resources in some cases by keeping a more balanced workload, although it increases the network traffic during creations. Regardless the allocation policy, the i-node of a regular file stores a reference to its data object by means of its GUDOID.

3.2 Implementation of Data Objects

FPFS internally implements data objects as regular files. When a data object is created, its DOID is generated as a random integer number. A string with the hexadecimal representation of that number is used as name of the regular file supporting the object. To avoid too large directories, which usually downgrade performance, files for data objects are distributed into 256 subdirectories.

An open() call on an FPFS file always returns a file descriptor in the OSD+ storing its data object to directly operate on the object. Current implementation supports read(), write(), fstat(), lseek64(), and fsync() operations. All of them operate on the data object whose descriptor is passed as argument. The open() call also returns a key (called *secret*) for the data object, so only those clients that have been granted access to the file can use the returned descriptor to operate on the data object.

3.3 Optimizing the Implementation

If the default allocation policy for data objects is active (i.e., a directory entry for a regular file and its corresponding data object are stored in the same OSD+), we can speed up the creation of files and other operations. For instance, when a file is created, the target OSD+ internally creates an empty file in the directory supporting its directory object. This empty file acts as dentry and embedded i-node (see Sect. 2). But because data objects are also implemented as files internally, that empty file can also act as data object. Consequently, creation is quite fast, and atomic too: the three elements will either exist or not after the operation. File systems with separate data and metadata servers (at least, from a conceptual point of view) incur in a noticeable overhead due to independent operations in different servers, and the network traffic generated to perform those operations and guarantee their atomicity.

The overlap between a dentry-inode and its data object disappears, however, in a few cases: (a) when a directory object is moved, (b) when a file has several data objects, and (c) for hard links. First case occurs when a directory object is migrated from an OSD+ to another due to a rename, or when a directory becomes huge and it is distributed (only dentries are moved, data objects remain in their original servers). Second case appears when a file has several data objects, each on a different OSD+ device. In this case, those objects will exist by themselves right from the start. Finally, third case happens when there exist files having more than one link. For each of these files, FPFS creates an *i-node object* that also has a GUDOID and stores all the file's attributes (except size and modification time, as explained), references to its data objects, and a link counter. The directory entry for a new hard link simply stores the new file name and the GUDOID of the i-node object of the source file.

4   Experimental Results

We analyze FPFS's performance, and compare it with that of OrangeFS 2.9.6 and Lustre 2.9.0. This section describes experimental environment and results.

4.1   System Under Test and Benchmarks

The testbed system is a cluster made up of 12 compute and 1 frontend nodes. Each node has a Supermicro X7DWT-INF motherboard with two 2.50 GHz Intel Xeon E5420 CPUs, 4 GB of RAM, a system disk with a 64-bit CentOS 7.2 Linux distribution, and a test disk (SSD Intel 520 Series of 240 GB). The test disk supports the OSD+ device for FPFS, and the storage device for OrangeFS and Lustre. Interconnect is a Gigabit network with a D-Link DGS-1248T switch.

We use Ext4 as backend file system for both FPFS and OrangeFS, while Lustre uses its Ext4-based file system. We properly set the I/O scheduler used by the test disk, and the formatting and mounting options used by Ext4, to try to obtain maximum throughput with FPFS and OrangeFS. Lustre, however, sets these parameters automatically, and we do not change them.

We configure the three parallel file systems to shared out directories among all the available servers right from the start. This is because OrangeFS crashes for relatively small values (<1000) of its `DistrDirSplitSize` parameter, and because Lustre does not allow a dynamic distribution of directories.

We use the following scenarios of version 1.2.0-rc1 of the HPCS-IO suite [5]:

- Scenario 4: there are 64 processes with 10 directories each. Processes create as many files (with sizes between 1 kB and 64 kB) as possible in 50 s.
- Scenario 8: there are 128 processes, each creating a file of 32 MB.
- Scenario 9: a single process issues `stat()` operations on empty files in a sequential order.
- Scenario 10: like scenario 9, but `stat()` operations are issued by 10 processes (this small number of processes is imposed by the scenario).
- Scenario 12: like scenario 10, but operations are issued by 128 processes.

Scenarios 9, 10, and 12 operate on 256 directories, each containing 10 000 empty files, so they use 2 560 000 files altogether. We discard scenarios that involve large or shared files (we do not support multi-dataobject files yet), and scenario 11 (we obtain results identical to those obtained for scenario 9). Processes in the different tests are shared out among four compute nodes.

Some scenarios of HPCS-IO place synchronization points among the processes, so achieved performance is not as high as it could be. They do not operate on a single directory either, so benefits of distributing hugedirs are not clear. Due to this, we also run the following benchmarks, where there is no synchronization among processes, and a benchmark finishes when the last process completes:

- *Create:* each process creates a subset of empty files in a shared directory.
- *Stat:* each process gets the status of a subset of files in a shared directory.
- *Unlink:* each process deletes a subset of files in a shared directory.

Results shown in the graphs are the average of five runs. Confidence intervals are also shown as error bars (95% confidence level). Test disks are formatted before every run of the scenarios 4 and 8, and the preprocess for scenarios 9–12 of HPCS-IO. Test disks are also formatted before every run of the create test. For the rest of the benchmarks, disks are unmounted/remounted between tests.

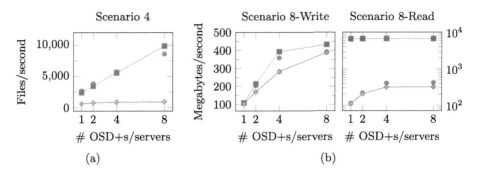

Fig. 3. HPCS-IO scenarios 4 and 8. Results for FPFS (—•—), Lustre (—■—), and OrangeFS (—◆—). Note the different Y-axis labels and ranges, and the log scale for the Y-axis in the read test of scenario 08.

4.2   HPCS-IO

Figure 3(a) depicts the results obtained for scenario 4 of HPCS-IO. We see that the performance provided by FPFS competes with that provided by Lustre, and it is almost one order of magnitude better than that of OrangeFS when 8 servers are used. Moreover, OrangeFS hardly improves its performance by adding servers. Since this scenario creates many small files, we conclude that FPFS and Lustre deals with data and metadata operations much better than OrangeFS.

Figure 3(b) shows results for scenario 8. When there are only a few files and large data transfers, results of each file system depend on its implementation and features. Lustre implements a client-side cache that provides significantly better aggregated read rates. Lustre is also implemented in kernel space and uses the interconnect in a more optimized way, introducing a smaller overhead that allows it to obtain higher aggregated write rates. On the contrary, FPFS and OrangeFS are implemented in user space and provide no client-side caches. Despite this, FPFS still obtains a higher aggregated bandwidth than OrangeFS: up to 23,5% for writes and 4 servers, and up to 34% for reads and 8 servers. Note that rates hardly increase when the number of servers grows to 8, because network interface cards (NICs) in the clients are saturated with 8 servers.

Figure 4 depicts results for HPCS-IO scenarios 9, 10, and 12, which only issue `stat()` operations on 2 560 000 empty files. In scenario 9, only one process carries out operations, so performance does not increase with the number of servers. FPFS achieves around one order of magnitude more operations/s than OrangeFS, and around 4× the throughput achieved by Lustre. FPFS and Lustre provide a steady performance regardless the number of servers, while OrangeFS's performance slightly decreases when there are more servers.

In scenario 10, FPFS's performance is more than 12× better than OrangeFS's and more than 4× than Lustre's. All the file systems provide a quite steady performance, regardless the number of servers. The situation changes for FPFS and Lustre in scenario 12, where they greatly improve their performance, which also scales up with the number of servers. OrangeFS, however, does not change

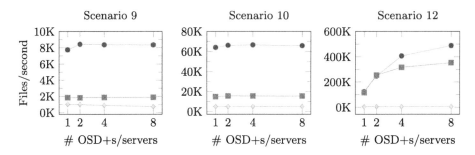

Fig. 4. HPCS-IO scenarios 9, 10, and 12. Results for FPFS (—•—), Lustre (—■—), and OrangeFS (—♦—). Note the different Y-axis ranges.

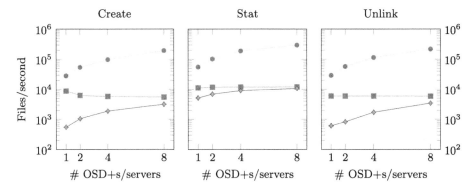

Fig. 5. Shared huge directory. Weak scaling when the number of files per server is set to 400 000. Results for FPFS (—•—), Lustre (—■—), and OrangeFS (—♦—). Note the log scale in the Y-axis.

its behavior, and basically provides the same performance as in scenario 10. Due to this, FPFS gets more than 95× operations/s than OrangeFS. Note that Lustre hardly improves its performance with more than two servers. After analyzing the network traffic, we have seen that Lustre puts different requests for a server in the same message. This "packaging" adds delays that downgrade performance.

4.3 Single Shared Directory

Figure 5 shows performance achieved, in operations per second, when 256 processes, spread across four compute nodes, concurrently access a single shared huge directory to create, get the status and delete files. Processes work on equally-sized disjoint subsets of files. The directory contains $400\,000 \times N$ files, where N is the number of servers. The directory is distributed right from the start. Files are uniformly distributed among the servers, which roughly receive the same load.

Graphs show the huge performance of FPFS with respect to the other file systems. FPFS always gets, at least, one order of magnitude more operations/s, but it is usually much better (up to 70× more operations/s than OrangeFS, and 37× more than Lustre, in some cases of the unlink test). It is worth noting that, with just 8 OSD+s and a Gigabit interconnect, FPFS is able to create, stat, and delete more than 205 000, 298 000 and 221 000 files per second, respectively.

These performance differences between FPFS and the rest can be explained by the network traffic generated by each file system and some serialization problems. Lustre and OrangeFS generate a high network traffic that even increases with the number of servers. Both also usually have a metadata server that sends and receives much more packets than the rest. Consequently, Lustre and OrangeFS present serious scalability problems that limit their performance.

5   Related Work

This section focuses only on some of the existing file systems that use a metadata cluster, support the distribution of directories, and use OSD or similar devices.

Ceph [11] stores data objects in a cluster of OSD devices that work in an autonomous manner to provide data-object redundancy for fault tolerance, etc. Contents of directories are written to objects in the OSD cluster, and metadata operations are carried out by a small cluster of metadata servers. Each metadata server adaptively splits a directory when it gets too big or experiences too many accesses. Despite all these features, setting a stable metadata cluster in Ceph has been no possible (we still have to test latest releases), so we have discarded this file system in our benchmarks.

OrangeFS [10] also uses a cluster of data servers. They are not OSD devices, but play a similar role. OrangeFS has supported several metadata servers for quite a long time, but only recently has introduced the distribution of a directory among several servers based on ideas from extendible hashing and GIGA+ [8]. When a directory is created, an array of *dirdata objects* (each on a metadata server) is allocated. Directory entries are then spread across the different dirdata objects, whose number is configurable per directory.

Lustre [7] offers a cluster of data servers through OSD devices. Latest versions of this file system also allow to use several MDTs in the same file system. A directory can also be shared out among several servers, but this distribution is static, and it is set up when the directory is created.

FPFS shares some important features with all the above file systems: existence of several data and metadata servers, use of OSDs or similar devices, data objects, distributed directories, etc. However, design and implementation aspects determine the performance and scalability of all of them. For instance, all but FPFS separate data and metadata services, which makes it difficult, when not impossible, to optimize some operations that involve both data and metadata elements. OSD+ devices deployed in FPFS also add a small-overhead software layer that leverages the underlying local file system to provide an efficient service.

6   Conclusions

In this paper, we describe the implementation of data objects in an OSD+ device. We show how OSD+s can internally optimize their implementation to speed up some common file operations. This kind of optimizations are not possible in other file systems like Lustre, OrangeFS or Ceph, where data and metadata elements are, from a conceptual point of view, managed independently.

We add support for data operations to our OSD+-based Fusion Parallel File System, and compare its performance with that achieved by Lustre and OrangeFS. Results show that, for metadata-intensive workloads such as creating, stating and deleting files, FPFS provides a throughput that is, at least, one order of magnitude better than that achieved by the other file systems, and up to 95× better than OrangeFS's, and 37× than Lustre's. For workloads with large data transfers, FPFS can obtain up to 34% more aggregated bandwidth than OrangeFS, while can compete with Lustre for data writes. Results also show serious scalability problems in Lustre and OrangeFS that limit their performance.

Acknowledgements. Work supported by the Spanish MEC, and European Commission FEDER funds, under grants TIN2012-38341-C04-03 and TIN2015-66972-C5-3-R.

References

1. Avilés-González, A., Piernas, J., González-Férez, P.: Scalable metadata management through OSD+ devices. Int. J. Parallel Program. **42**(1), 4–29 (2014)
2. Avilés-González, A., Piernas, J., González-Férez, P.: Batching operations to improve the performance of a distributed metadata service. J. Supercomput. **72**(2), 654–687 (2016)
3. Bent, J., Gibson, G., Grider, G., McClelland, B., Nowoczynski, P., Nunez, J., Polte, M., Wingate, M.: PLFS: a checkpoint filesystem for parallel applications. In: Proceedings of the Conference on High Performance Computing Networking, Storage and Analysis (SC 2009), pp. 1–12 (2009)
4. Brandt, S.A., Miller, E.L., Long, D.D.E., Xue., L.: Efficient metadata management in large distributed storage systems. In: Proceedings of the 20th IEEE Conference on Mass Storage Systems and Technologies (MSST 2003), pp. 290–298 (2003)
5. Cray Inc.: HPCS-IO, October 2012. http://sourceforge.net/projects/hpcs-io
6. Dilger, A.: Lustre metadata scaling, April 2012. http://storageconference.us/2012/Presentations/T01.Dilger.pdf. Tutorial at the 28th IEEE Conference on Massive Data Storage (MSST 2012)
7. OpenSFS, EOFS: The Lustre file system, December 2016. http://www.lustre.org
8. Patil, S., Ren, K., Gibson, G.: A case for scaling HPC metadata performance through de-specialization. In: Proceedings of 7th Petascale Data Storage Workshop Supercomputing (PDSW 2012), pp. 1–6, November 2012
9. Skeen, D., Stonebraker, M.: A formal model of crash recovery in a distributed system. IEEE Trans. Softw. Eng. **9**(3), 219–228 (1983)
10. The PVFS Community: The Orange file system, October 2016. http://orangefs.org

11. Weil, S.A., Brandt, S.A., Miller, E.L., Long, D.D.E., Maltzahn, C.: Ceph: a scalable, high-performance distributed file system. In: Proceedings of the 7th USENIX Symposium on Operating Systems Design and Implementation (OSDI 2006), pp. 307–320 (2006)
12. Wheeler, R.: One billion files: scalability limits in Linux file systems. In: LinuxCon 2010, August 2010. http://events.linuxfoundation.org/slides/2010/linuxcon2010_wheeler.pdf

Author Index